CB 245 .G7

THOMAS H. GREER
Michigan State University

A Brief History of Western Man

BEE COUNTY COLLEGE LIBRARY
3800 CHARCO ROAD
BEEVILLE, TEXAS 78102
(512) 354-2740

D0884946

6722

Harcourt, Brace & World, Inc.
New York | Chicago | San Francisco | Atlanta

LIBRARY
BEE COUNTY
COLLEGE

COVER

Detail of *Apoxyomenes* by Lysippos. By courtesy of the Vatican Archives, The Vatican Museum, Rome.

Detail of *Abendmahlgruppe* (*Last Supper*) by Tilman Riemenschneider from Heiligblutaltar in Rothenburg/Tauber. Photo: Helga Schmidt-Glassner.

Detail of *The Family Group* by Henry Moore. Reproduced by courtesy of the Trustees of the Tate Gallery, London, and the artist.

MAPS BY J. P. TREMBLAY

Figures 11–2, 13–2 permission S.P.A.D.E.M.
by French Reproduction Rights, Inc., 1967.

© 1968 by Harcourt, Brace & World, Inc.

All rights reserved.
No part of this publication may be reproduced or transmitted
in any form or by any means, electronic or mechanical,
including photocopy, recording, or any information storage and retrieval system,
without permission in writing from the publisher.

Library of Congress Catalog Card Number: 68–11244

PRINTED IN THE UNITED STATES OF AMERICA

Preface

Man is surely the most complex of all the beings on earth. This would be a true statement even if we spoke only of the cave man, who was innocent of most of what we call "civilization." For man, whether of the cave or the spaceship, possesses unique powers of response and creativity: thought and language, spiritual and moral sense, political awareness, and aesthetic capability. Civilized man is, of course, the most complex being of all.

Inscribed on the temple of Apollo at Delphi was the motto *Know thyself*. But if we are the most complex beings on earth, how can we come to know ourselves and, what is still more difficult, know our fellow men? Biology, psychology, and anthropology can tell us important things about man—but what they tell us applies about as well to the cave man as to modern man. To understand what distinguishes us as *civilized* men, we must look elsewhere. Fortunately, the "elsewhere" is not far to seek. It lies in the actual *experience* of our forefathers—experience that can be reconstructed (in substantial measure) from the records of history, religion, philosophy, literature, and art.

My aim in this book is to present a clear and concise view of the main course of Western history, focusing on the most significant human experiences. I have concentrated on the major events, institutions, ideas, and creative works that have shaped (and expressed) our civilization. Some understanding of these will help to explain how Western men have come to think and feel, believe and dream, act and create as they do. Thus, if my hopes are fulfilled, this book will help the reader to "know *himself*" and will prepare him for further intellectual exploration.

Western man has never lived in isolation. Today, more than ever before, he lives in constant interaction with other peoples of the world. This book deals directly, however, only with *Western* civilization, for we must understand ourselves before we try to understand others. The need for broader knowledge—of all cultures and civilizations—remains an insistent challenge. But time and mind have their limits; we progress step by step, not all at once. For these practical reasons this book holds to the familiar paths of Western man—from the trails blazed by the ancient Greeks to the nuclear crossroads of the twentieth century.

Perhaps the most satisfying way of exploring the past is through direct contact with great ideas and creative works. The student should find the reading of Homer, Plato, Augustine, Shakespeare, and Darwin (for example) a fruitful and inspiring experience. This book, while complete in itself, is designed as a guide and companion to such reading. It may also serve as a suitable guide to appropriate secondary readings.

The author of a general book such as this is deeply indebted to the scores of teachers and scholars from whom he has learned. In addition, I wish to thank all those who have aided me directly in the preparation of this book. Among my colleagues at Michigan State University, I am grateful especially to Professor Stebelton H. Nulle, who read the entire manuscript with critical acumen and who collaborated in preparing the "Recommended Further Reading." Other colleagues who read individual chapters and contributed helpful suggestions are Professors Werner Bohnstedt, J. Bruce Burke, Nelson Edmondson, Petr Fischer, R. Craig Philips, John Reinoehl, and Karl Thompson. Their assistance does not, of course, relieve me of responsibility for all statements of fact and interpretation.

I wish to thank, too, the All-University Research Committee of Michigan State University for its grants of financial assistance. My appreciation goes also to Jann McGiveron and Edie Starr for their expert and faithful services in typing the manuscript. The ultimate word of gratitude is reserved for my wife, Margarette M. Greer, whose personal sacrifice during my years of writing the book far transcended the call of duty.

THOMAS H. GREER

Contents

I. The Ancient World

B.C.	Art and Architecture	History and Literature	Religion and Philosophy	Political, Social, and Economic Developments	B.C.
4000–2000	First temples and palaces	Invention of writing	Sun worship in Egypt	Earliest civilizations in Egypt and Mesopotamia	4000–2000
3000–1400	Palace at Knossos (Crete)	Development of alphabet		Minoan civilization Achaean migration into Greece	3000–1400
1200			Moses and the Covenant	Dorian invasions of Greece Trojan War Rome founded "Homeric Age" of Greece (1200–800)	1200
1000			David and Solomon	Hebrew kingdoms (1000–600)	1000
800		Homer	Amos First Olympic games honoring Zeus	Greek city-states founded Greek colonization of the Mediterranean	800
600	Greek archaic style of sculpture	Greek drama emerges	Zoroaster (Persia) Thales Second Isaiah		600
500	Classical style Phidias Parthenon Myron	Aeschylus Herodotus, Thucydides Sophocles Aristophanes Euripides Xenophon	Parmenides Growth of mystery cults (Greece) Protagoras and Sophists Socrates Plato	Roman Republic founded Twelve Tables of law Persian Wars in Greece Athenian supremacy and empire Peloponnesian War	500
400	Praxiteles		Aristotle	Philip of Macedon Alexander the Great	400
300	Hellenistic style		Epicurus Zeno	Hellenistic kingdoms Punic Wars and Roman Con-	300

Timeline — The Roman World

Date	Architecture	Literature	Religion & Culture	Political & Historical Events
B.C. 200		Polybius		...quest of the Mediterranean world; Reforms of the Gracchi in Rome
B.C. 100		Vergil, Horace, Ovid	Cicero, Lucretius	Civil disorders in Italy; Julius Caesar's conquest of Gaul; Overthrow of the Roman Republic; Augustus and the foundations of the Roman Empire; Pax Romana (27 B.C.–180 A.D.)
A.D. 100	Colosseum, Trajan's Forum, Pantheon	Plutarch, Suetonius, Tacitus, Juvenal	Birth of Christ; Peter; Paul; Marcus Aurelius	Trajan
A.D. 200	Pont du Gard; Baths of Diocletian		Last great persecutions of the Christians; Anthony; Rivalry of Mithraism and Christianity	Diocletian
A.D. 300			Toleration decreed for Christians; Council of Nicaea; Christianity becomes official Roman faith	Constantine; Theodosius; Germanic invasions begin
A.D. 400			Jerome and Vulgate; Augustine; Recognition of papacy in the West	Sack of Rome by Goths; Sack of Rome by Vandals; End of western half of Roman Empire
A.D. 500			Benedict and his monastic rule	Roman law codified by Eastern emperor Justinian

The Greek Beginnings

1

Western man and civilization itself appeared very recently in human history. Man roamed the earth for nearly a million years before developing the rudiments of civilization—town life, orderly government, written language and law, the division of labor, and the beginnings of the arts and sciences. Civilized man emerged only six or seven thousand years ago, and his civilization is but a thin veneer on an ancient groundwork. Not until the last thousand years has civilization covered a major portion of the globe.

ORIENTAL ORIGINS OF CIVILIZATION

The earliest known beginnings of civilization were in the great river valleys of the Near East, a region that lies, roughly, between the eastern end of the Mediterranean Sea and the head of the Persian Gulf (FIG. *1-1*). The communities of the ancient Near East, from which Western civilization derives so much of its heritage, had many characteristics in common. Both of the earliest civilizations, those of Egypt and Mesopotamia, arose along the course of great rivers, the Nile and the Tigris-Euphrates. Which of the two appeared first is still disputed, but both emerged when their Stone Age villages gave way to more highly organized social units. It is with the fortunes of these communities that the story of early civilization begins. Out of the incessant conflicts between neighboring communities the first unified kingdoms emerged: in the Nile Valley the process was completed, about 3000 B.C., with the formation of the united kingdom of Upper and Lower Egypt; in Mesopotamia the Babylonian plain was first brought under the rule of one king about 2200 B.C.

The rise of each of these great kingdoms, Egypt and Babylonia, was accompanied by the growth of royal administration. In each

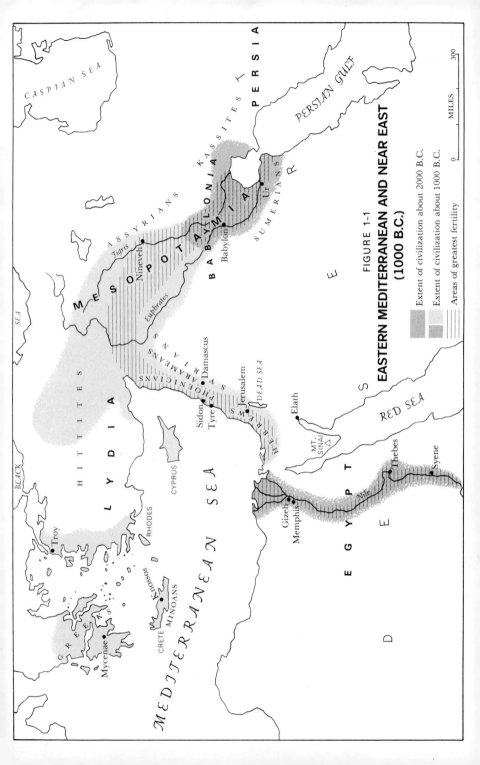

FIGURE 1-1

**EASTERN MEDITERRANEAN AND NEAR EAST
(1000 B.C.)**

Extent of civilization about 2000 B.C.

Extent of civilization about 1000 B.C.

Areas of greatest fertility

0   300
MILES

kingdom, too, political power was closely identified with supernatural forces (as interpreted by a well-organized priesthood). Gods were thought to be patrons of the kingdom and defenders of the social and moral order. In Mesopotamia the ruler was regarded as the viceroy of the gods; in Egypt the ruler was believed to be himself a god. In both, the monarch claimed absolute power and demanded the unquestioning reverence and submission of his subjects.

Royal power was exercised through a centralized bureaucracy, with deputies of the king performing important functions in the local communities. Their principal responsibility was to collect taxes. The various offices of the central government clustered about the royal palace in a vast compound that included the temples, with their privileged priesthoods, and the residences of royal officials. Complexes such as those at Memphis or Babylon, where divine and human powers were brought together, formed the earliest capitals.

In both the Egyptian and Mesopotamian kingdoms, the will of the ruler was enforced through a standing army, which was also the instrument of royal ambition. Military conquest, leading to the establishment of the first empires, was accompanied by commerce. The combined demands of government and of widening trade led in turn to the invention of writing—first ideograms, in which signs represented some idea or object, then syllabic writing, and finally the earliest alphabet. Here was one of the most precious of all human inventions, making possible not only the preservation of records and documents, both public and private—on papyrus, baked clay, or stone—but the growth of literature and science.

The expansion of government and commerce also gave rise to written laws, at least in the Babylonian kingdom. There, about 1800 B.C., King Hammurabi issued one of the earliest codes of civil law. There, too, emerged the methodical observation of the skies, especially by the priests, that led to the rise of astronomy and astrology—companions for centuries to come. Mathematics and geometry, the indispensable tools for understanding and controlling man's environment, date from these early centuries. Uniform weights and measures also came into being, as did the calendar, with a twelve-month year, a seven-day week, and a twenty-four-hour day.

The Mesopotamians are further distinguished by the introduction of metal coinage, the first use of the arch and the dome, and the building of flood-control and irrigation systems, which kept their arid land fertile for centuries. Finally, they pioneered in the arts of geography and medicine.

THE AEGEAN BACKGROUND
OF WESTERN CIVILIZATION

But the sources of Western civilization are not to be found in the
Near East alone. Between 3000 and 2000 B.C., a third distinct civilization—known to us as Minoan (from Minos, a legendary ruler)—
arose under Near Eastern influences on the island of Crete. The
ruins of sumptuous palaces, especially at Knossos (where the palace
was equipped with baths and plumbing), testify to a rich, refined
civilization. That civilization rested on control of the surrounding
seas and on widespread, thriving trade. Its artistic remains suggest
a peaceful, pleasure-loving society in which women played a prominent part and a people devoted to spectacular games and the worship of a fertility goddess.

By 1600 B.C., versions of this civilized way of life were flourishing
along the coast and on the islands of the Aegean Sea (FIG. *1-2*).
These civilized societies, the first to appear on the continent of
Europe, are known as Mycenaean after the name of the earliest
mainland site to be discovered in modern times. The Mycenaean
settlements, in contrast to the Minoan sites, were fortified with massive walls and citadels, and their inhabitants carried on both trade
and warfare. For a time they struggled with the Cretans for control
over the commerce of the eastern Mediterranean; the rivalry ended
after the mysterious destruction of the Minoan towns around 1400
B.C. (For many years historians believed that the destruction was
the work of invaders from the Greek mainland, but recent investigations indicate that the towns were inundated by a tidal wave following the explosion of a volcano on the island of Santorini, some
seventy miles to the north of Crete.) Thereafter precise knowledge
of Minoan civilization was lost until archaeological investigations
were launched at Knossos about 1900 A.D.

It was after the disaster in Crete that the Greeks, the people who
were to lay the true foundations of Western civilization, began to
assert themselves. Apparently of mixed Nordic and Alpine stocks,
speaking an Indo-European language, they had begun to wander
southward with their flocks after 2000 B.C. from the region of the
lower Danube. The earliest of them, called Achaeans, played some
role in both the Minoan and the Mycenaean societies, though the
details are unclear. But after 1200 B.C. fresh waves of more warlike
Greeks, called Dorians, overran the Aegean world; around 1150
they sacked "golden" Mycenae. Shortly before this event, an expedition of allied Greek forces had besieged and captured the flourish-

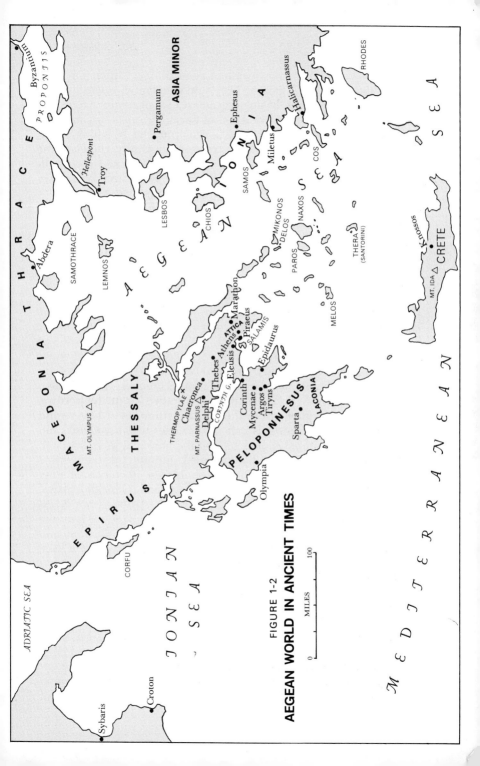

FIGURE 1-2
AEGEAN WORLD IN ANCIENT TIMES

ing city of Troy, on the northwestern coast of Asia Minor (FIG. *1-2*).
The destruction of Mycenae, Troy, and many other towns marked
the eclipse of civilization in the Aegean area for nearly four centuries
—a period known as the "Dark Ages" of Greek history (1150–800 B.C.).
The Dorian conquerors had come down from the North as a barbarian folk. Their society centered around the family, the clan, the
tribe, and the village; their economy was simple and largely self-
sufficient; they had neither written law nor machinery of government.

During the period of the Dark Ages a mingling of populations
occurred that produced the Greek of classical antiquity, and the
essential character of classical Greek civilization was forged. Starting
with the remnants of Minoan and Mycenaean achievement, joining
them with their simpler ways brought down from the North, and
adding elements derived from contact with the civilized Near East,
the Greeks succeeded in creating their own distinctive culture. By
the eighth century B.C., it extended from the mainland to the
Aegean islands and the western coast of Asia Minor. This is the
culture we sometimes call "Homeric." (The poet Homer is believed
to have lived in the eighth century.)

The Greeks, through their trade relations with the Near East,
acquired an alphabet and important new techniques. Among them
were innovations in pottery-making, sculpture, and architecture.
But of even greater moment to the future civilization of Greece and
Europe were those features of oriental societies that the Greeks did
not adopt: the divinized monarchy and the powerful priesthood.

The country the Greeks had invaded and settled they called
Hellas, after their mythical forefather, Hellen. It consisted of a
mountainous mainland—with narrow valleys, few rivers and plains,
many bays and harbors, and hundreds of rocky islands strewn across
the Aegean Sea. This arm of the Mediterranean was, in fact, the
geographical center of the Greek world, bounded on the west and
north by the European land mass, on the east by the coast of Asia
Minor, and on the south by the island of Crete, which lies like a
breakwater between the Aegean and the Mediterranean. Though
the climate was mild, Hellas was poor in natural resources. As the
Greek nomads settled on the conquered land, they turned to herding and farming; barley, grapes, and olives were the main crops.
But the rocky soil provided most farmers with only a meager livelihood, and some of them, during the long summers, supplemented
their income by trade—which often meant piracy.

Geographical variety and the surrounding sea encouraged movement and innovation among the Greeks. Unlike the Babylonians

and Egyptians, who clung to their narrow river highways, the Greeks became a daring and venturesome people. From the Black Sea westward to the coast of Spain, the Mediterranean's shores came to be dotted with Greek colonies. And yet, both at home and in their colonies, the Hellenes (as the Greeks called themselves) maintained their sense of "oneness." As early as 776 B.C., according to tradition, they celebrated the first Olympic games. The contests were part of a Pan-Hellenic gathering (i.e., for all Greeks) in honor of the god Zeus. This celebration was held every fourth year thereafter, and it served as one of the binding forces in Hellenic life.

THE CITY–STATE

Soon after the first Olympic celebration, the social and political unit known as the city-state began to emerge out of the simple family and clan organization of earlier times. This development was not unique to Greece. The early centers of civilization in the Near East had been temple-states or city-states before they were merged into larger political units. The major Greek city-states, however, remained independent during their most creative period and developed a distinctive spirit and way of life. It is impossible to separate the idea of the city-state from Greek civilization itself.

The mature Greek city-state, or *polis* (source of our words "metropolis" and "political"), was more than just a government, a trading center, or a place to live. It ranged in extent from a few square miles to an area almost as large as Rhode Island. When possible, the city proper was built around a protecting hill, with a fortress, or acropolis, crowning the summit (FIG. *1-3*). The surrounding

FIGURE 1-3. The Acropolis. (Alison Frantz.)

countryside, the mountains, and the sea nourished the city with agriculture and commerce. The population (of both town and country) ordinarily numbered only a few thousand, though Athens, after absorbing its smaller neighbors, may have reached three hundred thousand. Each city-state regarded itself as a sovereign unit of government: it was *the* government, the *sole* law for the politically privileged and responsible people—the citizens.

Yet the law was not something that was forced upon the citizen; he did not view it as an infringement on his private life and liberties. Although various types of government emerged, from kingship to democracy, the Greeks always believed that the city-state was a community enterprise and that its affairs belonged to all. The source of this spirit, which prevailed even in such large city-states as Athens, lay in the origins of the city-state itself. Each city was believed to have been founded and developed by a family or a clan— a kinship group—and most of its citizens could trace their ancestry back to common forefathers. In other words, they could think of themselves as distantly related members of one big family. They saw no more reason for conflict between the state and the individual than between the family and the individual. The "good life" for the individual was a life of active participation in civic affairs.

The city-state was also the people's church. Although Greeks everywhere believed in the same pantheon (group of gods), they paid special reverence to the particular god or goddess who was associated with their own city. Local legend almost invariably held that the founder of the community was divine or semidivine and that a certain deity bestowed favor and protection on the city. The goddess Athena, for example, was the patroness of Athens, and all Athenians were therefore united in a special faith and ritual. The temple priests, moreover, did not form a class apart from the state; rather, they were civic functionaries.

Finally, the city was the citizens' school, recreation center, and club. There was no classroom education for adults; instead, the citizens exchanged and discussed ideas daily as they talked in the marketplace, gymnasium, assembly, and civic festivals. These, rather than the home, served as the main social centers (which explains in part why the citizens paid far more attention to public architecture than to private dwellings, as we will see later).

It is not surprising that the Greek cherished his city-state, with its harmonious design for living. True, it was in a sense a narrow and artificial unit, poorly suited to an expanding world of trade and politics. And, in the end, the tiny states destroyed each other through endless rivalry, jealousy, and war—for each had its own armed force as well as its own law. By failing to join together in larger political units, they exposed themselves to foreign conquest. But the Greek was unwilling to accept any reduction in the independence of his city-state. He valued it even more highly than Westerners value the nation-state today; for to him it was not only the object of patriotic fervor but an extension of himself and his family, a place of livelihood, learning, and pleasure—and a thing divine. Although the Greek city-states had many features in common, each was individual in character and had its own personality. Athens brought forth in the course of a century more enduring creations of the human mind and spirit than any other city before or since. Yet Athens was by no means the only center of creativity; there were, for example, Miletus and Ephesus in Asia Minor and Thebes, Argos, and Corinth on the mainland. But the power that contended with Athens in the climactic struggle for Greek supremacy was Sparta. Though both were city-states, their particular institutions and temperaments were strikingly different. Before examining the remarkable achievements of Athens, we will look at its polar opposite in the Greek world.

Sparta: the military ideal

The Spartans were the chief descendants of the warlike Greeks (the Dorians) who had conquered the southern mainland. The land surrounding Sparta, known as Laconia, is one of the few broad and fertile plains of Greece. It forms part of the Peloponnesus, a hand-shaped peninsula attached to the mainland by the Isthmus of Corinth (FIG. *1-2*).

The Spartans were, in a sense, the victims of their own history. They began in Laconia as a small ruling minority, but, as they expanded their conquests, the number of people they subjugated came to exceed their own by about ten to one. A proud and aloof people, the Spartans were unwilling to dilute their citizen body by granting the vanquished any of the rights and privileges of citizens. Instead, they compensated for their small number by cultivating physical excellence, by exercising constant vigilance, and by subjecting themselves to the strictest discipline. They rarely wavered from this self-imposed regimen. The word "Spartan" has aptly become a byword for courage, stamina, stern living, and determination.

Sparta's failure to move on through the stages of political growth experienced by other Greek communities was due largely to the Spartans' fear of change. Since their power over subjugated peoples was precarious at best, they hesitated to tamper with any of the institutions on which that power rested. They kept their dual kings, for example, long after kings had disappeared elsewhere in Greece—though they did limit the royal powers. While the kings continued to command in battle, the chief governing functions came to be exercised by a council of elders. This consisted of the kings, along with some thirty other members chosen for life from among the leading families. But the elders had to be at least sixty years of age, and the five powerful ephors (overseers) who were elected annually by the citizens were usually old men, too. Hence, the affairs of the city were conducted by elderly, conservative men who resisted innovation. In most of the other Greek cities the popular assembly, which was open to all adult male citizens, became a genuine lawmaking body. But in Sparta the members of the Assembly were not permitted to debate. Instead, the Spartan elders drew up all proposals and then presented them to the Assembly for approval or disapproval only—and this was given, not by vote, but by a shout.

The Spartans tried to seal off their city from outside influences. Compared with other Greek cities, Sparta had little contact with foreigners: she had no port, she discouraged trade, and she showed visitors little hospitality. Her citizens feared that "subversive" ideas might upset the delicate internal balance, and they resorted to secret police and isolation to keep them out. (The Spartans were not the first—or the last—to fear the power of ideas.) But they were not motivated simply by fear; most Spartans *wanted* to preserve intact their system of government, their way of life, their ideal of virtue.

Spartan men were required by law to serve as professional soldiers; all other occupations were closed to them. Property was fairly evenly divided among them, and any tendency to luxury was frowned on as a sign of softness. Farms were worked for the Spartans by the conquered people, called helots (serfs), while a middle class of aliens were permitted to conduct such little business as existed.

One of the most curious features of the Spartan social system was the family life (or lack of it) among the ruling class. The men, when they were not out fighting, lived in barracks until their children were born. They might then have some home life with their wives and children, but they were still required to take their chief meal each day at a public mess. Infants who showed any sign of weakness were abandoned to die of exposure. Boys were taken by the state at the age of seven; they were taught the manly graces and reading and writing and were launched on a lifelong regime of physical toughening and military instruction. Girls were required to participate in mass drills and exercises designed to develop them into healthy, child-bearing women. Celibacy was punished, and the state encouraged mating and breeding by the best human specimens. All this regimentation, this denial of personal choice and decision, was directed toward one main goal: the maintenance of Spartan supremacy.

Although the Spartans paid a high price for security, their system did exactly what they wanted it to do. For centuries Sparta dominated the Peloponnesus, and, in the desperate struggle with democratic Athens, the Spartans came through weakened but victorious in 404 B.C. Their way of life had its compensations, too—for the master class, at least: the men spent their days exercising, hunting, fishing, fighting, drinking, and eating; the women had few housekeeping chores; and the boys spent their time in physical contests, war games, and outdoor living.

Athens: the glory of Greece

But to the Athenians, such a life was not worth living. One of their favorite quips was that the kind of life the Spartans led explained their willingness to face death. The Athenians sought a more balanced life. While they grudgingly admired the Spartans' physical prowess, they insisted that man had other potentialities that were equally or more important. The Spartan had a reputation for action rather than speech; the English term "laconic" (from Laconia) means "sparing of words." The Athenian, on the other hand, gloried in talk, though he could also act. From Athens flowed the daring speculation, the glorious literature, the stunning creations of the mind that have so enriched our heritage. Athens, rather than Sparta, is nearer to our idea of the Greek—though one reason may be that the Athenians wrote most of Greek history.

The contrasts between the two cities are endless. Sparta was agricultural and landlocked; Athens carried on a prosperous commerce and had access to the sea. Sparta had the more powerful army; Athens' chief strength was her navy. Sparta desired cultural isolation, while Athens welcomed foreign ideas and visitors. Where Sparta had been founded on swift conquests and was ruled by the sword, Athens was the product of a gradual and less violent development.

The Athenian homeland lay about a hundred miles northeast of Sparta (Laconia), in the central portion of ancient Greece where the peninsula of Attica juts into the Aegean Sea (FIG. *1-2*). Here a band of Greeks had settled some time after 2000 B.C. (the date is uncertain). We know that by 800 B.C. the neighboring communities of Attica had merged into the Athenian city-state. This gradual and

comparatively easy development led to a stable condition that was
not charged with the tensions of Laconia. While war and discipline
were common to both Laconia and Attica, the inhabitants of Attica
enjoyed relatively greater freedom and leisure. In this situation
Athenian culture came to flower in the fifth century B.C.

The turning points in the life of Athens and the rest of Greece
were two, both military. The first was the Persian Wars, in which
Athens led the Greek city-states to victory over a mighty oriental
empire. This exhilarating success was followed by the Age of
Pericles (460–430 B.C.), a period of highest confidence, power, and
achievement in Athens. That period, in turn, was cut short by the
second turning point, the Peloponnesian War, between Athens and
Sparta (as we will see). Let us now view Athens at her best. The
signal that raised the curtain on her glory was the Persian attack.

Persia (Iran) lies to the east of the Tigris-Euphrates Valley, one
of the birthplaces of civilization. In the sixth century B.C., its rulers
had succeeded in overrunning Babylonia, Syria, Egypt, and Asia
Minor and had welded together the largest empire known up to
that time. The "Great King," Darius, determined (about 494 B.C.)
to extend his control into Greece, for the Athenian upstarts had
recently abetted a rebellion against him by their sister cities in Asia
Minor. Darius sent several expeditions by land and sea against the
stubborn Greeks, losing the first decisive battle to the Athenians at
Marathon in 490 B.C. (The original "marathon" was run by the
messenger of victory, who sped the twenty-six miles to Athens to
break the news.) Sparta, which shared with Athens the leadership
of the Greek defense, also contributed to the defeat of Persia; the
Spartans' stand at Thermopylae (480 B.C.) has become a symbol of
heroism. But in the course of the long war Athens made the greater
sacrifices and was recognized by the Greek states as the leader of
their confederation. By 445 B.C., when peace was made with Persia,
Athens was the controlling power of the Aegean Sea.

The courageous and resourceful little state had demonstrated surprising capacity in fighting the Persian forces. The Athenians had
twice fled their homes and watched the enemy burn their city to
the ground. But with their victory came a new-felt power. How had
they, so few in numbers and so limited in wealth, turned back the
power of the Great King, with his millions of slavish subjects? To
the Athenians, flushed with confidence and pride, there could be
only one answer: they and their free institutions were *superior*. As
they rebuilt the temples of their Acropolis, this time in marble
rather than wood, they worked with a sense of mission and assurance. The structures they erected (including the Parthenon) show

their genius. And the same spirit infuses the sculpture, drama, and philosophy of these remarkable years. True, the Golden Age of Athens had been for centuries in gestation, but it was the crisis successfully met, the quickened pulse, the thrill of triumph that brought it to splendid birth.

Pericles, whose name is synonymous with the Golden Age, was the leader of Athens after the victory over Persia. It was largely through his initiative and guidance that the ambitious public-works program on the Acropolis was carried through. An aristocrat, a man of wealth and learning, Pericles nevertheless identified himself with the "popular" faction in politics. By virtue of his personal influence and his long tenure in important elective offices, he acted as the city's guiding force during the thirty-year period of Athenian supremacy in Greece. His death in 429 B.C., soon after the start of the Peloponnesian War, signaled the end of the Golden Age.

Under Pericles, Greek democracy came to fulfillment. Athens, which had started as a monarchy, had passed through several stages in its political growth. But through all these stages—including, for a time, rule by tyrants—there was one clear trend: the extension of political power and participation to all adult male citizens. (Citizenship was a matter of birth; the status of a father normally determined that of his children.)

By the fifth century B.C., monarchy had long since disappeared, and the principal power resided in the Assembly of male citizens. All major decisions were taken there: for peace or war, for sending forth expeditions, for spending public money, and for the general control of public affairs. Meetings were held about once a week, and the number of citizens present was usually less than five thousand. Although many more were eligible to attend, the men who lived in the country districts of Attica were often unable to come to town. At first the Assembly met in the marketplace (agora) of Athens, later on the slopes of a nearby hill (Pnyx), and still later in an open-air theater. Although it could draw up laws on its own, ordinarily it discussed proposals put before it by a committee of the Council of Five Hundred. The latter body was chosen annually by lot to draft the laws and to supervise their administration.

Debates in the Assembly were often spirited. Naturally, those with a talent for public speaking enjoyed a great advantage over their fellows. The members of the Assembly, highly critical and not always polite, might express their disagreement with an argument by jeering or whistling. But a shrewd and skillful orator like Pericles could win and hold the favor of the Assembly. And once he had done so, he became the most powerful man in Athens, for the decisions of the Assembly were final. Voting was by a show of hands, and a simple majority carried the vote.

The Athenians insisted on direct democracy not only in making laws but in administering them as well. There were more than a thousand public officials in Athens—tax-collectors, building inspectors, and the like—and all but a few of them were chosen annually by lot. Since these officials were paid for their services, poor men as well as rich could afford to hold office. Here was a system of "rule and be ruled," the full application of a deep faith in the political capacity of every citizen.

The Athenians did not, however, trust to lot in selecting their *chief* executive officers. These were the Ten Generals (*Strategoi*), who were chosen each year by vote of the male citizens. They commanded both the army and the navy, managed the war department, and had extensive control over the treasury. The Ten Generals were, in fact, a kind of "cabinet," or board of control, for the city; they chose their own chairman, who served as the chief officer of the government. The popular Pericles was elected general by the people and chairman by the board for sixteen years in succession.

The laws of Athens, then, were made and administered by the citizens. Who passed judgment on alleged violators of the laws? The citizens themselves. Athenian courts differed from American courts in several respects. They were much larger in size, ranging from a hundred to a thousand members. The reason for this was to make bribery difficult and to guarantee a broad cross-section of citizen judgment. Jurors for each trial were chosen by lot from a long list of names. There was no officer, like our judge, to decide questions of law; the Athenian court was judge and jury combined. By majority vote, it ruled on all issues of procedure, legal interpretation, guilt or innocence, and form of punishment. There were no lawyers, either. Every citizen argued his own case—another reason that the ability to speak effectively was so valued in Athens.

The Athenians practiced what they preached about political democracy. In fact, they invented democracy (as well as the word itself). Civic and political participation was part of the Athenian way of life, at least the life of the adult male citizens. We have no statistical records, but estimates suggest that during the Age of Pericles the number of adult male citizens was only about 40,000 out of a total citizen population of perhaps 120,000. Beneath them in status were resident aliens, chiefly tradespeople, who may have numbered 50,000. At the bottom of the social structure were the slaves, who were perhaps equal in number to the citizen class. Thus the estimated 40,000 male citizens controlled the government of a state of possibly 300,000 inhabitants. And even though aliens and slaves were excluded, there were doubtless more individuals actively participating in government in Athens than in any other city of comparable population before or since.

Slaves were found in all the city-states. They were chiefly non-Greeks, descended from captives of war. The Athenians (including the philosopher Aristotle) justified slavery by arguing that Greeks were superior to non-Greeks and that it is good and right for superiors to rule inferiors. By taking over the dull and heavy tasks, the slaves freed their masters for greater leisure. Most of the slaves in Athens were household servants; some worked in the fields; many were craftsmen; about ten thousand of them worked in the silver and lead mines of Attica. The mine-workers were driven cruelly, but the others seem to have been treated humanely. Slaves were legally the property of their owner, and they worked and lived pretty much as he chose. Some were permitted to rise to positions of considerable importance in Athens, and many were set free as a reward for faithful service. At any rate, there were no slave revolts such as those that occurred in Laconia and in most other places where slavery has existed. The orator Demosthenes claimed that Athenian slaves enjoyed greater freedom than the citizens of many other lands, and he was probably right. A favorite taunt by the Spartans (in a way, a compliment) was that on the streets of Athens one could not tell a citizen from a slave. As a matter of fact, the Athenians did not stress social and economic differences. The great majority of citizens were men of limited means: small farmers, merchants, and artisans.

But the Athenian economy was diversified and balanced. Its chief products were wine and olive oil, though by the fifth century Athens had become well known also as a manufacturing center. Free men and slaves, working in small shops, produced excellent metal weapons, crockery, and hand-wrought articles of silver, lead, and marble. Most of these were sold abroad in return for grain, meat, fruit, textiles, and lumber. Many citizens made their living by building or sailing ships, for Athens was a leading maritime power. Wages and profits were generally low, but so was the cost of living.

And the Athenian had simple needs. Wrap-around garments and a single pair of sandals made up his wardrobe. He took but one main meal each day. Recreation was free at the many civic festivals, which included athletic contests, dances, and dramatic performances. What the Athenian citizen sought most of all was not wealth but leisure: time for talk, for exercise and games in the public gymnasium, and for engaging in the affairs of his city. Living standards did vary, of course, and there was always some feeling of hostility

between rich and poor—hostility softened, however, by common devotion to the community and by the fact that the wealthy paid for
festivals, dramatic shows, and ships for the navy.

Women apparently did not enjoy the general freedom of Athens.
In fact, they had fewer rights than the women of Sparta or of
ancient Egypt. Respectable Athenian girls and women seldom went
into the street except to attend religious celebrations. Women could
not own property; marriages and divorces were negotiated by male
relatives; and banquets and entertainments were usually for men
only. The wives of citizens spent virtually all their time managing their households and raising their children. But if the men
found their wives dull they might (if they could afford it) take
female companions (*heterae*). These women, usually noncitizens
from Asia Minor, were schooled in the arts of entertainment and
conversation. The most famous of them was the cultivated and
charming Aspasia, consort of Pericles. Marriage, obviously, was
viewed as a practical partnership for producing heirs and keeping
house. The female figure was a favorite subject in Greek sculpture,
but such statues as the famed *Venus de Milo* represented idealized
women—not wives, but goddesses.

The Athenians lavished great care upon their children. Though
the girls received little formal training, private tutors instructed the
boys in manners, modesty, and music. They were taught to exercise,
to play games, to compete in sports; they were also instructed in
reading and writing, in the popular legends, and in the poems of
Homer. When youths reached eighteen years of age, they were assigned to special companies for two years of military and civic training. But the city itself was the principal school for young and old.
Talking in the marketplace, the Assembly, and the courts; listening
to music and dramas; visiting the temples; and participating in athletic contests—in these ways the male Athenian could approach the
classical ideal of "a sound mind in a sound body."

The city-state way of life

In Athens we find the culmination of Greek genius, but there
were scores of other city-states in which the way of life was similar.
And, though Greek civilization expressed itself through these independent city-states, we should not lose sight of the "oneness" of
their culture. Each city paid special respect to its favorite gods, but
all sacrificed to the same chief deities, just as they shared common
shrines and oracles and celebrated all-Greek festivals such as the
Olympic games. All claimed a common ancestor, Hellen, and all
had a common inheritance in the heroes and history of Homer.

The same language bound these freedom-loving peoples together and set them apart, in their own view, from outsiders. Those who did not speak Greek they called barbarians (*barbaroi*). This was not necessarily a term of discredit or blame, for the Greeks applied it to refined and sophisticated Orientals as well as to rude and untamed tribes. It meant simply that these outsiders could not speak Greek, from which it followed that they could not think Greek, hence know or live the Greek way.

What was this Greek way? How did it differ from the oriental way? The cardinal distinction lay in the Greek view of the *individual*. In the ancient cultures of the Near East the ordinary man was of small account. The valley of the Nile teemed with people, and life there was cheap. The ruler of Egypt, the pharaoh, owned and regulated the land and its inhabitants through divine right. Guided by priests and working through an army of agents and bureaucrats, he ordered the pattern of existence. The idea of personal liberty had little meaning to the mass of his subjects, and no one in authority regarded them as capable of governing themselves.

The Greeks would be slaves to no man and to no state. They believed in law and in an orderly society guaranteed by the gods, but they generally insisted upon a substantial measure of freedom and political participation. The city-state was more than a means of government; it was in itself a way of life—the only "good life" for man. And, the Hellenes believed, all free and intelligent Greeks were capable of enjoying this good life. They did not take the view, characteristic of the Orient, that the individual must resign himself abjectly to a fate beyond his control. In a qualified way, the Greeks were optimistic about the world and about what man could do on his own—if he did not presume too far. During the Golden Age, at least, they showed tremendous zest for living. The struggle, the contest, the game—even when lost—seemed exciting and challenging.

GREEK RELIGION

While the Greeks' view of life was reflected in their politics, it was expressed most fully in their religion, philosophy, and art. Greek religion by the Age of Pericles (fifth century B.C.) had become a well-developed institution of the state. It ordered the daily lives of citizens, inasmuch as the community undertook no important act without giving thought to the gods, but there was no authoritative body of dogma, no "Word of God," and no special class of priests. Prayers, rites, and festivals were rooted in customs that traced back to the misty beginnings of Greek history and were preserved in the works of early poets. The greatest of these poets, Homer (p. 32), drew portraits of the gods and told colorful tales about them. Another poet, Hesiod, wrote more directly about the genealogy of the gods and the creation of the universe. These works and those of several lesser writers were generally accepted by the Greeks as highly respected accounts of the divine scheme of things.

Gods and goddesses

The Greeks believed, not in a single, all-powerful god, like the God of the Jewish and Christian faiths, but in hundreds of deities. This type of religion, which is called polytheism (belief in many gods) as distinguished from monotheism (belief in one god), has been common to many cultures. The Greek religion was also anthropomorphic, which means simply that the Greeks visualized their gods in the guise of men. They did not regard the gods as mortal, of course, but saw them as glorified (and undying) men—"human beings writ large." Other religions have thus personified the forces of nature and fortune, but the Greek poets and artists surpassed all others in their appealing imagery. The creations of their mind and spirit survive gracefully and lustily in Greek sculpture, painting, and mythology.

The gods lived close by—the great ones on top of Mount Olympus, the highest peak of Hellas (FIG. *1-2*). There, behind a veil of clouds, Zeus, father of the gods, presided over his divine family. The Olympian deities were usually perfect and beautiful in form, but they displayed human frailties and emotions. They knew ambition, pride, and jealousy, and they took an active interest in the affairs of men. Though they were not all-powerful, they merited the deference of mortals, who took pains to win their favor by sacrifices, honors, and prayers.

Zeus (Jupiter),* whose special zone was the sky, shared overlordship of the world with two of his brothers: Poseidon (Neptune) ruled the sea, and Hades, or Pluto (Dis), ruled the underworld. The underworld was a dark, forbidding place, where shades of departed men lingered for an uncertain period. There was no expectation of immortality for humans and no system of rewards and punishments after death. But the gods could inflict their power for good or ill on a man during his life on earth. Many a Greek who had offended Zeus had been struck by his thunderbolt, and every sailor knew the fury of the sea when Poseidon was angered. In this fashion the elements of nature were personified and interpreted by the Greeks.

* The names of deities in parentheses are those of Roman gods later identified with the Olympians.

LIBRARY
BEE COUNTY
COLLEGE

6722

As Zeus embodied the patriarchal, or fatherly, principle, his wife Hera (Juno) embodied the matriarchal, or motherly, principle. She was regarded as the protectress of womanhood and marriage. But she was also something of a shrew, and Zeus found solace in other amours, which resulted in numerous divine offspring. His favorite daughter was Athena (Minerva), a spirited virgin noted for her wisdom, armed and martial in bearing, the consoler of maids, and the patroness of Athens. The Athenians raised many monuments in her honor; the most perfect was the temple of the Parthenon (Virgin), which still crowns the acropolis of Athens.

The legends of the love affairs of Zeus and of other gods had doubtless grown up as an anthropomorphic way of explaining the special character of individual deities and their traditional relationships to one another. But the Greek poets gave extraordinary color and vigor to these legends. They told, for example, how Leto, one of the consorts of Zeus, had presented him with a splendid pair of twins—the handsome Apollo and his sister Artemis (Diana). Apollo, later associated with the sun, was widely worshiped as the god of poetry, music, art, and manly grace. Artemis, associated with the moon, was the goddess of wild nature, a huntress, and the model of athletic girlhood.

A female of quite another type was Aphrodite (Venus), goddess of beauty and love. Aphrodite tried her charms on many men, among them the bluff and powerful Ares (Mars). But the god of war, "the curse of men," preferred the thrill of killing to the pleasures of lovemaking. More companionable was the fleet Hermes (Mercury), messenger of the gods and patron of athletes. He had the lithe, virile form of a perfect runner, and he glided on winged sandals over land and sea. Dionysos (Bacchus) was a son of Zeus by a mortal woman. It was, in part, this mixed parentage that made him so popular and beloved among the Greeks. Many legends were mingled in Dionysos: he was the god of wine and indulgence; he was also associated with the fertility principle in nature, with the suffering of death, and with the joy of rebirth. It is not surprising that mysterious cults promising personal immortality grew up in connection with his worship.

Priests and oracles

The Greeks had no churches—neither organizations nor buildings —as we think of them. And, since they had no prescribed doctrine, a man could believe what he pleased so long as he did not openly deny or blaspheme the official deities. The temple, the chief place of public worship, was designed as a shrine for the personal use of the god it honored. A statue of the god was normally placed in the interior, which was seldom seen by ordinary citizens. The temple priest was responsible for the care and protection of the image and the sacred precincts.

Ceremonies in honor of the god were usually performed in front of the temple, where the worshipers presented the priest with gifts—pottery, garments, whatever might be pleasing to the god. They also offered up prayers and animal sacrifices to win divine favor and assistance. After the sheep or pig had been roasted and the aroma had reached the nostrils of the god, the priest and the worshipers ate the meat in a common sacred meal. The god's own food and drink were limited to ambrosia and nectar, which were believed to nourish immortality.

Some priests and priestesses claimed that they had the power to communicate with the gods. The Greeks took special interest in these seers (oracles) and paid them high honor and respect. The most famous oracles in all Greece were the priestesses of Apollo who dwelt at Delphi. Politicians, generals, heads of families—the mighty and the lowly—went or sent to Delphi for advice on such matters as whether or not to embark on a military campaign or what they must do to end a plague. A priestess would fall into a trance, relay the question to Apollo, and then utter the answer received from him. The utterance was usually unintelligible and had to be interpreted for the questioner by a priest. The Delphic oracles won a high reputation for accuracy, partly because the advice and predictions were cast in such vague, ambiguous terms that they could be made to fit almost any subsequent event.

The official religion thus offered mortals a glimpse of the divine will. It also explained the mysteries of nature and provided men with a means of gaining the favor and help of superhuman forces. What it did not provide was consolation to those who lost the game or suffered misfortune. Nor did it hold any promise of life other than this one on earth; only the gods enjoyed life eternal. As if to balance these shortcomings, various cults grew up alongside the conventional religious beliefs and practices. Since their rituals were usually known only to the initiated, these were known as mystery cults.

Dionysos, the central figure of worship in most of these cults, was associated with seasonal death and rebirth (winter and spring). His followers believed that they could identify themselves with the god, and thus share his rebirth, by means of ritualistic experiences; these included undergoing severe physical tests, becoming intoxicated with wine or drugs, eating a sacred meal, and witnessing a dramatic representation of the god's death and resurrection. At the end of such ordeals the worshiper sensed a mystic union with the god and assurance of everlasting life. The mystery cults supplemented, rather than replaced, the conventional religion, and probably only a minority of the citizens underwent the initiation rites.

Other Greeks were more interested in the relation of religion to morality. The gods of Homer had shown slight concern for conventional moral standards, but by the time of the Golden Age they had become more closely identified with concepts of right and wrong. Zeus was regarded as the upholder of justice, especially of the sanctity of oaths. Human crimes were frowned upon by most of the Olympians, and divine punishment would surely descend on the murderer, perjurer, blasphemer, or arrogant man. Even so, the official religion, with its accounts of strange and questionable acts performed by the gods themselves, did not fully satisfy the moralists. Greek dramatists and philosophers began to challenge traditional religious beliefs, insisting that religion should encompass a definite moral order. Failing to find it in the Greek legends, they either rejected the gods or made them subordinate to a higher abstract justice.

THE FOUNDERS OF WESTERN PHILOSOPHY

The earliest Greek philosophers (sixth century B.C.) began by criticizing the prevailing nature-myths. They found it hard to believe that earthquakes were caused by the stamping of Poseidon or that lightning was a bolt from Zeus. They made the crucial intellectual leap from a primitive, anthropomorphic view of nature to a rational, analytic view.

Pioneers of rational thought

One of the basic questions they sought to answer through rational analysis relates to the composition of the physical universe: What are the elements from which all material things are made? Around 600 B.C., Thales of Miletus (in Asia Minor) hypothesized that water is the basic ingredient, which was a logical inference, since water seems to be present, in various forms, throughout the world of space and matter. It fills the sea, rivers, and springs; it falls from the sky; it is found in the flesh and organs of animal bodies. And under varying conditions of temperature and pressure, it changes from a liquid to a solid or a vapor. Thales was no doubt aware that his hypothesis did not explain all the varied appearances of matter; but he and other Greek thinkers were convinced that nature, in its unseen essence, is far simpler than it appears to be.

Though later philosophers rejected Thales' belief that everything can be reduced to water, they agreed that he was on the right track. Some believed the prime substance to be air or fire; others concluded that there are four basic elements: earth, air, fire, and water. But during the fifth century B.C. Democritus of Abdera (in Thrace) developed the hypothesis that all physical things are formed by combinations of tiny particles, so small that they are both invisible and indivisible. He called them atoms. Democritus' atoms are identical in substance but differ in shape, thus making possible the great variety of perceived objects in the world. They are infinite in number, everlasting, and in constant motion. They account, said Democritus, for everything that has been or ever will be. Democritus offered no empirical evidence to prove the existence of atoms, but the fact that he could conceive this remarkable hypothesis demonstrates the far-reaching achievement of Greek rational thought.

By sheer logic another philosopher, Parmenides of Elea (in southern Italy), convinced himself that everything in the universe must be eternal and unchangeable. Change requires motion, he reasoned, and motion requires empty space. But empty space equals nonexistence, which by definition does not exist. Therefore, he concluded, motion and change are impossible. Parmenides readily admitted that some things *appear* to move and change; but this must be an illusion of the senses, he said, because it is contradicted by logic. And logic, thought the Greek philosophers, is the most reliable test of truth.

Logic did not always lead to the same answers, however. While Parmenides satisfied himself that matter was unchanging and permanent, another Greek reached the opposite conclusion. Heraclitus of Ephesus (in Asia Minor) insisted that the universe, instead of standing still, is in continuous motion. He declared that a man cannot step into the same river twice—in fact, the river is changing even as the man steps into it. This doctrine proved most disturbing, for if everything is constantly changing (including ourselves), how can we gain true knowledge of anything? By the time our mind has been informed, the object of our attention is no longer what it was!

Discomforting suggestions such as these led many Greeks to abandon the effort to find absolute or final truth. As philosophic inquiry began to center in Athens during the fifth century B.C., serious thinkers there turned away from baffling questions about physical matter, permanence, and change to the more immediate and engaging problems of human existence. A group of professional teachers, called Sophists because they claimed to make men wise (*sophos*), played a leading part in this shift. Most prominent among them was Protagoras, who lived and taught in Athens. He declared, "Man is the measure of all things, of what is and of what is not." Completely skeptical of general truths, even about the gods, he insisted that truth is different for each individual. What was true (or right) for a Spartan might well be false (or wrong) for an Athenian. Furthermore, as Heraclitus had suggested, our bodies and minds are changing every moment, and our perceptions and ideas change with them.

The Sophists concluded that it is pointless to look for absolute truth about nature or morals. Since truth is *relative* to each man, it is important only to know what one finds agreeable and useful, such as the arts of persuasion and how to succeed in life. As news of this teaching circulated in Athens and elsewhere in Greece, the more conservative citizens became shocked and alarmed. It smacked of blasphemy and threatened to subvert the laws and moral code of the state. The Sophists protested that their theories did not call for the denial of authority (anarchy), and they cautioned their pupils, "When in Athens do as the Athenians." Social order, they agreed, requires reasonable conformity to the laws of the community, whether or not they are absolutely true or right. But the conservative elders were not reassured. It was upsetting to them to think that one man's ideas are as "true" as another's. And the laws of gods and men, they argued, cannot be properly respected and upheld unless the citizens believe them to be true and just—in an *absolute* sense.

Socrates and Plato

The greatest teacher of the fifth century was Socrates, who met the Sophist view of how to get on in life with the full force of his intellect and will. He was not a defender of the Olympian religion or of traditional morality; he was convinced, rather, of the existence of a higher truth. Socrates did not claim to know this truth but spoke of himself only as a seeker after knowledge. Because of his skeptical approach, he was often mistaken for one of the Sophists. He believed that knowledge must proceed from doubting, and he was forever posing questions and testing the answers people gave him. The Athenians resented having to justify their ways and ideas to Socrates, and he became increasingly unpopular. But he persisted in his arguments and discussions, for, he felt, "The unexamined life is not worth living."

Socrates believed that a technique of careful questioning can lead to the discovery and elimination of false opinions, which often pass for "truth." He cross-examined his associates on their definitions of justice, right, and beauty, moving them constantly toward answers that seemed more and more certain. This "Socratic method," sometimes called the "dialectic method," is simply a procedure for reaching toward truth by means of a dialogue or directed discussion. Socrates did not believe it necessary to observe and collect data in order to find absolute knowledge; he had a deep conviction that truth is implanted in the minds of men but becomes obscured by erroneous sense impressions. The function of the philosopher is to *recover* the truth that lies buried in the mind.

Socrates' theory of knowledge is closely related to his idea of the soul (the seat of the mind). Almost all we know about his idea of the soul, as well as his other views, comes to us through the writings of his brilliant pupil, Plato. In the dialogue of the *Phaedo,* Plato describes the final hours of his great teacher. Condemned to death by an Athenian jury on charges of corrupting the youth and doubting the gods, Socrates faces his fate cheerfully. He does so because he believes the soul is immortal, though during life it is hindered by the troubles and "foolishness" of the body. Death brings release for the soul and the opportunity to see the truth more clearly than before. And for Socrates the real aim of life is to know the truth, rather than to seek the satisfactions of the body. His devotion to the search for truth persisted unto death.

It is difficult to say where the ideas of Socrates end and those of Plato begin. Plato wrote masterly literary works in the form of dialogues in which Socrates usually appears as the chief speaker. It seems clear that Plato took up the main thoughts of his teacher and carried them through a full and positive development. It is even possible that Socrates would have challenged some of the conclusions reached by his pupil. Plato, after traveling widely through the Mediterranean lands, founded a philosophical school at Athens (385 B.C.). The Academy, as it was called, became the most influential intellectual center of the ancient world. It endured after its founder's death for over nine hundred years, and it served as a model for similar schools in other cities.

Plato continued the Socratic attack on the Sophist theory of relative truth. He refused to admit that the world consists of nothing more than imperfect nature in a constant state of flux. Turning back to the conjectures of the earlier Greek thinkers, who had been concerned with the "stuff" of the universe and with the question of permanence and change, Plato felt that the imperfect surface of things conceals a perfect, absolute, and eternal order. With daring imagination, he constructed a picture of the universe that satisfied the demands of his intelligence and his conservative temperament.

In his famous "Doctrine of Ideas," Plato conceded that the *physical* world is just what Heraclitus and the Sophists suggested: imperfect, changeable, and different in appearance to every man. But the physical world is superficial, possibly only an illusion of our senses; above and beyond it, Plato asserted, is the "real" world of *spirit*. This consists of perfect Ideas, or Forms, which exist unchanged through all the ages. There are, for example, the Ideas of man, horse, tree, beauty, and justice. These exist but can be known only through the mind (soul). The physical objects that our senses report to us are at best imperfect reflections or copies of the master Ideas. Hence, though they offer clues to the Ideas themselves, they have no intrinsic value. The philosopher should shun these distractions and turn his mind to the discovery and contemplation of the perfect, the eternal, the real. It is in the realm of Ideas that he will discover absolute truths and standards.

Plato and thinkers of similar outlook have found this conception sublimely illuminating and satisfying. It is a possible explanation of the universe, though not a convincing one for persons who place faith primarily in their senses. Many arguments can be marshaled to support it, and centuries later Plato's view was to prove adaptable to the teachings of Christianity. For the Christians, also, subordinated physical things and urged men to think upon the world of spirit—the "other" world of divine order and perfection.

Affairs on earth, according to Plato, are best guided by absolute principles as interpreted by true philosophers. Partly to provide a model of an ideal society and government, he wrote the best-known of his dialogues, the *Republic*. The book is rich with suggestions on education, literature, and the arts, but its major influence has been on social and political thought. Plato believed that human institutions should aim, not at complete individual freedom and equality, but at social justice and order. Justice, to Plato, meant *harmony of function* within each individual and among the individual members of a society. An aristocrat by birth and inclination, Plato had contempt for democratic ways. The foot should not try to become the head, he would say—nor the head the stomach. Every part of the human body and every member of the body politic should do the job it was designed to perform. Only then can friction, envy, and inefficiency—the chief sources of human and social sickness—be eliminated. Only then can mankind achieve health and happiness.

To reach this objective, Plato felt, society had to be structured according to natural capacities. The bulk of citizens would make up the class of Workers (producers), who would be sorted into various trades according to their aptitudes. Above them would be the Soldier class, which would be trained in the arts of war. From this disciplined class would be chosen, with the greatest care, a ruling group of Guardians. While the Workers would be permitted to live "naturally," procreating and raising families, the Soldiers and Guardians would follow a most austere and regulated life. Matings among them would be arranged by the state, to ensure the production of superior offspring. Any infant showing a physical defect would be left to die of exposure, and normal infants would be taken from their mothers and placed in a community nursery. Parents would not be permitted to know their own children, nor would they be allowed to possess personal property. Such extreme measures are necessary, thought Plato, if rulers are to become truly selfless and dedicated to the welfare of the whole community.

The education of Soldiers and Guardians was to be closely controlled. Only the "right" kind of music, art, and poetry would be taught, so that pupils would receive the desired moral indoctrination. Men and women chosen to be Guardians would have additional training in philosophy and would serve a period of political apprenticeship before taking their place as directors of the state. The Republic of Plato remains to this day a model for believers in aristocracy, planned society, and state control over education and the arts. It was the first of a series of utopias, or ideal states, that have offered radical solutions for the problems of human society.

Aristotle

Plato's own pupil, Aristotle, combined the brilliant imagination of his master, who had made mind the sole reality, with a sense of the reality of the physical world. Born in Stagira (in Thrace), Aristotle made his way early to Plato's Academy in Athens; years later he founded a school of his own there—the Lyceum (335 B.C.). Far more than his teacher, Aristotle was interested in the evidence of the senses. He was, in fact, the greatest collector and classifier in antiquity. His interests ranged from biology to poetry and from politics to ethics.

Aristotle accepted Plato's general notion of the existence of Ideas, but he held that physical matter also is a part of reality and not to be despised. Matter, he thought, constitutes the "stuff" of reality, though its shapes and purposes come from the Ideas, or Forms, that Plato had described. By logical thinking, men can gain knowledge of the purposes of things and of their interrelations, knowledge that will give meaning and guidance to their lives and bring them at the same time closer to God—whom Aristotle conceived as pure spirit and the source of Ideas. To Aristotle, logic is the indispensable key to truth and happiness. For this reason, he worked out precise and systematic rules for logical thinking, rules that have been respected for centuries.

In his study of society and government, Aristotle began by examining existing constitutions and states. In his classic work, the *Politics,* he analyzed and evaluated the major types of political organization. He did not derive from these an ideal organization, suitable for all cities; rather, he recognized that there are differences in local conditions and classes of inhabitants. Aristotle identified three basic forms of government: rule by the one, the few, and the many. Each of these forms, if dedicated to the general welfare, is legitimate, but any one of them becomes a "perversion" when the rulers pursue their own interest alone. The worst government of all, he thought, is a perversion of rule by the many. What Aristotle favored is, when conditions permit, a version of his second pattern: constitutional rule by the "middle-class" minority of citizens. The more numerous poor, he stated, lack experience in directing others; the very rich are not used to obeying. The middle class knows what it is both to command and to obey and may be counted on to avoid political extremes.

The same spirit of moderation—"nothing in excess"—marks Aristotle's comments on what constitutes the "good life" for man. In accordance with his theory that all things have a purpose, he taught that every organ and organism should function according to its *design.* The function of the eye is to see; the function of the ear is to hear; the function of man is to live like a man. This last calls for a harmonious balance of faculties, of both body and mind. But, since the mind is the crowning and unique part of man, it is clear that man should be governed by his reason rather than by his appetites. Further, Aristotle insisted, it is not enough just to be a man; the "good life" must be *nobly* lived, with every act and faculty aimed at excellence.

But what makes an act excellent (virtuous)? Aristotle admitted that this is a difficult question that cannot be answered by any exact rule. Excellence is more than a matter of knowledge or science; it is an *art* that each individual must develop through practice. He advised that, in general, excellence in a particular faculty lies somewhere between extremes. In battle, a warrior should exhibit neither a deficiency of nerve (cowardice) nor an excess (foolhardiness). Rather, he should strike a happy medium (courage). A work of sculpture or architecture should be judged by asking whether it might be improved, either by taking something away or by adding something to it. If it cannot, the work is "just right"—excellent.

Aristotle warned that his advice did not apply to things that were good or bad in themselves. Truth and beauty, for example, should be sought in the highest degree, while murder, theft, and adultery are evil in any degree. But in most affairs each man should find for himself, through trial and self-criticism, the desired mean between extremes. This insistence on moderation has come to be known as the philosophy of the Golden Mean. It does not signify a pale average, or mediocre, standard; rather it calls for the *best* performance of mind and body working together in harmony.

GREEK LITERATURE

Aristotle did not invent the Greek ideals of excellence, but he did reflect and express them. Everywhere around him, especially in literature and art, he observed the products of Greek genius. Our Western drama, prose, history, and poetry are Greek in origin; our painting, sculpture, and architecture have sprung, too, from Hellenic models.

Epic poetry

The Greeks recognized and made use of various types of poetry suited to different moods and purposes, but the earliest and greatest was the epic. Almost every nation has at least one major epic: the English *Beowulf,* the French *Song of Roland,* the Spanish *Poem of the Cid.* An epic, by definition, is the story of great deeds and men. It is a narrative in poetic form, usually sung to the accompaniment of a stringed instrument. With the passing of time it becomes a legend, common to all the nation and evocative of patriotic feeling.

The father of the epic, and of all Western literature, is Homer. His *Iliad* and *Odyssey* were known and recited by every Greek of the Golden Age. Respected as fountains of wisdom, they provided succeeding Greek writers with countless plots, themes, and characters. No one knows exactly who Homer was, though his authorship of the two epics is firmly established by tradition. It is believed that he lived in one of the Greek cities on the coast of Asia Minor, perhaps about 800 B.C. He gave classical formulation to tales that had been in circulation for several centuries before him. The general setting of his poems is the Trojan War, a struggle between early Greeks and the defenders of Troy (Ilium), which took place in the twelfth century B.C. (p. 10).

Later writers gave a full account of the war and its aftermath in a collection of poems called the Epic Cycle. But in the *Iliad,* Homer concentrates on the decisive point of the struggle, during the tenth (and last) year of the war: the wrath of Achilles and its consequences for the Greeks and Trojans. Homer's sequel, the *Odyssey,* passes over the actual overthrow and destruction of Troy and tells a story of high adventure, the return of the Greek war heroes to their homes. The central figure is the wily and brave Odysseus, king of Ithaca.

The *Iliad* is much more than a bloody tale of war. It is imbued with the Greek zest for living, desire for glory, and high sense of personal honor. In brief, it relates the angry quarrel between King Agamemnon, leader of the Greek expedition against Troy, and Prince Achilles, the mightiest warrior of the Greeks. Achilles sulks and refuses to fight, because Agamemnon has deprived him of a beautiful slave, his prize in battle. Neither man will give in. The Trojans, led by the powerful Hector, take heart upon learning that Achilles has quit the field. Only after his dearest friend, Patroclus, is slain and dishonored, does Achilles return to the battle to seek vengeance and to avert disaster. With the help of the goddess Athena, the Greek hero succeeds in killing Hector. The loss of their leader seals the fate of the Trojans.

Homer depicted the human traits of courage, pride, envy, sacrifice, and love with telling realism. But the gods, too, are very much a part—if not the leading part—of the epic. Homer thus sketched, in the story of Achilles, a typically Greek view of men and gods, morals and fate. That view was to be restated, many times over, in classical literature, drama, and art.

Drama: tragedy and comedy

Though Aristotle admired Homer's epics, he believed that tragic drama is a higher form of art. In addition to being read or sung, Greek drama was acted out. It was "theater," involving dancing, pageantry, and spectacle. Further, it was more concentrated than the epic; its tighter structure gave it superior unity and impact. Classic tragedy remains an unsurpassed device for placing human affairs before our eyes—for both our inspection and our sympathy. It enables the audience, with a sense of detachment, to see themselves and others and their common destiny.

Greek tragedy grew out of traditional religious ceremonials. It began in the sixth century B.C. as part of the annual spring festival in honor of the god Dionysos. On those occasions it was customary for a choral group to sing hymns about the gods and heroes of Greek legend. As the chorus sang, it danced in dignified fashion around a circular plot of ground, called the orchestra (derived from the Greek word for dance). Drama was born when the leader of the chorus was permitted to step out from the group and to carry on a kind of discourse (in song) with the chorus.

By the beginning of the fifth century B.C. the choral dramas might have several individual characters, though no more than three actors (plus the chorus) took part at any one time. Thus the ancient, repetitive ceremonial became a medium for expressing new ideas. Gradually the cultic connection with Dionysos faded away, and writers of tragedy were allowed to choose whatever themes suited their purpose: themes such as human pain and anguish, crime and punishment, justice and vindication. The religious origins were not forgotten, however, and tragedy remained serious and moral in purpose and character.

Comedy, the other form of Greek drama, grew from a complementary side of the Dionysiac tradition. Dionysos personified the annual "death" and "rebirth" of plant life, but he was also known as a god of fertility, joy, and mirth. The periodic rites in his honor (both spring and winter) included not only somber dances and chants but raucous processions and frenzied revels. It was out of these joyful celebrations that Athenian comedy was born. The earliest comedies were crude slapstick performances, but gradually they became sophisticated and biting satires. Aristophanes, the only writer of comedy whose works have come down to us, used his plays to lampoon local politicians, poets, and philosophers with whom he disagreed. Ridicule was his weapon of criticism. A good example is his *Clouds* (423 B.C.), a hilarious satire on the teachings of the Sophists.

The comedies and tragedies were presented during the Dionysiac festival seasons in open-air theaters. The theater of Athens was located on a slope of the Acropolis. Rows of seats, arranged in a semicircle, descended from the top of the hill to the orchestra, a level, circular plot where the chorus danced. (The best-preserved Greek theater, at Epidauros, is shown in FIG. *1-4*.) Beyond the orchestra, across the open end of the theater, stood a *skene,* or actors' building; in front of it was a porch, or platform, from which the speakers usually recited their lines.

The Greek actors (all men) wore masks that identified their roles and were shaped to help them project their voices. The performances were rich and colorful, with grand speeches, music, graceful dancing and singing, elaborate costumes and headdresses. The effect was more that of opera than of modern stage-acting. The author himself wrote the music as well as the text, and also trained the cast.

During the standard three-day festival of Dionysos, dramatic performances began each morning and lasted until nightfall. There was no curtain or lighting and very little scenery. Usually, three play-

FIGURE 1-4. Theater at Epidauros. (Spyros Meletzes.)

wrights competed on successive days, and a prize of great honor was awarded to the one who was judged best.

Three of the greatest playwrights of Western history were Greeks. They all lived in one century, the fifth century B.C., and in one city, Athens. Aeschylus, Sophocles, and Euripides wrote nearly three hundred plays, although only about thirty have survived. The earliest tragic dramatist was Aeschylus, whose plays transform suffering and death into exaltation and the will to live. That, in fact, is the measure of true tragedy. A play that merely presents pain and grief with a sense of despair or baseness may be "dramatic" and "pathetic," but it is not "tragic." The Greek play, and its successors in the tragic spirit, generally show a hero of high rank, a great struggle, and intense suffering. But justice triumphs in the end, and there is reason beneath the suffering. One leaves Aeschylus with the feeling that men pay for their crimes—that the gods and the moral law are hard—but that men can face fate bravely and nobly.

In the Orestes trilogy—*Agamemnon,* the *Libation Bearers,* and the *Eumenides*—Aeschylus' central theme is the family crimes of the royal house of Atreus. The plot, well known in Greek legend, revolves around the murder of King Agamemnon by his wife when he returns from the Trojan War. Wife, son, and daughter are implicated in the crimes that follow; all of them can justify their acts, but all are nonetheless guilty. To Aeschylus, these crimes and the sufferings they bring are divine retribution for breaches of the moral order. In the final play of the trilogy, Athena herself intervenes to protect the murderer Orestes, son of Agamemnon, and to stop the awful cycle of crime and punishment. Retribution is transformed into justice, and Orestes is restored to grace.

Because Sophocles reflected the Greek ideal of "nothing in excess," he has been called the "most Greek" of the three playwrights. He addressed himself to the consequences of exaggerated pride and self-confidence. In the tragedy *Oedipus the King*, Oedipus thinks he can avoid his fate, which has been foretold by the Delphic oracle of Apollo. A man of good intention, he tries to escape from a shocking decree of the gods (that he will kill his father and marry his mother). But in the end the truth of his moral crimes, which he has committed unknowingly, are brought to light by his own insistent searching. He realizes at last the folly of his conceit and savagely blinds himself as punishment for the foulness of his deeds.

Euripides, the youngest of the great Greek tragedians, probably had the deepest insight into human character. He has been called "poet of the world's grief." He was considered something of a radical, for he challenged the traditional religious and moral values of his time. He opposed slavery and showed the "other side" of war. Greek poetry had glorified the exploits of the mighty warriors of the Trojan War, but in Euripides' *Trojan Women* the battle ends with a brokenhearted old woman sitting on the ground, holding a dead child in her arms. Euripides was keenly sensitive to injustice, whether of the gods or of men, and he pleaded for greater understanding, equality, and decency.

History

The Greeks rank high in historical writing as well as in dramatic literature. The "father of history," Herodotus, was born in 485 B.C. in Halicarnassus, a Greek city on the shore of Asia Minor. A great traveler, he visited Babylonia, Syria, Egypt, and Greek colonies from the Black Sea to southern Italy. Having lived through the time of the Persian Wars, which ended in the triumph of Athens and her allies (p. 16), he decided to set down a record of that struggle and of the events that led up to it.

Herodotus called his work the *Historia,* which means, in Greek, "investigation." Until his time, the legends of poetry had been accepted as true accounts of the past. He set out to distinguish fact from legend, to write an account based on direct observation and evidence. The sources he used, to be sure, were not all reliable, but he usually warned his readers when he was passing along doubtful information. The major portion of the *Historia* is a survey of the ancient world: political and military affairs, social customs, religious beliefs, and leading personalities. We owe much of our knowledge of the early history of Greece, Persia, and Egypt to Herodotus. In the final portion of his work he tells the story of the Persian Wars in a manner sympathetic to both Persians and Greeks, but he presents it as a dramatic contest between slavery and freedom.

A generation later the Athenian Thucydides lifted the writing of history to a much higher critical level (though at some sacrifice of literary charm). In the first "scientific" history, he wrote about the long and cruel war between Athens and Sparta that had broken out soon after their joint victory over Persia. An exiled general of Athens, he had traveled widely to gather information during the war.

His subject is far more limited than that of Herodotus, but his account has greater unity and depth. And he excluded all suggestion of supernatural interference; history is made by *men*. Thucydides was convinced that human nature could be understood through careful historical study and that the knowledge so gained could be used as a guide in the future. He presented his facts coldly, from both sides, showing the reader the causes, motives, and consequences of the war. But his work is more than military history; it deals shrewdly with the questions of imperialism, democracy, and the broad fabric of social relations.

ARCHITECTURE AND SCULPTURE

The words of Thucydides, Aeschylus, Plato, and Homer tell us a great deal about the Greeks, but they cannot tell us the whole story. For there are many creations of the human spirit that manifest themselves visually. The most prominent and impressive of the visual arts—and another glory of ancient Greece—is architecture.

As we have seen, the Greeks regarded community activities as more important than private affairs; hence, they put their best efforts into public structures. The temple, which represented the strongest bond between religious and patriotic feeling, was their supreme architectural achievement. But they constructed other types of public building as well: there were the open marketplaces, enclosed on four sides by a covered colonnade; the outdoor theaters

(FIG. *1-4*), used for dramatic festivals and public gatherings, including those of the assembly; the great gymnasiums, race courses, and stadiums. The Greeks were least interested, apparently, in private dwellings, which were small, simple, and built of light materials.

Up to the sixth century B.C. even the most important buildings were usually made of wood. Gradually, however, limestone and marble took the place of timber in public structures. This was a natural development, because the country's forests were thinning out, and there were ample supplies of stone. The Greeks used the post-and-lintel method for supporting the roofs of their buildings, meaning, simply, that the horizontal members (beams or lintels) rested on vertical posts or columns. A series of columns placed at close intervals could support a roof of considerable weight.

Temple building: the Parthenon

The Greek temple represents the perfection of post-and-lintel construction and of the refinements of the column. The early buildings had a rather heavy appearance, as in the sixth-century temple at Paestum, Italy (FIG. *1-5*). Gradually, however, the proportions of the temple, and of the columns especially, were modified. The culmination of this process of refinement was the Parthenon of Athens (FIG. *1-6*). In this shrine of Athena a perfect balance of the elements

FIGURE 1-5. Temple of Hera at Paestum. (Alinari.)

FIGURE 1-6. The Parthenon. (George Holton, Photo Researchers.)

was achieved. The supporting columns give the feeling of strength, grace, and ease.

The exterior columns of the Parthenon, which form a continuous colonnade on all four sides of the temple, are of the Doric order. This was the earlier of the two basic styles, Doric and Ionic, that the Greeks developed. The differences lie in the shaft, base, and capital of the columns and in the entablature (horizontal structures) that they support. The Greeks later developed a third order, called Corinthian; it was the same as the Ionic except for the column capitals, which were decorated with leaves and fronds.

The floor plan of the Parthenon is simple. It divides the interior into two rectangular enclosures. The principal enclosure (cella) contained the cultic statue of the goddess and had but one portal, facing east. The smaller cella, whose portal faced west, contained the treasury of Athens. The roof of the building, which was gabled, was closed at the west and east ends by a triangular section called the pediment.

The Parthenon was designed about 450 B.C. by the architect Ictinos, as part of Pericles' plan for rebuilding the Acropolis after the Persians had destroyed the ancient wooden structures there. Though ravaged by time and war, it still embodies the Greek ideal of the Golden Mean. It is not a huge structure (one hundred by two hundred feet), but it was ideally suited to its purpose and position. The pediments and portions of the entablature were decorated with sculpture, and pastel paints were applied to add warmth and interest. The paints have long since faded, but the weathered marble now provides attractive color of its own.

The wonder of the Parthenon derives, in part, from the painstaking details of its design. Subtle curves, rather than straight lines, avoid any impression of stiffness. Each of the supporting columns, for example, consists of grooved marble drums so carefully joined that they give the appearance of a monolithic shaft. The diameter of the column diminishes gradually as it rises to its capital, in a slightly curving line (*entasis*). The Greek builders had discovered that a perfectly straight profile makes a column look too rigid. They had also found that by adjusting the spacing between columns they could enhance the visual effect of the entire structure. Hence, in the Parthenon the interval between each corner column and its adjacent columns is less than the normal interval between columns, which lends a feeling of extra support at critical points of stress. The fact that the builders went to such pains to satisfy the demands not only of engineering but of aesthetics as well is testimony to their desire for excellence.

Images of gods and men

Little has survived of Greek painting except on pottery vases. But the Greeks' passion for beauty, interest in man, and striving for the ideal are magnificently preserved in their sculpture. Only a few originals—and those in mutilated condition—have come down to us, but hundreds of copies of Greek statues, produced by the Romans, still survive. The Greek originals, or what we know of them, have served through the centuries as models for Western sculptors.

Early Greek statues reveal an Egyptian influence. The Egyptians sought solidity and permanence in their figures; they did not aim to reproduce natural appearances. This same purpose is apparent in the many statues of young men, commonly called "Apollos," that have been unearthed in Greece (FIG. *1-7*). But the Greeks grew dissatisfied with this kind of representation and turned steadily toward greater naturalism, movement, and grace in their figures. Classical sculpture found its most perfect expression during the fifth century B.C., at the time of the building of the Parthenon. The statues carved in that period were chiefly of gods and goddesses; like the deities themselves, they resembled mortals—not actual individuals, but idealized men and women.

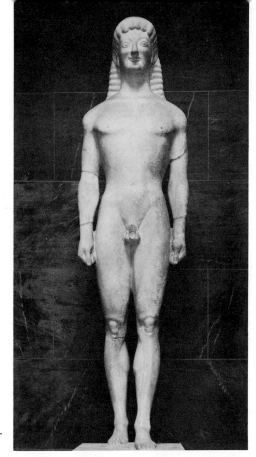

FIGURE 1-7. *Youth from Tenea. Ca.* 600 B.C. Glyptothek, Munich. (Marburg-Art Reference Bureau.)

Phidias, the most highly respected sculptor of Athens in the Age of Pericles, was put in charge of the Parthenon sculptures. It was he who carved (from wood) the gigantic statue of Athena that was placed in the main cella. Although the original was lost long ago, apparently it was richly decorated with ivory, gold, and jewels. Phidias also planned and supervised the marble carvings of the temple pediments and of the sculptured frieze (band) that ran around the outside of the cella walls. Fragments of this sculpture are still in existence, most of them in the British Museum in London. These fragments (FIG. *1-8*) show that the frieze was sculptured not "in the round" but "in relief." They form parts of a carved procession of maidens and men, some on horseback, moving toward a platform on which various deities are seated. The sense of ease and motion, the impeccable proportion and form, are evident even in these fragments.

FIGURE 1-8. *Horsemen in procession.* From western frieze of Parthenon. British Museum, London.

FIGURE 1-9. *Discus Thrower.* After Myron. Terme Museum, Rome. (Alinari.)

FIGURE 1-10. PRAXITELES. *Hermes with Infant Dionysos.* © Deutsches Archaologisches Institut, Athens.

Better known is the *Discus Thrower* by Myron, another sculptor of the time of Phidias (FIG. *1-9*). The original bronze casting has been lost, but the figure was so much admired that many marble copies were made for the Romans (by Greek artisans). In this statue, Myron chose to portray the athlete at the moment before he made his supreme effort, so that he would appear dynamically poised and in full self-control. The statue is not an accurate picture of a real discus-thrower; rather, it is an ideal representation of the male figure—a masterpiece of line and form.

After 400 B.C. Greek sculptors tended toward greater delicacy and gracefulness, producing by our standards of perception a more effeminate impression. The leading developer of this style was Praxiteles. Only one of his original statues has survived—*Hermes with the Infant Dionysos* (FIG. *1-10*). Although this figure lacks the masculine power of the *Discus Thrower*, it is a supreme expression of ease, smoothness, and relaxation. The famous *Aphrodite of Melos*, also known in modern times as the *Venus de Milo* (FIG. *1-11*), is thought to be a copy of an original from the time of Praxiteles (fourth century). For centuries this Venus stood as the model of female beauty in the West.

FIGURE 1-11. *Venus de Milo* (copy). Louvre. (Alinari.)

Along with the trend toward greater delicacy there developed an interest in portraiture, emotional expression, and representation of ordinary people—street vendors, dancers, and common soldiers. The sculptors of the fifth century had carved only gods and heroes. They had also avoided showing facial expression and, generally, any indication of pain or suffering. But with the passing of centuries exact likenesses came into vogue, and more and more statues showed intense emotion. Probably the most famous example of works of the latter kind is the marble group known as *Laocoön and His Sons* (about 50 B.C.). This group represents a Trojan priest and his young sons being crushed by two deadly serpents (FIG. *1-12*). According to

FIGURE 1-12. *Laocoön and His Sons.* Vatican Museum, Rome. (Alinari.)

legend, the gods had punished the priest in this cruel manner for having warned the Trojans not to accept a gift from the Greeks— a giant wooden horse—during the siege of Troy.

THE DECLINE OF THE GREEK CITY–STATES

Art during and after the fourth century B.C. reflected an attitude toward life that was considerably different from the attitude of Greeks during the Age of Pericles (fifth century B.C.). The change was an outgrowth of the Peloponnesian War and its consequences. The Persian Wars brought confidence and glory in their wake; the Peloponnesian War left disillusionment and decay. Most of the Greek city-states were caught up in the conflict, but the principal antagonists were Athens and Sparta. Writing as an Athenian, the historian Thucydides called it the "Peloponnesian" war, because the chief enemies of Athens were Sparta and her allied cities of the Peloponnesus (FIG. *1-2*). There had been earlier conflicts between Sparta and Athens, but the long struggle that opened in 431 B.C. and lasted until 404 B.C. ended with the final defeat of Athens.

The Peloponnesian War

The underlying cause of the Peloponnesian War, and of the interminable wars that preceded and followed it, was inherent in the Greek city-state system. Each city had its own military forces and asserted its complete independence of any higher authority. When differences developed that could not be settled by mutual agreement, either party might resort to war. Some cities managed to subdue their neighbors temporarily by force of arms, but the defeated communities refused to be absorbed and waited patiently for a chance to regain their independence. Hence the Greek world was in a constant state of war. The cities refrained from fighting one another only when it was necessary to league together against a foreign foe. It was through such a general alliance that they had met the Persian threat in the first half of the fifth century B.C.

Soon after Athens became the leader of the anti-Persian alliance in 477 B.C., the Athenians began to use that alliance for their own purposes. They sponsored the formation of the Delian League, which consisted of most of the Greek cities on the Aegean coasts and islands. Members of the league contributed money to a common treasury to pay for the construction of warships (which were placed under Athenian command). After the Persian threat had passed (445 B.C.), the member states announced that they would make no more payments. But Athens threatened to use force should they cease sending money. What had been contributions for the common defense against Persia were thereby transformed into tribute to Athens.

All Greece was aroused by the Athenians' behavior. The smaller cities appealed to the Spartans, who were themselves uneasy, to put a check on Athens. At last the Spartans decided to support Corinth, which had become involved in a naval war with Athens. The Athenians, with their league of allies (both forced and voluntary), took up the challenge.

In the course of the war (431–404 B.C.) the Athenians, at first under the wise guidance of Pericles, showed themselves superior to their foes. Their most serious reversal during the early phase of the war came not through force of arms but through disease. A terrible plague struck the city in 430 B.C., and Pericles himself was one of its victims. This misfortune weakened the Athenians and sapped their confidence, and control of the city passed into the hands of willful and reckless politicians. While the Spartans on several occasions offered terms of compromise and "peace without victory," the Athenian leaders spurned the offers and held out for absolute triumph. A major disaster befell Athens with the defeat of a naval expedition sent against Syracuse, an ally of Sparta, in 415 B.C. Even after that setback Athens won some surprising battles at sea, but her fate was sealed when Sparta secured financial aid from Persia, the common enemy of Greece. Now the Spartans were able to equip a powerful fleet, which succeeded at last in overcoming the navy of Athens. Stripped of the protection of their warships, the Athenian citizens were starved into surrender (404 B.C.). They gave up all their outlying possessions, pulled down their walls, and became forced allies of Sparta.

But Athens was not alone in defeat. The victors as well as the vanquished were critically weakened by the loss of men and resources. Greek civilization in its traditional form never recovered from the ruinous struggle, even though Athens retained its cultural leadership for another century. The pattern of Greek life, best exemplified by Athens in the Age of Pericles, could not be restored. Sparta for a while, then Thebes, tried unsuccessfully to exercise leadership and maintain order. But it was only a matter of time until the Greek cities were to fall before foreign powers (first Macedonia, then Rome) and to surrender for good their cherished independence. When the city-state lost its old meaning, the core of Greek life itself disintegrated, for the city had been the focus of the citizen's loyalty, his pride, his love. Henceforth, the individual tended to turn inward, to regard politics and civic affairs as things apart from himself and his family.

The average citizen lost faith not only in his city-state but in its religious and moral principles. Athena had failed to save the city of her name from disaster and humiliation. The Olympian gods may have defended the Greeks against the Persians, but they had not preserved them from self-destruction. And the citizens who survived found little solace—no promise of a better world to come—in their traditional religion. Many of them turned to more personal and hopeful faiths.

Disillusionment spread in other directions as well. The search for truth, the appeal to reason, and the counsel of moderation had not brought the anticipated satisfactions and happiness. Democracy itself came in for a share of blame, because the leaders of democratic Athens were held chiefly responsible for starting and prolonging the fatal war. Sparta and her league of allies, on the other hand, had leaned toward aristocracy. The military triumph of the Peloponnesians bolstered aristocratic attitudes and weakened the democratic cause throughout Greece. And in every city where democratic and aristocratic factions still vied for power, the struggle was intensified by bitter memories of social division and civic betrayal.

The rise of Macedonia

Meanwhile, to the north of the weakened city-states, a new power was rising. Macedonia was a backwater of Greek civilization, several centuries behind Athens in its cultural development. But Philip, who became king of Macedonia in 359 B.C., admired the Greeks and longed to associate himself with them. A shrewd man of broad vision, he determined to gain control of the weak and divided city-states and to lead the Greeks and the Macedonians in a united force against the weakening empire of Persia. First, he consolidated his own position in Macedonia, strengthened his army, and made careful plans for infiltrating and conquering Greece.

Philip's agents worked to prevent the city-states from joining forces against him. One eloquent Athenian, Demosthenes, recognized the peril and repeatedly warned his fellow citizens. But the traditional reluctance of the city-states to work together, combined with their failure to take the new menace seriously, played into Philip's hands. At last he was ready to move. Through diplomacy, intrigue, and military pressure, Philip thrust into northern and central Greece. The Athenians, aroused at last, formed an alliance with the Thebans in an attempt to stop him. But it was too late. At the Battle of Chaeronea (338 B.C.) the Macedonians won a decisive victory. What remained of Greek independence was lost; the land and culture of Hellas lay open to Philip.

The Macedonian king, a barbarian by Greek standards, used his new-won power wisely. After advancing into the Peloponnesus, he established himself as president of a league of Greek states. He treated the Greek cities considerately and left them autonomous except in the conduct of foreign affairs. Philip, now at the head of a formidable alliance, promised to avenge the ancient insults and damages visited on the Greeks by invading Persians. But as he stood at the very brink of fulfillment, Philip was assassinated in 336 B.C. His son, Alexander, only twenty years old, succeeded him. This inexperienced youth seemed unequal to the task of carrying out his father's grand design.

ALEXANDER THE GREAT
AND THE WIDER SPREAD
OF GREEK CULTURE

Those who knew the young Alexander—men like his one-time tutor, Aristotle—were not surprised by his display of authority and determination. He first dealt with disturbances in Macedonia and Greece that had broken out after his father's death and then crossed into Asia Minor (334 B.C.) and launched the campaign that was to make him the greatest conqueror in history. True, the Persian empire had declined in military power, but Alexander's daring and generalship proved successful beyond anyone's expectation. His small but well-disciplined army, consisting of about thirty-five thousand Greeks and Macedonians, broke the power of the Persian king within four years. Asia Minor, Syria, Egypt, and Mesopotamia fell before him (FIG. *1-1*). Pushing on through Persia to the frontiers of India, he was checked only by the grumbling and protests of his own men. At the age of thirty-three, Alexander died of a fever in the city of Babylon, which he had chosen for his imperial capital.

Alexander's dream of one world

Although Alexander left no adult son to succeed him, he had established certain principles of government for his new "world-state." He hoped that his conquests would lead to an ultimate fusion of East and West and put an end to the struggle that had started two centuries earlier with the clash between Persians and Greeks. Though he believed in the superiority of Greek culture, Alexander had no intention of destroying the culture of the East. Rather, he had hoped to fuse the best features of each civilization into a new culture. To achieve this end he had founded cities in the regions he conquered. Their military garrisons would serve to maintain order in the surrounding countryside, and the cities themselves would serve as cultural "melting pots." He made Greek the official language and distributed Greek books and works of art throughout his empire; he hoped by these means to spread Hellenic ideas and standards, at least as a veneer, over the oriental pattern of life. He encouraged intermarriage and led the way himself by marrying a daughter of the Persian king. But there were not enough Greeks to go around! The hoped-for fusion of cultures never became more than an imperfect mixture, and the ways of the East persisted substantially as in the past.

Alexander's "one world" was divided after his death among his top generals. After a succession of dynastic conflicts, three major states emerged from Alexander's conquests and survived until the Romans took over the eastern Mediterranean. These states were based, respectively, on Macedonia, Egypt, and the remains of the Persian empire in western Asia.

Although Alexander's dream was never fulfilled, it had a profound effect on the development of the West. The culture of Greece, which had formerly been limited to the Aegean area, was broadcast throughout the entire Near East. Since Athens and the other centers of Hellenic culture were to be overrun again and again by invaders in the centuries ahead, most Greek works of art and literature would probably have been lost forever had it not been for the wide diffusion that Alexander made possible. The Greek legacy was passed on to the West, not by the city-states of Hellas, but by the libraries and museums of the Alexandrian world.

The Hellenistic states

The mixed culture that emerged in the Near East was, of course, markedly different from the culture that had flourished in Athens in the Age of Pericles. To describe this fusion of Greek ways with oriental ways, historians have invented the term "Hellenistic." The term suggests that the culture was "Greekish"—not wholly Greek. And the political forms of the Hellenistic world were actually more oriental than Greek. After Alexander, the independent city-state became virtually extinct, for now men were thinking in terms of a much larger unit of power—the great state, or empire—and of loyalty to a personal ruler, not to a community. Democracy, that remarkable Greek achievement, was submerged in the new order of things. Absolute rule by divine-right monarchs, a concept that was sanctioned by the traditions of the Orient, was accepted as the only effective means of governing large domains. Alexander's vision of a unified world-state and culture lived after him and served as a model for later conquerors and statesmen of the West—for Caesar, Charlemagne, Napoleon.

The economy of the Hellenistic age was also markedly different from that of earlier times. The new and more extensive political units encouraged large-scale production and trade. The Greeks had carried on a far-flung commerce, ranging from the Black Sea to Gibraltar, but now the gates were opened eastward—as far as India. The vast new market stimulated enterprise: huge fortunes were made, banking and finance were expanded, and a thriving capitalism was established. The heads of the great states took a keen interest in business affairs. They promoted commerce by aiding navigation and transport, and their expenditures were more than recouped through taxation of enterprises. The Ptolemies, rulers of Egypt, also set up hundreds of state-owned factories and shops for the direct support of their dynasty.

Although wages and general living standards remained low, the growth of industry and trade created many new jobs in the cities. As a result, thousands of peasants moved from the countryside into the urban centers of the Near East. The typical Greek city-state had been a community of perhaps five or ten thousand citizens, but the metropolis now became the central unit of social organization. Many large cities grew up around the centers Alexander had tried to establish. The greatest and most renowned was Alexandria, which he had founded at the mouth of the Nile, in Egypt. Its population may have approached a million by the time of Christ, and it rivaled imperial Rome in size and magnificence. Alexandria was the economic and cultural hub of the eastern Mediterranean; for centuries its marvelous library and museums were centers of scholarship and scientific study.

When the Romans conquered the Hellenistic states (in the second and first centuries B.C.), they recognized the richness and sophistication of these cities. Here they found the culture—the philosophy, literature, and art—that they were to absorb and pass on to western Europe. The Hellenistic world submitted to the Romans and paid tribute to them, but it was otherwise little affected by the conquest. It remained a distinct cultural section of the Roman Empire; and after the empire began to break apart (fourth century A.D.), the Hellenistic portion continued for many centuries as an area of prosperity and advanced civilization.

The Roman Triumph and Fall

2

As the Greeks were the most brilliant originators of Western civilization, the Romans were the most notable organizers and preservers. By force of arms and statesmanship, the Romans linked the proud cultures of the Hellenistic East with the less sophisticated cultures of the western Mediterranean. Embracing Alexander's dream as their legacy, they made the idea of "one world" a reality.

THE RISE OF ROME

The question of why Rome "fell" has intrigued scholars for centuries. But an even more fascinating question is how Rome rose from the status of a small Italian city-state to become master of the world. Athens and Sparta had failed to maintain power in the limited area of the Aegean, and Alexander's conquests fell into pieces soon after his death. But Rome built an enduring order of astonishing dimensions. How did the Romans achieve what had never been done before and has not been equaled since?

Italy and its peoples

While the Dorian Greeks (p. 8) were moving down into the Aegean basin, tribes speaking another Indo-European dialect were making their way into central Italy. There they mingled with earlier settlers to form the Latin stock. Around 1000 B.C. some of them settled by a ford in the Tiber River (FIG. 2-1). At first only a cluster of huts built on low-lying hills along the river—the famed Seven Hills of Rome—this crude settlement was destined to grow into a great city-state. By 500 B.C. Rome had emerged as the chief power of the surrounding area of Latium.

The resources of the Italian peninsula, though not rich, are superior to those of Greece. Most of the land is mountainous, with the Apennines forming a spiny barrier from the Po Valley in the north to the very toe of the Italian boot. But there are extensive

FIGURE 2-1

ROME IN ITALY

Roman territory about 325 B.C.

Territory controlled by Rome at the start of the second Punic War, 218 B.C.

0   MILES   150

pasture lands and fields, and the peoples who settled this country were self-sufficient from the very first.

Rome itself was strategically situated on the peninsula. Lying fourteen miles from the sea, the city was fairly easy to defend, and it was even better adapted to offense, for it controlled the principal routes of travel. The Italian peninsula itself was to serve later as a superb base for Rome's far-ranging conquests. Astride the Mediterranean, it commanded east and west, north and south.

The Romans did not have the peninsula to themselves, however. Early in the fifth century barbarian Gauls invaded the Po Valley; later, around 390 B.C., they moved southward and burned the city of Rome. More important were the Etruscans and Greeks, both latecomers to Italy (FIG. *2-1*). The Etruscans, whose background is mysterious, apparently arrived about the ninth century B.C. After seizing control of the north-central portion of the country in the seventh century B.C., they struck out in all directions.

They conquered Latium, and for a time their kings ruled Rome itself. Around 500 B.C. the Etruscans were ejected from Rome by an uprising. Their power was short-lived, because they failed to conciliate or assimilate the people they conquered. But they carried with them a superior, urban culture that was readily absorbed by the Romans. From the Etruscans the Romans learned a great deal about war, politics, religion, and agriculture, and adopted such specific features as a street plan for cities, the insignia of authority (fasces), the triumphal procession, the gladiatorial combat, and the masonry arch.

The Romans also borrowed freely from the Greeks. As early as the eighth century B.C. the city-states of Hellas had begun to plant colonies in southern Italy, where the heel of the Italian boot lies only fifty miles from the Greek coast. So extensive was this colonization that the Romans, like the Greeks before them, came to call Italy and Sicily "Great Greece" (*Magna Graecia*). Among the earliest settlements were Cumae, Naples, Tarentum, and Syracuse (in Sicily). From Cumae the Latins first learned the alphabet and something of the Olympian gods. And in dealing with the Greek colonies they came into direct contact with the civilized life of the Greek city-state. The Romans, realizing that this civilization was more advanced than their own, gradually absorbed Greek ideas and arts into their own culture.

The government of the early republic

Under the cultural tutelage of the Etruscans and the Greeks, the Romans acquired the skills that enabled them to build their unique political institutions. For several centuries they were governed by kings whose authority resembled that of the rulers of Homeric Greece. The king served as high priest of the state religion, military commander, supreme judge, and chief executive. He was advised by a council of elders (the Senate) composed of the heads of the leading families (the patricians). When a king died, his successor was chosen by the Senate from among its own members, subject to approval by the popular assembly of citizens.

Around 500 B.C., when the Etruscans were expelled and the monarchy was abolished, executive power was transferred to two chief magistrates (consuls), elected annually by the assembly. The Romans created this plural executive as a guard against tyranny, and they empowered each consul to veto any action proposed by the other. This was not an unprecedented arrangement, for the conservative Spartans had always reposed power in two kings. But the Romans extended this practice by appointing two or more men to all the important offices of the republic (*res publica,* or commonwealth). Those who shared a given office were required to act in concert. This principle of divided responsibility, or administration by checks and balances, proved a two-edged sword. It guarded against hasty action and undue concentration of power, but it sometimes led to costly delays, even paralysis. To correct this weakness the republic permitted the appointment of a "dictator" in time of emergency. The dictator was chosen by the consuls with the advice of the Senate, and his term was limited to six months.

The evolution of government under the republic reflected the serious social struggle that was taking place among the Romans. On the one side were the upper-class citizens, the patricians, who belonged to the oldest and noblest Roman families and who alone could perform the religious rituals on which the safety of all depended. These families could be traced back, through the male line, to the earliest leaders of the community—to the military chieftains and the wealthy owners of land and flocks. On the other side were the common citizens, the plebeians, whose origins are not entirely clear. They appear to have been subject to the patricians, in varying degree, from the very beginning. Some may have been descendants of the earlier native population that had been suppressed by the invaders in the dim past. Some had fallen into dependency because of debts, while others had come, no doubt, as fugitives and immigrants from surrounding cities.

By 500 B.C. the line between these classes had become sharply drawn. The patricians, though they made up only a tiny fraction of the total citizenry, dominated Roman politics. The popular assembly, which included the plebeians, held the powers of ratifying laws and electing public officials; but officials could be named only from the patrician class, and they were obliged to act under senatorial guidance. The Senate consisted of a fixed number (about 300) of the heads of patrician families; senators were appointed for life by the consuls.

The plebeians, who felt that they were being treated as second-class citizens, were determined to win equal rights. They resorted to various means of putting pressure on the patricians—including acts of passive resistance and threats to secede and start a rival settlement. Since they managed, however, to stay within the bounds of law and order, the republic was not subverted.

Among the chief complaints of the plebeians was that they lacked legal protection. Before the fifth century B.C. there had been no written code of law to which an accused person could turn for guidance or defense. The sacred traditional laws were interpreted by judges, who were of course patricians. Understandably, the plebeians protested that they were not receiving equal treatment in the courts. About 450 B.C., in response to their demand, the laws of Rome were set down in writing. The new code was engraved on twelve bronze tablets and mounted in the Forum for all to see. These Twelve Tablets defined private and public rights and penalties and served as the foundation for the elaborate system of Roman law that grew up in the centuries to come.

The plebeians also demanded admission to the major public offices (magistracies), especially the consulship. Although the patricians firmly resisted this demand, they did agree to let the plebeians elect officials of their own, called tribunes. Immune from interference when in the pursuit of their duties, the tribunes had power to protect any citizen who they thought was being wronged by a patrician magistrate. Later, they acquired the right to initiate laws in the popular assembly.

This compromise, like others that gradually admitted the plebeians to greater power, was characteristic of the Roman approach to politics. Instead of abolishing or radically altering an old institution, the Romans preferred to install a counterweight. This habit exasperates modern political scientists who try to analyze precisely how the republic worked, but the Romans themselves were little disturbed by the welter of checks and balances, the contradictions between political form and reality, and the unplanned accretion of offices. They had a lingering affection for traditional ways, and their system showed a flexibility and resilience often lacking in more logical political structures.

By 250 B.C., the plebeians had won the main objectives in their contest with the patricians: eligibility for *all* public offices, the right to marry into the patrician class, and admission to the Senate itself. These changes did not bring about democracy, however. Control of the republic still rested in the hands of the Senate, which was now an aristocracy of wealth. After the third century B.C. senators were appointed from the list of ex-consuls, and politicians could win a consulship only after they had been elected to a succession of lesser offices. Campaigning was expensive, and the elective offices paid no salary. So only the well-to-do could afford to work their way up to the Senate.

Those who did reach the top sat in the seats of the mighty, for the Senate was a permanent body of enormous prestige and influence. The consuls, tribunes, praetors (judges), and other officials were elected by the popular assembly for one-year terms. But they looked to the Senate for guidance. And they hoped that they themselves might one day be admitted to that august body.

In conducting the endless wars that Rome waged during these centuries, the Senate earned a reputation as a "council of kings." The senators possessed tested political experience and wisdom, and they demonstrated a patience, canniness, and will that carried Rome to victory over a succession of powerful foes. They set long-range policies and made immediate decisions on pressing matters. They appointed and instructed the military chiefs of the republic, received foreign emissaries, and concluded treaties. They supervised finances and investigated high crimes. The powers of the Senate grew not so much by legal enactment or decree as by assumption and consent. The magistrates and popular assemblies (a second assembly had been set up in the fifth century B.C. to express the plebeians' will more fully) continued to perform their duties, but the Senate was the balance-wheel in the complex mechanism of the state. Until the closing century of the republic, it governed both firmly and well.

Roman expansion

The Romans were, above all, a military people—patriotic farmer-soldiers. The first campaigns that we know much about were essentially defensive—against the Etruscans, Gauls, Greeks, and competing Italic tribes. Then, as the Romans secured their position at home, they began to reach out for territories and allies. Along the way they encountered ever more enemies, for across each new frontier stood a new danger. The Romans, of course, lost as well as won battles, but they invariably won the war.

In addition to the toughness of its soldier-citizens and the shrewdness of its Senate, Rome had a superior military organization. Its manpower was based on conscription—all male citizens were liable for either field or garrison duty. At first they served without compensation, usually for short periods. Later, the state began to pay them in order to permit longer campaigns and better training, and a professional corps ultimately replaced the citizen army.

The Roman army was made up of legions, whose organization and tactics were an innovation in the Mediterranean world. Each legion consisted of some four thousand infantrymen organized in maneuverable units of about a hundred men (centuries). The soldiers and the rugged centurions who led them carried light armor, helmet, and shield. For weapons they had a short sword, lance, and javelin. But what most distinguished the Roman army was its iron discipline. Penalties for cowardice or dereliction of duty were severe and cruel; on the other hand, there were generous rewards and promotions for the brave and the victorious.

The Romans applied this same incentive-deterrent system to the peoples they conquered in war. They avoided the mistake of treating all their vanquished foes alike, for they found it more profitable to convert their former enemies into friends and allies than to make them permanent slaves. The rule of conquest, booty, and massacre that had prevailed generally in the ancient world was supplanted by a new formula: in exchange for cooperation, the Romans offered protection and self-rule. Those who remained loyal and contributed most were given the highest privileges; those who wavered or deserted were punished or destroyed.

The new conquerors refrained from interfering with local laws, religion, and customs, insisting only that the defeated communities submit to Rome's direction of external relations and provide troops for the Roman forces. They tightened their control over the Italian peninsula by creating a network of colonies in which the settlers enjoyed political rights almost equal to those of Roman citizens. These colonies served both as garrisons and as working models of Roman civic organization.

Roman methods of conquest and administration were shrewd, flexible, and judicious. They paid handsome dividends, for by 250 B.C. all of Italy south of the Po Valley was in Roman hands. The City of the Seven Hills had compounded its resources until they included the peninsula and most of its peoples. The conquered, too, began to appreciate the advantages of Roman rule. In place of bloody anarchy, the victors brought peace, order, roads, and prosperity. It was this principle of two-way benefit that the Romans would extend, step by step, to the whole Mediterranean world. The army was the foundation of Roman power; but the conquered domains were cemented to Rome by *mutual* interest and service.

No sooner had the Romans secured their position on the peninsula than they were challenged by a major power beyond the sea. That power was Carthage, a rich empire with its capital on the north coast of Africa. The city had been founded about 700 B.C. by colonists from Phoenicia (modern Lebanon), a trading folk of Semitic origin who had built up a thriving commercial civilization. Organized as an aristocratic republic similar in form to Rome, Carthage spread its influence across North Africa, southern Spain, Sardinia, Corsica, and Sicily. It was the Carthaginians' interest in Sicily, lying between Africa and Italy, that brought them into conflict with the Romans. The Greek city-states of the south had for centuries been struggling with Carthage for control of the island, and the Romans had inherited the struggle when they assumed responsibility for protecting their Greek allies. Thus began the fateful Punic Wars (264 B.C.–146 B.C.), which catapulted Rome into the position of a "world" power. (The term "Punic" derives from Poeni, the Roman name for the Carthaginians.)

After some opening skirmishes between Rome and Carthage, it became clear that more was at stake than the harbors and hills of Sicily. These two proud and aggressive antagonists were vying for command of the whole western Mediterranean. The struggle was fought on land and sea in three vicious rounds, but Rome's system of alliances proved strong enough to meet the test. The loyalty of the Romans' allies and the perseverance of their own forces enabled them to triumph over the formidable Carthaginians. In a final act of vengeance, the victorious Roman general razed to the ground the city of Carthage, solemnly condemned it to permanent desolation, and sold the survivors into slavery.

The former possessions of Carthage became the first Roman provinces (Sicily, Spain, Africa). These administrative units did not enjoy the status of Rome's allies in Italy; instead, they were ruled as conquered lands by senatorial appointees (proconsuls). They paid tribute to the Roman state and provided opportunities for influential Roman citizens to build up private fortunes. (It was not until the time of Augustus, after 27 B.C., that the provinces began to share the benefits of Roman order.)

The conquerors found their new wealth and power very much to their liking. Even before the defeat of Carthage venturesome Romans were looking eastward for new areas to exploit. The prospect in that direction was promising, for the Hellenistic world was in ferment.

Rome's first involvement was in Greece, and it grew out of a special invitation. Around 200 B.C. ambassadors from various Greek city-states appealed to Rome for aid in resisting the king of Macedonia, who had been in league with Carthage. Moved by admiration for Hellenic culture, as well as by grosser motives, the Romans obliged by sending an army. Their professed aim was to secure the liberties of the proud and quarrelsome Greek cities and then withdraw. But they soon became entangled in the politics and conflicts of the Near East. In the course of endless maneuvering and fighting, the Romans carved one province after another out of the Hellenistic kingdoms, until, by the time of Christ, they were supreme in the eastern Mediterranean. From Gibraltar to Suez fell the shadow of mighty Rome.

THE OVERTHROW OF THE REPUBLIC

Rome's triumphs abroad had a profound effect on society at home. In former days, the farmer-soldier had been the backbone of the state. But the social and economic revolution that followed the Punic Wars and Rome's adventures in the East changed all this.

The impact of war and conquest

During one phase of the Punic Wars the Carthaginian general Hannibal had marched up and down the Italian peninsula for years. Thousands of Roman farmers had been slain and their fields ravaged. And then, after Hannibal's defeat, new calls were made on the farmer-soldiers to serve in Greece and Asia. Many never came back; those who did often found their farms spoiled by neglect. Some farmers remained stubbornly on their land, but most gave up and drifted into the cities, especially Rome. There they became dependents (clients) of the well-to-do and began to look to the politicians for security and amusement.

While the small, independent farmers were disappearing, a new social class was rising to prominence in Italy. It consisted of war profiteers of various sorts—contractors to the armed forces and dealers in booty. They used their wealth to buy up the ruined farms, restocked them, and turned them to new purposes. The small plots on which the independent farmer had raised grain were now merged into large tracts of pasture land, vineyards, or olive groves. The new owners, who operated their holdings as capitalistic enterprises, had little interest in the displaced farmers either as tenants or as hired hands. Most of the labor was now performed by slaves, who had become plentiful and cheap as a result of Rome's conquests overseas.

By 150 B.C. the social composition of Rome and the peninsula as a whole had undergone a drastic change. The important element of farmer-citizens had withered away; at the same time there had appeared the new capitalist class, a growing population of urban poor, and increasing numbers of slaves. The senatorial class, which had guided Rome through its long wars, still held power. But insidious forces were at work to pervert the character of this ruling aristocracy.

From the early days of the republic the noble families of Rome had valued honesty, simplicity, and high-mindedness. But few could resist the lure of the riches that now poured into Rome from across the seas. Senators were required by law to hold most of their property in land and were forbidden to engage in business. Many of them, however, found ways of sharing in the new opportunities for profit—especially those who secured appointments as provincial administrators. Gradually the old republican virtues were eroded by the temptations of affluence. Austerity and rectitude gave way to indulgence and corruption.

The failure of virtue at the top was in time communicated to the rank and file of the population. Patriotism and respect for law and order declined among civilians, and to the soldiers discipline and bravery now seemed less compelling than the chance for promotion and spoils. Polybius, a Greek scholar who wrote around 150 B.C., had foreseen this general decline. Carried to Italy as a hostage after a Roman campaign in the East, he had been freed by his captors to write a history of their conquests. He wrote a fair-minded account, in which he analyzed the factors underlying Roman success. But he warned that the fruits of victory would lead to the deterioration of the republic.

One result of the deterioration was a worsening of Rome's relations with its provinces and its Italian allies. Until the Punic Wars, Rome had enjoyed a reputation for judicious treatment of conquered foes. But during the final century of the republic (150 B.C.– 50 B.C.) its allies complained of unfair dealings, and the provincials cried out against Roman plunder.

Thus began the republic's time of troubles. Some Roman moralists held that the growing influence of Greek attitudes and ideas was responsible for Rome's plight. But this influence was probably of minor significance. The fact is that the Romans had become subject to powerful new forces within themselves; their change in moral outlook was a direct consequence of their rise to imperial fortune.

The republic paid for this fortune with its life, for the new wealth, corruption, and acquisitiveness upset the political balance of Roman society. Had the Senate been able to meet the host of problems that came crowding in on Rome, its position could have remained secure. But the senators, absorbed in the pursuit of personal gain and privilege, proved unequal to the broader challenges of their times. New leaders, meanwhile, contemptuous of ancient traditions, were seeking to enlarge their own influence. In so doing they ran into fierce opposition from the senatorial class, and civil strife ensued. As one legal procedure after another was violated, the life of the republic degenerated into a contest for personal power. It became clear, at last, that the old political arrangements were hopelessly obsolete; only a major revolution could save Rome from collapse.

The first sign of political breakdown had appeared in the latter part of the second century B.C. Tiberius and Gaius Gracchus (the Gracchi), sons of a patrician family, thought that a partial solution to Rome's troubles would be to resettle the city's poor on small farms and to provide a subsidy of grain for those who remained in Rome. Such a program, they hoped, would restore the independent farmers and reduce the gap between rich and poor. Though unable to win Senate support for these measures, the Gracchi proposed them directly to the popular assembly. Tiberius, who was elected tribune of the people in 133 B.C., initiated the reform effort. But the office of tribune, limited by tradition to a one-year term, allowed him insufficient time to carry through his long-range program. Moreover, the Senate attacked him as a demogogic threat. Tiberius decided to break tradition and stand for reelection as a tribune; in so doing he gave the aristocracy an excuse to instigate and condone his murder. His younger brother, Gaius, carried forward the reform crusade; he too fell under attack by the Senate and met a violent death (121 B.C.).

In a sense the Gracchi were reactionaries, for their reforms would have turned back the clock of Roman history. And even if they had succeeded, they would have corrected only part of the republic's difficulties. Actually, they set in motion a chain of events that was to destroy respect for legality, lead to the rise of standing armies and class war, and culminate in the overturn of the republic itself.

The turn to monarchy: Julius Caesar

The agent of the final collapse was Julius Caesar. Of an old patrician family, he had entered the city's politics as a young man. His early ambitions were doubtless for personal fame and power, but as he grew in maturity and experience he also came to identify Rome's key problems both at home and abroad. In the class struggles he sided with the poor and used his influence with them to advance his own cause. By 59 B.C., when he was first elected consul, he had begun to evolve grandiose schemes for his future. In view of the ineptitude of the Senate and the endless intrigues among the members of the governing class (of which he too was a member), he decided that the only way to bring about the reforms Rome so desperately needed was to gain absolute power. Thus he might fulfill both his personal aspirations and his reform ideals.

His opportunity came in 58 B.C., when he won an appointment as proconsul in Gaul. Now he had a military command, which was indispensable to the building of personal influence. For eight years he remained in Gaul, reducing the inhabitants to obedience and laying the foundations for the spread of Roman culture. His brilliant campaigns ranged from the Alps to the Rhine and into Britain. By 50 B.C. he had built a powerful army that was personally devoted to him; he was ready to challenge the Senate and its partisans.

When Caesar was recalled from Gaul by the senators, he decided to return with his army. This was contrary to law. As he crossed the River Rubicon, the southern boundary of Gaul, he declared fatefully, "The die is cast." A rival general, Pompey, was hastily commissioned to defend the Senate, but his forces proved no match for the veterans of Gaul. Forced to flee from Italy, Pompey was later defeated by Caesar in Greece. After subduing his opponents in various other provinces, Caesar returned to Rome in triumph in 46 B.C. The Senate, which had once branded him an outlaw, now hailed him as the "father of his country."

Caesar moved swiftly to consolidate his position and launch his program of reform. Publicly he rejected the offer of a royal crown, but by devious means he gathered to himself the authority of a monarch. He assumed the republican office of consul, then that of dictator (for life). He had himself appointed to the offices of tribune, censor, and pontifex maximus (chief priest of the state religion). He altered the functions of most of the republican institutions, though he was careful to preserve their form. The popular assembly, for example, continued to exist, but under Caesar it did little more than endorse his proposals. He showed his respects to the Senate but treated it as a mere advisory body.

Caesar used his new powers to attack the grave problems facing Rome. He revived the agrarian program of the Gracchi by resettling war veterans on farm lands in Italy and the provinces. He extended Roman citizenship to portions of Gaul and Spain, appointed provincials to the Senate, and tried to make Romans more conscious of the world beyond Italy. By reducing the barriers between the city and the provinces, he initiated the historic union of Rome and her dominions in a single commonwealth.

Romans at home and abroad applauded the deeds of Caesar. He gave them splendid public buildings and roads and introduced reforms into every department of administration. The Senate, now augmented by his own appointees, paid him noble compliments and vowed to risk death in defense of his person. But there remained a stubborn core of older members who were irked by Caesar's successes. Their personal prestige and privilege had been diminished, and they saw Caesar as a threat to the republic.

Caesar himself grew ever more imperious in manner. He permitted a religious cult to be established in his honor and wore the purple robe of the ancient kings. These acts were in defiance of republican tradition, and the die-hard aristocrats found them intolerable. At last, some sixty of his enemies entered into a conspiracy to assassinate him when he visited the Senate House on the Ides of March (March 15), 44 B.C. In spite of urgent warnings, Caesar appeared, unarmed and unguarded, according to his custom. The conspirators, crying "Tyrant!", struck him down with their daggers.

The murder of Caesar did not restore the republic. It served only to disrupt political reconstruction and to throw Rome again into civil disorder. Cassius and Brutus, the ringleaders of the senatorial plot, spoke of themselves as liberators; but the populace and the army, urged on by Caesar's fellow consul, Mark Antony, turned against them. Antony was soon joined by the youthful Octavian, Caesar's grandnephew and adopted heir. The senatorial forces were defeated in battle, and Octavian and Antony for a short while held the Roman world between them. Their partnership soon turned to hostility, however, and, after a decisive naval engagement near Actium (in Greece) in 31 B.C., Octavian emerged as sole master.

THE IMPERIAL FOUNDATIONS

Octavian completed the reforms and reconstruction begun by Caesar. Familiar with civil strife from an early age, he matured rapidly into a shrewd and subtle statesman. Once in sole command, Octavian set about advancing the new order at home and abroad. Soon after his triumph at Actium, the Senate conferred upon the young man the title of "augustus" (revered), which had formerly been reserved to the gods. The main lines of the "Augustan settlement" had emerged by 27 B.C., the year generally accepted as the beginning of the Roman Empire.

We should notice that the word "empire" may be used in two senses. It can mean the dominion of one state over others; in this sense, the Roman Republic exercised imperial power as early as 250 B.C. (by which time it had established control over the Italian peninsula). In its second sense, the word "empire" means a form of internal government in which supreme authority is vested in a single ruler. After Caesar's overthrow of the republic, Rome became an empire in *both* senses. Augustus developed and refined the new institutional arrangements, which worked satisfactorily until 180 A.D. After that, when the government fell into less competent hands, the Roman Empire entered a period of civil war and near-anarchy.

The Augustan political settlement

Though Augustus completed the founding of the Roman Empire (in *fact*), he took pains to deny it. He recognized that sentiment for the republic persisted, especially in high places, and he chose to utilize that sentiment rather than resist it. He also knew that Rome and her subjects were eager for peace—for an end to the violent conflicts of rival factions. He could have ruled, as others had before, by military force alone. Instead, having employed ruthless means to secure power, he chose to use that power to establish a peaceful world of "law and justice." The Roman citizens, for their part, recalling the fate of Caesar and the shameful disorders that followed his death, felt that the time had come for tolerance and compromise rather than defiance and conspiracy.

After celebrating his military triumphs in traditional style, Augustus announced that his aim was to restore peace and the republic. He refused the offer of regal honors and referred to himself simply as "princeps" (first citizen). By arrangement with the Senate in 27 B.C., Augustus accepted election or appointment to the principal republican offices (including consul, censor, and pontifex maximus). In return, he permitted the Senate to supervise Italy and the city of Rome and to administer certain provinces. He kept for himself control of the major provinces and continued as commander in chief (imperator) of the armed forces. Every soldier swore obedience to Augustus personally and looked to him for pay and maintenance.

Augustus kept all his arrangements flexible, but no one doubted where the real authority lay. By cloaking his authority in traditional trappings, he gained the backing of conservatives, thereby strengthening his power and reducing the danger of assassination. His prudence brought genuine harmony to Rome. After removing hostile aristocrats from the Senate, Augustus consulted it frequently and treated it generously. The popular assembly, meanwhile, faded into oblivion. In contrast to the royal manner affected by Caesar, Augustus wore the toga and insignia of a consul and lived like any other wealthy patrician. Although he was essentially an innovator bent on creating a new world order, in his own time Augustus was known as a divine restorer and preserver of the republican tradition.

Augustus strove for peace throughout the empire as well as for harmony at home. He halted the continual advancement of Rome's frontiers, the lengthening of lines of military supply, and the mounting burden of arms expenditure. Up to this time, no one had given serious thought to fixing the boundaries of the empire. Augustus marked defense lines that could readily be held and then deployed adequate forces to man them. He wanted the army to serve no longer as a vehicle of personal adventure and exploitation; he limited its role to keeping the Roman Peace (Pax Romana).

Reforms and reconstruction

After his victory over Mark Antony, Augustus found himself in command of some sixty legions (about three hundred thousand men). These soldiers were professional volunteers recruited chiefly from the lower classes of society. They had fought for one commander after another during the death throes of the republic and had developed a taste for spoils and political influence. In short, they were a potential danger to peace and order. Augustus quickly cut the troop strength in half. He provided pensions for the discharged men and left the rest on a volunteer basis, with fixed rates of pay and long terms of service. In addition to the regular legions, which he stationed on the frontiers, Augustus created an elite corps (the Praetorian Guard) to protect himself and the city of Rome. Although this privileged corps gave loyal support to Augustus' immediate successors, it later discovered that it possessed the power to make and unmake rulers.

One of Augustus' aims was to bring just administration to the empire's far-flung territories. During the days of the republic, as we have seen, the provinces had suffered under grasping governors and dishonest officials, when, with only token supervision from Rome, the provincial administrators had amassed private fortunes at the expense of the people they governed. Caesar had made a start at correcting this injustice; Augustus instituted a whole series of carefully devised reforms.

First, in appointing governors for the imperial provinces, Augustus chose men of demonstrated ability and loyalty and paid them ample salaries. Second, he entrusted imperial administration more and more to career bureaucrats rather than to political appointees. Third, in order to make tax assessments more equitable, Augustus ordered a census of the provinces at regular intervals. (This census is referred to in the Gospel of Luke [2:1]: "In those days a decree went out from Caesar Augustus that all the world should be enrolled.") And he sent inspectors to make sure that the tax-collectors were behaving honestly.

During the course of numerous personal tours of the provinces, Augustus showed his respect for existing institutions and encouraged the provincials to exercise their political responsibilities. Control over the affairs of the empire as a whole he kept in Rome, but control over local affairs he left to the provinces themselves. Finally, he strengthened the economy of the empire by driving the brigands and pirates from the seas, by building new roads, and by extending the postal service.

It is hardly surprising that Augustus was revered in Rome and worshiped in the provinces. In the East especially, people were soon looking upon him as a divine being. Tradition had long accustomed them to worship demigods and god-kings, such as the Egyptian pharaohs and the Greek Alexander; Augustus was quickly given a place among the countless deities of the Hellenistic world. Temples were built in his honor, and cults of worship sprang up throughout the Eastern provinces. Augustus sanctioned these cults and promoted their spread to the Western provinces. Emperor-worship was thus established as part of the state religion. Whatever Augustus himself may have thought about his divinity, he realized that this strong religious sentiment would foster loyalty and unity throughout the empire. Veneration of the emperor subsequently became a symbol of civic respect and obedience, and those who refused to bow before the imperial statues were suspected of treason.

Augustus also tried to restore the ancient Roman virtues, which, as we have seen, had been corroded by the spoils of conquest. Through personal example he strove to guide the Romans back to the virtuous paths of the old republic. He had strict laws passed on personal behavior, on adultery and divorce, and he encouraged poets to extol high-mindedness, noble conduct, and love of country.

In these efforts, however, Augustus was less successful than in his other undertakings.

THE APPROACH TO ONE WORLD: PAX ROMANA

The very success of the reforms introduced by Augustus raised in men's minds an ominous question: Who would take his place when he died? The simplest solution would have been for Augustus to establish a family dynasty based on hereditary succession. But it was the suspicion that Caesar was plotting just such a scheme that had led to his assassination. Augustus disavowed any dynastic ambitions, insisting that his sole aim was to restore the republic. This meant that legally and constitutionally he held his immense powers simply as a gift of the Senate.

The lack of a definite arrangement for orderly succession was a serious flaw in the Augustan settlement. The problem grew out of the contradiction between the *fact* of monarchy under Augustus and the *form* of the republic through which it operated. Theoretically, when the princeps died, power would revert to the Senate until that body named his successor; during the interregnum, the door might well be opened to civil strife. Augustus was able to provide only for his immediate heir. He brought his stepson, Tiberius, into the government and appointed him to a series of important public offices. He trusted that the Senate, after his death, would respect his intention and proclaim Tiberius as his successor. When Augustus died in 14 A.D., the Senate declared Tiberius the new princeps, and he assumed full authority without challenge.

Most of the emperors who succeeded Tiberius during the first century A.D. were designated in a similar manner. The rulers of the second century, in contrast, preferred to pick successors from outside their own families, presumably on the basis of merit alone. Each of these men, by "adoption and designation," became a junior colleague of the ruler during his lifetime and took full charge when he died. The custom never became formally incorporated into law, however, and the choices of later emperors (of the third and fourth centuries) were often ignored after their deaths. Perhaps no single factor contributed more to the ultimate downfall of the Roman Empire than the absence of a sound and accepted rule of succession.

And yet the administration of the empire continued to run smoothly for nearly two centuries after Augustus. Even when the capital at Rome was torn by intrigue and violence, life in the provinces remained relatively serene. The governing structure that Augustus had built proved remarkably stable, and a growing class of career bureaucrats, in partnership with local agencies of self-government, tended to the daily business of empire.

The empire: extent and composition

The empire reached its greatest extent during the second century A.D. (FIG. 2-2). Actually, the area under continuous control was limited by the natural frontiers Augustus had chosen: the African desert to the south, the Atlantic Ocean to the west, and the Rhine-Danube line to the north. To the east, where there were no natural barriers, the Roman frontier between the Black Sea and the Arabian desert shifted back and forth for centuries. Most of Asia Minor, however, and Syria and Palestine were kept under Roman control. The chief antagonist in the East was the kingdom of Persia (later, Parthia), which, though a stubborn foe, was only a minor state compared with the empire itself. The only other great power of which the Romans were aware was China, then under the Han Dynasty. But China was a remote land, known to the Romans only through the occasional reports of traders.

From west to east the empire measured some three thousand miles; from north to south, about two thousand. Its population was perhaps fifty million, and during its most prosperous period (the second century) the population may have risen to nearly seventy million. The peoples of the empire fell into three broad cultural groups, each of which embraced many dialects, religions, and ways of life. The Eastern group, which was least affected by the Roman overlordship, consisted of Egyptians, Jews, and Syrians. These Easterners had learned long ago how to adjust to foreign domination, and they persisted in their traditional ways. The second group, the Hellenic, spread over the Aegean basin and southern Italy, was influenced only slightly by Rome. The third cultural group occupied the largest geographical area: the Western, or "Romanized," section of the empire. Here the stamp of Rome was unmistakable. From Italy northward to the Rhine and Danube rivers, the once-barbarian lands were gradually civilized by Roman armies, governors, and colonists. This section included Spain and North Africa as well as distant Britain.

Cities of the empire

Although the empire was administered through some forty provinces, the basic unit of government and of social and economic life was the city (*municipium*). In fact, the Roman Empire has been

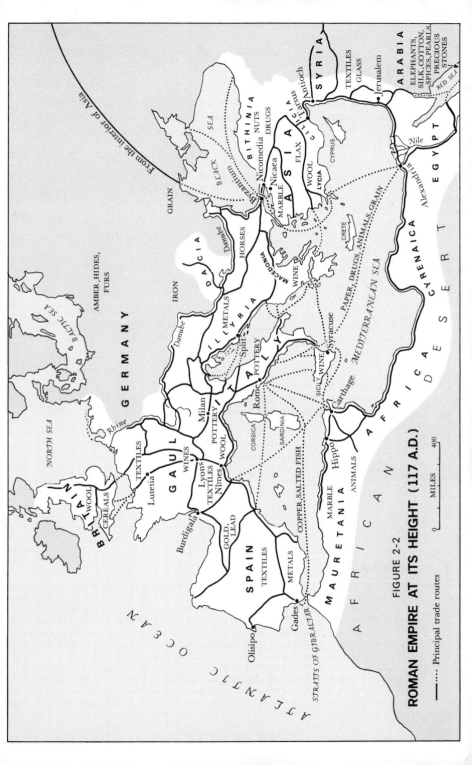

ROMAN EMPIRE AT ITS HEIGHT (117 A.D.)

FIGURE 2-2

- - - - - Principal trade routes

0   MILES   400

called a league of cities. It was more than that, of course, but the imperial structure was superimposed upon a foundation of city-states. Rome itself was the city-state triumphant, and its patterns of social organization were imitated everywhere. Where cities existed in conquered territories the Romans sustained them as centers from which to control the surrounding districts; where there were no cities the Romans created new ones in the image of Rome. In contrast to the self-destroying independence of ancient Athens or Sparta, there was an even balance between municipal self-government and centralized power under the early empire.

The cities of the empire were bound together by a network of sea lanes and highways, with Rome, the magnificent capital, at the center. During the prosperous second century, nearly a million people lived there. *Roma Æterna* was stamped on the imperial coins, and the city has indeed stood through the centuries as a timeless glory of Western civilization. Augustus is said to have found Rome a city of brick and to have left it a city of marble. And the emperors who followed him lavished their munificence upon the capital, erecting temples, forums, arenas, monuments, public baths, and palaces to honor themselves and to please the populace. True, not everyone lived in villas; the poor lived in wretched tenements. But Rome gave a stunning impression of affluence and grandeur.

Only a few cities approached Rome in size. Whether large or small, the cities of the empire were alike in their social and political organization. In each city a senate managed local affairs, and in each there was a rigid structure of social classes. In the oriental and Greek cities, the old patterns of society persisted. But the cities of the West—in Italy, Gaul, Spain, and Africa—strove to copy Rome. Each had its forum and senate house, its baths, arena, and temples. The water supply and sewage systems were excellent, with fresh water being piped in by way of aqueducts. The remains of these admirably planned cities are still to be seen, notably at Pompeii (Italy), Segovia (Spain), and Timgad (Africa).

The meaning of the Roman Peace

During the second century the empire was favored by a line of able rulers who succeeded one another by the rule of "adoption and designation." The great Spaniard Trajan, who became emperor in 98 A.D., was the first; he had been picked by a wise predecessor, Nerva. His selection reflected the widening base of political participation, for he was the first non-Italian to sit on the imperial throne. Trajan, in turn, exercised sound judgment in selecting Hadrian (another Spaniard) as his junior colleague and ruler-elect. Hadrian was followed by the prudent Antoninus and the philosopher-statesman Marcus Aurelius. These conscientious, intelligent men demonstrated the full merits of the Roman imperial system when it was directed by able rulers.

What was the world like in the century of Trajan and Marcus Aurelius? For one thing, it was a peaceful world. From the dawn of history the Mediterranean lands had been convulsed by wars, pillage, and looting; the Pax Romana brought political and social stability. Now men could live without fear. Productive forces—agriculture, industry, and commerce—could advance without disturbance, and the empire cleared the broadest area of trade known until that time. The flow of people, goods, and ideas was stimulated by the extension of Roman citizenship—first to Spain and Gaul and later to the East. Finally, in 212, Emperor Caracalla decreed that Roman citizenship be bestowed on all free-born inhabitants of the empire. Protection under a universal and equitable system of law thus became the birthright of every freeman.

The Romans built an empire, but they permitted all the races and nations that lived within it to participate in its administration. Provincials could become judges, senators, generals, emperors. There were no barriers of color or religion, and interracial marriage was widespread and legal. It is small wonder that ancient tribal and communal loyalties were transcended by a new sense of belonging to the human family. The Greek biographer Plutarch, writing in the second century, remarked, "I am a citizen, not of Athens or of Greece, but of the world."

ROMAN CHARACTER AND THOUGHT

Unless we dismiss the Romans' achievement as a mere accident of history, we must conclude that it was in some measure the product of their character. What was the "inner" nature of those remarkable conquerors and governors?

Religion and morality

The Romans, from earliest times, accepted the existence of powers outside themselves that had to be treated with respect. They regarded themselves neither as completely free agents nor as pawns of supernatural forces. In their primitive period, they had viewed the world as teeming with spirits (*numina*), each with a special function. There were protective spirits of the hearth, the cupboard, the house;

other spirits were active in the fields, the woods, and on battle-
grounds. The Romans propitiated these forces by appropriate rites,
prayers, and sacrifices; the father of the family (paterfamilias) usually
acted as priest. Home and family were a more intimate part of life
in Rome than in Greece; the father was responsible for the education and devotions of his children and, in theory at least, was absolute master of his household.

When the Italic peoples began to associate with the Greeks of
southern Italy (after about 300 B.C.), they encountered a more sophisticated religion than their own. Their beliefs gradually came to
reflect the anthropomorphism of Greek religion, and their deities
took on distinctive personalities. Educated Romans, in particular,
began to identify their sky spirit, Jupiter, with the Greek lord of
the sky, Zeus; their Juno with Hera, their Venus with Aphrodite,
and so on through the pantheon.

The Roman view of the deities, however, remained within the
bounds of their traditional values. They could not accept as proper,
for instance, the rather disreputable image of the gods and goddesses
portrayed by Homer. For the Roman character was marked by rectitude. And what the Romans held to be moral was, generally, what
had been done—what was embodied in the tradition of Rome's heroic farmer-soldiers. Even during the late republic and the empire,
when Roman morality declined, this conviction did not wholly disappear. Certainly the noblest and truest Romans embodied the
"high old virtues" of the early republic.

The moral quality most valued by the Romans was *virtus*. This
meant, literally, "manliness," but it carried the special sense of bravery in battle. This quality was considered of such importance that
the term came to suggest, ultimately, the character of goodness as a
whole; hence, our general word "virtue." Manliness was tempered by
pietas, a disciplined acceptance of the authority of higher powers,
both human and divine. Also valued was *gravitas,* a sense of responsibility and seriousness; every matter at hand, however small, had to
be weighed with care. The best Romans might be good humored
and easy in manner, but they were rarely light minded or impulsive.
A related quality was *simplicitas,* the ability to look at things clearly
and directly.

Literature as moralistic expression

Roman literature reflects these qualities of mind and action. It is
less speculative than Greek literature; and, though it includes striking examples of sensual and emotional writing, a substantial portion
is sober and moralistic in tone.

Among the first Roman writers was Livius Andronicus, a poet of Greek origin who wrote in the third century B.C. It was Livius who translated the *Odyssey* into Latin. Roman poets were soon writing epics and dramas of their own; during the second century B.C., for instance, Plautus and Terence authored comedies that are still being produced. The republican age also produced two brilliant poets during the first century B.C.: one was the philosopher Lucretius, whom we will speak of again; the other was Catullus, a writer of sensitive and passionate lyrics.

The greatest prose writer of the first century B.C. was Cicero. A distinguished figure in public life during the last days of the republic, he was best known for his speeches in the law court and the Senate. In addition, he wrote long philosophic essays on the art of government, justice, and theology in which he provided digests of the best Hellenistic thought. These essays gave Romans a literature of philosophy that they had hitherto lacked, and they made Greek thought accessible to future generations.

Three outstanding poets adorned the reign of Augustus (27 B.C.– 14 A.D.): Vergil, Horace, and Ovid. Vergil was the eloquent spokesman of the Romans' spiritual tradition and of their love for the soil. He was also the prophet of Rome's mission and destiny. Writing at a time when the old republican order was lying in ruins, his desire was to promote a regeneration of patriotic values. Although the spirit of Vergil's masterpiece, the *Aeneid,* is Roman, he took Homer's epic form as his model, and the adventures of his hero, Aeneas, parallel those of Odysseus after the fall of Troy. Guided by the gods, Aeneas wanders to Italy, where he and his companions found the city of Rome.

The lyric *Odes* of Horace range over a variety of moods: trivial, moralizing, and amatory. His patriotic odes consistently reflect the spirit of the Augustan revival and sing of the destiny of Rome. Ovid's erotic poems, published under such titles as *Loves* and the *Art of Love,* deal in a playful, witty, adult manner with the life of the senses. In an age when official policy was committed to the restoration of morality, these poems seemed highly immoral. It was partly for this reason that Augustus banished Ovid to a remote province of the empire.

Though the literature of the century after Augustus' death is usually judged inferior to that of the century preceding, it was not lacking in distinction. The Greek Plutarch, a man of cosmopolitan tastes, wrote *Parallel Lives,* some fifty short biographies of Greek and Roman statesmen and generals. Appearing about 110 A.D., these served to remind his readers of the glory of ancient Greece and to equate the talents of the best Greek and Roman leaders. Plutarch's Roman contemporary Suetonius wrote short biographies (*The Twelve Caesars*) of the successive Roman rulers from Julius Caesar to Domitian (who died in 96 A.D.). Unlike Plutarch, Suetonius refrained from speculation or interpretation, confining himself to personal details and anecdotes, many of them of a scandalous nature.

The scandals of the empire provoked blistering attacks from the satiric poet Juvenal (who wrote after 100 A.D.). In his verse we find once more that recurrent trait of Roman literature, a nostalgic yearning for the past and its ideals. Juvenal, in his satires on profligacy in high society, the depravity of women, and the oppressiveness of life in the great metropolis, pointed again and again to the "good old days" of early Rome.

Roman Epicureanism and Stoicism

The Romans borrowed freely from Greek philosophy as well as from Greek literature. But it was not the thought of Plato or Aristotle that attracted them. Rather, they were drawn to the more individualistic philosophies of the Hellenistic period. One of these was Epicureanism, which enjoyed a vogue among educated Romans. Epicurus, who had taught in Athens around 300 B.C., concentrated not on cosmic problems but on ways of achieving individual happiness. The chief exponent of his teachings in the West was the Roman poet Lucretius (first century B.C.), who articulated them in his eloquent *De Rerum Natura* (*On the Nature of Things*). This poem is also a hymn to Epicurus himself, whom Lucretius praises for having liberated men's minds from superstitious fears.

Epicurus had presented a "scientific" view of the universe. Setting aside the naive mythological explanations, he endorsed the principle of Democritus of Abdera (p. 26), which reduces all matter to atoms. To Epicurus, all forms of existence are temporary combinations of minute, imperishable particles; death and dissolution occur when the atoms separate. Only the laws of motion and chance determine the shape and character of things, and there is no governing "purpose" on earth or in the heavens.

In such a universe, Epicurus believed, the only logical aim for the individual is to strive for personal happiness. The individual is powerless to change the material world, and he has no obligation to try. As a guide in the search for happiness Epicurus formulated this basic equation: happiness equals pleasure *minus* pain. He suggested that the major potential for securing happiness lies in decreasing the pain factor rather than in increasing the pleasure factor. Though he conceded the existence of bodily aches, Epicurus taught that fear, the ache of mind and heart, is the deepest source of human pain; and fear feeds upon ignorance and superstition.

Religious teachings, Epicurus had charged, were designed to frighten simple-minded believers with tales of terror and punishment. Priests and sorcerers played on the fear of death, a fear that is natural to man, in order to serve their own purposes. Epicurus was no atheist; he did not deny the existence of the gods (whom he conceived as made of atoms). But, he insisted, the gods live remote from men and have no concern for them. Prayer is useless, for one cannot expect help from the gods. Yet there is some consolation in believing, as Epicurus did, that the gods do no *harm*.

To dispel man's dread of death, Epicurus insisted that death is *nothing*—simply a separation of atoms: "Death, usually regarded as the greatest of calamities, is actually nothing to us; while we are, death is not, and when death is here, we are not." Epicurus' assertion may have reduced men's fear of death, but it offered little emotional reassurance.

The pursuit of pleasure—the other factor in Epicurus' "happiness equation"—is an art more difficult than the avoidance of fear. Epicurus warned that bodily pleasures are usually self-defeating, for they stimulate appetites that act as fresh sources of pain (until they have been satisfied). Such pleasures as eating and drinking, which arise from the satisfaction of hungers, Epicurus classified as "dynamic" (restless) pleasures. Rather than indulge these appetites, he thought it wiser to discipline them and to reduce their influence on our behavior.

Epicurus urged that men cultivate the "passive" (quiet) pleasures, those agreeable experiences that do not arise from hunger satisfaction. These include the pleasures of literature, recollection and contemplation, personal friendship, and the enjoyment of nature. He shunned the pursuit of wealth or public office, for it often brings disappointment, trouble, enmity, and pain. Epicurus valued, above all, calmness, poise, and serenity of mind. (It is ironic that his name has become linked with pleasures of the appetites and that a connoisseur of fine food and drink has come to be known as an "epicure.")

Epicureanism has had only limited appeal as a way of life, for its successful application demands solitary courage, intellectual resourcefulness, self-control, and refined taste. The great majority of Romans—those who frequented the arenas and banquet tables—preferred the grosser thrills to the gentle pleasures recommended by

Epicurus and Lucretius. Nevertheless, Epicureanism attracted some leisured devotees in the Roman world, and its ethical teachings served, indirectly, as a moderating influence on the times.

The most influential of the philosophies Roman intellectuals imported from the East was Stoicism. One reason, no doubt, is that its ethical code paralleled the traditional Roman virtues. We might almost say that the Romans had practiced Stoicism before hearing of it. The term itself derives from the portico (stoa) in Athens where Zeno, the founder of Stoicism, had taught (about 300 B.C.). Zeno, like Epicurus, had a materialistic conception of the universe. But passive matter, he held, contains within itself an active principle known variously as "divine fire," "providence," "reason," "nature," and "God." The universe is not chaos; rather, it functions according to a benign plan. Although man cannot control what is beyond himself, he is master of his own being: he can hold himself ignorant, he can rebel against nature, or he can live in harmony with it.

Harmony and happiness, taught the Stoics, are achieved by striving for virtue rather than pleasure. Virtue, according to their definition, consists of understanding nature through reason, accepting by self-discipline the cosmic purpose, and living in accordance with duty, truth, and natural law (justice). They regarded all men as inherently equal, since all men share, in common with God, the spark of reason. Consequently, since all men are brothers, the individual should tolerate, forgive, and love his fellows. The ideal Stoic is self-sustaining, dutiful, compassionate, and calm.

Because Stoicism spoke to men of all classes and stations in society, it had universal appeal. While Epicureanism found most of its adherents among members of the aristocracy, Stoicism appealed to thoughtful men of all ranks: Cicero, the noble lawyer and senator; Seneca, a wealthy writer and adviser to the Emperor Nero; and Epictetus, once a learned slave in Nero's court. But the Roman who espoused Stoicism most ardently was an emperor himself—Marcus Aurelius. The last of the "good emperors" of the second century, he embodied Plato's dream that kings should be philosophers, or philosophers kings. Day by day he set down his inmost thoughts in a little book, commonly called the *Meditations*.

The work of God (providence), wrote Marcus Aurelius, is in its *totality* good. But specific events may seem harmful to the individual who is immediately affected by them. In order to live in wisdom and harmony, the individual must learn to accept such events as necessary to the total good. Then personal suffering will actually give him a sense of participation in the greater works of providence. No matter what his lot, he will bless God and conduct himself with serenity.

Stoicism, as formulated by Aurelius, was quite in accord with the ancient Roman virtues. "Let it be your hourly care," he advised, "to do stoutly what the hand finds to do, as becomes a man and a Roman, with carefulness, unaffected dignity, humanity, freedom, and justice. . . . Perform every action as though it were the last of your life, without light-mindedness, without swerving through force of passion from the dictates of reason." Every man, whether emperor or slave, must do his duty as it falls to him. Thus nature's plan is served, and the individual blends his life with that of the cosmos.

To weary men burdened with care, Aurelius said, "Trouble not yourself by pondering life in its entirety." The individual should live one day at a time, leaving the past to itself and entrusting the future to providence. He should strive to avoid "distractions"— elegant clothing, stylish homes, the opinions of others—and concentrate on his own mind and character.

Stoicism made a significant mark on Roman times and influenced the future; it provided a noble standard of conduct and in its ethics anticipated Christianity. Perhaps the most direct influence, however, was on Roman jurisprudence, in which the Stoic idea of "natural law"—law identical with reason and God—was of cardinal importance.

ROMAN LAW

Although in literature and philosophy the Romans were essentially preservers and disseminators of Hellenistic culture, in the development of law they were genuine originators. In fact, their most enduring contribution to Western institutions was in the practice and theory of law.

The evolution of Roman law

In the later republic the Romans gradually developed the notion that the law of the state should reflect what is right according to universal reason. Hence they used the word *justitia,* which is related to *justus,* or "right." According to Cicero's definition, "Law is the just distinction between right and wrong, made conformable to most ancient nature." As we have seen (p. 55), the "customary" laws that the patrician judges had been observing were recorded in

the Twelve Tables during the fifth century B.C. That early code
remained the basis of Roman law for centuries. Although its provisions were harsh and rigid, the judges gradually modified them
through interpretation. The rulings of the courts thus conformed
ever more closely to *justitia*.

After 366 B.C. a special magistrate, called a praetor, was elected
annually to administer justice to the citizens of Rome. He was expected to abide by the code of the Twelve Tables but was given
some freedom in interpreting it. Each praetor, at the start of his
term, was required to announce his own interpretation of the law.
Through this interpretative decree and through his daily decisions,
he adapted the original Tables to the cases before him. By 246 B.C.
another praetor had been established to deal with disputes between
Roman citizens and aliens. This official had a still wider basis for
interpretations, for he could draw on the various foreign laws, as
well as Roman law, in arriving at fair decisions and settlements.
Thus there grew up, in the days of the republic, two distinct bodies
of law: the law of citizens (*jus civile*) and the law of peoples (*jus
gentium*).

Since the law of peoples had a broader base than the law of citizens, the praetor for citizens tended to be guided more and more
in his interpretations by the *jus gentium*. By the first century, the
basic provisions of the two bodies of law had been brought close
together; after 212, when all free inhabitants of the empire were
declared Roman citizens, the dual system disappeared. From that
time on—in theory, at least, and usually in practice—one system of
law prevailed throughout the empire.

Under the empire, the ancient statutes of the republic were
further augmented by the decrees and interpretations of rulers and
by the opinions and commentaries of legal experts. The praetors
themselves were not always professional lawyers, and even during
the first century B.C. they had established the custom of consulting
men who were "skilled in the law" (*jurisprudentes*). The emperors
regularly commissioned outstanding legal scholars to advise magistrates on specific cases. As the Romans had profound respect for
the law, and for experts in law, the commentaries carried considerable authority. The judicial traditions of the West owe much to the
clarifying and humanizing influence of these detached and dedicated scholars.

The idea of "natural law"

Most of the jurists were well-educated men who felt at home with
Stoic philosophy. They observed that the laws of nations had many

elements in common and that the laws themselves were gradually merging into the single law of the empire. This similarity in legal ideas among the peoples of the empire coincided nicely with the Stoic belief that there was one law in nature, the law of reason. From this the jurists inferred the reality of "natural law" and concluded that human rules could and should conform to this "higher law." Thus, the Roman experience, buttressed by Hellenistic philosophy, gave rise to the doctrine of natural law (*jus naturale*).

This doctrine, which has deeply influenced legal theory in the West, is the basis of the conception of law and human rights enshrined in the Declaration of Independence. Cicero, in the *Laws*, observed: "Law and equity have not been established by opinion, but by nature." The regulations of states that do not conform to reason, he declared, are not truly *laws* and do not deserve obedience. Clearly, this doctrine is a two-edged sword: It gives added sanction to those laws that citizens regard as right. But for those they believe wrong, it opens the door to disobedience (and rebellion).

Codification of the laws

Over the centuries several emperors tried to bring a degree of order into the mounting accumulation of laws, interpretations, principles, and procedures. But it was not until the sixth century (after the division of the Roman Empire) that a definitive codification was carried through, under the Emperor Justinian (p. 139). Justinian's *Corpus Juris Civilis* (*Body of Civil Law*) consists of several parts: the *Digest,* a summary of judicial opinions and commentaries; the *Code,* a compilation of statutes from Hadrian to Justinian; the *Novels,* a collection of measures enacted after the publication of the *Code;* and the *Institutes,* a brief treatise on legal principles, designed for students. Justinian's great codification became the foundation for the legal systems that were subsequently devised throughout Europe. Hundreds of millions of people today live under systems that were modeled, in whole or in part, upon Roman law as distilled in the *Corpus.*

ARCHITECTURE AND ENGINEERING

The Romans built their state, their law, and their public structures for eternity, and there is no more impressive proof of their sense of power and permanence than their architecture. After centuries of erosion and vandalism, the ruins of hundreds of Roman buildings still stand upon three continents—from the shores of the eastern Mediterranean to the Scottish border. Although the architects of Rome borrowed and adapted techniques from a wide variety of styles, the primary influences were Etruscan and Hellenistic. The Romans built on a larger scale than the Greeks, however, for where the Greek *polis* had to provide public structures for only a few thousand citizens, the population of Rome numbered hundreds of thousands. The Romans, moreover, developed a taste for grandeur, elegance, and display, and they indulged this taste freely in their architecture.

Construction materials were readily available: the Italian peninsula had plenty of timber and stone, as well as good clays (for brick) and lava and sandy earth (for concrete). Other materials, such as decorative marble, were often imported. Brick and concrete faced with stucco or marble veneer were the materials most commonly used in Rome itself.

Architectural forms and aims

Although the Romans made some use of the post-and-lintel method of construction (p. 38), their preference in large undertakings was for the arch, vault, and dome. They realized that an arch formed of bricks, stones, or poured concrete would carry a far heavier load than a pair of columns. And they discovered that a

FIGURE 2-3. Pont du Gard. (French Government Tourist Office.)

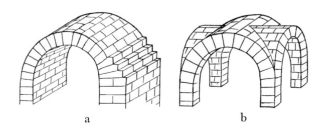

a   b

FIGURE 2-4. Roman vaulting systems. a. Barrel vault, b. Cross vault.

series of arches placed side by side could carry a bridge or an aqueduct across deep valleys (FIG. 2-3).

The vault is actually an extension of the arch. The typical tunnel, or barrel, vault is an arch extended in depth to produce a tunnel-shaped enclosure of the desired width and length (FIG. 2-4). Since this type of vault admits light only at the two ends, however, it is of limited usefulness in public structures. To overcome this difficulty, Roman architects devised the cross-vault plan, which permits light to enter from the sides as well. It consists of one or more short vaults intersecting the main vault at right angles (FIG. 2-4). This kind of structure can be carried to a substantial height and can be made to enclose a huge space with no need for supporting members between floor and ceiling.

Another architectural device used by the Romans to provide an uncluttered enclosure was the dome, which is simply a hemisphere resting on a cylindrical wall or on a circle of supporting arches (FIG. 2-5). A large dome was built up of a series of progressively smaller horizontal rings of brick, stones, or concrete. When completed, the parts formed a single unit firmly set in place.

A highly practical people, the Romans were particularly ingenious in devising structures for utilitarian purposes. To provide their cities with water for public baths and ornamental fountains and also to assure a good supply of drinking water, they built great aqueducts leading down from distant mountain springs. Much of the way, the water descended through pipes or channels in the mountains or hills, but across a valley or a plain it flowed through a channel carried by an aqueduct. Since the Romans had no mechanical pumps, the aqueduct was engineered so that the water flowed steadily by force of gravity alone.

The famous Pont du Gard (FIG. 2-3) is part of the Roman aqueduct that originally carried water across the Gard River to the provincial city of Nîmes in southern France. The lower level served, and still serves, as a bridge; the upper level, one hundred eighty feet above the river, carried the water channel. This giant bridge, nine hundred feet long, is built of stone blocks without mortar.

Perhaps the most impressive utilitarian achievement of the Romans was their wide-ranging network of roads. Their military expansion demanded a swift and reliable means of overland movement. Over the centuries, they built or improved some fifty thousand miles of roads, reaching out from Rome to the farthest corners of the empire. The standard roadbed was fifteen feet wide and five feet deep. Broken stone and gravel were tamped down to form a foundation, which was then surfaced with thick blocks of hard stone. Sections of these remarkably durable highways are still in use.

The army had priority in the use of the strategically planned system of roads, but they were open to public travel and served as the basis for a postal system operated by the state. The roads were regularly patrolled, and guide books were issued to travelers. On the major arteries there was a stable every ten miles and a hostel every thirty miles. No road system comparable to the Roman highways was to be undertaken again until the twentieth century.

In domestic architecture the wealthy Romans found their model in the dwellings of the ancient Etruscans. The basic plan of the Roman villa, with its central court (atrium) partly open to the sky, was Etruscan in origin. Such homes were extremely comfortable and luxurious, as we can tell from the remains of the splendid houses at Pompeii, south of Rome. (An eruption of Vesuvius in 79 A.D. buried the city in layers of lava and ashes, thus preserving it virtually intact). Excavations have revealed the well-designed homes, with their fountains, sculptures, wall paintings, mosaics, and metalware. The great mass of the urban populations, however, lived in flats and tenements. Examples of these have recently been uncovered at Ostia, a port and suburb of Rome.

Civic architecture and monuments

It is in the public buildings, however, that we find the grandest and most enduring monuments of Roman architecture. In the major cities of the empire there was always a public square—a forum—that served as a civic center. The Forum Romanum, for example, was a marketplace in the early days of the republic, but it was gradually transformed into an impressive meetingplace with handsome statues, temples, and halls of government. Overlooking the Forum was the sacred Capitoline Hill, topped by the temple of Jupiter, while across the Forum, on the Palatine Hill, stood the official residences of the emperors.

Successive rulers also constructed imperial forums in Rome as memorials to themselves. One of these, the Forum of Trajan, was built early in the second century A.D. on a spacious site near the Capitoline Hill. Symmetrically laid out, it included a large area for shops, an imposing hall (basilica), a library, and a temple dedicated to the deified emperor. Dominating all the rest was the gigantic marble Column of Trajan, with a spiral band of sculptured relief (three feet wide and six hundred and fifty feet long) depicting the emperor's conquests.

Most of the public meeting halls in Rome and the other cities of the empire were built in the style of the basilica. This was a rectangular building constructed either on the cross-vault principle or with a roof supported by columns in the Greek manner. In either case, there was a wide central aisle running the length of the building, with narrower side aisles. By lifting the roof of the center aisle higher than the roof of the side aisles, the architects were able to admit light through a series of clerestory windows. A semicircular area, called an apse, was joined to one end; sometimes there was an apse at each end. Covered by a half-dome, the apse was often partitioned from the central hall and used as a chamber for courts of law. In the fourth century, when the Christians were finally permitted to build public houses of worship, they adapted the basilica to their own needs. The congregation stood in the open rectangular area, and the apse was used to house the altar and sanctuary. This plan of church architecture persisted for centuries.

Religious shrines did not occupy the preeminent place in Roman architecture that they did in Greek. The usual Roman temple resembled the Greek, but it followed more precisely an Etruscan plan. Though columns were used to support the roof, the Roman temple stood on a higher base (podium) than the Greek and faced in only one direction. The most impressive of all Roman temples, however, has a design unlike that of earlier structures. It is the Pantheon in Rome (FIG. 2-5), a temple dedicated to all the gods (*pan theoi*). The present building is actually a reconstruction ordered by the Emperor Hadrian about 120 A.D. to replace the original temple, which had been destroyed by fire. It was converted into a Christian church (St. Mary of the Rotunda) in the seventh century and has been used continuously since then as a place of worship.

The Pantheon consists of a round central hall, or rotunda, capped by a vast concrete dome. To carry the great weight of the dome, the rotunda wall was built twenty feet thick. The height of the dome and its diameter are identical (one hundred forty feet), assuring geometrical balance; and the dome is pierced by an eye (*oculus*),

FIGURE 2-5
a. The Pantheon,
exterior. (Alinari.)

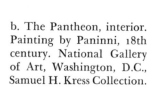

b. The Pantheon, interior.
Painting by Paninni, 18th
century. National Gallery
of Art, Washington, D.C.,
Samuel H. Kress Collection.

thirty feet across, which serves as the source of light. Originally, it is believed, statues of the seven "planetary" deities stood in the seven niches cut into the wall. There is a single doorway, which is approached through a Greek-style portico. From the outside, the Pantheon has a squat, heavy appearance. But the interior gives a dramatic impression of space and buoyancy. The Pantheon has served as a prototype of a noble line of domed structures, including St. Peter's in Rome, St. Paul's in London, and the Capitol in Washington, D.C.

The civilization of the empire, as we have seen, was predominantly urban, and elaborate structures were erected to satisfy the recreational needs of the city populations. Particularly popular were the public bathhouses (thermae), which were equipped with steam rooms and pools filled with hot, tepid, or frigid water. The emperors also courted popular favor by donating magnificent pleasure palaces that housed not only baths but large indoor and outdoor swimming pools, gymnasiums, gardens, libraries, galleries, theaters, lounges, and bars. Since these recreational centers were especially attractive to the lower classes and to idlers, their reputation in polite society was not altogether savory.

The best-preserved pleasure palace in Rome is the complex of buildings known as the Baths of Diocletian, built in the late third century. Its main hall, which once enclosed a huge swimming pool, is constructed on the cross-vault principle. It is three hundred feet long, ninety feet wide, and ninety feet high. In the sixteenth century, Michelangelo converted this great room into the central section of a Christian church, St. Mary of the Angels. The church is still standing, along with a series of huge tunnel vaults and half-domes that formed portions of the original baths. It is estimated that the baths could accommodate three thousand bathers in lavish surroundings of gilt and marble.

One of the most popular pastimes of the Romans was watching the chariot races of the circus and the gory combats of the arena. Although every city of the empire had facilities for mass entertainment, the most famous arena was the Colosseum of Rome (FIG. 2-6). This huge structure, which covers about six acres and seated more than fifty thousand spectators, was the largest of its kind. The crowds made their way to their seats through some eighty entry vaults, and the stairways were so arranged that the stadium could be emptied in minutes.

A variety of materials was used in the construction of the Colosseum. Key areas of stress, such as archways and vaults, are generally of brick; other sections are of concrete and courses of broken stone.

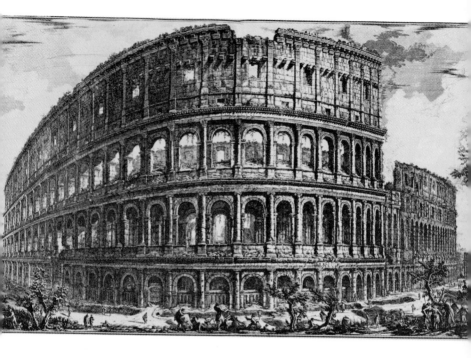

FIGURE 2-6. The Colosseum. Engraving by Giovanni Piranesi. (Courtesy of the Prints Division, New York Public Library.)

The façade is divided into three stories and a high wall, built of masonry blocks. Between the arches on each story stand attached Greek columns, with Corinthian pilasters standing above them in the high wall. Sockets set into the high wall accommodated great poles, on which protective awnings could be mounted. A facing of marble originally covered the exterior of the Colosseum, but the marble (and other building materials) have been carried away, over the centuries, for use in other structures.

Underneath the arena floor, which was made of wood covered with sand, lay a labyrinth of corridors, chambers, and cells, where the men and animals scheduled for combat awaited their turn on the program. These contests were usually fought to the death, but the crowd's appetite for violence was hard to satiate. "Roman holidays" were long affairs, lasting from early morning till dark. Wealthy donors seeking popular acclaim usually footed the bill, including the cost of food and refreshments.

To impress the citizens and the thousands of visitors who flocked to Rome, the emperors ordered monuments raised in their own honor—triumphal arches, columns, and statues. These are still to be found in profusion in the Eternal City, as well as in the provinces. Like the mighty Column of Trajan (already described) they convey a sense of pride, power, and permanence. To the Roman rulers, works of sculpture were also viewed as media of propaganda. They might relate the events of a military campaign or present, simply, the unaffected portrait of a man. Figures of gods and goddesses were based on Greek models, and the same idealized style might be used to represent the rulers themselves. Most Roman portraits, however,

FIGURE 2-7. *Portrait of a Roman. Ca.* 80 B.C. Palazzo Torlonia, Rome. (Alinari.)

are emphatically lifelike (FIG. 2-7). In the National Museum of Naples there is a superb collection of original busts of emperors, each of which bears the mark of individual personality.

DIVISION OF THE EMPIRE
AND FALL OF THE WEST

The great age of the Pax Romana ended with the death of Marcus Aurelius in 180 A.D. The third century was a time of revolts and civil wars and fierce attacks on Rome's distant frontiers. In the fourth century, however, the empire made a recovery, largely through the reforms instituted by the emperors Diocletian and Constantine. These reforms extended the life of the empire for another two hundred years, but eventually the disintegrating forces proved too strong to be overcome. First the administration of the empire was divided between East and West, and then the western portion succumbed to Germanic invaders. The last emperor in the West (a puppet of German mercenaries) was deposed by another barbarian (Odoacer) in 476.

The nature of the Roman fall

The disintegration of the Roman Empire was a gradual process marked by intermittent periods of recovery. Even during the final centuries, the average citizen had no sense of sudden catastrophe; despite the many ills that beset the empire at home and in the provinces, life went on much as usual. Although scholars have written hundreds of volumes on the "cause" of the fall of Rome, the evidence suggests that many debilitating forces were at work both at the heart of the empire and along its borders.

The economic deterioration of the western portion of the empire was one of these forces, perhaps the most significant of all. After the Punic Wars of the second century B.C., Italy was no longer self-sufficient—though it was able, for a long time, to live off the profits of conquest. But as Augustus and his successors lifted the burdens of tribute from the provinces, Rome and Italy gradually lost their favored position. But the appetite for high living did not abate; imports (especially from the East) continued to exceed exports.

As government revenues from the provinces tapered off, taxes had to be raised in Italy. But higher taxes added to the cost of doing business and thereby discouraged producers. As marginal operators were forced under, taxes on those remaining had to be boosted still further in order to maintain an adequate flow of government revenue. After 200 A.D. the economic situation was made even worse by a decline in population in Italy and a rise in military expenditures (to meet fresh threats on the frontiers). The inevitable consequences were a drying up of capital, low productivity, inflation, and inadequate revenues for defense and administration.

In the eastern portion of the empire, the population was larger and more productive. This fact persuaded the emperor to transfer his headquarters in 284 from Rome to Nicomedia in Asia Minor. He wished to be nearer the major economic resources of the empire, and the East was strong enough to support and defend itself. The West, left thereafter to its own resources, proved unable to sustain itself for long against the attacks of the barbarians. The differential in their population and wealth is the fundamental reason the eastern half of the empire survived for many more centuries, while the western half succumbed.

Still, the whole empire might have survived had there been an effective mechanism for ensuring able leadership. As we have seen, the gravest weakness of the imperial system was the lack of a sound and certain means of selecting new rulers. During the second century, the method of "adoption and designation" was used with success. But Marcus Aurelius chose to name his own offspring, the worthless Commodus, as his successor. Commodus was murdered after twelve years of irresponsible rule, and the ensuing disturbances opened the way to succession by force of arms.

During the turbulent third century even the pretense of legitimacy was discarded. The Praetorian Guard in Rome and the provincial armies vied with one another in advancing their favorite candidates. One ruler after another was assassinated, and the succession was determined by the clash of legions. Surprisingly, many of the emperors so chosen proved to be forceful and competent leaders. But this did not save them from violent death, and their terms of office were generally short. At a time when the empire was crying out for wise leadership, its human resources were being squandered.

Reconstitution of the empire
by Diocletian and Constantine

At last, in 284, a ruler came to the throne who was determined to rescue the faltering empire. Diocletian is often credited with undertakings that were begun before his time, and many of his innovations were carried to completion by his successor, Constantine. Nonetheless, he was the principal agent in shoring up the crumbling foundations of the empire.

In many ways Diocletian was a typical third-century man. Born in Illyricum (modern Yugoslavia), the son of a freed slave, he enlisted in the ranks, worked his way up, and was at last proclaimed emperor by his troops. Rivals contested his claim to the throne, but he subdued them all. Though he himself had secured power by illegitimate means, Diocletian set out to restore legitimacy to the empire. After a reign of some twenty years, he retired voluntarily to a palatial estate at Spalato (Split) in his native Illyricum.

We might say that Augustus had relied on his personal power in launching the empire at the very outset. Yet he had also made effective use of the ancient republican institutions (especially the Senate) and of the Italian citizen class. Moreover, he could count on the cities of the empire to carry much of the burden of local administration. But Diocletian found that most of these traditional sources of support had been undermined by the calamities of the third century. And so he was obliged to utilize and strengthen the only means left to him: the army, the imperial bureaucracy, and his personal authority. Consequently, the "late empire" took on a centralized, regimented, and militarized character.

Diocletian's first major step was to overhaul the civil administration. The empire was now too big, he decided, for one man to administer; so he divided it in two. In theory, Diocletian was still monarch of the entire empire; but he moved his capital to Nicomedia, taking direct charge of the eastern portion, and in 286 he appointed a fellow general, Maximian, as joint ruler to govern the western portion from Milan. After 293 the two *augusti,* as they were called, were each assisted by a junior colleague (a *caesar*), who was assigned to rule a specified portion. Thus began the separation of East and West, which became complete and permanent in 395.

Diocletian reduced the size of the individual provinces (and increased their number) and placed them under closer supervision. The one hundred twenty provinces were grouped into twelve units called dioceses; the dioceses were in turn grouped into four prefectures, each ruled by one of the *augusti* or caesars. This hierarchical arrangement ensured stricter control from the top and reduced the possibility of provincial revolts, which had plagued the third century.

In his reform of the military establishment, Diocletian stripped the provincial governors of their traditional command of troops. Armed forces stationed in the provinces were decreased, and powerful mobile armies were concentrated near each of the imperial capitals. The total number of soldiers, more and more of whom were barbarian recruits, was expanded to five hundred thousand, all under the command of the imperial co-rulers. Thus, Diocletian succeeded in restoring authority and order within the empire and on the frontiers.

Diocletian was less effective in his economic measures. He ordered a new survey of the empire's population and wealth, revised taxes, and reformed the coinage; but neither the ruler nor his advisers knew enough about economics to cope with the deeper problems. A tough old soldier, Diocletian knew how to deal with barbarian invaders. But what to do about unemployment, lack of capital investment, and rising prices? In a heroic attempt to check inflation, he issued an "edict of maximum prices," which froze the price level of all basic commodities. This, however, only compounded the difficulties of producers and traders. The death penalty, which he decreed for violations, was rarely imposed, but the threat had a depressing and stagnating effect. Eventually, all efforts to enforce the edict collapsed, and prices continued to soar.

Thousands of men who were still trying to carry on business grew discouraged in the face of mounting difficulties and simply gave up. They made their way to the large cities, already beset by food and housing shortages, and swelled the indigent mobs there. Alarmed by this trend, which threatened to reduce production still further, Diocletian took a desperate measure. He ordered that critical occupations be made hereditary and that all persons remain at their jobs. This sweeping decree destroyed the mobility of the labor force, weakened what was left of individual incentive, and made workers virtual slaves to their jobs. Strict enforcement proved impossible, though substantial efforts were made to put the order into effect. This measure did not solve the basic economic problems, but it did check the descent into complete economic collapse.

From the beginning of his reign, Diocletian realized that he would have to strengthen the respect and obedience of all his subjects if he was to hold the empire together and win compliance with his reform decrees. Following the trend of centuries, he transformed the imperial office into a sacred monarchy. The affected simplicity of Augustus was superseded by undisguised absolutism. The title of "princeps," preferred by Augustus, gave way to "dominus" (lord). The few men who were admitted to the presence of the emperor no longer offered the republican salute; they were obliged to prostrate themselves before his sacred person.

At Nicomedia, Diocletian built a two-thousand-room palace of oriental splendor, set in a vast park. From the Persian monarchs he borrowed regalia dating back to the Great King, Darius. On state occasions the emperor sat on an immense throne beneath a canopy of Persian blue and the glittering emblem of the sun. He wore a magnificent costume, gold fingernails, and a crown of pearls. Visitors, after being screened by the secret police, were brought to the throne room through a labyrinth of chambers, doorways, and corridors. This arrangement served not only to protect the emperor from assassination but to overwhelm his visitors with a sense of mystery and majesty.

Diocletian's successor, Constantine, and the rulers who followed them, recognized the effectiveness of these devices. The tradition of seclusion, secrecy, and sumptuous display persisted in the Eastern empire until the fall of its capital in 1453. In the West also, the oriental court model was later studied by those who would wield absolute authority. Examples of its influence are the splendid court of the Renaissance papacy at Rome and the court of the French monarchy in the eighteenth century at Versailles.

Diocletian succeeded in reestablishing imperial authority. But, like his predecessors, he failed to solve the troublesome succession issue. He had planned an orderly procedure, with the junior rulers becoming *augusti* as the senior rulers retired or died. But when one of Diocletian's successors died, a struggle broke out among various claimants to power. After years of dreary struggle, one of them—Constantine—emerged as sole victor. By 324 he had disposed of all rivals, and for a brief period there was again one empire and one emperor.

Constantine carried forward most of Diocletian's reforms. His major departure was in the imperial policy toward Christians—a departure for which Christian historians have styled him "the Great." (We shall discuss in the next chapter the rise of the Christian Church.) Diocletian had persecuted the Christians in the belief that they were undermining his efforts to save the empire. His suspicions are understandable, for the Christians met together in what appeared to many to be secret societies, they opposed military service, and they refused to recognize the emperor as divine. Diocletian persecuted them, not because of their strange beliefs (he supported the idea of religious toleration), but because of their seeming disloyalty to the state.

Constantine, however, observed that persecution had failed to crush the determined and well-organized sect. Instead, martyrdom seemed only to nourish its growth. At last, in 313, Constantine personally accepted Christianity and subsequently decreed complete freedom of worship throughout the territories under his control.

Although he continued to tolerate other faiths after 313, the emperor showed his preference for Christianity. When he founded his new capital on the Bosphorus (New Rome, later called Constantinople), he made it a Christian city from the start. His religious policy may be seen as a culmination of the Pax Romana. A world of one law and one citizenship called, logically, for one faith. The pagan cults survived for another century or more, but most citizens followed the emperor's example.

Constantine exercised shrewd statesmanship in taking the Christian Church into partnership. To him, it was always a junior partner, however, for the emperor remained supreme. And the long line of Eastern emperors who succeeded him at Constantinople continued to subordinate the Church to the imperial will.

The binding power of a single faith came too late to keep the once unified Roman world from separating. It did not stop the economic decline of the West or the mounting threat of barbarian invasions. In 381 the Emperor Theodosius made Christianity the official state religion and outlawed all other religions. But he was the last to rule a united empire; before he died in 395, he decreed a permanent legal division. Theodosius split the empire along the lines established by Diocletian, naming one of his sons emperor of the West (at Rome) and the other emperor of the East (at Constantinople).

Germanic invasions of the West

Meanwhile, fierce Germanic tribes were pressing more and more insistently against the frontiers. Until the fourth century the emperors had managed to hold these barbarians in check north of the Rhine-Danube line, an area in which they had been wandering about for centuries. They were nomadic, pastoral peoples, constantly searching for new forage areas and shifting their settlements from one place to another. From the time of Julius Caesar, small groups of them had been filtering down into the empire; many had joined auxiliary forces of the Roman army, and a few had even enlisted in the legions themselves. Occasionally, fairly large groups had been permitted to settle on the Roman side of the frontier, as a buffer against further encroachments. These people were readily assimilated as citizens, and some of them rose to high rank in the army and the civil service.

During the fourth century a new Germanic tribe, the Goths, appeared along the lower Danube. The Goths had originated in the Baltic area, but they had subsequently settled north of the Black Sea. During the third and fourth centuries a great horde of Huns swept out of Asia and drove the Goths from their settlements. On the move once again, the Goths turned toward the frontiers of the empire, and in 376 they crossed the Danube and advanced toward Constantinople. Not far from the capital, they won a crushing victory over the imperial troops at Adrianople and wrested a substantial grant of land from the Eastern emperor. The Goths were by no means satisfied, but the rulers at Constantinople succeeded, through diplomacy and bribery, in persuading them to move westward.

The emperors in the West, with fewer resources at their disposal, were less successful in resisting the invading barbarians. Alaric, a Goth, shook the Roman world in 410 by sacking the Eternal City itself. (This was the first time in eight hundred years that Rome had been taken by outsiders.) Later, a small but aggressive tribe called the Vandals swept across the Rhine, through Gaul and Spain, and down into North Africa. From their base there, they made a sea raid on Rome in 455, leaving their name in history as a synonym for looters and destroyers.

By the end of the fifth century, the Western empire had been carved up into a number of Germanic kingdoms. The Vandals held

Africa; the Goths held Italy and Spain; the Franks had penetrated Gaul and the Rhineland; the Angles and the Saxons had sailed across the North Sea to occupy Britain. Most of the tribal leaders accepted the nominal overlordship of the emperor at Constantinople, but in practice they ruled autonomous states. They assigned portions of the conquered lands to their military chieftains, who collected taxes on those lands and maintained some semblance of order there. But the administration was poor, and there was a good deal of violence and pillage. Roads and aqueducts were abandoned, and public services virtually ceased. For most people daily life became a wretched struggle for food and shelter; personal security was almost nonexistent. The fall of the Western empire was a blow from which Europe was to emerge only slowly and painfully.

The disaster might have been even more severe had it not been for the preserving influence of the Christian Church. The barbarians respected Roman ways and proved willing converts to Christianity. The empire dissolved, but the organization of the Church held firm, serving as a bridge between Roman and barbarian, Christian and heathen, conquered and conqueror. The moderating influence of a bishop was often all that stood between a rapacious band of warriors and a defenseless community. Thus, though much of the ancient culture was lost, a precious remnant was saved.

New Roots of Faith: Christianity

3

The Church as an institution matured in the declining years of the empire, but the origins of Christianity were older than the empire itself. The product of centuries of human experience, Christianity arose in Palestine and then spread throughout the Roman world to embrace many diverse peoples. By the Emperor Constantine's time it had become a truly universal faith. And when the empire disintegrated in the West, the Church provided a base for the continuance of civilization.

SOURCES OF CHRISTIANITY

Christianity had first appeared as a sect among the Jews. The disciples of Jesus embraced him as the Christ, the Messiah, for whom the tribes of Israel had been waiting for centuries. Indeed, for many years the pagan Romans made no distinction between Jews and Christians. To the Christians, those who persisted in their Jewishness were brethren who failed to recognize Christ.

Judaism

Before we can understand Christianity itself, we must be aware of its intimate relationship with Judaism. Though other cultures and other religions influenced Christianity, its foundations were essentially Jewish. Jesus, of course, was born a Jew, as were his twelve disciples. His very words, as we find them in the parables and teachings, reflect rabbinic traditions. The elements common to both Jews and Christians are so familiar to us that we sometimes overlook them: the faith in one almighty God; the account of Creation; Adam and Eve and their disobedience; the Ten Commandments; ethical precepts stressing righteousness and love; and the expectation of a Messiah (Savior). The Hebrew holy books make up the Old Testament of the Christians and are accepted by them as the word of God.

To uncover the beginnings of Judaism, we must go back about two thousand years before the birth of Christ, to the time traditionally associated with the patriarch Abraham, legendary "father" of the Jews. His people were a small tribe of Near Eastern nomads. Though their origins are obscure, we know that by 1200 B.C. they had settled in the hilly country west of the River Jordan, known as Palestine. The career of these courageous, indestructible people was marked by trouble and affliction. Caught between the power centers of Egypt and Mesopotamia, they refused to be assimilated and yet were too small to preserve their independence.

A decisive historical event, according to Hebrew tradition and scripture, was the liberation of a community of Jews who had settled in Egypt and had there fallen into servitude. Some time in the thirteenth century B.C., they were led across the Red Sea by the prophet Moses, who had been called to his liberation mission by the Jewish deity Yahweh (Jehovah). On the slopes of Mount Sinai, south of Palestine, Moses then received the Law from on high and renewed God's Covenant with Abraham. In this Covenant, Yahweh promised the Jews protection and favor as his Chosen People in return for their pledge of exclusive allegiance and obedience.

The subsequent history of the Jews is one of temporary victory in the promised land of Palestine, followed by centuries of struggle to preserve their identity, of recurrent persecutions, and of a persisting sense of frustration as the Chosen People. When they at last despaired of overcoming their enemies through their own efforts, their prophets preached that ultimate redress yet would come through a divine deliverer, the Messiah. This unyielding faith in their destiny in the face of setbacks and humiliations produced one of the most extraordinary chapters of history. Countless tribes and peoples in various parts of the world have emerged, been assimilated, and disappeared—the Trojans, the Philistines, and the Romans, to name only a few. But the Jews have held their culture intact for some four thousand years. This habit of perseverance, passed on to the Christians, undoubtedly helped them, in turn, to survive their ordeal of persecution.

What was the source of the Jews' uncommon will? It is true that for a brief but splendid period around 1000 B.C. the Jews, under the rules of David and Solomon, tasted military triumph and worldly power of their own. On Mount Zion, in the heart of Jerusalem, they raised a magnificent temple and palace. Thus, Zion became a symbol of both holiness and glory in Jewish hearts and minds. But other peoples have experienced grandeur and have then slipped into oblivion. What was it that gave the Jews their exceptional will to persist?

There seems to be only one answer: their unique religious experience. At first, when they were still a nomadic people, they thought of Yahweh (Jehovah) as a fierce and jealous God who would support them against hostile tribes and gods. When they moved into Palestine, the local deities of the region began to compete with Yahweh for their allegiance. Some of the Jews succumbed to this temptation, but most remained faithful to Yahweh. After the eighth century B.C., when Assyria and then Babylonia conquered and dispersed the Jews, many of the faithful concluded that the gods of foreigners—gods like the Assyrian Assur—were stronger than Yahweh. Once again, however, the more devout Jews refused to forsake their God. But they had to answer this question: If their God was all-powerful, and if they were his Chosen People, why had he abandoned them to their enemies?

For generations the prophets had been warning the Jews that they were straying from righteous living and were neglecting their loyalty to Yahweh, but many refused to listen. The devout Jews now construed their troubles as a vindication of both the prophets and their deity. This rationalization found its boldest expression in the writings of the "Second Isaiah" (written about 540 B.C.). The disaster that had fallen on the nation, Isaiah asserted, was not an occasion for despair but rather a proof of Yahweh's power. The Jews had not been overcome by foreign gods; rather, they were being castigated by Yahweh, the one and almighty God, for violating his commandments. The Assyrians—in fact, all peoples and all nations—were simply his instruments. Once the Jews had turned their hearts back to God, had cleansed themselves of sin, and had returned to the path of virtue, they would be restored to power and granted victory over their enemies.

Thus, under the guidance of their prophets, the Jews were the first people to arrive at a clearly defined, exclusive belief in one God. Their monotheism proved to be a precious heritage, for it is a kind of faith that is especially strong in adversity. A polytheist, who worships several gods, is likely to interpret disaster as a sign that his gods are weak, indifferent, unfriendly, or nonexistent. But for one who firmly believes that only one god exists and that he directs the universe according to his own benign and secret purposes, *nothing* can happen, logically, that will contradict the believer's faith and take away its comforts.

There is a corollary to this line of reasoning. If disaster strikes (as it had struck the Jews), and if the deity cannot be blamed, then the fault must lie with the people themselves. This conclusion gave the Jews a deepened consciousness of sin and its consequences—and a stronger feeling of individual moral responsibility, which was passed on to the Christians. The Jews were at the same time uplifted by a sense of historical mission. Surrounded by "unenlightened" Gentiles (nonbelievers), they saw themselves as unique witnesses to the one true God. This gave them a feeling of superiority, which, along with their faith, has sustained them ever since.

Hebrew literature provided a further source of strength. The best of it is included in the Holy Scriptures, which, unlike the literary works of most cultures, were read by all classes of Jews. The Hebrew Scriptures consist of three parts: the Torah (the story of the Creation and the Law), the prophetic books (Jewish history and ethics), and the writings (proverbs, psalms, and moralistic narratives). Thus, in every Jewish home there was a source of poetic beauty and a revered document embodying the nation's history and purpose. The Scriptures have a message for all peoples, but to the Jews that message is peculiarly personal.

Persian religious ideas and practices

Other oriental religions also had a profound effect on Christianity, though their influence is less obvious than that of Judaism. In fact, some of the concepts from these religions seem to have come to Christianity by way of Jewish thought. During the sixth-century exile (the so-called Babylonian Captivity) following the conquest of Israel by Assyria and Babylonia, many Jews lived in daily contact with Mesopotamian culture. When Cyrus the Persian overthrew Babylonia in 538 B.C., he permitted those Jews who desired to, to return to Palestine. He imposed his rule upon their country, however, as he did on the rest of the Near East; thus, for the next two centuries (c. 500–300 B.C.) Jews everywhere came under Persian influence. It was during this time that Persian religious ideas made their impact on Jewish thought.

The greatest figure in Persian religion is Zoroaster, who lived in the seventh century B.C. Zoroaster transformed the ancient beliefs and superstitions of his people into a noble and inspiring faith in one God, the author of good and evil. His followers turned this faith into a dualism which taught that the world was the scene of two contending forces: Ahura Mazda, god of goodness and light; and Angra Mainyu, demon of evil and darkness. At the end of time Ahura Mazda would triumph, Angra Mainyu would be cast into the pit, and the dead would be resurrected and judged according to their merits. All this was written down in the Avesta, the Persian holy book.

There is an unmistakable similarity between Zoroastrian and subsequent Christian ideas about "things to come" and the idea of evil personified in Satan. At the approach of the last days a Messiah would appear, miraculously born, to prepare the way for the Judgment. Moreover, Zoroastrianism was an ethical religion that extolled truthfulness, love, and the "Golden Rule" and denounced pride, lust, and avarice. Whether a man went to heaven or hell after death was determined by his conduct during life. All men, however, would ultimately be saved by Mazda's pervading goodness; unlike Christian damnation, the Persian hell was not eternal.

With the sweep of Persian conquest in the sixth century B.C., the religion of Zoroaster, much altered since his time, was carried to all the peoples of the Near East. For several centuries it worked its influence in those lands. Alexander the Great, after defeating the Persians about 325 B.C., tried to undermine the religion by destroying copies of the Zoroastrian holy books. But he could not destroy the faith; and when Persia revived, during the period of the late Roman Empire, the religion of Zoroaster regained its position as the state religion of Persia.

Zoroastrianism, mingling with Greek and oriental polytheism, won adherents throughout the Roman world. An especially popular offshoot was Mithraism, which spread westward from Asia Minor after the first century B.C. through military and commercial contacts. It flourished in the empire, particularly among the legions, until Constantine threw his support to Christianity in 313.

The divine Mithra was believed to be a lieutenant of Ahura Mazda, but he attracted worshipers in his own right. According to legend, he was born of a rock and was first attended by shepherds. (Long before Christ, December 25 was celebrated as the date of his birth.) Mithra was also associated with the sun, and his followers marked Sunday as his day of worship. They called it the "Lord's Day," for Mithra was known to them as Lord. Only men were admitted to the cult, and initiates had to undergo secret and terrifying rituals designed to instruct them and to test their will. Among the milder ceremonies were baptism in holy water and the partaking of a sacred meal of bread and wine. After passing through successive ordeals, converts were "reborn" in Mithra. This experience charged them with new hope, for, though Mithra had ascended to heaven, he had promised to return and bring life everlasting to his loyal followers.

· In the competition for souls during the troubled third century

(p. 89), Christianity found a formidable rival in Mithraism. The ancient gods of the Greeks and Romans had lost their attraction, but "mystery" religions like Mithraism had a powerful appeal in those trying times. People were casting about for a message of hope and consolation, for a promise of better things—if not in this life, then in the next. They were particularly responsive to the tales of the miraculous that clustered around such deities as the Persian Mithra, the Phrygian Cybele, and the Egyptian Isis.

All these mystery cults originated in ancient vegetation myths; all told of a god who had died and was resurrected, as the cold death of winter is succeeded by the warm life of spring. And all taught that the individual worshiper, through initiation and ritual, might win eternal life. These religions interacted with Christianity for several centuries and influenced its developing traditions.

Greek philosophical thought

Greek philosophy, too, had an effect on Christianity, especially as the new sect began to expand beyond Palestine into more thoroughly Hellenized lands. Plato's Academy, founded in the fourth century B.C., continued to train scholars far into the Christian era, and the impact of Plato's thought on Christianity was immense. Plato had been the first to elaborate the concept of an eternal "soul" distinct from the body. In his "Doctrine of Ideas" he spoke of a permanent spiritual order of perfection, presided over by the Idea of the good (God). He considered the human body a source of distraction and evil, a view that reinforced the ascetic strain in Christianity.

Stoicism also exerted a strong influence on Christianity. Belief in a universe ruled by providence, emphasis on the brotherhood of men and on the virtues of justice, compassion, and restraint—all were central to its teachings. Stoicism was widespread among the educated classes of the Roman Empire, and its numerous parallels with Christianity helped pave the way for the new faith.

THE LIFE AND TEACHINGS OF JESUS

After we have sifted through all the historical antecedents and influences, however, we must recognize Christianity as a religion with its own integrity and power. Jesus is not a vague, mythological figure (like Mithra) but a person who lived and taught in Roman times. And it is his life, character, and message that stamp the Christian faith with its unique meaning.

What is known of Jesus' career is contained in the four Gospels: Matthew, Mark, Luke, and John. Scholars are not certain as to the actual authorship and dates of composition of these books, but they were obviously written by zealous believers. In explaining the relationships of the Gospels to one another, scholars generally agree that Mark (and possibly another, undiscovered book) was used as a source by Matthew and Luke. John's account, which was written later (at the close of the first century), reflects a more developed theology, with emphasis on the divine nature of Jesus and his affirmations of immortality.

The "nature" of Jesus

But there are gaps even in this composite biography. The Gospels concentrate on the birth of Jesus, the brief years of his ministry, and his death and reported resurrection; the disciples felt no need to set down all the details of his life, for to them the "good tidings" required no "historical" proof. Faithful converts would accept him as the Christ (Messiah), the true God in human form (incarnate). They would believe that his sacrifice on the Cross atoned for the sins of men and that his resurrection promised life eternal to all who loved him. Thus, the Cross became and remains the dominant symbol of Christianity.

An objective scholar looking for the historical Jesus will not find his answer as simply and clearly as does the believer. To begin with, since the Gospels were written by avowed disciples of Jesus, the story is colored by their personal relationship to him. Moreover, though the Gospels agree in general outline, they differ in their accounts of Jesus' personality and identity. Did he, for example, represent himself as God (or the Son of God)? Some Gospel passages appear to say this explicitly, but at least one passage indicates that Jesus did *not* identify himself with God: "Why do you call me good? No one is good but God alone" (Mark 10:18). Perhaps, suggest some scholars, Jesus' claims to divinity were introduced into the narratives only after converts accustomed to savior-gods had accepted him as divine.

The nature of the historical Jesus, then, is shrouded in doubt. Was he Son of God, son of man, divine prophet, religious reformer, humanitarian idealist—or, as the Jewish scribes insisted, a blasphemer and imposter? A final answer, acceptable to all, cannot be drawn from the available sources. The orthodox Christian belief, of course, is that Jesus *is* God.

The Sermon on the Mount

The ethical teachings of Jesus are most clearly summarized in the Sermon on the Mount (Matt. 5–7). In his account the disciple Matthew brought together the best-remembered sayings, parables, and moral admonitions of his master. What manner of life is most pleasing to God? What virtues does he value most highly? Jesus answered these questions directly and precisely, in the context of his own place and time. During the three years of his ministry, he was challenged by particular sects and tried to refute their points of view. He opposed, for example, the Pharisees and scribes, who stressed Jewish exclusiveness and strict observance of the rites, regulations, and holidays prescribed by the Law. And he criticized fellow Jews who had given over their lives to the pursuit of power and wealth. So he spoke, not as an aloof divinity, but directly to the people with whom he came in contact.

Blessed are the meek, he declared, the merciful, the peacemakers, and the pure in heart. In other words, he was telling his listeners to turn away from the warrior ideal exemplified by Achilles, Alexander, and Caesar, since righteousness and love are more precious in God's sight than worldly success and honor. Moreover, Jesus assured his listeners that there was no conflict between his teaching and that of the Hebrew prophets of old, that he came not to destroy "but to fulfill." His moral demands, indeed, were based on the traditional ethics of Judaism, but he carried them almost beyond human reach. Obeying the Law and the Commandments was not enough. In the new testament that Jesus taught, one must love not only the Lord but one's *enemies;* one must refrain not only from adultery but from lustful *thoughts;* one must not only give up the search for material goods but give away all possessions; one must "resist not evil" but "turn the other cheek."

This code of conduct made inordinate demands on the human spirit. Did Jesus really expect men to live up to it? To this question, too, there is no clear-cut answer. A few Christians have taken his injunctions literally, pledging themselves to an ascetic life and straining to measure up to Jesus' "unnatural" standards. Others have discounted the code as idealistic, beyond the grasp of real men in the real world. The view generally taken by the Church is that Jesus' precepts constitute an ideal toward which all should strive but which none can attain. Therefore, all will fall short—yet all may be saved by repentance and God's mercy.

When Jesus himself was seized on charges of posing as king of the Jews, his very disciples failed him. Judas betrayed him, Peter denied him, the others abandoned him in terror and despair. Thus even the saintly twelve fell short of their master's expectations. But the faithful did not founder on the rock of Calvary. According to the Gospels, Christ rose from the tomb and appeared several times to his disciples before ascending to heaven. The Resurrection renewed the faith of his followers and gave them the will to obey his last instruction: "Go ye into the world, and preach the gospel to every creature" (Mark 16:15).

THE EARLY CHURCH AND ITS EXPANSION

The Acts of the Apostles, which tells the story of the early Church, reveals that the disciples were at first dismayed by Jesus' command to set forth as missionaries. How could they, a handful of despised and humiliated men, succeed in such a task? They were simple and unlettered Jews, with little knowledge of foreign lands or tongues. So they waited patiently, according to Jesus' admonition: "But ye shall receive power, after that the Holy Ghost is come upon you" (Acts 1:8).

Missionary beginnings: Pentecost

According to tradition, the missionary work started at Pentecost (fifty days after the Resurrection), when, Acts relates, the Holy Ghost descended upon the disciples as "a mighty rushing wind" (2:2). The Spirit bestowed upon them the gifts of wisdom, tongues, and healing, thus distinguishing them from other men and preparing them for their task. But the mission was not easy. Three thousand souls, the Scriptures say, were baptized in the faith on Pentecost. These first converts, however, were all Jews, and soon the apostles were faced with a thorny question: Could they break bread with Gentiles, contrary to Jewish law, and baptize them directly in Christ? Or must Gentiles first become cleansed as Jews (subject to circumcision, dietary restrictions, and prescribed observances)? Peter, the first disciple of Jesus, leaned toward the latter view. But a vision taught him his error, and he began to baptize Gentiles in company with Jews. The issue was finally settled by a council of apostles and elders at Jerusalem in 48 A.D., which decreed that Gentile converts were not to be bound by the Law.

Peter continued to hold that those who had been born to the Law should abide by it, but the trend was steadily away from the observance of the Law by all Christians. Easter, for example, displaced the Jewish Passover, which commemorated the deliverance of the ancient Hebrews from Egyptian bondage. This event was the high point of Jewish history as told in the Torah; but in the Christian view it was eclipsed by the Resurrection, which promised salvation to *all* men. Thus Easter became the climactic day of the Christian year. Similarly, the Jewish Sabbath (seventh day) gave way to Sunday as a day of rest and worship, for it was on the "first day of the week" that Christ arose from the dead.

The apostle Paul

Paul, the "apostle to the Gentiles," led the way in differentiating Christianity from Judaism. Going beyond Peter, he asserted that the Law was no longer valid—even for Jews. No man can be saved by the Law, taught Paul; the Law can only bring a man to an understanding of his dependence upon Christ. A Christian of passionate conviction, Paul undertook the religious conquest of the non-Jewish world.

Of all the apostles, he was perhaps the best qualified for this mission. He was not one of the original twelve, not even a native of Palestine, but a Jew born in the city of Tarsus, in Asia Minor. He claimed Roman citizenship and apparently came from a well-to-do, cultivated family. Trained in both Hebrew and Greek, he was familiar with the religions and philosophies of the Hellenistic world, and, as a member of the orthodox sect of Pharisees, he shared the prophetic hope that Yahweh would one day be acknowledged by all men. Yet he knew at firsthand how reluctant the Gentiles were to accept the burden of the Jewish Law.

While studying at Jerusalem, Paul witnessed the first Christian martyrdom. Stephen, one of the early converts, was preaching against dependence on the Law and was urging Jews to accept Christ. The assembled Jews charged Stephen with blasphemy and stoned him to death. Paul, then full of zeal for the Law, condoned the killing and sought out other Christians to hale before the Jewish court. While he was engaged in this undertaking on the road to Damascus, in Syria, Paul was suddenly converted. Acts tells us that he was blinded by a great light and heard the voice of the Lord asking why Paul persecuted him. At last Paul's eyesight was restored, and God announced that he had become a "chosen vessel" to bear the name of Christ to the Gentiles.

The Epistles of Paul, in the New Testament, reflect the enthusiasm and skill he brought to his missionary task. He had become convinced that Christ represented the culmination of historic Judaism —but a Judaism made pure and universal. With the barrier of the Law taken away, the true religion could now be carried to the Gentile world.

Though Paul was not one of Jesus' companions and, indeed, at first appeared as an enemy, he is ranked by the Church as a leading apostle, second only to Peter. This recognition speaks eloquently of his accomplishments. Primarily an organizer, he made arduous journeys by land and sea and founded numerous congregations in Asia

Minor and Greece. His task was made easier by the existence of the Pax Romana and the imperial roads and by the fact that the Greek language was universally spoken in the eastern parts of the empire. Still, these means would have been worthless had it not been for his fearless devotion to the cause of Christ.

In the course of his missionary work, Paul became of necessity an interpreter of the faith, for Jesus had left few dogmas and no developed theology. When Paul carried the Word to the curious and speculative Greeks, he was met by all kinds of questions—many of which are recorded in his Epistles, or Letters. He answered the questions humbly, explaining that he spoke only as the Lord gave him power.

The First Epistle to the Corinthians illustrates the manner in which Paul set forth interpretations. The congregation at Corinth had asked him several questions: Is virginity more seemly to God than the married state? How is the Lord's Supper to be partaken? In what kind of body will believers be raised from the dead? In his patient answers to these and countless other questions, Paul enunciated beliefs and attitudes that were to carry down through the centuries.

Paul was convinced that in order to transform Christianity from a Jewish sect into a universal faith, Jewish observances and rites would have to be discarded. In winning souls for Christ, he was admittedly "all things to all men" (I Cor. 9:19–23). He demanded no particular mode of life, no legalistic rule of conduct, no special ceremonies. It was sufficient for men simply to have faith in Christ as their Savior.

Hence Paul laid the foundation for the belief that salvation depends exclusively on faith rather than on observance of the Law (or "works"). This belief was to raise a dilemma in Christian ethics and discipline, because one may well ask, "Why, then, bother to obey the rules and precepts of the Church?" Paul's answer would be that good works will flow naturally from faith, but it is *faith*, not works, that saves one. The Church, traditionally, has been fearful of the consequences of this interpretation when carried to the extreme, and theologians have had serious trouble explaining the relationship between faith and works.

Paul's position led him unavoidably to another problem: How do men receive faith? Do they earn it through their own efforts, or is it a gift freely granted by God, for his own secret reasons? Paul believed that faith was a gift of God, a conviction that was confirmed by his own experience. Why had Paul, a stony-hearted enemy of Christ, been chosen by the Lord to see the light of conversion? The only answer, Paul felt, lay in God's secret will. As Paul expressed it in his Epistle to the Romans, "So then he has mercy upon whomever he wills, and he hardens the heart of whomever he wills" (9:18). This view, variously referred to as the doctrine of "predestination" or "election," was to become a source of controversy within the Church. Augustine (in the fifth century) and Calvin (in the sixteenth) are among those who have pursued Paul's line of thought most vigorously, but the idea that some human souls are excluded from all hope of salvation has proved unacceptable to a majority of Christians.

Paul did not labor alone in his efforts to bring Christianity to the Gentiles. Tradition holds that Peter reached Rome and founded the congregation there. Other missionaries were busy in Egypt, Syria, and Asia Minor. The most prominent apostolic churches (those founded by apostles) were at Jerusalem, Alexandria, Damascus, Antioch, and Rome. By the end of the first century there were more than fifty Christian congregations, and during the next hundred years the gospel was carried to every province of the empire.

Persecution of the Christians

But the early Church was met everywhere by popular and official hostility. It is often difficult for modern Christians to understand why the followers of Jesus, with their teachings of love, peace, and brotherhood, should have been persecuted. Yet for some three hundred years, beginning with the crucifixion of Jesus himself, the faithful were distrusted by Jews and Gentiles alike. Stephen was stoned to death by the Jews; Paul was beheaded by the Romans; and the twelve apostles (and countless Christians who followed them) met violent deaths.

The long roll of martyrs was partly the product of rumors and misunderstandings regarding the new religion. Since the Christians spoke out against established institutions—such as the Jewish Law and the Roman cult of emperor-worship—they were widely thought to be contemptuous of the whole existing order. They often refused to associate with pagans, and they condemned such popular amusements as the public baths and circuses. The respected Roman historian Tacitus concluded that they harbored "hatred for the human race."

Many of the accusations made against the Christians—such as cannibalism and incest—sprang from prejudice and ignorance. Other charges, however, sprang from the actual nature of the Church. Christianity was truly a revolutionary movement that aimed to turn conventional life upside down. Understandably, people of conservative learnings considered the missionaries "subversive"—unpatriotic, fanatical, and atheistic (in relation to the pagan deities). Moreover, the Christians often assumed an air of spiritual superiority and exclusiveness. It is little wonder that the resentment of their contemporaries sometimes flared into violence.

The attitude of the Roman government was somewhat different. Ordinarily, Roman officials refrained from interference in local affairs and observed religious toleration throughout the empire. The imperial government outlawed Christianity as early as the first century, however, on the grounds that it was a secret sect dangerous to the state. But enforcement of the ban was lax and irregular; persecutions occurred only when the populace became aroused against the Christians or when the emperor needed a scapegoat to divert attention from internal problems.

The government continued to look upon the sect with disapproval, however. Christians refused to burn incense before the emperor's statue, they would not serve in the army, and they seemed utterly lacking in public spirit. Worse, they were constantly causing trouble by their denunciations of rival faiths and their efforts to proselytize all nations. Consequently, the more conscientious rulers concluded that the Christians, by their efforts to subvert established institutions, had forfeited their right to toleration. Accordingly, they sought to compel Christians to renounce their faith—or at least to pledge homage to the emperor. When the faithful refused to take the required "loyalty oath," they were sentenced to death.

Practices of the early congregations

But persecution did not check the spread of the gospel. There was a yearning, especially among the common people, for the "good news" the Christians brought. Most of the early converts were of the poorer classes—men who had found a home in Christ. They were predominantly city-dwellers; the conservative peasants (*pagani*) held stubbornly to the ancient cults. Moreover, many of the converts, looking forward to the imminent Second Coming of Christ, sold what little they possessed and gave the proceeds to their congregation. This urge toward community property began to fade during the second century, however, when it appeared that the Savior's return would not be as speedy as was at first expected.

Since the Christians found the doors of Jewish synagogues closed to them, and since the government forbade them to build temples of their own, they usually met in private homes or halls. There, accepting one another as brothers, they prayed, sang psalms, and took part in simple rituals. Though the ceremonies were not at first uniform, two were performed by every congregation. One was baptism, the purifying rite of Christian initiation; the other was the partaking of bread and wine, in keeping with the Gospel story of the Last Supper. This second ritual came to be known in the Greek service as the Eucharist and in the Latin service as the Mass. (In Protestant services it is commonly called Holy Communion or the Lord's Supper.)

THE GROWTH OF CHRISTIAN ORGANIZATION AND DOCTRINE

From such rudimentary beginnings, the Church had developed an elaborate system and structure by the time of the Emperor Constantine. The Eucharist remained the central ritualistic act, but a host of companion rites and practices evolved. The developing liturgy—that is, the forms of worship—reflected the influence of Judaic tradition and of the Greek and oriental mystery cults. Incense, bells, and vestments came into use, along with holy water, oil, candles, and prayer beads. And gradually the religious calendar, with its cycle of fasts and feast days, was worked out. From birth to death the Church provided the faithful with guidance through a ceaseless round of services and observances. In short, the idea of Christianity became thoroughly institutionalized.

The rise of the priesthood and the emergence of bishops

It would have been impossible to accomplish all this without strong leadership and organization. In the beginning little formal structure was necessary; but, as the gospel spread throughout the Roman world, a need arose for organized supervision and direction. Moreover, unity among the scattered congregations served as a defense against persecution. The first step toward formal organization was the emergence of a corps of Church officers set apart from the ordinary members of the congregation. So long as the congregations were small and the Second Coming was still believed to be near at hand, all the members probably shared in the management of local affairs. But as the congregations grew larger and as ritual became more complex, it was natural to develop a specialization of talents and responsibilities. Those who were assigned special functions came to be known as the "clergy"; the rest of the congregation was called the "laity."

A differentiation in levels of authority began to evolve at about the same time. Though the early groups viewed all their members as equal in authority, they accorded special status to the twelve apostles. The twelve were reported to have been filled with the Holy Ghost at Pentecost, thereby gaining the powers of tongues, wisdom, and healing. These powers, it was believed, could be passed on to others by the solemn act of the "laying on of hands." Thus, according to Acts, Matthias was chosen to take the place of the betrayer Judas (1:26), and Paul received the power of the Spirit at the hands of the disciple Ananias (9:17).

The theory of ordination that grew out of these traditions justified the special role and authority of the priesthood. The priests, by virtue of the "laying on of hands," were believed to have received the power to perform the miraculous rites of the Church. This theory strengthened the clergy's authority over the laity and ensured, at the same time, that unauthorized persons would not be able to assume roles of leadership.

At first the priests and lesser officers were elected (or approved) by their congregations; but as time passed the clergy grew more and more independent of the laity. They sensed the need for closer association among themselves and for superior levels of authority. Only by these means could they hold the scattered congregations together against external attacks and internal divisions. And so there grew up over the years a system of ascending ranks and jurisdictions —the hierarchy of the Church.

Before the end of the second century, each city in which there was a Christian congregation had a chief priest who was recognized as its overseer, or bishop. He was selected by the priests of his community, aided at least in theory by the laity, and he held his position for life. Responsibility and authority in local affairs gravitated increasingly to the bishop. He was ordained to the office by other bishops, and the theory gradually developed that the bishops together constituted the successors of the original apostles. (The church of every bishop, by tradition, was believed to have been founded by an apostle or by the companion of an apostle.) The bishops alone possessed the power of ordination. They taught that priests, deacons, and lesser clerics received, through the bishops, a *portion* of apostolic authority, but that only the bishops possessed it in full. This doctrine came to be known as the doctrine of "apostolic succession."

Since control of the Christian communities in the second and third centuries rested largely in the hands of the bishops (*episkopoi*), the system is referred to as the episcopal form of church government. This form still prevails in the Roman Catholic Church, the Greek Orthodox Church, and the Anglican churches. It was not seriously challenged until the time of the Reformation, when Protestant leaders like Martin Luther and John Calvin adopted the presbyterian system, which puts control in the hands of assemblies of ministers and elders (presbyteries) elected by the congregations.

A third-century bishop was a busy man. He oversaw the preaching of the gospel, the performance of religious rites, the care of the sick and poor, the management of church property, and the nurturing of Christian morals. He spoke for the faithful in dealings with civil authorities and represented them at religious councils. His area of jurisdiction, known as a diocese, normally included the city in which his church was located and the surrounding district. The diocese was divided into parishes, each with its local congregation and priest (pastor). Since both clergy and laity were obliged to obey the bishop, he held full control over the Christian community.

In coordinating their religious activities, the bishops turned to the model of Roman administration. As Diocletian grouped several provinces into a civil diocese, the bishops (reversing the terms) grouped several dioceses into a province. Over this larger jurisdiction reigned the bishop of the largest city in the province. Since a great city was known as a metropolis, this bishop assumed the higher title of "metropolitan" (later, archbishop).

By the time of Constantine there were five leading metropolitans: the bishops of Jerusalem, Alexandria, Antioch, Constantinople, and Rome. Their preeminence led to their being designated as "patriarchs," a status above that of other metropolitans. Thus, from the parish priest upward there were four distinct levels in the Christian hierarchy, just as there were in the hierarchy of the late empire. Both church and state achieved, at about the same time, closely supervised and authoritarian regimes.

Roman supremacy: the Pope

The final step in the organization of the Church was the establishment of a "monarchy." The theory of apostolic succession ensured a framework of legitimate authority, which could settle differences and enforce discipline at the local level; the bishops exercised control within their jurisdictions by assuming the right to excommunicate—that is, to exclude individuals from church fellowship and services. But when issues arose that divided the bishops themselves, serious troubles ensued.

A question had come up, for instance, about 150, regarding the correct day for celebrating Easter. The Gospels were contradictory on this point; the churches of Asia observed one date, the churches of the West another. It seemed incongruous, if not unholy, for one group of Christians to be feasting while another was fasting. Later in the second century, Victor, Bishop of Rome, decided to settle the question by excommunicating the Asian churches, presumably on the grounds that the authority of the Roman bishop was superior to that of all others. In any event, the Asian churches accepted Victor's date for Easter, and the excommunication was lifted.

Thus unity of practice was achieved through the assertion of a higher *authority*. And many Church-leaders felt that the only way to solve the countless other issues, of a more serious nature, that divided the Church was to recognize a final authority at the apex of the hierarchy. But each of the five patriarchs believed that the top position rightly belonged to him. Alexandria, Jerusalem, Antioch, and Constantinople offered impressive arguments, but Rome seemed to have the strongest claim. The Roman bishop had several decisive advantages: the Eternal City still enjoyed great prestige among the communities of the empire; Rome was the scene of the missionary work and martyrdom of the two leading apostles, Peter and Paul; and, according to tradition, the Roman bishopric had been founded by Christ's first disciple, Peter.

Roman bishops made the most of this Petrine tradition. They interpreted a passage in the Gospel of Matthew (16:18–19) to mean that Christ had founded his Church upon Peter and had entrusted to him alone the "keys to the kingdom of heaven." This, they insisted, made Peter supreme among the apostles. And, since each Bishop of Rome was the direct successor to Peter, the bishop of Rome was clearly supreme among the bishops of the world.

The rival patriarchs rejected Rome's claim to supremacy, pointing out that such a sweeping presumption could hardly be justified by a brief passage appearing in only one of the Gospels. They argued, further, that during the early days of the Church all important decisions were made by a council in Jerusalem, a council in which Peter had participated but which he had not ruled. Paul had made no references to Peter as the supreme head, and Peter had made no such claim for himself.

Nevertheless, the position and dignity of Rome and its association with both Peter and Paul won for it a place of *primacy* in the Christian world. The patriarchs of the East conceded that the successors to Peter had a right to sit at the "head of the table," so to speak. The Roman bishop, however, was not satisfied with this concession; he continued to insist on his *supremacy*, on being recognized as absolute monarch, the "vicar of Christ" on earth.

In the West, where there was no rival, Rome achieved that supremacy. By the fifth century the Roman bishop had begun to reserve to himself the title of *papa* (pope). This word, meaning "father," had formerly been used to refer to any bishop or priest, but henceforth it was used only for the Bishop of Rome, in the broader sense of "father of the Church." And from this usage arose the term "papacy" to refer to the office of the pope.

After the Germanic invasions of the West, the bishops of the East separated themselves from the Bishop of Rome—partly because of their continued unwillingness to recognize him as supreme. After numerous and tedious efforts to reunite the Latin and Greek branches of Christianity, a final schism occurred in 1054. The Bishop of Rome excommunicated the Patriarch of Constantinople, who had attained primacy among the Eastern bishops; the patriarch, in turn, excommunicated the Bishop of Rome, on the ground that his exaggerated claims made him a usurper. This deep split on the fundamental issue of organization and authority has persisted ever since. The Greek Church still denies the supremacy of the pope, while the Roman Church admits of no other possibility.

The Eastern clergy contended that ultimate power reposes in the council of Christian bishops. This conciliar theory of authority, generally accepted until the fourth century, continues to be upheld by the Greek Church. In the Roman Church, the conciliar theory, though it has reappeared from time to time, was eclipsed by the monarchical theory of Petrine supremacy.

The canon of Scriptures

The administrative authority invested in the Church hierarchy was paralleled by the development of Biblical authority. At last, in the fourth century, the canon (that is, the authorized list) of Scriptures was established. Previously a great many "holy" books and epistles had been in circulation, but the bishops agreed that if the unity of the Church was to be preserved these writings would have to be screened for certification. How were they to decide which had been inspired by God and which had not? Some of the bishops objected to accepting the Hebrew Scriptures, but these writings were so well established by tradition that it was finally decided to endorse them. The Greek translation of the Hebrew writings (the Septuagint) was taken as the canon for what Christians now call the Old Testament.

For other writings (the New Testament) there was no such guide in tradition, so the bishops resorted to authority as their criterion. They agreed that only writings by apostles or their companions would be admitted. Although this rule at once eliminated many disputed books of uncertain origin, it did not work automatically. For example, when a certain gospel attributed to Peter was found to favor a doctrine offensive to the bishops, they simply declared that Peter could not have been its author. On the other hand, books and epistles that struck the bishops as "right" in doctrine were readily attributed to an apostle—and thereby included in the canon.

This practice may seem to violate modern rules of critical scholarship, but it was hallowed by ancient tradition. The Jews had made Moses the author of all the sacred books on law, David the author of the psalms, and Solomon the author of the books of wisdom. And so, in the final analysis, it was the judgment of the bishops that determined whether a particular writing was admitted into the canon. Historically, the Church *preceded* the Bible and, in a real sense, authorized it.

The bishops did not reach final concurrence on the canon until near the end of the fourth century, when the pope proclaimed that Jerome's Latin translation (p. 125) was the Bible of the Church. In the West, where Latin was the language of the common people (*vulgus*), Jerome's translation became known as the Vulgate. It remains to this day the official version for Roman Catholics.

Doctrinal differences: orthodoxy and heresy

Notwithstanding the development of its hierarchy and canon of Scriptures, the Church was rent by serious disputes over doctrine. These ranged over a broad area: the liturgy, rules of Christian conduct, and the tortuous field of Christian theology—that is, explanations of God, the Creation, man, sin, and salvation. For centuries, the espousal of conflicting positions harassed the leaders of the Church. If there is to be one Church, there must be one doctrine; if truth is single and absolute, then differing views must be *false*. Committed to these assumptions, the Church Fathers could not rest while heresy stirred.

"Heresy" may be defined as any belief that deviates from the "true," or orthodox, doctrine as taught on the authority of the Church. All deviations disturbed the Church, some more deeply than others. One of the earliest, most persistent, and most radical of the heresies was Gnosticism (from *gnosis,* or knowledge). The Gnostics were a religious-philosophical sect with origins distinct from those of Christianity. Many of them, however, found their way into the Church, where they formed coteries and held to secret teachings that made use of certain Christian ideas. Had their influence proceeded unchecked, they might have revolutionized Christian doctrine.

Gnostic thought was a curious blend of Greek and Near Eastern speculation. It revolved around a *dualistic* conception of the universe, similar to that which runs through Platonic thought. According to the Gnostic view, the universe is divided between spirit and matter. Spirit is the only true good; matter came into existence as a kind of casting-off from spirit when the physical world, including human bodies, was created. The body (as Socrates had taught) imprisons the soul and is the source of evil; the true aim of life is to gain knowledge, by which the soul may liberate itself and join with the universal spirit. But, said the Gnostics, this knowledge cannot be attained through reason; it comes only as *mystical* insight, which the initiate achieves after passing through secret rites. Similar notions had appeared in Persian thought, particularly in Zoroaster's dualism.

Gnostics who had become Christians interpreted Christ as the Savior who would emancipate mankind from the prison of the flesh (sin). Moreover, since Christ is all-good, he could not have had a body; hence, the Incarnation, Jesus' life as a man, and his human suffering were only appearances. They could not have occurred, logically, for goodness consists of pure spirit.

This view clearly ran counter to basic Christian dogmas, and it alarmed the Church-leaders. During the second and third centuries, the bishops struck hard at such unauthorized teachings. When the Gnostics declared that their wisdom had come to them through "chosen" agents, the bishops replied that no one but the apostles and their successors could speak for the Church. The ordained bishops stood firm, and at last the Gnostics were suppressed as heretics. In varying forms, however, the central idea of this heresy continued to plague the Church. It cropped up in the fourth century as Manicheism, and again in the thirteenth as the Albigensian heresy.

The persistence of such deviations arises from the fact that the orthodox Christian position itself rests on a precarious balance between spirit and matter, soul and body. This position holds that both exist and that both are essentially good, for both are the handiwork of a perfect deity. Yet there is a clear tendency in Scripture, in the preaching of Jesus and Paul, to place spirit above matter, although *how far* above is not made clear. Given this lead, some Christians have tended to exalt the soul as the true home of God and to abase the body as the "devil's workshop." Those who follow this line to the extreme show contempt for *all* worldly things, including food and drink, sexual activity, and care of the body. A practical outlet for this impulse, within the limits of the Church control, is monasticism (which we will discuss later in this chapter).

No sooner had the Gnostic threat been suppressed than a heresy of a different sort cropped up: the Donatist heresy, named after Donatus, Bishop of Carthage. This heresy jeopardized the organization and functioning of the Church rather than its basic dogmas. It gave rise to a particularly bitter feud, partly because North Africans still harbored traces of the resentment Rome had generated by her destruction of Carthage centuries before. Consequently, many Africans supported Donatus out of provincial sentiment. (Not infrequently in history, movements of this sort have sprung from a combination of religious and sociopolitical protests.)

The religious issue was simple: Are the rites and ordinations performed by a priest or bishop valid if the ministrant is a sinner or not in good standing in the Church? During the persecutions under Diocletian, some African bishops had given up their holy books at the demand of imperial authorities, thereby saving their own lives. Their capitulation was regarded as an act of treason to the Church, and, although the authority of Rome reinstated the offenders after they had shown due repentance, many members of the African Church refused to accept them. Worse, Donatus and his adherents insisted that all the rites performed by the bishops after their sinful acts were invalid. Thrown into question were ordinations of Holy Office, marriages, baptisms—all the sacred rites of the Church. Here was a challenge that could not be ignored.

A council of bishops at Arles in 313 considered the question and decided against the Donatists. They declared that priests who had surrendered to persecution might be restored and that their ritual acts were in no wise affected by personal guilt or nonguilt: "Once a priest, always a priest." The power given through ordination was indelible and could not be erased. This reasoning is logical, and, for practical reasons, it appears to be the only position the Church could have taken. If the council had ruled that a priest must be in a state of goodness (grace) in order to discharge his functions, the validity of any ceremony he performed would be open to doubt. The decision at Arles sealed the powers conferred by ordination and set at rest the apprehensions of the faithful. The Donatists, however, stubbornly refused to abide by the ruling, and the heresy smoldered until the seventh century. It disappeared at last when the Islamic tide rolled over North Africa, engulfing orthodox and heretical Christians alike.

The Council of Nicaea and the "Nicene Creed"

The doctrinal dispute that came nearest to splitting the Church was over the "nature" of Jesus and his relationship to God. We have already seen that the Gnostics believed Jesus to be pure spirit and denied his human nature. In direct opposition to that view was the idea that Jesus was only a man, although a man of superior moral stature, who had been adopted by God for his divine purposes. Between these extremes were countless other points of view, most of which subordinated the Son in some manner to the Father. All the variety and subtlety of Hebrew and Greek tradition were brought into play in this crucial theological debate. For how could Christians worship as one body unless they agreed on the nature of the godhead?

The argument was still raging three centuries after the birth of Christ. By the early fourth century, however, opinions had become polarized. One view was propounded by Athanasius, Bishop of Alexandria, and the other by Arius, an erudite priest of the same city. Athanasius held that Father and Son were two equal persons but *one substance*. Arius insisted that, since Christ had been "begotten," there must have been a time when he did not exist. Since he was not coeternal with the Father, he could not be coequal.

When the Emperor Constantine learned of this religious division, he was deeply distressed. After accepting Christianity in 313, he had given the Church legal status, fully expecting that it would serve as a unifying force in the empire. But now he found it instead a source of discord. Most of the East leaned to Arius; the West supported Athanasius. How could he heal the breach and restore Christian unity?

Constantine knew that the dissension could not be bridged by means of reason, for logical arguments were being spun out endlessly by both sides. Realizing that, as in matters of discipline, the final resort would have to be to authority, he summoned the hierarchy of the Church to a meeting at Nicaea (in Asia Minor) in 325. This was the first ecumenical (worldwide) council of the Church, and more than three hundred bishops attended. On the question put before them, the majority sided with Athanasius. A formal creed of belief, embodying his view, was drawn up in a carefully worded statement that excluded all forms of "subordinationism." The statement also stressed the dual nature of Christ as *both* man and God, thus striking at Gnostic teachings.

This "Nicene Creed," slightly modified by subsequent councils, remains the orthodox view. It declares that the Son is of one being, or essence, with the Father. It hurls the anathema upon those who say that there was a time "when he was not" or that he is of "another substance or essence." The creed also includes the Holy Spirit in the statement, thus completing the concept of the godhead as a trinity: one *substance* in three equal but distinct *persons*.

The Council of Nicaea did not immediately succeed, however, in restoring Christian unity. When Arius and several other priests at Nicaea refused to sign the creed, Constantine banished them. The power of the state, formerly employed against Christians, was henceforth used to support orthodoxy against heresy. Ten years later, an Eastern council at Tyre reversed the decisions of Nicaea and exiled Athanasius instead of Arius. Constantine's successors held divergent opinions on the issue, and for some forty years the banishment and recall of bishops turned on the caprice of imperial politics; Athanasius was banished six times in all. Finally, a new emperor, Theodosius, reunited the empire and summoned a second ecumenical council. This meeting, held at Constantinople in 381, reaffirmed the Nicaean decision and put an end to the exhausting debate. The Arian heresy, nevertheless, persisted stubbornly among the converted Goths and in corners of the East.

THE WORLDLY VICTORY OF THE CHURCH

The early leaders of the Church guided Christianity through the critical period of the first three centuries and made possible its ultimate triumph. Had it not been for their devotion to unity, all the efforts to establish doctrine and organization would have led to nothing. From each persecution and heresy the Church emerged stronger and wiser than before.

The conquest of the state

The rise of Christianity was aided by the shortcomings of rival faiths and the troubles that befell the empire. In fact the Church made its great leap forward during the third century, when Roman rule was degenerating into an endless struggle over the succession. The new emperors raised up by the troops were usually too busy looking out for their own safety to be much concerned about the Christians. At the same time, many Romans of the middle and upper classes had grown weary of civil strife and had begun to look with sympathy and respect upon the outlawed faith. Membership in the Church, once restricted to the poorer people, now cut across society. The number of converts mounted swiftly; by the time of Constantine, probably 10 per cent of the population were pledged to the Cross.

The last persecutions, which took place in the third century, were failures. Many martyrs earned their reward, but public opinion had shifted from contempt to compassion for the Christians. It was clear that the Church could not be broken. At last, when Constantine came to power and was won over, people everywhere knew that the Cross had conquered the crown and had actually enlisted it as an ally against the pagan rear guard. In 381 Theodosius legalized the victory by making Christianity the official religion of the empire and by proscribing all others. Now the tables were turned. Mobs attacked pagan temples, smashing idols and assaulting worshipers. By the end of the fourth century, pagans (and Christian heretics) were being sentenced to death. The Church, which had once vilified emperors for their intolerance of Christianity, now joined with the state to stamp out rival faiths.

The worldly success of the Church was due to a combination of forces. At a moment in time when old beliefs had grown stale, Christianity appeared as an appealing new religion. It placed faith in one God of justice and mercy, taught brotherhood and love, and promised life eternal in a better world. Though the synthesis itself was unique, it contained elements that had been made familiar by Judaism, the mystery cults, and Greek philosophy. Hence, Christianity's ideas were easier to explain and to accept than if they had been totally strange. Its ritual satisfied the emotions; its theology challenged the intellect. Because of its many-sided appeal, it attracted superior leadership and loyalty. The Church also benefited from the limitations and weaknesses of its competitors. Most of its rivals were local or national in outlook, while Christianity aimed at universality. The pagan religions lacked organization and zeal; the Christians were well-disciplined, aggressive, and uncompromising. Their abiding faith in ultimate victory sustained them through the dark and bloody years of their persecution.

Augustine: the philosopher of Christian victory

Augustine, one of the Fathers of the Church, symbolizes the Christian triumph. His own life, with its pagan beginnings and ultimate acceptance of Christ, is a recapitulation of the larger struggle within the empire. Born of a Christian mother and a pagan father, Augustine was attracted at one time or another by the leading cults and philosophies of his day, and he watched the steady progress of Christianity until at last it became the established religion under Theodosius. About 387 Augustine was himself converted and rose swiftly to a position of eminence in the Church. A man of extraordinary intellectual power, he influenced succeeding generations even more than his own, for his ideas have helped to forge the theology, morals, politics, and philosophy of the Western world. A prolific writer, he set down his major thoughts in the *Confessions* and the *City of God*.

Augustine grew up in a small town in North Africa. He was sent for schooling in rhetoric to cosmopolitan Carthage, a Roman city that had been built on the ancient Punic site. There he plunged into the study of classical literature and the arts of logic and disputation, which were to serve him later as an advocate of Christian doctrine. During those same years he indulged his taste for pleasure and immersed himself in pagan thought. When at last he felt the pull of Christianity, he discovered that he could not make his way to God by himself; the *Confessions* tells the story of his inner struggle.

Augustine's youthful association with Manicheism (an extreme version of Gnosticism) gave him a lifelong bias toward dualism, which influenced his interpretations of his personal history and of world history. He saw the struggle within himself as categorical: his love of worldly things versus his love of the Lord. Ultimately, by God's grace, the higher love won out, and the tortured young man was baptized a Christian. Thanking the Lord for this gift, Augustine confessed, "For so completely didst thou convert me to Thyself that I desired neither wife nor any hope of this world, but set my feet on the rule of faith." He became a priest and, later, Bishop of Hippo, in North Africa.

From his personal experiences Augustine concluded that bodily appetites (as well as false philosophies) distract men from the contemplation of God. He denounced as sinful, therefore, even the simplest of physical pleasures, and he inferred that all men bear an enormous burden of sin. Their only hope for salvation is to pray for God's help in bringing them to repentance and self-denial. Augustine himself gave up wife and child and lived like a monk. The power of his intellect, will, and example thus came down on the side of Christian asceticism.

His experience also led him to embrace Paul's doctrine of predestination—that the Lord chooses those who are to be saved. The original sin of Adam, wrote Augustine, condemned all men to eternal punishment—but "the undeserved grace of God saved some therefrom." Thus Paul was chosen from among the Pharisees and Augustine from the Manicheans to become servants of God. Neither felt he had earned grace through his own behavior, and so both gave full credit to the Lord's mercy.

Augustine expanded this concept of the "elect" and the "nonelect" into a comprehensive, and profoundly simple, philosophy of world history. Following his inclination to view matters in a dualistic way, he declared that all mankind—the dead, the living, and the unborn—are divided into two communities. The first is moved by love of self, the second by love of God. These allegiances, he argued, transcend the superficial attachments to race, nation, and class. He called one community, metaphorically, the Earthly City and the other, the Heavenly City (the City of God). Though the members of these two communities are intermixed in the present world, they are destined for separate fates. The first will suffer everlasting punishment with the devil, and the second will reign eternally with God. History, Augustine wrote, is a drama planned by the Lord and centered upon a continuing tension and struggle between the two cities.

It was in this cosmic light that he explained the sacking of Rome by the barbarian Goths in 410. This calamity, occurring only a generation after Theodosius had made Christianity the state religion, shocked and dismayed many Christians, and surviving pagans whispered that it was a sign of retribution by their gods. Augustine indignantly refuted their claim and began to write his monumental book, the *City of God,* which put the fall of Rome into a universal perspective. With prodigious labor he catalogued the earlier reverses and disasters of Rome, thus "proving" that the city's troubles were not the result of its having embraced Christianity. If Rome was being punished again, it was because of its ancient crimes: paganism, conquests, enslavements, and the persecution of Christians.

Augustine assured the faithful that the sack of Rome was, in truth, a spectacular confirmation of basic Christian teachings: it demonstrated that even the most powerful of earthly cities must sooner or later crumble and fall. The only *true* Eternal City is the City of God, and the whole earthly show of history is a passing thing. To some men, Augustine's interpretation implied that they should simply stand by and let events take their course ("God's will be done"). But he reminded them that the empire, whatever its past sins, was now a Christian state and a bulwark of order; he therefore urged all its citizens to resist the barbarians who were bringing pillage and anarchy.

But, some critics objected, are not fighting and killing contrary to the commandments of God? Augustine, interpreting Scripture, answered that the rule against killing applies only to personal behavior. A war declared by officials of the state can be morally "right," and in a "just war" killing is permissible. Augustine's premise of the "just war" carried with it an inescapable implication: if our side is just, then the enemy must be unjust. He thus laid the foundations for the Christian sanction of wars among states and the "good"-versus-"evil" stereotype in interstate relations.

Along with his explanations of history, the Bishop of Hippo offered his view of the future beyond history: while sinners endure unending torment, the elect (the saints) will enjoy the perpetual presence of the Lord. Augustine's picture of heaven was inferred from his reading of the Scriptures, but it also reflected his deep feelings about man's nature. He believed that the citizens of heaven are furnished (as Paul had written) with incorruptible bodies. These are not unruly as the physical body is but behave according to the commands of the will. As a special gift God rewards the saints (in heaven) with the *inability to sin.* Thus, they come to know true freedom—the freedom of God himself, who cannot sin. Augustine's concept of the hereafter and his philosophy of history guided Christian thinking for centuries to follow. More immediately, his ascetic example and teachings lent support to an emerging institution of the Church—monasticism.

EARLY CHRISTIAN MONASTICISM

The way of life observed by a monk or a nun often strikes the modern mind as eccentric and unnatural. Yet monasticism has been a recognized way of life in Western culture for centuries, answering the needs of a sizable minority of people. Today there are some two hundred religious orders in the Roman Catholic Church alone, with a membership of nearly a million and a half men and women.

The words "monasticism" and "monk" derive from the Greek *monachos,* meaning "one alone." The basic motivation of the monastic is to escape from society, to pray and contemplate in solitude, and so to come nearer his desired spiritual goal. The urge is older and broader than Christianity; there were "holy" hermits in ancient Egypt and Greece and ascetic communities in Palestine, and the recently discovered Dead Sea scrolls describe the rules of discipline in the Qumran monastery near Jerusalem, before the time of Christ. In other parts of the world—especially the Far East —the monkish life has attracted millions of men over the centuries.

The ascetic ideal

There is no simple explanation for the appeal of monastic life. The walls of a convent have always offered a haven to those who wish, for whatever reason, to remove themselves from the world. They may be prompted by disgust, fear, failure, or the urge to repent. Sometimes a severe personal tragedy will induce a man or a woman to retreat to the cloister, and some are attracted by the security it affords. None of these reasons, however, was central to the rise of Christian monasticism. Its primary motive was the desire to lead a "purer" life, as understood through faith. This desire, in turn, sprang from two forces: love for God and fear of damnation.

The holy life, in the Christian view, is not easily attained. It requires, above all, self-discipline—strict control over the natural self and appetites. The very term "ascetic" is derived from the Greek word for the exercise practiced by a trained athlete. Just as the discus-thrower must discipline his muscles, so the "perfect" Christian must gain control over his entire body and mind. Only then will he be free from sinful thoughts and acts—free to follow Christ's commands and, perhaps, to know the ecstasy of heavenly visions.

No mortal can expect to succeed in emulating Jesus, but some have experienced a keen urge to perfection. Not content to abide by the minimum requirements of Church and Scripture, they have preferred a harder road—to suffer, even as Christ suffered. They have adopted a more rigorous code than they could observe in worldly surroundings and have voluntarily withdrawn from human contacts in order to gain, in solitude, mastery over the flesh.

Why have some Christians conceived of perfection in such "unnatural" terms? In most cases they have taken their lead from the example of Christ. Jesus was no monk, but his teachings had a decidedly ascetic quality. As we have seen, his ethical precepts called for a degree of selflessness that few humans have been able to achieve: "If you would be perfect, go, sell what you possess and give to the poor, and you will have treasures in heaven; and come, follow me" (Matt. 19:21). Added to this original emphasis was the influence of Paul. He distinguished two standards of Christian conduct, the permissible and the heroic, and set the second above the first. While conceding, for instance, that it is "better to marry than to be aflame with passion" (I Cor. 7:9), he ranked virginity above the married state. "It is well," Paul admonished, "for a man not to touch a woman" (7:1). Finally, the impact of Gnostic views, which identified the body with evil, further reinforced the dualistic tendency in Christianity.

The hermit monks: Anthony

In the early days of Christianity, a man who aspired to the ascetic ideal simply abandoned civilization. In Egypt, where Christian monasticism was exceedingly popular during the third century, this was an easy matter, for the empty desert was close at hand. There, exposed to the burning heat and sand, the hermit could punish his body and strengthen his will. One of the most celebrated hermit monks was Anthony, whose biography by Bishop Athanasius was widely read throughout the empire. The son of an aristocratic family of Alexandria, Anthony became a devout Christian about 270. After selling all his possessions, he headed for the desert and spent the rest of his life subjecting his body to increasingly severe discipline. So famous did he become that thousands sought him out, hoping for cures and advice from this "holy man." To preserve his privacy, he was forced to move deeper and deeper into the desert.

Anthony's hardest struggle was with sexual desire. His biographer reported that the devil would appear to him at night, in the "form and deportment of a woman." But Anthony stubbornly resisted, and at last he cried out so fiercely that the devil "fled in terror." Other monks, too, were bedeviled by the sexual urge, which, more than any other, symbolized to them the insidious appetites of the body. Monastic chronicles are full of anecdotes about the monks' torments of desire and their efforts to dispel them. One way was to keep from looking at a woman. But, as Anthony discovered, this did not shield the mind from provocative imaginings. A surer way was to keep the body weak, bruised, and exhausted—a solution that also enabled the monk to display his contempt for the flesh.

Anthony was a model Christian hermit, fasting constantly and wearing a hair shirt beneath his leather outer garment. He never washed his body and was at pains to keep even his feet out of water. His solitary life of prayer and contemplation was frequently rewarded, we are told, by divine visions. This way of life must have agreed with Anthony, or else he was of very hardy stock: at the age of a hundred, writes Athanasius, the hermit fell ill and died in his desert cell.

Stirred by the example of Anthony and other world-renouncing anchorites, a multitude of Christians throughout Egypt and the East began to abandon the cities and take up a solitary life. Though most of them were sincere, there were many faddists among them. The behavior of a few was quite alarming. We are told of men grazing in the fields like animals, rolling naked in thorn bushes, and living in snake-infested swamps. One of the most famous of all the hermits was Simeon Stylites of Syria, who built a sixty-foot pillar, climbed to the top, and squatted there for thirty years until he died.

The Church could hardly ignore such excesses, even though they were not typical. The bishops decided that it was unwholesome for men to live in solitude and that the ascetic impulse, though good in itself, must be tamed. Solitary life should be combined with community living. And so in time the first monasteries were founded. Here each monk had a private cell for devotions, but during certain hours of the day he joined his fellow monks for common meals and labor.

Regulated communities: Basil, Jerome

The first religious "houses" were organized in the fourth century. One of the earliest was founded by Pachomius, who built a crude compound on an island in the Nile. A former soldier, Pachomius laid the place out like an army camp and imposed a strict schedule and discipline. Somewhat later his rule was taken over and modified by Basil, a bishop of Asia Minor. The Basilian Rule became the basis of monasticism in the East and has remained so to the present day.

The ascetic impulse spread westward across the Mediterranean world, spurred by the changing relationship between Christianity and the empire. Constantine's recognition of Christianity, which put an end to persecutions, was followed by Theodosius' decision, in 381, to make Christianity the empire's official religion. By making it safe to practice the faith, these measures brought into it large numbers of converts who lacked the sincerity and conviction of earlier Christians. In other words, as the Church advanced into the world, it became more worldly. Even the clergy began to succumb to corruption and ambition as the doors to wealth and power opened before them.

Christians who wished to emulate Christ and the venerated martyrs were dismayed and repelled by the growing worldliness of the Church; after the fourth century many of them chose monasticism as a substitute for martyrdom and as a refuge from the distractions of secular affairs. The Latin Fathers gave warm support to this ascetic trend. Augustine established a monastic community in North Africa and practiced rigid self-discipline himself. The scholarly Jerome, Augustine's contemporary, gave up a comfortable life in Rome to become a recluse.

The early hermits had shown contempt for all books other than the Scriptures. Anthony, for instance, was an uneducated man who believed that all a devout Christian needed was a sound mind and the inspiration of the Spirit. His attitude was in keeping with the teachings of Jesus, which might be characterized as anti-intellectual. And Paul, like Jesus, had put faith and love above reason and learning. Jerome, however, could not bear to leave his library at home, and so he carried it with him to the Holy Land. But his passion for the classics filled him with spiritual remorse, and he decided at last that he must be either a "Ciceronian" or a Christian.

He determined to give up his attachment to pagan literature. As soon as he stopped studying, however, he was tormented by visions of Roman dancing girls. Like Anthony, he tried to beat down his lustful thoughts by starving and mortifying his body. Nothing availed, however, until he hit upon the idea of learning Hebrew. As Hebrew was the language of Scripture, this study was pleasing to the Lord, and it required such mental concentration that his tantalizing visions began to fade.

Eventually Jerome was able to look at women without desire. When he was called to Rome on church business, he took the opportunity to spread the gospel of asceticism among the noble ladies of the city and persuaded many of them to turn their lives to Christian purity. "Marriage fills the earth," he counseled: "virginity fills heaven." On his return to Palestine, he founded, in partnership with a rich widow named Paula, several monastic communities in Bethlehem—some for men and some for women.

Jerome's most famous literary work, completed about 410, was a translation of the Bible into Latin from the original Hebrew and Greek sources. Jerome decided to set the monks and nuns to work on scholarly projects also. His success in harnessing the energy of monasticism to productive literary enterprise established an important precedent. During the Middle Ages monasteries helped safeguard the cultural heritage of the West by preserving and copying manuscripts and by providing rudimentary schooling for the clergy.

Benedict and his rule

The most influential founder of European monasticism was Benedict of Nursia. The son of a noble Italian family, he began early in life to follow Anthony's example. Sickened by the vice he saw in Rome, he fled to the nearby hills and imposed on himself a regimen of fierce self-punishment. So famous did the austere hermit become that he attracted other young men who wished to share his way of life. Convinced at last that asceticism was better practiced in groups, he left his solitary cave and established several small communities for his disciples.

The monastery at Monte Cassino, which Benedict founded about 529, served as the center of his work. It has been rebuilt many times (most recently, after the Second World War), and it still stands on a towering hill overlooking the town of Cassino, between Rome and Naples. There Benedict drew up a set of rules to govern the lives of his monks. This Benedictine Rule reflected the ideals of love, humanity, and piety that inspired the life of its author. It struck a balance between solitary meditation and group activities. The rule proved so successful that it became the model constitution for all other religious orders in the West, and within a few centuries nearly forty thousand monasteries and nunneries were governed by it. Since then, many millions of lives have been subject to its daily regulation.

Any free man or woman was eligible to commit his life to the rule. After spending a probationary year to ensure that he was equal to its rigors, the novice took three perpetual vows: chastity, poverty, and obedience. In addition, he pledged "stability," which meant that he had to confine himself to the monastery premises unless he received permission to leave. The monk thus surrendered sexual gratification, private property, and personal freedom for the chance of living a life more pleasing to God and of achieving salvation through discipline.

Benedict felt that monarchical rule made for the greatest serenity and harmony within the monastic community. Consequently he granted authority over the monks to a superior known as an abbot. The abbott was chosen by the monks to serve for life, and Benedict advised the utmost care in his selection. He also gave the abbot advice on how to govern. The abbot, said Benedict, ought "rather to be of help than to command"; he should "exalt mercy over judgment . . . and strive to be loved rather than feared." He should always be aware of his own frailty and should keep himself from becoming troubled and anxious; if he grows jealous or suspicious, he will have no rest. He should use moderation in assigning labor to his monks: "He shall so temper all things that there may be both what the strong desire, and the weak do not shrink from" (*Rule,* LXIV).

On all matters of importance, Benedict urged, the abbot should consult the assembled brethren and weigh their advice seriously. "Do all things with counsel, and thou shalt not thereafter repent" (*Rule,* III). At the same time he warned the abbot against shutting his eyes to the vices of the monks. In dealing with a recalcitrant monk, the abbot should first rebuke him and then exclude him from association with his brothers. If these steps, supported by prayer, did not bring the offender to repentance, the abbot was authorized to use the lash, and, as a last resort, expulsion from the monastery. "Remove evil from you, lest one diseased sheep contaminate the whole flock" (*Rule,* XXVII).

Though Benedict left the abbot some measure of discretion, he set down in detail the standard monastic routine. The most important activity of all was the saying of Divine Office (obligatory daily prayers); eight times a day, the toll of bells called the monks to their knees. During meals the monks were to observe the rule of silence, while one of them read from the Scriptures. Certain hours of the day they were to spend alone in their cells, reading and meditating. To Benedict, the monastery was a "school for the service of the Lord."

As each monastery depended on its own resources, the monks had to spend much of their time growing and preparing food and providing for their other material needs. From four to eight hours a day were set aside for manual labor, which, thought Benedict, would provide a wholesome balance to their intellectual and spiritual activities. The monks cleared new land for cultivation, learned the arts of agriculture, and preserved ancient handicrafts in their workshops. Their services to Western civilization during the Middle Ages were immense, for in addition to performing manual chores they served as missionaries among the heathens and carried on scholarly tasks after the example of Jerome.

Yet direct service to God remained the primary aim of the Benedictine houses and of the religious orders that arose later. The monks devoted their life to prayer and charity, providing a model for Christians outside the cloister. To some degree their example moderated the brutality and crassness of a turbulent world. They also exercised a corrective influence on the more worldly priests and bishops of the Church. During the fifth and sixth centuries, when the moral level of the clergy outside the monasteries declined sharply, the exemplary behavior of the monks led to their being recognized as a distinct branch of the Church. Since they lived under a special rule (*regula*), they were designated as the "regular" clergy. Clerics who were free to move about in the world (*saeculum*) came to be known as the "secular" clergy.

By the sixth century, the very existence of the Church depended heavily upon the regular branch. Acting as the conscience of the secular clergy, its members began to regard themselves, in moments of suspended humility, as a spiritual elite. Some of the most vigorous and devoted leaders of the Church came up through the rule—men like Gregory the Great, who became Bishop of Rome in 590 and served as architect of the medieval papacy. After the collapse of imperial power, the survival of Western civilization itself rested largely on the three organized forces within Christianity: the papacy, the secular hierarchy, and the monastic orders. Ironically, it fell to the Church, whose primary mission was to open the way to the *next* world, to safeguard the civilization of *this* world.

II. Medieval Civilization

	Art and Architecture	History and Literature	Religion and Philosophy	Political, Social, and Economic Developments	
500				Kingdom of the Franks established by Clovis Justinian's temporary reconquest of the western Mediterranean	500
600	Hagia Sophia		Mohammed and the Koran	Islamic conquests of Near East and Mediterranean world Rise of Carolingian Dynasty	600
700			The Hegira	Charles Martel and repulse of the Moors	700
800	Palace at Aachen		Donation of Pepin ("States of the Church")	Charlemagne declared "Roman Emperor" Division of Islamic conquests Break-up of Charlemagne's empire Invasions of western Europe by Norsemen, Moslems, and Magyars	800

Date	Art & Architecture	Literature	Religion & Learning	Political & Social
900			Monastic reform movements: Cluny	Emergence of feudal and manorial systems; Partial recovery of central authority
1000		Growth of vernacular literature; *Song of Roland*	Ecclesiastical reform: Gregory VII; College of Cardinals; Separation of Latin and Greek Churches; Cistercian order	Revival of trade; Norman conquest of England; Rise of towns and guilds
1100	Romanesque style of architecture; St. Trophîme Cathedral (Arles)	Chivalric romances; Goliardic poetry	Rise of universities	The crusades (1096–1204)
1200	Gothic style; Chartres Cathedral		Papacy at height of power: Innocent III; Franciscans and Dominicans (friars); Thomas Aquinas; Scholastic philosophy dominant; Papal Inquisition	Magna Carta; Origins of Parliament
1300		Dante; Chaucer	Decline of papal power: Boniface VIII	

The Creation of Europe:
Political and Social Foundations

—————————— *4* ——————————

The passing of Greece and Rome brings us to a new phase of Western history. Geographically the focus shifts from the Mediterranean basin to Europe—that favored region jutting into the Atlantic from the Eurasian land mass. Britain, Gaul, Germany, and Italy formed the matrix of what was to become a distinctly European culture. In the seventh century the rest of what was once the Roman Empire split into two different domains: Byzantium and Islam. Byzantium (heir to the eastern portion of the empire) embraced Greece and Asia Minor, while the power of Islam rolled across the rest of the Near East and the southern rim of the Mediterranean, then north through Spain to the Pyrenees. Thus, the "one world" of the Pax Romana was broken into three separate parts (FIG. *4-1*).

Later in this chapter we will look briefly at Byzantium and Islam in their role as long-lived neighbors of the West. But our attention will center on Europe, for it was here that Western civilization was reconstituted and here that it expanded into a worldwide force. The nascent European culture was not just a duplication of the old Graeco-Roman culture, though many of the same ingredients were present. Rather, it emerged as a *new* compound of classical, Christian, and Germanic elements.

The Church was the principal agency of rebuilding of the West, and it set the tone of European civilization for many centuries. The ascetic, otherworldly view of Christianity displaced the more down-to-earth attitude of the ancient Greeks and Romans. This shift, which had set in during the twilight of the empire, became irreversible once Constantine accepted the Cross in 313, and the ascetic ideal persisted in Europe for nearly a thousand years. If one considers the "modern" period, with its materialistic emphasis, to have

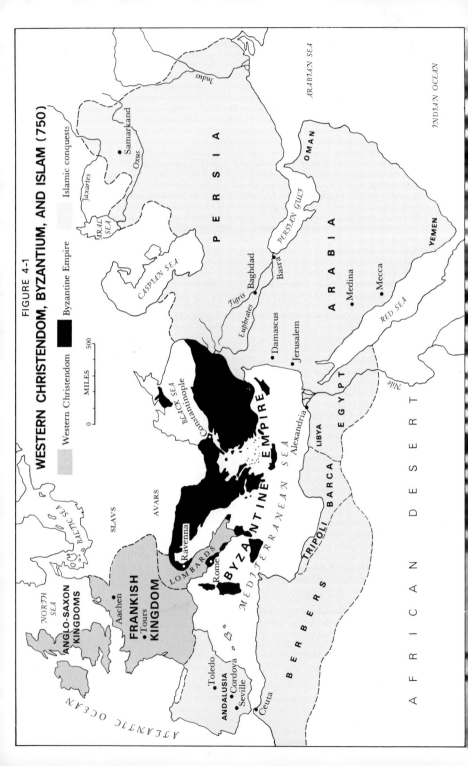

FIGURE 4-1

WESTERN CHRISTENDOM, BYZANTIUM, AND ISLAM (750)

Western Christendom   Byzantine Empire   Islamic conquests

begun around 1500, then the period between it and the ancient world is aptly called the Middle Ages, or the medieval world. (Both terms apply only to the unfolding of Western civilization and are meaningful only in relation to the history of Europe.)

EUROPE IN THE EARLY MIDDLE AGES

After the fall of the Roman Empire in the west, conditions of life remained at a low ebb there for several centuries. The barbarian invasions brought devastation to lands already in a chronic state of neglect. With the drying up of trade the cities virtually disappeared, and most of the inhabitants sought security and sustenance on the great landed estates. The urban civilization of Rome thus gave way to a rural culture. The decline in population that had commenced in the late empire continued, and the struggle for survival made men forget most other concerns. Education, literature, and the arts languished. Though the rudiments of civilization survived, the early centuries (500–800) are often called the Dark Ages. It was not until after 1000 that the new social institutions of Europe matured. Upon these foundations, the West achieved stability and moved into a brilliant era of creativity.

The Germanic barbarians

We have already discussed the Roman and Christian ingredients of medieval civilization (in Chapters Two and Three). Now let us look at the new element—the Germanic. The Germanic barbarians constituted the last major wave of northern invaders to engulf the civilized lands of the south. Among their predecessors were the Greeks, who overran the Aegean lands before 1000 B.C., and the Italic tribes, who had centered their empire on the Tiber. To their victims, all these invaders were "barbarians"; all were nomadic peoples with cultures far less advanced than that of the urban civilizations they enveloped.

The word "German" (or "Germanic") applies to countless tribes that spoke closely related languages. They appear to have shared similar physical characteristics as well, tending toward tall stature, blue eyes, fair skin, and blond hair. Before historic times, they lived in Scandinavia and northern Germany, but by the time of Caesar some had migrated southward into the broad area between the Baltic and North seas and the Rhine-Danube frontier. One of the first of these tribes to cross the Rhine (in the third century B.C.) was called the Germani. The Romans applied this name to the tribes in general and spoke of their homelands as Germania.

When the invaders moved into the Roman domains, they took with them their ancestral habits and institutions, which reflected a relatively simple society based on hunting, herding, farming, and pillaging. Although most of the Germans were ordinary farmers, each tribe had a nobility based on birth. In addition there were some men who were bound to do labor for others in payment for debt, and there were slaves who had been captured in battle.

The Germanic tribes lived in mud huts built close together in villages. Each village held a monthly assembly, open to all free males, which served both as a council and a court. (There were no written laws.) The tribal military organization was the *comitatus*, a war band made up of warriors who pledged themselves to follow a chieftain (king) and who swore to defend him with their lives. The chieftain, in turn, supported the warriors and gave them a share in his spoils. Thus, in the conquered Roman territories a new landed nobility came into being alongside those native landlords who might be permitted to remain.

Our sources of information about the early Germans are meager: Caesar's *Commentaries* (first century B.C.) and Tacitus' *Germania* (first century A.D.) are the most notable. But the records, inadequate though they are, give us a consistent picture of these warriors. Similar to Homer's Greeks, they were fierce, proud, and independent, with a passion for warfare. Tougher than the Romans, who from the second century onward hired them as mercenaries, they eventually inherited the empire.

Though the Germanic tribes retained many of their own traditions after coming into contact with Rome, they respected civilized ways and sought to imitate them. The manner and place of contact were of critical importance here. Germans who had lived for generations in close association with the Romans were completely assimilated. But those who made quick thrusts into the collapsing empire were less influenced by Roman ways. This was also true in peripheral areas like Britain, where Roman roots had not penetrated very deeply.

The missionary work of the Church helped to civilize the Germans both before and after their entry into the empire. As early as the fourth century Bishop Ulfilas was sent out from Constantinople to convert the Goths. Their own religion, about which we have only sketchy information, seems to have had no strong hold on them, and they responded readily to the message brought by the missionaries. Most of the tribes accepted the new faith without a struggle.

What information we do have suggests that the indigenous Germanic religion was polytheistic, not unlike that of the early Romans. The Germans did service to nature spirits, who were thought to reside in trees, rivers, mountains, and animals. They also worshiped a number of higher deities: the sky-god, Thor, held a position similar to that of Zeus in the Greek pantheon. Although the tribes abandoned their pagan deities after embracing Christianity, the old traditions persisted in German folklore and symbolism. Indeed, the climactic day of the Christian calendar took its name from Eastre, the ancient German goddess of spring.

The kingdom of the Franks

All through the fifth and sixth centuries, numerous German tribes slipped across the unmanned frontiers of the empire to find new lands for themselves. In addition to the Goths, Vandals, Franks, and Anglo-Saxons, there were countless others that were absorbed and lost their identity. Actually, only two succeeded in building permanent states: the Anglo-Saxons and the Franks. From the vicinity of modern Denmark, the Anglo-Saxons sailed over the North Sea and invaded Britain during the fifth century—after the Romans had withdrawn their protection from that distant province. The Anglo-Saxons subdued the native Britons, who were quarreling among themselves, and established several kingdoms of their own. (Scotland and Wales alone retained their independence.) Finally, in the tenth century the separate Anglo-Saxon states were merged into a single kingdom, which came to be known as England (Angle-land). Within this territory the Teutonic (German) language and customs had taken firm root.

The most powerful state to arise in the West was that of the Franks, who were to give their name to modern France. When the epic invasions began in the fifth century, the Frankish tribes were joined together in a loose confederacy that controlled an extensive area along the lower Rhine. One of their chieftains, Clovis, welded the confederacy into a unified force and then (in 486) launched simultaneous campaigns against neighboring Germanic kingdoms and against the Romans in Gaul.

The victorious Clovis and his successors pushed south to the Pyrenees and eastward from the Rhine. Unlike the other barbarian tribes, the Franks never abandoned their base on the lower Rhine; as a result, their forces were never cut off, surrounded, and absorbed. The eastward thrust was particularly significant, for it closed a large gap (between the Alps and the North Sea) through which repeated barbarian invasions had come.

Clovis now tried to build a stable system for governing his territories. Instead of overthrowing the Roman political institutions he found in operation, he simply put them under the control of his Frankish followers. His position was strengthened by his early conversion to Roman Catholicism, which won him the support of native Catholics against rival tribes that had accepted the Arian heresy. The Arians, who rejected the orthodox doctrine of the Trinity, had been branded as heretics by the pope. And the clergy encouraged Clovis to regard himself as the preserver of Christian and Roman traditions. Thus, though the level of state protection and administration declined considerably, a certain continuity of order was maintained. The alliance between the Church and the Franks provided the West with a new base of power to replace the shattered authority of Rome.

When Clovis died, however, much of what he had done to restore stability was destroyed. Following Germanic custom, he divided his kingdom among his four sons, treating political authority as though it were private property. This practice was to plague the Frankish kingdom throughout its life, since the sons usually quarreled over their legacies and gave the landholding nobility a chance to play one brother off against another. The nobles (who by now included many bishops and abbots) connived to gain crown lands for themselves and to govern those lands without interference from the king.

The Frankish rulers, who had neither adequate revenue nor adequate means of administration, were gradually obliged to surrender their authority to the nobles. In the seventh century, after years of civil warfare, the king was compelled to legalize earlier usurpations of crown lands by the nobles and to grant them additional lands as well. At the same time he had to accept as his chief minister ("mayor of the palace") the leader of the rebellious landlords. By 700, with the king thus reduced to a figurehead, the main elements of the feudal state had been established; in succeeding centuries, they were to be refined and formalized.

THE RIVAL CULTURE OF BYZANTIUM

While the Franks, with the help of the Church, were seeking to restore order in the West, the emperors at Constantinople continued to claim authority over East and West alike. (The Greek name for the site of Constantinople was Byzantium, and this name has been used by Western writers to refer to the empire and the culture of which Constantinople was the capital.) Byzantium could not make good its claims to authority over the West, but it remained powerful in the eastern Mediterranean. The strength of the eastern empire rested on foundations that had been laid by Diocletian and Constantine. Centralized control was assured through an absolute monarchy sustained in oriental splendor at the grand court of Constantinople. The emperor commanded a professional bureaucracy and well-trained armies and navies. Moreover, his productive realm provided him with sufficient revenues to support administration and defense. He was supported, too, by the powerful Eastern (Greek) Church, of which he was the formal head.

Justinian

Several Byzantine emperors tried to recapture portions of the West. In the sixth century, a grand, if somewhat foolish, effort was made by the energetic Justinian. This man of extraordinary talent and determination, who came to the throne in 527, took seriously his role of God-appointed despot and determined to strengthen and expand his empire. One act of enduring value was his codification of Roman law, known as the *Corpus Juris Civilis* (p. 79). The emperor also took firm command of the Byzantine Church, appointing its presiding bishop, or patriarch, deciding theological disputes, and enforcing clerical discipline. The Eastern (Greek) and Western (Latin) branches of Christianity had drifted far apart in their relations to the state, as well as to each other. While the Roman popes, in response to the decline of civil authority in Italy, became more and more independent of the state, the patriarchs at Constantinople fell under the domination of the Byzantine emperors. Both the emperors and the patriarchs rejected the claim of the popes to supremacy in religious matters.

Justinian's driving desire was to reconquer the imperial territories in the West. At severe cost in men and resources he succeeded in wresting Italy from the Goths and northwest Africa from the Vandals. His armies and navies also won the western Mediterranean islands, including Sicily, and gained a foothold in Spain. The Mediterranean world became, once more, the province of the "Romans." The popes, though threatened by Justinian's stance as protector of Italy, managed to preserve their independence, and after Justinian's death in 565 the peninsula slipped from Byzantine control.

Justinian's fleets and garrisons had been spread too thin, and the lengthened perimeter of empire invited attack at many points. The Persians, renewing their ancient feud with Rome, launched a vicious assault on Justinian's successors. The onslaught was eventually checked, and the Persians were driven from Syria and Egypt. But the imperial troops were so exhausted that those lands fell easy prey to the Arabs a short while later. Meanwhile, the withdrawal of Byzantine forces from the West (to meet the Persian threat) exposed Italy to a fierce Germanic tribe, the Lombards. The popes were finally rescued from this new menace by the Frankish kings, as we will see. Byzantium managed to hold a few coastal areas of Italy and thereby preserved some direct points of contact with the West.

Byzantium's historic role

In spite of Justinian's ill-advised strategic policy, he did manage to strengthen the internal administration of his empire. And his successors, though harassed on every side, succeeded in keeping the machinery of government running. This was fortunate for Europe, since Byzantium guarded the continent against attack from the East. Another key to imperial strength was the superb defensive position of the capital itself, which was surrounded by water on three sides. Though Byzantium slowly yielded her Asiatic provinces to invaders from the East, she kept the invasion door to Europe shut until 1453. Persians, Arabs, and Turks were brought to a halt before the gates of Constantinople.

Byzantium also served as the custodian of classical culture when the Western world was being ravaged by barbarism. The rich literature of Hellenism was conserved in archives and libraries, and Byzantine scholars enriched their heritage by compiling their own commentaries and compendiums. Greek learning continued to serve as the foundation of education in the empire. Though Justinian, in his role as Christian advocate, closed the philosophical schools of Athens, a great university grew up in Constantinople.

Some critics have alleged that the Byzantines were so preoccupied with conserving the culture they had inherited that they devoted little energy to creating a culture of their own. Even so, their accomplishments were impressive—particularly in the decorative arts and architecture. Byzantine craftsmen devised superb objects in gold, silver, and enamel of exquisite color and design. Visitors from the West were dazzled by the sumptuous beauty of the "city of cities."

Justinian himself had launched an ambitious building program for the capital. The principal monument, to the glory of God (and the pride of the emperor), was the mighty church of Hagia Sophia (Holy Wisdom). An elaborately conceived structure, it employs domes and half-domes to create a vast interior space. The most striking feature is the main dome, over one hundred feet in diameter and one hundred eighty feet in height. It does not rest, as does the dome of the Pantheon, upon a cylindrical wall. Instead, it rests on four giant arches, which mark off a central square beneath the dome. The arches carry the downward thrust to four corner piers, which are reinforced by massive stone buttresses on the outside. Arched windows, piercing the base perimeter of the dome, crown the interior with a halo of light (FIG. *4-2*).

Built in only six years' time, under the urgings of the impatient emperor, Hagia Sophia is one of the world's architectural wonders. It combines the building principles of the Romans with the decorative splendor of the Persians. The columns of the interior are of richly colored marbles quarried in various parts of the Mediterranean world. The vaultings are covered by multicolored mosaics, which have survived the whitewash of Moslem conquerors. This temple provokes, in its own fashion, the sense of marvel and holy mystery that the cathedrals of Europe were to achieve centuries

FIGURE 4-2. Hagia Sophia. Lithograph by Gasparo Fossati. (Prestel Verlag, Munich.)

later. It has served as a model for thousands of churches in Near-Eastern lands.

After the Germanic tribes had migrated to the west, new groups of barbarians moved into the areas they had vacated. The largest group consisted of Slavic peoples, who were related to the Germans in race and language. (The Slavs were unheard of in the Roman world until nearly 200 A.D., when they were reported to be living in the region of the Pripet Marshes, between Poland and Russia.) In the sixth and seventh centuries, having been checked in their descent upon Constantinople, the Slavs settled most of the present countries of eastern and central Europe.

The Byzantine clergy set out to bring these new barbarians into the Christian fold. Conversion of the Slavs was completed by the tenth century, but the influence of Byzantium continued among them in other ways. Monks from Constantinople devised the Cyrillic alphabet for writing the Slavic languages, thus making it possible for the rudiments of civilization to pass northward. In short, the Greek Church tutored Eastern Europe (including Russia), just as the Latin Church was tutoring the West. Cultural divergences between the two areas—divergences that exist today—may be traced in part to this difference in tutelage.

The Arabs, as well as the Slavs, were to learn from the Byzantines. When they swept out of Arabia, as we will shortly see, they were an unlettered people. In a less direct way, Byzantium also contributed to the education of Western Europe. All through the Middle Ages, there was constant interchange between East and West—by way of clergy, warriors, pilgrims, traders, and scholars. Though there was more antagonism than affection between the two, both were heirs of Hellenism. And it was Byzantium that guarded their common cultural endowment.

THE BOOK AND SWORD OF ISLAM

At the beginning of this chapter, we mentioned that the one world of the Pax Romana split into three parts: the West, Byzantium, and Islam (FIG. 4-1). We have spoken briefly of the influence of the Byzantine Empire; we will now turn to Islam, the third heir to the Roman world.

About 400, a period of mass migration and head-on collisions set in throughout Eurasia; Germans, Slavs, Mongols, and countless others were caught up in a restless stirring. Tribal wanderings had been going on for centuries, of course, but the Roman world was not affected by them until the Rhine-Danube defenses cracked open.

Then, as one tribe after another passed through, they left living space into which others pushed. The break in the Roman wall thus served as a stimulus to movements in areas as remote as central Asia.

The Arabs and Mohammed

Two centuries later a second incursion into the Mediterranean world developed from a different quarter. The weakening of Byzantine defense resulting from Justinian's military adventures opened the way to an invasion from Arabia. Before the seventh century little had been heard of this extensive, largely arid peninsula, lying like a giant hinge between Asia and Africa. Now its inhabitants charged suddenly into the main stream of history and with the swiftness of their horsemen created a far-reaching empire. The Arabs (or Saracens, as the Romans called them) brought a crusading faith and succeeded in building a brilliant and distinctive culture. Their religion and their culture are known by the name of *Islam*.

At the opening of the seventh century most of the Arabs were barbarians. Since they conquered and assimilated an advanced civilization, there is a parallel between their role in the Mediterranean world and that of the Germans in western Europe. There are significant differences, however. For the Arabs, instead of being converted by the Christians they conquered, were fired with a religious zeal of their own and sought to impose what they considered to be a superior spiritual truth upon the peoples they overcame.

The founder of the faith was Mohammed (the Prophet), a man who was destined to transform the lives of millions. Born about 570 in Mecca, a trading center near the western coast of Arabia, he apparently grew up with no formal education. He did, however, learn something of the teachings of Judaism and Christianity, which had sifted down from Palestine and Syria. When he was about forty, he turned from his life as a merchant to become a religious ascetic. Spending days in lonely meditation, he began to experience visions that he believed to be direct revelations from God (Allah). In one of these visions the archangel Gabriel directed him to convey these messages to his people, and from that time on he abandoned all other pursuits.

Most of the Arabs, however, were polytheists who worshiped idols and nature spirits, and Mohammed soon found himself a prophet "without honor in his own country." His insistence that "there is no God but Allah, and Mohammed is his Prophet" proved offensive to them. He became especially unpopular in the city of Mecca, the site of a building known as the Kaaba, which housed idols and a Black Stone that the Arabs considered holy. When he denounced this shrine, he was branded a blasphemer and a disturber of the peace. Faced with this opposition, Mohammed left Mecca in 622, "shaking its dust from his feet," and fled northward to Yathrib (later renamed Medina, "City of the Prophet"). There he was able to preach freely, and his band of disciples began to grow. The year of his flight (Hegira) is regarded as the beginning of the Moslem era.

Mohammed's purpose was to wipe out primitive superstitions, put an end to tribal feuds, and unite the Arabs under a single pure faith. This could be done only if the Arabs would surrender to the will of Allah as revealed by the Prophet. The Arabic word for submission is *islam*, and the word for one who has submitted is *moslem*. These are the terms used to identify, respectively, the faith and the believer.

Though Mohammed viewed himself as a spiritual leader, he became a political and military chieftain as well. His disciples responded to his words without question; and he was persuaded, through revelation, that he should use force, if necessary, against unbelievers. Soon he was leading his followers on raids against Meccan caravans, an activity that turned out to be highly profitable. He justified these hijackings by declaring that the infidels deserved no better, thus giving rise to the Moslem concept of "holy war" (jihad). The proud Meccans were at length obliged to yield, and the Prophet returned to Mecca in triumph. He ordered that all the idols in the city be destroyed, but he preserved the Black Stone as a symbol of the new faith. Attracted by his militant methods and by his vision of bringing the whole world under Islam, the desert tribes began to flock to his leadership. By the time of his death, in 632, he had extended his personal control over a large portion of Arabia.

The Saracen empire

Once the pattern of Moslem expansion had been established, the movement spread with lightning speed. Mohammed, though many times married, had left no son to inherit his mantle, so his disciples chose a successor (caliph) from among his close relatives. Family connection with Mohammed was accepted from the beginning as a mark of political legitimacy. Under the first two caliphs, Abu Bakr and Omar, the Arabs carried their holy war to the neighboring peoples of the Near East. Within a decade their hard-riding horsemen had conquered Egypt, Syria, Mesopotamia, and Persia. Though outnumbered in almost every battle, the crusaders for Islam succeeded in routing their opponents. At the end of two generations, their empire stretched from Gibraltar in the West to India in the East. By 720 they had wrested Spain from the Christianized Goths and were sending raiding parties across the Pyrenees into France. Near Tours, in 732, they were repulsed by Frankish warriors under Charles Martel (FIG. *4-1*).

How can we explain these phenomenal conquests? They were due, in part, to the zeal that sparked the Arabs. Every Moslem warrior knew that he would share in a rich booty if his side was victorious, and he believed that if he fell in battle his soul would fly straight to paradise. But there are other reasons. Persia and Byzantium, the only substantial powers in the area, had weakened each other in years of bitter warfare and could offer no effective resistance to the onslaught. Further, many of the peoples of the Near East and Africa were discontented under their rulers and welcomed the Saracens as liberators. Syrians and Egyptians, for example, tended to look with satisfaction at the overthrow of the Greek and Roman hegemony that reached back a thousand years to the time of Alexander the Great. They also resented the heavy Byzantine taxation and the unrelenting persecution of Christian heretics. The Saracens, in contrast, held out the promise of religious toleration and a unified world of prosperity and peace (*Pax Islama*).

Although the Saracens were eager to convert all people to their faith, they did not believe in doing so by force. They were satisfied to be the masters; Jews and Christians who paid a head tax were free to follow their own religious practices. Within a few generations, however, most Christians in the conquered territories embraced Islam. There were legal and social advantages in becoming Moslems, and the religion had an intrinsic appeal to many Christians. The conversion was to prove enduring; except for Spain, the lands that fell to the Arabs are still the lands of the mosque.

Islam and Christianity

What were the teachings of this new faith? Mohammed never claimed divinity for himself, though his followers would no doubt have accepted him as divine. A radical monotheist, he insisted only that he was the last and greatest of Allah's prophets. He set his revelations in the context of Judaism and Christianity, identifying Allah with Yahweh (Jehovah) and accepting the line of Jewish prophets from Abraham through Jesus. Instead of claiming that he was introducing a new religion, he insisted that his work was the culmination of the old. His position with respect to Judaeo-Christianity was similar to that of Jesus with respect to Judaism. His message, as recorded in the Koran (Book), might be viewed in this light as a sequel to the Old and New Testaments.

Christian theologians of the Middle Ages concurred, in a sense, with the Prophet's conception of his relation to Christianity. While denouncing him as an instrument of Satan, they classified Islam as a heresy or schism, rather than as a wholly new religion. The learned Dante put Mohammed in one of the lower circles of his Inferno, among the sowers of division. (Mohammed's punishment, symbolic of his alleged crime, was to have his torso repeatedly axed down the middle.)

The central spiritual appeal of Islam was its stress on the oneness of God. Most of the Koran is given over to describing and praising Allah, who alone is the supreme reality, all-knowing and all-powerful. The true believer must submit unreservedly to Allah's will as expressed through the Prophet. This could be done simply and without perplexity; unlike Christianity, Islam raised no abstruse questions concerning the nature and persons of the godhead.

Similarly, there were no arguments over what constituted the sacred canon. Mohammed's revelations were memorized by his disciples and written down in final form shortly after his death; this original Koran, in Arabic, remains the only authorized version. Shorter than the New Testament, it is a poetic book of moderate length, which thousands have committed to memory. Though today Moslems are outnumbered by Christians two to one, the Koran is undoubtedly the most-read book in the world. It serves not only as a record of divine inspiration but as a guide to morality, law, and science—and as a text from which young Moslems learn their Arabic.

Islamic social and ethical ideas

Mohammed's ethical teachings are in the Judaeo-Christian tradition, and the Koran repeats many of the proverbs and stories of the Bible. Since the Prophet had a practical mind, the model life that he described is within the reach of the faithful. While stressing love, kindness, and brotherhood, he did not insist on an asceticism that was beyond the capabilities of most people. He saw no inherent virtue, for instance, in sexual abstinence. He did, however, try to moderate the prevailing Arab practice of polygamy. Repugnant to Christian doctrine (though not to all Christians), polygamy had arisen chiefly from the imbalance in the number of men and women among the Arabs, whose tribal feuds resulted in a chronic shortage of men. One means of providing security for the surplus females was to permit each male to take several wives. The practice had eventually led to sexual promiscuity, however, and the Prophet declared that a man should have no more than four wives at a time. (The quota did not apply to Mohammed himself, who was exempted by a special revelation.) No limit was set on the number of concubines a man might have.

A conservative reformer, Mohammed did not condemn profit-making so long as the profit was reasonable and honest. Once a merchant himself, he did not feel that business dealings are intrinsically displeasing to Allah. Islam thus did not give rise to the tension between commerce and religion that has troubled the conscience of the West.

A characteristic of Islam that appealed to many was the absence of a priesthood. Every Moslem stands as an equal before Allah. There are no saints or prelates mediating between man and Allah; and since there are no priests, there are no mysterious rites that only priests can perform. To enhance the worshiper's concentration on Allah, statues and images are banned from Moslem art. The place of worship—the mosque—is devoid of anything that resembles an idol.

All this contrasted sharply with the Byzantine (Christian) Church, with its apostolic succession, its distinctions between laity and clergy, its elaborate rituals, and its veneration of saints and icons (holy images). The dedicated Moslem felt that his faith was spiritually purer and more democratic than Christianity. He scorned the Byzantines as men addicted to wrangling over doctrine, content to worship three or more divine figures, and cloaked in pagan superstition.

Obligations of the faithful

The religious duties of Moslems, known as the Five Pillars of Faith, are clearly defined in the Koran. The first is the familiar profession of belief, "There is no god but Allah, and Mohammed is his Prophet." By accepting and repeating these words, the convert is initiated into the faith.

Daily prayer—at dawn, midday, midafternoon, sunset, and nightfall—is the second duty. At the appointed hours, from atop slender minarets, the muezzins (criers) call upon the faithful to bow down. The posture of the body and its orientation (toward Mecca) are prescribed, and the prayer must be said in Arabic. The prayer itself, which is not unlike the Lord's Prayer, usually includes the short opening verse of the Koran, praising Allah and asking for guidance along the "straight path." This formula is reiterated many times each day. The only public religious service is the noon prayer on Fridays, which must be attended by all adult males. Inside the mosque, standing in self-ordered rows, the congregation prays aloud in unison; then the leader, a layman, delivers a brief sermon. After the service, normal secular activities may be resumed.

The third duty is giving to the poor. At first, alms-giving was practiced as an individual act of charity, but it gradually developed into a standard levy. In the Islamic states the money was collected through regular taxation and was used to help the needy and to build and maintain the mosques. The usual levy was one-fortieth of the individual's income. (This may be compared with the tithe—one-tenth—which the Christian Church expected from its members.)

Fasting, the fourth pillar of faith, ordinarily is confined to Ramadan, the ninth month of the Moslem lunar calendar. It was during Ramadan that Allah gave the Koran to Gabriel for revelation to Mohammed. For thirty days no food or drink may be taken between sunrise and sunset. Fasting, which was not practiced by the Arabs before Mohammed, was adopted from Jewish and Christian custom.

Finally, every Moslem who can afford it must make a pilgrimage to the shrine of Mecca at some time during his life. Over the centuries this practice has had a unifying effect on the diverse peoples that embrace Islam. Rich and poor, black and white, easterner and westerner—all fraternize in the Holy City. Although the majority of Moslems are unable to fulfill this obligation, many millions make the journey. In the early stages of Moslem history a sixth duty was required of all able-bodied men: participation in the jihad (holy war). It was this requirement that sparked the first explosive conquests of the Arabs. Each caliph believed it his obligation to expand the frontiers of Islam and reduce the infidel "territory of war."

The Pillars of Faith are only the minimum requirements of Islam. In all things the true believer must seek to do the will of Allah as revealed in the Koran. He must also subscribe to the belief that God has predestined the ultimate fate of all men, to be revealed in the Last Judgment. Mohammed left vivid descriptions of hell and heaven. Unbelievers will burn eternally in a great pool of fire; believers who die in sin will also suffer there for a time but will finally be released. In the end, *all* Moslems—all those who have accepted Allah—will enjoy the pleasures of paradise. Mohammed, drawing on Persian sources, pictured paradise in sensual terms as an oasis of delight, with sparkling beverages, luscious fruits, and dark-eyed nymphs.

Religious and political divisions

In spite of the simplicity and clarity of Mohammed's teachings, they were subjected to conflicting interpretations as the years passed. The major disagreements arose over the principle of succession to the caliphate, religious doctrines, and the proper way of life for Moslems.

Since Islam had no authoritative hierarchy for dealing with internal differences, a large number of rival sects evolved. The main division was between the Sunnites and the Shiites. The Sunnites were associated with the Ommiad Dynasty, which seized the caliphate in 661 and moved the capital of Islam from Medina to Damascus, in Syria. They accepted as valid certain traditions (Sunna) which had grown up outside the Koran. The Shiites, on the other hand, abided strictly by the Book and held that only descendants of the Prophet could become caliphs. The Abbassid family, of the Shiite sect, gained power in 750 and moved the capital again, this time to Baghdad.

After the eighth century, the Saracen empire began to break up. The ousted Ommiad family established itself in Spain and broke off political connections with Baghdad (FIG. *4-1*). Similarly, a descendant of Fatima (Mohammed's daughter) later declared himself an independent caliph in control of Egypt, Syria, and Morocco. Provinces in Arabia and India also fell away, until by 1000 the Abbassid ruler controlled only the area surrounding Baghdad.

The Moslem legacy to the West

Despite all these political divisions, Moslem civilization reached its height in the ninth and tenth centuries. To this the Arabs, who themselves were culturally backward, contributed little. But the unifying faith, the common language, and the relative stability that they provided served to bring about a renaissance in the Near Eastern world. The Islamic achievements of this period are a blend of various traditions, especially Hellenic, Syrian, and Persian.

Dramatic advances were made in agriculture and commerce. Routes of travel were made secure, and merchants traveled from Spain to China and the East Indies. Arab rulers supported studies of geography and navigation and encouraged popular education and universities. There is hardly a branch of learning that was not advanced by the Moslems. Perhaps their most fruitful contribution was the introduction from India of what we now call Arabic numerals—an innovation that freed mathematicians from the awkward Roman system. One way of suggesting the range of Moslem influence is to mention some of the thousands of Arabic words that survive in our vocabulary: zero, algebra, alcohol, chemistry, zenith, nadir, admiral, arsenal, traffic, check, muslin, bazaar.

Greek scientific works were translated into Arabic and circulated the length and breadth of Islam. Great centers of learning sprang up, notably at Cairo and Toledo, where scholars studied Aristotle and Plato and tried to reconcile their writings with Mohammed's religious teachings. Gradually, European scholars made their way to Spain and Sicily to study the scientific and philosophic works of the Greeks. As the Moslem tide receded from those areas after 1000, the Christians of the West seized on the rich intellectual deposit and made it their own. After having lost for centuries many of the

FIGURE 4-3. Taj Mahal. (Bob and Ira Spring.)

treasures of Greek learning, Europe recovered them through Arabic translations.

Western artisans and builders were also impressed by what they discovered in Moslem countries. In the tenth century, when most of Christian Europe was busy trying to fend off attacks from every quarter, Moslem Spain was enjoying unequaled prosperity. Its capital, Cordova, the largest city of Europe after Constantinople, boasted magnificent mosques and palaces, public baths, colleges, libraries, and private homes. Cordovan leather, textiles, and armor were famous everywhere. Scholars, poets, and musicians were generously patronized by the rulers.

Moslem architecture, a blend of Persian and Mediterranean styles, was distinguished by its graceful variations of the Roman dome and arch—typically pointed or in the shape of a horseshoe. Walls were richly decorated with marble, precious stones, and glazed tiles. Since Mohammed had forbidden the representation of human or animal figures, painting and carving were marked by intricate geometrical and floral designs (arabesques). Spanish architecture still reflects this Moslem influence.

The triumph of the Islamic architectural style, however, is to be found not in Spain but in India, in the seventeenth-century mausoleum at Agra (FIG. *4-3*). Built by a wealthy ruler as a mausoleum for his favorite wife, the Taj Mahal stands as one of the most perfect works by the hand of man.

After the Christian crusades (to be discussed in Chapter Five) and the later Mongol invasions of the Near East, Moslem culture fell into a decline from which it never recovered. But until the thirteenth century it was in most respects superior to that of Europe. Though there was fierce hostility between Christendom and Islam, the developing civilization of the West gained much of value from the Moslems.

THE EMERGENCE OF MEDIEVAL INSTITUTIONS

Now that we have spoken briefly of the contemporaneous cultures of Byzantium and Islam, we return to western Europe. The Franks, it will be recalled, were the only Germanic tribe to establish what promised to be a viable kingdom on the Continent. By 600, however, the Frankish monarchy had fallen into impotence. The landholding nobles had usurped the king's authority and had installed their own leaders as "mayors of the palace."

The rise of the Carolingian Dynasty

The mayors of the palace succeeded in making their office hereditary, thus establishing the dynastic line that, in 768, would produce
Charles the Great (Charlemagne), ruler of the Franks. (Since the
Latin for Charles is Carolus, the term "Carolingian" is usually applied to the period and the family.) The mayors, adding control
over the crown lands to the wealth of their private estates, soon
aroused the fear and envy of the Frankish nobles. A frightful civil
war broke out between the mayors and the nobles that raged unchecked for some fifteen years. The country was ravaged; farms,
villages, and whole towns were ruined. At last the Carolingian family gained the upper hand, and by 700 they were firmly in charge of
the kingdom. With the legal monarchs thrust ever more into the
background, the *de facto* rulers turned to the grim work of reconstruction.

In the midst of these troubles the Moslems swept north from
Spain and made forays into the Frankish kingdom. They found the
richest booty in the treasuries of churches and monasteries, and in
732 they were riding toward the abbey of St. Martin of Tours, the
richest in the country. Charles Martel (the Hammer), the current
mayor of the palace, commanded a defense force that consisted of
foot soldiers supported by a small number of mounted knights. The
Saracen horsemen had superior mobility and striking power, but
Martel maneuvered them into launching an attack on a staked fort.
The raiders, badly hurt by a shower of arrows and javelins, decided
to pull back to Spain.

Martel was hailed as a hero, the savior of the West. But he
knew that more attacks were coming and that he must convert his
army into a mounted force in order to withstand them. He knew,
too, that the thousands of horses and armed riders he needed could
be assembled only at great expense. Since wealth existed mainly in
the form of land, he began to look about for available property.

The Church caught his eye at once. Bishoprics and monasteries,
as a result of generous gifts and legacies, now held from a third to
a half of all the land in the realm. Charles Martel tried to persuade
church officials to part with some of their holdings so that he could
assign them to noblemen in exchange for service as mounted warriors. Though the clergy knew that they would suffer if the Saracen
raids continued, they rejected his appeal. Martel then took matters
into his own hands: he seized many church properties and distributed them as military grants (benefices) to certain noble warriors. In return, each warrior bound himself to supply a body of

armed cavalry when called upon. Thus was laid the basis of the "feudal contract," in which the use of land was exchanged for military equipment and service.

Within a century the Frankish army had been converted into a force of mounted knights, or chevaliers (horsemen). Infantry largely disappeared, and for the next five centuries the cavalry was to be the "queen of battles." So long as physical defense depended on the service of mounted knights, and so long as land remained the principal source of wealth, landholding would be closely associated with the corps of chevaliers.

The alliance of the Franks and the papacy

Charles Martel's son, Pepin, decided that the time had come for the *actual* power in the kingdom to be recognized as the *legal* power. For more than a century the Carolingian family had assumed responsibility for the defense and administration of the realm; the Frankish monarchy had become a mere shadow. But it was not a simple matter to wrest the crown from the descendants of Clovis. Though they were only figureheads, they were respected as the rightful possessors of the kingship and were consecrated in office by the Church.

Pepin, anxious to avoid another civil upheaval, tried to win the Frankish bishops over to his side before deposing the reigning monarch. But the bishops were still smarting from Martel's seizure of church lands and had no intention of supporting Martel's son. So Pepin went over their heads and appealed directly to Rome. The pope, for his own reasons, approved the deposition, and in 751 Pepin had himself anointed king of the Franks.

Later it was Pepin's turn to do the pope a favor. Almost two centuries before, in 568, the Lombards had invaded Italy, defeated the Byzantine forces stationed there, and threatened the independence of the papacy. They were restrained for a while, but during the eighth century it began to appear that they would extend their control over all of Italy, depriving the popes of their power in Rome and adjacent territories. Since the Byzantine rulers still claimed Italy, the pope, Stephen II, might have appealed to Constantinople for aid. But the schism between the Latin and Greek churches had strained relations between East and West; moreover, the Eastern emperor had military problems of his own. So Stephen turned to Pepin for protection. He journeyed to the Frankish court in 754, reanointed the king, and won promises of military help.

Two years later Pepin discharged his obligation to the papacy by crossing the Alps, defeating the Lombards, and transferring a strip of territory across central Italy to the governing authority of the pope. Thus, by the so-called Donation of Pepin, the States of the Church came into being as a sovereign political entity. They remained so for over a thousand years—until the unification of Italy in 1870.

Either before or immediately after Pepin's gift, the papacy justified its right to govern this territory with a far bolder claim. It asserted that the Emperor Constantine, when he moved to Byzantium, had bequeathed *all* of the West to Pope Sylvester and his successors. As proof of this claim, the papal court produced a signed document. The Donation of Constantine, as this paper came to be known, also declared the pope to be the superior of all other bishops and of the *emperor* himself. In the fifteenth century the document was shown to be a forgery, but in the meantime it served to buttress the pretensions of the papacy.

For centuries the Donation of Constantine and other spurious documents were accepted as part of canon (church) law. In the long run, they would prove harmful to the Church, for the papacy could not make good its claims to secular supremacy. And in seeking worldly power the medieval popes often neglected their spiritual mission. The Donation of Pepin, however, was genuine enough and had immediate results: it sealed the alliance between the Frankish state and the papacy, the two strongest forces in the West. The fruit of this alliance was the empire of Charles the Great.

Charlemagne

Charles, Pepin's son and Charles Martel's grandson, stands as one of the towering figures of history. Through the force of his personality and the circumstance of a long reign (forty-six years), he contributed mightily to the evolution of Europe. After centuries of near-chaos he restored some semblance of unity to Western Christendom and advanced its frontiers. Charles personified the merging of Germanic, Roman, and Christian elements into a powerful compound.

Tall and blue-eyed, Charles was proud of his German heritage. His given name was Karl, and, though he knew Latin, he preferred to speak in his native Frankish tongue. The French language and nation were yet to emerge, and the name "Charlemagne" did not appear until more than a century later. Nevertheless he is usually referred to in French and English narratives as Charles or Charlemagne (Charles the Great).

Brought up as a Roman Catholic, he was a champion of the Church and pushed the boundaries of Christianity eastward by military force. He embraced the Roman ideals of universality, law, and justice and sought to make them realities in Europe. During his lifetime he created a kind of reincarnation of Roman power in the West, but since conditions were not favorable to its survival his empire faded soon after his death. Even so, he revived the idea of a strong central state and laid the foundation for many European political institutions.

Charlemagne was almost constantly at war. Ruthless and cruel in battle, he fought, not primarily for spoils, but for what he considered to be the higher goals of Christianity and universal order. When advised by the pope that the Lombards were again threatening papal territory, he led his armies into Italy in 774 and broke the Lombard power. Now he styled himself king of the Lombards as well as king of the Franks and extended his authority over most of Italy (FIG. *4-4*).

His most arduous campaigns, which lasted some thirty years, were against the Saxons. These virile warriors, some of whom had crossed the North Sea to Britain in the fifth century, occupied the region north and east of the Frankish boundaries (as far as the Elbe River). The only Germanic tribe as yet unconquered by the Franks, they clung stubbornly to their primitive heathenism. Charles, encouraged by the Church, was determined to transform the Saxons into loyal Christian subjects. He succeeded, but only after laying waste to Saxony, massacring countless captives, and relocating thousands of families in other parts of his empire. At last the Saxons accepted Christianity, and the Frankish clergy moved in to establish bishoprics and monasteries.

With the subjugation of Saxony, Charles' power extended to the borders of the heathen Danes (FIG. *4-4*). Instead of invading their territory, however, he created a military zone, called a march, or *mark,* along the frontier. This barrier between Christianity and heathenism stood for more than a century. In the eleventh century, after the Danish king had been converted, the kingdom came to be known as Denmark (*Dane-mark*).

Other European states developed from military zones along other stretches of the Frankish borders. The *Nordmark,* set up on the eastern frontier of Saxony as a defense against the Slavs, was to become the duchy of Brandenburg (later, the state of Prussia). Charles colonized still another area, the East March (*Ost-mark*), in order to deny the Mongolian Avars access to the Danube Valley. On this territory the duchy of Austria was to emerge.

South of the Pyrenees, Charles erected the Spanish March as a wall against the Moslems. From this foothold Christianity gradually

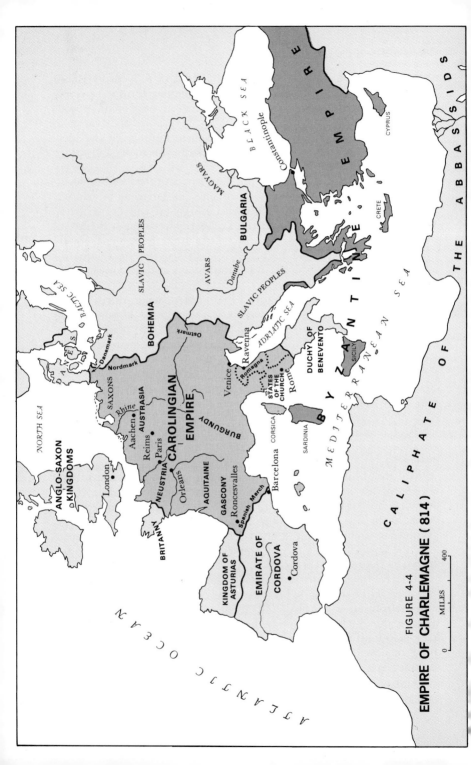

FIGURE 4-4

EMPIRE OF CHARLEMAGNE (814)

expanded into the kingdoms of Aragon and Castile. The setting up
of the Spanish March had literary as well as political consequences.
Returning from a sally below the Pyrenees, Charlemagne's rear-
guard was ambushed in the pass of Roncesvalles by the mountain-
dwelling Basques in 778. Commanded by Roland, nephew of the
king, the Frankish warriors fought bravely but were finally wiped
out. Their heroism passed into legend and ballad, finally emerging
as the epic *Song of Roland.*

Charlemagne concerned himself with domestic matters as well
as with military campaigns. Recognizing the Church as the only
institution that was accepted by all his subjects, he strove to
strengthen its leadership and extend its activities. Though a devout
and submissive Christian in private life, he believed that, as king,
he must act as head of the Church. Regarding the ecclesiastical
structure as an integral part of his royal administration, he appointed bishops, issued reform orders to the clergy, and assumed,
in general, the attitude the Byzantine emperors took toward the
Greek Church. He treated bishops and abbots as agents of his government and saw to it that they received copies of his secular
decrees.

Aside from canon law and imperial decrees, Charles imposed no
common legal code on his sprawling territories, leaving the various
peoples—Franks, Lombards, Saxons, Romans—to govern themselves
according to their own laws. This attitude was typical of Charles'
administration; he chose for the most part to accept existing institutions as he found them. One regular feature of his government, inherited from earlier kings and late Roman rulers, was the role
played by his counts (companions). Each count represented the
crown in a given region, called a county. He presided over a court
that met once a month, collected fines, and, in time of war, assembled the knights of his county for military action. Sometimes,
for purposes of defense, several counties were grouped into a larger
unit headed by a duke (leader). Both counts and dukes were selected
from the local landed nobility. Their counties and duchies eventually became the historic provinces of France (Brittany, Champagne,
Flanders, Burgundy, Gascony, Poitou, and so forth).

As a check on the honesty and efficiency of these officials, Charles
appointed royal inspectors (*missi dominici*) who visited all his territories once a year. Traveling in pairs (a nobleman and a clergyman),
they investigated the performance of the counts and dukes and reported their findings to Charles. By acting vigorously in response to
this intelligence, he succeeded in holding together his sprawling
domains.

Since there was no general system of taxation, Charles had to draw most of his revenue from the crown lands, which he shrewdly kept as his own. He held thousands of estates, most of them concentrated between the Seine and Rhine rivers. Understandably, he was keenly interested in the efficiency with which his properties were managed, and he prepared detailed instructions for the guidance of his royal stewards.

Charles made his capital at Aachen, which was surrounded by productive crown lands in the heart of the ancient Frankish territories. His palace chapel at Aachen, which still stands, was the first important stone building to be erected north of the Alps after the fall of Rome. This fact in itself symbolizes the belated recovery of the West. The chapel was modeled on the church of San Vitale in Ravenna, a Byzantine outpost on Italy's east coast. San Vitale, in turn, was built in the same general style as the grand Hagia Sophia. Charles was so impressed when he first saw San Vitale—a rich church, glistening with mosaics—that he directed his builders to duplicate the plan in his own capital. Thus, the art of Constantinople found its way to Aachen and the Frankish heartland.

By importing artisans and artists from Italy, Charlemagne stimulated the development of the arts in northern Europe. He was concerned as well over the distressingly low level of education and scholarship in his realm and issued a decree instructing bishops and abbots to improve the training of the clergy. In Aachen itself he set up a palace school, which became a center of intellectual activity. The school was under the guidance of a monk named Alcuin, the leading scholar of his day, whom Charles had called from the cathedral school of York, in England.

Alcuin trained a staff of expert scribes, who rejuvenated the monastic tradition of reproducing ancient manuscripts. He also established a curriculum, based on contemporary instruction in monastic and cathedral schools, for selected young men of the Frankish nobility. The faculty of the school at Aachen was made up of distinguished scholars drawn from all over Europe. Many of their pupils became outstanding teachers themselves in other intellectual centers of Germany and France. Though Charlemagne's empire barely survived him, the "Carolingian renaissance" of the arts and scholarship provided a lasting impetus to the cultural development of Europe.

The restoration of the "Roman Empire"

The most dramatic event of Charles' reign—a stroke that captured the imagination of Europe—was his coronation as "Charles Augustus, Emperor of the Romans." The event took place on Christmas Day, 800, while the Frankish king was attending Mass in St. Peter's Basilica in Rome. Apparently, Charles had not planned the coronation beforehand; his biographer, Einhard, reports that Pope Leo III, without warning, placed the diadem on his head and pronounced him emperor.

The pope had his own reasons for taking this historic step. Now that he could no longer call on the Byzantine (Eastern) emperor for help, he needed a strong protector in Italy. Pepin and Charles had defended the papacy from the Lombards in years past, but the pope was eager to win a guarantee for the future. Further, there was the possibility that the Franks themselves might prove dangerous. By taking the initiative in 800, the pope succeeded in defining the relationship between the restored (Western) empire and the Church. By setting himself up as a *donor,* he secured the superior position: Charles received the crown from the hand of the pope, thereby putting the emperor under obligation to the papacy. The action also gave force to the subsequent claim that the papacy had a right to withdraw what it had given. Later popes, standing on this claim, would depose emperors.

Though Charles may have been disconcerted by the circumstances of his crowning, there is no evidence that he was displeased. From the time of Clovis' conversion to Roman Catholicism in the fifth century, there had been close ties between the Franks and the papacy. Together, they had worked to spread the faith and to reestablish order in the West. By Charles' time the Frankish state had become extensive enough and substantial enough to qualify as a successor to the Roman Empire. The pope now recognized and blessed the Frankish king as *augustus,* and the new emperor pledged himself to defend and champion the Church.

The restoration of the empire in the West demonstrates the historical force of an idea. Through four centuries of struggle and near-anarchy, the *idea* of universal law and order had lived on. At the first sign of its becoming a reality, the "restoration" was proclaimed—even though an "Emperor of the Romans" had been sitting in Constantinople since the fourth century. (The pope may have chosen to act when he did because at that moment a woman, Irene, was reigning over Byzantium. Since in the Roman tradition females were considered ineligible to rule, the pope elevated Charles to a "vacant" throne.)

In any case Charlemagne's empire incorporated the three major elements of medieval civilization: the *Roman* idea of universality and order, the *Christian* religion, and *Frankish* military power. In extent it was substantially less than even the western half of ancient Rome; missing were North Africa and Sicily, Spain, and Britain. On the other hand, territories east of the Rhine that had never been controlled by Rome were part of Charlemagne's domain.

There were other significant differences between the two empires. In Charles' territories there was no single citizenship, no unified law, no professional bureaucracy. There were few cities, since few had survived; and the roads had fallen into disrepair. Christianity, which had become the state religion in the closing years of the old Roman Empire, was the main integrating force in the new, and yet the agencies of the Church could not make up for the absence of firm political institutions. Charlemagne's empire was held together chiefly by the strength of his personality. Soon after his death in 814 the empire disintegrated—leaving but a fiction of unity and an ideal.

The dissolution of Charlemagne's empire

The ninth century was a time of unprecedented ordeal for western Europe. The promise of order and stability held out by Charlemagne faded in the dusk of renewed civil wars and invasions. Yet, in a sense, this was a return to "normal" conditions. The turbulent centuries from 500 to 1000 were marked in both Europe and Asia by grand disintegrations, transcontinental migrations, and clashes of crusading faiths. For a time Charlemagne had checked the forces of chaos. After his death, however, those forces rose again, and under his successors the Carolingian empire dissolved. Yet out of the conditions that accompanied the collapse emerged the peculiar institutions of medieval Europe that would govern Western life and thought until the fifteenth century.

The troubles of the ninth century sprang in part from the inherent weaknesses of the Frankish kingdom and in part from external pressures. Charles' son, Louis the Pious, preferred the company of clerics to that of soldiers and administrators; but his fatal mistake was to divide the kingdom among his three sons. The eldest, Lothar, was named emperor-elect and received the Middle Kingdom, including Lotharingia (Lorraine) and Italy. The second son, Louis, received the portion of the empire east of the Rhine, which would become, in time, modern Germany. Charles, the youngest son, inherited the western third of the empire, which was destined to become France.

But France and Germany were centuries away from nationhood, and with the strong hand of Charlemagne removed, the dukes, counts, and archbishops of the empire transformed their jurisdictions into independent domains. In the west, the east, and the Middle Kingdom, these provincial lords usurped royal prerogatives, collected their own revenues, and administered their own justice. They converted their offices and landholdings into hereditary family possessions. Within a short time the Middle Kingdom disappeared altogether. The Carolingian heirs carved up Lorraine, some of it going to the western realm, some to the eastern, and some to independent men powerful enough to seize what they wanted.

The disintegration of Charlemagne's empire was speeded by ferocious attacks from the outside. One arm of invasion came from the Mediterranean, where Moslem raiders from North Africa had established themselves in Sicily and Sardinia. They preyed on shipping, struck at the coastal towns of Italy and southern France, and made off with everything they could carry. In 846 they captured Rome itself and pillaged the surrounding countryside. In desperation, Pope Leo IV built a wall around the heart of Rome. The rest of the city, however, lay open to the Moslems when they returned some years later.

On the eastern frontier the barbarian Magyars, who had settled down on the plain of Hungary, sent plundering expeditions into Germany during the ninth and tenth centuries, striking as far as the lower Rhine. Until they were beaten decisively by the German king Otto in 955, they kept much of central Europe in turmoil.

By far the strongest blows, however, came from the North. During the ninth century the warriors of Scandinavia—heathen Vikings who had not previously appeared in Western history—struck out on a bold campaign of expansion. This was the first great barbarian invasion of western Europe since the Germanic migrations of the fifth and sixth centuries. But there was an important difference: the Germans had been in contact with civilized peoples long before they burst into the empire, whereas the Vikings had had no such association.

The culture of the Norsemen was similar to that of the ancient Germans. They were more of a seafaring people, however, and turned readily to the prizes of piracy. Their long, high-prowed vessels, driven by sails and oars, began to appear along the coasts of the English Channel after 800. The fierce warriors who leaped ashore demanded tribute from the inhabitants or else carried off what they could seize. They did not remain content with coastal raids, however, and soon they were sailing up the rivers, raiding deep into the interior. Finally, the Anglo-Saxons were forced to cede a large portion of Britain (the "Danelaw") to the invaders. The Frankish monarchy, similarly, was compelled to yield a substantial area along the Channel; it was called, after the Norsemen, the duchy of Normandy. (The dukes of Normandy were destined to play an important role in European history: William of Normandy conquered England in 1066.) Still other Norse leaders turned southward, seizing lands in Italy and Sicily.

The incursions of the Norsemen accelerated the weakening of central authority in western Europe. King Charles the Bald, who had inherited the western portion of the Frankish empire, tried to check the invaders by building blockhouses at key points. But the nobles, who were interested only in saving their own properties, refused to serve in them. In desperation, the king agreed to grant royal lands adjacent to the blockhouses to nobles who would fight in them. This concession solved the immediate problem, but repeated grants of this nature reduced what was left of the king's power and bolstered the independence of the nobility.

Confronted by violence and danger, and with no central government to turn to for protection, men did what they could to protect themselves. Blockhouses and crude wooden castles began to appear on hilltops and other defensible sites. Open villages and estates were fenced in with sharpened stakes. The walls of ancient Roman towns were repaired and extended, and ramparts were built around churches and monasteries. Many peasants, unable to defend themselves, offered their labor in return for military protection, thus reducing themselves to serfdom.

The warrior nobles sought to enlarge their landholdings and increase the number of fighting men at their disposal, thereby strengthening their position. Some resorted to open warfare, others to advantageous marriages and alliances. During the ninth and tenth centuries many new men, as well as the scions of established families, joined in the scramble for properties and offices. Some of the most famous titled families of later times could trace their ancestry to these troubled decades.

Yet even in the middle of the tenth century, when both property and person were exposed to countless hazards, there were signs of a revival of central authority. The last of the Carolingian rulers in the western Frankish kingdom died in 987; he was succeeded by the Count of Paris (Hugh Capet), a member of the leading noble family of the country. Capet's dynasty brought fresh vigor to the monarchy. In the eastern Frankish kingdom the succession fell to the dukes of Saxony. The ablest of this family, Otto the Great, reclaimed the imperial title, which had fallen into disuse, and was crowned emperor in Rome in 962. Actually, Otto's domains included only Germany and Italy, but he perpetuated the universal political ideal of

Augustus and Charlemagne. Though his assertion of authority was continued by the German emperors throughout the Middle Ages, the basis of law and order remained localism and feudalism.

FEUDALISM

Today we find the ancient Greek city-state and the Roman universal state closer to our experience and easier to understand than the feudal state of the Middle Ages. Feudalism was not a tidy, unified system spelled out in any decree or constitution. Rather, it showed marked variations in time and place and was a curious mixture of fact and theory. Nevertheless, the system did afford some measure of security and justice to millions of Europeans for more than five hundred years. Feudal systems similar to that of medieval Europe have grown up in like circumstances in other parts of the world—in China, Japan, and India, for example—following the collapse of central government.

By the eleventh century there were three principal feudal states in Europe: the "Holy Roman Empire," revived by Otto the Great; the kingdom of France, ruled by the Capetian monarchs; and the kingdom of England, consolidated by William the Conqueror, a Norman. In each of these realms the monarch claimed sovereignty over the whole state, even though his actual power was limited by the extent of his personal landholdings (the royal domain). In each country most of the land was held by dukes, counts, archbishops, abbots, and warrior nobles of lesser degree, who owed certain obligations to the king as their overlord. Except for these obligations, they governed their territories without royal interference.

The barons (a general term for those who held property directly from the king) were unable to exercise their control without assistance. In order to gain military aid and to administer their duchy, county, or bishopric, they found it expedient to distribute part of their holdings to other warriors. These warriors, in return, became bound to the barons in more or less the same fashion in which the barons were bound to the king. But all relationships were personal and variable, the chief arbiter being local custom. What existed, in fact, was a host of miniature governments, loosely associated for mutual defense and self-interest.

The feudal compact

At first the feudal relationship was extremely vague, consisting essentially of an unwritten bond that was subject to a wide range of interpretation. By the eleventh century, however, the feudal contract had evolved into a fairly standard form prescribing the exchange of *property* for *personal service.* The king or the duke —whoever granted property to another—stood in the position of "lord"; the recipient of the property was his "vassal." Property in the Middle Ages nearly always meant real estate, for land was the main source of wealth. A piece of land granted by a lord to a vassal was called a "fief," and the vassal was entitled to the income from it so long as he discharged his feudal duties.

The fief carried with it certain political functions as well as economic benefits. The vassal was expected to protect the inhabitants of the fief, collect revenues, and dispense justice. Thus, under feudalism, political authority was linked to landholding. Since only professional warriors could provide physical protection and undertake the obligations of fief-holding, political and economic power remained in the hands of a military aristocracy (the nobility).

Each vassal, in return for the benefits of his fief, owed important obligations to his lord. Chief among these was military service. Every vassal was expected to serve his lord in person, and the holder of a large fief was required, in addition, to furnish a body of armed men. In this way the kings and the barons, who found it impracticable to support standing armies, were able to raise their fighting forces. At first the extent of the vassal's obligation to fight when called on by his lord was unlimited, but gradually it was set by custom at about forty days' service each year.

The holder of a fief was obliged also to serve on the lord's court, which was usually held once a month. Medieval justice was simple and harsh by modern standards. It rested upon custom, derived chiefly from ancient barbarian practices. One element of Germanic origin, for example, was the testing of the accused by "ordeal." When conclusive evidence was lacking, the court might require an accused person to walk barefoot over hot coals or to thrust his arm into a pot of boiling water or to risk personal injury in some other obvious fashion. It was believed that God would save him from harm if he was innocent. But serious bodily damage from the test was interpreted as proof of guilt, and the court then imposed the customary penalty for the alleged crime. Not until the thirteenth century did the Church withdraw its support of trial by ordeal. By that time, the more humane procedures of Roman jurisprudence were being revived.

Under the feudal compact a vassal was required to make certain payments to his lord. Upon receiving his fief, for example, he normally turned over the first year's income. This payment was called "relief," a sort of transfer or inheritance tax. He also owed his lord "hospitality." For a given number of days each year, the lord and his retinue could demand food, lodging, and entertainment from the vassal. On certain occasions—the knighting of the lord's eldest son, or the marriage of his eldest daughter—the vassal was required to make a special contribution. Finally, if the lord was captured in battle, his vassal was obliged to pay ransom for his release.

It may seem that all these duties must have been onerous. Yet we should remember that the vassal enjoyed the security of his fief and the military protection of his lord. If any man threatened his land or his person, he had a right to call upon the lord for help. In those violent and dangerous centuries, the feudal compact served as a vital alliance for the defense of life and property.

Homage and knighthood

The granting of a fief, with all its implications, was solemnized by the vassal's swearing a pledge of personal loyalty to his lord. This was called the act of "homage." Usually the vassal knelt down, put his hands between those of his lord, and offered himself as the lord's man (*homo*). The lord accepted the vassal's homage, bade him rise, and embraced him. Next, it was customary for the vassal to take a Christian vow of fealty in addition to his pledge. The lord, in exchange for the declaration of vassalage, customarily presented his vassal with a clod of earth or some other symbolic object to serve as the "investiture," by which he "invested" the vassal with the right to govern and use the fief.

The feudal contract remained in effect so long as lord and vassal honored their mutual obligations, or until one of them died. By custom, the eldest son of each came to enjoy the right of succession to his father's position with respect to a fief (the law of primogeniture). But whenever a lord or vassal died, new pledges of homage and new acts of investiture were necessary.

Only warriors (knights) could become vassals and fief-holders. Before a young man could qualify for knighthood, he had to serve an apprenticeship as squire to his father or some other fighting man and then undergo severe tests of courage and military skill. Once he had passed these tests, he was ready for the knighting ceremony.

There is no record of such ceremonies before the eleventh century, and the early ones noted seem to have been simple affairs. Within a century or so, however, knighthood took on more of an aura of romance and idealism. The ritual of knighting was the initiation of a young man into a professional caste, marked by the presentation of a sword to him by a qualified knight.

This ceremony, originally secular, soon developed spiritual and religious overtones. By the middle of the twelfth century, the knight's sword was usually placed upon an altar before the presentation, implying that the knight was obliged to protect the Church. By the thirteenth century, the ritual was normally performed in a church or a cathedral, rather than in a manor house or a castle. The initiate spent a night of vigil and prayer before the day of the ceremony, emerging from the ritual as a "soldier of Christ." The purely secular view of the knight and his role did not disappear, however, and the behavior of the warriors seldom measured up to the ideals of the Church. Yet the transformation of the knighting ceremony into a religious ritual tended to improve the conduct of Europe's military aristocracy.

When a vassal died and left an heir who was not a qualified knight, special arrangements had to be made. If the heir was a son who had not yet attained his majority, the lord would normally serve as guardian until the youth could qualify as a knight and become his vassal. If the sole heir was a daughter, the lord would serve as guardian until he found her a knightly husband. Then her husband, through the act of homage, would receive the fief as the lord's new vassal. Such marriages were one of the chief means of expanding individual and family power during the feudal age. When a vassal died leaving no heir, the fief reverted to the lord, who could keep it for himself or grant it to a new vassal on the same terms.

The feudalization of the Church

Not all the land of western Europe was held in fief during the Middle Ages. Certain properties were owned outright, with no obligation of vassalage. But most of the usable land, including that held by the Church, was bound up in the feudal pattern. Church lands were held as fiefs by archbishops, bishops, and abbots who had sworn fealty to counts, dukes, princes, and kings. But how, one may ask, could men of the cloth perform military duties and kill enemies on the field of battle? They were not qualified knights, and canon law forbade the shedding of blood by the clergy.

The ranking clergy were usually the sons of noblemen, familiar with the ways of war. During the ninth and tenth centuries, in fact, they often ignored the canonical prohibition and engaged in personal combat. Archbishop Turpin, in the epic *Song of Roland*, wields his sword against the infidel and dies a hero's death along with Charlemagne's lay vassals. With the clerical reform movement of the eleventh century (which we will discuss in the next chapter), however, ecclesiastical lords were directed to satisfy their military obligations by assigning portions of their properties as fiefs to warrior nobles. The warriors pledged, as vassals of the ecclesiastical lords, to perform the required military services. This arrangement illustrates how, by a series of adaptations to circumstance, feudalism developed as a viable system of government for western Europe. Lay and spiritual lords became intimately associated at all levels of authority.

MANORIALISM

In medieval society the clergy, as guardians of men's souls, were regarded as comprising the "first estate" (class). The nobility, as protectors of life and property, were ranked as members of the "second estate." All other men fell into the "third estate" and were considered "commoners." Though they made up about 90 per cent of the population of Europe, these commoners had little political voice and even less social prestige. It is to their life, work, and forms of community that we now turn.

The manorial estate

Since land was the basis of wealth in medieval Europe, most of the people were farmers, or peasants. They did not, however, work on individual private farms. For the principal unit of agricultural production was the manorial estate, or manor. Every great fief was subdivided into hundreds of these estates, which also served as the basic social units of the Middle Ages.

To the peasants who worked on a particular estate, the limits of the manor were the limits of their world. Ordinarily they were not allowed to leave the manor at all, and only rarely did they go beyond the nearest town or fair. Travel, even when permitted, was seldom undertaken because of its perils. Roads were poor, hostels few, and banditry widespread. Manorial estates ranged in size from a minimum of perhaps three hundred acres to a maximum of about three thousand. The average estate was probably about a thousand acres. The estate had to be large enough to sustain the manorial community and to enable its lord to fulfill his feudal obligations, but it could not be so large as to be unmanageable as a farming unit.

The productive heart of the manor consisted of the arable fields, and more than half the total estate was normally used for crops. This portion was divided into three planting areas—in the so-called three-field system. In a given year one of these areas would be sowed in the spring, another in the fall, and the third left fallow. In the succeeding year the fallow area would be planted in the spring, the previous "spring" section would be planted in the fall, and the previous "fall" section would be left fallow. Thus, each year, two-thirds of the arable lands were in use, while one-third was lying fallow. This simple conservation measure saved the land from wearing out.

A peculiar feature of medieval land cultivation was the strip system. A peasant who held land, or who was bound to work certain land, did not have a compact area assigned to him. Instead, he held long, narrow strips in each of the three planting areas (FIG. 4-5). Although the origins of this system are obscure, several reasons for its widespread use suggest themselves. In the first place, the system allowed the farmer to operate, at any one time, in each of the planting areas, thus allowing his continuous employment. Second, since work animals were scarce and small, plowing and harvesting had to be done on a cooperative basis; large unfenced fields, where the strips lay side by side, were easier to work in this manner than smaller fields enclosed by fences or hedges. The strip system also made it possible to distribute the good and poor lands equitably among the peasants on each estate. And it guarded against disastrous loss to a particular farm family. If blight or crop failure struck one sector of the estate, the peasants suffering losses would have strips elsewhere to help carry them through.

The shape of the strips was apparently governed by the techniques of cultivation. One long furrow could be plowed more efficiently than several short ones. The typical strip was a rod wide (about seventeen feet), allowing ample turning space for a team of oxen, and forty rods long (a furlong, or one-eighth of a mile). A unit of these dimensions could be plowed comfortably in a morning or an afternoon, which meant that the workday could be conveniently planned. The lord of the manor, according to his privilege, usually retained a special plot of land for his exclusive use (the "close"). This, together with his strips in the open fields, was known as the lord's "demesne." Other strips were set aside for the benefit of the parish priest ("God's acre").

In addition to the arable lands, supporting areas were essential to the functioning of the estate. There was a common forest or wood lot where the peasants were permitted to gather fuel, a common meadow to provide hay for the work animals, and a pasture where the sheep and cattle grazed. A water source (usually a stream or a pond) was indispensable, as well as an area for dumping refuse. Only a small section of the estate was occupied by the village itself, while

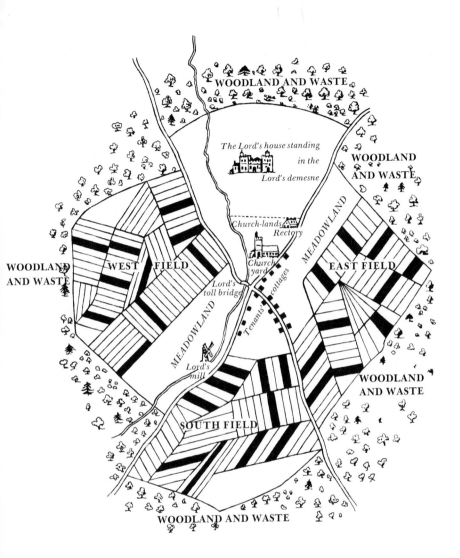

WOODLAND AND WASTE

The Lord's house standing in the Lord's demesne

WOODLAND AND WASTE

Church-lands Rectory

WOODLAND AND WASTE

WEST FIELD

MEADOWLAND

Churchyard

Lord's toll bridge

Tenants' cottages

EAST FIELD

MEADOWLAND

Lord's mill

WOODLAND AND WASTE

SOUTH FIELD

WOODLAND AND WASTE

FIGURE 4-5. Plan of a manor. From *An Introduction to English Industrial History,* by Henry Allsop, G. Bell & Sons, Ltd.

the lord's residence (a manor house or a castle) was usually situated on a commanding site some distance from the flimsy huts of the peasants. The barns and outbuildings of the manor, in fact, were likely to be more substantial than the thatched, wattled homes of the village. Around their huts the villagers kept small vegetable gardens and raised a few hens or pigs to supplement their diet. The food grown in the open fields consisted chiefly of staples: wheat, rye, oats, barley, peas, or beans.

Every village had a church and a parson's house. In addition, the lord usually provided (for a fee) a grinding mill, a bake oven, and a wine press to serve the villagers. A limited specialization of labor provided such services as metalworking and shoemaking. The manorial community, consisting usually of about two or three hundred people, was almost entirely self-sustaining. Until the later Middle Ages it produced little surplus for exchange, depending on home manufactures for almost all its needs.

The people of the manor

The records of village life prior to the thirteenth century are meager. But we do know that in those mute centuries the basic habits of work, law, worship, and festival evolved into established custom. And we have abundant evidence that village life as it existed in the thirteenth century persisted with little change for the following five hundred years. The rise of trade and the growth of cities, the emergence of national states, the struggles between religious factions—all seem to have had slight effect on the basic patterns and rhythms of rural life.

Although the lord of the manor was presumably guided by the rules of God and by custom, his word had the effect of local law. Whether a simple knight or a noble of high degree, he was often away from home for long periods of time. For he was a warrior as well as a landlord and had his feudal obligations to fulfill. When he was not performing these duties, his favorite pastime was hunting. He typically took little direct interest in farming and left the management of his lands to overseers.

From his own demesne and from payments in kind from the peasants, the lord normally took about half the total produce of the estate. This may appear excessive, but we must remember that as a mounted knight he had to support retainers as well as the members of his own family. In addition, he was obliged to make certain payments in kind to his overlord. Finally, he maintained a reserve of grain in his barns, so that in years of blight or crop failure he would be able to provide the peasants with rations. He could not allow them to starve, for, aside from humane considerations, they represented his labor force.

Most of the peasants were serfs, whose special obligations and ties to the soil were inherited. During the turbulent times of the early Middle Ages, whole communities of farmers had been subjugated by, or had offered their labor to, some powerful man in return for protection. And it was always possible, even later, for a man to commit himself and his descendants to perpetual servitude in return for a piece of land to cultivate. The lord could free a serf whenever he chose, but otherwise serfs were legally held to their obligations.

Serfs were bound to work on their assigned strips of land and to turn over to the lord a stipulated share of their crop. They also had to cultivate and harvest the lord's demesne and the strips set aside for the parish priest. In addition, they could be called on to build roads, clear forests, and do other work whenever the lord demanded. The serf's children were likewise bound to the manor; no member of his family could leave the estate or get married without the express consent of the lord.

Men whose ancestors had managed to avoid serfdom enjoyed the status of freemen. This did not necessarily mean that they were better off; some, in fact, lived on the edge of starvation. If the freeman farmed land, he did so as a farm tenant, paying rent to the lord in the form of a share of his crop. The lord could evict a freeman whenever he saw fit, whereas a serf could not legally be separated from his land.

In the later Middle Ages, many landlords began to find tenancy a more flexible and satisfactory arrangement than serfdom; the serfs, for their part, were glad to escape the degradation of servitude. Whether free or servile, the peasants of a manorial village shared a common life. They knew little of the outside world, save for news and gossip brought by the lord, the priest, or itinerant peddlers and clerics. The course of their lives was shaped by the pattern of labor, the turn of the seasons, the cycle of religious holidays, and the round of marriages, births, and deaths.

THE RISE OF TRADE AND TOWNS

While the manor remained the principal unit of European society until the eighteenth century, the seeds of "modern" civilization were being nourished as early as the eleventh. With the rise of trade routes and marketing centers came the emergence of the towns that were destined to convert Europe from a rural to an urban society. The lords and peasants who remained on the manorial estates played a negligible role in the growth of towns. An entirely new cast of characters appeared, consisting of merchants, entrepreneurs, bankers, lawyers, artisans, and unskilled laborers. In the thirteenth century these groups comprised but a fraction of Europe's population (less than 10 per cent), but their numbers were destined to grow until, by the twentieth century, they would be a majority.

Origins

There was little resemblance or connection between the city-states of the ancient world and the new communities of western Europe. Athens, for example, was founded by warrior-landholders under the patronage of a goddess. The Greek *polis* (or the Roman *civitas*) was conceived as a sacred and sovereign community, whose leading members lived in town but held properties in the surrounding countryside. It was loyally supported by urbanites and rustics alike as an integrated kinship unit. Medieval towns, by contrast, were isolated from rural society. They sprang from the revival of commerce, and their immediate aims were narrowly materialistic. Their founders were generally not warriors, nobles, or kings—but landless commoners, most of whom came originally from manorial villages. The townsmen had to struggle for many generations to wrest from the landed aristocracy a degree of political autonomy for their communities.

The stimulus for the revival of trade came from the Mediterranean world. Byzantium and Islam were vigorous commercial societies and manufactured elegant articles for export. Their merchandise was brought to western Europe by overland routes through Spain, or, more commonly, through Venice and other port cities of Italy (FIG. 4-6). Constantinople was the main source of luxury goods, which found a growing market among European aristocrats. Those who could afford them sought spices (pepper, ginger, and cinnamon) to relieve the monotony of medieval cooking; silks and satins; precious jewels; statues, rugs, and tapestries. It was the desire of the well-to-do for such luxuries that set in motion the wheels of commerce in Europe and thus led to the rise of towns.

Gold and silver had largely disappeared in the West, and the Europeans had to sell goods in order to pay for their imports. Their commodities included woolens and linens, horses, weapons and armor, timber, and furs. Caravans carried these items from all parts of Europe, across the Alps, to Milan and other centers on the Lombard plain. There they were taken over by merchants from the Italian port cities for shipment to the East. Northern Italy thus became the focus of the reviving commerce between West and East.

This trade was relatively insignificant in the eleventh century but grew rapidly during the twelfth and thirteenth. It was accompanied by a rise in population and in production. With some assurance that surplus crops could be marketed, peasants and nobles had a new incentive for increasing farm produce, which led to improvements in agricultural techniques and the opening of new lands to

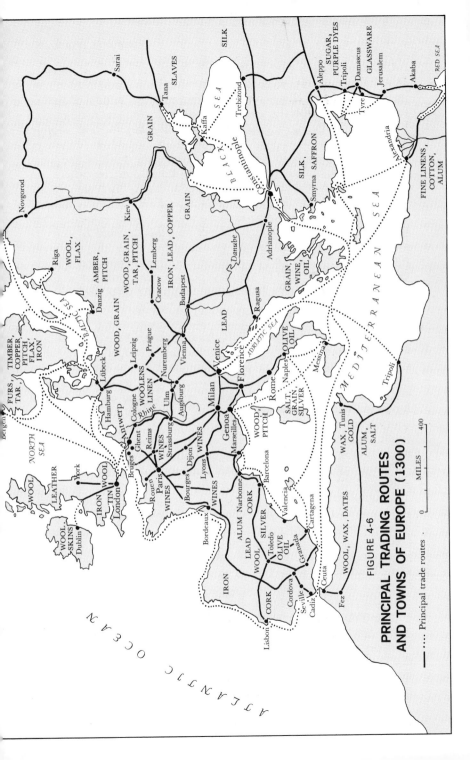

FIGURE 4-6

PRINCIPAL TRADING ROUTES
AND TOWNS OF EUROPE (1300)

—— Principal trade routes ·
····· Principal trade routes ·

cultivation. Secular and ecclesiastical lords, who had formerly received their income in goods and services, now demanded money instead. Gold and silver were being coined again and were passing into circulation with the acceleration of trade. Money, little used in the early Middle Ages, was now seen as the key to new comforts and delights.

The wool and textile industries provided the bulk of European exports. These industries centered in the Low Countries, where conditions were favorable to sheep-raising. In time this region gained fame also for its woolen manufactures, and Flemish entrepreneurs finally had to turn to outside sources of raw wool to satisfy their needs. English farmers and landlords met this demand by converting part of their holdings into pasture land. After the thirteenth century, both in England and on the Continent, there was a ready-cash market for wool. The simplest peasant, with only a few sheep, might thus become a participant in the trading revolution.

The location and appearance of towns

The early towns were essentially trading posts where local produce could be sold and foreign merchandise purchased. Traveling merchants, moving along established land and water routes, carried their wares from northern Italy to such trading sites as the junction of highways, the confluence of rivers, or the capital of a duchy or a kingdom (FIG. 4-6). Ancient Roman cities that happened to be strategically located reawakened as bustling towns. The community surrounding a cathedral (that is, the seat of a bishop or an archbishop) might also develop into an important trading center.

Physical protection for the merchants was, of course, a necessity. They usually set up their shops in the shadow of a castle or a fortified compound and then raised walls around their "new" town, linking it to the old. The English word "town" derives from the Anglo-Saxon *tun* (enclosure). And the widely used suffix "burg" (French *bourg*) originally meant a fortified community. As a town grew outward from its nucleus, successive walls were constructed to afford continuing protection. The remains of these walls may still be traced in many of the old cities of Europe.

Understandably, space was at a premium in these medieval towns. Streets and passageways were kept as narrow as possible, so that a maximum number of buildings could be erected. And the buildings themselves had as many stories as safety would permit (sometimes more!). There was very little town planning, and sanitation was notoriously poor. From the very earliest times, European cities faced problems of congestion, traffic control, public health, and slums.

Nevertheless, there was a certain orderliness in most medieval towns. By the thirteenth century, a typical pattern began to emerge. The town was usually dominated by the spires of its main church. Next in importance were the town hall and the buildings of the various trading and industrial organizations (the guilds). The heart of the town was the central marketplace, with the adjacent shops. At first most of these were the places of traders, but artisans of all kinds (weavers, smiths, bakers) soon found they could sell their services in town, and they set up workshops there. Industry (handicrafts) developed side by side with trade.

The new towns presented an avenue of escape to men and women who were seeking release from the drudgery and routine of the manorial village. This was especially true for the serf who longed to cast off his inferior status. He could, if he grew desperate enough, run away from the manor and lose himself in a distant town. According to the custom of the period, he was legally free if his lord failed to recapture him within a "year and a day." (Later in the Middle Ages, he could gain his freedom by making a cash payment to his lord.)

A new social class: the bourgeoisie

Yet life in town was by no means a guarantee of absolute freedom, for the towns had a social structure of their own—though one not quite so rigid as that of the manor. At the top were the leading merchants and moneylenders and the masters of the craft organizations. Beneath them were skilled artisans and clerks, and at the bottom were apprentices and unskilled laborers.

The members of the highest group dominated civic affairs and came to be known by the end of the Middle Ages as the *bourgeoisie* (townsmen). They constituted, in fact, a new class in European society, a class that gained in wealth and power as the centuries passed. Even so, the bourgeoisie were regarded as commoners, legally and socially inferior to the nobility and the clergy. They later were referred to as the middle class; this term placed them *between* the nobility and the mass of commoners.

Since the whole pattern of life in the towns was different from that of the feudal estate, a new mode of government had to be devised for the new communities. The townsmen sought special charters that would free them from the customary obligations of the feudal relationship and would permit them to establish appropriate rules of their own. These charters, which were granted by the king, nobleman, or bishop holding jurisdiction over the area, recognized the citizens of the town as a political body, or corporation, with legal privileges and powers. In return for these privileges, and in lieu of feudal services, the corporation made regular payments of money to the grantor. The form of government differed from one town to another, but in most places control resided in the hands of a governing council and a titular official called a mayor or burgomaster. Though voting rights were often quite liberal, it was uncommon for any but the leading families to hold important offices.

Economic theory and control: the guilds

The governing council imposed strict political control on the community. Legally, the citizens of a town were free individuals, but the idea of collective responsibility and regulation permeated town and countryside alike. Economic activities in the town were subject to close supervision. Authority over trade and industry was delegated to special corporations, called guilds, which acted in accordance with certain general principles: that production and sale of goods were *common* ventures limited to members of the guild, that standards of business practice and quality of merchandise must be upheld, and that the price of every commodity should be pegged at a "just" figure corresponding to the amount and character of labor that produced it.

Each guild enjoyed a monopoly over a given field of business, and its members had to obey the guild's regulations. The principal organization in most towns was the merchant guild, which established rules governing the marketplaces. These rules controlled the times and places at which goods could be sold, the standard weights and measures, and the grades and prices of the commodities sold.

At first the merchant guild included most of the entrepreneurs in a given town. With growing specialization, however, one group after another split off from the parent unit to form craft guilds: weavers, dyers, tailors, carpenters, masons, silversmiths, bakers, barbers, and the like. The number of separate craft guilds differed from place to place; by the thirteenth century there might have been as many as thirty or forty guilds in a single town.

The primary function of a craft guild was to supervise the production of goods and the training of artisans. Craftsmen were classified as masters, journeymen, or apprentices. Only the masters had the right to operate workshops and train others; they alone were voting members of the guild and directed its policies, and their coveted status was attained by other craftsmen only after long experience and proof of excellence. Before the masters certified a candidate to their rank, they customarily required him to submit an example of his workmanship. This effort, the finest he was capable of, was called his "masterpiece." Journeymen were licensed artisans who had served their apprenticeship. They were employed by masters and were usually paid at a fixed rate per day (*journée*). Before becoming a journeyman, a man was obliged to work for a specified period of time, ranging from two to seven years, as an apprentice in the shop of a master. In return for his labor, he received only food and lodging.

Although the guilds were primarily economic units, they also performed personal and social functions. If a member fell sick, was put in jail, or got into some other kind of trouble, he could count on help from the guild fraternity. The guilds ceremonialized births, marriages, and funerals, conducted social affairs, and celebrated church festivals as a body. Each one, moreover, honored a particular Christian saint who was associated by tradition with a given craft. (St. Joseph, for example, was honored by the carpenters.) The guilds often dedicated altars or chapels in the town church to their patron saints. In all their varied activities they embodied the corporate and community spirit so characteristic of medieval society.

The Flowering of Medieval Culture

5

During the eleventh century, as the near-anarchy of earlier centuries passed, the political and economic institutions of western Europe took on strength and stability. The order that emerged was to endure for some five hundred years. Feudalism and manorialism, the towns and the guilds, furnished a foundation on which Western man could build a rich and distinctive culture.

THE MEDIEVAL CHURCH

In the preceding chapter we concentrated on the material side of life in the Middle Ages. But medieval men were more concerned with what lies *beyond* this world; they looked toward life eternal. And since the central role of the Church was to guide souls to everlasting salvation, the Church was regarded as the primary institution in society.

So widespread was the Christian faith, and so confident the expectation of a better life after death, that the era is often called the Age of Faith. Never before had the Church been so dominant in the affairs of Western men, nor has it been so since. Though priests and bishops looked toward eternity, they paid close attention to what happened on earth. For what men did in the "here and now" would determine their fate in the hereafter. Consequently, the Church felt obliged to examine the heart and deeds of every Christian and to ensure that human institutions reflected the will of God.

The sacraments

The extraordinary power of the medieval Church rested solidly upon the trust of the people. Rich men willed the Church generous legacies, and bishops and abbots thereby acquired vast properties in land, serfs, animals, and buildings. And wealth brought influence. The strength of the Church had deeper and broader sources, however—among them, the direct and intimate relation of the Church to every inhabitant of the "Christian commonwealth." For the Church was held to be the sole door to salvation; a bishop, by his authority to open or close that door to each person under his jurisdiction, exercised a mighty persuasion.

The sacraments (instruments of God's grace) were in the custody of the Church. A general theory of the sacraments, as well as an accepted explanation of each of the rites, had emerged by the eleventh century. It ran as follows: Adam's Original Sin against God's will has stained all human beings with guilt. Although this guilt can be washed away through the rite of baptism, men, by their sinful nature, continue to fall into disobedience and unseemly acts. Only through divine aid (grace) can they be strengthened and forgiven. And the Lord in his goodness has created the sacraments as the means for transmitting that grace. Priests alone can administer the sacraments, for priests acquire miraculous power through the rite of *ordination*. By this rite they receive a portion of the powers originally vested by the Holy Ghost in the twelve apostles.

Seven sacraments, counting *ordination* itself, were recognized by the hierarchy. Through *baptism* the individual was initiated into Church membership and cleansed of the stain and penalty of past sin. The second sacrament was *confirmation*. Whereas baptism was customarily administered to infants, this rite was administered (by a bishop) only after a man had received religious instruction and had expressed his willingness to live as a Christian. Through it, he was confirmed in his acceptance of Christ and was strengthened in his faith by the Holy Ghost. Since ordination, baptism, and confirmation each left a special mark upon the soul that was believed to be indelible, these sacraments were administered only once during a person's lifetime.

The other four sacraments could be repeated. Foremost among them was the *Eucharist* (Mass), which was held to provide indispensable nourishment for the soul. The Church taught that at a certain moment in the rite the bread and wine were transformed (transubstantiated) into the body and blood of the Savior. The partaker received thereby the strength of Christ himself, which would assist him in doing good and resisting evil. Christians were enjoined to partake of the Eucharist at least once each year. But the Eucharist was beneficial only if it was received worthily—that is, only if the communicant was in a "state of grace," absolved from past sins. To prepare for the Eucharist, the communicant had recourse to the sacrament of *penance,* which consisted of the following steps: after inward repentance for his misdeeds, oral confession, and acceptance of a penalty, he was absolved by the priest. When it appeared that a Christian was on the point of death, he was given the sacrament of *extreme unction* (last rites), which granted him final forgiveness for the sins of his lifetime.

The seventh sacrament was *matrimony,* the joining of husband and wife. The clergy compared the matrimonial bond to the union between Christ and the Church and held it to be indissoluble so long as the two partners lived. Should one of them die, the survivor could take another spouse by repeating the matrimonial rite. This sacrament and that of ordination were not essential to the individual's salvation. But the other five were mandatory, and the clergy taught that only through them could a Christian reach heaven.

Christian devotional life

The sacraments were central to the spiritual life of medieval men. They were part of a complex of religious observances that revolved around the calendar and the clock. The Christian liturgy included all the formal worship services of the clergy and the laity; the most important of these services was the liturgy of the Mass. Though Masses were performed every day, the main service was on Sunday, when attendance was required of all Christians. In the larger churches this became an elaborate performance, with the chief priest and his assistants wearing rich and colorful vestments. The appeal to the senses was heightened by the use of music, incense, and gold and silver vessels. These sights and sounds combined to create an atmosphere of mystery and awe.

The experience of the Mass strengthened the bonds of association in the Age of Faith. Clergy and laity were joined in a common, dramatic experience as men and women of all social classes participated together under one roof. They were taught that the sacrament was a mystic union—a holy communion—between Christ and themselves. No other ritual has symbolized so completely the intimate association between human and divine beings.

In addition to conducting worship services, the clergy had the further obligation of saying daily prayers, or the Divine Office. They followed an authorized book of prayers (breviary) that prescribed which ones were to be recited at certain hours of the day (the canonical hours). Prayers consisted, for the most part, of praise and thanksgiving to God, together with pleas for guidance and aid. The Divine Office also served as a continuing reminder to the clergy that they should dedicate their whole lives to praising the Lord and fulfilling his will. The laity believed that the offering of prayers by the clergy brought benefits to the entire society of Christians.

Around these formal devotions clustered a multitude of informal practices, which made up the popular religion of the times. These practices grew out of the beliefs, fears, and aspirations of the common man. While such developments were sometimes regulated by the priesthood, they often exceeded the bounds of official doctrine, as we shall see.

The cult of the Crucifixion, for example, was not, at the outset, at least, the result of priestly teaching. It grew out of a deep and spontaneous sympathy for Jesus as a *man*. In earlier centuries, theologians had tended to stress the role of Jesus as *God*. His life, death, and resurrection were seen as part of a grand design by which the Lord overcame the devil and opened the path of human salvation. The Crucifixion, in this view, was an act of divine majesty—above the fears and pains of ordinary men. In early Christian art, the Savior had been generally portrayed as the risen Christ sitting in august dignity upon the heavenly throne. Sometime after 1000, a new conception of the Lord's life on earth began to predominate. This view emphasized Jesus' human experiences—his struggles, indignities, and physical sufferings. Both theologians and the common people drew fresh meaning from the Passion of the Lord, recognizing in his agony and humiliation their own anguish and miseries. Artists increasingly represented the dying Christ hanging heavily from the Cross. Gradually the crucifix, which aroused in pious hearts the deepest feelings of compassion and love, became the most popular devotional object.

Interpretations of the Gospel were subtly influenced by this more human view of Jesus. The changes are reflected most clearly in Christian sculpture and painting: the infant Jesus in early portraits appears as a regal figure, but during the Middle Ages he was made to look like any infant held in the arms of his loving mother. And Mary herself was depicted in a manner ever more tender and human.

The cult of the Virgin was exceedingly popular in the Middle Ages. The monasteries played a leading role in developing the cult, but ordinary people responded warmly to the appeal of Mary. Aside from her role as the mother of God, she personified the Christian ideals of womanhood, love, and sympathy. During an upsurge of religious fervor in the thirteenth century, many of the great new cathedrals were dedicated to "Notre Dame" (Our Lady). A rich literature and a host of legends came into being that told of the countless miracles of the Virgin. She was pictured as loyal and indulgent toward all who honored her and ready to bestow earthly benefits and heavenly rewards on those who prayed to her. From time to time the higher clergy grew concerned over the intensity of the Marian cult. There was always the risk that homage to the Virgin might compete with worship of God. The bishops nonetheless encouraged the cult as part of the general veneration of saints.

Mary was the most exalted of the saints, but there were hundreds of lesser figures who also attracted prayer and devotions. It is difficult to understand this phenomenon except in terms of the medieval man's compelling will to believe. Faith in marvels, omens, and supernatural intervention was nearly universal, devils and demons were thought to lurk everywhere, and miraculous cures and resurrections were reported almost daily. These wonders, many of which were attributed to the saints, fired the imagination of the unlettered and erudite alike.

The saints were the heroes of the Middle Ages, as the epic warriors had been the heroes of classical Greece. They included the twelve apostles and the early martyrs, as well as a host of later figures. Their fame as preachers, ascetics, and workers of miracles became established by tradition, though it was not until after the Middle Ages that the popes began to identify them formally as saints (through canonization). The bishops, from early times, required Christians to show the saints the special honor of veneration. Though it was taught that veneration should not become *worship* (which was reserved for the deity), medieval Christians addressed a large share of their devotions to the saints.

The Church taught that saints have the power to perform miracles after their death as well as during their life on earth. In heaven, by virtue of their privileged position, they can win divine aid for mortal petitioners by interceding with God. Moreover, some of their power was thought to persist on earth in their physical remains (relics). Hence immense value was placed on the bones, teeth, and intimate possessions of departed saints. No church or monastery was without its hoard of relics—its "spiritual endowment." To this day the treasuries of many European churches are rich with golden reliquaries and their precious contents.

Hardly any act was undertaken in the Middle Ages without first invoking the saints. Oaths and treaties were sworn on saintly remains; townsmen carried them in processions; before setting out on a dangerous journey or campaign, men prayed to a saint and touched his relics; knights often inserted holy remnants in the hilts of their swords. The skulls, bones, and hairs of saints were the most common relics, but some exotic items were preserved as well: the sweat, tears, and umbilical cord of Jesus; St. Joseph's breath; and the Virgin's milk. Fragments of the "true" Cross seemed to be everywhere—enough, it was said later, to build a ship. Several heads of John the Baptist were enshrined, as were the whole skeletons of many lesser saints. The genuineness of these relics was not questioned by the faithful, and the number of relics throughout Europe ran into the millions. At last, by the close of the Middle Ages, some devout Christians began to doubt their authenticity.

Monastic reform movements: Cluny and the friars

In addition to providing spiritual guidance, the medieval Church ministered to society in numerous other ways. The "secular" clergy (p. 127) acted as counselors and administrators for civil rulers; bishops and archbishops functioned as vassals of kings and emperors. Homelier services were performed by the "regular" clergy, who populated the great monastic houses. After the founding of Monte Cassino in 529, monasteries began to appear all over western Europe, most of them independent houses pledged to the Benedictine Rule. Although their primary function was to serve as a refuge for ascetics seeking to devote themselves to God, the monks answered the needs of the times by assuming important social functions as well.

The regular clergy preserved and copied manuscripts and provided elementary schooling for youths planning to enter the clergy, thus keeping literacy and learning alive. At the same time they preserved in their workshops the useful arts of weaving, pottery-making, and metalworking, and in the fields they developed more efficient techniques of farming. Over the centuries the religious houses became large landholders, and, though the monks themselves were bound by vows of poverty, the corporate wealth of the monasteries rose steadily.

As a result of this growing wealth the monastic establishments became more and more involved in the affairs of the world. The head of a monastery—the abbot—held the monastery's property as a fief from some overlord, and he had the usual military, financial, and political responsibilities of a vassal. He met his obligations, in part, by granting some of the monastery's lands to knights, who, as vassals of the abbot, performed the required military duties. From the ninth to the twelfth century military contingents from monastic fiefs were important components of feudal armies.

The kings and the feudal barons frequently chose their administrators from among members of the regular clergy (as well as the seculars). At a time when few men were literate, the regulars furnished a valuable supply of civil servants. Since the monasteries from which they came were well rewarded for these services, the houses became richer and richer, and the monks became more deeply involved in secular affairs. These developments enhanced the stability of the government and the economy, but they tended to impair the ascetic way of life once so characteristic of the regular clergy. By the tenth century some ecclesiastical leaders had become alarmed by the growing divergence between monastic ideals and practices.

Wealth brought the ways of the world into the cloisters themselves. Some abbots lived as elegantly as barons, and ordinary brothers enjoyed the fruits of prospering estates. Indulgence in food and drink led to a broader pursuit of pleasure. Obedience to monastic rules weakened, the vow of chastity was taken less seriously, and physical labor grew less attractive. The monks tended, at the same time, to neglect the arts of reading and writing.

Standards of learning and conduct fell to an even lower level among the secular clergy. The appointment of bishops and archbishops was generally controlled by powerful nobles, who often sold the offices to the highest bidder. Some of these "successors to the apostles" were more intrigued by politics than by spiritual matters. Many parish priests also fell short of their responsibilities; some were unable to read; some had wives and families. The popes, as the monarchs of the Church, might have tried to correct these incongruities, but they were as subject as other bishops to the influences of the times. They, too, sought to extend their wealth and power, and some of them owed their very office to the efforts of local nobles or the Holy Roman emperor (p. 163).

Distressed by the widespread corruption within the Church, a few conscientious rulers, bishops, and abbots launched a program of reform. The most far-reaching of these efforts was undertaken in the Burgundian monastery of Cluny, founded in 910 by the Duke of Aquitaine. In order to insulate themselves from local interference, the Cluniac monks placed themselves under the direct authority of the pope. The first abbot, Berno, set out to revive the strictness of the Benedictine Rule. From Cluny the impulse toward reform spread to all parts of the clergy.

Though Cluny aimed at restoration of the Church as a whole, it launched a notable innovation in monastic organization. Formerly each Benedictine house had been independent; now the abbots of Cluny proceeded to found "daughter" houses subject to the "mother" house. Their purpose was to protect individual houses from falling under local secular influences. Within a century there were some three hundred Cluniac houses spread across western

Europe. Only the mother house was designated a *monastery*. The daughter houses were called *priories*, and the priors (subabbots) who governed them were appointed by the Great Abbot of Cluny.

Heads of the older Benedictine houses also came under the influence of the reform spirit; bishops, too, and the papacy itself were caught up in this revival of Christian purpose and discipline. The Cluniac movement was a striking success. Monastic life was restored to something like its original rigor, simony was exposed and reduced, and the rule of priestly celibacy was more strictly enforced. Part of Cluny's success can be attributed to a series of extraordinary abbots. Moreover, since her monks came chiefly from noble families, Cluny took on an aristocratic style and enjoyed generous support and gifts from the landed classes. In the end, Cluny's very success brought about its decline as a model of reform. By the twelfth century, surrounded by mounting wealth and influence, the monks of Cluny slipped into the ways of material ease.

Repeating the Cluniac pattern, a new order now appeared. It, too, ran its puritanical course and then fell into laxity. This order arose in a barren area of Burgundy, with the founding of an abbey at Citeaux (Cistercium) in 1098. Its daughter houses expanded spectacularly under the leadership of the saintly and magnetic Bernard of Clairvaux, who was to promote the Second Crusade in 1146. The Cistercians, as they were called, wore white robes to distinguish themselves from the black of the Benedictines. There was acute rivalry between the two orders, with the Cistercians at first deploring the wealth and ostentation of Cluny. But the white robes, too, became soiled by economic success, gifts, and temporal power. Within a century of the abbey's founding, the Cistercians had succumbed to the comforts of affluence.

A third reform effort followed a similar course. Early in the thirteenth century a young Italian, Francis of Assisi, felt himself called to live his life in imitation of Christ. The son of a wealthy merchant, Francis gave up his home, his fine clothing, and the security of his family to travel about in voluntary poverty—sustained by alms alone. Soon he was joined by companions of like mind, forming a company of twelve. Rejecting the routine of monks in some remote cloister, they chose instead to work among the needy of the towns. In the expanding centers of trade the Franciscans preached and ministered to the poor, stressing the theme of Christian love and brotherhood.

Francis was reluctant to found an order, for he believed that formal organization tends to suppress individual spontaneity. He also feared the effect of wealth—even collective wealth—on the ideal of holy poverty. The papacy, however, was apprehensive about what Francis and his followers would do if they were permitted to carry on their activities without close supervision by the Church. Consequently, the papacy authorized Francis to establish an order subject to his direct control. Soon, the brothers (friars) of the new order, who had previously supported themselves by begging, began to accept gifts of property and buildings. Within a century the Franciscans became a wealthy order, and their devotion to poverty and simplicity gave way to concern for material things.

The Franciscans originally had little use for books or education. Francis himself was a mystic—one who sought God's truth through inner inspiration and revelation. He and his fellow mystics, who had substantial influence in the Middle Ages, were skeptical of book learning and human reason. Of a contrary spirit was the Spaniard Dominic, a contemporary of Francis. Dominic was an austere intellectual who saw God's truth as a rational ideology, and the order of friars he founded was devoted chiefly to scholarship and teaching. Alarmed by the spread of heretical doctrines, Dominic believed he could best serve the Lord by guiding the thoughts and education of men. Francis appealed to men's hearts; Dominic appealed to their minds. Both the gray friars (the Franciscans) and the black (the Dominicans) became familiar figures on the streets and highways of Europe.

The papal monarchy

The most significant reforms of the medieval Church were associated with the papacy itself. For centuries the feudal nobles of Italy had vied with one another for control of the office. In the tenth century, after the east Frankish king, Otto, became Holy Roman emperor, he subdued the Italians and set German bishops on the throne of St. Peter. Conscientious leaders of the Church, spurred by the Cluniac reform, strove to lift the papacy out of the arena of imperial politics to a position of independence. In a very real sense, the effort to cleanse the Church as a whole hinged on the success of this endeavor.

The Italian Hildebrand, who was destined to become Pope Gregory VII, was the chief architect of papal independence. As Archdeacon of Rome, a key office in the Church's administration, he proved himself a shrewd planner and tactician. In 1059, with one masterful stroke, he brought into being a new system for the election of popes—the College of Cardinals. Prior to that time popes had been elected, theoretically, by the entire clergy of the Roman diocese, subject to the approval of the city's populace. This arrangement had lent itself readily to manipulation by local nobles and foreign monarchs.

Hildebrand corrected the situation by restricting the papal electors to the cardinal clergy—a small number of the ranking priests of Rome. The cardinals were appointed by the pope, and when one pope died they met in seclusion to name his successor. Since they usually chose from their own membership, the body automatically furnished select candidates for the papal office. In subsequent centuries the College of Cardinals was expanded to include leaders of the Church throughout the world. Except for rare occasions when foreign military forces were present in Rome, or when the Church suffered from schism, the electoral system has functioned remarkably well. It has brought to the highest office of the Roman Catholic Church a notable succession of leaders whose ability, on the average, has surpassed that of any line of hereditary rulers.

In 1073 the cardinals chose Hildebrand as pope (Gregory VII). Conditioned by his earlier training at Cluny, he applied himself to a sweeping reform of the Church. One of his main objectives was to strengthen the papacy, to make it a monarchy in fact as well as in theory. Under his guidance the central administration of the papacy came to be handled through a number of bureaus, departments, and assemblies—called, collectively, the papal curia. The officers in charge of these agencies were usually chosen from among the cardinals and formed, in effect, a kind of pope's "cabinet."

Beyond Rome, papal authority reached into every diocese of Christendom. According to the doctrine of apostolic succession (p. 109), the bishops constituted the core of the Church. But all were subordinate to the supreme bishop, the successor to Peter: the pope. He kept in touch with them through regular correspondence—the papal letters run to thousands of volumes. Bishops (and archbishops) were also required to make periodic visits to Rome, which often involved arduous travel. In order to enhance his influence outside Italy, Gregory initiated the practice of sending forth papal legates. These deputies of the pope came to be assigned more or less permanently to the capitals of Europe. Each legate conducted inquiries and oversaw the Church hierarchy in the territory where he resided.

In addition to the income from their extensive properties in Italy, the popes received large revenues from all over Europe, including such special levies as "Peter's pence," an annual tax on Christian families in England. The popes also collected a substantial sum from every newly appointed prelate. Countless other payments flowed to Rome: fees for appeals from bishops' courts, for exemptions from canon law, and for papal indulgences. The latter were certificates, issued through agents of the pope, that purportedly reduced the penalties (now and after death) due to sin. All these revenues were used for various purposes—administrative and political as well as religious, charitable, and artistic.

Papal influence over medieval society was reinforced by sweeping disciplinary power. The pope and the bishops could excommunicate Christians under their jurisdiction and thus deprive them of the benefit of the sacraments. Since observance of the sacraments was essential to salvation, excommunication was regarded as a most fearful penalty. The threat of excommunication was used to induce obedience from clergy, noblemen, and commoners alike, and not infrequently it was invoked against recalcitrant kings and emperors.

If excommunication did not bring a ruler to his knees, the pope could resort to the interdict. This was an order closing the churches and suspending the sacraments in a particular area or realm. A ruler, no matter what his own religious convictions, could scarcely ignore the interdict. For the faithful, fearing that their souls were in jeopardy, would press the ruler to yield so that the churches might be reopened. Moreover, with the appearance of any sign of revolt, the pope could supplement the interdict by declaring the ruler deposed and releasing his subjects from obedience.

The disciplinary power of the pope had certain limits of effectiveness, however. A person who had been excommunicated could beg forgiveness; if he showed evidence of genuine penitence, the pope was virtually obliged to lift his ban. And, extreme measures like the interdict often boomeranged. If a ruler who was in dispute with the pope enjoyed the sympathy and support of his people, the interdict might cause them to rally to the ruler's side.

Nevertheless, through the innumerable channels and agencies of the Church, the papacy could exert a powerful influence on popular thought and behavior. By means of proclamations, letters, and speeches, for example, the Bishop of Rome could disseminate his ideas and exercise active leadership. Serving as his instruments were the ecclesiastical hierarchy, the religious orders, and the church schools—all of which were in contact with the people. The sacrament of penance, with its oral confession, kept the priesthood in touch with the inmost thoughts and feelings of men and women. And the bishops, especially, were on the alert to spot signs of heresy and to stamp it out.

Their efforts were reinforced in the thirteenth century by special courts of inquiry set up by the papacy. These courts, known as the Inquisition, were introduced to many areas of Europe, but the most active of them was the one established in the south of France after heresy and revolt had gripped that region. The Grand Inquisitor, who sat at Carcassonne, had deputies in other towns and cities to ferret out unorthodox beliefs. They used torture to wring confessions from reluctant suspects, and they denied accused persons the right to counsel and the right to confront witnesses. Proceedings were usually conducted in secret. A lucky prisoner would confess early, repent, and forfeit only his property. If he proved stubborn, or if he lapsed again into heresy after repenting, he was excommunicated and turned over to the civil authorities for more severe punishment.

Canon law forbade the clergy to take life, but the civil authorities suffered no such inhibition. Since heresy was often associated with popular discontent or rebellion, they regarded it as tantamount to treason and set the penalty of death for convicted heretics. If a responsible official failed to apply that penalty, he was himself liable to punishment. The most common means of execution was burning at the stake—a means that gave the heretic a chance to make a final repentance as the flames reached higher and higher. He might then have time to beg for God's forgiveness and the salvation of his soul. But in no case would the fire be quenched; the body of a "confirmed" heretic was already forfeit.

The procedures and penalties of the Inquisition appear cruel and inhumane to modern minds. In the view of medieval churchmen, however, the end (rooting out heresy) justified the means. Even the "Angelic Doctor" of the Church, Thomas Aquinas, held that extreme punishments were necessary to protect souls from the contamination of false beliefs. His was no doubt an honest argument. But the Inquisition was open to the foulest abuses. To level the accusation of heresy became a convenient way of injuring or getting rid of personal enemies, and the accusers were never identified by the court. Despite the justifications proffered by its apologists, the Inquisition was generally abandoned after the seventeenth century.

The struggle for supremacy over the state

Gregory VII, as we have seen, strove to strengthen the control of Rome over the hierarchy and to free the Church from secular interference and corruption. To the extent that he accomplished these goals, he fulfilled the aims of the pervasive Cluniac reform movement. But Gregory aspired to go beyond the cleansing of the Church. Cluny had concentrated on the reform of the clergy and had tended to accept the secular world as it was; Gregory sought to alter the equilibrium between church and state. Where Cluny aimed to set the Church *apart* from the state, Gregory desired to place it *above* the state. He would thus give to the Church—and to its monarch, the pope—the responsibility and the power to purify the whole of Christian society.

Before Gregory's time, Christian teaching had attributed to civil monarchs a sacred character as well as secular authority. Their prerogatives were sanctioned by God; they defended the Church and were blessed by it. The Emperor Charlemagne, who was held up as a model, had appointed bishops and abbots to their offices and had employed clergymen as administrators and as teachers in his palace school. Mutual support between the nobility and the clergy existed at all levels of feudal government. It was this relationship that Gregory and his successors sought to change.

On various historical pretexts, including the spurious Donation of Constantine (p. 154), Gregory claimed to be the overlord of the rulers of western Europe. He asserted, for example, that the Holy Roman emperor, Henry IV, was his vassal, on the ground that Charlemagne, Henry's predecessor, owed his crown to Pope Leo III (p. 159). He objected particularly to Henry's control over the election of German bishops, who were important fief-holders and vassals of the emperor. Henry was exercising a traditional right when he influenced their selection and invested them with their symbols of office. Gregory insisted, however, that bishops were spiritual officers and could be invested with ring and staff, the symbols of their religious authority, only by the pope. What he sought, of course, was papal control over the elections themselves. This *investiture* issue set off a prolonged conflict between Rome and the European monarchs, but it was only one aspect of the papal bid for supremacy.

Gregory employed every means at his command to bring Henry down. He intrigued with the emperor's enemies in Germany, subjected him to excommunication and deposition (1076), and turned to the Normans in southern Italy for military assistance against Henry's forces. But Gregory lacked sufficient armed power to transform his occasional triumphs into lasting victory. Though he brought civil war and ruin to Germany—and to Italy as well—he failed to win control over the Holy Roman Empire. The investiture argument itself was settled later by compromise: Henry's successor agreed in 1122 to relinquish the investiture of religious symbols to the pope, but he retained the emperor's traditional influence over episcopal elections.

Gregory's successors carried on his struggle. During the reign of Innocent III the papacy reached its height of prestige and power. Its ascendancy was symbolized by the humbling of King John of England, who, after a bitter dispute with Innocent over the election of the Archbishop of Canterbury, was forced to submit. John was deposed; then he was granted the realm of England *as a fief from Rome,* but only after pledging homage to the pope (1213).

Papal assertions were carried still further by the aggressive Boniface VIII. He met his master, however, in King Philip (the Fair) of France. Philip, who was waging war against England, levied a tax on church properties in 1296. This bold move, contrary to existing law, was answered by Boniface with angry denunciations. The violent dispute reached its climax a few years later when Boniface issued a papal bull (pronouncement) titled *Unam sanctam,* which incorporated the most extreme claims of Gregory and other papal supremacists. Boniface declared that all secular rulers were subject to the pope and that the pope could be judged by God alone. He concluded, audaciously, "We declare, state, define, and pronounce that it is altogether necessary to salvation for every human creature to be subject to the Roman pontiff." Yet Boniface's words did not prevail over Philip's deeds. Philip, realizing that no peaceful solution could be reached with Boniface, sent a military force across the Alps to seize the aged pontiff. Roughly treated and humiliated by the French soldiers, Boniface died of shock soon afterward (1303).

These events set the stage for a rapid decline of the papacy. The popes had overreached themselves in their pursuit of secular power, and their absorption in politics had caused them to neglect the spiritual affairs of the Church as a whole. The fourteenth and fifteenth centuries would see the unhappy consequences of papal extremism.

CHRISTIAN ART

Despite the later decline of the papacy, the Church was a powerful creative force throughout the Middle Ages. Nowhere is this force displayed more clearly than in the arts. Faith in God and hope for salvation held a central place in the hearts of medieval men, and the artisans of the age dedicated their best efforts to creating works for the Church.

For several centuries after the Germanic invasions of the West, the unsettled conditions of society had proved inhospitable to the arts in general and to architecture in particular. Until the tenth century most new buildings north of the Alps were built of timber; the first stone structure of importance was Charlemagne's chapel at Aachen, completed around 800. With the return of stability and security in the eleventh century, architecture began to revive, and the first truly European "style" emerged. This style, known as the Romanesque, predominated from about 1000 to 1200 and found expression in painting and sculpture as well as in architecture.

The Romanesque style

The term "Romanesque" is somewhat misleading, for this first European style was based only partially on Roman examples. The relationship is most apparent in architecture, where the round arch and the vault served as basic structural elements. But the builders of the Middle Ages used these elements in a manner quite different from that of the ancient Romans. Moreover, they adhered to no unified style; instead, characteristic styles developed from region to region. Byzantine, oriental, and barbarian influences were also evident in the Romanesque.

The monastic-reform movement that originated at Cluny provided an impulse for widespread building activity during the eleventh and twelfth centuries. Though secular structures of various kinds were erected, the most important building of this period was of monastery churches. And these churches reflect a surprising variety of styles, notably the styles of Normandy, Burgundy, Provence, and Lombardy.

Wealthy as the monasteries were in corporate property, the individual members were committed to the ideal of poverty. This ascetic goal, along with the missionary zeal of the monks, impressed itself upon the architectural spirit of the times. Religious houses and churches were built of thick stone walls with narrow apertures. The effect, from the outside, was forbidding; inside, one felt withdrawn and protected from the secular world. Although the architectural designs were well planned and aesthetically satisfying, little attempt was made to give the buildings any elegance or sensuous appeal.

The earliest Christian churches (of the fourth century) had been modeled on the Roman basilica, a lofty hall in which legal or financial business was transacted. The typical basilica had a rectangular floor plan divided longitudinally into a central aisle (nave) and two or more side aisles. At one end of the building there was customarily a small, semicircular extension (the apse) covered by a half-dome. Here the Romans sometimes built a dais for the chair (cathedra) of the presiding official.

Although at first the Christian bishops simply adapted the basilica to the needs of their congregations, certain liturgical developments during the Middle Ages induced a shift to the cruciform (cross-shaped) plan (FIG. 5-1). The nave and the side aisles were retained, but the apse was enlarged, and chapels were built into its perimeter.

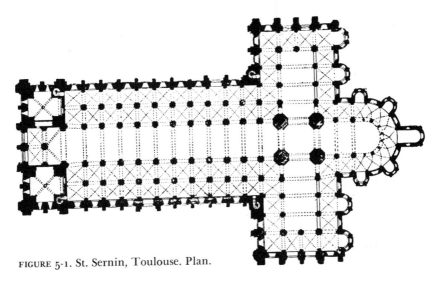

FIGURE 5-1. St. Sernin, Toulouse. Plan.

A transept, or cross-arm, was introduced at right angles to the nave, with portals at either end. This new plan provided more space for the clergy participating in the Mass, for members of the choir, and for worshipers making their private devotions. It became, with numerous variations, the favored plan for large churches throughout the West.

Aside from its functional merit, the cruciform plan had obvious symbolic meaning. When the faithful entered the church, they were "returning to the Cross." The façade (front) of the building usually had three main portals, symbolizing the Trinity. Whenever possible, the axis of the cross was oriented so that the nave ran from west to east, with the altar at the eastern end. Thus the worshipers faced more or less in the direction of Jerusalem. Symbolic cues of this sort were of particular value in an age of general illiteracy.

Reminders of the classical style of architecture were visible in the rounded doorways and windows of Romanesque churches and in the variations in the modified Roman arches and tunnel vaults used to support the roof. The roofs of earlier churches had generally rested on a framework of timber; the Romanesque architect, seeking greater permanency, chose stone. But how could the massive weight of a stone ceiling be supported? One way was to bridge the nave by means of a tunnel vault (FIG. 5-2). Such a vault subjected the supporting masonry to severe stress and usually had to be buttressed by half-vaults built over the side aisles. It also followed that the size of apertures was strictly limited, for large openings would have made the walls dangerously weak. Hence, scant daylight found its way into the nave.

To admit more light, medieval architects often divided the nave into a series of rectangular spaces, or "bays." The stone ceiling over each bay was formed by a Roman-type cross-vault (p. 81). This type of construction permitted larger openings in the clerestory portion of the nave—that is, the part rising above the side-aisle roofs.

The round dome, which also goes back to Roman times, was frequently used by Romanesque builders. More characteristic of the Romanesque style, however, was a new architectural feature: the tower. The earliest known towers in western Europe date from the fifth century A.D. and were used chiefly for hanging bells; the bell tower thereafter became closely associated with church architecture. In Italy, the graceful campanile stood by itself a few feet away from the church; elsewhere in Europe the tower was an integral part of the main building. It was sometimes built over the "crossing," where the nave and the transept intersect, but more commonly a tower or a pair of towers formed part of the façade. Though of all shapes and sizes, they generally followed a regional pattern. In some areas, for example, they were capped by a soaring spire. Church towers remain to this day a symbol of Western Christianity.

Sculpture, an art on which the Greeks and Romans lavished their genius, had fallen into decline with the triumph of Christianity in the fourth century. The Church linked sculpture with the pagan worship of idols, and this bias put a temporary end to life-size works in western Europe. Artistic activity during the Dark Ages was limited mainly to small-scale carving and manuscript illumination. With the beginning of the Romanesque period, around 1000, full-size painting and sculpture were revived. The renewed interest in these art forms was prompted by the accelerated pace of ecclesiastical building; in fact, painting and sculpture remained subordinate to architecture until the close of the Middle Ages. Sculpture was used exclusively for religious purposes: the glorification of God and the instruction of the faithful. Transcending the barrier of illiteracy, each medieval church was virtually a "Bible in stone."

Nowhere is the atmospheric contrast between the medieval world and the ancient world more sharply displayed than in sculpture (FIG. 5-3). The idealistic style of the Greeks and the naturalistic style of the Romans are both absent, in part because few ancient statues were available to the sculptors of the eleventh and twelfth centuries. They took as their models the illustrated figures of medieval manuscripts, the only art form that continued uninterrupted throughout

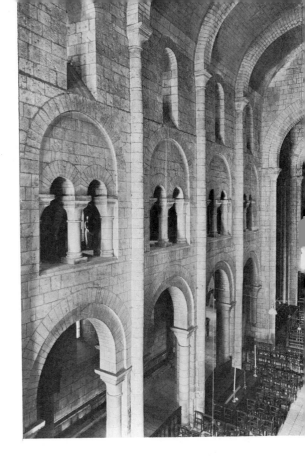

FIGURE 5-2. St. Etienne, Nevers. (Marburg-Art Reference Bureau.)

the medieval epoch. These miniature figures were crudely drawn, with little regard for anatomical accuracy. Their purpose was to fulfill a design of line and color and to "support" a story or a moral.

The grotesque animal figures that appear in Romanesque sculpture came directly from the northern barbarian tradition. Numerous books were available describing hundreds of imaginary beasts, and sculptors rendered them in stone. Romanesque churches were studded with frightening monsters and demons, which looked all too real, no doubt, to the congregation.

Romanesque sculptors mingled the natural and the supernatural, the earthly and the unearthly. Hence the real may look unreal, and the unreal real. To ensure that the idea or story they were illustrating would be correctly interpreted, sculptors relied heavily on symbols. Although they might depict St. Peter in a num-

FIGURE 5-3. Tympanum, St. Trophime at Arles.
(Marburg-Art Reference Bureau.)

ber of guises, they inevitably identified him by giving him a set of keys. Matthew was consistently shown as an angel, Mark as a lion (FIG. 5-3). Having identified his subject by the appropriate symbol, the artist then treated it in an individual manner.

This freedom presented an opportunity for creativity quite unknown in classical art. The Romanesque sculptor, though often showing inferior technique, was not bound to exacting artistic rules or to naturalistic representation and thus enjoyed greater scope in trying to create his own images. Liberation from literal representation also permitted him unusual freedom of composition—a freedom shared by painters and other artisans of the period.

The Gothic style

One of the features of Western civilization that distinguishes it from the Eastern is its dynamic quality. Styles of art in the East have lasted thousands of years, but in the West constant change has been the rule. The Romanesque style marked a break with the past, but in less than two centuries it had begun to give way to yet another style. Out of the Romanesque, in response to emergent social, spiritual, and technical forces, came the climactic style of the Middle Ages—the Gothic. This style showed itself first in architecture, around 1150, reached its prime by 1300, and declined in vitality with the closing of the Middle Ages.

Whereas the Romanesque style had flourished in the monasteries, the Gothic style flourished in the towns. Now abbots and their churches gave place to bishops and their cathedrals. Though the Christian faith was still the leading force in Western society, the ascetic spirit was now overshadowed by a more worldly one. Insecurity gave way to a new confidence: Gothic cathedrals were built to the glory of God, but they reflected the pride of man.

The term "Gothic" was applied to the style only in later centuries, by men who had come under the spell of a classical revival. They abhorred the disruption of the classical tradition and derogated the medieval period as the Germanic (Gothic) interlude. We can see now that they failed to recognize medieval culture as a unique amalgam of German, Roman, and Christian elements. This culture reached its full development around 1300, and the Gothic style was its grandest expression.

Gothic architecture incorporated brilliant technical innovations. Although the cruciform ground plan of the Romanesque church had proved suitable enough to the Christian liturgy, the bishops and laymen of the later Middle Ages grew dissatisfied with the massive, earthbound appearance of Romanesque buildings. They sought something lighter and loftier, with a soaring, vertical movement. Their fulfillment of this desire has been interpreted as a mark of the liberation of northern (Germanic) aesthetic ideals from the Roman forms to which they had long been subject.

The main effect of the shift from the Romanesque was to foster a heightened sense of interior space. Romanesque churches were heavy with masonry, and their walls gave a feeling of confinement. But any attempt to alter this pattern raised a difficult technical question: How could architects lift the stone roof to a greater height and at the same time lighten the fabric of the supporting structure? They found their answer in "rib" vaulting.

In the twelfth century Romanesque builders had developed a better system than cross-vaulting for supporting a heavy roof. They divided the nave into rectangular bays, each marked off by four masonry pillars. From the top of each pillar they connected ribs of arching stone to the tops of the other three; then they filled in the ceiling areas between the ribs with light brick. Thus they con-

FIGURE 5-4. Amiens Cathedral, vault. (Clarence Ward.)

structed a *framework* of stone (FIG. 5-4) on which they could rest the roof of the nave. The thrust of the gabled roof (which was generally tiled) was transmitted to the ground by the stone framework. Consequently, no force was exerted on the areas between the pillars.

Gothic architects developed the full potential of the new method. This revolutionary plan of construction enabled them to lift roofs to soaring heights and to convert the walls of the clerestory into glowing sheets of stained glass. They could discard the idea of a building as a stone mass enclosing static space and conceive it instead as a web of stone, with space and light flowing freely through it. Among the innovations and refinements they advanced to carry out their idea were the pointed arch and the flying buttress.

The graceful pointed arch, which resembles a pair of hands touching in prayer, is a hallmark of the Gothic style. Although the builders no doubt appreciated its spiritual and aesthetic quality, they also had practical reasons for using it. It accentuated the vertical lines of their structures and lifted the vaults to greater heights than could be achieved with the round arch. With the pointed arch, the direction of thrust is more downward than outward, decreasing the danger that the supporting pillars will collapse. Moreover, the pointed arch is far more adaptable to rib vaulting, for the steepness of its curve can be fitted to varying lateral distances between the pillars, whereas the round arch follows a fixed curve.

To make the soaring vaults safer, French architects devised external buttresses of masonry. They could not build supports directly against the pillars of the nave, because the side aisles, with their separate, lower roofs, stood in the way. So they erected massive stone piers at intervals *outside* the side aisles. The piers rose almost to the level of the nave ceiling and were connected to the pillars of the nave by stone ribs, or spokes. (An early example of this may be seen at Chartres, FIG. 5-5.) Since the ribs seem to be suspended over the side aisles, they are commonly termed "flying" buttresses. Though they support the stone framework at critical points, they interfere only slightly with the flow of light through the great clerestory windows.

The Gothic cathedral, pointing to heaven, stood high above the houses huddled in the town (FIG. 5-6), symbolizing the commanding position of the Church in the lives of medieval men. As travelers approached a cathedral town, the first sight they saw on the

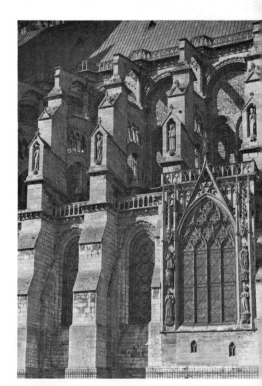

FIGURE 5-5. Buttresses, Chartres Cathedral, nave exterior from south. (Archives Photographiques.)

FIGURE 5-6. Salisbury Cathedral.
(Aerofilms Ltd., London.)

horizon was the spire, or spires, reaching hundreds of feet into the sky. Then the body of the cathedral would gradually come into view. If the travelers were pilgrims, they would approach the west façade and reverently prepare to enter.

Set into the façade were stone sculptures representing figures from the Bible. Gothic sculptors were more naturalistic in style than their Romanesque precursors. Although the figures could still be identified by conventional symbols, they looked more lifelike than the Romanesque (FIG. 5-7). The artisans of this period relied less on copybook drawings and looked more to live models. Their technique and general craftsmanship rose steadily in excellence.

Inside the cathedral, the emphasis was on space, light, and color (FIG. 5-8). Here one forgets the calculations and engineering wisdom that made possible the complicated thrust and counterthrust of arches, vaults, and buttresses. One is absorbed by the vastness, rhythm, and splendor of the interior. Stained glass is the special glory of the Gothic. By daylight, the upper levels of the interior glow with luminous blues, reds, greens, and golds. The windows, of varying shape and size, consist of mosaics of colored glass. The glass

FIGURE 5-7. Reims Cathedral, Annunication and Visitation, central portal, west façade. (Archives Photographiques.)

FIGURE 5-8. Amiens Cathedral, nave looking east. (Clarence Ward.)

pieces are held together by lead strips and bars, creating geometrical designs. The function of the windows, like that of the sculpture, is to illustrate Biblical events, but the figures are often absorbed into the broader patterns of line and color.

THOUGHT AND EDUCATION

Medieval education, as well as the arts, was dominated by the Church. At no other time in Western history have the channels of communication and education been so completely in the hands of one institution. The members of the clergy, who made up the only literate and educated class of society, manned virtually all the schools, libraries, and centers of higher learning. Almost all manuscripts and books were produced in the monastic scriptorium, or copyroom, and the principal means of oral communication was the pulpit. Every idea expressed inside or outside the Church was subject to the scrutiny and judgment of the ecclesiastical hierarchy.

The result of this intellectual supervision was not so stultifying as one might suspect. The feudalistic and provincial character of the times counterbalanced what was, in theory, the monolithic force of the Church. The methods of long-distance communication were primitive, and the Church itself was split into many jurisdictions, orders, and factions. Although basically only a Latin Christian point of view could be professed in western Europe, a wide range of intellectual inquiry and debate was still possible.

During the troubled centuries immediately after the fall of Rome, there had been a real danger that learning and scholarship would vanish from Europe. The monasteries then arose as the repositories of precious manuscripts and transmitted at least the rudiments of education to the clergy, the only class of society that was thought to need it. Around 800, Charlemagne gave strong impetus to the revival of interest in intellectual matters. Though advance was slow, it may be said that by 1200 Western civilization had achieved again the level of learning of ancient times and had begun to match that of the Moslems. The monasteries still provided elementary education, and cathedral schools were beginning to respond to a growing desire for education in the towns. But the most significant development was the rise of the universities.

The rise of universities

The earliest steps toward higher education were taken in southern Europe. Formal medical instruction started at Salerno (Italy) in the twelfth century, and training in the law began about the same time at Bologna. The universities founded at these centers were professional in nature. They were stimulated by the persistence of Moslem learning in Sicily and by the demand for physicians and lawyers to serve Italian princes and merchants. The word *universitas* was simply the Latin word for a body or corporation, such as a guild. When a number of teachers (or students) in a given place joined together as a legal body, a university came into existence.

The university movement spread northward from Italy to Montpellier and Paris. It was in Paris during the thirteenth century that Europe's foremost institution of learning was established. Its faculty was made up of professors drawn from the cathedral school and from local monastic schools, along with lay lecturers in law and medicine. Paris was the first university to offer the four major curriculums that have become identified in the West with the idea of a university. Whereas Salerno and Bologna limited themselves initially to professional training in medicine and law, Paris offered instruction in all the recognized fields of knowledge. The university was divided into four faculties: medicine, law, theology, and liberal arts. The last two earned for Paris its paramount reputation. From Paris, which served as the model in the North, the movement spread to England, Germany, and the rest of western Europe. By 1500 the total number of universities, many of which are still in existence, exceeded eighty.

Each university operated under the protection of a charter granted by a ranking official of the Church or the state (usually the pope or a king). Thus the universities were freed, for the most part, from the jurisdiction of local courts and local clergy. One justification for this exempted status was that teachers and students came from all over Europe, making the universities truly international. Moreover, most students held minor clerical rank and therefore could claim immunity from civil authority ("benefit of clergy"). In the Middle Ages the word "clerk" (cleric) usually meant "scholar."

The organization of a typical university paralleled that of a craft guild. The masters (professors), who managed the affairs of the university, had the sole right to award "degrees." The apprentices (students), after earning the appropriate degree, were then eligible to become masters in a teaching corporation (university).

The liberal-arts curriculum of the university was normally a prerequisite to the professional courses. Its outlines had been developed in the monastic schools, which in turn had followed late Roman educational practices. The liberal-arts subjects were seven in number: grammar, rhetoric, and logic (the trivium); arithmetic, geometry, astronomy, and music (the quadrivium). Grammar, of course, meant Latin grammar. This was the language used by members of the clergy, lawyers, physicians, and scholars all through the Middle Ages. But the trivium went beyond the mechanics of language; it involved the analysis of works of philosophy, literature, and history. The quadrivium was based on the study of ancient texts and was almost entirely theoretical. Today we refer to the subjects of the trivium as humanistic studies and to the subjects of the quadrivium (excepting music) as mathematical studies.

The students in medieval universities did not enroll for course "credits" or "units." In order to earn a degree they did not have to complete a given number of courses with at least a "C" average. Instead, degrees were granted on the basis of comprehensive oral examinations. After attending lectures and reading for several years in the subjects of the trivium, a student would ask to be examined by the members of the faculty. If he performed satisfactorily, he was granted the preliminary degree of bachelor of arts (B.A.). This degree was of no particular use in itself, except as a prerequisite for going on to the quadrivium. After several additional years of study, the student would present himself for examination once again. If he passed, he was awarded the degree of master of arts (M.A.), which certified that he was qualified to teach the liberal-arts curriculum.

The higher degrees were, similarly, *teaching* degrees. The Latin word "doctor" (teacher) was customarily used for the degrees in theology, law, and medicine. Each of these degrees normally required four or more years of study beyond the master's. Again, however, the award was based, not on the time spent in study or the number of credits earned, but on the candidate's performance in a rigorous examination. The candidate usually presented a "thesis," or proposition, which he explained and defended orally before a faculty board.

Student life was quite different from what it is today. Since girls were thought to have no need for a formal education, the universities were for boys and men only. There was no campus of the sort that Americans are accustomed to today. Professors lectured—at least at first—in their homes or in hired halls, and students lived independently, according to their means and tastes. This unregulated life sometimes led to ill-health, vice, or both. As a corrective, private donors established residential "colleges" for scholars at many universities.

The first such college was founded about 1250 by Louis IX's chaplain, Robert de Sorbon; he provided it with a dormitory, in which theology students at the University of Paris could live. Later, faculty members were assigned to the college, and lecture and library facilities were made available. Thus the "Sorbonne" became a separate living-and-learning unit under the university's general jurisdiction. The same pattern was adopted for students in other curriculums at Paris, and it gradually spread to universities beyond France. It took firm root in England (at Oxford and Cambridge), where it has persisted until the present time. Elsewhere in Europe the "college" system has since been abandoned.

During the Middle Ages students had few books and no laboratories. They inscribed their lecture notes on wax tablets and then transferred them to sheets of parchment. More stress was placed on memorizing and analyzing a small number of "authoritative" sources than on extensive reading. Of special interest to scholars were some of the ancient classics that had reappeared in the West during the eleventh and twelfth centuries. Growing contact with Constantinople and the Moslem world prompted Latin translations from Greek or Arabic of many of the works of Aristotle, as well as books of Hellenistic science, mathematics, and medicine. These were accompanied by original writings and commentaries by leading Moslem scholars, who had hitherto been unknown in western Europe.

Scholastic philosophy

The stimulus from the East lifted the intellectual life of Europe beyond the level of earlier monastic and cathedral education. The creative response by scholars (schoolmen) gave rise to the major philosophical system of the Middle Ages, called scholasticism. The scholastics were primarily interested in religious matters. Thus Anselm, a learned Italian monk and one of the first scholastic philosophers, fashioned arguments to prove, logically, the existence of God. In another treatise (about 1100) he explained why God had chosen to assume human form as Jesus. In defense of his studious efforts, Anselm asserted that *understanding* was a legitimate supplement to Christian *believing.*,

In the twelfth century, the French scholar Abelard argued that the authorities of the Church should not be read without questioning, for they often contradicted one another (*Sic et Non*). He insisted, therefore, that all writings be subjected to the rigorous scrutiny of logic. "By doubting," he observed, "we come to examine, and by examining we reach the truth." Thus Abelard had returned to the position of Socrates, who had sought knowledge through persistent questioning. Abelard sought to replace the general medieval habit of credulity with an insistence on critical examination; no subject henceforth would be shielded from the light of reason.

Though theological matters remained the focus of scholastic concern, medieval philosophers debated every subject under the sun—some grand and divine, some trivial and profane. One of the most absorbing issues was that of "universals." Do "man," "horse," "beauty," and "justice" exist, independent of particular things? Or are these terms merely convenient symbols for referring to various classes of objects and characteristics? The argument paralleled the classical one between Plato and the Sophists. Plato believed that Ideas (Forms) had a perfect and independent existence, while the Sophists thought that only particular things existed. In the Middle Ages, those who held that "universals" were real were called "realists"; those who declared that they were just names (*nomina*) were called "nominalists."

The argument was (and is) of critical importance to one's philosophical outlook. The extreme realists attached little importance to individual things and sought by sheer logic or revelation to apprehend the universals. The extreme nominalists, by contrast, perceived *only* discrete objects and refused to admit the existence of unifying relationships among the infinitude of particulars. The realists tended to ignore the observed world; the nominalists could scarcely comprehend it.

Most schoolmen took a middle position on this question. Among the moderates, Abelard expressed a view which approximates that of most scientists today. It is called "conceptualism." Abelard held that only particular things have an existence in and of themselves. The universals, however, are more than mere names. They exist as concepts *in individual minds*—keys to an understanding of the interrelatedness of things. Thus, the concept "horse" exists in our minds and adds something to our perception of all quadrupeds of a given general description. Once we have identified such a creature, we can attribute to it the specific characteristics derived from our concept. By means of many such concepts, inferred from individual observations, we can make the world (to a degree) comprehensible, manageable, and predictable.

Thomas Aquinas, the greatest of the scholastic philosophers, was a moderate realist. Born near Monte Cassino (Italy) of an aristocratic family, he joined the order of Dominican friars in 1244. A brilliant pupil, he studied at Cologne and Paris and spent his adult life teaching at Paris and Naples. He wrote a prodigious number of treatises. Reflecting the medieval desire for unity, or oneness, scholarly works, the most significant of which were his systematic Aquinas sought to harmonize various approaches to truth and to integrate all knowledge. In his most comprehensive work, *Summa Theologica* (*Theological Compendium*), he clarified and integrated the Roman Catholic teachings about the nature of God and man. (His conception of theology embraced the full range of divine and human affairs.)

Following the lead of Anselm, Abelard, and other scholastics, Aquinas set a high value on the faculty of reason. By this time the full impact of Aristotle and the new learning from the East had struck the schools and universities of Europe, and Christian dogmas were being challenged by pagan, Moslem, and Jewish logicians. Instead of meeting these attacks by denying the validity of reason, Aquinas adopted Aristotelian logic and turned it to the defense of his faith. He sought to demonstrate that revealed truth is never in conflict with logic, *properly exercised.* Both faith and reason, he argued, were created by God, and it is illogical to hold that God could contradict himself.

Aquinas' methodology is most plainly set forth in the *Summa Theologica,* in which he divided each major topic into a series of questions. For each, he marshaled the arguments *pro* and *contra,* in accordance with the conventional scholastic mode of presentation. The arguments are generally deductive in form and rely heavily on both pagan and Christian authorities. Thus, in an effort to support a particular point, Aquinas may couple a generalization from Aristotle's *Politics* with Jesus' Golden Rule. He presented his own conclusion for each of the questions he posed—a conclusion that generally accorded with the orthodox teachings of the Church.

The *Summa* is an ingenious combination of scriptural allusion, formal logic, and "common sense." It pays scant attention to observation and induction and none to experimentation. Aquinas conceived of truth as a closed system, complete and unchanging. Though his grand synthesis does not meet modern scientific criteria for validation, it stands as an impressive monument to the discipline and resourcefulness of the human mind.

By the end of the thirteenth century, the intellectual life of the West had achieved a new vigor. The communities of university scholars had succeeded in their efforts to preserve and advance learning. Though lacking in originality, the scholastic philosophers had refined the methods of logical thought and had laboriously collected, compiled, and classified sources of information. Above all, they had established the essentials of scholarship: comprehensive research and precision of expression.

Modern science owes much to these medieval seekers after truth. They built upon classical learning, reconciled it with Christian teachings, and absorbed new ideas from the Moslem world. Bernard of Chartres once compared himself and his fellow scholars with the

philosophers and scientists of ancient times. "We are like a dwarf,"
he said, "standing on the shoulders of a giant." There is modesty in
this statement, but also pride—pride in the fact that he and his colleagues could see a bit farther than their intellectual ancestors.

LANGUAGE AND LITERATURE

The language common to Europe during the Middle Ages was
Latin. A legacy of pagan Rome, it had been carried beyond the
ancient Roman frontiers by the Church. Although it persisted as the
formal language of education, law, medicine, and commerce, Latin
began to disappear from spoken discourse. It was gradually supplanted by a variety of regional dialects (vernaculars), from which
the modern European languages were to develop. By the thirteenth
century the vernaculars had gained predominance in popular literature as well as in everyday speech.

Latin writings

Medieval Latin failed to maintain the classical standards of Cicero
and Vergil. Jerome's translation of the Bible remained the official
version and was regarded as a model of style for the clergy. But
Jerome was only one model, and the study of pagan writers was
viewed, generally, with suspicion. Chiefly as a result of this bias,
classical norms tended to be neglected, and a vulgarized Latin
evolved.

The finest creations in medieval Latin were the prayers and hymns
of the Christian liturgy. Some of these were incorporated into the
Mass and are notable for their poetic beauty (*Stabat Mater* and
Dies Irae). Latin was also used in new forms of religious drama:
"Passion" plays (which grew out of the Easter ritual), dramatizations
of the lives of the saints, and Christian "morality" plays. Classical
dramas were not performed in the Middle Ages and did not begin to
influence European literature until the fifteenth century. By then a
secular branch of dramatic literature had grown out of the religious
performances and had detached itself from the Church.

Though Latin was the language of worship, it was sometimes
used to express dissent from Christian ideals. A substantial body of
verse written by wandering scholars began to appear in the twelfth
century, the best of which is known as Goliardic poetry since it was
dedicated to a mythical patron, Saint Golias. Although few of the
poets have been identified, it is clear that they were men of learning, schooled in Latin and familiar with the classics. One Goliard
refers to his band as a "vagrant order" of runaway students and

clerics. Their verses were mainly satirical, aimed at the clergy and the ascetic ideal. They were pagan in spirit, lauding the pleasures of drinking, eating, and lovemaking. One of the Goliardic poets, called the "Archpoet," declared,

> My intention is to die
>   In the tavern drinking;
> Wine must be at hand, for I
>   Want it when I'm sinking.
> Angels when they come shall cry,
>   At my frailties winking:
> "Spare this drunkard, God, he's high,
>   Absolutely stinking!"*

Vernacular writings

Goliardic verse could be understood only by the educated few who knew Latin, but the vernacular tongues were more suitable for the circulation of secular ideas. These tongues fell into two broad groups: the Romance (Romanic) and the Teutonic (Germanic). The boundary between the two was roughly the frontier of the ancient Roman Empire. In those areas that had long been occupied by Rome, colloquial Latin served as the foundation of the vernacular tongues. It was modified only slightly as a result of the Germanic invasions and evolved, as living languages do, into local dialects. In areas north and east of the imperial frontiers, the Teutonic-speaking peoples continued to use their age-old tongues. Western Europe to this day is divided into these linguistic groups: the national languages of Italy, Spain, and France are derived from the Roman; those of the Netherlands, Germany, and Scandinavia from the Teutonic.

England is a special case. It was less thoroughly Romanized than the other provinces of the empire, and the Anglo-Saxon invaders were able to impose their Teutonic dialect upon the native Britons. Subsequent Danish and Norman conquests brought additional linguistic influences. By the middle of the fourteenth century Anglo-Saxon had become modified into what we now term Old English. Out of this evolved modern English, a mixture of Teutonic and Romance elements.

As early as the eleventh century the spoken vernaculars began to be set down in writing. As might be expected, these writings reflected secular interests, for strictly religious works were written in

---

* From George F. Whicher, *The Goliard Poets.* Copyright 1949 by George F. Whicher. Reprinted by permission of New Directions Publishing Corporation.

Latin. They appealed chiefly to the nobility and exercised some modifying influence, no doubt, on the values and behavior of those rough warriors. The "literature of chivalry" was in part a reflection of and in part an influence upon the changing character of knighthood (pp. 165–66).

The epic *Song of Roland* (*Chanson de Roland*) had been recited by minstrels for a century or more before it was written down in the dialect of northern France (about 1200). A long heroic poem by an unknown author, it recounts the legendary exploits of Charlemagne. Its chief actor, Count Roland, nephew of the king, personifies the warrior ideals of valor, loyalty, and military prowess—and the Christian faith in God and salvation. The tradition of the Greek epic can readily be seen in this poem. It glorifies France and her heroes as Homer had glorified the champions of Hellas. Roland is the counterpart of proud Achilles; the field of battle runs red with the blood of the courageous; and Roland's fellow vassals observe strictly the code of honor and revenge. Other national epics were written at about the same time in neighboring countries: the *Nibelungenlied* (*Song of the Nibelungs*) in Germany and the *Poema del Cid* (*Poem of the Cid*) in Spain.

But the troubadours (professional singers) of the Middle Ages did not confine themselves to epic tales. They also sang of courtliness and romantic love. For the first time since the days of the pagan authors, a poetry of passion appeared in Europe. But it was, for the most part, passion on an "elevated" plane. The romantic knight placed his ideal woman on a pedestal and adored her from afar—with thoughts of physical fulfillment repressed or deferred. This "cult of love" also brought forth elaborate manuals of behavior for lovers. Courtly love, it should be noted, was a pastime for the nobility only; commoners were considered unsuited to the delicate art of romance.

Clearly, the hearty, masculine culture of the early Middle Ages was giving way to a more tranquil, confident, and leisurely society. The noble's castle was becoming less of a barracks for fighting men and more of a theater for refined pleasures. Aristocratic ladies were accorded more and more attention and were able to exercise greater control over the men.

The feudal society of the later Middle Ages is splendidly portrayed in the so-called Arthurian romances, a cycle of prose stories composed in the twelfth and thirteenth centuries by French and Norman writers. The central figure of these stories is King Arthur, a Celtic chieftain of sixth-century Britain who fought against the Anglo-Saxon invaders. But the legends of Arthur's Round Table are told in the manner of the late Middle Ages; they are tales of forbidden love, knightly jousts, and colorful pageantry. Successive poets and musicians have turned again and again to Camelot, the legendary site of Arthur's court; Guinevere (Arthur's queen), Sir Lancelot, and Sir Galahad have become familiar characters in Western literature.

But the European bourgeoisie, finding little of their own life in the knightly romances, preferred another type of secular literature. This, too, originated in France, and consisted of fabliaux (fables). Unlike the heroic and idyllic tales of chivalry, the fabliaux were about everyday life. Frank, sensual, and witty, they ridiculed both courtly and priestly life. One of the most popular fables was *Aucassin and Nicolette,* in which the hero, Aucassin, spurns knighthood in order to pursue his passion for a beautiful young Moslem captive. He is indifferent to his soul's salvation and subordinates everything to his desire for union with Nicolette. He even prefers hell to heaven, on the ground that the company there will be more attractive and entertaining.

The peasantry—the largest element of the population—could not read books of any sort. But they could listen to folk tales, legends, and ballads and could learn to recite them. A typical hero of folk literature was Robin Hood, a glorified English yeoman (freeman) who stole from the rich and gave to the poor. Robin's deeds corresponded to the commoners' desire for adventure, rebellion, and social justice.

Two works of the late Middle Ages rise above ordinary classification. One is the *Canterbury Tales* of Geoffrey Chaucer, written in the fourteenth century. This collection of stories is in the general spirit of the fabliaux but encompasses all classes of society and expresses a broad range of themes. Born of a merchant family, Chaucer spent most of his life in the service of the English aristocracy. He read broadly and traveled extensively on the Continent. His outlook was cosmopolitan and urbane, and he exhibited a rare combination of scholarship, sophistication, insight, and humor. In the *Tales,* a group of people exchange stories as they ride on pilgrimage to the shrine of Canterbury. The stories, of "good morality and general pleasure," appealed to all literate classes in fourteenth-century England. In them, as in a mirror, they could see themselves and their fellow men.

The other monumental work of the period is the *Divine Comedy* of Dante, which is regarded as the masterpiece of Italian literature. More profound than Chaucer's work, the *Comedy* is a grand synthesis of medieval theology, science, philosophy, and romance. Dante, a

Florentine scholar and poet, was immersed in the political and intellectual currents of his time. His heroic poem is constructed as an allegorical tale, describing the experiences of human souls after death. Escorted by the Roman poet Vergil, Dante travels in his poem through the regions beyond the grave. He descends into the terrible Inferno (hell) and then moves on to Purgatory, where the souls of absolved sinners are struggling ever upward. At last he is permitted to enter Paradise (heaven), where the blessed enjoy, in appropriate degrees, the gifts of God. For this final portion of the journey, Dante must leave the pagan Vergil behind. Now he is guided by the pure Beatrice, his ideal of Christian womanhood, who represents the fusion of romantic and spiritual love that leads Dante at last to a climactic vision of God.

Dante called his work a comedy, because he believed the story suggested a happy ending for all men who choose to follow Christ. (Later admirers added the compliment "divine.") Although in outline it appears to be an abstract theological treatise, it is a moving and intensely personal testament. At every turn of the narrative, Dante makes incisive comments on the characters of history and myth, who serve as dramatic symbols for his moralizing. Above all, the poem is a marvel of word imagery.

WEST AND EAST: THE CRUSADES

The flowering of European literature and art reflected the mounting self-confidence of the West. Latin Christendom had come a long way from the troubled, precarious days of the ninth century, when western Europe had been a besieged fortress, struggling to hold out against determined invaders. By the end of the tenth century the tide of history had begun to turn. As medieval institutions grew stronger, relations between West and East were bound to alter.

The western counteroffensive

Having withstood heavy blows from the Saracens, Magyars, and Norsemen, the men of the West began to push outward in all directions. The ground for this counteroffensive had been laid by Charlemagne, who founded military zones (*marks*) along the perimeter of his empire. From the tenth century onward, Charlemagne's imperial successors pushed eastward from the *Nordmark* against the Slavs. The struggle was long, bloody, and bitter—reminiscent of Charlemagne's offensive against the Saxons. It was a contest between an "advanced" culture and a "backward" one, between Christianity and paganism.

The German knights who led this eastward thrust viewed it as a crusade, just as urgent as the expeditions that were being mounted against the Moslem infidels in the Holy Land. With the vigorous backing of German bishops, traders, and colonists, their forces at last swept along the southern shore of the Baltic to overrun Prussia and Esthonia in the thirteenth century. The indigenous cultures of the area were virtually obliterated, Latin Christianity was imposed on the natives, and the Germans became masters of the land. In achieving their conquests, the Germans provoked a hostility among the Slavs that persists to the present day. The zone between the Elbe and the Russian border remains a kind of no man's land between West and East, German and Slav.

More decisive, historically, was the Christian counteroffensive to the southwest. Charles Martel had checked the Saracens at the Pyrenees in 732, and Charlemagne had created the Spanish March as a base from which to clear the Iberian peninsula. It was not until the troubles of the ninth century were past, however, that the West could proceed to run the Moslems out of Europe. The Christian kingdoms of Aragon and Castile, which had been carved out of the Spanish March, pushed relentlessly against their enemy. By the close of the thirteenth century, only the region of Granada remained in Moslem hands, and this, too, was wrested from them in 1492.

During this same period control of the western Mediterranean also reverted to Christian hands. The Saracens had won Sicily and the other islands lying between Italy and Spain, and their shipping had dominated the surrounding waters for several centuries. But Norman invaders conquered Sicily in the eleventh century, and the Italian city-state of Pisa seized Sardinia and Corsica. Thus the western Mediterranean was cleared for the rising commerce of Europe.

Triumph and tragedy in the Holy Land

The crusades against the Slavs and the Moslems of Spain were regional efforts, but all of Western Christendom was stirred to action against the Moslems in the Holy Land. The "great" crusades—aimed at recapturing the birthplace of Christianity—constituted an international mass movement. For two centuries (1095–1270) they fired the imagination of all classes of Christian society. Though they failed to achieve their declared aim, they provided a dramatic expression of the confidence and zeal of a reviving West.

It was the preaching of Pope Urban II that set Europe off on the First Crusade. But the response to his call can be comprehended only in light of long-standing tensions that may be traced back as far as the fourth-century division of the Roman Empire. Latin

Christendom and Byzantium, though linked by Christianity, were intensely hostile toward each other. Each regarded itself as the true heir of Caesar and Christ and saw the other as a usurper. To the Westerners the Byzantines seemed decadent, pompous, and effete. They, in turn, looked upon the Europeans as rude and grasping barbarians. In the long centuries between the fall of Rome and the launching of the crusades, relations between the West and Byzantium had gone from bad to worse.

The relations of the West with Islam were less complicated. The Saracens were openly recognized as enemies who had long fought the Christians in Spain and in the western Mediterranean. Though the Moslem religion was known to Westerners only in caricature, it was condemned by the Church as a diabolical heresy. Western prelates remained continually fearful lest Islam resume its expansive sweep of earlier centuries. Nevertheless, until after 1000 there were few signs of general hostility on either side: the Christian faithful who remained in Moslem countries continued to enjoy freedom of worship, and pilgrims to the Holy Land were permitted to proceed without interference. As more and more pilgrims visited the precious shrines, however, there was mounting resentment among Christians that these places should be held by infidels.

The series of events that precipitated the crusades had its beginning, actually, in central Asia. During the ninth century a militant nomadic people, the Turks, had entered Persia from the north. They were quickly converted to Islam and for more than a century exercised control over the Abbassid caliph at Baghdad (p. 149). In the eleventh century another Turkish invasion of the caliphate occurred, led by an even more aggressive dynasty, the Seljuk. The new leader assumed the title of "sultan" (ruler) and thereafter governed in form as well as in fact. Members of his family pushed westward from Baghdad into Syria, Palestine, and Asia Minor. They established themselves as sultans of several autonomous states in those areas and reversed the tolerant policies of their predecessors. Having crushed one Byzantine army in Asia Minor, the Turks began to move toward the imperial capital itself. It was this emergency that caused the Eastern emperor, Alexius, to send an urgent appeal for help to the West. Thus was triggered the European movement known as the crusades.

Pope Urban II heard the plea of Alexius' ambassador early in 1095 and found the idea of sending a rescue force to the East well suited to his own strategic aims. Heir to the Cluniac reform movement and to the policies of Gregory VII (p. 187), Urban realized that a successful holy war against the Turks would do more than free Palestine and reopen the roads of pilgrimage. It would in all likelihood compel the Byzantine emperor, in repayment, to recognize the supremacy of the pope over the whole Christian Church. Moreover, the triumph would lift the prestige of the papacy to such a height that the Cluniac ideal of church supremacy over the state would surely be realized.

Urban used the Council of Clermont, in central France, as his forum for launching the First Crusade. His speech, a masterpiece of shrewdness, appealed to both the highest and the lowest motives of men. As he addressed the assembled clergy, he was really speaking to all the classes and interests of Europe. He knew that some of the churchmen listening to him at Clermont had a deep aversion to violence. Yet his call for action was so effective that, as he ended the oration, his listeners shouted, "God wills it!" This became the battle cry of the crusaders.

In his speech the pope kindled ugly prejudices and fanned them into a flame of hatred for the Turks. He recounted, in horrific detail, atrocities that the "vile" and "accursed" race had allegedly committed against Christians. In the name of Christ, Urban exhorted men of all ranks, rich and poor, to exterminate the infidels. He reminded his listeners that such a response would be in keeping with the grandest traditions of Latin Christendom: Charlemagne, for example, had proved his manhood and achieved glory by destroying paganism and extending the territory of the Church. The same objectives could be accomplished once more—and with a guarantee of safety for the soul of each participant. The pope, citing his authority as vicar of Christ, declared that all who died while journeying or fighting on this "holy pilgrimage" would be automatically absolved of sin.

Urban was aware, however, that it would take more than fervor to defeat the Turks. He aimed his appeal directly at the military class—the knights and landholders. Quoting Scripture, Urban told them that they must not hold back because of their concern for family or possessions. "Everyone that hath forsaken houses, or brethren, or sisters, or father, or mother, or wife, or children, or lands for my name's sake shall receive an hundred-fold and shall inherit everlasting life." Then Urban observed that Europe was a narrow and confined space—too small to support its growing population. For this reason, he explained, you "murder and devour one another" in endless private warfare. Let your quarrels and hatreds cease, the pope concluded: "Enter upon the road to the Holy Sepulchre; wrest that land from the wicked race, and subject it to yourselves. That land which, as the Scripture says, 'floweth with milk

and honey,' was given by God into the possession of the children
of Israel."

Thus presented, the crusade appealed to men's desire for wealth,
for Christian unity, for personal honor and sacrifice, for excitement
and adventure, and for spiritual salvation. The Italian merchants,
though Urban had not been addressing them directly, saw a special
advantage to themselves in the crusade. They would gain profit by
providing ships and supplies. And if the crusaders succeeded,
fabulous commercial opportunities would be opened to them.

Of the successive expeditions to the East, by land and by sea, the
First Crusade was the only one to attain (temporarily) its professed
goal. French noblemen, responding to the call of Urban (who was
himself French), constituted the main body of crusaders. Godfrey,
Duke of Lorraine, joined by other dukes, counts, and barons, set
out in 1096 with an army of some fifteen thousand knights. They
took the land route to Constantinople and then crossed into Asia
Minor to confront the Turks.

The crusaders suffered severe hardships and losses, but at first
they were victorious. Their leaders, having turned back the Turkish
threat to Constantinople, proceeded to establish dukedoms in Asia
Minor and abandoned their original plan to march on to Jerusalem.
The survivors of lesser rank, however, insisted that the crusade be
resumed. Responding at last to their demands, Raymond, Count of
Toulouse, advanced on Jerusalem and took the city, after a six-
week siege, in 1099.

The crusaders' entry into the Holy City was an orgy of killing and
looting. One crusader reported in his journal,

> The amount of blood that they shed on that day is incredible . . . .
> Some of our men (and this was more merciful) cut off the heads of their
> enemies; others shot them with arrows, so that they fell from the towers;
> others tortured them longer by casting them into the flames. Piles of
> heads, hands, and feet were to be seen in the streets of the city . . . .
> It was a just and splendid judgment of God that this place should be
> filled with the blood of unbelievers, since it had suffered so long from
> their blasphemies.

With the help of fleets from Venice, Genoa, and other Italian
cities, the crusaders moved on to take the coastal towns of Palestine
and Syria. (For this aid the Italians received, as they had hoped,
rich privileges in the trade of the Levant.) The various conquered
territories were then drawn together into a loose feudal state called
the Latin Kingdom of Jerusalem. Godfrey of Lorraine was chosen
as its first overlord and enjoyed the homage, fealty, and services of

the landholding nobility. The feudal system of western Europe was thus transplanted to this Christian enclave in the Near East. But the kingdom proved short-lived. Half a century later, having rejuvenated and reunified their forces, the Turks launched a counter-offensive from surrounding territories. They pursued the struggle successfully, despite the arrival of Christian reinforcements from Europe. In 1187 Saladin, their resourceful leader, recaptured Jerusalem, and for all practical purposes the Latin Kingdom was dead.

There were countless other expeditions, or crusades, to the East, only some of which have been given a number by European historians. Even before the First Crusade was launched, a motley crowd of commoners had set out from southern Germany for Constantinople. Their enthusiasm, sparked by the pope's call to arms, was whipped to a fury by a maverick preacher known as Peter the Hermit. The Peasants' Crusade, as it came to be called, distinguished itself chiefly by the massacre of Jewish communities along the way. Lacking provisions of their own, these commoners lived off the country as they marched. When they at last reached Constantinople, the Byzantine emperor grew alarmed and hastily ferried them across the Bosporus to Asia Minor. There the Turks made quick work of the misguided peasants.

The Second Crusade (1146) was inspired by a reforming monk, Bernard of Clairvaux (p. 185). An extraordinarily persuasive man, he induced two monarchs and thousands of fighting men to "put on the Cross." The main force of this expedition was cut to pieces as it moved across Asia Minor. Bernard, convinced that his cause was just, concluded that the failure must have been due to the sinfulness of the crusaders.

Bernard's diagnosis was accepted by his more ardent followers. Some of them went still further: they reasoned that if purity of soul was a requirement for victory, young children would be the most favored of all crusaders. Somewhat later, in accordance with this notion, thousands of innocent German and French boys marched off on a Children's Crusade (1212). They never reached the Holy Land, however, for they fell victim to accident and disease or were captured by slave-dealers along the way.

The abortive Ninth Crusade (1270) was the last one whose express purpose was to retake Palestine. Expeditions continued, however, until the end of the Middle Ages. Though papal propaganda continued to stress the recovery of the holy places, the principal motive of the later expeditions was to guard against the rising power of the Turks.

Actually, the crusades had increased the vulnerability of Europe by undermining the Byzantine Empire. When Emperor Alexius called for aid in 1095, he had hoped that the Western knights would help his armies eject the Turks from Asia Minor and restore imperial control over that strategic area. But, as we have seen, the feudal lords had different intentions. The counts and dukes indulged their private ambitions and divided Asia Minor and Syria into principalities for themselves. These fell like houses of straw when the Turkish storm broke again in the twelfth century.

The cruelest blow to Byzantium occurred during the Fourth Crusade, which was turned against the city of Constantinople itself. The crusade was organized by prominent French barons and was to have gone by sea from Venice to Egypt. But the leaders, while en route, intrigued with the Venetians to divert the expedition from its original objective. They knew that Constantinople was a richer prize than all the Holy Land—and that it could be taken more easily.

The imperial capital was stormed in 1204 by the very men whose forefathers had promised rescue a century before. Untold treasures of gold, silver, and holy relics were seized during the subsequent pillage and rape. Vandalism and fire consumed irreplaceable works of Greek art and literature. The city and the European portion of the empire were then divided among the chieftains of the crusade, and these mutilated remnants were constituted as the Latin Empire of Constantinople. The Count of Flanders was proclaimed its first emperor, and a new patriarch of the Eastern Church was installed— one who was loyal to the pope in Rome. Venice secured special trading privileges, and the hinterland was parceled out in feudal fashion to the plundering knights. Thus, long-coveted and ill-concealed goals were momentarily realized by the papacy, the Venetians, and the French aristocracy—all at the expense of Byzantium.

The Latin Empire of Constantinople was a freak of history, and its life was even briefer than that of the Kingdom of Jerusalem. What the Western forces really accomplished by this infamous crusade was a fatal weakening of Europe's key point of defense against the Turks. A Byzantine emperor in exile persevered at Nicaea, clinging to a remnant of territory in Asia Minor, and in 1261 even managed to regain Constantinople and the land around it. But Byzantine power had been so shattered that it proved unable, in the fifteenth century, to check the Turkish sweep into Europe.

THE MEDIEVAL SYNTHESIS

The crusades are a dramatic expression of the contradictions that characterized medieval civilization. The impulse that sent many of the knights to the Holy Land, at great personal sacrifice, was noble and genuine, but personal valor and high-mindedness were often overshadowed by baser motives. These contradictions marked European society as a whole. Though every civilization reveals some gap between ideals and reality, in the Middle Ages the gulf was excessively wide. The Christian goals of peace and love were generally professed, but the years were heavy with strife and war. Asceticism and voluntary poverty were lauded as holy virtues, but the most admired of living men were fiercely proud and acquisitive. The idea of a "Christian commonwealth" was preached, but the actuality was a narrow provincialism and constant struggle between church and state.

Yet, despite such contradictions, there existed a great deal of common ground. There was but one "true faith" in the Latin West, with one Church and one supreme head (the pope). The Church, notwithstanding its human failings, errors, and internal conflicts, offered a unified and comprehensive conception of man and the universe. This served to relate all medieval institutions and to give them meaning and sanction. Moreover, there was but one political system (feudalism) and a dominant economic system (manorial agriculture). There was a single social structure, too, made up of clergy, nobility, and commoners, each with its assigned functions and legal status. Education, from the elementary level through the professional curriculums of the universities, followed a set pattern. Art forms, also, were remarkably consistent and culminated in the universal Gothic style.

What, in human terms, were the strengths and weaknesses of this medieval synthesis? First, there was a strong sense of security, of "belonging." This does not mean physical security, of course, for probably at no other time in Western history were person and property more vulnerable. But there was psychological security. The individual seldom had reason to feel isolated or rejected. His Christian faith told him that his role in life, whether high or low, was divinely ordained, and all that was required of him was to live out his days according to custom. Moreover, his life was an enterprise shared with others: he belonged to a village, a guild, a town, a fellowship, or an order. Finally, though there existed a hierarchy of privilege and power in this world, all souls were considered equal before God. Hope of a better life to come compensated for everyday privations; consolation lay in the belief that whatever is, is the will of God.

The slow rate of change in the Middle Ages also spared most men the stress of having to make continual adjustments in their modes of living and thinking. Paternalistic control in both spiritual and temporal matters relieved them of the burden of making many important decisions. At the same time, the upper classes enjoyed a good deal of independence, and authority was not exercised so thoroughly as to extinguish freedom of mind and spirit altogether. Proof of this lies in the impressive spontaneity and creativity of medieval men. Though they were living in a rigid society, they steadily improvised, improved, and invented. This was as true in farming, commerce, and warfare as it was in law, education, literature, and the arts.

These admirable features have led some modern writers to adopt a nostalgic attitude toward the Age of Faith. There is, however, another and darker side of the coin. No amount of romanticizing can obscure the medieval record of famine, disease, and violence. Such experiences, in turn, coarsened feelings and turned many men to pillage and killing. Banditry and private wars ravaged the countryside, and through all these centuries, in fat times or lean, dirt and squalor were commonplace.

But probably the most crippling deprivation lay in the sphere of the intellect. Most individuals of all classes (except the higher clergy) were sunk in ignorance. Literacy and education were not a right of every man but only a requirement for specific vocations. And even the educated few believed in many crude superstitions. Their image of reality was blurred by ancient errors and by an exaggerated belief in the miraculous. Virtually all minds were closed to systematic empirical investigation. Though the medieval philosophers were thorough and well disciplined, they held to a static concept of truth that was too narrow to encompass the expanding world of Western man.

III. The Coming of Modern Times

	Political, Social, and Economic Developments	Religion, Science, and Philosophy	History and Literature	Art and Architecture
1300	Emergence of capitalism Growth of banking Hundred Years' War (1337–1453) Decline of feudal and manorial systems	Renaissance humanism (1350–1600) "Babylonian Captivity" (1309–76) Great Schism (1379–1417) Wiclif	Petrarch Boccaccio	Florence Cathedral Giotto Brunelleschi Renaissance style of architecture Donatello
1400	Domestic system of production (1400–1750) Fall of Constantinople Expulsion of Moors from Spain Age of despots in Italy: Cosimo de' Medici Francesco Sforza Jacob Fugger	Hus Neo-Platonism (Florentine Academy) Ficino Gutenberg	Valla Gutenberg	Masaccio Van Eyck Ghiberti Botticelli

Date	Art	Literature	Thought / Science / Religion	Politics / Events
1500	Da Vinci	Erasmus	Pico Machiavelli	Overseas exploration Columbus Da Gama Establishment of European colonial empires Cortez
	Michelangelo Titian	Castiglione More	Luther (Beginning of Protestant Reformation) Calvin	Rise of national monarchies: Henry VIII, Francis I
	St. Peter's Basilica Holbein	Rabelais Cellini	Pope Paul III (Beginning of Catholic Reformation) Copernicus Loyola and Society of Jesus Council of Trent	Charles V, Holy Roman Emperor Philip II Spanish Armada
	Brueghel	Montaigne		
	Escorial Palace Baroque style			
1600	Rubens	Shakespeare Jonson	Bacon Galileo Descartes Kepler	Elizabeth I Religious Wars
	Rembrandt Bernini			
1650	Versailles Palace			Peace of Westphalia Louis XIV

The Transformation and Expansion
of Europe

6

Unlike the Roman world, medieval civilization did not come to an abrupt end. There were no waves of invading barbarians, no collapse of civic order and commerce. On the contrary, western Europe at the "close" of the Middle Ages displayed a remarkable vitality and an expansive zeal. It moved, without a perceptible break, across the threshold of "modern" times. So we cannot point to any historical event or series of events and say, "Here ended the Middle Ages." We might even contend that our present civilization is an extension of medieval times, for the evolution of Western institutions has been continuous over the past thousand years, and the seeds of each new era are nurtured in the old. Clearly, though, the *pattern* of Western life has changed profoundly. And the beginnings of this change were present as early as the thirteenth century.

DISSOLUTION OF THE MEDIEVAL SYNTHESIS

The "modern world," as that term applies to the West, was several centuries in maturing. In some parts of Europe it arrived sooner than in others. But for Western civilization as a whole, the medieval pattern had begun to dissolve by 1400, and by 1650 a new pattern had come into being.

The forces that dissolved the old synthesis and created the new were varied but related. When a change began in one sphere of human affairs, it was reinforced and accelerated by responses in others. The primary force appears to have been economic. The relatively static, agrarian economy of the Middle Ages steadily gave way to a dynamic, commercial economy, and economic change produced social change. New social ranks appeared; serfdom grew obsolete; the entire class structure became more fluid. The bonds of caste and group were thereby loosened, and the freedom of the *individual* was enhanced. With economic and social change came political change. As stability and prosperity returned to Europe, monarchs found that they could exercise a larger measure of direct authority over their kingdoms. Feudal regimes gradually gave way to despotic national states.

With the world altering in so many ways, ethical and philosophical views were bound to alter too. In the sharpened competition for wealth and power, the medieval ideals of asceticism, poverty, and humility were thrust aside by the "modern" aspirations for pleasure, money, and status. On the plane of formal thought, the scholastic approach to knowledge was challenged and discredited. (We will treat the new view of man and its expressions in philosophy, art, and literature in Chapter Seven.)

The breakup of the medieval pattern proceeded, for the most part, in a gradual, undramatic fashion. Many of the changes were hardly noticed when they took place, and few men could tell where they were leading. But one change was observed by all: the seamless garment of Western faith was rent by the Protestant movements of the sixteenth century. These movements set in fairly late in the course of the medieval dissolution, and they served to convince reflective men that a new epoch had arrived. For, if the Church had been the core of European life, its division confirmed the end of the traditional synthesis. (We will consider the forces underlying this religious upheaval in Chapter Eight.) In the present chapter we will examine the complementary factors—economic, social, geographic, and political—that transformed the civilization of the West.

THE NEW ECONOMY

We have seen that the rise of trade and towns was a crucial development of the Middle Ages. But by 1400 European commerce had begun to take on a new look. Medieval guilds and merchants had generally operated within limited areas and had been subject to local regulation. The masters of the workshops paid money wages and hoped to make a profit from their enterprises, but most prices were fixed, and the scale of business was small. As a result, the master's profit was seldom large, and whatever he made usually went to the upkeep of his shop and the care of his family. Though capital was used in trade and industry, very little capital surplus could be built up. The entrepreneur still thought primarily in terms of "production for use" in a static economy; he had not yet grasped the idea of the unlimited accumulation and expansion of capital. The true capitalist had not yet emerged.

The birth of modern capitalism

The Italian merchants had taken the lead in the revival of trade in the eleventh century, and in the fourteenth and fifteenth they pioneered the development of capitalism. They dealt chiefly in luxury goods from the East, which were highly valued in Europe, and many of them made quick fortunes in their dealings. Finding that they could not spend all their profits immediately, they hit upon the idea of reinvesting the surplus.

This novel idea made it possible for the successful trader to launch new, more ambitious enterprises. Soon he was no longer traveling about as an ordinary merchant but was minding his account books at home as a "capitalist." He directed his energies to extracting profits from his varied enterprises and reinvesting them to gain *more* profits. Thus emerged the features that have characterized the "capitalist system" for the past five centuries: its boundless profit-seeking and its dynamic spirit.

For merchants to accumulate really substantial capital surpluses, they had to expand their trading activities constantly. What the Italians achieved as the middlemen between Europe and the Levant the merchants of the port cities of Germany achieved in the Baltic. They found that by pooling their resources they could build fleets and win joint trading privileges abroad, and by the fourteenth century the leading towns of northern Germany had formed an effective commercial league (the Hanse). The cities of the Hanse monopolized the foreign trade of northern Germany and set up outlets in the trading centers of Russia, Norway, England, and the Low Countries. From these far-flung outposts, rich profits flowed in to the capitalists of northern Germany.

The merchants of the Low Countries prospered, too. To the wharves of Bruges and Antwerp came a steady stream of Italian ships carrying oriental spices and silks, and vessels from the eastern Baltic loaded with furs, timber, and herring. The industries of England and the Rhineland also funneled their products into the Low Countries. By the fifteenth century a truly international commerce had evolved—extensive enough to provide for the accumulation of profit surpluses and for the growth of a capitalist class.

Innovations in business organization

The new leaders of enterprise scrapped many of the traditional methods of doing business. In the Middle Ages the masters of each guild, collectively, had served as its directing force, and within a well-established framework of rules individual masters had run their own shops. After 1400 several industries cast off the shackles of the guild. Still the entrepreneur found that he could seldom go it alone. Commerce was becoming more extensive and complex, requiring a pooling of capital and of managerial talent. Gradually the *partnership* came into vogue as a unit of business organization. A special form of partnership, the family firm, was the most common. A group of relatives could best handle matters demanding secrecy and mutual trust and could assure the continuity of the enterprise.

The displacement of guild control is best illustrated by the woolens industry, in which the traditional association of master weavers, journeymen, and apprentices had disappeared in most areas by 1400. The industry was taken over by enterprising merchants, who bought the raw wool and put it out to semiskilled laborers for processing—first to spinners and then to weavers, dyers, and shearers in succession. The workers were paid by the piece, or by measure, but the ownership of the materials stayed with the merchant. He sold the finished cloth (or garments) in the international market at whatever price he could get.

The wool merchants thus reaped the profits of both industry and commerce. They paid the laborers at a meager rate and permitted them no say in the conduct of the business. Moreover, the laborers were forbidden by law to organize or strike. This "putting-out" or "domestic" system was the dominant mode of production in early modern Europe. It destroyed the fraternal relationship between master and journeyman that had existed in the medieval guilds. It made profit the sole concern of the entrepreneur and diminished the worker's sense of creativity. The fierce antagonisms that grew up between capitalists and workers foreshadowed the conflicts that were to mark the modern industrial world.

The rise of banking and bankers

As Europe moved from a largely self-sufficient economy to an economy geared to trade, the old techniques of exchange and finance proved inadequate. Relatively little money had circulated in the Middle Ages; most exchange was by barter. During the fourteenth and fifteenth centuries the supply of coins grew steadily. However, the expansion of enterprise depended not so much on money itself as on new instruments of exchange and credit.

Perhaps the most important substitute for money payments was the bill of exchange, which was similar to a modern bank draft or check. A merchant with branch offices in various countries usually made a side business of selling drafts that were payable by his firm in some other city. A Venetian who bought linen from Antwerp, for example, would find it inconvenient to ship money to the Low Countries every time he placed an order. Instead, he could go to a Venetian firm that did business in Antwerp and purchase a draft payable by its office there. The seller of the linen in Antwerp was perfectly willing to accept this bill of exchange, for he knew he could collect on it in his own city. Rather than demand cash for it, however, he would probably endorse the bill and use it as a means of payment in a subsequent business transaction.

The first bankers were successful merchants who had accumulated a profit surplus and who wished to reinvest it. They found that moneylending, though risky, could be highly lucrative. Although some merchants, kings, nobles, and popes had borrowed heavily during the Middle Ages, moneylending did not become big business until the fourteenth and fifteenth centuries. One reason was that the Church had condemned all interest-taking as usury. As a result, moneylending was viewed as an unseemly occupation.

With the expansion of commerce, people came to realize that lending was a useful and defensible business. The traditional argument against taking interest payments was based on a revulsion against imposing high rates on individuals in distress. But loans to businessmen engaged in profitable enterprises were obviously of a different nature. These loans were *productive,* and they exposed the lender to risks that justified some reward. Seen in this light, lending (banking) gradually became a respectable pursuit for Christian capitalists.

Italian merchants had moved into the banking business as early as the thirteenth century. In the next century, Florence became the leading center of international finance. The Bardi and Peruzzi families, for example, advanced huge loans to Edward III, king of England. Later Edward repudiated the loans and forced those families into bankruptcy. But in the fifteenth century a new house of bankers, the Medici, emerged in Florence. This family restored the financial power of the city and came to dominate its political and cultural life.

Banking spread north from Italy to the rest of Europe. Jacques Coeur, a French merchant who had made a fortune in trading with the Levant, was appointed royal treasurer by Charles VII, king of France (1439). Taking advantage of his position at the court, Coeur acquired extensive holdings in mines, lands, and workshops and emerged as one of Europe's most powerful international bankers. He used his enormous wealth for the benefit of his family and built a palace worthy of a king in his native town of Bourges.

The wealthiest and most famous banker of the period was Jacob
Fugger of Augsburg. Southern Germany, in the fifteenth and sixteenth centuries, was sharing richly in the prosperity of growing
commerce and had the added resource of profitable copper and
silver mines. Some years earlier, capital had entered the mining
industry for the first time, permitting miners to dig more deeply and
more efficiently with improved tools. The leading entrepreneurs of
the industry soon took control of smelting and metalworking as well
as the mines, concentrating the direction of all operations in a few
hands. The workers, who formerly had been independent producers,
now became voiceless employees of the capitalists.

The Fugger family wrested immense wealth from these and other
enterprises and channeled their surplus into banking. Jacob pushed
the family business beyond Germany and opened branch offices in
the major commercial centers of Europe. He ventured into buying,
selling, and speculating in all kinds of goods, and he rendered financial services to merchants, prelates, and rulers. One of his more
spectacular operations was to lend half a million gold florins to
Charles, the Habsburg king of Spain, who wanted to "buy" the
imperial title. When Jacob died in 1525, he left a fortune of about
a quarter of a billion dollars. A good capitalist, he was also a good
philanthropist. He and his brothers built, as evidence of their piety
and generosity, an attractive group of dwellings for the "righteous"
poor of Augsburg. It still stands, near the center of the city, as a
memorial to the Fuggers' wealth and charity.

The impact on social structure and values

The forces released by the rise of capitalism disrupted European
society and economic life by undermining the guilds and rendering
the manorial system moribund. The customs associated with manorialism had seemed almost unbreakable, even in the later Middle
Ages; they survived long after the reasons for their existence had
vanished. Even so, important features of manorialism were altered
by the emerging capitalistic economy.

The most pervasive change, which affected all relationships between nobles and peasants, was the substitution of money for payments in goods or services. During the Middle Ages the lord of the
manor had received, in lieu of rent, a share of the crops from his
peasants' strips. In addition, the serfs had been obligated to cultivate the lord's demesne, the land reserved exclusively for his benefit.
The forced labor of serfs was not very efficient, however, and the
lord cared little about better management. Toward the close of the
medieval period, the nobles often found it advantageous to rent

their demesnes to free tenants, who were now able to sell their produce at nearby markets and pay their rents in cash. The feudal landlords had also been entitled to extra labor in return for the serfs' use of the common fields and woodland. This service, too, was gradually converted into fixed money payments. The serfs preferred this arrangement because it released them from onerous work; the lords preferred it because they could usually find cheap day labor and still have cash left over from the serfs' payments.

The next step was the emancipation of the serfs. Now that the nobles no longer depended on obligatory labor, they were quite willing to grant the serfs freedom. In most instances the freedman remained on the land as a tenant and in exchange for his freedom paid his lord a lump sum or extra rent. But he surrendered his hereditary right to stay on the land, which meant that he could be ousted when his leasehold expired.

By 1500 serfdom had disappeared from England and had become a rarity in western Europe. The medieval seigneur, with his rights to the produce and services of the peasantry, had become a capitalist landowner living off his rents. Though many of the great estates remained intact, the pattern of relationships had been transformed. In short, the spirit of commercial enterprise had spread to the countryside. Merchants began to buy estates and play the role of landed aristocrats, while intermarriage between bourgeois and landed families further blurred the old distinctions. Serfs were becoming free men, merchants were becoming landholders, and noblemen were becoming agrarian capitalists, or *rentiers*.

This social change, like other significant changes in history, brought loss as well as gain. The sense of personal security and community solidarity waned, but no longer was one class arbitrarily subjected to another. Equality of opportunity did not arise immediately, for the new circles of privilege were tightly drawn, but there was greater freedom of movement, both upward and downward.

Dislocations in society engendered dislocations in ethics. Capitalism has been called the major heresy of the Middle Ages, for it was directly opposed to some of the central teachings of Christ. The merchants and bankers of the modern period made profit their immediate and constant concern and divorced commercial dealings from Christian ethics. In their desire for gain they differed only in degree from the landlords and rulers of medieval times. The latter, however, could camouflage their activities under the cloak of feudal and regal rights and customs; the upstart bourgeoisie had no such camouflage at their disposal. Materialism came to be openly approved and systematized, leading to an overturn of traditional values. Pride, envy, and avarice—identified by the Church as cardinal sins—were now regarded as the mainsprings of economic life. The religious ideals of meditation, prayer, and giving were superseded by the goals of hard work, punctuality, and saving.

One might suppose that the Church would have mobilized its forces against this challenge to its ancient ideals. With its widespread organization and its control over public opinion, it could certainly have done so. But it no longer wanted to. Though it continued to profess its attachment to spiritual goals, the Church itself had in large measure succumbed to materialism. Nowhere was this more apparent than in the top ranks of the hierarchy. The popes, like almost everyone else in Europe, were dazzled by the new riches and became obsessed with wealth, elegance, and power.

The active carriers of the new morality were the bourgeoisie, or middle class. Some members of this class, like Jacques Coeur and Jacob Fugger, attained high levels of influence, equal to that of counts or princes. The position of the class as a whole, however, advanced much more slowly. The bourgeoisie enjoyed one long-run advantage in their competition for power with the landed nobility: they controlled the *movable* assets of the economy (commodities, ships, and money), and these assets were growing in value, while the nobility controlled the *fixed* assets (mainly land), and these assets were declining in value. Money, furthermore, was infinitely more flexible than land, and with it middle-class men could buy the goods and services that secured influence.

Several centuries were to pass before the bourgeoisie attained social dominance. The nobility maneuvered to retain its inherited privileges, and the weight of tradition retarded the advance of the middle class. But from the sixteenth century onward, the ideals of the bourgeoisie had a growing influence on society as a whole. Bourgeois "virtues" included, in addition to the habits of work and thrift, the qualities of probity, reliability, and inventiveness. These competed successfully against the romantic ideals of the nobility: physical prowess, courage, chivalry, and tradition. Middle-class aspirations and manners, by the middle of the nineteenth century, would become the modes of Western civilization.

THE NEW GEOGRAPHY

The impact of capitalism and materialism was magnified by expansion overseas. The epochal voyages of Columbus, Da Gama, and Magellan gave Western man a vision of ever expanding markets and fathomless riches. The expansion of Europe was more than just economic, however. It was a climax to the outward thrust of Western civilization that dated back to the tenth century (p. 212).

Had the mariners of ancient Greece, or of early medieval Europe, crossed the Atlantic and discovered America, it is almost certain that nothing would have come of their discovery. (Leif Ericson's reported finding, around 1000, made a negligible impression on the West.) The fact is that Europeans learned about the New World at the very moment when expansionist forces were rising. And by an accident of history the explorations took place at a time when the Europeans held decisive technological advantages over the peoples of the rest of the world. Nothing in the history of world relations has proved more fateful than this far-flung (and unequal) encounter between Europe and the other continents.

The impulse to overseas expansion

Before 1500 few Europeans had given very much thought to the regions beyond their shores. They knew the Baltic area and its eastward extension into Asia. The crusades had carried Europeans to the Near East and had excited their curiosity about the lands beyond. They knew the Black Sea and, of course, the Mediterranean. But the areas to the west and southwest of Spain were great blanks on their maps—reaching, perhaps, to the edge of the earth.

Popular conceptions of what the rest of the world was like were full of fanciful notions. Tales of sea monsters abounded, and sailors, wary of the unknown, hugged the coasts in their tiny vessels. There was, however, a considerable body of reliable information about the world, and crude instruments of navigation were in use. Though geography was not taught in the schools or universities (none of the applied sciences was), cartography and seamanship were well-developed arts. Most of the information had been handed down from ancient times. The Greeks had concluded that the earth was a sphere and had computed its circumference with extraordinary accuracy. Oddly, the Hellenistic scientist Ptolemy (150 A.D.) substantially reduced their estimate. His error was passed on to medieval geographers, with interesting consequences for later mariners. (Columbus, for example, accepted Ptolemy's figure.)

Marco Polo, a thirteenth-century merchant of Venice, contributed more than anyone else to Europe's awareness of exotic lands. Members of the Polo family, after establishing trading contacts with the Tartars (Mongols) in western Asia, decided to journey to the far side of the Tartar empire. A long trek by caravan took them from the Black Sea to the Chinese city of Peking, where Kublai Khan held court as emperor. The Polos were welcomed with courtesy, and

Marco remained there for many years. When he returned to Italy
he wrote of his travels and revealed to astonished Europeans the
fabulous wealth of the Orient.

Through the Near Eastern trade, the West had for several centuries tasted sweets, spices, and other luxuries from afar. Now the
desire grew to acquire these goods directly, without paying a middle-
man's profit to Moslem merchants. The desire was especially strong
in countries outside the Mediterranean area. The Italian cities, as
sole carriers of the profitable spice trade to the West, were quite
content with things as they were. But the merchants of Spain,
France, and England dreamed of bypassing *both* the Italians and
the Moslems.

By the fifteenth century a race was under way to find new sea
routes between western Europe and the Far East. Europeans knew
that no water passage existed between the Mediterranean and the
Indian Ocean; hence only two possibilities lay open. One was to
try the way south, around Africa, then eastward to India. This was
a relatively conservative plan, since ships could hold close to land
during most of the voyage. The other was a bolder, more theoretical plan: sailing due west across the open Atlantic. Though Africa
and the Indian Ocean appeared on contemporary maps of the
world, the Atlantic was uncharted. Geographers agreed that China
must lie on the farther side, but none knew for sure what distances
or barriers might have to be crossed before reaching it.

Both alternatives were costly and risky to test, and European merchants, though eager to find new routes, were reluctant to finance
voyages of exploration. This could better be done, in any case, by
governments, because to set up commercial routes and bases would
require political and military power. The ambitious monarchs of
Europe grasped the opportunity. They saw that by bringing wealth
to their lands they could strengthen the economic base of their
regimes and enhance their personal glory. In backing these ventures,
the kings had the blessing and encouragement of the Church. For
the prelates, responding to their obligation to spread Christianity,
were eager for new converts. Thus three central motives combined
to launch the brave sailors and their ships: the aspiration of the
clergy to spread the gospel, the desire of the monarchs for power
and glory, and the hunger of the merchants for gold.

The voyages of discovery: the New World

The little kingdom of Portugal took the lead in sponsoring exploration. It had only a short history of independence, having
emerged when the Moslems were being expelled from the Iberian

peninsula. Portugal had been a fief for a period, subject to the Christian rulers of Castile, but in the twelfth century its count proclaimed himself a king. The Portuguese monarchy reached the apex of its power during the sixteenth century. With astounding will, enterprise, and ruthlessness, the Portuguese exploited vast territories and hosts of people overseas. Portugal became the prototype of that species of cultural aggression known as Western imperialism.

The Portuguese favored the proposed route around Africa. In the course of developing it, their forces occupied Madeira and the Azores and opened the slave trade along Africa's western coast (Guinea). At last, in 1498, Vasco da Gama rounded the Cape of Good Hope and sailed across the Indian Ocean to the west coast of India (FIG. 6-1), thereby linking Europe with the Orient. The Portuguese, having won that race, moved swiftly to secure their prize.

Meanwhile, a Genoese mariner named Christopher Columbus was seeking support for a plan to sail west to China and Japan. The son of a weaver, he had turned to the sea and to dreams of fame and fortune. Finding his way to Lisbon, the center of activity in geography and navigation, Columbus went into the business of making maps and charts. On occasion he accompanied ship captains on voyages down the African coast. He also gained sufficient social status to marry a daughter of the governor of Madeira, thereby gaining access to the royal court of Portugal.

When Columbus described his bold project to the king and asked for ships and provisions, the royal advisers pronounced his plans unsound. Columbus' scheme was based on the inaccurate calculations of Ptolemy and on an exaggerated notion of Asia's eastward projection; the king's advisers correctly reckoned that China was too distant to be reached by sailing westward across the Atlantic. Columbus believed China to be about 3,000 nautical miles west of Lisbon, while his critics put the figure at about 6,000. The actual distance is more than 12,000 miles.

Though disappointed, Columbus was not a man to give up. He turned next to the Spanish rulers, Ferdinand and Isabella, who were now driving the last of the Moslems from the Iberian peninsula. His proposal was at first rejected by a commission of experts for the same reason that had been advanced by the Portuguese. However, when the queen learned that Columbus was journeying north to offer his plan to the French king, she called him back. Attracted by his winning personality, Isabella decided to give him her personal support and agreed to an extravagant contract whereby Columbus was to become governor of all the lands he discovered and was to receive one-tenth of the wealth he extracted from them.

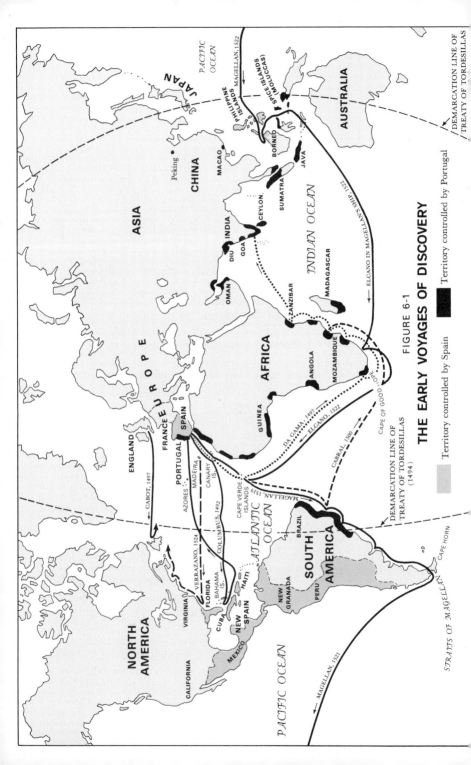

THE EARLY VOYAGES OF DISCOVERY

FIGURE 6-1

Territory controlled by Spain

Territory controlled by Portugal

Further, he was to be known as "Admiral of the Ocean Sea, Viceroy, and Governor."

Columbus personified the modern spirit. A modest capitalist, he invested some of his own money in the venture. When his tiny vessels dipped below the horizon in 1492, they carried with them a transcendent faith in the individual—and a passion for wealth, power, and glory. His courage brought him to the discovery of the New World, though he never understood the true nature of what he had found. By a bizarre coincidence, he sighted land (the Bahama Islands) at precisely the point where he expected to find the shores of Asia. This convinced him that his geographical theories and calculations were correct and that he had reached his true destination. Yet if an unknown continent had not lain across his path, the admiral would have returned to Spain empty-handed—or sailed on into oblivion.

Still seeking Japan or China, Columbus spent several months exploring the Caribbean, whose islands he mistook for the "Indies." He sighted and claimed Hispaniola (Haiti) as well as Juana (Cuba). On three subsequent voyages he strengthened Spain's claim to the Western Hemisphere. He died in 1506, still believing he had opened a westerly route to Asia.

After 1500 most geographers were convinced that Columbus had not reached Asia but had stumbled across a land mass hitherto uncharted. They decided to name it for another explorer, one who first discovered the true nature of Columbus' discovery. Amerigo Vespucci was a Florentine adventurer and mapmaker who was once connected with the banking firm of the Medici. Although his activities are uncertain, he apparently took part in several Spanish and Portuguese voyages along the mainland coasts of the hemisphere, from Brazil to Florida. Vespucci wrote colorful letters about what he saw and coined the term "New World." Copies of his letters were widely circulated in Europe, and literate persons were soon discussing the "land of Amerigo" (America).

Conflicts quickly arose over the rival overseas claims of Spain and Portugal. To avert trouble the monarchs of the two countries agreed, in 1494, to draw a line of demarcation between their spheres of interest. In the form of a circle of longitude, the line passed through a point approximately 1500 miles west of Cape Verde, the westernmost tip of Africa. The Portuguese were to confine their claims to trade and territories east of the designated meridian, while the Spaniards would limit themselves to the west. The Spaniards believed that this division would give them all the lands in the area of Columbus' discoveries; they had miscalculated the eastward extension of the southern continent. As it turned out, a large portion of it (Brazil) reached into the Portuguese zone. Lisbon thus gained, unexpectedly, a claim in the Western Hemisphere.

With the discovery of the Pacific by Vasco Nuñez de Balboa (1513), Europeans came to realize that beyond the New World lay another great stretch of water. The Spanish were disappointed that Columbus had failed to reach the Orient and still hoped that portions of it might fall within their treaty sphere. It was mainly with this in mind that Ferdinand Magellan set out in 1519 to find a passage to the Pacific through which he might sail on to Asia.

Magellan, a Portuguese in the service of Spain, guided his fleet of five ships down the coast of South America. After a false start up the broad Plata River, he continued his search until he entered the straits near the southern tip of the continent. He managed the hazardous passage into the Pacific and then sailed northwestward into the greatest of oceans. Following a frightful crossing of about a hundred days, during part of which his men lived on leather and rats, Magellan reached the island of Guam. With fresh provisions, he sailed on to the Philippines, claiming them for Spain. There he was killed in a skirmish with the natives, but the expedition pushed on to the Spice Islands (the Moluccas), and the one remaining vessel, with a remnant of the original crew, finally returned to Spain by continuing westward around Africa (FIG. 6-1). Magellan's expedition thus revealed that there was a water passage around the New World and demonstrated that a westerly route could be followed from Europe to Asia. More significant, it proved conclusively that the earth was round, it dramatized the vastness of the Pacific, and it gave men a truer idea of the globe's size.

Though Spain and Portugal felt that the overseas world was to be shared by them alone, the northern countries of Europe did not intend to stand idly by. The English and French kings were also seeking routes for direct trade with the Orient. A Genoese mariner, whom the English called John Cabot, was sent out in 1497 to seek a "northwest passage" to the Indies. Cabot touched the shores of the New World somewhere around Labrador and Newfoundland and thereby provided England with a claim to North America.

Shortly afterward a Florentine, Giovanni da Verrazano, explored the North Atlantic coast for the king of France. Neither he nor anyone else ever discovered another water passage, but the search led to a close examination of the hemisphere's eastern shores from Labrador to the Straits of Magellan. It was only after hope of finding a passage had been virtually abandoned that the French and English took steps to settle the northern lands.

The colonial empires

The Portuguese had won the race to the Orient when Vasco da Gama brought his ship into the harbor of Calicut. They perceived their goal clearly, attained it, and exploited their victory to the full. What they wanted was a monopoly over the richest trade in the world, and this they held for more than a century. When the Portuguese landed in India they found a heavily populated land with substantial resources. Its culture was rich, but it was painfully divided in religion, class, and politics. Consequently the inhabitants raised no effective resistance against the European intruders. Moving in with superior ships and weapons, the Portuguese quickly established permanent trading settlements along the western (Malabar) coast.

The next strategic step was for the Portuguese to wipe out Arab shipping, which for centuries had carried luxury goods from the Indian ports to the Near East. Having seized this lucrative trade from the Arabs, they extended their operations eastward to the Spice Islands and entered the ports of China and Japan. Here, too, they sought to monopolize commerce, reserving the transport of silks, lacquer, and spices to their own ships and restricting all sea trade in the area to ships licensed by the Portuguese crown.

The cost of maintaining naval vessels, bases, and men was high, but the crown and a few chosen companies reaped sensational profits—for a time. The Portuguese were too small a people to colonize the oriental lands, and their grip on strategic positions was tenuous. When the Dutch and English cut into the spice trade during the seventeenth century, the golden empire began to crumble. Nevertheless, some five centuries after Da Gama, Portugal still clings to the dwindling remnants of her overseas possessions.

The Spanish looked on enviously as the Portuguese piled success on success. The demarcation treaty of 1494 had tied their hands east of the meridian, and Columbus' failure in the west had destroyed their dream of breaking through from that direction. True, Magellan had finally reached the Orient, but the miseries of his journey only proved the infeasibility of the route. At first the New World appeared to the Spaniards as a monstrous obstacle to their ambitions.

The Caribbean natives were peaceful enough, but they offered little of value to European traders. The only hope left to the Spanish adventurers was to fall upon some precious store of wealth— gold, silver, or gems. This they did in a manner and on a scale that surprised even those hardy soldiers of fortune. It was Hernando Cortez who first struck it rich. Attracted by rumors of wealth on the mainland, he organized and equipped a small expeditionary force in Cuba. He debarked in 1519, without authorization from his superiors, and made his way to Mexico, where he had his soldiers proclaim him the legitimate ruler of the land, subject only to the king of Spain. Then he scuttled his ships, so that his men had no means of escape.

Cortez' conquest of the Aztec empire is a remarkable chapter of history. The Aztecs, like the Mayas before them (and the Incas of Peru), were by no means primitive. In the Caribbean islands the Spanish had looted and destroyed as they pleased, but in Mexico they found an advanced civilization, capable of resistance. The Aztecs suffered serious disadvantages, however. They had not developed the wheel, could not make iron utensils or weapons, and lacked horses and cattle. The government was oppressively theocratic and constantly threatened by tribal unrest.

Cortez played upon the natives' superstitious fears, drew up his cannon (recently developed in Europe), and set one tribe against another. In the face of constant personal danger, he succeeded in overthrowing the emperor, Montezuma. He then destroyed the Aztec capital and laid out a new one on the old site, which later became Mexico City. Home to the Spanish court came rich prizes, and the king recognized Cortez as captain-general and governor of New Spain. Within a decade his lieutenants had subjugated most of Central America, from Panama to the Rio Grande.

This caesar of the New World had many freebooting companions and rivals, though none surpassed him as a conquistador (conqueror). South of the Panamanian isthmus, the most notorious adventurer was Francisco Pizarro, who, hearing of gold and silver in the Inca territories (Peru), organized an expedition with royal approval. He discovered that the Inca empire was torn by internal unrest and, like Cortez, made the most of the situation. Armed with superior weapons, Pizarro's men captured the ruler and held him for an exorbitant ransom. After Pizarro had received tons of gold and silver, carried in from all parts of Peru, he had his prisoner baptized a Christian and then had him strangled. He next marched to the Inca capital of Cuzco, looted it, and took over the empire (1534).

The success of these European adventurers was to be repeated over and over again in the New World. Small bodies of armed and determined men were able to overturn impressive civilizations. They did so under exceedingly difficult conditions, operating far from their homelands with little knowledge of the terrain or of the native languages and cultures. But they had decisive advantages on their side. While the native leaders and peoples were usually divided among themselves, the conquistadors were united by their purpose of plunder.

Their greed was accompanied by a driving sense of superiority and a fanatical conviction that Christianity was the one true faith and that they were responsible for spreading that faith. Priests accompanied the invaders; missionaries and bishops followed in their wake. The superior equipment and weapons of the Europeans provided them with the tools of victory, and through a combination of force, guile, terror, and treachery they subdued the New World.

The court of Spain was elated with the wealth that had been wrested from Mexico and Peru. The king received his royal share, and nobles close to the throne were granted vast estates in America. But soon it became evident that the quick-and-easy prizes of the New World had been consumed. The monarchy now had to adapt itself to demanding, long-range enterprises in its overseas territories.

Gradually the Spaniards came to realize that Columbus' legacy was an asset of unmeasured dimension, infinitely richer in wealth than all of Europe. But that wealth—which existed in the form of land and people—had to be cultivated in order to be harvested. By 1550 the monarchy had begun to lay the foundations of royal administration in the Americas. The era of conquest and plunder was over, and the long period of construction and development had begun. Thus, driven by the twin desires for exploitation and Christianization, the Spanish proceeded to impose the institutions of Western culture on the New World.

After 1600 the Portuguese, too, turned their attention from commerce alone to the longer, harder task of developing the wealth of America. They established in Brazil a system of autocratic control similar to the Spanish. In both colonial empires the natives were forced into virtual serfdom, working huge estates (*encomiendas*) for the white landlords. Since the Indians were not well suited to certain types of labor, the Spanish and Portuguese brought large numbers of African slaves into the Western Hemisphere. In the Caribbean these slaves quickly replaced the natives, who succumbed to the white man's maltreatment and diseases. Negroes and mulattoes comprise, today, about one-sixth of the total population of Latin America, while whites constitute about one-quarter, and most of the remainder are a mixture of white and Indian (mestizo). From early times, the Spanish and Portuguese permitted intermarriage between Europeans and Christianized natives.

The extension of European culture to North America started about a century after the colonial beginnings in Central and South

America. The English, French, and Dutch had set out in search of lucrative trade, but they, too, had been obliged to switch to settlement and development. The results of these several national efforts were a transformation of the entire New World and a profound alteration of the Old.

Consequences for the conquered

The impact of the conquests on Europe was perhaps more significant than their impact on America. For Europe after 1500 became the heart of an expanding system that reached into all parts of the world, and changes occurring at the center of the system reverberated in far-off places. Yet we must be mindful of the direct effects of conquest upon the conquered. The initial European penetrations into America were more disturbing than any comparable incursions in recorded history. The killing, burning, looting, raping, and enslaving were not unusual. But there was, in addition, a rare psychic shock, arising in part from the clash of highly divergent levels of culture.

The trauma was intensified by the unprecedented suddenness and strangeness of the encounter. The Indians had no knowledge of the existence of the white men and no warning of their coming. When the conquerors stepped ashore from the great ocean—with their pale skin and unfamiliar dress—it was as if they had descended from another planet. They rode animals never before seen, wore armor stouter than anything known to the natives, and spoke in the name of the "one true God" who was stronger than all the rest. The hapless Indians trembled when the white man's cannon roared. Gripped by fear and superstition, they fell into terror and confusion.

After the conquests were over, the routine of exploitation was less painful (except for the continuing outrage of the slave trade). The Spanish and Portuguese monarchies, in intimate collaboration with the Church, endeavored to bring a rational order of existence and Christian salvation to their subject millions. On the whole, considering the perversities of human nature and the immense geographical distances involved, they succeeded remarkably well. The *Pax Hispanica* covered an area far broader than the Roman Empire. And, while Rome imposed her civilization upon only a portion of her domain, Spain (and Portugal) were determined to Christianize and Westernize the whole of Latin America.

The Spaniards, in a sense, carried the historic Roman mission to the New World in the sixteenth century. Heirs to Rome, they would build as well or better than their forebears. During three centuries of rule they organized cities and towns, churches and missions, plantations and industries. They constructed fine bridges, aqueducts, and highways. The Spanish (and the Portuguese) brought to America, long before anyone else, the European legacy of art, literature, and learning. True, these fruits of civilization were enjoyed mainly by a privileged few—the Iberian-born whites. For the colonial administrations differed from the Roman Empire in one vital respect: Rome permitted the native peoples to participate in imperial prosperity; Spain viewed them primarily as property, to be used for the benefit of the crown.

Consequences for Europe

What effects did the overseas expansion have on Europe itself? The most immediate motive for the explorations had been economic, and their first effect was economic: expansion nourished the institutions of capitalism. As trade with the Orient and the Americas increased, profits accumulated, and the huge investments demanded by the long voyages and the colonial ventures brought long-range gains to bankers and capitalists. The flow of gold and silver from the New World stimulated general business activity. By 1600 the volume of money in existence in Europe had risen to nearly a billion dollars (in current terms). This more adequate coinage facilitated trade and strengthened the incentive of all classes to produce for the market, and it also created price inflation. This, in turn, gave an added push to business, for merchants and investors are eager to buy goods and properties when they see that prices are moving upward.

The overseas trade brought an abrupt shift in the geographical distribution of prosperity and power. Venice, Florence, Genoa, and the smaller Italian cities had long enjoyed a strategic position between the Near East and northern Europe. Italy had sparked the revival of trade in the eleventh century and had nurtured the growth of early capitalism. But after the Portuguese reached the sources of oriental commerce in the sixteenth century, the Mediterranean routes dwindled in importance, for the countries of western Europe, facing upon the Atlantic, now had the advantage of geographical position. Venice, the queen of the Adriatic, fell into decline.

Antwerp, Amsterdam, and London were to emerge, in turn, as the leading financial centers of expanding world commerce. These cities had the first organized "money markets" in which large private and government loans were floated. Exchange houses arose there for trade and speculation in commodities, currencies, bonds, and stocks. Stocks began to appear in the seventeenth century with the creation of joint-stock companies, the forerunners of the modern corporation, which made possible the raising of large sums of capital for long-term investment. Though limited at first to commercial ventures, joint-stock companies were later formed in the mining and manufacturing industries.

The triumph of capitalism was assured by the acceleration of trade and production. The wealth of Europe mounted steadily, and the variety and quantity of goods increased with every day. Commodities and habits hitherto unknown in Europe were introduced from both Asia and America. New foods added nourishment and novelty to European diets, notably potatoes, Indian corn, tomatoes, citrus fruits, chocolate, coffee, and peanuts. Chinaware, oriental furnishings, and exotic works of art began to appear in the homes of the privileged classes. The taste for luxuries had been whetted by medieval commerce, and the well-to-do could now indulge it to the full.

The significant fact is that after 1500 the world became virtually the treasure house of the West. Europe, whose people constituted a tiny fraction of humanity, was in a position to appropriate and exploit vast areas of the globe. In no other period of history has a major cultural group enjoyed so favorable a ratio between its population and available resources. Although the Europeans were to squander this advantage on endless wars, it served to elevate their standard of living and their sense of power.

This success in winning the riches of the world had a profound effect on the outlook and psychology of Western men. By corroborating the usefulness of curiosity, daring, and ruthlessness, it enhanced the value they placed on these traits. It intensified materialism by making more widespread the enjoyment of wealth and the prospect of acquiring it. It broadened the intellectual horizons of Europeans to some degree, but it contributed little to their respect for non-Western ideas and institutions. On the contrary, their startling successes in conquering oceans and continents fortified their optimism and strengthened their faith in their own superiority.

Most important of all, the overseas penetrations triggered the expansion of European civilization into a *worldwide* civilization. For the first time in history, a civilization was to leap every barrier of race and geography and spread its influence around the globe. Some areas, of course, would be touched only superficially, but European values and ideas would become familiar almost everywhere. And within the emerging world of associated cultures, the West would continue to serve as the chief carrier, catalyst, and transformer of ideas and institutions.

THE NEW POLITICS

Intimately bound up with economic evolution and expansion were new developments in the patterns of government. The feudal system, with its divisions into small, loosely related political units, gave way to larger units of centralized power. Had it not been for this trend, well under way in the fifteenth century, overseas exploration and settlement could not have been adequately supported. The successes of Spain and Portugal in the New World rested in part on their new political strength. As the monarchs of France and England consolidated their positions, they too began to press their claims overseas. Political power thus promoted expansion, capitalism, and wealth; wealth, in turn, strengthened the hands of the rulers. The new politics and the new economy reinforced each other.

Absolutism in practice: Italy

Italy did not achieve national statehood until the nineteenth century, but it was in the Italian city-states that the practice and theory of strong government developed in the early modern period. The Italian city-states also pioneered in the practice of diplomacy and in the development of the law that was to become the foundation for international relations.

One reason for the belated unification of Italy was the long struggle that took place between the popes and the Holy Roman emperors. Each party wanted to win overlordship of the Italian peninsula and was willing to sacrifice the country and its people to gain that end. The region under the direct rule of the popes had derived from the Donation of Pepin (p. 154), which had granted the papacy a substantial portion of Italy. With Rome as its capital, the States of the Church cut across the peninsula, dividing it in two (fig. 6-2). Lesser states were to rise and fall in Italy, and the Holy Roman emperors were often preoccupied north of the Alps. But until near the close of the nineteenth century the pontiffs of the Roman Church proved to be unrelenting foes of Italian unity.

Reinforcing the popes' opposition to unification were Italian particularism and factionalism, fierce and persistent forces deeply rooted in history. Like the ancient Greeks, the Italians identified strongly with the city of their region, rather than with any broader territorial unit. The city was near and familiar; it was worthy of reverence and sacrifice. Dante, for example, was more a Florentine than an Italian. As a result of this attitude, Italy had emerged from the Middle Ages as a collection of rival city-states struggling among

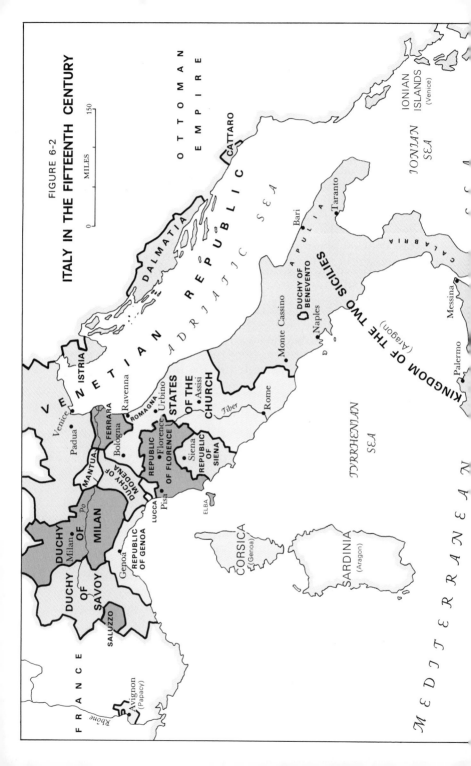

FIGURE 6-2

ITALY IN THE FIFTEENTH CENTURY

MILES

0   150

themselves for survival and mastery. By the middle of the fifteenth century, the stronger ones had expanded their boundaries, absorbing their weaker neighbors. A kind of "balance of power" developed among the five leading states: Milan, Florence, the States of the Church, Naples, and Venice.

During these turbulent years significant changes occurred in the internal politics of the Italian cities. By the end of the thirteenth century, most of the cities had won autonomy from the feudal nobility and had emerged as independent republics. Their citizens, however, proved incapable of stable self-government. The usual source of trouble was the rivalry of factions: the bankers and capitalists, rising rapidly in wealth, tried to wrest political control from the more numerous petty merchants, shopkeepers, and artisans. At the same time, wealthy families competed for special advantage.

Out of the struggle, which was marked by corruption and violence, political "strong men" had emerged during the fourteenth century. Sometimes they were invited to assume power by one or another of the factions looking for an alternative to chaos; sometimes they invited themselves. In the main they supported, and were supported by, the bankers and capitalists. The rest of the citizens submitted (except for occasional plots and uprisings), for they too preferred stability and order to the turbulence of freedom.

The new rulers, generally known as "despots," had been schooled in the arena of Italian politics. Men of few illusions, they trusted no one, yielded nothing, and resorted to any means to advance their interests. They put power first. In the past, weak governments had given rise to rebellion and disorder; the despots used an iron hand to restore peace and economic well-being and relied on hired soldiers to preserve their power. Since there was no citizen militia to speak of during this period, professional warriors became the final arbiters in conflicts within and between cities.

The soldiers were organized in armed bands (mostly cavalry) led by enterprising captains (condottieri). The condottieri, in the spirit of the times, were a special sort of "merchant"—their merchandise was military service. With no sentimental attachments, they generally sold their services to the highest bidder. (The bankers usually made the best offers.) On occasion they turned down all bids and seized power for themselves. These hardened and wily adventurers, thirstier for money than for blood, remained an uncertain force in the politics of Italy.

One of the most famous was Francesco Sforza, who made himself ruler of Milan in 1450. Assuming the title of "duke," which a preceding despot had purchased from the Holy Roman emperor, he governed from his moated *castello* (fortress-palace). Under the shrewd policies of Sforza and his heirs, Milan enjoyed a half-century of peace and prosperity. In the fashion of the times, the despot patronized the arts and attracted scholars to his city.

The city of Florence, though it had experienced numerous upheavals and short-lived tyrannies, remained a republic. In 1434 authority settled in the hands of Cosimo de' Medici, scion of a wealthy banking family. He and his successors held no political office, but through persuasion, manipulation, bribery, and force they controlled the machinery of government. The Medici advanced their own financial interests and the interests of their faction and treated opposing factions harshly. Despite their methods, they enjoyed the support of the citizens, for they put an end to riot and confusion in the city. The most illustrious member of the family, Lorenzo the Magnificent, was a man of extraordinary ability and taste. Under his rule, in the latter part of the fifteenth century, Florence became the cultural center of Italy.

The States of the Church belonged to the popes, but the pattern of despotism there was barely distinguishable from that in the rest of the country. The popes hired condottieri to reduce subject cities to obedience, engaged in wars and alliances, and used their office to further the wealth and rank of their families. The Borgia pope, Alexander VI, was notorious for his faithlessness and debauchery; Julius II had a fondness for waging war; and the Medici Leo X was an elegant connoisseur of the arts. Such qualities were hardly those of Peter the fisherman, but they were typical of the secular despots of the new era.

South of Rome, the development of commerce had been interrupted by successive military conquests. The Byzantines and Moslems had invaded this area (including Sicily), and the Normans had established a feudal state there in the eleventh century. French and Spanish claimants had fought over the territory during the thirteenth and fourteenth centuries, and at last, in 1435, the larger portion of it (the kingdom of Naples) was taken by Alfonso of Aragon, who already held Sicily. His joint realm, called the Kingdom of the Two Sicilies, was equal in area to all the rest of Italy (FIG. 6-2). Though the south Italian countryside was agrarian and backward, under Alfonso's "benevolent" despotism cultural life flourished in the capital at Naples.

The only major city to escape the trend toward despotism was Venice, whose government had been stable since the beginning of the fourteenth century. A small group of rich merchants managed to keep political control over the city and saw to it that the rest of the citizens were excluded from participation. The constitution of Venice, the envy of her less fortunate rivals, provided that the city be governed by councils and committees elected from and by the merchant oligarchy. The titular head of state was a doge (duke), who was chosen for life by the patrician families. Though the doge was treated with deference, he had no independent authority.

The theory of absolutism: Machiavelli

Fifteenth-century Italy was throbbing with individualism—in commerce, in learning, in the arts. And yet in politics there was a pronounced tendency, as we have seen, to curb individual freedom. The citizens of the city-states were proud and competitive men who by no means relished submitting themselves to absolute authority. But their long experience with factional rivalries and political instability had been disheartening. And so one city after another had accepted the rule of a despot. This submission to political authority did not check individualism in other spheres, however; Italy's "age of despots" was also the age of her greatest artistic flowering.

In the judgment of many Italians, their whole nation would benefit from a unified, absolute government. Despotic rule had put down internal dissension in Milan and Florence, for example, but in the relations between city and city, anarchy still reigned. If a despot could bring all of Italy under his rule, these wasteful conflicts would cease. After 1500 the argument for unity grew stronger. The French and Spanish monarchs found that they could sweep into the peninsula and easily subdue the divided cities, which were protected only by corrupt mercenaries. The invaders, with their loyal, well-equipped armies, kept Italy in turmoil for a century.

The most articulate spokesman for Italian unification and political absolutism was a Florentine, Niccolo Machiavelli, a one-time diplomat and a close observer of Italian affairs. He set down his basic views in a kind of manual, which he intended as a guide for the despot who would one day liberate Italy. *The Prince,* written in 1513, was dedicated to the Medici rulers of Florence.

Machiavelli's book marks a sharp turning in Western political thought. Medieval philosophers had seen government as one aspect of God's administration of human affairs: the Church and its officers direct man toward *spiritual* salvation, which is eternal; the state looks after his physical well-being, which is *temporal.* Yet both branches of authority are subject to divine law.

Thomas Aquinas had discussed this matter in his *Summa Theologica.* He reasoned that temporal power is invested by God in the people as a whole, who delegate it to suitable persons. The state, then, whether monarchical, aristocratic, or democratic, is not a power in itself. It derives its authority from God (through the people), and it must exercise that power for Christian purposes and in a Christian manner. To be sure, medieval practice often seemed to contradict this doctrine, but deviations were explained away as the result of human frailty or error.

Machiavelli met the doctrine head on, repudiated it, and stated formally the "modern" view of politics and the state. He felt no compunction about breaking away from traditional Christian precepts. He blamed the papacy for keeping Italy divided and felt that Christian teachings, in general, did not contribute to good citizenship. In his commentary on the ancient Roman Republic (*Discourses*), Machiavelli observed that the pagans had encouraged civic pride and service, whereas the early Christians had urged men to detach themselves from public affairs.

The state, he thought, does not rest on any supernatural sanction. It provides its own justification, and it operates according to rules that have grown out of the "facts" of human nature. He thereby removed politics from Christian ideology and placed it on a purely secular level. As we noted earlier in this chapter, economic life had already become secularized, and literature, art, and science were soon to follow. This trend toward the secularization of life heralded the arrival of a new epoch.

Machiavelli's view of government won general acceptance in European thought and practice. Largely through his influence the word "state" came into use to designate a sovereign political entity. And the evolution of European states from the sixteenth century onward moved in the direction suggested by Machiavelli. The state was to become the central force of modern times, a law unto itself, subjecting both institutions and individuals to its will.

Means, as well as ends, were a matter of concern to Machiavelli. As he saw it in *The Prince,* the central problem of politics is how to achieve and maintain a strong state. Much depends on the character of the citizens. He admired the Romans of the ancient republic and the self-governing Swiss of his own day, but he concluded that a republican form of government could prosper only where the citizens exhibited genuine civic virtue. This he found lacking in sixteenth-century Italy. And, in giving advice to his ideal despot, he wrote in the context of his own time and place. His book was not a blueprint for utopia; it was a manual for action.

His advice to rulers is geared, therefore, to a particular view of human nature. The Italians of his day were men of exaggerated defects and exaggerated virtues. Machiavelli regarded them as corrupt beyond correction (except, possibly, by a strong prince). He wrote that they were, in general, "ungrateful, voluble, fakers, anxious to avoid danger, and covetous of gain; they offer you their blood, their goods, their life, and their children, when the necessity is remote; but when it approaches, they revolt."

With citizens of such character, how was a state to be founded and preserved? Machiavelli advised that a ruler first turn his attention to military strength. The prince, he believed, must devote himself to the training and discipline of his troops and must keep himself fit to lead them. He must practice maneuvers and study the decisive battles of the past; it was thus that Caesar had learned from Alexander. Machiavelli had only contempt for the condottieri and their hirelings, as they had proved ruinous to Italy and incapable of defending the country from invasion. He advised the prince to build an army of citizens, drawn from a reserve of qualified men under a system of compulsory military training, for their interests would be bound up with his own. Machiavelli thus introduced to modern Europe the ideas of universal conscription and the nation in arms.

Military strength is not enough in itself, however. For the prince must be both "a lion and a fox." The lion, Machiavelli explained, cannot protect himself from traps, and the fox cannot defend himself from wolves. A ruler, in other words, must have both arms and cunning. Machiavelli noted that the most successful princes of his time were masters of guile. They made agreements to their advantage, only to break them when the advantage passed. He asserted that the ruler should hold himself above any norm of conduct, Christian or otherwise—that the only proper measure for judging the behavior of a prince is power. Whatever strengthens the state is right, and whatever weakens it is wrong; for power is the end, and the *end justifies the means.*

Machiavelli cautioned the prince never to reveal his true motives and methods, for it is useful to appear to be what one is not. Though the prince must stand ready, when necessary, to act "against faith, against charity, against humanity, and against religion," he must always *seem* to possess those qualities. Machiavelli summarized his advice to the aspiring despot as follows:

> Let a prince therefore aim at conquering and maintaining the state, and the means will always be judged honorable and praised by everyone. For the vulgar is always taken in by appearances and the issue of the event; and the world consists only of the vulgar, and the few who are not vulgar are isolated when the many have a rallying point in the prince.

Building the national monarchies:
France and England

The rising monarchs of Spain, France, and England were cut to the Machiavellian pattern. Their efforts to build state power were aided, in each country, by emerging national sentiment. In Spain, the spirit of patriotism had been ignited during the fierce struggle to expel the Moslems. When the kingdoms of Castile and Aragon, which had led the fight, were linked through marriage in 1469, the way was open for a unified Spain. Though the Portuguese remained independent, the rest of the people of Iberia welcomed the consolidation of territories once ruled by the Moslems. With popular backing, the young King Ferdinand broke the independence of the feudal lords, who had taken over most of the lands from the defeated enemy. He also reformed the Spanish Church, gaining the right to name its bishops. So vigorous were the centralizing efforts of Ferdinand (and his queen, Isabella) that the foundations of royal absolutism were completed by the close of his reign (1516).

In France the nobles were more firmly rooted, and the challenge to the monarchy was correspondingly greater. France was also the richest and most populous kingdom of Europe, with some twelve million inhabitants. As France became increasingly unified, she would move irresistibly to the forefront of European power and culture. As early as the twelfth century, local and regional sentiments had begun to yield to attachment to the broader community. Even the feudal barons of the *Song of Roland,* in their moment of truth, had called out to "fairest *France.*"

The most powerful stimulant to French national feeling was the Hundred Years' War (1338–1453), an intermittent struggle with the English that arose out of conflicting feudal claims. William of Normandy, after conquering England in 1066, had left his heirs holdings in both France and England. Through marriage and inheritance, other provinces of France (Aquitaine and Gascony) were later acquired by the English crown. These provinces, however, were held as fiefs, subject nominally to the overlordship of the French monarchs. In the thirteenth century King Philip Augustus of France declared the fiefs forfeit and incorporated most of them into his royal domain. He was motivated in part by a desire to extend his own power and in part by a growing sense of national identity among the French. Medieval fiefs had generally been granted and held without reference to nationality, but Philip now resented English control over *French* soil.

In the fourteenth century the English leaders, stronger than they had been earlier, decided to recover the lost fiefs. Their king, Edward III, laid claim to the throne of France as well. (The succession was in doubt, and Edward was himself the grandson of a French king.) And so the long campaigns began. By 1420 the English had triumphed, and most of France north of the Loire was ceded to Henry V, whom the French forces accepted as heir to their throne.

This humiliation at the hands of foreigners provoked a surprising reaction among the French people, who traditionally had been indifferent toward feudal struggles. They found an inspiring leader in a peasant girl called Joan of Arc, who in 1429 persuaded Charles, the disinherited son of the French king, to march to Reims, the ancient crowning place of French monarchs. Claiming divine guidance, Joan herself took command of a small military force and vowed to drive the English from the soil of France. The young prince, responding to Joan's appeal, was crowned in Reims Cathedral as Charles VII and went on to lead his armies to victory over the English (1453). Joan did not live to see that day, however. Soon after the coronation she fell into the hands of the English, who tried her as a witch and burned her at the stake. The martyred Joan has been revered for centuries as the glorious symbol of French patriotism.

The Hundred Years' War was frightfully destructive to France and interrupted the growth of royal authority. But when it was over the French monarchs were able to proceed more rapidly than before with the work of political centralization. The nobles, great and small, had been reduced in number and power, and a new spirit of national consciousness had spread through the land. The majority of the people, especially the bourgeoisie, now looked to the king for security and economic well-being. Charles VII and his son, Louis XI, completed the building of a strong national state.

In their struggle with the feudal nobility, the kings of France were able to take advantage of dramatic new developments in the techniques of waging war. During the Middle Ages, mounted knights had been virtually invincible in battle. As we have mentioned, the Frankish kings had shared their lands and their power with the warrior class in their efforts to build up a strong cavalry force. So long as the monarchy depended on the services of these nobles, neither their independence nor their lands could be taken away from them. But during the fourteenth and fifteenth centuries new weapons came into use: first the longbow and the crossbow (which could penetrate the armor of mounted knights) and then gunpowder and cannon (which could penetrate their walled castles). The noble cavalrymen were reduced to auxiliaries, and battles were now fought mainly by foot soldiers supported by artillery. Once the feudal warriors had become obsolete, Charles could build and maintain a standing army (mostly infantry) that was more than a match for his aristocratic opponents. He also subjected his soldiers to strict military discipline, something that had been lacking in feudal military units. Charles' new army became a prototype for other European rulers.

To maintain a standing army required more revenue than the monarch had ever received through ordinary feudal dues, but Charles succeeded in raising this revenue. In preparing for his final thrust against the English, he summoned the Estates-General of France in 1439. This body, which represented the three estates (classes) of France, had the sole prerogative to authorize general taxes. In a burst of patriotic fervor, the Estates-General approved Charles' national army and authorized a permanent tax for its support. This tax was called the *taille* (cut); it was a kind of income tax levied on all persons in the realm. With this substantial new revenue, supplemented by income from his own estates, Charles could now afford to act independently of the nobles. He proceeded by intrigue, threats of force, and marriage alliances to bring the great fiefs back into the royal domain. He permitted the lesser nobles, if they were cooperative, to remain on their ancestral estates and to keep their inherited titles. But he eliminated feudal functionaries from the government and replaced them with royal administrators recruited from the nobility.

Charles' son, Louis XI, pursued his father's methods and more than doubled the size of the royal domain. His final victory was to win back the duchy of Burgundy, which had long been a powerful autonomous state even though it was nominally subject to the French crown. Its last independent duke, Charles the Bold, had tried to expand his dominions into a major state between France and Germany. But his plans had miscarried, and when he died without a male heir Louis took over the duchy (1477).

In their contest with the refractory nobles, the kings of France enjoyed the support of the middle class. The merchants and capitalists had much to gain from a secure national market, and they despised the pretensions and arrogance of the aristocracy. Wealthy individuals rendered financial aid to the monarchs. (Jacques Coeur, it will be recalled, was fiscal minister for Charles VII and financed his later military campaigns.) And the burgeoning towns became firm allies of the king.

The success of the monarchy in consolidating the realm transformed the role of the nobility. The nobles had no choice but to submit to the new regime. By the end of the fifteenth century, most of them had adjusted to their altered condition and had begun to seek lucrative positions as military or civil officers of the king. They abandoned their notions of independence and consoled themselves with the privileges and favors of the court. The monarch, for his part, now had at his disposal the services of an elite class.

The Estates-General lingered on, meeting from time to time at the request of the crown. It might have developed into a constitutional body of importance, as did Parliament in England, but class and sectional rivalries, coupled with skillful manipulation by the monarchy, prevented this from happening. The Estates-General never became a serious challenge to royal authority, and it was to be swept into the dustbin of history in 1789.

Nothing now inhibited the king's control over secular matters. But absolute power, to be absolute, must embrace ecclesiastical matters as well. While taming the nobility, Charles did not overlook the clergy. In some respects the spiritual lords were more formidable than the lay aristocracy. The archbishops, bishops, and abbots held vast properties in France and had a pervasive influence over the people. The members of the hierarchy generally supported the king in his efforts to centralize authority and end feudal warfare. They were jealous, however, of their own prerogatives, and they wavered in their loyalty between king and pope.

After the secular ambitions of the papacy collapsed at the end of the thirteenth century (p. 191), the French clergy had tended to act independently of Rome. Although the French bishops and abbots had no thought of subverting traditional ecclesiastical doctrines and institutions, they resented papal interference in local administrative affairs. The popes, however, continued to insist on the right to fill important ecclesiastical offices, a privilege that brought them handsome fees. They also siphoned off a substantial proportion of church revenues to Rome.

As national feeling grew in France, there was mounting sentiment for a legally autonomous "Gallican" Church. In 1438 the clergy, with Charles' approval, formally declared its administrative independence of the Pope at the Council of Bourges. The decree limited papal interference and forbade payments and appeals to Rome. This move gave clear control of the Gallican Church to the French hierarchy, under royal protection. Louis XI revoked the decree, however, and his successor, Francis I, struck a bargain with the pope that extended the influence of the crown over the Church. In a treaty with the pope (the Concordat of 1516), Francis secured the right to appoint French bishops and abbots. In return for this right, the papacy was to receive the first year's income of ecclesiastical officeholders in France. The pope thereby gained additional revenue and the alliance of a powerful monarch; the king, outflanking his own clergy, brought the Church within his grip.

The rise of despotic monarchies contributed to the general ascendancy of secular forces in Europe. During the Middle Ages, when governments were weak and decentralized, the popes had aspired to supremacy over them. Having failed then, their chance had slipped away forever. Rulers of the new states were waxing in power and sought to exclude every sort of external influence; they became increasingly hostile to a *universal* Church, which could not be entirely subject to their control.

The despots were also good Machiavellians, however. They had themselves crowned with ecclesiastical pomp and declared their zeal for a unified Christendom. But behind these ceremonial demonstrations they nourished their real interests and intentions. Thus, Francis, the "Most Christian King" of France, allied himself with the infidel Turks against Charles, "His Most Catholic Majesty of Spain." Henry VIII of England, whom popes had dubbed "Most Christian King" and "Defender of the Faith," denounced the papacy in 1534 and proclaimed himself the supreme head of the Church of England.

Before Henry VIII ascended the throne, England, like France, had been forged into a strong monarchical state. The Hundred Years' War had had an effect on England quite different from its effect on France. Though it had strengthened the national feeling of the English, it had weakened the position of the monarch. For one thing, it had permitted the nobles to build up large bands of armed men, who subsequently became their personal retainers. Moreover, in order to raise the substantial sums of money needed for the expeditions to France, the kings of England had been obliged to make concessions to Parliament.

The origins of Parliament go back to 1295. In that year Edward I, seeking to enlarge the base of his support in the country, summoned representatives from the shires (counties) and boroughs (towns) to meet with his feudal council of barons. During the next century Edward's successors convened Parliament frequently in their quest for additional funds to carry on the war in France. Parliament evolved into two chambers: the House of Lords and the House of Commons. In the former sat the great barons and ecclesiastics of the country—lords who held fiefs and offices directly from the crown. In the latter sat representatives of the landed gentry (knights and squires) and of certain towns. The Lords were the dominant branch for several centuries, but the Commons would ultimately have the upper hand.

Since the king was obliged to turn to Parliament for approval of new revenues, its members took advantage of the situation to gain privileges and redress of grievances. It will be recalled that the Estates-General, the corresponding body in France, authorized a royal income tax without demanding concessions from the monarch. Parliament did not agree so readily to the desires of the monarch and kept a firm hold on the purse strings.

Its control over lawmaking and general administration came only slowly, however. By 1399 Parliament had won the right to determine the line of succession to the throne. It chose the Lancaster house, and the monarchs of that line (who reigned from 1399 to 1461) worked closely with Parliament. At the close of the Hundred Years' War, however, England was overtaken by a series of calamities. Confidence in the crown was shattered by the defeat in France, and the nobles proceeded to slaughter one another in a civil struggle called the Wars of the Roses. When Henry VII, of the Tudor family, at last emerged victorious in 1485, the strength of the nobles had been broken, and the nation was yearning for peace and unity.

Henry restored law and order and put an end to private feuding. Aware of the value of the bourgeoisie to the nation, he supported measures to protect home industries and commerce from foreign competition and, by means of treaties, extended markets abroad. As the influence of the nobility declined, that of the middle class rose. And the English middle class, like the French, rallied to the service of the king as its position improved.

The sixteenth century, the century of Henry VIII and Elizabeth I, was an era of despotic power in England. Parliament, however, unlike the Estates-General, did not sink into oblivion. In fact, in the century to follow, it was to replace royal absolutism with parliamentary government.

The eclipse of the universal empire: Germany

Elsewhere in Europe strong central government did not come for centuries. Neither Germany nor Italy became a unified state until 1870. The reasons for this contrast with the rest of western Europe are many and complex, but the main one is the long conflict between the Holy Roman emperors and the popes during the Middle Ages. The emperors, distracted by their campaigns in Italy, failed to give sufficient attention to building a solid political foundation in Germany. Over and over again they made concessions of authority north of the Alps in order to win support for their expeditions to the south. As a result, the German princes became so entrenched and so independent that they could not later be reduced to obedience. Another reason was that the emperors did not identify strongly with any national group. Traditionally they were German, but the office was elective and theoretically open to any European candidate. Further, so long as the emperors asserted *universal* claims, they could not build a viable *national* state.

As a consequence, while Spain, France, and England were growing into strong centralized powers, Germany lingered on as a patchwork of hundreds of fiefs. It was a pleasant and prosperous country (except for the interminable quarrels) but politically archaic. There were landed nobles with a bewildering array of ranks and titles, affluent dignitaries governing free cities under imperial charters, and powerful ecclesiastical lords. The ranking princes of the empire had won the status of permanent "electors" as the result of an imperial decree of 1356 (known as the Golden Bull). Three of the electors were ecclesiastical: the archbishops of Cologne, Mainz, and Trier. Four were lay: the Count Palatine of the Rhine, the Duke of Saxony, the Margrave of Brandenburg, and the king of Bohemia. When an emperor died, these seven men met to choose his successor. This was often an occasion for protracted haggling and bargaining; for the imperial office, though its power was on the wane, remained the political position of highest prestige in the West.

Dynastic considerations, more than concern for national sentiment, guided the politics of central Europe. The family that played the dynastic game most skillfully was the Habsburg, whose influence on the Continent endured for centuries. Rudolf of Habsburg, a south German prince, had been elected Holy Roman emperor in 1273. The main reason for his being chosen was that he was a minor figure who could be counted on not to create trouble for the independent-minded barons and bishops. And in fact he took his imperial responsibilities lightly, choosing to concentrate on expanding his family holdings. In a struggle with a defiant vassal (Ottocar of Bohemia), Rudolf won the duchy of Austria and surrounding territories. He assigned these lands to his sons as imperial fiefs, and Austria thus became the base of the family properties.

The Habsburgs' aggrandizement caused apprehension among the electors, who, when Rudolf died, chose an imperial successor from another, less affluent family. For nearly two centuries the Habsburgs were then passed over, but in 1438 another member of the family was named emperor. Thereafter, until the dissolution of the Holy Roman Empire in 1806, the Habsburgs managed to keep the office in their possession, meanwhile extending their wealth and power by means of carefully arranged marriages.

The family holdings reached their greatest extent when they

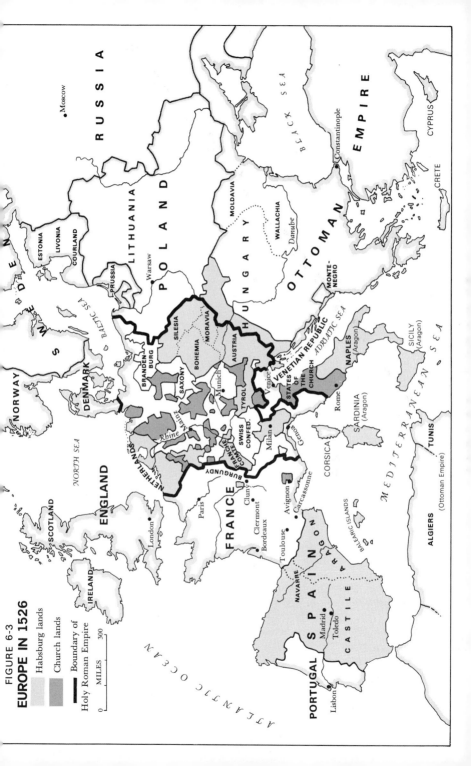

FIGURE 6-3
EUROPE IN 1526

Habsburg lands

Church lands

Boundary of
Holy Roman Empire

MILES   300

0

passed to the young man who was to become Emperor Charles V. His inheritance embraced the ancestral Danubian lands, Luxembourg and the Netherlands, Spain, Sardinia, and Naples and Sicily. When he secured the imperial title in 1519 (by buying the votes of the electors), he added to his family domains the overlordship of Germany and northern Italy. This constituted the greatest aggregation of territory under the control of one man since the rule of Charlemagne (FIG. 6-3).

But the aggregation existed largely on paper. Charles' amorphous empire was a hodgepodge of territories, like those of the Middle Ages. The emperor encountered an endless series of political, military, and personal frustrations, and he at last retired to a monastery in 1556. Before abdicating, Charles divided the Habsburg properties into a western and an eastern portion, but each of these was destined to crumble. The future lay with the rising national states and their despotic monarchs.

The Renaissance: Upsurge of Humanism

7

The political and social changes that swept over Europe after the end of the Middle Ages were accompanied by fresh ideas about the nature of man and his place in the universe. To continue our examination of the transition from medieval to modern times (1400–1650), we will now look at the mind and spirit of Western man as expressed in the world view, literature, and art of the era and then, in the next chapter, round out the picture by viewing the concurrent reformation of the Church.

THE RENAISSANCE VIEW OF MAN

So arresting were the emerging ideas about man that some observers felt civilization itself was being "reborn." In fact, some historians later used the word "Renaissance" (rebirth) to describe the era as a whole. Modern scholars, however, tend to restrict the use of that term to the revival of interest in classical literature, art, and values. Thus limited, the Renaissance was but one aspect of the transition to modern times; its central core was an upsurge of humanism.

The revival of interest in the classical world

Humanism can be generally defined as a view that puts man (*humanus*) at the center of things and stresses man's creative, rational, and aesthetic powers. This view is at least as old as the Greeks and Romans. Although the word "humanism" was not used in the classical age, Cicero referred to *humanitas* as the quality of mind and spirit that distinguishes human beings from mere animals. That quality, he thought, is best nurtured and expressed through literature (including history, philosophy, and oratory). Renaissance scholars, following Cicero's lead, identified the study of classical literature (both Greek and Latin) with humanism, and they applied the term "humanist" exclusively to classical scholars.

We should note that interest in the classics had not altogether disappeared during the Middle Ages. By the twelfth century many schoolmen had made themselves familiar with works of antiquity, and Dante and Chaucer drew heavily from the Latin poets. Before the fourteenth century, however, there had been little to equal the enthusiasm of Renaissance scholars for classical writings. It was in those works that they caught their "new" vision of man. Moved by their discovery, they searched eagerly for ancient documents and developed a veneration for the literary culture of antiquity. Their rising enthusiasm was not caused primarily by dramatic finds of material; it resulted, rather, from a quickening change in the European state of mind.

The medieval intellect, steeped in a God-centered, otherworldly view of the universe, had been largely closed to the naturalistic, pagan spirit. The schoolmen fingered classical manuscripts through thick gloves, so to speak; their religious inhibitions kept them from a truly sympathetic contact. But with the waning of the Middle Ages the ideals of asceticism and Christian poverty receded before advancing worldliness. The theological approach to life—with its sterile handmaiden, scholasticism—occasioned growing distaste.

This distaste was most pronounced in the developing towns. The bourgeoisie, finding medieval ideals increasingly uncongenial, were looking for standards closer to their hearts. They discovered them in the culture of the ancient world, which they could glimpse through the classics. There they saw a wealthy elite, not unlike themselves, devoted to secular pursuits. They hoped, by imitating the best in ancient thought and behavior, to recreate classical standards in their own times. They failed to bring back the past, or even to imitate it faithfully, but their efforts to do so helped shape modern values.

To Renaissance humanists the classical view of man was the proper view. They, like the ancients, saw man as an aspiring egoist whose interests were centered in the here and now. If the humanists seldom renounced religion, they tended to regard it as a formality or as an extension of man's knowledge and power.

The good life, they thought, is the life that is pleasing to man's senses, intellect, and aesthetic faculties. Everything human is inherently good, though it needs to be cultivated and proportioned. The greatest wrong, to most Renaissance humanists, was negation, the absence or repression of spontaneous human expression. Their attitude was doubtless a reaction against the long centuries of ascetic idealism and inhibitions of caste. Each man, they asserted, should be free and proud. He should strive for mastery of all the worthy arts, because his ultimate value would be measured not in humility but in talent and accomplishments. The successful man, as the Italian humanists put it, possesses *virtù* (manliness, virtuosity). His mind is so filled with thoughts of this world that he has little chance (or reason) to contemplate the next.

The ideas of the humanists plainly ran counter to many Christian teachings. They seemed to reject the dogma of Original Sin and natural depravity. They elevated the status of man and suggested that he could perform mighty deeds without divine assistance. And yet (especially in the North) a Christian humanism developed alongside this secular humanism. Some pious scholars shared the growing enthusiasm for the classics and ancient languages. They shared, too, the heightened appreciation of man's capabilities, especially his powers of reason and creativity. But they insisted that all human powers were a gift of God—and that this life, though rewarding, fell short of the glory of heaven.

The new scholarship: Petrarch, Boccaccio

It is no accident that the Renaissance arose in Italy (as did capitalism and absolutism). The forces of social change were farthest advanced there; the development and spread of urban life, for example, had progressed further in Italy than they had in northern Europe. There was another reason, however, independent of those forces: the growing consciousness of *nationality*. While this consciousness did not produce a unified state in Italy (as it did in Spain and France), it caused Italians to embrace their past more warmly than ever before. As Italian humanists delved into the Latin classics, they began to dream of restoring the grandeur of ancient Rome. Their countrymen had never forgotten those glories, for their land was strewn with eloquent reminders. The humanist "road back to Rome" was shortest in Italy, and it was traveled by patriotic pilgrims.

Francesco Petrarca (Petrarch), who is regarded as the founder of Renaissance humanism, was born in 1304 of an exiled Florentine family. Urged by his bourgeois father to study law, he came upon the works of Cicero in the course of his reading. His admiration for Cicero's philosophy and style led to a passion for all the classics, and when his father died Petrarch gave up his study of law and turned to a life of scholarship.

It was Petrarch who first undertook the collection of ancient manuscripts. He persuaded others to join him in a search through monastic and cathedral libraries that took him all over Italy and into France and Germany as well. Among his finds were some lost orations and letters of his beloved Cicero. He employed copyists in his home and built up an admirable collection of pagan documents and books. His private library, the first of its kind, became a model for scholars and educated gentlemen.

Petrarch's enthusiasm was contagious. Following his example, many sons of the well-to-do took up the search and began to build their own libraries. Wealthy patrons became interested and by the fifteenth century had founded such famous libraries as the Laurentian in Florence, St. Mark's in Venice, and the Vatican in Rome.

Petrarch set the style as a scholar as well as a collector. Though he led a busy life and spent much of his time in cities and at the courts of aristocrats, he expressed a love of solitude and the peace of nature. But this was a different solitude from that prescribed by the ascetic ideal; it was closer to the ancient Roman model. He spent his private hours, not meditating and praying, but studying literature, for isolation without books, he declared, was "exile, prison, and torture." He alternated writing with reading, in the fashion of the modern scholar. What a glory it was, thought Petrarch, "to read what our forerunners have written and to write what later generations may wish to read . . . ."

He preferred to write in classical Latin, for he had only contempt for the vernacular tongues and the corrupted Latin of the Middle Ages. Many of his writings were in the form of epics, dialogues, and letters slavishly patterned after the style of Cicero and Vergil. He is hardly remembered for these efforts. More successful were his love poems (sonnets), which he deigned to write in Italian. He addressed most of them to Laura, a beautiful young matron whom he loved and idealized. A record of his most intimate thoughts upon seeing her and thinking of her, these sonnets to Laura became a model for many generations of romantic poets.

Petrarch lived only a generation after Dante, the supreme poet of the high Middle Ages, but in these two figures we can see the shift from medieval to modern times. Though Dante knew the classics, philosophically he remained a medieval man. Petrarch knew them better and more warmly embraced pagan values. His irrepressible pursuit of fame culminated in his being crowned with the laurel wreath in 1341 and thus becoming the first poet laureate of modern times. Originally the laurel wreath had been bestowed as a prize on victors in the Pythian games honoring Apollo; later it was conferred on outstanding public officials and artists of Greece. The Romans had adopted the custom, and it was revived late in the Middle Ages. Dante, significantly, refused the offer of a laurel crown, but Petrarch was pleased to strengthen the link with antiquity and to bask in the "immortal glory" of the prize. After a formal examination before King Robert of Naples, he was crowned in a classic ceremony in Rome.

One of Petrarch's followers, Giovanni Boccaccio, was among the first Westerners of modern times to study the Greek language. The son of a Florentine banker, Boccaccio grew bored with the humdrum of credits and debits and set out to learn Greek. Once he had done so, he instructed his tutor to translate Homer into Latin and thus helped to introduce his contemporaries to their first reading of the *Iliad* and the *Odyssey*. Like Petrarch, Boccaccio searched far and wide for ancient manuscripts. One of his prized discoveries was a work of the historian Tacitus, which he uncovered in the monastery library at Monte Cassino. When he first saw the neglected condition of the archives there, he broke into tears.

Though Boccaccio was nominally a Christian, his own writings are markedly pagan in spirit. *Fiammetta,* which is sometimes called the first psychological novel of the West, makes no reference to the world of Christian faith and morals. When the heroine is torn by the question of whether to give herself to her lover, she is answered, not by the Virgin, but by Venus. The characters in the *Decameron,* Boccaccio's best-known work, are similarly un-Christian in outlook and behavior. The tales in this collection, which Boccaccio borrowed from various countries of Europe and the Near East, feature sensual escapades, deceits, and ingenious revenges.

Now other Italian scholars began to study Greek, aided by refugee scholars from Constantinople, who had begun to flee the city before its fall to the Turks in 1453. These scholars offered Italians instruction in Greek, Hebrew, and Arabic. Moreover, they brought thousands of manuscripts from Byzantium for safekeeping in the libraries of Florence, Venice, and Rome. By 1400 nearly all the Greek authors had been recovered by the West and translated into Latin and Italian. This was an intellectual transfusion of singular importance. While medieval scholars had become familiar, through Arabic, with many of the works of Aristotle and the Hellenistic scientists, they had no direct knowledge of Greek literature. It was the humanists who restored to our Western heritage such luminous names as Homer, Herodotus, Thucydides, Aeschylus, Sophocles, Euripides, and Plato.

Humanistic education and the "gentleman"

This new body of knowledge challenged the traditional patterns of education and thought. In conjunction with new social forces and the rising secular spirit, it precipitated a revolution in European schooling. Medieval education had been almost exclusively by and for the clergy; even the rudiments of reading and writing had been considered essential mainly for priests and monks. Professional training in law and medicine had been introduced into Italian universities during the Middle Ages and thence had spread to the North. But for medieval Europe as a whole, theology remained the focus of higher learning. The trivium and quadrivium centered on Scriptural texts, the writings of the Church Fathers, and the logic of Aristotle.

The Italian humanists made up the first substantial body of *secular* scholars in Europe. Most of them were sons of the middle class or the nobility and had no connection with the clergy. Nor had they any use for the arid scholasticism that still dominated education; in fact, they regarded it as irrelevant to the new society. In Greek and Roman literature they saw the means of providing students with a truly liberal education.

It was fairly easy to eliminate scholasticism from the Italian universities, for it had never taken deep root there. The new learning was introduced in its place by humanist professors of rhetoric whose lectures drew enthusiastic students from all over Europe. The humanists were not welcomed at most northern universities, however. In the scholastic strongholds of Paris, Cologne, and Heidelberg, the faculties looked with disdain upon the unfamiliar Greek studies. Some Oxford masters condemned them as "dangerous and damnable." Not until the end of the sixteenth century did Greek and Latin literature—the "classics"—supersede scholastic philosophy as the foundation of liberal education in the North.

Humanism reached into elementary as well as higher education. The private schools that arose in the towns to serve sons of the well-to-do were secular in tone and concentrated on Latin and Greek studies. But they aimed at more than the cultivation of the intellect. The schoolmasters saw in Pericles and Cicero models to inspire young men to lives of fruitful citizenship. The Greeks and Romans had lived in cities and had enjoyed a sophisticated social life, so it was their example, rather than that of the monks and saints, that seemed pertinent to the new society. Literature and moral edification were balanced by regular training in music and athletics. The Greek ideal of the well-rounded man, mentally and physically fit, was at the heart of humanistic education.

During the sixteenth century this pattern of education spread from Italy throughout western Europe. The private secular school largely replaced monastic and cathedral schools in the education of Europe's leaders. Like the classical model on which it was based and the privileged society it served, the private school was aristocratic in purpose and style. (Its most famous descendants are the public schools of England, notably Eton, Harrow, and Winchester.)

Although the curriculum of Greek and Latin studies often became rigid and sterile, it helped shape a new type of personality: the "gentleman." As an ideal, the gentleman now supplanted the medieval knight and the ascetic holy man. Whether of noble or bourgeois background, the ideal gentleman was a man of refinement and self-control. Just as chivalry had tamed the warriors of the Middle Ages, humanistic education taught the new landowners and capitalists the ways of urbane, sophisticated living.

The true gentleman possessed a disciplined mind, graceful manners, and impeccable taste. For those impatient to acquire such virtues, manuals of proper behavior began to appear; the most influential of them, *The Courtier,* was published in 1528 by an Italian nobleman, Baldassare Castiglione. As Machiavelli counseled rulers on the art of statecraft, Castiglione advised young aristocrats on education and manners. The gentleman was to flourish as an admired type in the West for some three hundred years. (In the twentieth century he seems to have been replaced by the "expert" and the "organization man.")

Philosophy: the vogue of neo-Platonism

Though the recovery of Greek learning revolutionized European education, its influence on philosophy was comparatively modest. Its main effect was to put Plato in Aristotle's place as the foremost philosopher. Aristotle had ruled over the medieval universities because his methods of logic proved so useful to the scholastic dialecticians. His works were better known than Plato's, and his moderation appealed to men like Aquinas. But the humanists found his writings formidable and devoid of literary appeal. As the complete dialogues of his teacher, Plato, became available during the fifteenth century, the humanists were struck by their charming style. Here was philosophy that was at the same time literature, and literature that was philosophy. Plato became the new master.

Florence was the leading city for Platonic studies. Cosimo de' Medici, a scholarly despot who was keenly interested in Plato, founded the Platonic Academy there about 1450. The Academy served as a center for the translation of Platonic and neo-Platonic writings and for discussions of Plato's philosophy. Just as Christians of the Middle Ages had striven to reconcile Aristotle with their religious doctrines, so the Italian humanists tried to reconcile Plato with Christian thought.

The Academy was more of an intellectual club than a school. It consisted of only a few select scholars, subsidized by the Medici, and their circle of friends. Their talk and writings were of a rarefied sort that meant little to ordinary people. And yet the influence of the Academy was substantial—especially in art and literature. Almost every artist of the later Renaissance was touched by Platonism, and some, like Botticelli and Michelangelo, became deeply absorbed in it. Through them the Platonic influence passed on to later generations—ultimately to such nineteenth-century writers as Goethe and Wordsworth.

Marsilio Ficino was the shining light of the Academy. Chosen by Cosimo at an early age, he was carefully educated and then installed in a villa in the hills near Florence. From that time until his death, he devoted himself to translating Plato's writings and expounding his doctrines. He presided over polite seminars at the villa and corresponded with notables all over Europe, striving to demonstrate that the Platonic teachings could be correlated with Christianity. For those who could not accept religion on the basis of dogma, he suggested that Plato could open another way.

Pico della Mirandola, a disciple of Ficino, went beyond his master and attempted a synthesis of *all* learning, Eastern and Western. This prodigy of the age knew Arabic and Hebrew as well as Greek and Latin, and he studied Jewish, Babylonian, and Persian records. He refused to ignore any source of truth merely because it was not labeled Christian. He felt that by employing all the records and resources of contemporary scholarship he had achieved a comprehension of man and the universe transcending that of scholastic philosophy. Actually, Pico added little to the view of the world shared by his contemporaries. He did, however, emphasize man's freedom and capacity for learning, and by breaking through the bounds of medieval theology he opened a door to the study of *comparative* religion and philosophy.

Like the other members of Cosimo's circle, Pico embraced the neo-Platonic view of creation and existence, which held that by some accident of prehistory man had become separated from his divine home of pure spirit. Though the soul (spirit) had fallen prisoner to matter (the body), it struggled for liberation and a return to God. This view corresponded to the Christian doctrine of the Fall and man's longing for salvation.

An interesting corollary to this concept had a profound effect on the arts. The feeling for natural beauty, said the Platonists, derived from the soul's remembrance of the divine beauty of heaven. Hence aesthetic expression and enjoyment took on a religious cast. Finally, the Platonists related the emotion of physical love to the higher urge that moves man toward his divine source (Platonic love). These teachings elevated the arts, even when they dealt with secular subjects, to a lofty plane. According to the Florentine intellectuals, art stimulates sensitivity to beauty and love, and love brings the individual closer to his ultimate goal of spiritual reunion with God.

The widespread acceptance of this doctrine helps to explain the Renaissance "cult of beauty" and the toleration by devout Christians of a frankly sensual art. It reinforced, ironically, the naturalistic thrust of humanism and the rising secular taste of the times. Thus by the fifteenth century most painters and sculptors had turned their back on the otherworldly style of art and had plunged eagerly, sometimes ecstatically, into realistic representation.

The critical spirit and the beginnings of empiricism

Beyond its influence on aesthetics, the Platonic revival had only a limited effect on European philosophy. Of greater importance were the methods of scholarship that were introduced by the humanists, although the philosophical implications of those methods were not fully recognized at the time. Petrarch, Boccaccio, and the others who collected classical manuscripts sought to create, from documentary remnants, accurate texts of the ancient authors. Their intention was simply to reassemble old learning, but their method of doing so opened new paths of creative scholarship. Their textual analysis led to a more critical attitude toward the written word and a greater attention to observed facts, while the downfall of scholasticism, with its system of truth based on authority and reason, freed scholars to seek truth by empirical investigation.

The Roman humanist Lorenzo Valla was a pioneer of modern textual criticism. An expert on Latin style, he abhorred the slovenliness of medieval writers and was bold enough to attack even the Latin of the Vulgate (the Bible as translated by Jerome). He also challenged the popular belief that the Apostles' Creed, the traditional confession of Christian beliefs, had actually been composed by the apostles. His most shocking discovery, in 1440, was that the Donation of Constantine (p. 154) was a forgery. This document, which served as a basis for papal claims to secular supremacy over the West, had stood unchallenged for centuries.

Using his new tools of scholarship, Valla demonstrated that the language of the Donation could not have been that of the fourth century but was more likely that of the eighth or ninth. Going beyond grammatical analysis, he pointed out (as a careful scholar should) that the manuscript contained terminology of a period later than the date it was supposedly written. In the words of the Donation, the Emperor Constantine confers vast rights upon Pope Sylvester *before* leaving Rome to build a new capital at Byzantium. Yet he declares that the pope shall have supremacy over all patriarchs, including the one at "Constantinople." How could this be, asked Valla, when at that time Constantinople was not yet a patriarchate or a city, nor yet known as Constantinople? So conclusive was Valla's criticism that the Donation was recognized by all as a fraud.

It is indicative of the spirit of the age that the reigning popes took no punitive action against the iconoclastic Valla. On the contrary, they solicited the scholar's services. He was secretary to King Alfonso of Naples when he published his exposé of the forgery. Afterward, Pope Nicholas V hired him away and brought him back to Rome to translate Thucydides. Nicholas, a patron of humanism, put scholarship above orthodoxy and founded the Vatican Library as a depository for ancient manuscripts.

Valla was bold, critical, and independent, but as a practicing humanist he limited his attention to what could be learned from the literature of the past. Niccolo Machiavelli went further. He wanted to see what could be learned through direct observation of the world around him. As we noted in the preceding chapter, Machiavelli's work was a watershed in the history of political thought. We have seen how his view of the state contrasted with that of Thomas Aquinas, but even greater was the contrast in the methodology of the two scholars. Aquinas, the scholastic philosopher, had sought truth mainly by reasoning from authority (deduction). Machiavelli sought it by generalizing from collected data (induction). He drew his facts from recorded history *and* personal experience. Though he was without the system, precision, and control that characterize modern social scientists, Machiavelli was clearly moving toward a new conception of knowledge and its verification.

He was not alone in his pursuit. Leonardo da Vinci, a fellow citizen of Florence, grew discontented with bookish learning and determined to see things for himself. Though Leonardo is best known for his great paintings, his love of art was matched by a desire to unlock the secrets of nature. In order to improve his skill in drawing human and animal bodies, he dissected cadavers and set down his on-the-spot sketches and comments in notebooks. He found dissection difficult and distasteful, but he insisted that observation was the only means to true knowledge. He also experimented with mechanics and drew up plans for ingenious practical inventions. A man of his times, Leonardo both typified Italian humanism and foreshadowed the age of empiricism.

Christian humanism: Erasmus

So far we have spoken only about humanism in Italy, without tracing its spread beyond the Alps. During the fifteenth century a number of northern scholars journeyed to the Italian centers of learning and carried home with them the seeds of the new scholarship. But the soil of the northern countries produced a different variety of humanism—the pagan flavor, so strong in Italy, was missing.

When humanism came to the North, the intellectual leaders there were imbued with Christian piety and were eager to reform the Church. Dissatisfied with the sterility of scholasticism, they seized on the rediscovered classics of antiquity. Unlike the urbane scholars of Italy, however, they were not looking for models of sophisticated secular life. Rather, they sought guides to a purer religion and identified in the ancient writings those ideals that would encourage spiritual reform.

Humanism as represented by Pico and his circle was an outlook based upon many faiths and systems. In the North, however, it emerged in a strictly Christian framework. The northern leaders believed that the example of disciplined and balanced living found in Cicero and the Stoics could well be incorporated into a sensible Christian life. Above all, they sought to use the new linguistic and textual skills developed by the Italian humanists as a means of establishing a "truer" Bible. They hoped with these tools to cut away the "false growths" of medieval religious practice and to restore thereby a "pure" Christianity.

There were many devout and vigorous humanists in the North, especially in Germany and England. But the greatest of them all was Desiderius Erasmus. Born in Rotterdam in 1466, he was a cosmopolitan scholar, at home in many lands. His learning and scholarship won him acclaim throughout Europe as the "prince of humanists."

Erasmus, an illegitimate child, had little knowledge of his family background. His father, of middle-class origin, was a priest at the time of Erasmus' birth. Little is known of his mother. The boy was sent off to school at a tender age, so he lacked the comfortable bourgeois background characteristic of the Italian humanists. His school was supervised by an order of devout laymen, the Brethren of the Common Life. The Brethren, who were dedicated to a pious, mystical Christianity, taught that individual lives should be modeled

on the example of Jesus. While subjecting themselves to rigid spiritual discipline, they emphasized the ideals of service and love. Erasmus was deeply touched by this early influence, and he adopted the
"philosophy of Christ" as his lifetime ideal.

After Erasmus left school he was persuaded to enter an Augustinian monastery, where he received little formal instruction but was
free to read as he pleased in the classics, both Christian and pagan.
At the age of thirty, aspiring to wider and deeper scholarship, he
secured a release from his monastic vows. He went to the University
of Paris, where he completed a course in theology. From then on he
devoted his life to research and writing, visiting the major centers of
learning. Though he was ordained a priest, Erasmus never served a
parish. He lived, sometimes meagerly, on the support of patrons and
on income from his books.

In the classics Erasmus found models of behavior that could well
be followed by genuine Christians. Socrates, Plato, and Cicero were
worthy, he thought, of a place among the saints. But he read the
ancient writings as a firm believer, and he was persuaded that a
man's studies should serve to strengthen his faith, not undermine it.
He mastered Greek, for example, not in order to find a truer Homer
or Thucydides, but to discover a truer Christ.

Erasmus used his scholarly skills to prepare a more accurate version of the New Testament. Like Valla, he felt certain that the
Vulgate, venerable though it was, contained accumulated errors.
After collecting a number of the earliest available New Testament
manuscripts in the original Greek, he produced a fresh version based
on a comparison of the texts. He finished this work in 1516, along
with his own Latin translation and commentary, hoping that these
efforts would lead to a clearer understanding of the message of Christ
and to translations in the vernacular tongues. He was one of the first
to believe that the Bible should be read by the people themselves.

Erasmus also prepared improved texts of the writings of the Greek
and Latin Church Fathers as well as revised editions of pagan authors. He carried on an extensive correspondence with fellow scholars, and the influence of his ideas, expressed in lucid, polished Latin,
was extraordinary. He was feared by suspicious conservatives among
the clergy but was welcomed everywhere by admiring humanists.
Unlike many of them, however, Erasmus was not content to bask in
the adulation of an elite; he wanted to make his thoughts available
to all literate people.

He published a great many works, often satirical, through which
he tried to call attention to the need for reform. He wished to
cleanse the Church and society of selfishness, cruelty, hypocrisy,

pride, and ignorance—and to replace them with tolerance, honesty, wisdom, service, and love. Repelled by violence and disorder, he hoped that appeals to *reason* would bring about peaceful change. But he sometimes doubted if reform could be achieved peacefully. His most widely read and most entertaining work, the *Praise of Folly,* is filled with ironic skepticism. Paraded before the reader are the devotees of Folly, a character that personified for her creator the ascendant elements in human nature.

Erasmus has Folly sing her own praises: "Without me the world cannot exist for a moment. For is not all that is done among mortals, full of folly; is it not performed by fools and for fools?" Men find happiness in lightheartedness and lightheadedness—in spontaneous, animal-like behavior. They delight in deceiving and in being deceived. Society rejects the man who pulls off the masks in the comedy of life; the "well-adjusted" person adapts to the game, mixes with people, and indulges their delusions.

At one point Folly observes that sober reason puts an unwelcome damper on natural impulses. The preacher's congregation yawns when he discusses a serious matter but perks up when he tells some silly anecdote. And man's behavior is governed less by reason than by his emotions. According to Folly, anger holds the citadel of the breast, and lust rules "a broad empire lower down."

Erasmus spoke of the foolishness of war and war-makers and the peculiar conceits of individuals and nations, but he reserved most of his barbs for ecclesiastics. The Church, he thought, had grown unduly fond of Folly and had drifted far from the precepts of Christ. He criticized the hair-splitting theologians, the vain and ignorant monks, and the power-loving prelates. He also ridiculed the excesses of the popular cult of relics, the invocation of saints, and the purchase of indulgences (pp. 187–88).

The *Praise of Folly* appeared in 1509. Although Erasmus spoke with tongue in cheek, contemporary events tended to confirm what he said. The literate men and women who read his books were impressed and amused, but neither they, nor the Church, nor society at large was much changed by his sharp words. His criticism of ecclesiastics, it is true, helped to bring on the Reformation, but it did so in a manner repugnant to him. What he hoped for was a peaceful reform of Christianity as a whole. He wanted a purified Church, not a divided one.

Erasmus was just as critical of the passions and violence aroused by Martin Luther as he was of the errors of the popes. This made him appear in the eyes of Protestant reformers as a moral and physical coward who would not stand up for his convictions. Actually,

Erasmus stood fast upon his convictions that Christian unity should be maintained, reason pursued, and rebellion shunned.

THE REVOLUTION IN ART

The spirit of humanism could not be confined to literature and philosophy and, as early as the fourteenth century, burst forth splendidly in the visual arts. It appeared first, as one might suspect, in Italy—in Florence, the capital of humanism, which remained for some two hundred years the leading center of European art. Few places on earth, over a comparable period, can match that city's production of painting, sculpture, and architecture. The miracle of Florence is often likened to the miracle of ancient Athens.

The pioneer of naturalism: Giotto

In point of time, Giotto di Bondone was a medieval man, a contemporary of Dante. But he was, in fact, a transitional figure who foreshadowed the modern spirit. In his own day (the early fourteenth century), Giotto was hailed by the citizens of Florence for having wrought a revolution in artistic technique.

In 1305 he was commissioned to paint, on the inside walls of the Arena Chapel in Padua, the New Testament story of Mary and Christ. This was an enormous task, calling for some thirty-five separate scenes. Giotto worked in a common technique known as fresco. Each morning a small area of the wall, covering the space the artist planned to finish that day, was plastered fresh (fresco). The paint, consisting of powdered pigment mixed with water, was applied to the wet plaster and became part of the wall surface when it dried. Because of its scale and quality, the Arena composition was a milestone in European painting. Succeeding artists would be commissioned to follow Giotto's grand example, their efforts culminating in Michelangelo's stupendous work on the ceiling of the Sistine Chapel.

Giotto's paintings reveal the new techniques that were just beginning to emerge. He was not satisfied with the flat look of medieval altar panels and illuminated manuscripts. These served well enough to tell a story, and they were often superb in color and design. But Giotto wanted to recreate an actual scene, to give the viewer the feeling of being an eyewitness. In order to accomplish this, he sought to produce the illusion of depth (perspective) on a plane surface and to make the figures look solid and real. This he did by skillful use of light and shadow, by modeling the faces and figures, and by foreshortening the hands and feet. He also gave careful attention to

FIGURE 7-1. GIOTTO. *Lamentation*. Arena Chapel, Padua. (Alinari.)

the composition of each scene, arranging individual figures and groups in the fashion of a tableau. Finally, he suggested the emotional state of his subjects through the sensitive rendering of facial expression and gesture (FIG. 7-1).

Later painters were to go beyond Giotto in the development of naturalism. But he was the pioneer, and his contemporaries recognized him as such. His tomb, in the cathedral of Florence, bears this epitaph: "Lo, I am he by whom dead painting was restored to life, to whose right hand all was possible, by whom art became one with nature . . . ." Giotto's influence touched every artist of the Renaissance and extended beyond mere technique. He established himself as a model to aspire to: the artist as hero, a famous individual. Medieval painters and sculptors had rarely identified

FIGURE 7-2. Cathedral of Florence. (Alinari.)

themselves, but Giotto, in the new spirit of the times, signed his paintings and amiably accepted popular acclaim. He demonstrated, further, the humanist ideal of the many-sided genius, the person of *virtù*. A man of many skills, he became the official architect of Florence and designed the graceful campanile of the cathedral (*duomo*). Rising some four hundred feet above the piazza, it overlooks his beloved city and the valley of the Arno (FIG. 7-2).

New artistic techniques: Brunelleschi, Van Eyck

Giotto bequeathed a technical challenge to his successors: How could painting be made *more* naturalistic? It was not until a century later that a significant advance in this direction was made. Again it was a Florentine, Filippo Brunelleschi, who pointed the way. A master of sculpture and architecture as well as painting, he designed the stunning Gothic dome to complement Giotto's tower. But he shared with his fellow humanists a distaste for medieval forms and set out, after a close study of Roman ruins, to create a new style. Adapting classical forms to the needs of his day, he achieved a distinctive, charming style that marked many of the churches and palaces of Florence (FIGS. 7-3 and 7-4) and set the tone of Renaissance architecture.

Brunelleschi made a unique contribution to drawing and painting through his study of *perspective*. He was the first to lay down the mathematical rules governing the reduction in size of represented objects as they recede into the background of a picture. The ancient Romans, and Giotto, had been skillful in suggesting depth and dis-

FIGURE 7-3. BRUNELLESCHI.
Santo Spirito, interior.
(Alinari.)

FIGURE 7-4. MICHELOZZO.
Medici-Riccardi Palace.
(Alinari.)

FIGURE 7-5. MASACCIO. *Trinity with the Virgin, St. John, and Donors.*
Soprintendenza alle Galerie, Florence. (Anderson-Art Reference Bureau.)

tance, but they did not have at their command precise mathematical
laws. Brunelleschi formulated them by means of observation and
measurement, the "new tools" of Renaissance learning.

One of the first painters to make use of the laws of perspective
was Masaccio, a younger contemporary of Brunelleschi. In 1427 he
finished a fresco in the church of Santa Maria Novella (Florence). It
was a startling innovation. The subject matter was conventional
enough: the Holy Trinity, with the Virgin, St. John, and the donors
of the painting (FIG. 7-5). What was striking about it was that it
presented the illusion of a Roman tunnel vault reaching back
through the church wall. The placement and handling of the figures
enhanced the sense of depth. Perspective drawing is familiar to us
today, but its unveiling in the fifteenth century provoked amaze-

ment. As the viewer stood back from the wall, he must have gasped at what seemed to be a group of sculptured figures placed within a classical, three-dimensioned chapel.

In northern Europe, artists were taking a different approach to naturalism. Among the most influential was Jan van Eyck, a painter of Flanders (in the Low Countries). The Flemish towns, it will be recalled, were thriving in the fifteenth century as centers of the expanding international trade. Well-to-do patrons began to appear there, as in Italy, and Flemish art set the style for northern Europe during most of the Renaissance period.

Van Eyck, less radical than Masaccio, observed most of the traditions of late Gothic painting. But he carried to an unprecedented degree the recording of precise detail. He worked, for example, on the famed "Ghent Altarpiece" (completed in 1432), a complex, folding triptych containing twelve wooden panels, with the *Sacrifice of the Mystic Lamb* as its central subject. The painting was conventional in style, but Van Eyck was far more exact in his rendering than any previous painter had been.

Van Eyck's realism was distinct from that of the Italians. Giotto and Masaccio sought to give their figures roundness and solidity, set against a receding background, whereas Van Eyck treated objects in the background of his paintings with the same meticulous attention that he gave to those in the foreground. His work has been described as both microscopic and telescopic. In the detail from one of his por-

FIGURE 7-6. JAN VAN EYCK. Detail from *Arnolfini and His Bride.* Courtesy of the Trustees of the National Gallery, London.

traits, *Arnolfini and His Bride* (FIG. 7-6), he seems to have counted every hair on the little dog, and he shows each one in a precise gradation of light and shadow.

In his efforts to achieve such effects, Van Eyck experimented with various media. He was among the first to develop and exploit oil paints. Before this time, painters had mixed powdered pigments with water (for frescoes) or with a white-of-egg liquid (called tempera). The latter gave fairly good results, but it dried out rather quickly. Van Eyck discovered that by mixing his pigments with linseed oil he could work more slowly and produce the special effects he desired. The quality and brilliance of his painting, as well as its accuracy, soon led most European artists to follow his lead.

The liberation of sculpture: Donatello

Sculpture, even more than painting, lends itself to the faithful reproduction of nature. The sculptor has no need to create an illusion of depth, for he is working in three dimensions. Yet medieval sculptors usually had to fit their figures into the narrow spaces assigned to them by architects and were therefore unable to realize the full potential of their art. Donatello, a contemporary of Masac-

FIGURE 7-7. DONATELLO. *Feast of Herod*. San Giovanni, Siena. (Brogi-Art Reference Bureau.)

cio and Brunelleschi, restored sculpture to an independent status and also stamped upon his art the character of naturalism and humanism.

Donatello made a careful study of the remains of Roman sculpture. Discarding the copybook methods of medieval workmen, he also began to work (as the Romans and Greeks had) from live models. One of his earliest statues, a marble *St. George* (1416), reveals the contrast between the new technique and that of the Middle Ages. The young warrior, standing by his shield, does not have the otherworldly look of most medieval figures: his feet are planted firmly on the ground; he looks straight ahead with an expression of readiness and resolution. The realistic appearance of this figure reflects Donatello's painstaking observation of the human body.

Donatello's fame spread swiftly from his native Florence. And just as Giotto had been called to Padua to paint the murals of the Arena Chapel, so Donatello was commissioned to work in one city after another. (The rival city-states of Italy competed with one another not only in arms and politics but in art as well.) Near the close of his life, Donatello spent some ten years in Padua, which was then part of the Venetian Republic. There he produced a monumental equestrian statue in bronze (*Gattamelata*). The man on horseback is a Venetian condottiere, with the astute, assured look of a caesar. The first equestrian statue to be made since Roman times, it was modeled after a monument to the Roman emperor Marcus Aurelius. That splendid work, the only one of its kind to survive from the ancient world, was discovered by humanists in the fifteenth century.

The *Gattemelata,* which still stands in the cathedral piazza, was Donatello's largest free-standing statue. He created smaller carvings and relief sculptures as well. His most striking relief is the *Feast of Herod,* a bronze panel for the baptismal font of Siena's cathedral (FIG. 7-7). In the Biblical scene depicted, King Herod is being presented with the head of John the Baptist. Herod had ordered John's execution reluctantly, at the urging of his stepdaughter Salome. Now he and his guests, seated at the banquet table, recoil in horror. Though Donatello's panel measures only about two feet on each side, it is rich in dramatic detail. Having learned the trick of perspective from his friend Brunelleschi, he created a wondrous illusion of depth. One can look through the rounded arches to Herod's musicians and beyond, through other archways, into the remote background.

Though less revolutionary, Lorenzo Ghiberti surpassed Donatello as a sculptor of reliefs. His fame rests on the gilded bronze doors

FIGURE 7-8. GHIBERTI. *Meeting of Solomon and the Queen of Sheba*. Baptistry, Florence. (Alinari.)

of the cathedral baptistery at Florence, on which he labored for nearly thirty years. Michelangelo later called them fit to stand as the "Gates of Paradise," and so they have been known ever since. They are divided into ten large panels, each presenting a scene from the Old Testament. One of the panels, the *Meeting of Solomon and the Queen of Sheba* (FIG. 7-8), exemplifies the artist's mastery of composition, perspective, and dramatic effect. The "Gates of Paradise" were hung in 1452, an event that may be regarded as the crossing point in Renaissance art between the period of revolution and the period of culmination.

Art triumphs over nature: Leonardo

The painters and sculptors of the late fifteenth and early sixteenth centuries were challenged by a task even greater than that of their predecessors. Masaccio, Van Eyck, and Donatello had shown the way to naturalistic representation—an impressive achievement, made possible by intensive study and technical innovation. But once naturalism had been established it revealed some inherent limitations. A literal rendering of subject matter did not necessarily result in harmonious composition. It did not always convey a message, mood, or emotion in the most effective way. Finally, if it was a perfect imitation of reality, it could not, as art, *transcend* nature.

Sandro Botticelli, a fifteenth-century Florentine, wanted to preserve the liveliness and realism typical of the work of the Renaissance pioneers, and yet he wanted to create an art that would be more beautiful than nature itself. This meant taking liberties with the actual appearance of things, subordinating literal fidelity to form and color—even injecting elements of mystery. One of his most successful efforts was the *Birth of Venus* (FIG. 7-9).

Botticelli was among the first painters to use figures from classical mythology in a major work. During the Middle Ages the Church, the chief patron of art, had forbidden the glorification of pagan traditions. The humanists admired antiquity, however, and during the neo-Platonic revival in Florence the Greek myths rivaled the Christian epic in popularity. In fact, Botticelli was commissioned by one of the Medici to paint the *Birth of Venus* for his private villa.

The work is full of color, movement, and grace. In the center, being wafted to shore on a seashell, stands the goddess of love. The picture is harmonious and unified, and it conveys the mystery of beauty that so intrigued the Florentine intellectuals. It will be recalled that these men associated love of beauty with man's desire for reunion with the divine. Venus, symbolically, was the fountain of beauty and love. Though Botticelli used a flesh-and-blood model, his Venus appears detached, unearthly. She represents a transcendent spirit—an *idealized* beauty.

FIGURE 7-9. BOTTICELLI. *Birth of Venus.* Uffizi Gallery, Florence. (Alinari.)

The cult of beauty encouraged patrons and artists alike to select pagan themes. Even when the myths were not completely understood, the humanists assumed that they contained occult wisdom. Under this cloak of intellectual respectability some artists went on to portray their subjects in a frankly sensual fashion. The Venetian painter Titian is a notable example. His *Venus of Urbino* (FIG. 7-10), which he painted in 1538, concentrates the viewer's attention on a recumbent, seductive nude. This is not the ethereal Venus of Botticelli but an enticing woman who seems aware of her naked loveliness and the eyes of the viewer. Titian's remarkable technique is revealed in the flesh tones and textures. His works were to serve as models for every painter of nudes from Rubens to Renoir.

The innovations in treatment and technique were, indeed, more significant than changes in subject matter. And the leading experimenter, both in art and nature, was Leonardo da Vinci, who fulfilled the humanist ideal of the "universal genius." His *Notebooks* demonstrate the astonishing breadth of his curiosity. He began his artistic training toward the end of the fifteenth century as an apprentice in a Florentine workshop, where he learned, under the guild system of supervision, the standard methods of observing and sketching models and objects. He studied the optics of perspective, the mixing of colors, and the techniques of metalwork. But when he left the shop of his master, Leonardo had only started his education. For he was less interested in the surface appearance of things than in what lay underneath, and so he undertook his ceaseless exploration of anatomy, physiology, and nature.

He left many of his projects unfinished. We have only a few of his major paintings, and some of these are in poor condition. In those we have, his genius is manifest. He resolved the difficulties of combining lifelike representation with artistic form and an element of mystery. By comparison, the mirror-like paintings of Van Eyck appear rigid and lacking in focus. In his use of light and shadow, Leonardo found that shading lends grace and softness to facial features and reduces stiffness of line. By blurring his contours, especially at the corners of the mouth and eyes, he provoked the imagination of the viewer. Hence, each time we look at his *Mona Lisa* (FIG. 7-11), her expression (and thought) seem to change.

Leonardo's most famous painting is the *Last Supper,* completed in 1497 (FIG. 7-12). This sacred subject had been treated countless times before. How could an artist do anything arresting or original with it? Most earlier paintings had shown Christ and his disciples quietly seated around the supper table in varying settings and modes of dress. Leonardo introduced drama and excitement. He

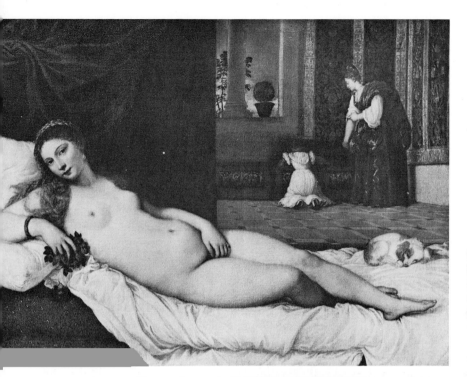

FIGURE 7-10. TITIAN. *Venus of Urbino*. Uffizi Gallery, Florence. (Alinari.)

FIGURE 7-11. LEONARDO DA VINCI. *Mona Lisa*. Louvre, Paris. (Anderson-Art Reference Bureau.)

chose the precise moment after the Lord had said, "One of you will betray me" (Matt. 26:21–22). While Christ sits calm at the center of the picture, waves of disbelief, amazement, and distress sweep to the right and left of him. Only Judas, among the disciples, is motionless. And even with the agitation and tension of the recorded instant, the painting forms a harmonious whole.

The artistic climax: Michelangelo

Though Leonardo was the most versatile of Renaissance figures (artist, musician, and scientist), he was overshadowed as an artist by Michelangelo Buonarroti. Leonardo observed and investigated nature as a whole; Michelangelo concentrated on anatomy, convinced that the inmost urges and sensitivities of man could best be expressed through the human figure.

Michelangelo preferred to represent the body in the three dimensions of sculpture, but he was destined to execute numerous commissions as a painter. In 1508, he was called to Rome from his native Florence by the pompous and militant Pope Julius II. The pontiff, desiring a monumental tomb for himself, had turned to Michelangelo, the best sculptor of his day, to execute it. Complications arose, however, and Julius asked Michelangelo to paint the ceiling of his private chapel instead. The chapel had been built by Pope Sixtus IV (hence the name Sistine), and its walls had been painted by an earlier generation of masters (including Botticelli). The ceiling vault, however, remained blank.

Michelangelo, disappointed when his sculpturing commission was

FIGURE 7-12. LEONARDO DA VINCI. *Last Supper.* Convent of Santa Maria della Grazia, Milan. (Alinari.)

FIGURE 7-13. MICHELANGELO. Detail from *The Creation of Adam*. Sistine Chapel, Vatican, Rome. (Alinari.)

deferred, accepted the new task with reluctance. But having once decided to undertake it he plunged into the work with his customary vigor. Some four years later the fresco was finished. It covers about ten thousand square feet and includes over three hundred figures. In conception, execution, and magnitude no other painting in history (by a single individual) has surpassed it.

In the Sistine Chapel painting, as in all his creations, Michelangelo expressed his deep philosophical concern about man. Tormented by a sense of sin, his own and that of the human race, he suffered from a feeling of personal frustration, of unfulfilled aspirations. His conviction that man struggles helplessly against destiny led him to a tragic view of life. He felt that man's spirit, which is of divine origin, desires to return to God but is held fast by the flesh and by the sins of the flesh. In the *Last Judgment,* which he painted late in life on the end wall of the Sistine Chapel, he portrayed a muscular and implacable Christ condemning crowds of sinners to the eternal fires of hell.

Michelangelo was profoundly influenced by the neo-Platonism of the Academy. In an effort to reconcile his Christian convictions with the teachings of the Platonists, he merged the two philosophies in his overall design for the chapel vault. The main feature, on the ceiling proper, is a series of nine panels depicting the Hebrew-Christian epics of the Creation and the Flood. (The Biblical story from Noah to Christ had already been painted on the lower walls.) Perhaps the most appealing of the panels is the *Creation of Adam* (FIG. *7-13*). The Father, borne by the heavenly host, is about to bring the inert Adam to life by the touch of his finger. Evident here is Michelangelo's capacity to suggest latent power, to infuse light and movement.

After finishing his backbreaking labor on the Sistine scaffolds, Michelangelo returned to his first love, sculpture. He began to carve, from solid blocks of marble, several figures for the projected tomb of Julius. The peculiar quality of his sculpture can be understood in part by his attitude toward the stone: before taking up his chisel,

FIGURE 7-14. MICHELANGELO. *David*. Accademia, Florence. (Alinari.)

he always visualized the human form within each block. He then proceeded, with furious energy, to "liberate" the form from the stone.

One of his finest works, carved some years earlier, expresses the spirit of athletic youth. His eighteen-foot-tall *David* (FIG. 7-14) was at first placed in the main piazza of Florence. A copy stands there today, but the original is housed in a Florentine museum. The *David* shows the influence of Greek sculpture on Michelangelo's work. Later creations, such as the figures for Julius' tomb, show the influence of neo-Platonism. In one of these, known as the *Dying Slave*, Michelangelo depicts a mature, powerful body falling into repose as death approaches, releasing the slave from life's futile struggle. Among Michelangelo's other sculptural works are a *Pietà* (the sorrowing Virgin mourning for the dead Christ) and a wrathful, monumental *Moses*.

Later in life, having won fame as a painter and a sculptor, Michelangelo turned his attention to architecture. Here too he was without peer. He continued the development of the distinctively Renaissance style that had been initiated by Brunelleschi. Much of his work was done in Rome, and the touch of his hand is revealed there in countless places: the Farnese Palace, the church of St. Mary of the Angels (which he converted from a great hall that had once been part of the Baths of Diocletian), and the Campidoglio (a piazza atop Capitoline Hill, enclosed by civic buildings).

His last masterpiece was the dome of St. Peter's. The new St. Peter's (there had been a series of churches on the same site) was conceived early in the sixteenth century by the tireless Julius II. He wished to erect, over the tomb of the first apostle, a structure that would surpass all others in Christendom. Several architects had a hand in the design, but in 1547 Michelangelo was put in charge. During the remaining years of his life he devoted most of his energies to planning the mighty basilica.

The floor plan was for a colossal square church laid out in the form of a Greek cross. A central dome was to be its crowning feature. Earlier schemes had called for a shallow dome modeled on that of the Pantheon. But Michelangelo wanted something loftier for the "capitol" of Christendom. Inspired by Brunelleschi's dome in Florence, he planned one even steeper and higher—one that would tower over every other building in the Eternal City.

Although he died before St. Peter's was completed, the dome was finished according to his designs. The square plan of the basilica, however, was altered into a conventional (Latin) cruciform plan (p. 192), which meant that a long nave had to be constructed. As

FIGURE 7-15. MICHELANGELO. St. Peter's. (Alinari.)

a result, the view of the dome from the front of the church is partially obscured. The view of St. Peter's from the rear (FIG. 7-15) shows the dome as it would have appeared from all sides had the original plan been carried out.

The magnificent dome, the largest in the world, has been copied by architects everywhere. Equal in diameter to the Pantheon, it rises three hundred feet higher. It stands as a splendid symbol of Christianity and a fitting monument to Michelangelo.

LITERATURE AND DRAMA

While the visual arts of the Renaissance reached their climax in Italy, the greatest accomplishments in literature appeared beyond the Alps. The genius of the north could not produce the equal of the best painting and sculpture of the south. It was superior, however, in the written word.

The invention of printing

The influence of scholars and writers was vastly extended by the invention of printing and the introduction of paper. During the Middle Ages literature had to be copied by hand on parchment (sheepskin). Books were therefore rare and expensive and could be afforded only by the wealthy. The art of making paper had originated in China before the birth of Christ. The Arabs, in the eighth century, had learned it from the Chinese and had carried it with them to their conquered lands. Cheaper than parchment, paper was coming into use in western Europe when John Gutenberg of Mainz began printing with movable metal type in 1447.

Printing by woodcut blocks had been known for centuries. A whole page of text and illustrations could be carved out of a single block, and the block could then be inked to print on paper. But this process was slow and wasteful, since each block could be used only for a single purpose. Gutenberg's invention of individual letters cast in metal meant that the characters could be arranged and rearranged as many times as desired. By drastically reducing costs, the new method of printing wrought a revolution in communication and education. By 1500 there were more than a thousand printers at work in Europe, and nearly ten million books had been printed.

The early printers aspired to match the artistic standards of medieval scribes, and most of these "cradle books" (incunabula) were of excellent quality in type, paper, and binding. As the reading public grew, however, and as price competition became more pressing, the general quality of printing declined. Still, the influence of the printed word was infinitely greater than it had ever been before. The invention of movable type made possible, ultimately, free public libraries, mass education, and cheap newspapers and magazines. Its immediate effect was to accelerate the spread of humanism by making the classics more readily available.

The libertarian humorist: Rabelais

Printing also brought a wider readership to humanist authors. Erasmus probably had more contemporary readers than any previous writer. In France the most popular author was François Rabelais, an enthusiastic humanist with a talent for satire and parody. Though his books were condemned by religious and civil authorities (the issue of censorship arose soon after the invention of printing), they had a warm appeal to readers. Rabelais was (and still is) a most popular author.

Like Erasmus, who was born a generation earlier, Rabelais knew the Church and the universities from the inside. Of middle-class family, he had entered a Franciscan monastery in order to become a scholar. But he was a rebel from the beginning; his absorption in the classics disturbed his superiors and led to trouble. He switched from one religious order to another, for a time wore the garb of a priest, studied at various universities, and later took up law and medicine. His career, like his writing, followed no visible plan. With a vast appetite for life and learning, he was the personification of a vigorous and spontaneous humanism.

Though Rabelais loved the classics and knew them intimately (especially the Roman), his own temperament was by no means classical. It was the content rather than the style of the classics that appealed to him. He wrote in colloquial French rather than classical Latin, and he detested all rules and regulations. Each man, he insisted, should follow his own inclinations. Rabelais thus represented a humanism that did not copy classical models (or any other) but stood as a purely individualistic philosophy. Rejecting the dogma of Original Sin (and most other dogmas), he stressed natural goodness; he held that most men, given freedom and proper education (in the classics), will pursue happy and fruitful lives.

This philosophy is central to Rabelais' great work, *Gargantua and Pantagruel*. The story, about two fictitious giant-kings, was published in several volumes over a period of years (beginning in 1538). Rabelais often used the giants, father and son, as spokesmen for his own views. He wrote the work primarily for amusement, because he believed that laughter (like thought) is a distinctively human function. However, in narrating the heroes' education and adventures, he voiced his opinions on the human traits and institutions of his time. In a tumble of words, erudite and playful, he mingled serious ideas with earthy anecdotes and jibes.

Monasticism was a prime target for Rabelais, as it was for most humanists. Its stress on self-denial, repression, and regimentation was to him inhumane and hateful. He had Gargantua endow a model institution that violates monastic practices in every conceivable way. At this "abbey of Thélème," with its fine libraries and recreational facilities, elegantly dressed men and women are free to do as they please. Monks, hypocrites, lawyers, and peddlers of gloom are explicitly barred from the abbey; only handsome, high-spirited people are admitted.

Rabelais disliked pretense and sham and extolled the natural instincts and abilities of free men. Rejecting the ascetic ideal, he expressed secular humanism in its most robust and optimistic form.

In a true sense, he anticipated the modern appetite for unlimited experience and knowledge.

The skeptical essayist: Montaigne

Michel de Montaigne, born a generation after Rabelais, lived through the same troubled times of religious struggle between Protestants and Catholics and shared Rabelais' fervent interest in the classics. But some critical difference of personality turned him toward quite another kind of humanism. His temperament was nearer that of Erasmus. Both men remained loyal to the Roman Catholic Church and both were dedicated scholars, but Montaigne was more secular-minded and detached than was Erasmus. He had no strong desire to reform society, and he was insensitive to what other people thought of him. (His *own* opinion was all that mattered.) The son of a landed family near Bordeaux, Montaigne received a superb education. His father held public office, traveled abroad, and believed in a humane upbringing for his children. When he died, Michel inherited the family estate and was able to retire at the age of thirty-eight to his library of a thousand books.

Privacy and leisure, which Montaigne treasured above all else, gave him an opportunity to read and reflect. He chose only those books that gave him pleasure—pleasure in the Epicurean sense (p. 75). These were the Latin authors (and some Greeks in translation), whom Montaigne considered superior in style and content to medieval or contemporary writers. From his reading, he developed a desire to mold his personal life according to classical norms and, like Petrarch, began to record his own thoughts and observations.

Out of this activity came the first two volumes of *Essays* (1580). Unlike Rabelais' books, these were models of lucid French prose. They were immediately popular, and Montaigne was encouraged to publish a third volume soon afterward. Altogether, he wrote more than a hundred essays on such topics as the emotions, superstition, customs, education, marriage, scholarship, and death. His usual manner was to begin with the opinions of authorities on the topic, inserting quotations from their works, and then to conclude with his own views. Frequently, he would present opposing answers to a question and then suggest a compromise solution—or, perhaps, no answer at all.

Montaigne's essays constituted a new form of literature. They were not treatises of the sort written by the ancients but simply *essais* (attempts). He did not commit himself to drawing conclusions or persuading his readers to accept his views but wrote, in large measure, for his own intellectual satisfaction. And since the essays were based on his own experiences and thoughts, they also represent a form of autobiography. The notion that every man of worth should pass on to posterity some record of his own life and ideas became widespread during the Renaissance. The ebullient Florentine artist, Benvenuto Cellini, was among those who accepted this idea; he dictated his engaging *Autobiography* in 1560. Gradually the essay and the memoir became standard literary forms, additional expressions of the individualism and self-confidence of a vigorous age.

In one of Montaigne's most notable essays on the subject of knowledge and reason (Vol. II, Essay 12), he revealed himself as a philosophical relativist and skeptic. He spoke of the limits of reason in man's efforts to comprehend the universe. Neither theology nor science can provide answers to the "big questions"; all knowledge is subject to uncertainty and doubt. The human mind, observed Montaigne, is erratic; and the senses, which are unreliable, often control the functioning of the mind. Beliefs, no matter how firmly held, cannot be regarded as constant, for they, too, have their seasons, their birth and death. Ethics are a matter of custom and religion a matter of geography.

Montaigne did not imply that men should not use their minds. On the contrary, he thought that every individual capable of reason should seek answers satisfactory to himself. The thinking man should never embrace the ready-made views of others, no matter how impressive their authority, but ought to entertain various theories, then choose for himself. And if he feels unable to make a choice, he should remain in doubt. The uncertain character of knowledge ought to teach us, above all, that dogmatism is unjustified—and that persecuting men for unorthodox beliefs is wrong.

Montaigne made his eloquent plea for tolerance in the midst of the frightful struggles between religious fanatics that raged through sixteenth-century France. He could see that war and homicide are often the outcomes of absolutistic thought and belief. Like Erasmus, Montaigne was a political conservative and opposed to violence; he felt that firm authority was indispensable to peace and order. Though he cherished independence of thought, he did not rebel against established institutions, hoping, rather, that those who held power would see the light, ultimately, of moderation and decency. In any event, he adhered to his personal philosophy—a blend of skepticism, Epicureanism, and Stoicism—and remained aloof from his fellowmen. In the quiet and security of his library, Montaigne could meditate on one of his favorite maxims: "Rejoice in your present life; all else is beyond you."

Rabelais and Montaigne were among the few writers on the Continent whose devotion to humanism was not disturbed by the religious upheavals that broke out around 1520. Another was Miguel de Cervantes, the greatest author of Spain. He began his masterpiece, *Don Quixote,* in 1605 as a satire on the tiresome tales of chivalry that were still being written (and read) in his native land. His hero is a caricature of the romantic knight; he imagines windmills to be evil giants and vainly tilts against them. While Don Quixote is a hopeless idealist, his squire, Sancho Panza, sees the world in simple-minded, down-to-earth terms. Cervantes succeeded in demolishing chivalric literature and revealed, through the Don's intriguing adventures, the Spain of his day. On the philosophical level, the contrasting universes of Panza and Quixote remind one of the relativity of truth that Montaigne had noted in his essays.

The master dramatist: Shakespeare

Humanism came late to England. It had hardly been established there by 1500, and it might even have vanished in the religious turmoil that erupted shortly thereafter. One of the casualties, indeed, was Sir Thomas More. A dedicated scholar and a friend of Erasmus, he wrote the visionary *Utopia,* in which he set down the characteristics of a truly rational society. But he later paid with his life for refusing to swear loyalty to the king as head of the Church of England (1535). Humanism and the secular spirit proved hardy, however, and attained their full expression in literature around 1600. The leading genius of this expression was William Shakespeare.

Shakespeare was not a classical scholar. He had "small Latin and less Greek," but he was familiar (in the original or in translation) with many of the ancient authors. Moreover, he was imbued with the *spirit* of humanism, which characterized the Elizabethan age (1550–1600). For England this was a period of rising national strength, bourgeois prosperity, and lusty living. Shakespeare's plays contain elements of the classical and the timeless, but they speak in the special accents of the Renaissance.

The roots of Elizabethan drama go back to the Romans and the Greeks, for during the Middle Ages there had been only religious pageants and the Passion and morality plays. But the classical revival of the fifteenth century stimulated the reenactment of Roman dramas at the courts of Italian rulers, and in time a new form of secular drama, based on the Roman model, came into being and spread across Europe.

Although the Italian playwrights adhered to the classical tradition of lengthy recitations, a chorus, and little action, the English introduced modifications to suit their national taste. They also began to build permanent theaters for dramatic performances; none had existed in medieval times. When Shakespeare arrived in London in 1590, both the new drama and the new manner of designing theaters were approaching maturity.

The Globe Theater of his day is a good example of the Elizabethan playhouse. Octagonal in shape, it faced inward on a large courtyard. The stage, or platform, occupied one side of the octagon and projected some ten feet into the yard, and there were three tiers of balconies, or covered boxes, ringing the open space. Those who could not afford boxes stood or sat in the yard below.

The stage itself lacked the scenery and equipment found in contemporary theaters. A curtained area in the rear could serve as a chamber or an inner room; when closed off, it became the backdrop for a setting on the main stage. The front of the platform often served as a street or passageway. Since there was no main curtain, the script had to provide action to clear the stage at the end of each scene.

A balcony directly above the stage could represent the window of a house, the deck of a ship, or the top of a castle wall, while trap doors in the floor and roof of the stage enabled witches and spirits to ascend or descend. Lighting was no problem, since this was an open-air theater and performances were given in the afternoon. Though much of the setting was left to the viewer's imagination, the Elizabethan theater proved remarkably flexible and enabled the actors to establish close contact with their audience. As in classical drama, all the roles were played by men or boys. (The stage was not considered a fit place for females.)

The dramas themselves still bore the mark of the classical tradition. The length of the plays, their division into acts, and the general conception of characters and themes derived from ancient comedy and tragedy. Greek plays were known in Elizabethan times only through their Roman versions, particularly those of Seneca, a Stoic writer of the first century A.D. Drawing from well-known Greek myths, Seneca had written gruesome dramas peopled by crudely drawn characters, ghosts, and phantoms and dealing with themes of betrayal, revenge, and madness.

Renaissance drama differed from ancient drama in significant ways, however. It was not associated with religious festivals, as Greek drama had been, and, though it often dealt with moral issues, its spirit was markedly secular. Supernatural touches were occasionally introduced (the audience expected them), but the plays were emphatically of "this world." Though Shakespeare himself was nominally a Christian, his dramas lack any doctrinaire Christian tone; in some of them there are even hints of religious skepticism and fatalism.

The range of Shakespeare's themes and locales is greater than that of classical dramatists. "All the world's a stage," declares one of his characters, speaking to an audience who had daily reports of remarkable exploits in newly discovered lands. Many other features of his work reflect the characteristic values and concerns of humanism. The urge to power, which lay at the root of Renaissance absolutism, is the central theme in many of his plays, and the rising sense of nationality, or patriotism, permeates his historical dramas. Shakespeare's deep interest in character and psychological subtleties relates to the Renaissance concern with individualism. Many of his passages reflect, too, the contemporary emphasis on materialism and sensuousness. Finally, he demonstrated the same concern for realism that motivated the humanist painters and sculptors.

Hamlet, one of Shakespeare's greatest tragedies, illustrates his dramatic methods. The story derives from a medieval chronicle, though Shakespeare probably based his work on a play written during the sixteenth century. *Hamlet* is a tragedy of revenge, a type of drama that was popular at the time. Shakespeare artfully endowed it with the elements of conflict, suspense, violence, and poetic imagery that his audience enjoyed. Since his public consisted chiefly of educated men and women, he was able to introduce moral and philosophical ideas into the course of the dramatic action.

As a character, Hamlet typifies the ideal "gentleman" of the new Europe. He also embodies the conflict between meditation and action that intrigued the intellectuals of the age. Hamlet knows that it is his duty to avenge his royal father, but he insists on using the humanistic tool of reason to guide his action. As he procrastinates a series of miserable deaths occurs. Shakespeare left it to his audience to decide whether reason should bow to custom, and whether man is the master of his destiny.

We know little about Shakespeare's life except that he prospered in London and retired to his native Stratford some years before his death (1616), but we do have the legacy of his works. No man had a surer feeling for the sense and sound of the English language. In addition to his poetry, he left some forty plays, among them several masterpieces. These make superb literature as well as fine theater; his collected writings have been referred to as the "English secular Bible." The Renaissance, which admired the individual genius, produced such a man in Shakespeare. Moreover, as his friend Ben Jonson observed, he was "not for an age, but for all time."

The Reformation:
Division and Reform in the Church

8

As with all major cultural movements, it is difficult to say precisely when the Renaissance began or when it ended. The influence of the classics on art and literature, so marked in the Renaissance, has continued with diminishing force into the twentieth century. Humanism, as a general point of view, has persisted, too, but by 1600 it was no longer a leading influence in European life. Other ideas (and systems)—capitalism, absolutism, and national self-consciousness—continued to grow in strength. And added to these in the sixteenth century was the explosive force of religious revolt and reform. The resulting division of the Church completed the dissolution of medieval civilization.

The bitter religious struggles that broke out in 1520 did not subside until about 1650. They so absorbed Europe's attention and energies that the years between came to be known as the era of religious reformation and religious wars. The Reformation was a complex phenomenon. The primary impulses behind it were, of course, religious, but religious matters were intimately bound up with political, social, and economic matters. And actually there were *two* concurrent reformations: the Protestant, which was carried out in defiance of papal authority, and the Roman Catholic, which had papal approval. The former led to separate Christian denominations, each with its own organization and doctrines; the latter was limited to the correction of "abuses" and to a reinvigoration of Catholic spiritual life.

BACKGROUND OF THE REFORMATION

In relation to the established church organization, the Protestant reformers were heretics who successfully defied the pope. Differences on matters of doctrine had arisen early in the life of the Church, but for many centuries ecclesiastical unity had been maintained in the West. (The Eastern, or Greek, Church went its separate way after the breakup of the Roman Empire; the "final" separation occurred in 1054). To preserve that unity, the hierarchy had exercised continuous vigilance and strong discipline. During the Middle Ages, thousands of heretics had been burned at the stake in the name of Christian purity and unity. How was it that the Protestant heretics survived where their predecessors had perished? One reason is that the late medieval Church had suffered a fateful deterioration.

Decay of the Church

During the thirteenth century the medieval Church had reached its zenith of power and influence. This was when the great cathedrals were built, when powerful reform orders were founded, and when scholastic philosophy achieved its greatest influence. Under Pope Innocent III the papal monarchy had dominated the secular rulers of Europe as well as the ecclesiastical hierarchy (p. 190). But the fourteenth and fifteenth centuries saw a steady fall in the condition of the Church, and by 1500 the organization had reached its nadir.

The fortunes of the Church as a whole were closely tied to those of the papacy. Medieval popes like Gregory VIII and Innocent III had done much to strengthen the ecclesiastical structure. But the popes of later centuries had been less successful in their undertakings, and their failures affected the entire institution. Boniface VIII, for example, was defeated in his struggle with the French king Philip the Fair (p. 191). After Boniface's death (in 1303) Philip moved to avoid future trouble with Rome by forcing the election of a French bishop as the new pope. Thus the papacy was drawn into the orbit of French politics. The new relationship was manifested shortly thereafter when the pope (Clement V) transferred his court from Rome to Avignon.

Avignon was a papal fief, on the lower Rhone River, just across the border from France. Clement went there voluntarily, chiefly because conditions in Rome were turbulent and unsafe. But his move confirmed a widespread feeling that the papacy had become a captive of the French monarchy. Clement created a French majority in the College of Cardinals, and for some seventy years a succession of French popes reigned at Avignon.

Outside France, these popes were looked upon with suspicion and hostility. Since the papal office was tied to that of Bishop of Rome, it seemed incongruous that the pope should reside anywhere but in the Eternal City. The English, who were then at war with the

French, regarded the papacy at Avignon as the ally of their enemy. Actually, the popes acted quite independently during these years, but that did not prevent the Italian humanist Petrarch from labeling their stay at Avignon as the "Babylonian Captivity" (a reference to the forced removal of the ancient Jews to Babylonia).

More serious embarrassments to the Church were yet to come. In 1377, Gregory XI decided to restore the papal court to Rome; upon his death there, the Roman populace coerced the cardinals into choosing an Italian as pope. But the French cardinals fled the city, pronounced the election invalid, and chose another prelate. This pope, with his supporting cardinals, removed to Avignon, while the Italian pope, with his cardinals, stayed in Rome. Each declared the other to be a false pope and excommunicated him and his followers.

The Great Schism, as this division was called, lasted some forty years (from 1378 to 1417). Europe now endured the spectacle of a Church divided into opposing hierarchies, with two popes and two colleges of cardinals. Conscientious Christians were distressed, for they had no way of being certain who was pope and who was "antipope." Secular rulers supported whichever side seemed more useful politically. Thus France and her allies recognized Avignon, while England and the German princes recognized Rome. The schism was at last settled by a general council of the Church, which deposed both popes and elected a new one. But by this time the papacy had suffered irreparable damage. The fulcrum of papal power had previously been its immense moral authority. That authority was now gravely weakened, opening the way to contempt and defiance.

The humiliation of the papacy contributed to the decline of the clergy as a whole—a decline that had begun to set in after 1300. Worldliness and laxity had swept the Church once more, and the brave reform efforts of earlier centuries were forgotten. The monastic orders, traditionally the conscience of the clergy, fell into disarray, their ascetic spirit eroded by comfortable living. Many of the seculars (priests and bishops) also succumbed to self-indulgence, lust, and greed. While there doubtless remained thousands of honest, chaste, and pious clerics, the situation was nevertheless scandalous.

Vigorous reform of these abuses became imperative. But the popes of the fifteenth century, themselves steeped in worldliness, were not interested in reform. The Renaissance princes of the Church were more interested in politics and wealth than in spiritual affairs. The Medici pope Leo X is reputed to have said after his election in 1513, "As God has seen fit to give us the papacy, let us enjoy it!"

The awakening reform spirit: Wiclif, Hus

Many devout Christians realized that the moral reform of the Church would have to start at the top of the hierarchy, but they feared that the papacy lacked the will to reform. As a consequence, they began to turn *inward* in their devotions. The fifteenth century saw a fervent revival of mysticism and pietism in the North. A characteristic response there was the founding of the Brethren of the Common Life (p. 271), whose members turned away from the formalism of established rituals. They joined together in quasi-religious communities, stressing Christlike simplicity, purity of heart, and direct communion with God.

The revival of mysticism and piety was one reaction against an ecclesiastical system that had become meaningless or repugnant to conscientious believers. If the system could not be changed, they reasoned, one could simply withdraw into *oneself*. They were also moving toward a new concept of the visible Church, taking as their model the "primitive" Christianity that was practiced during the first century after Christ.

John Wiclif, a leading Oxford scholar and teacher, was among the first to question openly the need for a priestly hierarchy. His ideas, expounded late in the fourteenth century, provided a foundation for later Protestant doctrines. After a lifetime of study, Wiclif concluded that the Church was suffering from more than just the misbehavior of some of its clergy. He challenged the established role and powers of the clergy itself—arguing that God and the Scriptures are the sole sources of authority.

Wiclif made an English translation of the Vulgate and urged laymen to read it for themselves. Every individual, he said, can communicate directly with the Lord and can be saved without the aid of priests or saints. For challenging the prevailing doctrines of authority and salvation, he was condemned and forced to retire from teaching. (Civil disturbances in England and the Great Schism in the Church saved him from more drastic punishment.) Wiclif was thus silenced, but his ideas were not.

Most of Wiclif's followers in England (who were known as Lollards) were extirpated as heretics. John Hus, the hero of Bohemia, met the same fate. Hus was a priest and a professor at Charles University in Prague, capital of the kingdom of Bohemia. Already active in efforts to reform the clergy, he was inspired by the writings of Wiclif to launch stronger, more radical attacks. Hus had the support of most of his compatriots, partly because many of the prelates he criticized were Germans. (National feelings, here and elsewhere, revealed themselves in the religious disputes.)

Bohemia was part of the Holy Roman Empire, and the Emperor Sigismund had grown disturbed by the mounting disaffection among the Bohemians. When Hus was summoned by the Council of Constance in 1414 to stand trial on charges of heresy, the emperor promised him safe conduct to and from the trial. After a long and cruel imprisonment in Constance, Hus was tried and found guilty. The emperor did not fulfill his promise of protection, and Hus, refusing to recant his beliefs, went to his death at the stake. The reaction in Bohemia was instantaneous. Anti-German and antipapal sentiments were inflamed, and a bloody uprising erupted in the country. This was but the beginning of a long series of political-religious wars in Europe.

During the fifteenth century, the criticisms by heretics like Wiclif and Hus were reinforced by the writings of the Christian humanists. Erasmus poured ridicule on the hierarchy, monasticism, and popular devotional cults. But his intellectual approach did not stir the common people, and he never challenged the authority of the Church. For these reasons, and because of the humanist leanings of the Renaissance popes, Erasmus escaped personal harm.

Nevertheless, there was a link between the Christian humanists and the rebels against authority. The leaders of the Protestant revolt found justification for their actions in Erasmus' call for a purer religion, one freed from ritualism, superstition, and pagan embellishments. They were prepared, of course, to go much further than Erasmus: they would defy authority and split the Christian community if necessary in order to achieve their goals.

The influence of political and social forces

By 1500 the ideas for religious reform were in broad circulation. All that was needed was the opportunity to start an effective *movement*. A century after Hus the political, economic, and social conditions in Europe were shifting in such a way as to present that opportunity. The new situation would permit the rise of religious founders instead of religious martyrs.

National sentiment and political absolutism, whose growth we discussed in Chapter Six, were working against the principle and practice of the universal Church. As distinctively national cultures evolved, people grew increasingly conscious of belonging to a particular nation—a nation independent of all others. The citizens of the northern countries, especially, came to regard the popes as "foreigners" who had no proper business outside Italy.

This popular feeling supported the desire of despotic kings and princes to gain control over the Church in their respective territories and to build *state* churches. By 1520 the monarchs of Spain and France had virtually achieved this end by securing the right to appoint bishops within their kingdoms. One reason for the failure of heresies in those two nations is simply that their kings had nothing to gain from religious disturbances. In Germany and England, however, where the kings and princes expected to enlarge their powers in the event of a religious break with Rome, heresies were to prove successful.

The higher social classes also began to sense that they might benefit from a break with Rome. In Germany the Church was immensely wealthy, holding from one-fifth to one-third of the total real property. The landed aristocrats looked on those holdings with covetous eyes, and members of the middle class, though not particularly interested in acquiring land, disliked the fact that church properties were exempt from taxes. Their own tax payments would be reduced, they reasoned, if church holdings were shifted to private hands. And all classes of German society deplored the flow of ecclesiastical revenues to Rome; the feeling that the "foreign" papacy was draining the homeland of wealth thus created another source of support for a religious revolt.

These economic, social, and political circumstances must be kept in mind if we are to understand the nature and success of the Protestant reform movements. The reformers, to be sure, did not act upon a calculation of these circumstances; they acted, rather, in response to the urgings of their minds and hearts. But this had been true also of the less fortunate heretics who preceded them. The success of the Protestant leaders was due primarily to the new alignment of political and social forces. The time was ripe for religious revolt in northern Europe; the division of the Latin Church was at hand.

THE REVOLT OF LUTHER: JUSTIFICATION BY FAITH

The reformers did not intend, at the outset, to divide the Church or to found new churches. Each believed that he had the correct vision of the *one* true church, and he set out to convert (or force) all Christians to his point of view. (The Protestant leaders, to the dismay of Erasmus, were to prove as dogmatic and intolerant as the papacy.) But, since no one of them managed to dominate the others, the end result was the division and subdivision of the Church.

The provocation: the sale of indulgences

In 1517 Martin Luther struck a spark that set religious passions aflame. The event did not appear at the time to have far-reaching significance, but it started a chain reaction of dissent and rebellion. A Dominican friar named Tetzel, who was selling papal indulgences in Germany, had set up shop near the Saxon town of Wittenberg. According to Catholic teaching, indulgences may reduce or eliminate temporal penalties imposed for individual sins, both on earth and in purgatory. (Purgatory, in Catholic doctrine, is a temporary state after death for the cleansing of absolved souls on their way to heaven.) Tetzel, however, made extravagant claims for indulgences, implying that they would automatically remit the sinner's *guilt* as well as his penalty.

Tetzel's claims were unacceptable to the local professor of theology, an Augustinian priest named Martin Luther. In protest, he nailed to the door of the Wittenberg Castle church a long list of criticisms of the sale of indulgences (the "Ninety-five Theses"). Luther charged that the proceeds of Tetzel's sale of indulgences were going to Rome for the building of a new basilica for St. Peter's. (He resented having Germans pay for an undertaking that would be of no benefit to them.) He also challenged indulgences in general, implying that they were of dubious validity. His charges provoked an immediate outcry from the clergy. They struck a sympathetic chord with the laity, however, and copies of the "Ninety-five Theses" were distributed throughout Germany. The revolt from Rome, aided by the new technique of printing, was under way.

The pope, Leo X, directed that a reply be made to Luther's theses. In answering this reply, and in the series of exchanges that followed, Luther began to question the basic authority of the papacy and the whole ecclesiastical system. When it became clear that his views could not be reconciled with the doctrines of the Church, Luther chose to stand by them rather than retract. Unlike Erasmus and other humanists, he did not hesitate to defy authority in matters of personal belief. He would obey only his conscience. When he was warned that his unyielding position might lead to "division, war, and rebellion," Luther answered that *one cannot compromise on what one believes to be true.*

Luther's spiritual search: his doctrine of salvation

The force of Luther's personal conviction was due in part to his temperament. He relished a fight and was capable of quick, violent, and sustained anger. He was also a man of instinctive frankness and courage. But his beliefs were mainly the product of a long spiritual pilgrimage marked by doubt, agony, and, finally, conviction.

Luther was of peasant stock. His father, who had once been a miner, made wise investments and became a respected member of the bourgeoisie. He wanted his son to study law in preparation for a career as a middle-class bureaucrat. But Martin, who had attended a school run by the Brethren of the Common Life, had fallen into deep spiritual anxiety in his early years. By the time he completed his liberal-arts course at the University of Erfurt (in Saxony), he had decided to abandon secular life and enter a monastery. His decision was sealed, he later explained, when he was caught in a violent thunderstorm and, terrified, interpreted the thunder as a call from God.

Luther took his vows at an Augustinian monastery in Erfurt. Fearing that his soul was in danger of damnation, he hoped that an ascetic life would afford him a better chance of salvation. But he found no peace of mind either as a monk or as a priest. No matter how diligently he fasted, prayed, and punished himself, his sense of unworthiness persisted. The Church taught that "good works" helped to "justify" man's soul before God. But Luther continued to be obsessed by the fear of God and despaired of doing *enough* good works to gain his favor. While he was in the throes of this torment, he was sent by his superior to a new university in Wittenberg that had been founded by Frederick, the Elector of Saxony. After receiving his doctor's degree there in 1512, he stayed on as professor of theology.

At Wittenberg Luther began to discover his path to spiritual peace. While he was preparing some lectures on the Bible, he was struck by certain passages that seemed to suggest an answer. In Paul's Epistle to the Romans, for example, Luther read, "The just shall live by faith" (1:17). After days and nights of pondering, Luther reached the conclusion that the justice of God meant "that righteousness by which through grace and sheer mercy God *justifies* us through *faith*." The whole of the Scripture, he explained later, then took on new meaning for him. Whereas the "justice of God" had formerly filled him with hate, it now became "inexpressibly sweet in greater love. This passage of Paul became to me a gate to heaven . . . ."

Now Luther understood why his own penances and works as a monk had availed him nothing. Man, by his nature, cannot please God without faith, but faith, a free gift of God's mercy, "justifies" a man and ensures salvation. We are saved not by works, concluded

Luther, but by *faith alone.* The man who accepts Christ unreservedly as his Savior has the right to feel that true faith has been given him. From his love of God, he will freely perform good works—not because he *needs* to, but because he *wants* to.

These ideas afforded Luther immense personal relief, but when he began to apply them to the institutions of the Church, he grew troubled. If men received faith according to God's secret judgment, of what use was the ordained priesthood? If every Christian was, in effect, a priest, were not the pretensions of the hierarchy absurd and hateful? And what justification was there for the special vows and way of life undertaken by monks and nuns? If works were no help to salvation, what was the benefit of penances, pilgrimages, and papal indulgences?

In 1517 Tetzel's selling of indulgences brought Luther face to face with what he regarded as a flagrant distortion of religious truth. Up to this point he had shared his views only with his students; now he felt compelled to speak out. And so it was that he posted, in formal academic fashion, his "Ninety-five Theses."

The widening breach with Rome

As the dispute over indulgences dragged on, Luther busied himself with writing theological pamphlets in which he broadened his attack on the Church, especially the papacy. At the same time he appealed to the nobility, and to German laymen in general, by speaking of the "priesthood" of *all* baptized Christians. Ordained priests and bishops, he argued, had no more *inherent* powers than other Christians; they were simply fulfilling the duties of their office (as princes fulfilled theirs). He also attacked monasticism and declared that priests should be permitted to marry.

In addition to challenging the doctrines of apostolic succession and "good works," Luther struck directly at the number and meaning of the holy sacraments (pp. 178–80). Of the seven traditional sacraments, he asserted that only *two* were warranted by Scripture: baptism and the Eucharist. And, contrary to doctrine, he insisted that in the Eucharist there was no miraculous change of substance (transubstantiation) from bread and wine to the body and blood of Christ.

Pope Leo, whose main interests appeared to be in art, hunting, and politics, was annoyed by the excitement Luther had stirred up in Germany. He referred scornfully to the dispute over indulgences as a "squabble among monks." But when he realized how serious the implications were he moved against Luther—cautiously. One reason for his caution was that Luther, as a professor at Wittenberg, enjoyed the protection of the Elector Frederick of Saxony; and the pope, for political reasons, was trying to stay on friendly terms with Frederick.

Ultimately, however, Leo had to act. In 1520 he ordered Luther excommunicated. Luther responded by burning the bull (the papal document of excommunication) before the city gates of Wittenberg, thus demonstrating his defiance of Rome. The clergy now called upon the Holy Roman Emperor, Charles V, to seize Luther (it was considered the duty of the civil ruler to punish confirmed heretics), but Luther had such strong support among all classes of the laity that the emperor hesitated. The Elector Frederick then insisted that Luther receive a hearing before the imperial diet (assembly) of princes. At the Diet of Worms in 1521 Luther was afforded a last chance to retract his heresies. He refused, declaring eloquently that Scripture was the sole source of authority and that he must obey his conscience.

Luther had been guaranteed safe conduct on his journey to Worms. After he left the assembly, however, the emperor ordered him put under the ban—which meant that he was branded an outlaw. Subjects of the empire were forbidden to harbor him, and, if seized, he could be killed. Frederick, however, had planned for his safety in advance. His soldiers kidnaped Luther as he left Worms and took him secretly to Frederick's castle at Wartburg, where Luther remained for about a year, working on a German translation of the Bible. His "people's" version of Scripture helped shape the modern German language as well as Protestant doctrines.

Building the Lutheran Church

When Luther thought it safe, he returned to Wittenberg to lay plans for a reformed church. He spent the rest of his life, not as a rebel, but as an organizer and administrator. It was in this phase of his career that he met his severest tests. Many of his followers responded extravagantly to his pronouncements on the "priesthood of all believers" and the sole authority of Scripture, and some of them developed eccentric notions about Christian practices and radical ideas about the relation of religion to society. Numerous sects began to arise in Germany and to break away from Luther's guidance.

The largest group of deviants was the Anabaptists—various sects opposed to infant baptism. They insisted that baptism was meaningful only after someone old enough to comprehend Christian doctrines had made a free and knowing confession of faith. More troublesome were their social ideas. Applying New Testament teachings literally to the life of their times, they sought to establish a more equalitarian community. Some of them favored using force against impious persons and against officials who declined to punish them.

Luther, who was extremely conservative in his views on the social order, was alarmed by such proposals. He opposed any sort of rebellion against established *political* authorities, holding that they alone had the right to wield the sword. In 1524 he responded angrily to a peasant revolt that swept over Germany seeking relief from feudal and manorial burdens. (Germany had lagged behind France and England in abolishing serfdom.) He urged the aristocracy to put down the violent uprising without mercy, to slay the rebels as they would "mad dogs." He later admitted that it was he who commanded the slaughter of the peasants: "All their blood is on my head. But I throw the responsibility on our Lord God, who instructed me to give this order."

He was equally severe with preachers who disagreed with his doctrines. He considered them "blasphemers" and believed that they, like persons guilty of sedition, should be executed. Though claiming for himself the freedom to interpret Scripture, he denied it to those whom he judged to be not properly "qualified." The Lutheran Church developed an orthodoxy of its own, resting on the "Augsburg Confession" of 1530. This document, largely the work of Luther's friend and disciple, Philip Melanchthon, was a moderate statement of Luther's doctrinal views, including those on justification (salvation), sacraments, and the relation of faith and works.

The Emperor Charles, though distracted by war and politics outside Germany, still hoped to suppress the Lutheran Church by force. In 1529 Charles and the Catholic members of the imperial diet reaffirmed a decree prohibiting all new religious doctrines in Germany. The Lutheran princes (of northern Germany) protested this step and thus acquired the name "Protestant." In time, this name came to be used for all the rebellious creeds.

Soon Germany was split into armed alliances, Catholic states arrayed against Lutheran states. By the time the emperor could send his forces against the Lutheran princes, he found them too powerful to overcome. The result was a truce, known as the Religious Peace of Augsburg (1555), in which the members of the imperial diet agreed to leave each prince free to choose either Catholicism or Lutheranism for his realm. (Other sects were still prohibited.) Under the Peace of Augsburg religious warfare among the German states was suspended for some sixty years.

The people living in the Lutheran states found no great difficulty in accepting the decisions of their respective princes. Though the peasants had been embittered by Luther's harsh attitude toward them, their bitterness softened with time. For their part, the princes, nobles, and bourgeoisie enthusiastically supported the reformed church. It appealed to German patriotism by rejecting the Roman papacy, and its support of the established order pleased all who held office or wealth. The laity as a whole tended to feel comfortable in Luther's Church. According to his doctrine, all baptized Christians were on the same spiritual plane as their ministers; the devout man of property could feel equal, before God, to the ascetic, propertyless cleric. Secular society and values had won the sanction of the Church.

The kings of Scandinavia recognized the advantages of a Lutheran state church, and they, too, established the new creed as their official religion. In each Lutheran country the ruler appointed superintendents to oversee his ecclesiastical establishment—thus subordinating church to state. Religious buildings and their premises were assigned to the new churches, but the extensive landholdings of the Catholic bishops and abbots were seized by the crown.

In accordance with Luther's teaching, monastic orders were abolished in all these states, and ministers were permitted to marry. (Luther himself married a former nun, who bore him six children.) The veneration of saints and relics and all manner of formal "good works" were rejected. Luther did, however, retain the principle of ecclesiastical authority and many semblances of medieval religious practice. The liturgy, in German, was not far removed from the Catholic liturgy. Unlike some other religious reformers, Luther also kept art and music in his Church; he composed a notable book of hymns as well as several catechisms.

CALVIN AND THE ELECT: PREDESTINATION

Luther was by no means the only religious rebel at work during the 1520's. And, though he tried to impose his doctrines upon the others, he failed to do so outside North Germany and Scandinavia. The logic of his own thought, in fact, militated against a unified reform movement. He had taught that each man, guided by the Holy Spirit, must see the truth of Scripture according to his own conscience. While the papal theory of Petrine supremacy offered a logical basis for *one* interpretation of truth and for *one* church, Luther's theory led ineluctably to *many* churches. Once papal authority had been overthrown, there was no logical limit to the proliferation of creeds and denominations.

Of the countless separations that followed Luther's revolt, two require special attention because of their far-reaching historical influence. One of these is the Church of England, the most conservative of the major breaks from Rome. The other, initiated by John Calvin, departed more radically from the medieval tradition. Among the principal Protestant denominations, Calvin's moved the farthest from Catholicism in doctrine, spirit, organization, and ritual.

Calvin: the international reformer

Younger than Luther by some twenty-five years, Calvin was born and raised a Frenchman. Fear of persecution by the Catholic king forced him to flee to Switzerland, however, and he settled down in the city of Geneva in 1536. The city, which had just revolted from its feudal overlord (a bishop), was in the throes of political and religious turmoil. Within a short time, Calvin and his version of reformed Christianity achieved dominance in the community. For some twenty years, until his death in 1564, he controlled the church, the state, and the Academy (university) of Geneva.

Calvin's influence extended far beyond the boundaries of his city. He corresponded with rulers and theologians alike, and reformers from all over Europe came to Geneva to study his doctrines. When they returned to their homelands, they carried Calvinism with them. Calvinism thus became the leading Protestant force in France (the Huguenots), Holland (the Reformed Church), Scotland (Presbyterianism), and England (Puritanism).

Calvinism is important not only because of its international influence but because of its peculiar appeal to the bourgeoisie. Born to a middle-class family, Calvin accepted business as a normal Christian vocation. He took for granted (as Luther and the Catholic theologians did not) the functions of capital, banking, and large-scale commerce. Though admonishing entrepreneurs to be honest and reasonable in their dealings, he did not question the propriety of their activities. He was the first theologian to praise the capitalistic virtues: hard work, thrift, and the accumulation of capital. He lauded the creation of wealth through industry so long as that wealth was not used for self-indulgence. The businessman should be sober and disciplined, dedicated to the "service of the Lord."

It is not surprising that these ideas were warmly received in such commercial centers as Amsterdam, Antwerp, and London. (In Switzerland the mountain regions remained Catholic, while the urban cantons embraced Calvinism.) Calvin's faith was in accordance with the economic realities of the day and was attractive to the most progressive and venturesome class of Western society. Carried to New England in the seventeenth century, Calvinism contributed significantly to the shaping of American traditions. Three centuries after the founding of Massachusetts Bay Colony, a President of the United States would proclaim that "the business of America is *business.*" His name: John Calvin Coolidge.

As a young man, John Calvin had prepared for the priesthood in Paris and then, at his father's urging, had turned to the study of law. His legal training sharpened his logic and strengthened his ability to express himself, but he found a career in law distasteful. He became absorbed in humanistic scholarship and, after receiving his law degree, took up the study of Greek and Hebrew. His taste for the classics was reflected in a book he wrote about a work of the Stoic philosopher Seneca. A year later (in 1533) Calvin experienced a sudden conversion to the idea of religious reform. France, like the rest of Europe, was the scene of heated disputes about the Church; the writings of Erasmus and Luther had stirred the youthful Calvin. He remained a keen scholar all his life, but after his "conversion" Calvin the humanist gave way to Calvin the reformer.

He turned to a systematic exposition of his religious doctrines and finished the first edition of the *Institutes of the Christian Religion* when he was only twenty-six years old (1536). He wrote the original in Latin but soon produced a translation in French. This work was to stand as the principal statement of Protestant theology for some three hundred years and as such is comparable to the Catholic exposition by Thomas Aquinas (*Summa Theologica*).

The doctrine of God's omnipotence

Calvin was very close to Luther in his basic theology. He saw the Bible as the sole source of authority and rejected a priesthood based on apostolic succession. He agreed that salvation was determined by God's grace alone, unaffected by man's works. Like Luther, he too scorned monasticism and such "Romish" practices as the veneration of saints and relics, pilgrimages, and indulgences.

The difference between the two men, and it was a real one, lay in what each chose to emphasize. Luther was obsessed with his soul's salvation, and it was this that led him to his doctrine. Calvin, on the other hand, was obsessed with a sense of God's omnipotence and man's depravity. He argued that men must do what God wills, not as a means to salvation but *because God wills it.* Calvin's position may well have been a reaction to his contact with humanism, which stressed the importance of man and his physical world. But he drew his premise of God's glory and perfection directly from the Old Testament, and no other theologian has deduced with such relentless logic the implications of that premise.

The best-known and most controversial of Calvin's doctrines is that of predestination and election. God, declared Calvin, foreknows and determines everything that happens in the universe—even those events ordinarily attributed to chance. It follows that he certainly determines who shall be saved and who shall be forever lost. All men, because of Adam's sin and their own depravity, would disobey God if left to their own puny powers. But God gives to those he "elects" the grace (manifested by faith) to persevere in his service. The rest, for his own reasons, he allows to fall into perdition. Calvin unflinchingly defined this doctrine in his *Institutes:*

> Predestination we call the eternal decree of God, by which he has determined in himself, what he would have become of every individual of mankind. For they are not all created with a similar destiny; but eternal life is foreordained for some, and eternal damnation for others. Every man, therefore, being created for one or the other of these ends, we say, he is predestinated either to life or to death.

In his discussion of predestination, Calvin warned that the subject is dangerous and delicate, since it touches on an inmost secret of the Almighty. To the charge that God could not be so unfair as to condemn most of mankind to damnation, Calvin answered that no one deserves salvation and that it is only through God's gracious mercy that *some* are saved. Further, it is impious to question the plans and judgment of God. Man has only a worm's-eye view of Creation. Whatever God has willed is right, because he has willed it. Calvin admitted that the Lord's predestination was an "awful decree," but he held that all must nevertheless accept it.

But all men would not accept so harsh a doctrine. Luther, with his Pauline thinking, accepted it, though he did not stress it in his teachings. Most of the Calvinist sects, in time, would ignore or repudiate the doctrine for one of two reasons: it is too gloomy, and it denies free will. The Roman Catholics (including Erasmus) indignantly condemned Calvin's teachings, declaring that it reduces man to a mere puppet. They did not deny that God's grace is indispensable to salvation, but they implied that it is offered more generously than Calvin suggested. They also insisted that each individual can either cooperate (through good works) in achieving salvation or can refuse to cooperate. By refusing, a man chooses the path to hell, but this is his own doing. Calvin answered that the Catholic argument is an insult to God's majesty. It suggests either that God's will is not all-powerful or that his grace, if it must be supplemented by works, is inadequate.

In reply to the assertion that his doctrine would destroy all incentive for pursuing a worthy Christian life and that it would cause some people to throw themselves into dissipation, he made this reply: nothing in the doctrine of predestination excuses any person from striving to obey God's commandments. On the contrary, argued Calvin, no man knows for certain who is of the "elect" and who is "reprobate." Every man, therefore, should act as if he enjoys God's favor. If he does enjoy that favor, he should want his life to be a shining example to others; if he does not enjoy it, he should obey God anyway. It is surely the duty of those who feel moved by the Spirit to do God's will themselves and to see that others, whether or not they are to be saved, also honor God. The divine will can be clearly read in Scripture; men should mold their lives accordingly, regardless of the decree of predestination.

Calvinist ethics: the Puritan discipline

Calvin applied this line of reasoning with rigorous logic to the entire realm of Christian ethics. Though a person's behavior is not the means to his salvation, it must nonetheless be subjected to minute scrutiny. Puritanism as a social discipline was thus born of Calvin, for he wanted the behavior of all Christians to be held under strict control.

This aim reflected Calvin's own disposition and temperament. He was a slight and sickly man, humorless, and with little zest for the pleasures of life. In addition, the awesome doctrine of predestination colored Calvin's view of his surroundings. If most men are doomed to eternal fire, the world is indeed a "vestibule of Hell." (This thought in itself tends to drive off levity.) To Calvin, God is a righteous, severe judge under whose searching eye men should comport themselves humbly, piously, and soberly.

Calvin had a further rationale for his ascetic doctrine. If we would truly glorify God, we must first rid ourselves of the distractions of the flesh; we must achieve, in short, a contempt for the world. This belief followed that of Paul, Augustine, and the medieval ascetics; it was directly opposed to the humanism of Calvin's day. Yet his acquaintance with humanism gave him some appreciation of its values. He was even willing to tolerate, in theory, a moderate enjoyment of the fruits of earth (since they were part of God's creation). But, since moderate indulgence often leads to excess, he urged abstinence as a practical policy.

Calvin criticized any form of decoration lest it lead to ostentation and any form of card-playing lest it lead to gambling. The theater, because of its associations with paganism, was closed down in Geneva; art was seen as a distraction from God's word. Drinking was

condemned as a prelude to intoxication, and dancing was prohibited as a stimulant to desire. The clothing of women had to be plain
and ample; he regarded the display of ornament or the exposure of
flesh as a signal to carnal instincts. In living a "puritanical" life,
concluded Calvin, one follows the teachings of the Lord, who "condemned all those pleasures which seduce the heart from chastity
and purity."

To Calvin, a man's *conscience* is the prime defense against ungodly distractions and against sin itself. But the conscience commands perpetual "civil war in the breast." One should not yield to
"natural" inclinations to indulgence; they are in all probability the
temptings of Satan, and God wants us to overcome them. This compelling, inward sense of sin is difficult for modern minds to comprehend. Freud has suggested that physical urges need not be identified
with sin, and theologians have recently translated Satan from a live
demon into an allegorical concept. But in the sixteenth century the
sense of sin and the fear of its consequences haunted God-fearing
men and women. Luther himself confessed that he was harried by
the devil and once threw his inkpot at him.

If the individual could not avoid wrongdoing, Calvin believed, it
was up to other Christians to be their "brother's keeper." He used
his pulpit to admonish and frighten potential sinners. When his
sermons failed, he resorted to force in prohibiting unseemly acts
and words. The Consistory of Geneva was a special body of pastors
and lay elders responsible for public morals and discipline. Alleged
offenders were haled before this court, which might reprimand the
accused or impose bread-and-water sentences upon them. Common
offenses were blasphemy, intemperance, dozing in church, impugn-
ing ministers, dancing, and other "immoral" acts.

More serious acts were handled by the town council. One man,
who was accused of placing an insulting placard on Calvin's pulpit,
was tortured on the rack until he confessed to guilt; later, he was
beheaded. Accused heretics were also brought before the council for
judgment. The most notorious trial was that of the Spaniard
Michael Servetus, who challenged the doctrine of the Trinity. Calvin, after warning Servetus to stay away, had him arrested when he
visited Geneva. He then charged him with heresy, pushed through
his conviction, and had him burned at the stake (1553). With relentless logic Calvin justified the destruction of "false prophets" by
referring to the harsh thirteenth chapter of Deuteronomy:

> God makes plain that the false prophet is to be stoned without mercy.
> We are to crush beneath our heel all affections of nature when his

honor is involved. The father should not spare his child, nor the brother his brother, nor the husband his own wife, or the friend who is dearer to him than life.

Erasmus, now in his grave, was spared knowledge of Servetus' agony and Calvin's self-righteous brutality. The Protestant reformer had come full circle to the papal position of infallibility, dogmatism, and intolerance. By excommunicating "wrongdoers" from his Church, Calvin drove most of his critics from Geneva; refugees from Catholic persecution, meanwhile, kept drifting in from other lands. By the end of Calvin's reign (1564), the citizenry had thus been "converted" to firm support of his principles and policies.

Relations of church and state

Though Calvin controlled both religion and government in Geneva, he held no public office. He was opposed to the union of spiritual and temporal authority, and he desired to keep church and state constitutionally separate. But he desired separation only as a means of safeguarding the independence of the church and of assuring its domination over the state. In this he again followed papal policy, especially as manifested by Gregory VII (pp. 189–90): the ministers of the church must stand as the teachers and judges of civil rulers. To Calvin, the purpose of government was to regulate society according to the will of God, and the church was the appointed interpreter of God's will. "Great kings ought not to think it any dishonor to prostrate themselves before Christ, the King of Kings, nor ought they to be displeased at being judged by the church. . . . They ought even to wish not to be spared by the pastors, that they may be spared by the Lord."

Geneva was legally a republic whose principal governing organ was the town council. As we have seen, the council served to protect Calvin's Church against critics, schismatics, and heretics. And in the manner that Pope Gregory had held the threat of excommunication (and disgrace) over kings and princes, so Calvin held it over the politicians of Geneva. His Consistory watched their public and private behavior for the slightest evidence of impropriety.

For some twenty years, Geneva served as a model of theocracy (church-controlled state). The organized church, Calvin asserted, is essential for the supervision of the state as well as for the redemption of souls. This view, too, paralleled the papal pronouncement that individual salvation is possible only within the church. The idea of dependence upon church membership may seem to contradict Calvin's doctrine of predestination and election. If God has already determined that a person is to be saved, why must he remain in communion with Calvin's Church (or any other church)? This was a crucial question for both Luther and Calvin, because their very doctrines suggested that they themselves were dispensable. Yet "inner voices" told them that this could not be. Calvin's explanation was simple: it is God's will that the elect be saved *through* the church. And by means of its teaching and discipline the Heavenly City might be reflected on earth.

Calvinist ministry and ritual

Calvin saw nothing incongruous in adhering to many of the Roman Catholic principles. What he offered was not new doctrine concerning the role and prerogatives of the church but the *true church itself*. His teachings on salvation and "good works," however, were at variance with Catholic teachings, and so were the ministry and ritual of his Church. He accepted with Luther the "priesthood of all believers"; his Church attributed to its ministers no inherent powers that distinguished them from baptized laymen. Their authority derived from their assigned *office*, as did the authority of civil officials.

Calvin guarded against preaching by self-proclaimed ministers. A "legitimate ministry," he declared, is formed when suitable persons are appointed by the elders, subject to the approval of the congregation and other pastors of the community. In the administration of each church, the minister was assisted by elders elected by the congregation. Thus developed the presbyterian theory and practice of church government. (The Greek word *presbyteros* corresponds to "elder.")

Today, at each level of the Calvinist Church (local congregation, district, nation), control resides in the hands of ministers and elected elders. Thus, the ultimate power in Calvinist churches (and others that have followed its structural model) is the congregation of baptized believers. The ultimate power in the Roman Catholic Church, on the other hand, resides in one person—the pope.

Calvin insisted that church ritual be based exclusively on Scripture. He found, with Luther, that only baptism and the Eucharist are clearly established there as sacraments. Beyond the administration of these two rites, Calvin permitted little else except the singing of Psalms and the preaching of sermons. He regarded images of the saints as a distraction from the exclusive worship of the Almighty, and he barred their use.

He believed that music, art, and ornamentation had no place in the church; the great cathedrals, with their stained glass, gilt, and statuary, he branded as pagan temples. Jesus and Paul, according to Scripture, conducted their ministries in simple fashion by preaching. And preaching was the core of the Calvinist service. There were no processions, genuflections, embroidered garments, incense, or mysterious Latin chants. The minister wore simple black and spoke only in the ordinary language of his congregation (as Jesus had). The typical Calvinist service was once described as consisting of "four bare walls and a sermon."

HENRY VIII AND THE CHURCH OF ENGLAND

Calvinist austerity found little acceptance among Lutherans or among English reformers. While Protestant ideas from the Continent influenced the doctrine of the Anglican Church (Church of England), organization and ritual remained close to the Catholic tradition. Thus, the Anglican Church represented a sort of compromise between extreme Protestantism and Roman Catholicism. Radical reformers criticized it as a muddled and illogical institution, subservient to the state; Roman Catholics condemned it as schismatic and heretical. The Anglicans, however, insisted that theirs was the true church, that it was both Catholic *and* reformed. This is still the view of the worldwide Anglican Communion, which includes the Protestant Episcopal Church of America.

Although Wiclif had preached in England during the fourteenth century, there was no English counterpart to Luther or Calvin during the age of Reformation. Religious reform in England, though supported by numerous critics of the Catholic Church, was carried through by monarchs. From the time of Henry VIII, who initiated the reform, to the time of Elizabeth I, who completed it, changes were prompted primarily by considerations of state. The Church of England did not bear the mark of any one spiritual leader, though many devoted clergymen helped establish it.

The first Tudor monarch, Henry VII, had laid the foundations for royal absolutism and bourgeois prosperity (p. 257). His policies were vigorously pursued by his son and successor, the youthful Henry VIII. Henry proved to be a popular king, a robust Renaissance despot. He had had some training in theology, for as a younger son in the royal family, he had been started by his father upon an ecclesiastical career. The plan was dropped upon the death of his elder brother, Arthur, which left Henry heir to the throne. His interest in religious matters persisted, however, and after his coronation he formally defended the orthodox view of the sacraments against Luther's public attack (1521). As a reward, Leo X gave Henry the title of "Defender of the Faith."

Henry's desire for independence

Henry accepted Roman Catholic doctrine, but he soon came to resent Roman interference in the affairs of his realm. The rising tide of national feeling had already divested the pope of much of his influence in European states. In Spain and France the monarchs controlled the Church within their borders, but in England the pope still confirmed the appointment of prelates. Appeals from ecclesiastical courts (in keeping with canon law) and a portion of church revenues continued to go to Rome.

But it was a personal matter, related to the welfare of the state, that led Henry VIII to break with Rome. In order to preserve a dynastic alliance with Spain, he had married Catherine of Aragon, the widow of his elder brother. Because it was contrary to canon law to marry so close a relative, he had sought and received a papal dispensation permitting the union. In the course of their marriage, Catherine bore six children, but all except one were still-born or died in infancy. The single survivor, unfortunately, was a girl (Mary). The English had only recently emerged from a bloody civil war over the succession to the throne, and they feared that a female ruler might prove unable to maintain national strength and unity. When it appeared that Catherine would have no more children, Henry and his advisers began to think about his taking a new wife.

Henry's sense of duty was fortified by his fondness for Anne Boleyn, an attractive young lady-in-waiting to the queen. In 1527 he decided to marry her and directed his chancellor to get his marriage to Catherine annulled. The Church did not permit *divorce;* but if it found a marriage to be invalid, both partners were free to marry again. It was thought that Pope Clement VII, a Medici, would grant Henry's request, just as his predecessor had approved the original union. Since Henry's marriage to Catherine had been contrary to canon law, it would have been easy enough for papal lawyers to find some defect in the earlier dispensation.

But the infatuated Henry was to be disappointed. The Habsburg emperor, Charles V, was Catherine's nephew. He informed the pope that there were no valid grounds for annulment, and that such action would be cruel and insulting to his aunt and his family. Charles did not wish Henry to remarry, for his cousin Princess Mary was heir to the English throne. If Henry had no son, Mary would ultimately become queen, bringing another state into the Habsburg orbit.

Charles was engaged at the time in a campaign to win control of Italy, and his army happened to be in Rome when Pope Clement received Henry's appeal. Charles augmented his pressure on Clement by offering to restore the Medici family to power in Florence if the pope would refuse to grant the annulment. But Clement chose to do nothing, hoping that something would happen to extricate him from his dilemma. After nearly six years of waiting, Henry's patience ran out. He married Anne Boleyn in 1533, after his newly appointed archbishop, Thomas Cranmer, had declared his marriage to Catherine invalid. Clement promptly excommunicated the king and released Henry's subjects from the obligation of royal obedience.

Break with Rome: the Act of Supremacy

Infuriated by the pope's delaying tactics and by what he considered to be Clement's interference in state affairs. Henry determined to free himself of the pope once and for all. He was backed by both Parliament and the people, for the papacy had become exceedingly unpopular in England. Having first submitted the issue to the assembled English clergy, Henry had the Act of Supremacy passed by Parliament in 1534. This act declared that the king was the "only supreme head on earth" of the Church of England and endorsed his power to "repress, redress, and reform" all errors, heresies, and abuses in religion.

A series of supplementary acts made the break with Rome complete. Communication with the pope (who was now referred to as the "Bishop of Rome") was forbidden; payments to Rome were stopped; the crown was given sole right to appoint bishops and abbots; and any denial of the king's supremacy was labeled as treason. Sir Thomas More, a Christian humanist and former chancellor, refused to take the required oath of supremacy and was beheaded. Other men of strict principle followed him to the block, and some minor rebellions had to be put down. But Henry imposed his will upon the clergy, Parliament, and his subjects.

Henry's assumption of control over the Church of England did not mean that he wished to reform its *doctrine*. On the contrary, he disliked the Protestant tendencies that were abroad in the country and had Parliament pass the notorious Six Articles, which defined heresy. If an individual denied any of the "test" articles of faith, he could be executed. These articles included belief in transubstantiation, celibacy of the clergy, and the necessity of oral confession. Henry thus showed his determination both to rule the Church and to keep it orthodox. Those who challenged his authority were sent to the block as traitors; those who questioned Catholic doctrine were sent to the stake as heretics.

Henry's only important deviation from Catholic tradition was his suppression of monasticism. The monks had acquired an unsavory reputation in England, and as the core of the pro-papal faction they had aroused Henry's ire. Further, the religious houses possessed great wealth and extensive lands, and Henry was hard pressed for money. His obedient Parliament voted to close the monasteries and to turn over their property to the crown. The income from a portion of this property was assigned to the support of older monks, some of the property was converted to the king's own purposes, and the rest was distributed to his favorites and supporters.

Henry—a shrewd manipulator of men and institutions, a true Machiavellian prince—was thus able to create new ranks of landed noblemen who had a vested interest in his break with Rome. In those troubled times, moreover, many Englishmen (like many Italians) preferred despotic power to liberty and disorder. The success of Henry's undertakings, as well as his hearty manner, endeared him to most Englishmen despite his avarice, cruelty, and marital misadventures.

Three years after marrying Anne, he accused her of adultery and treason, had her beheaded, and then proceeded to take, in succession, four more wives. Anne Boleyn had borne him a daughter (Elizabeth), and Jane Seymour gave him a son at last. But the boy, Edward, proved frail. He succeeded to the throne when he was only ten years old (1547), and his powers had to be exercised by a guardian regent. He died before coming of age, and the crown passed, after all, to his elder sister Mary (the daughter of Catherine).

The struggle over doctrine: Protestant advance and Catholic reaction

During the regency period, Protestant factions in England brought about significant changes in the Anglican Church. Cranmer, Archbishop of Canterbury, had Lutheran leanings; after Henry's death, he led the way to reform by persuading Parliament to repeal the Six Articles and to pass an Act of Uniformity (1549). The latter required that all church services follow a uniform liturgy composed in English by Cranmer himself. The liturgy was prescribed in the *Book of Common Prayer,* which is still the basis of Anglican ritual. All subjects of the realm were enjoined by the act to attend services regularly; other forms of public worship were outlawed. Cranmer also issued a summary of doctrine, the Forty-two Articles, which constituted a moderate statement of Protestant theology.

When Mary succeeded Edward in 1553, the religious pendulum swung once again. Mary, who had been raised a devout Catholic, was determined to restore her realm to allegiance to Rome. She replaced Protestant-minded bishops with orthodox Catholics and compelled the clergy to renounce their wives. (Under Cranmer, priests had been allowed to marry, in accordance with the Lutheran practice). Latin replaced English in the services of the Church. When Mary invited Cardinal Reginald Pole to England as papal legate, he ceremoniously absolved her subjects from heresy and restored England to communion with Rome. Mary's most unpopular act was to wed her cousin Philip, heir to the Spanish throne and a dedicated enemy of Protestantism.

In the face of Mary's ruthless policy against heretics, most Englishmen adjusted their beliefs to avoid execution; but several hundred, including Cranmer, went to the stake for their convictions. The monarch thus earned the name (among Protestants) of "Bloody Mary." She was no more ruthless than her father, Henry, but she offended national feeling by subjecting the country once again to the pope and by marrying a despised foreigner. As Mary bore no child, her reign proved to be only a reactionary interlude whose net effect was to make Catholicism more unpopular than before.

The Elizabethan Compromise

Elizabeth, the daughter of Anne Boleyn, inherited the crown upon Mary's death in 1558. She had been raised a Protestant, but unlike her half-sister she was neither devout nor fanatical. During her early years, when Parliament pronounced her successively legitimate, illegitimate, and then again legitimate, Elizabeth must have developed a certain cynicism. And she could observe for herself the frequent shifting of individual allegiances in religion and politics. As queen, she stood firmly for a Protestant Church and independence from Rome. But her first concern was for the security of the crown and the unity of her subjects.

A true child of Henry, she managed Parliament and her ministers with astuteness. She had Mary's Catholic legislation repealed and the Act of Supremacy reenacted (1559). But she studiously avoided giving unnecessary offense to those of her subjects who were pro-Catholic. Her new laws embodied the Elizabethan Compromise (or Settlement), which remains to this day the foundation of the Anglican Church.

Parliament, with Elizabeth's approval, enacted a revised summary of official doctrine known as the Thirty-nine Articles. Similar to Cranmer's earlier statement, it was designed to satisfy all but extremists. The Thirty-nine Articles were explicitly Lutheran or Calvinist on certain matters, including the exclusive authority of Scripture, salvation by faith alone, the number of sacraments, and the freedom of the clergy to marry. But on many points the language was obscure, leaving a wide latitude of interpretation. There was also a firm injunction to respect the traditions of the Church, except those that were clearly "repugnant to the Word of God." Under the cover of tradition, pro-Catholics would continue to venerate the saints, go on pilgrimages, and engage in other "Romish" religious practices.

In internal organization the Anglican Church was very similar to the Roman Catholic. The monarch was its "Supreme Governor," but only in the sense that she was responsible, under God, for ruling all classes (religious and secular) in her realm. This idea was reminiscent of the priestly role of King David and King Solomon in the ancient Jewish state and of the position of Constantine, Theodosius, and Charlemagne in relation to Latin Christendom.

The actual ministering of the Word and the sacraments were restricted to the ordained priesthood, in accordance with the doctrine of apostolic succession. The Anglican bishops traced their authority back to the twelve apostles, as did the Roman Catholic bishops (and those of the Eastern Church). They rejected, however, the theory of Petrine supremacy, which was the cornerstone of papal claims to universal authority.

It is in the role of the bishops that Anglicanism differs most sharply from other Protestant denominations. This distinction is reflected in the designation "Episcopal Church" in America (*episcopus* is the Latin word for "bishop"). Most Protestant groups adhere to a presbyterian form of church government, a form we encountered in our discussion of Calvinism. The presbyterian form may be characterized as *representative,* the episcopal form as *aristocratic.* Roman Catholic polity (to complete our comparison) is *monarchical.*

The Elizabethan Settlement brought stability because most Englishmen (who by this time were weary of religious quarreling) were prepared to conform. Only a handful of the clergy—who had called themselves Catholic under Mary—now refused to accept the new Act of Uniformity. Elizabeth, who cared little about the private scruples and reservations of her subjects, was content with outward obedience. She would not tolerate open dissent, but penalties were softened and offenders were few. Not until the seventeenth and eighteenth centuries would new religious stirrings disrupt the established church in England. These would lead to further divisions of Christianity: Baptists, Quakers, Methodists, Unitarians, and others. But all that lay in the future. For the rest of the queen's long reign, her firm hand brought internal peace and prosperity.

The age of Elizabeth also brought England to the threshold of world power. Philip of Spain, who had become Philip II in 1556, sought the hand of Elizabeth after the death of his wife, Mary. Elizabeth had shrewdly held him off, so Philip ultimately decided to take her realm by force. (The pope excommunicated Elizabeth in 1570, declared her deposed, and thus opened the way to Philip's adventure.) In 1588 Philip sent a mighty fleet (the Spanish Armada) against England, expecting that once his soldiers had landed on the island, the thousands of unhappy Catholics in the country would rally to his banner. But the Armada was routed in the Channel by the English navy and was smashed by storms on its return home. With Spain, the leading power of the Continent, thus humbled, the English became conscious of their strength on the seas. Elizabeth's reign marked a turning point in the nation's history. Thereafter, English seapower, commerce, and diplomacy were to exercise a mounting influence over European and world affairs.

THE ROMAN CATHOLIC RESPONSE: REFORM AND REAFFIRMATION

So far we have been discussing the consequences of the Protestant movements—the revolt of religious leaders and civil rulers from the Roman Catholic Church. These movements grew out of a mixture of motives and were shaped by varying political and social conditions. But they all led to one result: the division of Western Christendom. Within half a century after Luther's challenge at Wittenberg, most of northern Europe had seceded from its allegiance to the papacy. Protestants dominated the urban cantons of Switzerland; they formed a militant minority in France; and a few had even penetrated the Catholic strongholds of Spain and Italy.

Finally the Roman Catholic Church, after hesitation and uncertainty, moved to check the spreading revolt. Too late to stop the major secessions, these efforts did recover some lost ground and kept the remainder of Europe in the Roman fold. The response took two main courses: reform within the Catholic Church and countermeasures against Protestantism.

Relation to Protestant movements

Catholic reforms were inspired, in part, by the same ideas and ideals that had motivated Luther and the other religious rebels. As we have seen, the condition of the late medieval Church had provoked widespread discontent and sharp criticism. The Christian humanist Erasmus was the most eloquent spokesman for reform without rebellion. Other sincere Catholics, both lay and clerical, hoped or worked for a deeper piety and the correction of abuses. A ground swell of reform, similar to that which had started the Cluniac movement in the tenth century, now began to rise. There can be no doubt, however, that Catholic reform in the sixteenth century was also prompted by the Protestant secession. The papacy, whose leadership was essential to effective action, had long remained indifferent. But when Paul III became pope in 1534 he was forced to respond to the ominous events in both Germany and England.

Though some aims were common to both the Catholic and the Protestant reform movements, there were crucial differences between them, for both orthodox and liberal factions among the Catholic leaders accepted the central doctrines, traditions, and organization of the Church. What the Catholic reformers desired was a purer Christian life within the established framework, which they achieved, in keeping with the Church's historic tradition of self-reformation. The Protestant leaders, on the other hand, were not content with purification alone. As we have seen, they wanted a reconstitution of the visible Church, in accord with deviant theories of authority, priesthood, and salvation.

While the Protestant movements arose in the North, Catholic reform efforts were centered in Spain and Italy. The Spanish reformation had begun in the late fifteenth century, led by Cardinal Ximenes (Archbishop of Toledo), with the full support of the monarchy. The Spanish reform served as a model for Catholic action elsewhere in Europe. This was reform distinctly in the medieval tradition: it included a rigorous campaign to improve the morals and education of the clergy, military action against infidels (the Moslems), and the persecution of all Christians who deviated from orthodox belief.

In Italy, too, some churchmen had urged the correction of clerical abuses and the restoration of Christian piety. But the Renaissance popes had dampened the zeal of reformers, and the secular princes of Italy were either indifferent or unwilling to make the necessary effort. As in the Middle Ages, however, new and reformed religious orders now arose to improve the quality of Christian life. One was the priestly order of Theatines, which was dedicated to education. Another was the order of Capuchins, a reformed branch of the Franciscan friars. The Capuchins modeled themselves upon Francis of Assisi and carried his message of love, piety, and simplicity to the common people.

Loyola and the Company of Jesus

One man and one order above all others, however, were to play a decisive role in the Catholic reformation and in stemming the Protestant tide. Ignatius Loyola, a Spanish nobleman and soldier of the king, was the founder of the new order. At about the time Luther was standing before the Diet of Worms (1521), Loyola was seriously wounded in a battle. His leg was shattered by a cannon ball, and he lay for months in painful convalescence, during which time he experienced a profound spiritual conversion.

Loyola was burdened, as Luther had been, by a sense of sin and unworthiness. After a long period of confession, fasting, and keeping vigil, visions of Christ and Mary appeared to him and relieved him of his anxiety. Now he resolved to give up all thought of resuming a secular life and enlisted himself as a "soldier of the Lord." He turned the strong military and chivalric tradition of his country to a spiritual purpose, dedicating his services to the Virgin, as a knight to his lady. And he held to the Spanish tradition of orthodoxy, finding satisfaction not in revolt but in absolute obedience to God and the pope.

Loyola realized that if he was to save souls from heresy or indifference he would need a thorough religious education. After preparing himself in Latin, he went on to the University of Paris, where he studied for some seven years, gathering about him a small band of devoted followers. Working at first as an informal association bound by common vows, they formed a regular order in 1540.

The order was named the Company of Jesus, and its members were commonly called Jesuits. Loyola was elected its general, or commander, for life, and he placed himself and his Company at the disposal of the pope. The general fashioned the internal organization along strict military lines, with a chain of command reaching down to the ordinary Jesuit "soldier."

The Jesuits imposed the usual monastic vows of chastity, poverty, and obedience and required, in addition, absolute acceptance of orthodox doctrines. In his manual for members, Loyola prescribed both "spiritual exercises" and rules of conduct. One of the rules stated, "To be right in all things we ought to adhere always to the principle that the white which I see I will believe to be black if the Hierarchical Church so rules . . . ."

The organization and discipline of the Company of Jesus were well suited to its broad purpose: "to employ itself entirely in the defense of the holy Catholic faith." The Jesuits sought to accomplish this goal chiefly through widespread education and preaching. They founded schools and colleges to inculcate young minds with the "true" doctrine, and they sent out missions to convert heathens and heretics. The Jesuits also strove (mainly through oral confessions) to keep wavering Catholics on the path of orthodox belief. And by serving as confessors and advisers to civil rulers, they tried to guide states in policies favorable to the Church. Though the Jesuits were highly effective in their education and preaching, their political activities ultimately brought them into international disrepute.

The reforming popes and the Council of Trent

When Loyola died in 1556, the Company had grown to nearly fifteen hundred members. All were carefully selected men, well trained and well disciplined, who could be counted on to support the pope without question. They proved especially effective in imposing papal control over the important Council of Trent in the mid-sixteenth century.

Paul III was the first of the reformation popes. Unlike his Medici predecessor, Clement VII, he was seriously committed to reform. A report by a committee of cardinals on abuses among the clergy he found so shocking that he decided to keep it secret. He did, however, launch an overhauling of papal administration, and he summoned an ecumenical council to deal with reform and heresy.

Many Catholics, as well as Protestants, felt that a Church council might help resolve the deep troubles of Christendom. The conciliar tradition was long and well established; the first ecumenical council, held at Nicaea in 325, had successfully faced a serious division over doctrine. The Council of Constance had faced an equally trying problem in 1417 with respect to the Great Schism of the Church. Some believed that another meeting of the prelates might once again restore unity and purity to the Church.

Others, however, though they favored a reform of practices, feared that a council might be drawn into a compromise on doctrine. The pope was apprehensive for an additional reason: past councils had tried to limit the papal monarchy and to establish the council itself as the supreme authority in the Church. Although Paul III at last summoned a council, he ensured that the papacy would control it.

The Council of Trent met, with interruptions, over a period of some twenty years (1545–63). The Jesuits at the council sought to keep a balance favorable to Roman policies; they were aided in this by the fact that papal legates presided over the sessions and Italian bishops outnumbered those of any other nationality. (The French clergy, who were committed to a "national" Church, did not participate fully.) Since the Italians (and Spaniards) were loyal to Rome, they could be relied on to support the papacy.

By the time the council opened, the pope had decided on a definite course of action. Earlier, a few of his advisers had recommended that some effort be made to bring about reconciliation with the

Protestants, but all overtures had proved futile. The pope settled instead on a program of reform and reinvigoration, while refusing to compromise on doctrine. He was willing, apparently, to accept the Protestant secession for the time being and to concentrate on keeping the rest of Christendom in the Roman fold. This, he thought, could best be done by correcting abuses and by defining and endorsing orthodox beliefs.

The Council of Trent submitted its final decrees to the pope, thereby reaffirming the supremacy of his authority. In general, the decrees gave the papacy what it wanted. They fell into two main categories: reform decrees and pronouncements on doctrine. Bishops were enjoined to restore strict discipline over their clergy in such matters as vows, morals, behavior, and dress. (Special attention was given to the problem of restoring continency and the putting away of concubines.) And they were required to provide better education for the priesthood by establishing a seminary in each diocese. Among the higher clergy, the abuses of selling offices (simony), taking the income of an office *in absentia,* and holding more than one office were forbidden. The *sale* of indulgences or of sacramental services was also outlawed. Had these reforms been launched fifty years earlier, they might have answered the criticisms of Erasmus and other conscientious Christians. In any case, Trent was a turning point in Catholic history, and the Catholic clergy and laity experienced a reawakening of piety and fervor.

Although the Protestant revolt no doubt stimulated the reform and revival of the Church, it also prompted a hardening of Catholic doctrine. The Council of Trent made no compromise with Luther or Calvin on theological issues; in responding to the Protestant challenge it not only reaffirmed traditional doctrines but stated them more distinctly. The result was to make orthodoxy clearer and narrower and to leave Catholic theologians with less freedom of interpretation than they had had before Trent.

The authority of the ordained priesthood, the indispensability of the Roman Church and the seven sacraments, the doctrine of transubstantiation, the veneration of saints and relics, the belief in purgatory and indulgences—all were specifically confirmed by the council. At the same time, the council explicitly condemned the opposing Protestant doctrines. Headed by the papacy, the Church was now prepared to execute the reform decrees of Trent and to restore orthodoxy throughout Christendom. Under the zealous popes of the second half of the sixteenth century, the Roman Church moved from stagnation and defensiveness to a bold offensive.

In addition to the Jesuits, two other agencies worked to crush

heresy and to keep the faithful safe in orthodoxy. The first was the
Inquisition, a medieval institution (pp. 188–89) that was now revived in Spain, Italy, and the Low Countries. Directing its efforts
against those accused of harboring heretical ideas, its secret trials,
torture, and burnings aimed at conformity through terror.

The censorship of books had been decreed by the Council of
Trent as another means of checking unorthodox beliefs. The council had provided for an Index (list) of prohibited books, including
all those that attacked the Roman Church or contained ideas contrary to its doctrines, and for a permanent Congregation of the Index
to be established in the Vatican to publish the list and keep it current. Church members were forbidden to read any work named in
the Index, which soon came to include much of the serious literature of Europe. Censorship, of course, had long been exercised by both
Catholics and Protestants, but the new effort was more comprehensive and was executed with greater energy than ever before. Although the prohibited books continued to circulate even in Catholic
countries, the Index no doubt contributed to a constriction of
thought.

The vigorous response of the Roman Church to the Protestant
challenge prevented further Catholic losses. Changes in religious
affiliation among Europeans were few after 1570, and the religious
divisions of that time (FIG. 8-1) persist today. Four centuries after
Trent, the antagonisms burn less fiercely, and there is rising sentiment for a closer association among all Christian faiths.

HISTORICAL SIGNIFICANCE
OF THE REFORMATION

Viewed from the perspective of the twentieth century, the struggles of the Reformation period seem strange in several respects. In
the first place, it appears incongruous that theological issues should
have called forth so much attention, energy, and bloodshed at a time
when religion, generally, was a declining force in European affairs.
(We have noted in the two preceding chapters the rise of materialism and secularism.) In the second place, while looking backward to
primitive Christianity, the Protestant movements actually drew
strength from contemporary social developments and gave them
strength in return. The growing sense of nationality, for example,
helped Luther's cause in Germany and was, at the same time, stimulated by Luther's revolt. The secessions from Rome furthered the
aspirations of power-seeking princes in northern Europe, while the
subordination of church to state in Lutheranism and Anglicanism

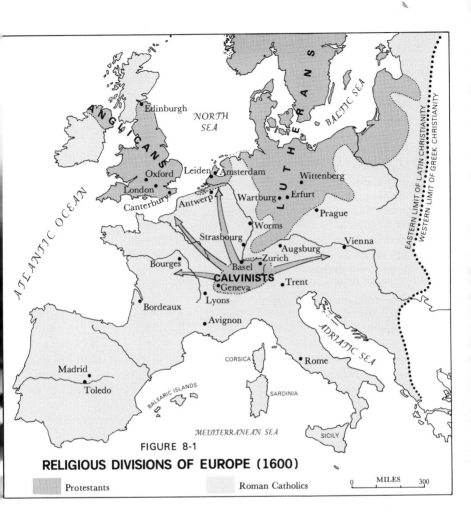

FIGURE 8-1

RELIGIOUS DIVISIONS OF EUROPE (1600)

Protestants   Roman Catholics

MILES
0   300

was both a response and a stimulus to the spirit of secularism. Also, Protestantism and capitalism tended to be mutually reinforcing. Calvin, for instance, though he urged businessmen to behave ethically, gave his blessing to their vocations. Thus, by praising the virtues of hard work and thrift, he sustained bourgeois morale and encouraged the accumulation of capital.

Perhaps the leading trend in Western culture from the close of the Middle Ages onward was toward *individualism*. It can be observed in the breakdown of the medieval social order, the growth of commercial enterprise, and the spread of overseas exploration (see

Chapter Six). The trend persisted in the Renaissance—in politics, art, literature, and society. The Protestant movements, too, reflected this tendency and gave it new impetus. Luther and Calvin stressed the right and power of each believer to read the Bible for himself and to communicate directly with God. True, both soon came to the position of imposing their authority on others. But the initial thrust of Protestantism—its spirit of rebelliousness and its appeal to individual conscience—could not be checked.

We see, then, that although the Reformation was in one sense reactionary, it was at the same time in harmony with "progressive" forces. It may, indeed, be interpreted as an *adjustment* of the Christian religion to the forward movement of national consciousness, secularism, capitalism, and individualism. But such an adjustment was by no means the deliberate aim of the reformers; they saw their movement, rather, as an adjustment, within the Church, to such strictly religious issues as ecclesiastical authority, doctrinal definition, and Christian discipline.

In any case, the Reformation radically altered the position of Christianity in Western civilization. The Christian Church, after the sixteenth century, could no longer speak with a single voice, and thoughtful men found it hard to accept absolute truth and absolute authority when the proponents of that truth and that authority contradicted and fought one another. This division brought dismay to many and led others to skepticism or atheism.

More than a century of wars over religion ended eventually in stalemate in 1650. The surviving religious denominations did not abandon their claims to absolute truth, but most people in western Europe came to agree that "truth" should no longer be imposed by force. And religious toleration, which thus emerged as a by-product of the Reformation, created a new intellectual climate of open questioning and independent reasoning. The abiding faith of medieval Christianity, with its intensity and its ecstasy, was gone forever. Religious doubt was to become a mark of modern man.

ART DURING THE REFORMATION

For many Protestants sacred paintings and sculpture were associated with Rome, and the revolt against "popery" was often accompanied by attacks (physical and verbal) on "idolatrous" images. Calvin, as we have seen, regarded works of art as a distraction from the word of God. He objected to any attempt to "paint or carve" subjects that transcended the realm of ordinary observation: "God's majesty, which is too exalted for human sight, may not be corrupted by fantasies which have no true agreement therewith."

The Protestant reformers (and some pious Catholics as well) were also offended by the sensuality so prevalent in Renaissance art. The "cult of beauty" had produced a number of works that were shocking to puritanical viewers, and a reaction now set in against the portrayal of nudity. Reforming popes of the sixteenth century ordered artists to paint clothes on the figures in some Renaissance masterpieces, and many of these works simply disappeared from public view.

The impact of Protestantism: Holbein, Brueghel

The Protestant artists of the sixteenth century faced two problems: they stood in the shadow of the Renaissance giants, and their main source of patronage had been cut off by the Reformation. In many areas, especially those under Calvinist influence, works of art were banned from the churches, and even for private homes paintings and decorations were frowned upon as frivolous. Erasmus, writing from the Netherlands in 1526, reported, "The arts here are freezing." For the individual painter or sculptor, the chill was often fatal. He might be deprived of income, acceptable subject matter— and useful work, which could be a psychic as well as a financial blow. The sense of alienation, characteristic of artists today, had its beginnings in the period of the Protestant Reformation.

The career of the German painter Hans Holbein is illustrative. Born in 1497, he mastered the techniques of his day and produced works that combined the best of the Italian and the northern styles. Most of his early paintings were designed for church altars, but with the coming of the Reformation Holbein was obliged to turn to portrait-painting. By good fortune, and with the help of Erasmus, he was able to move to England, where he secured commissions from the aristocracy and eventually became court painter to Henry VIII. He produced hundreds of lifelike portraits of the monarch, his family, and the royal courtiers. Working with oils and in the realistic tradition established by Jan van Eyck, Holbein usually showed his subject in a characteristic setting, surrounded by the symbols and tools of his office or profession.

Other Protestant painters explored the subject possibilities of landscapes and scenes of ordinary life ("genre" painting). The Flemish master of genre was Pieter Brueghel; though he produced many splendid landscapes, he is best known for his pictures of common folk. Brueghel was himself a townsman, but he exhibited

FIGURE 8-2. BRUEGHEL. *The Wedding Dance*. Courtesy of the Detroit Institute of Arts.

a keen understanding of simple, unsophisticated peasants. His persistent interest in rustic subjects shows itself in his paintings of peasants at work and at rest and in his scenes of hunting, feasting, and playing.

Brueghel's *Wedding Dance* (FIG. 8-2), painted in 1566 near the end of his life, is a striking example of perspective and organization. With its lively movement and rhythm, it suggests the hearty animal spirits of the dancers. Brueghel was one of the first artists to break with the aristocratic tradition of Renaissance painting to show us, bluntly and honestly, the ordinary men and women who made up the bulk of European society.

The development of the baroque: Rubens, Rembrandt

Although many Catholic painters were also skillful at depicting secular subjects, they were encouraged to direct their talents to religious art. The Catholic Church, after the Council of Trent, was eager to check the spread of Protestant ideas, and one way was to make the teachings of the Church immediately accessible to the faithful. Art had provided religious instruction during the Middle Ages; it was now called upon to renew its role in defense of orthodoxy.

The response was an outpouring of magnificent art ranging from the mystical to the sensual. Though the new artists built on Renaissance models, they threw off the restraints of classical rules. Their work came to be called "baroque"—meaning excessive, eccentric, or grotesque. But the movement generated its own standards and must not be measured by classical norms. At its best, baroque has an impressive originality and impact.

The exemplar of baroque art is the Flemish painter Peter Paul Rubens. In 1600, as a young man of twenty-three, he journeyed to Italy, where he learned to create heroic, large-scale canvases. After returning to his native Antwerp, Rubens combined the traditional Flemish attention to detail with his newly learned Italian style. He worked chiefly for the court of the ruling Habsburgs, the Flemish aristocrats, and the Church. A man of enormous energy and versatility, he created fine portraits, altar paintings, and huge murals for palaces and religious houses. His subject matter ranged from romantic and mythological subjects to the central mysteries of the faith.

Rubens was one of the few painters in history who was successful, prosperous, and respected in his own day. So great was the demand for his work that he set up a well-organized workshop in which he trained specialists to paint certain elements—heads, hands, animals, or backgrounds. He supervised the production of each work and finished the key features with his own hand. His paintings are notable for their breadth of conception, organization, color, and texture.

He was blessed by good fortune and a happy disposition, and his paintings are charged with movement and vigor. His well-nourished nudes reflect the spirit and vigor with which he viewed the world. In his treatment of a traditional subject from Roman legend, the *Rape*

FIGURE 8-3. RUBENS. *Rape of the Daughters of Leucippus.* Alte Pinakothek, Munich.

of the Daughters of Leucippus (FIG. *8-3*), he arranged powerful men, horses, and women into a tight group of solid masses. There is little philosophical probing in this kind of painting, but it combines exciting elements of form, color, and action.

As Rubens was the artistic master of Catholic Flanders, Rembrandt van Rijn was the master of Protestant Holland. But a greater contrast in personalities can hardly be imagined. A generation younger than Rubens, Rembrandt won substantial recognition early in his career. After his beautiful and well-to-do wife died in 1642, however, his fortunes began to decline. He fell into debt, his popularity vanished, and he became more and more introspective.

Yet it was in the dark days of tragedy and self-scrutiny that Rembrandt did his most profound work. He painted no longer for rich patrons but for himself. Although he often depicted religious subjects, all his paintings are suffused with a mysterious spiritual quality. Unlike Rubens, he usually drew his subjects from the middle or lower classes. He portrayed them with remarkable economy of line and without affectation or theatricality, shunning bright colors and extravagant movements and relying on contrasting lights and shadows. His colors appear dark or drab to those who see his paintings for the first time; he favored browns, dark reds, and golds. For he did not wish the surface of his canvases to blind the viewer to the

FIGURE 8-4. REMBRANDT. *Supper at Emmaus.* Louvre, Paris. (Giraudon.)

"inner" man. When we look closely at a Rembrandt portrait, we sense the essential personality of the subject.

Rembrandt spent most of his life in Amsterdam, but he incorporated into his technique many of the characteristics of Italian painting. These included careful organization and balance and, above all, psychological meaning (as stressed by Leonardo). An illustration of Rembrandt's religious painting is the *Supper at Emmaus* (FIG. *8-4*). A good Protestant, he was a devout reader of the Bible, and in this picture he dramatized a moment from the life of Christ as recounted in Luke (24:13–31). The Gospel states that on the day of the Resurrection, Jesus appeared, unrecognized, along a road. There he joined two of his disciples, who invited him to sup with them at an inn. Rembrandt showed Jesus at the moment when he blessed and broke the bread and was revealed to his disciples as the risen Christ.

Baroque sculpture and architecture: Bernini

The true center of the baroque style was in Rome, from which the Catholic reformation radiated. The climax of that style came during the seventeenth century in the work of the sculptor and architect Lorenzo Bernini (who died in 1680).

A leading characteristic of baroque artists was their effort to fuse architecture, sculpture, and painting into a single structure of grandeur and "truth." Bernini was trained as a sculptor, but he thought of himself as an artist who combined several talents. "I render marble as supple as wax," he declared, "and I have united in my works the resources of painting and sculpture." Bernini's most distinctive contribution was the revival of the Italian sculptural tradition, which had fallen into decline with the passing of Michelangelo. In the cold and hard medium of stone Bernini succeeded in catching the fleeting instant, the throbbing passion, the rhythm of movement.

He learned much from the intense, twisting figures of Michelangelo, but his work displayed even wider range and versatility. By means of extraordinary technical skill, he brought sculpture to new heights of drama and emotion. The *Ecstasy of Santa Theresa* (FIG. *8-5*), which Bernini prepared for the side chapel of a small Roman church, shows the mystical Spanish nun after her heart has been pierced by the arrow of divine love. As a smiling angel looks on, the face and body of the saint express ineffable rapture.

Bernini skillfully blended sculpture with architecture. Under Michelangelo's dome in the great basilica of St. Peter's, he devised an elaborate decoration for the apse; and directly above the central altar (which rests over the tomb of Peter), he built a huge bronze

FIGURE 8-5 BERNINI. *Ecstasy of Santa Teresa.* Church of Santa Maria della Vittoria, Rome. (Alinari.)

canopy, or baldachin (FIG. *8-6*). The scale and character of its eccentric, swirling columns epitomize the spirit of Catholic baroque.

Some years later, Bernini fashioned a dramatic setting for the exterior of St. Peter's to match what he had done for the interior. He designed the vast, elliptical piazza that stands before the largest church in Christendom. (More than a hundred thousand people crowd into the piazza on special days to await the blessing of the pope.) Enclosing two sides of the piazza, Bernini constructed a mighty colonnade (FIG. *8-7*) consisting of 284 Doric-style columns, four abreast. They carry a roof more than sixty feet high, surmounted by statues of heroic scale. Visitors entering the piazza from its open end are embraced, symbolically, by the "arms" of the Church.

Baroque architecture (like baroque painting and sculpture) was an adaptation of Renaissance models. Such classical elements as columns, pediments, and arches were used profusely, but the classical

FIGURE 8-6. BERNINI. Baldachin, St. Peter's. (Alinari.)

rules governing their use were either relaxed or ignored. From the late sixteenth century to our own day, many of the public buildings of Europe have been designed in this variable style. Catholic churches were the first to display baroque innovations in design and construction, often overwhelming the viewer with their size and magnificence.

The Catholic monarchs of Europe were quick to adopt the style for their own purposes. Philip II of Spain, the most powerful ruler of his time, started in 1563 to build a new royal palace and mausoleum, choosing for its site the village of Escorial, in the mountainous country near Madrid. Philip's architects laid out a vast complex of buildings and courtyards, with an elegant church at the center. Beneath its main altar was placed a burial crypt in which the Spanish kings and queens have since been entombed. The Escorial complex also included a monastery, a seminary, and a royal library. Its architectural style is generally severe, but its conception is baroque.

A more familiar monument to royal pretensions is the Versailles palace, built a century later by Louis XIV. The French monarchy had by then succeeded the Spanish as the dominant royal house of Europe, and Louis wanted to erect a residence and a center of government and the arts that would surpass all existing palaces. Like the Escorial, Louis' residence was built in the countryside (about twenty miles southwest of Paris). It was a culmination of the secular baroque style, combining architecture, landscaping, sculpture, painting, and the minor arts into a grand synthesis.

Built at staggering cost, Versailles matched Louis' pretensions. The roofed area covered seventeen acres and housed some ten thousand people. The formal gardens, courts, parade grounds, and surrounding woods stretched over many square miles. The overall plan was a masterly realization of the baroque idea of "integrated" design. While the exterior style of Versailles is restrained, the interior is lavish in the extreme. One of the most resplendent cham-

FIGURE 8-7. BERNINI. Colonnade, St. Peter's. (© 1962 Charles Rotkin from *Europe: An Aerial Close-up.* Lippincott.)

FIGURE 8-8. Hall of Mirrors, Versailles. (French Government Tourist Office.)

bers, located in the central part of the palace, is the Hall of Mirrors (FIG. *8-8*), a shimmering room designed to dazzle visitors to the French court.

In many respects, Versailles proved to be a highly "functional" structure. It helped the king to centralize his authority within France, and it strengthened the role and image of France as cultural leader of the West. A milestone in politics as well as in civic planning and in the arts, Versailles called forth a hundred imitations (on a lesser scale) by the monarchs and princelings of Europe.

IV. The Modern World

	Art and Architecture	History and Literature	Religion, Science, and Philosophy	Political, Social, and Economic Developments	
1600	Baroque style of architecture		Copernicus (died 1543) Bacon Galileo Descartes Kepler	Religious wars (Thirty Years' War in Germany) Peace of Westphalia	1600
1650	Versailles Wren St. Paul's Cathedral		Royal Society founded Hobbes Bossuet Locke Newton	English Revolution Cromwell Gotius and emergence of international law Mercantilism Louis XIV Age of absolutism	1650
1700	Watteau Reynolds Rococo style	Age of classicism Racine Pope Voltaire	The Enlightenment Deism Rousseau	Rise of Prussia and Russia: Frederick the Great Catherine the Great	1700
1750	Classical revival style David	Jefferson	Condorcet Smith Burke	Industrial Revolution and beginnings of factory system American Revolution French Revolution Napoleon and empire of the	1750

	Art & Architecture	Literature	Philosophy & Science	History & Politics	
1800	Goya	Age of romanticism Wordsworth	Utopian socialists St. Simon Fourier, Owen Hegel Comte	French Congress of Vienna Metternich System Spread of political and economic liberalism	**1800**
	Gothic revival style	Goethe			
	Houses of Parliament Romanticism	Balzac			
1850	Delacroix Turner Constable Courbet Daumier	Dickens Ibsen	Marx and Engels Mazzini Darwin Kierkegaard J. S. Mill Spencer Pasteur	Growth of nationalism German unification and empire: Bismarck Rise of corporate Big Business Rise of labor unions Urbanization of Western society The New Imperialism Triple Alliance and Triple Entente	**1850**
	Impressionism Monet Cezanne	Von Ranke			
	Expressionism Van Gogh	Dostoevsky Tolstoy Shaw	Einstein Freud Nietzsche		
1900	Organic style	Joyce	Rutherford, Bohr	First World War	**1900**
	Wright International style Gropius Mies van der Rohe		Lenin	Russian Revolution: communism Rise of fascism and nazism: Mussolini, Hitler The Great Depression (1930–40) Roosevelt Second World War Atomic bomb	
	Le Corbusier	Eliot	Existentialism Tillich		
	Picasso				
1950	Moore	Sartre	John XXIII Vatican Council	The Cold War Liquidation of colonialism	**1950**

Science and the New Cosmology

During the age of the baroque, beneath the flourish of grandiose artistic expression, new modes of thought were emerging that were to have a profound effect on the position of all established authorities. Even more important, the new ideas were to revolutionize man's concept of the universe and his means of comprehending it.

NATIONAL AND INTERNATIONAL DEVELOPMENT

Before we turn to the seventeenth-century revolution in science and philosophy, we will summarize political developments in Europe. By 1650 the transition from the political patterns of the Middle Ages had been largely completed. The principal new forms were absolute monarchy and the nation-state. And the monarchs of the seventeenth century, in addition to strengthening order within their own kingdoms, laid the foundations of modern international relations.

Foundations of the European state system: The Peace of Westphalia

A miniature model for the new European state system had appeared in Italy during the Renaissance, when city-states such as Florence, Milan, and Venice had devised a viable system of relationships among themselves as sovereign powers. They established embassies and agreed on diplomatic rules for peace and war; they made alliances and sought to maintain a "balance of power" inside Italy. As unified national states arose beyond the Alps, they drew on the Italian experience in shaping their own international relations.

The European state system grew out of a welter of forces, including dynastic ambition, national sentiment, and religious antagonism. In the Dutch revolt against Spain, for example, all three forces were present. The northern provinces of the Netherlands, which were part of the Habsburg domains, had embraced Protestantism, and their Catholic rulers had responded by imposing repressive measures upon the provinces. In addition to admitting the Inquisition to the area, the Habsburgs had introduced harsh political and economic restrictions. The Dutch provinces reacted by declaring their independence in 1581, and when Philip II of Spain tried to bring them back under his control he met with armed resistance. The defiant Dutch, with English help, fought the Habsburg forces on land and sea and at last compelled them to withdraw. In 1648, in the general Peace of Westphalia, the United Netherlands (Holland) was formally recognized as an independent state.

Religion and politics were similarly entwined in France, where the Catholic monarchy viewed the Calvinist minority (known as Huguenots) as disloyal. After the death in 1547 of Francis I, the country had been weakly ruled, and an aristocratic reaction against the monarchy had set in. Many nobles, seeking to regain their independence from the crown, had associated themselves with the defiant Huguenots.

The ensuing civil strife was mainly a contest between monarchists and the aristocratic faction in France; the religious convictions held by many on both sides tended to become submerged in the struggle. Henry IV, seeking a truce in the political-religious warfare, secured civil rights and religious tolerance for the Huguenots by his Edict of Nantes (1598). In the course of the seventeenth century, however, the royal government broke the military power of the aristocratic Huguenot faction, and Louis XIV revoked the edict in 1685.

In Germany religion and politics combined to produce the most tragic consequences. As we have seen, the Lutheran military revolt had ended in 1555 with the Peace of Augsburg, which left each German prince free to decide whether the religion of his subjects would be Lutheran or Catholic. This settlement had brought a kind of peace for sixty years, although divisive pressures mounted steadily. Guided by the Jesuits, the Catholic princes during these years stamped out the remnants of Protestant dissent in their territories. The zeal of the Lutheran princes, on the other hand, was dissipated in bitter squabbles with Calvinist minorities. Sensing danger, some of the Protestant princes joined together in an armed league in 1608, an action promptly countered by the formation of a Catholic league.

As each camp eyed the other, watching for any move that might upset the religious and territorial balance, revolt exploded in Bohemia, which was part of the Holy Roman Empire. The trouble in that proud Slavic land, whose people were both anti-German and anti-Catholic, had its roots in the Hussite rebellion of the fifteenth century (pp. 301–02). During the sixteenth century, the Calvinists of Bohemia had enjoyed some measure of toleration under moderate Catholic rulers. But when Ferdinand of Styria, a Habsburg and a fanatical Catholic, was forced upon them as king, they feared that their religious and political rights were in jeopardy. Accordingly, in 1618 the Bohemian nobles announced their open defiance of Ferdinand and chose a Calvinist prince of the Rhineland to be their king. The Catholic league of princes moved swiftly to help Ferdinand crush the poorly organized rebellion, and Ferdinand's election as Holy Roman emperor in 1619 gave him added strength.

But, as he proceeded to destroy Protestantism in Bohemia, other anti-Catholic and anti-Habsburg countries became alarmed. The king of Denmark decided to intervene in Germany in order to protect Lutheranism and to acquire territory for himself. He was promised help by the English and Dutch, who, for their own reasons, also wanted to check the advance of Habsburg power. Later, Sweden and France joined the struggle against Emperor Ferdinand, chiefly for political reasons. During this Thirty Years' War (1618–48) Germany was transformed into a ghastly battlefield occupied by mercenary armies. As time passed the aims of the warring powers grew ever more blurred and corrupted.

The Peace of Westphalia, which concluded the war, is a landmark in European history. With the militancy of both Catholics and Protestants eroded by the long struggle, the so-called religious wars came to an end. In Germany the terms of the Peace of Augsburg were restored and extended to include Calvinism as well as Lutheranism and Catholicism. Each prince retained the right to prescribe one of these faiths for his subjects, but conditions throughout the country were so wretched that none of them used force to compel conformity. Thus a kind of religious "coexistence" emerged from the debilitating struggle.

The end of the wars left Germany in a desperate condition. Having long suffered from political disunion, the country had then endured the worst ravages of warfare, plunder, and famine. The population had been cut by a third, and the loss of property had been severe. At the Peace of Westphalia, the German princes won recognition as independent sovereigns, and the Holy Roman Empire was thus reduced to a shell. Switzerland and the Netherlands, which had once been subject to the Habsburgs, now emerged as independent states. With the decline of Germany and of Habsburg power, the Bourbon dynasty (founded by Henry IV) became ascendant in Europe, and a century of French grandeur was at hand.

Thus Westphalia marked a shift in the balance of dynastic power and the emergence of the modern European state system. Gone were the vestiges of imperial and papal claims to authority over the political life of Europe; gone was the medieval idea of a unified Christian commonwealth. The settlement, whose principal provisions held until the Napoleonic Wars, transformed the Continent into an area of independent states (FIG. *9-1*), with each free to wage war or make peace and generally to act in a sovereign manner. The earlier Italian practices of diplomacy, alliances, and balance of power were now followed throughout Europe.

The seventeenth century also saw the emergence of an international law designed to regulate the anarchic relations among these independent states. Some rulers, of course, were more scrupulous in observing the law than others, but the law did provide standards that were widely respected. The classic statement of these standards is the *Law of War and Peace* (1625), written by the Dutch jurist Hugo Grotius—partly in response to the atrocities committed during the Thirty Years' War. Though Grotius recognized war as a "legitimate" state of affairs, he distinguished between just and unjust conflicts and laid down some guide lines for "humane" methods of waging war. Drawing on the ancient Roman principles of natural law (pp. 78–79), he spelled out the rights of neutrals and civilians and condemned such acts as poisoning wells, mutilating prisoners, and massacring hostages.

With subsequent extensions and refinements, Grotius' statement remained the standard authority on international law until the global convulsions of the twentieth century. Recent events appear to have made obsolete the "law of war and peace," the traditional concepts of sovereignty and neutrality, and the entire state system legitimized at Westphalia.

The absolute monarch: Louis XIV

By the end of the Thirty Years' War (1648), nation-states governed by absolute rulers had clearly shown themselves to be more powerful than city-states, principalities, and loose dynastic aggregations. France, the wealthiest and most populous of the nation-states, had moved steadily toward political centralization during the fifteenth and sixteenth centuries. After a temporary setback following the death of Francis I, the trend toward absolute monarchy proceeded apace during the seventeenth century. Cardinal Richelieu, the astute minister of Louis XIII, led the way in crushing provincial and aristocratic revolts and in fashioning effective instruments of royal power. His aim, he declared simply, was "to make the king

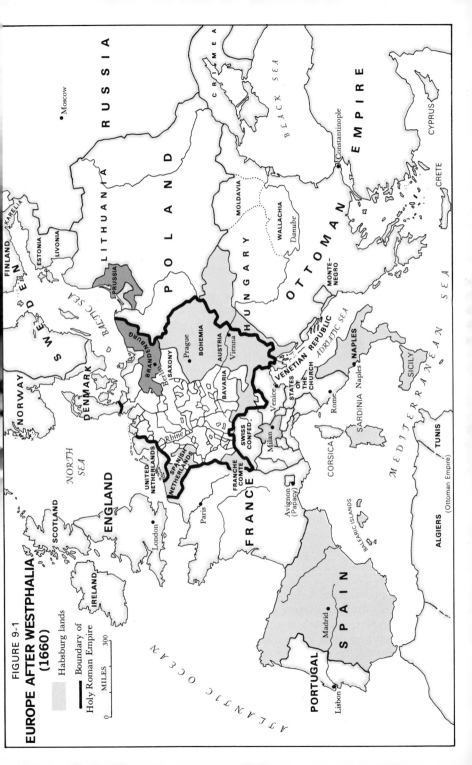

FIGURE 9-1
EUROPE AFTER WESTPHALIA (1660)

Habsburg lands
Boundary of Holy Roman Empire

MILES 0   300

supreme in France and France supreme in Europe." Richelieu died in 1642, but his work achieved fruition during the reign of Louis XIV.

The idea of absolutism was not new, but in Louis it found its most spectacular fulfillment. Having come to the throne as a boy in 1643, he took personal charge of state affairs in 1661 and held firm control for half a century, laboring ceaselessly at perfecting his royal image and performing his royal tasks. His style of governing became the model for all Europe, as did the French army, language, manners, and culture.

Louis ignored the traditional checks on royal power as he concentrated all authority in the crown, which became the symbol of national power (*"L'état, c'est moi"*). He overawed the nobles (whose fathers had entertained notions of regaining their independence) and used them as officers and ornaments of his court. His minister of finance, Colbert, strengthened the tax system and embarked on a paternalistic program of economic development. Internal trade was promoted by improved roads and waterways; colonies and trading companies were founded overseas; and home industries were fostered by means of protective tariffs and subsidies. State guidance and control of economic affairs (called "mercantilism") was thus well established in seventeenth-century France.

Louis had a passion for territorial expansion and an insatiable love of war and glory. By siphoning off the nation's wealth and manpower into costly military adventures, he negated many of the achievements of his long reign. His driving desire was to establish France's "natural" frontiers—the Rhine, the Alps, and the Pyrenees —and he bid, at last, to bring Spain into the French orbit. This bold challenge to the European balance of power provoked a Grand Alliance of the leading states against France. Despite the brilliance of his generals and the sacrifices of his subjects, Louis failed to realize his ambitions. Upon his death in 1715, France lay exhausted, her military power spent.

The rise of Prussia and Russia

England, which had been particularly effective in frustrating Louis' efforts to extend French control, was a potent force in European politics during the rest of the eighteenth century. Meanwhile, expanding states in central and eastern Europe began to make their weight felt in the power balance. The most important of these was Brandenburg-Prussia, whose ruling princes, the Hohenzollerns, gradually supplanted the Habsburgs as the most influential dynasty in central Europe.

The center of the Hohenzollern properties was the north German principality of Brandenburg, but the family also held the territory of Prussia to the east and claimed several smaller territories in western Germany. Through the Peace of Westphalia, the Elector Frederick William annexed adjacent Pomerania and then spent the rest of his life consolidating his control over the family's extended domains. Following the example of Richelieu in France, he built up a centralized treasury and bureaucracy and greatly strengthened his army. By the time Frederick William died near his capital of Berlin in 1688, Brandenburg-Prussia had become the most efficient state in Germany. His successor participated in the coalition against Louis XIV, and the allies accorded him the title of "King in Prussia" (in addition to Elector of Brandenburg). The higher title soon displaced the lesser one, and Prussia became the common name for the consolidated realm.

During the eighteenth century the Hohenzollern rulers continued to augment their dynastic power, regulating economic activities, raising ever larger and better-equipped armies, and demanding strict discipline from their soldiers and subjects. Prussia's landed aristocrats accepted the monarch's authority in return for complete control over their serfs. They also supplied the king with a hereditary officer caste. Since the army was essential to the survival of the Prussian state, it enjoyed high status and special privileges. It was at this time that the extreme militarism—"Prussianism"—emerged that was to mark Germany's destiny.

Frederick the Great, who was crowned king of Prussia in 1740, personified the new ideal of power. A product of the international anarchy and the political cynicism of his time, he became a master of the arts of war and diplomacy. With Machiavellian keenness Frederick expanded and consolidated his possessions to the east at the expense of a declining Austria and a dissolving Poland. He proved shrewder than Louis XIV, whom he took as his model. In his palace at Potsdam (whose design had been inspired by Versailles) he could boast at the end of his reign that he had made Prussia a power of the first rank in Europe.

Frederick was the most efficient of the eighteenth-century despots, but others sought to emulate him. His contemporary, the Habsburg ruler Maria Theresa of Austria, made some progress in centralizing control over her family's possessions in central Europe. Neither she nor her Habsburg successors, however, were able to achieve the cohesiveness and discipline that Frederick won for Prussia. Catherine the Great of Russia was still another of the autocrats of the eighteenth century. Like Frederick, she was keenly interested in literature, philosophy, and the arts; and like him she was a skillful practitioner of statecraft.

The expansion of Russian influence can be traced back to the fifteenth-century grand duchy of Muscovy (Moscow). The Slavs who inhabited this region were linked by religious and cultural ties to Constantinople, and Ivan the Great (who died in 1505) had married the niece of the last Byzantine emperor. Viewing himself as the heir to Byzantium, Ivan assumed the title of "tsar" (caesar) and referred to his capital as the "third Rome." Thus, from early times Moscow was impelled by a sense of imperial mission.

The feudal state of Moscow had long paid tribute to the Asiatic Tartars. Ivan's successors drove them east of the Ural Mountains, however, and then turned toward the west. By the end of the seventeenth century the Muscovites (now known by the broader term "Russians") were pressing toward the Baltic, and in the eighteenth century Peter the Great at last broke through. After a long war with Sweden, he won the Baltic provinces of Karelia, Esthonia, and Livonia (1721). In this region, at the head of the Gulf of Finland, Peter built a new capital, St. Petersburg (now called Leningrad). This "window on the West" was a symbol of his determination to Europeanize his empire.

When Peter died, a bitter struggle broke out between those Russians who supported a Western orientation and those who opposed it. Catherine, who became tsarina in 1762, looked toward Europe. Though she was the daughter of a German princeling, she devoted herself to the interests of her adopted country. Within the limits of her subjects' toleration, Catherine followed Peter's lead in encouraging Westernization. Forced to compromise with stiff-necked nobles, she never managed to secure the same degree of internal control that prevailed in France and Prussia. (Her sprawling empire, embracing many nationalities, was even more feudalistic than that of Prussia; nine-tenths of the population were serfs.)

It was in external affairs that Catherine the Great acted most nearly like her fellow despots. Intervening in Poland and the Ottoman (Turkish) Empire, she extended her territories to the west and south. By the end of the eighteenth century, Russia had emerged as a major force in the power balances of Europe and the Near East.

Rationales of absolutism: Bossuet and Hobbes

Absolutism was the predominant form of government in the seventeenth and eighteenth centuries. In the context of the times it appeared superior to other forms for very practical reasons; the despot was able to check civil strife within his realm, and in the struggles with rival dynasts he could command the full resources of his state. Nevertheless, no form of government enjoys the unquestioned respect and assent of every subject, and yet absolutism, by its very nature, was committed to strive for total control. Consequently the despots sought ideological justification for absolutism. They wanted to show why it was *right* for subjects to submit to their king—no matter what his policy or his demands.

The seventeenth-century monarchs might have elaborated the absolutist theory of Machiavelli, who had viewed politics as a purely secular art and science. This was indeed the thought and practice of the new monarchs, but they were themselves too Machiavellian to confess to his theory. (He had advised rulers to cloak their purposes in piety and religion.) For personal and political reasons, the despots preferred a "higher" justification of their authority: they found it in the doctrine of "divine right."

This was not, however, a return to medievalism. In the Middle Ages all authority was thought to be ordained by heaven, but authority was believed to be distributed and limited. The royal theorists of the seventeenth century went further: they sought to reconcile *absolutist* concepts and practices with traditional Christian doctrine. James I of England, the Stuart king who succeeded Elizabeth I in 1603, did not hesitate to speak out for himself. "The state of monarchy," he lectured Parliament, "is the supremest thing on earth, for kings are not only God's lieutenants upon earth, but even by God himself are called gods." Parliament, however, was not to be won over; in fact, time was running out for English advocates of absolutism. (The English Revolution will be discussed in Chapter Ten.)

It was in the France of Louis XIV, the "Grand Monarch," that divine right truly held sway. The theory was stated most precisely by a favored bishop of the court, Jacques Bossuet. In a treatise prepared about 1670 for the instruction of Louis' heir (*Politics Drawn from Holy Scripture*), Bossuet set down the royalist propositions in traditional scholastic form. Citing the Bible as the ultimate truth, he supported his points with appropriate quotations. Royal authority, he concluded, is sacred, paternal, and absolute. The king's judgment is subject to *no* appeal, and the king must be obeyed for reasons of religion and conscience. Whoever resists the king's command in reality resists God. For, declared Bossuet, "the royal throne is not the throne of a man, but the throne of God Himself."

The monarchs of France and other European states found these ideas appealing and, having heard them from childhood, may even have believed them. They were less enthusiastic about the secular argument for absolutism devised by Thomas Hobbes. An English scholar and philosopher, Hobbes was a royalist who supported the Stuart kings. His writings (around 1650) did them little good; nevertheless, his analysis proved significant for later generations.

Hobbes broke completely with religious traditions and drew instead on the mathematical and scientific advances of his time. (These will be discussed in the next section of this chapter.) In a sense, Hobbes took up where Machiavelli had left off; accepting politics as a purely secular matter, he tried to make of it a deductive *science*. His general philosophy rests upon materialism and mechanism and "reduces" man to a physical organism, the product of complex motion and countermotion. From this it follows that the physiology and psychology of human beings are the true bases of political organization, and, consequently, the true bases of the state.

Hobbes postulated the instinctive drive of every organism for self-preservation. The individual cannot achieve this goal once and for all, but he can move constantly to enlarge his *means* of security. As Hobbes wrote in his classic study, *Leviathan,* "I put for a general inclination of all mankind, a perpetual desire of power after power, that ceases only in death." In a "state of nature," with no governing (coercive) authority, the general human condition is a "war of every man against every man." To Hobbes such a life was "solitary, poor, nasty, brutish, and short." He did not turn to history or primitive cultures to verify such generalizations; his method was logical rather than empirical, deductive rather than inductive. His dismal picture of man's original (precivilized) condition derived from his postulates regarding man's physical constitution.

Fortunately, asserted Hobbes, men have a rational faculty that enables them to devise an alternative to the anarchy of nature. Because they are selfish egoists, unable to trust one another, they cannot create a cooperative society of equals. What they can do is agree to surrender their personal strength to a higher authority, which alone will have the power to curb individual aggression. Hobbes believed that human society, the state, and civilization itself arose from this hypothetical contract of each man with all others:

> I authorize and give up my right of governing myself, to this man, or to this assembly of men, on this condition, that you give up your right to him, and authorize all his actions in like manner. . . . This is the

generation of that great Leviathan, or rather (to speak more reverently) of that Mortal God, to which we owe under the Immortal God, our peace and defense.

Once civil government is established in this hypothetical manner, all subjects are bound by their covenant to *obey* it. They do so, not for moral or religious reasons, but, again, because of the under-lying motive of self-interest. Law is preferable to anarchy—because it better serves the *individual*. Hobbes supported absolute monarchy, or any other authority, on these grounds. But it is clear why his logic was not appreciated by the monarchists of his day. He de-molished their claim to divine right and brushed aside all moral arguments, appeals to tradition, and personal sentiments. Though a royalist, Hobbes was in fact a most radical Englishman. Paradox-ically, while defending the old, he turned men's minds toward the new. Though his thought contains numerous errors and confusions, it represented a breakthrough in the study of human behavior. It also provided a basis for the modern mechanistic concept of man—and for the modern authoritarian state.

THE SCIENTIFIC REVOLUTION OF THE SEVENTEENTH CENTURY

We will turn now to the intellectual changes that conditioned Hobbes' ideas and that were to have such a profound effect on Western life and thought. By comparison with these changes, the development of political institutions (which absorbed the atten-tion of kings and ministers) were of passing importance. The scien-tific revolution of the seventeenth century produced a radically different view of the universe and a new mode of thinking.

The methodology of modern science seems natural enough to edu-cated persons of the twentieth century. Because we are accustomed to it, we do not appreciate how *un*natural it is and how difficult it was to achieve. Yet our scientific method is unique in world history, a very special creation of the human mind. Science may be defined as a series of interconnected concepts and conceptual patterns re-lated to "irreducible and stubborn facts." It represents a fruitful union of precise observation, mathematics, and general principles. Through science, men have penetrated the operational mysteries of nature and have learned to predict and manipulate it.

Man's unaided "common sense" could never have produced science (any more than it could have produced theology or philoso-phy). In fact, one of the greatest barriers to scientific thinking was the proclivity of men to accept as truth the judgment of their senses. The fantastic world that science reveals to us is belied by its natural appearances. Through countless centuries, in every corner of the globe, men accepted the "obvious: that the earth for example, stands still, while the sun and stars whirl past. It was only through a rare combination of circumstances and high creative impulse that science was "invented." The methodology has not been perfected even yet, but it had its principal beginnings during the seventeenth century. The fertile minds of that time produced the supreme intellectual triumph of our civilization and made the West the tutor of the world.

This achievement rested, of course, on a rich intellectual heritage, starting with the science of the Greeks, which had been recovered in the late Middle Ages. The scholastics added refinements in logic and strengthened the idea of a rational, ordered universe. Then Renaissance men undertook geographical exploration and stressed the precise observation of nature. During the sixteenth and seventeenth centuries, instruments for observation were invented or improved; and mathematics, that indispensable tool of the mind, was sharply advanced. Equally important, the founders of science displayed the ability to see old things in new ways. The result was the overthrow of a universe—that of Aristotle and Aquinas. As the new universe was devised, the methods that had produced it evolved into a new scheme of thinking.

Discoverers of a new cosmos: Copernicus, Kepler, Galileo

The Aristotelian system must be understood before the revolution of the seventeenth century can be appreciated. That system was far more in harmony with the world of appearances than was the system that supplanted it. As adapted by Ptolemy, a second-century Alexandrian astronomer, the Aristotelian scheme placed the solid, immovable earth at the center of things. Rotating about the earth, in perfect circular motion, were the luminous heavenly bodies, which were embedded in successive crystalline (transparent) spheres. Closest to the earth was the sphere that carried the moon; then, at successive intervals, were the spheres of Mercury, Venus, the sun, Mars, Jupiter, Saturn, and the fixed stars. Beyond the sphere of the fixed stars was the Primum Mobile—a ninth sphere whose daily rotation from west to east drove the other spheres in their motion from east to west. Beyond the Primum Mobile extended the Infinite Empyrean (the highest heaven).

This ancient construct was incorporated into Christian thought and went unchallenged until the sixteenth century. It fitted the ordinary observations of men, and by means of ingenious adjustments it could be made to correspond to observed data. Moreover it accorded with man's awe of the heavens and his instinct for hierarchy by placing the heavenly bodies in a "higher" zone, distinct from the zone of earth. Scholars taught that imperfection and decay ruled over man's habitat but that the revolving spheres were governed by a superior set of laws. This explained the apparent permanence of the celestial bodies (in contrast to the ephemeral nature of things on earth)—and the regularity and harmony of their motions.

It should be noted that Ptolemy was aware of a heliocentric theory of the universe that had been taught by Aristarchus in the third century B.C. According to this theory, the apparent motion of the heavenly bodies was due to the earth's rotation on its axis. Ptolemy rejected this theory, as did other astronomers, because it did not fit his recorded observations so well as the geocentric theory. Further, it was impossible to reconcile Aristarchus' notion of earthly rotation with existing beliefs about motion. Again, the authority of Aristotle was decisive. He had held that earthly objects remain in a *state of rest* unless they are moved by a force and that sustained motion requires sustained force. As it was understood that these rules did not apply in the weightless celestial realm, the rotation of the crystalline spheres presented no difficulty. But, in the lower realm, motion depended on force; and the astronomers could discern no existing force strong enough to keep the earth's bulk turning. On this ground, and on the sensory evidence that the earth stood still, the heliocentric theory had failed to convince the ancient thinkers.

Nevertheless, Nicolaus Copernicus revived it in the sixteenth century. A learned Polish cleric with a passionate interest in astronomy, Copernicus grew dissatisfied with the geometrical complexities and discrepancies of Ptolemy's system. He allowed himself to imagine various celestial patterns and found that the heliocentric one offered the simplest geometrical explanation of observed movements. His major work, *Concerning the Revolutions of the Celestial Bodies,* was published in the year of his death (1543). Although other astronomers of the time shared his dissatisfaction with the Ptolemaic system, they did not accept the Copernican theory.

Copernicus' book was condemned by religious leaders, including Luther and Calvin, on the grounds that it contradicted Scripture and thus offended God. In one respect his hypothesis was but a limited departure from orthodox concepts: it did not challenge the celestial mechanics of Aristotle. Copernicus accepted the notion of revolving crystalline spheres and exchanged only the positions of sun and earth. This crucial alteration, however, upset the traditional view, for it transposed the earth into the zone of "celestial" laws and forces—and that made his hypothesis unacceptable.

A further objection was that Copernicus could furnish no observational proofs for his theory. If, as he thought, the earth revolved around the sun, then the positions of the fixed stars should show a shift when sighted from opposite sides of the earth's orbit. As astronomers know now, they do shift; but the shift is so small (because of the enormous distances) that Copernicus could not detect it. Copernicus also faced a problem that had baffled Aristarchus. How could he account for a force sufficient to keep the earth in rotation? He offered an answer, but it was hardly persuasive. He argued, in medieval fashion, that it was the "nature" of spheres to revolve and that the earth could not keep from turning.

It was more than a century before the Copernican theory gained substantial endorsement. Religious criticisms were not the only impediment; a great deal of observational work had to be done before its validity could be properly assessed. We should remember that Copernicus had no telescope to use in seeking proof for his theory; he worked from the ancient observational data handed down by Ptolemy. His mathematical mind constructed a neater system into which to fit the data, but he failed to reconcile his system with the prevailing physics.

Though Copernicus was unable to free himself from the bonds of traditional science, he nonetheless inspired later generations to resume the search for a simpler and more satisfying truth. Toward the end of the sixteenth century, a Danish astronomer, Tycho Brahe, made new and more comprehensive observations of the universe. These were assembled and analyzed by his co-worker, the brilliant German mathematician, Johannes Kepler. As a test of the Copernican thesis, Kepler tried to fit Brahe's data on the planets to postulated circular courses around the sun. When that effort yielded a negative result, he tested the hypothesis that the planets move in *elliptical* orbits. This he found to be so, and the finding came to be known as Kepler's First Law (1609).

Kepler next studied the data for mathematical relations that would prove the consistency of all planetary motions. His resulting Second and Third Laws held that every planet, though traveling its course at varying speeds, sweeps out equal areas of its elliptical plane in equal times, and that the square of the time a planet takes to complete its orbit is proportional to the cube of its mean distance from the sun. Kepler thus appears as the first man to operate in the manner of modern scientists: he first formulated hypotheses and then tried to verify their deduced consequences empirically. He also bridged the supposed gulf between celestial bodies and the earth by demonstrating the consistency of mathematical relationships throughout the solar system. Of still broader significance, he was the first to glimpse the universe as a vast, intricate machine subject to *exact and knowable* laws.

Though Kepler described the movements of the planets in precise mathematical terms, he was less successful in explaining what made them move. He assumed that some force must be holding the planets in orbit and moving them continuously along their courses. This force he concluded to be the sun. Basing his theory largely on the experiments of William Gilbert, an English physicist, Kepler suggested that the planets were magnetic. The sun, he held, was a giant rotating magnet; as it turned, it pulled the planets along in their orbits. Here Kepler was clearly reaching toward the modern concepts of universal gravitation and inertia. But it was left to the Italian genius Galileo Galilei to complete the overthrow of Aristotle, to confirm the heliocentric theory, and to bring the laws of motion to the threshold of a grand synthesis.

Galileo, a contemporary of Kepler, was less a mathematician and more an observer and experimenter. An astronomer as well as a physicist, he was the first, in 1609, to construct a telescope that could be used to examine the heavens. (The instrument had been invented a few years earlier by Dutch lens-makers.) Galileo's telescope was a lead tube about three feet long, with a two-inch glass. Crude and low powered by modern standards, it nonetheless revealed a world hitherto unknown to man.

In his excitement, Galileo saw that the planets were not mere points of light but bodies of dimension like the earth and the moon. Venus showed "phases" that corresponded to her position with respect to the sun and earth; this phenomenon disproved the prevailing notion that the planets were luminous and proved beyond doubt their heliocentric arrangement. By discovering the moons of Jupiter, Galileo provided support for the idea that there could be more than one center for heavenly orbits. And as he peered into the depths of space, looking past the fixed stars (which remained but points of light), he was overwhelmed by the incredible distances revealed by his telescope. Tens of thousands of stars, previously unseen, came into view in his telescope, and he was convinced that uncounted millions lay beyond. The comprehensible, closed universe of the Greek and Christian worlds vanished forever; earth and man were now seen as wanderers through the dark infinitude of space.

The Catholic Church was quick to condemn Galileo's views. Since its authority and doctrines were linked verbally to the Ptolemaic system, it regarded the new ideas as a menace to Christian truth and salvation. To the Church it mattered not that Copernicus, Kepler, and Galileo were deeply religious men, awed by God's wonders; their teachings contradicted both Scripture and sacred tradition.

Warned to forsake his view that the "earth moves," Galileo managed to keep his convictions private for some time. But he fell into trouble after publishing his *Dialogue on the Two Chief Systems.* In 1633 he was charged with heresy and brought before the Roman Inquisition; threatened with torture, he formally recanted. Through the *Dialogue,* however, his devastating attack on the conventional astronomy continued to spread. The book was placed on the Index (p. 328), along with the works of Copernicus and Kepler, where it remained until 1835. But the proscription of a book could not alter the order of the heavens.

After his ordeal before the Inquisition, Galileo was allowed to work quietly in a villa near Florence. During these years he turned to a subject that in itself would not disturb the ecclesiastical authorities—but that opened the way to the ultimate victory of the new view of the universe. The subject was *motion.* Though Aristotle's picture of the heavens was by now entirely discredited, his concepts of motion were still accepted. It was clear that the overthrow of his cosmic scheme must include the rejection of his mechanics, but no one had yet shown how that was to be done.

Earlier in his life Galileo had experimented with falling bodies. He later built special structures in order to study the acceleration of polished balls rolling down frictionless wooden planes. These devices permitted him to make more precise measurements of time and distance than he could make when objects were dropped through the air. In 1638 he published the results of his experiments and set forth his general conclusions on the subject of mechanics. He rejected the traditional beliefs that objects are "normally" in a state of rest, that there are "natural" directions of motion for certain substances, and that heavy objects fall faster than light ones.

His observations convinced him that a body in motion (with friction disregarded) continues at a constant speed without any sustaining force; a *change* in either velocity or direction requires a force. He found that the distance covered by any falling body is proportional to the square of its time of descent. These conclusions, known today to any schoolboy, were revolutionary in the seventeenth century. Galileo did not quite perceive that his terrestrial law of falling bodies was the same law that kept the planets in their orbits. But he completed the overturn of Aristotle's cosmos and contributed the crucial concept of *inertia.*

Molders of Scientific Method: Bacon, Descartes

Though the most striking accomplishments of the scientific revolution were in astronomy and mechanics, swift advances were taking place along the whole frontier of knowledge. One of the most significant advances was the development of science itself as a *methodology*. Here two men stand out: Francis Bacon and René Descartes.

Bacon, born in 1561, in the England of Elizabeth I, was a man of wide interests, a public official as well as a scholar. But his engrossing concern was with the advancement of learning. He complained of the stagnation of knowledge, blaming the condition on undue reverence for antiquity—above all, on the tyrannical authority of Aristotle. While the ancient Greek's celestial system was being upset by Kepler and Galileo, Bacon struck at the root of Aristotelian (and scholastic) science—its methodology—thereby adding impetus to the general intellectual revolution.

Bacon favored the practices of observation and experiment that had sprung up during the Renaissance. Experiments in themselves were not new, but he saw in them the foundation of a planned structure of useful knowledge. He criticized Aristotle's reliance upon *deduction,* which he viewed as a mere manipulation of words. Bacon's proposed system called for repeated experiments that would lead to inferences of generality, i.e., *induction.* Following each induction, new observations and experiments would be undertaken that would permit further inductions to be drawn. In this fashion a total system of descriptive truth could be built up, he thought, in a relatively short time.

Bacon was mistaken in many of his own beliefs about nature, but he anticipated modern methodology in his expectation that future experiments would correct his errors. He also urged scientists to record their experiments and to exchange data, in the interest of mutual assistance. Bacon's empirical philosophy and practical suggestions provided a stimulus to the budding science of the seventeenth century. True, he subordinated the role of mathematics in the scientific enterprise, but that deficiency was remedied by Descartes.

The advance of science requires, indeed, *two* modes of thought. One of these is induction, stressed by Bacon; the other is deduction, emphasized by Descartes. Descartes' classic *Discourse on Method* appeared in 1637; along with Bacon's writings, which had been published somewhat earlier, this book gave new direction to both science and philosophy. Descartes and Bacon had at least one thing in common: they were dissatisfied with traditional learning and sought to construct a completely new system of truth.

Descartes was a brilliant mathematician, and his accomplishments in mathematics affected his approach to knowledge in general. A private scholar of independent means, he was disgusted by the absence of certainty and precision that he detected in most areas of study. He therefore tried to apply to other subjects the methods of geometry and arithmetic, which start with "clear and simple" propositions of unquestioned validity. From these intuitive propositions, all consequences are deduced; plane geometry, for example, is built upon a single axiom (which itself is a self-evident assumption): "A straight line is the shortest distance between two points."

In adopting the method of mathematics, therefore, one must commence by *doubting* all present ideas ("Cartesian doubt"); the slate must be wiped clean, so to speak. If an idea can be questioned for any reason at all, it must be discarded. Descartes did just that, reducing knowledge to a single idea that he could accept absolutely: "I *think*"—from which he deduced, "therefore, I *exist*." Upon this intuitive foundation he set out to construct, by a series of logical steps, a complete picture of the universe (including God).

In this ambitious effort, Descartes committed errors and fell short of success. But his general rejection of existing knowledge, intellectual authority, and traditional modes of reasoning undermined the old ways of viewing the world. Especially provocative was his vision of a mechanical universe subject to unvarying mathematical rules, which vision was to exercise a profound influence on philosophy and religion as well as on science.

The grand synthesizer: Newton

The final statement of seventeenth-century science was left to Isaac Newton, who perfected and refined the new cosmic system first delineated by Kepler and Galileo. It was Newton, also, who established the canon of scientific method as a lucid union of Baconian and Cartesian theory. Genius though he was, he could not have accomplished what he did without the knowledge and techniques developed by countless predecessors.

Newton was a simple country youth whose precocious talents won him a place at Cambridge University. After earning his degree he became deeply absorbed in mathematics and shortly developed the system of calculus, which is indispensable for the continuous measurement of complex variables. While still in his twenties, he was appointed professor of mathematics at the university, where he continued his far-ranging inquiries. Motivated by the pure love of knowing, he had little interest in publishing the results of his research. He soon turned his probing mind to the puzzles posed by the new astronomy.

Galileo had virtually established the principles of terrestrial motion but had failed to demonstrate how these principles applied to celestial bodies. Why did the planets move in curved orbits rather than in straight lines? Galileo mistakenly answered that curved motion was as "natural" as straight-line motion and therefore had its own inertia. The solution to the mystery, of course, lay in the pull of gravity. While Galileo recognized and gauged the earth's gravity in his observations of falling bodies, he did not make the stupendous leap to the concept of universal gravitation.

Ideas about the magnetic attraction of physical masses had begun to be formulated during the seventeenth century. Around 1600 William Gilbert had built a spherical magnet and had noted that its properties were similar to those of the earth. He reasoned that the heavenly bodies must also resemble the earth in this respect, each one exerting a pull toward its own center. The moon, he said, keeps the same face toward us because of its magnetic attraction to the earth. But the sun, the largest body in the solar system, is the focus of attractive power. It will be recalled that Kepler also held this belief and ascribed the motion of the planets to the sun's rotation.

Suspecting that the relation between inertia and gravitation was the key to celestial motion, Newton studied the problem over a period of years. In order to verify his hypotheses, he had to translate the component elements into mathematical terms. He succeeded in calculating the masses of the sun, the planets, and their satellites. One of the first important consequences of these calculations was his discovery that each planet would travel according to Kepler's laws only if the gravitational pull upon it was inversely proportional to the square of its distance from the sun. He next applied this gravitational formula to the motion of the moon around the earth. Treating the moon as a body with inertial movement in space, he theorized that its curved orbit was due to a continuous "falling" toward the earth. And after making due allowance for its distance from the earth, he concluded that the moon behaves in conformity with terrestrial falling bodies. Newton thus linked Galileo to Kepler, eliminated the barrier between earthly mechanics and celestial mechanics, and established by *empirical and mathematical proof* the existence of *universal* laws.

Such was the message of Newton's *Principia* (*Mathematical Principles of Natural Philosophy*), published in 1687. In this work he unraveled the mysteries of celestial motion and established the fact that man possesses the means to achieve far greater understanding. For he demonstrated that on the basis of experiments conducted in a tiny corner of the universe, and aided by the lever of mathematics, man had discovered the nature of gravitation *everywhere*. Newton was able to express this discovery in the most precise terms: "Every particle of matter in the universe attracts every other particle with a force varying inversely as a square of the distance between them, and directly proportional to the product of their masses." Newton also set down rules of scientific reasoning to guide others in finding the fundamental principles embodied in phenomena, in elaborating these principles mathematically, and in verifying them through observation and experiment.

Not surprisingly, Newton was hailed by his contemporaries as a lawgiver, a scientific Moses. As Alexander Pope put it:

> Nature and nature's laws lay hid in night;
> God said, "Let Newton be," and all was light.

Although the *Principia* was not so widely read as Descartes' more literary *Discourse on Method,* it soon became the undisputed source and symbol of science—the new testament of a new faith. Some of Newton's concepts of matter and motion have been modified by twentieth-century physicists, but his methodological principles remain a model.

The organization of science

The story of science since Newton has been one of continuous acceleration in the growth of knowledge. Even in Newton's time, discovery was proceeding in numerous fields, and findings in one subject suggested and aided investigations in others. Robert Boyle identified physical "elements" and thereby fathered chemistry. William Harvey explained the function of the heart and the circulation of the blood, thus grounding the science of physiology. The Greek physician Galen, whose authority had ruled for centuries, shared the demise of Aristotle; medicine and pharmacy now achieved a scientific foundation.

Rapid strides were also made in optics, and the development of the microscope (as well as the telescope) opened promising new vistas. The microscope paved the way for the sciences of botany and zoology and made clear to man that he stands near the median point on the universal scale of magnitude—halfway between the giant stars and the infinitesimal particles of matter. Along with optical devices, measuring instruments of various kinds were invented to provide experimenters with the precision they needed. And the idea of the laboratory, where experiments could be conducted under controlled conditions, had taken shape by the end of the seventeenth century.

These various developments reflected the growing *interdependence* of scientific investigators and their equipment. The isolated, casual experimenter of the Renaissance (like Leonardo) had given way to a new type. No matter how proud or contentious scientists might become, they fully recognized that science was a social enterprise. No one man or nation was alone responsible; the advance of science was an international achievement that depended on generally accepted procedures and continuous communication among investigators. Curiously, while religion and politics were breaking down into national and subnational units, science arose as a universal system.

The universities were painfully slow in promoting the new learning. Still in the grip of ecclesiastical and humanist traditions, they were generally hostile or indifferent to science. In the education of young men, two centuries were to pass before the "classical" curriculum would make room for scientific subjects, and new institutions had to be created for the support and coordination of experimental studies.

The earliest societies for the advancement of research were founded in Italy. Rome set up an academy in 1603 of which Galileo was a member; a half-century later the Medici established a scientific institution in Florence. More influential and longer lasting, however, was the Royal Society of London, which was chartered in 1662. It consisted of scientists and mathematicians as well as interested merchants, nobles, and clerics. In an effort to implement Francis Bacon's plan for the grand incorporation of all knowledge, the members of the society supported experiments, listened to learned discussions, corresponded with foreign societies, and published a scientific periodical.

The society was interested in the practical applications of science as well as in "pure" research. Bacon himself had asserted that the true goal of science was to endow human beings with greater power. And Robert Boyle, an early member of the Royal Society, confessed that he did not desire merely to discourse about nature; he wanted to learn to *master* it. Traditional philosophy, he pointed out, had been barren of practical advantage to mankind. Science, properly understood, would strengthen the useful arts and raise the levels of material existence.

This emphasis on practical applications attracted support from commerce, industry, and government on the Continent as well as in England. Louis XIV, at the suggestion of his finance minister, Colbert, endowed the Academy of Science in 1666, and similar institutions were founded in other European states. Thus pure science (the search for truth) was wedded to technology (the creation of material goods and control over nature).

THE IMPRESS OF SCIENCE ON PHILOSOPHY: THE ENLIGHTENMENT

The link between science and technology could be perceived readily in the increased output of workshops and arsenals. More subtle and complex was the influence of science on the general ideas, values, and attitudes of society. For science gave to educated Westerners a radically new view of their universe and the forces that move it. Most ordinary people, of course, continued to pass their days, as millions of people always have done, in childlike innocence of the world of science.

Even unlettered men, however, could not wholly miss the consequences of the change. A new intellectual climate enveloped Europe in the eighteenth century and spread outward to the ends of the earth. The generators of the new point of view were the educated classes of Europe, whose way of looking at life derived from their underlying beliefs about the nature of the universe. While only a few intellectuals were trained scientists, most of them accepted (sooner or later) the scientific description of natural phenomena. And from this base, they proceeded to construct a new philosophy and a new society.

A revised cosmology: the "world-machine"

The scientists themselves had little to do directly with the new philosophy that emerged during this era. Men like Kepler and Newton tended to be conservative in their religious and social views; Descartes, though an apostle of intellectual doubt, urged people to conform to traditional mores. Nor did professional philosophers play a very significant role. The movement was mainly the work of gifted amateurs, "literary" men; in France, where the transformation was centered, these intellectuals came to be known as the *philosophes*.

The *philosophes* were so dazzled by Newton's brilliance that they considered themselves living in an unprecedented age of "light." It was this notion that gave rise to the term "Enlightenment" as a name for the period that reached from 1687, the date of the *Principia*, to 1789, the start of the French Revolution. The men who glimpsed the new vision of the universe thought of themselves as the "enlightened" ones, and they were eager to spread the light to their fellow men.

The universe they held up to view contrasted sharply with the traditional Christian one. The most evident and disturbing differences were that the new universe was heliocentric and that it extended through boundless space. The devout Catholic mathematician Blaise Pascal had confessed, "I am terrified by the eternal silence of those infinite spaces." But the humanist as well as the Christian felt humbled and perplexed: man was no longer the *center* of nature's plan. The architecture of Newton's universe made man insignificant, both in time and in space. It was still possible to believe that a personal God existed, that he had a special plan for man, that human life had supreme value. But such a faith was no longer buttressed by the evidence of astronomy. It seemed, rather, to be contradicted by the extravagant dimensions of the cosmos.

Other supports for traditional beliefs collapsed. With Aristotle's laws of motion overthrown, no role remained for a Prime Mover, or for Moving Spirits. The hand of God, which once kept the heavenly bodies in their orbits, had been replaced by universal gravitation. Miracles appeared impossible in a system whose workings were automatic and unvarying. Governed by precise mathematical and mechanical laws, Newton's universe seemed capable of running itself forever.

Men had long been familiar with such complex machines as watches and clocks. Was it not logical, after Newton, to believe that the universe itself was a grand machine? Not all its rules of operation had yet been discovered, but scientists knew enough to be able to infer the nature of the whole. The French astronomer Pierre Laplace epitomized the mechanistic idea of the eighteenth century when he said: "Give me the present location and motion of all bodies in the universe, and I will predict their location and motion through all eternity."

The view of God

If the "enlightened" concept of the universe had profound implications for the meaning of human freedom, responsibility, and ethics, it raised even more disturbing questions about religious convictions. What was to become of the belief in God? Some scientists hailed the marvels revealed by science as a confirmation of the wonders of the Almighty, while others chose to keep their scientific knowledge locked in a tight compartment of their minds, completely insulated from their religious beliefs. But it was extremely difficult to bring the two systems together, to fit Christian precepts and practices into the new cosmology. The "world-machine" had no *need* for supernatural guidance, prayer, priests, sacraments, or penance; these seemed superfluous if not contradictory.

Churches and synagogues went on as before with large bodies of followers. The certainty of individual belief may have weakened somewhat, though there was no external evidence of this. Religious leaders at first denounced the new scientific concepts as untrue and subversive; later, when the concepts could no longer be denied, they asserted that such ideas made no difference anyway. These reactions illustrated a "law" that Newton had never mentioned: the inertia of belief systems.

Many scientists and intellectuals, however, persuaded that they could not logically reconcile Christianity with scientific truth, rejected the former. This does not mean that they necessarily gave up the idea of God. Newton had explained the *operation* of matter in motion, but he gave no hint of its *origin*. Since common sense still made it difficult for men to think of something as existing that had not been *made,* the question of creation remained unanswered. Here was a role for God that appeared reasonable to the *philosophes*. It also satisfied the urge to believe, which remained a part of their cultural inheritance.

Newton himself stated that the First Cause is not mechanical and suggested that God, "in the beginning," had formed matter in the particular way he desired. Thus God was referred to in scientific circles as the Creator, the Maker, or the Author. It was equally logical to believe that he had established the governing rules of the universe as well as its substance; hence, he was given such alternate names as the Great Mathematician, the Great Engineer, and the Governor. Though scientists like Newton and Boyle suggested that the Divine Watchmaker might occasionally intervene to correct an irregularity in the operation of the world-machine, the prevalent belief was that God had long since removed himself from the affairs of the universe. Only *nature* remains, so it is nature that must be understood and respected.

This was a religion of sorts, but it was clearly not Christianity, Judaism, or any other revealed system of belief and worship. Vaguely labeled "deism," this new religion had been launched in the seventeenth century. An Englishman, Lord Herbert of Cherbury, tried to make of it a universal faith that would incorporate and supplant all the others. He posed five basic truths as common to the foremost religions of the world—and not incompatible with science. These were: the existence of a Supreme Power, the necessity of worship, the requirement of good conduct, the efficacy of repentance of vices, and the existence of rewards and punishments after death.

Lord Herbert's efforts to synthesize the major religious systems ended in failure. He had dreamed of a cessation of sectarian strife and the beginnings of accord among all men of good will. Though deism became popular with such eighteenth-century intellectuals as Voltaire, Franklin, and Jefferson, for most churchgoers it was an inadequate replacement for conventional religion. It lacked mystery, ritual, emotional appeal, and discipline. And it was repugnant to the clergy of all denominations, for it challenged the unique authority of their sacred books, dogmas, and hierarchy.

Deism gradually lost its appeal even to the converts of science. By the close of the eighteenth century many of them had decided that there really is no need even for a Maker. Newton had shown that motion is as natural as nonmotion. Is not matter, then, as natural as nonmatter? Was it not old-fashioned to think that things must be *created?* The universe and its motion had always been and always would be. This line of reasoning led some to deny God absolutely (atheism); others said they could not or did not know whether God existed (agnosticism). Religious doubt was by no means new in Western civilization, but the scientific revolution gave it new vigor and new appeal. Though the number of doubters remained small (and the number of *professed* doubters even smaller), they were to exercise a steadily corroding influence upon traditional faith.

The view of man and society

If God played an inactive role (or none at all) in the cosmology of the Enlightenment, the place and powers of *man* were dramatically enlarged. The humanists, after recovering from the initial shock of Newton's astronomy, saw that man's role became more important as God's role declined. Writers began to emphasize the grandeur of man's reason, which had enabled him to fathom the mysteries of the universe. Though he could not control its movements, he had touched the cosmos with his mind. And he had, at the same time, vastly expanded his power over life on earth. Through science and technology he could improve his well-being and press nature itself into his service.

Man might be viewed as not only stronger but better. The *philosophes* did not deny the existence of evil in human affairs, but they generally blamed it on bad social institutions. Nature, as revealed by Newton, is orderly and harmonious. Because of ignorance, however, man had failed to follow nature's ways and had forged customs, laws, sanctions, and beliefs that twisted and shackled the individual. Man would regain his birthright and exhibit his true character when the chains of unreason were broken.

This growing optimism about man's prospects had its roots in the Renaissance, but it was strengthened by the new science. The dogma of Original Sin appeared out of place in the new cosmos, and the observed laws of motion, celestial and terrestrial, showed no inherent movement in the direction of evil. Within the boundaries of human freedom, it seemed plausible that man would choose good rather than bad—so long as he followed nature and reason. As knowledge advanced, man would become increasingly capable of good; and when at last he reached complete harmony with nature he would be judged perfect. Thus, thought most of the *philosophes*, man is not only good but *perfectible*.

No doctrine of the eighteenth century proved more controversial than this doctrine of human perfectibility. It runs counter to traditional Christian teaching and is hard to reconcile with much of human history. But most of the *philosophes* were undisturbed by doubts. Convinced of man's perfectibility, they set about to achieve it as quickly as possible. They became indefatigable reformers, aiming to remake social institutions according to the lights of reason. The "humanitarian" movement, as an organized force, was in large measure a product of their thought and work. Voltaire in France and Beccaria in Italy, for example, pioneered in advocating more rational ways of dealing with crime and punishment. The reformers focused attention too on helping the poor, the orphaned, the enslaved, and the afflicted; in these efforts they were often joined by Christians acting in the spirit of holy charity. The *philosophes* worked, above all, for broad freedom of expression, tolerance, and a cosmopolitan outlook.

Faith in nature and reason

The humanitarian and ethical goals of the Enlightenment were similar to those of Christianity, and the "rational" criteria of goodness derived, in fact, from the Judaeo-Christian tradition. But the core of the new cosmology was wholly alien to established religion. Whereas the latter grew out of centuries of human experience, the philosophy of the Enlightenment sprang directly from the vision and method of the new science. The essential differences may be summed up this way: Christianity rests its faith in the power of God as known through revelation; the Enlightenment put its trust in nature as understood through reason. The supreme goal of the one is heaven (spiritual bliss after death), of the other progress (physical happiness in life on earth).

To the ancient Greeks, as well as to the Christians, nature had been an uncertain, brooding force, more likely to be hostile than friendly. To the men of the eighteenth-century Enlightenment, nature had virtually supplanted God and had been shown to be regular and knowable. They believed that the secrets of nature could be unlocked and applied beneficently to mundane affairs—the farmer, for example, could make the soil more productive by observing and following physical laws. They believed, too, that legislators and judges could provide justice by applying social "laws" to human relations. This latter confusion of moral and social principles with physical laws was to lead to bitter disappointments.

The eighteenth-century cult of nature was an outgrowth of excessive awe and zeal. Respect for the harmony of celestial motion led some enlightened philosophers to an unscientific, sentimental attitude toward *all* manifestations of nature. Alexander Pope attributed a grand intelligence and benign purpose to nature as an entity:

> All Nature is but art, unknown to thee;
> All chance, direction which thou canst not see;
> All discord, harmony not understood;
> All partial evil, universal good.

Others turned to a romantic worship of wildlife. Jean-Jacques Rousseau inspired a "back-to-nature" movement that persisted into the nineteenth and twentieth centuries. He helped popularize hiking and camping as ways of bringing one nearer to earth, rocks, and scenery unspoiled by man. The cult went so far as to glorify some of the least civilized individuals and some of the lowliest occupations, on the ground that they were closer to nature. Even the French queen Marie Antoinette had a rustic village built for her near the lavish palace of Versailles. There, on sunny days, she and her ladies frolicked as milkmaids.

Most eighteenth-century intellectuals, however, kept their eye on the central idea: the extension of useful knowledge through the exercise of reason. Perhaps the most exhilarating discovery of the age was that nature behaves in a rational, even mathematical, manner; therefore its workings correspond to human logic. From this the *philosophes* concluded that reason is the key to nature's secrets and powers and is the proper means of judging and regulating human affairs.

An acceptable model for explaining the working of the mind was supplied by the versatile Englishman John Locke. Though interested in science, Locke followed the guide of common sense rather than rigorous methodology. He studied medicine, economics, political theory, and philosophy, and he associated with the leading political figures of his country. Perhaps because of his familiarity with practical affairs, his writings were readily received by the educated public, and several generations of hardheaded revolutionaries found reassuring rationalizations in his political tracts. His writings on the nature and derivation of human knowledge were especially persuasive, for he rested his arguments on the ordinary sense experience of his readers. Locke may not have been profound, and he was certainly not scientific. Nevertheless, his writings swept away many ancient assumptions and showed what the "new" reason could do when it was applied to questions about man and society.

In his *Essay Concerning Human Understanding* (1690) Locke asserted that all knowledge derives from experience. This was in line with Bacon's empiricism and challenged long-established convictions that knowledge is innate or revealed. Descartes, for instance, held that some ideas are implanted by God, while Socrates and Plato had taught that all knowledge is inborn. According to Christian doctrine, truth is revealed to man by God.

Locke's theory, however, rested on a very simple model of the mind, whose functioning depended on no occult or supernatural elements. The mind at birth, said Locke, may be likened to "white paper, void of all characters, without any ideas." The ideas that become inscribed on this paper come from but one source: *experience*. By this Locke meant not only immediate perceptions (sensation) but the operations of the mind in sorting and arranging those perceptions (reflection). Thus the intelligent person uses his senses with care and systematically arranges and compares the impressions he receives through them. These processes are the substance of both reasoning and knowledge, and they enable man to understand and control the world about him.

Though Locke's conception of the "thinking-machine" was naive, it did provoke further study. Physiologists and psychologists, especially those of the Freudian school, have since discovered that the mind is infinitely more complex than Locke imagined. Still, the Lockean theory proved useful; it suited the eighteenth-century view that man is warped by his environment. According to Locke, ideas are totally dependent on outside stimuli. Hence, if the correct environment is provided, the individual will receive only the "right" ideas. This suggests, in turn, that through the reform of institutions, especially education, rapid improvements can be made in human nature and society.

These beliefs help explain the devotion of eighteenth-century intellectuals to both science and education. To them ignorance had replaced sin and the devil as the principal enemy. Man was to be redeemed, not by the grace of God, but by human reason. Research had to be encouraged so that investigators could learn more; education had to be overhauled and extended so that the new knowledge could be carried everywhere. The *philosophes* threw themselves into these endeavors with the dedication of missionaries. They felt that education should be for adults as well as for children. As propagandists of "truth," they took to writing pamphlets, books, and encyclopedias. The world was never to be quite the same again; the belief in science and education became a feature of the modern world. In the United States, founded at the peak of the Enlightenment, that belief has remained an article of national faith.

The vision of progress

The more enthusiastic apostles of reason had no doubt that they were on the path to paradise on earth. No Christian millennium or heaven existed in their cosmology, but they found a counterpart in their vision of progress—a vision they expected to fulfill within a few generations.

Progress, as the *philosophes* understood the term, was a new idea in history. The ancients had been more "realistic" in this respect, for they believed that life on earth would always be hard and uncertain. If they wished to contemplate something better than their own lives, they had looked *backward* rather than forward—to an age of heroes or a Garden of Eden. Christianity had taught that depraved man must live in this world as a pilgrim awaiting perfection in the world to come. Even the humanists of the Renaissance, though their estimate of man was higher than that of the ancients, were far from believing in the inevitability of progress. Erasmus saw folly unending, and Montaigne sought the consolation of books. Perhaps their attachment to the classics confirmed such scholars in their pessimism.

But seventeenth-century science at last broke the spell of antiquity. Scientists began to point out how much more they knew than the ancients. They felt moved to say what was plainly true: it was the Greeks and Romans who were "children" in time; and it was the most recent generations, who had the advantage of man's accumulated experience, who were in fact the "ancients." Science thus dissolved the myth of classical superiority and, with its new tools, pointed the way toward a grander future.

The Marquis de Condorcet made an eloquent statement of this high faith in progress. A well-educated nobleman trained in mathematics and science, Condorcet served as secretary of the French Academy of Science. He is especially remembered for his *Progress of the Human Mind,* written, ironically, during a chaotic year of the French Revolution (1794). Though an active reformer, Condorcet had broken with the more radical leaders of the revolution and was in hiding as a fugitive. But he wrote that his sorrow over temporary injustices and barbarities was overbalanced by his vision of the future. Such contemplation, he said, was a refuge in which he lived "with his peers in an Elysium created by reason."

Condorcet's expectation of universal happiness on earth was to prove illusory, but his writing was nonetheless prophetic. He declared that nothing could stop the advance of knowledge and power "as long as the earth occupies its present place in the system of the universe, and as long as the general laws of this system produce neither a general cataclysm nor such changes as will deprive the human race of its present faculties and its present resources." He forecast that rapid technological advances would lead to a world in which "everyone will have less work to do, will produce more, and satisfy his wants more fully." He saw the eventual abolition of poverty and the ordering of economic affairs so that every individual, guided by his own reason, could enjoy true independence.

Condorcet proposed a social-security system and suggested that population growth would ultimately have to be inhibited through birth control. He also prophesied an end to colonialism and warfare, declaring that wars would "rank with assassinations as freakish atrocities, humiliating and vile in the eyes of nature." His vigorous optimism, characteristic of the eighteenth-century *philosophes,* marked the culmination of the rise of secular values and human self-confidence that had begun with the emergence of capitalism in the late Middle Ages.

THE RATIONAL SPIRIT
IN LITERATURE AND ART

The new ideas in science and philosophy had a marked effect on the literature of the seventeenth and eighteenth centuries. The prevalent culture fashion was "classicism," which was an extension of Renaissance ideals, given fresh impulse from the new stress on logic and universal laws. Bernard Fontenelle, who preceded Condorcet as secretary of the Academy of Science, called attention to the significance of mathematical principles for literature:

> The geometrical spirit is not so tied to geometry that it cannot be detached from it and transported to other branches of knowledge. A work of morals or politics or criticism, perhaps even of eloquence, would

be better (other things being equal) if it were done in the style of a geometer. The order, clarity, precision, and exactitude which have been apparent in good books for some time might well have their source in this geometric spirit.

Condorcet insisted that all expression must accept "the yoke of those universal rules of reason and of nature which ought to be their guide." The endeavor of writers and artists to apply such rules led to the curbing of the extreme individuality that had developed during the late Renaissance and baroque periods.

The leaders of classicism sought, through the use of reason, to devise a view of man (and of types of men) that would be universally valid. They also sought to perfect exact *forms* of expression, based on ancient models, and to give to modern languages the precision and felicity of classical tongues. Rejecting the force of contemporary usage in determining what is "correct," they looked instead to recognized arbiters of style and taste. Nicolas Boileau (in France) and Alexander Pope (in England) were venerated critics whose judgments were taken as literary law. Each aspired to be the Newton of his art.

The advocates of classical standards favored the founding of national academies to promote and enforce those standards. This idea appealed to the absolute monarchs of the period—Louis XIV, for example, created the Académie Française in 1635. As patronage flowed chiefly from the court and its dependent aristocracy, most writers now felt compelled to observe the official canons of style and taste. The Académie succeeded in imposing classical standards on French writers for more than a century.

Classicism: Racine, Pope

As we saw earlier in this chapter, France was the center of European power and culture during the seventeenth century. And in France classicism had its strongest roots, inspiring one of the richest periods in French literature. This period, marked by more than a reverence for Latin and Greek classics, was the time when the "classics" of the French language were fashioned. In addition to philosophical writers like Descartes and Pascal, there were outstanding men in every branch of letters. Chief among them was Jean Racine, France's greatest dramatic poet and a leading exponent of classicism.

Educated by a Catholic religious order, Racine received thorough training in Greek and Latin as well as in theology. His middle-class family wanted him to become a priest, but an urge to write poetry took him to Paris in 1663. When an ode written to Louis XIV brought him to the attention of the king, Racine's literary career was launched. He received a post at the court the following year and was elected to the Académie Française in 1673.

The plots of Racine's tragedies were drawn from classical themes and invariably centered on a single moral issue. Racine honored strictly the "dramatic unities" attributed to Aristotle (time, place, and action). Like other plays of the period, his were intellectual and introspective in nature, with long speeches and little action on stage. He relied on the spoken word to reveal character and passion under stress. The simplicity, precision, and dignity of his poetry provoked Voltaire's comment: "Beautiful, sublime, wonderful."

Classicism in a different mode was represented somewhat later in England by Alexander Pope. In his *Essay on Criticism* (1711) he set down his dicta for critics, and in his subsequent *Essay on Man* he propounded, in verse, a rationalistic view of the universe. Pope, a Catholic by birth but strongly influenced by deism, tried to reconcile the epochal discoveries of science with the idea of a benevolent God. He stressed the elements of order in nature, which had been confirmed by the mathematics of Newton. But, while acknowledging the power of reason, he urged men to restrain their curiosity and pride: God's works are ultimately beyond understanding; it is best to accept man's limited place in the scheme of things and to believe that "Whatever is, is Right." Although this advice was not entirely satisfactory either to scientists or to theologians, it endeared Pope forever to defenders of the social status quo.

Pope's *Essay on Man* was classical in form as well as substance, consisting of measured couplets, many of which were well-turned (and well-remembered) epigrams:

> Know then thyself, presume not God to scan;
> The proper study of mankind is man.
>
> . . .
>
> Hope springs eternal in the human breast;
> Man never is, but always to be blest.

The work as a whole illustrates the strengths and weaknesses of didactic poetry and the style of classicism. Strict form possesses a power and beauty of itself; at the same time, it may inhibit the free development of ideas and feelings.

Satire: Voltaire

Literature in the eighteenth century, responding to the stimulus of the Enlightenment, reached out to an ever widening public. The

French classicists had written mainly for the court and for a coterie of devotees. The *philosophes,* however, were less interested in the refinement of letters than in the circulation of new ideas. With literacy on the rise, they found that men and women of all classes, but especially the bourgeoisie, wanted to be informed. A special category of writers appeared whose main aim was to digest important ideas and put them in readable form for "the public." Along with encyclopedias, dictionaries, and surveys of knowledge, there was a rapid proliferation of newspapers and magazines.

The most successful and famous of the new writers was Voltaire; he was, in fact, one of the first men to make a fortune by his pen alone. The son of a Parisian notary, he was schooled by Jesuits, who evidently sharpened his talent for argumentation. Though formally trained in law in his homeland, his real education began in England. In trouble in France because he had insulted a nobleman, Voltaire accepted exile across the Channel in 1726. Through private study and conversation, he quickly absorbed the ideas of English philosophy and politics.

When Voltaire returned to France, he began to write all sorts of works—plays, histories, poems, scientific surveys, and philosophical essays. The best-known and most widely read of his more than a hundred books is the satirical novel *Candide* (1759), which reflects his reasoned outlook, his irony, and his strong convictions. The story is a swift-moving, rollicking caricature of an idea popularized by Pope—that "this is the best of all possible worlds." The protagonist, Candide, is an innocent young man who has been brought up to believe that everything is for the best. In the course of incredible misadventures, he learns differently. The story ends with Candide and his companions living on a small farm trying to shut out the stupidities and indecencies of the world. "Let us work without theorizing; 'tis the only way to make life endurable."

In the course of the novel, Voltaire struck out with rapier (and bludgeon) at many targets: the bigotry and hypocrisy of organized religion, the atrociousness of war, the inhumanity of man to man. He showed contempt for dogma and arbitrary authority and disgust with ignorance and prejudice. Though a man of the Enlightenment, he criticized many of the new ideas as well. He ridiculed pseudo-reason, which spins out unsupportable hypotheses and seeks to distinguish "cause" and "effect" in every event; scoffed at the nature cult; and turned the dream of progress into a nightmare. Voltaire was clearly the descendant of Erasmus, Rabelais, and Montaigne, but he surpassed them all in directness of approach, pungency, and cynicism.

And yet Voltaire had faith in the method of science and the power of reason. He stood courageously for freedom of expression: "I disagree with every word you say," he declared to one of his detractors, "but I shall fight to the death for your right to say it!" He admired simple honesty, moderation, tolerance, and humaneness. If he sometimes grew petulant and bitter, it was because the world seemed so full of what he hated and so empty of what he loved. Like Erasmus, he was no revolutionist, but he and his fellow *philosophes* nevertheless helped prepare the ground for revolution.

The architecture of reason: Wren, Jefferson

The Enlightenment was only partly reflected in the visual arts. On the Continent, the style of baroque architecture carried over into the eighteenth century and was gradually modified into the lighter, more delicate style of "rococo" (shell-like). Both styles were elaborate and elegant, suited to the pomp of monarchs and aristocrats. By 1750, however, the classical influence led architects back once again to the simplicity of Roman and Greek models.

In England, the baroque had been more restrained, and the return to classicism came earlier there than on the Continent. The most influential architect of the time was Christopher Wren. The Great Fire of London (1666) gave him a unique opportunity; as the king's principal architect, he was charged with replanning the city and rebuilding St. Paul's Cathedral. As might be expected, Wren was obliged to accept many compromises, and his master plan for London was never realized. He did, however, succeed in having many of the city's churches constructed according to his designs.

Wren's triumph was St. Paul's (FIG. 9-2), which was completed in 1710. Though the cathedral chapter wanted a tall Gothic building, he won approval for a plan that was essentially classical. Wren was influenced by Michelangelo's plan for St. Peter's and by later Italian architects, but he shunned the curving lines and extravagance of the baroque. He desired a simple though monumental structure, crowned by a unifying dome. In order to satisfy the clergy, he placed tall bell towers above his classical façade and a ninety-foot "lantern" on top of the dome. The result was something of a hybrid, though Wren strove to preserve the basic harmony of the plan.

In his designs for parish churches Wren again came into conflict with his clients. The churchmen wanted tall Gothic spires, symbolic of Christian striving. Wren wanted simple, classical structures. The problem of combining the vertical thrust of the Gothic with the horizontal line of the classical was formidable, but somehow he

FIGURE 9-2. WREN. St. Paul's Cathedral. (A. F. Kersting, London.)

managed to solve it. A well-preserved church of Wren's style and generation is St. Martin-in-the-Fields (FIG. *9-3*). This church, and others like it, became models for churches in both England and America.

FIGURE 9-3. GIBBS. St. Martin's-in-the-Fields. Engraving drawn by Thomas Shepherd, engraved by H. W. Bond. (Courtesy New York Public Library.)

Subsequently the trend was toward a stricter classicism. The preferred manual of taste was now a book by the Renaissance architect, Andrea Palladio, who had methodically measured ancient ruins. The "Palladian manner," with its porticos, rotundas, and domes, became the standard for eighteenth-century England. Noblemen who built villas in this style believed that their homes were a reflection of an age of reason—the reason of Newton and Pope. In the second half of the century, admiration for ancient architecture was further stimulated by the excavation of the Italian cities of Pompeii and Herculaneum (at the foot of Mt. Vesuvius). The beauty and grace revealed in those ancient buildings had a powerful effect upon the houses, furnishings, and dress of the well-to-do.

Thomas Jefferson was one of the many intellectuals who became enamored of the classical style. On a visit to France in the 1780's he saw the ancient Roman temple, the Maison Carrée (FIG. 9-4), in the provincial town of Nîmes. He reported that he gazed at it for hours at a time, "like a lover at his mistress." When Jefferson returned to America he designed numerous public and private buildings, thus popularizing the classical style in America. His plan for the Virginia state capitol at Richmond (FIG. 9-5) was inspired by the Maison Carrée, and his designs for the library of the University of Virginia and his home at Monticello were patterned after the

FIGURE 9-4. Maison Carrée. (Caisse Nationale des Monuments Historiques.)

Roman Pantheon. The public architecture of Washington, D.C., still bears the impress of Jefferson and the classical revival. The new nation's leaders were proud to demonstrate visually their enthusiasm for the Enlightenment and its ideals of reason and order.

FIGURE 9-5. State Capitol, Richmond, Virginia. (Virginia Chamber of Commerce, photo by Phil Flournoy.)

The leaders of the French Revolution also favored Roman and Greek models. And the revolutionary heir, Napoleon, continued to support the classical style for personal reasons: he thought it fitting to his role as a "modern Caesar," and he wished to distinguish his own monuments from the baroque structures of the Bourbon monarchs. Classicism thereby carried over to the nineteenth century. It gave way finally to the Gothic revival in architecture, which was a symbol, in turn, of the nineteenth-century reaction against the ideals of the Enlightenment.

Academy painting: portraits of aristocratic elegance

Painting, of all the arts, was least affected by the radical changes in science and philosophy. In the seventeenth century, classical rules had continued to govern; during the eighteenth century the rules became less rigid. The painters of France, sustained largely by royal and aristocratic patronage, were serving a doomed social order. But their works reveal no sign of an impending cataclysm and are marked by singular charm, repose, and grace.

The Belgian master Antoine Watteau was the finest representative of the eighteenth-century style known as rococo. He came to Paris in 1715 and went to work on various commissions for the nobility. As a designer of interior decorations for courtly festivals and pageants, Watteau caught the spirit of refined ease and gallantry associated with the aristocratic ideal. He began to create oil paintings of picnics in the woods, music parties, and mythical scenes peopled by graceful ladies and gentlemen in lustrous silks and satins. But these are not lifelike portrayals. They arise out of a dream world, where ugliness is absent and beauty pervades all.

Watteau worked, like his fellow artists in France, under the watchful eye of the Academy of Painting. Yet his paintings have an unmistakable individuality—an air of detached melancholy reminiscent of Botticelli. Destined to die in his thirties of tuberculosis, Watteau seems to have sensed the fleeting character of life and beauty. In viewing his canvases we have an intimation that all the elegance and beauty will shortly fade away (along with the aristocratic society for which he was painting).

More sensual and gay (but no more realistic) were the paintings of François Boucher and Jean Fragonard. These artists painted mythical subjects and the frivolities of the nobility in a delicate and delightful manner. Their works, corresponding to the aims and taste of their patrons, had no important function other than playful entertainment.

Painting in England was more sober and solid. The dominant figure there was Joshua Reynolds, who became the first president of the Royal Academy of Art (1768). Reynolds is best known for his portraits of the wealthy and for his advocacy of traditional "laws" of painting. "I would chiefly recommend," he told the academy, "that an implicit obedience to the Rules of Art, as established by the practice of the great Masters, should be exacted from the young students." He regarded the Italian Renaissance, rather than antiquity, as the "classic" source for the rules of painting. But he agreed with the classicists that there existed universal standards of taste and excellence.

The English nobility and gentry were willing to pay a good price to have their portraits painted in the grand manner. Reynolds felt that historical or mythological subjects offered a greater challenge to his intellect, but he made a fortune by obliging his aristocratic sitters. With high skill in texture and composition, he created hundreds of flattering portraits. His *Duchess of Hamilton* (FIG. 9-6) is typical of the English classical style.

FIGURE 9-6. REYNOLDS.
Duchess of Hamilton. The
Trustees of the Lady Lever
Art Gallery, Port Sunlight.

THE CLASSICAL AGE OF MUSIC

The seventeenth and eighteenth centuries, taken together, comprise the classical age of music, for it was during these centuries that most of our modern instruments and forms of composition were established. If, however, we use the term "classical" in a narrower sense—meaning the musical *style* corresponding to that of classical literature and architecture—we find that it applies to the eighteenth century only. The music of that century, as we shall see, echoed the pervading accent on order, balance, and restraint. Seventeenth-century music, on the other hand, is usually called baroque, because its diversity and power corresponded to similar elements in baroque art and architecture.

Music in Western civilization

Music has always been a vital part of the life and expression of Western man. If we have given it slight attention in our account of ancient and medieval civilizations, it is chiefly because we have so little information about the musical instruments and compositions of those times. Almost all the music and instruments we hear today go back no farther than the Renaissance. Yet we know that ancient and medieval peoples ascribed important powers to music and used it for both sacred and secular purposes.

In primitive cultures, music was regarded primarily as a vehicle of magic. Singing and playing on a variety of homemade instruments were intended to win supernatural assistance for the individual or the tribe. Certain types of music were presumed to lend strength in battle; others promoted fertility; still others preserved health or dispelled sickness. With the rise of early civilizations, music began to be viewed also as a medium of pleasure and edification. The development of music as an aesthetic art ranks, in fact, as one of the prime achievements of the human spirit.

Though we possess only a few fragments of Greek music, we know that music held a high place in the Greek scale of values. Belief in its power is symbolized by the ancient myth of Orpheus; his playing on the pipes tamed wild animals and even secured the rescue of his wife, Euridice, from the underworld. Music was customarily used also to heal sick bodies and minds and was thought to influence the development of character and temperament. Thus, we find that the study of music was fundamental to Greek education. Aristotle explained that some "modes" of music depressed the emotions, some inspired enthusiasm, while others produced a moderate mood.

Greek music, like that of the Orient, was primarily vocal, as might be expected of the Greeks, who were a highly verbal people. (Plato considered melody and rhythm useless, except as accompaniment for words.) Instrumental music was therefore neglected, and singing was confined to a simple tune (monophony) with no harmonizing chords. The monophonic pattern is still characteristic of music outside Western civilization, but complex melodic forms (polyphony) began to appear in the West around 1000 A.D.

Every good Greek was an amateur musician, but there were professional singers and players as well. Itinerant poets recited ancient legends to the accompaniment of the lyre (a primitive stringed instrument played like a harp). The only other standard instrument was the pipes, which usually consisted of two slender tubes joined at the player's mouth. Its sound, scholars believe, was something like that of the modern oboe. Playing and singing were indispensable to Greek religious and civic processions, and they were vital parts of the drama, that climactic achievement of Hellenic art and intellect. The actors chanted their poetic lines, and the chorus sang and danced solemnly according to set steps and patterns.

We know little about the music of ancient Italy, except that the Romans readily adopted Greek forms. We know, too, that they contributed a family of instruments, the military horns. Later, the Roman papacy was responsible for transmitting a portion of the musical heritage of antiquity to western Europe. Pope Gregory the Great, the leading figure in the founding of the medieval Church, assembled and codified Christian sacred music in the sixth century.

This music had originated in a variety of oriental sources, chiefly Hebrew. Exclusively vocal, it was used only in liturgical services (the Mass) and canonical prayers (the Offices), and it was sung by the priest, the choir, or the congregation. It consisted of a monophonic chant, or plainsong. The music collected by Gregory, or attributed to him, is known as the Gregorian chant. For centuries it has been the principal sacred music of the Roman Catholic Church.

We have reason to believe that secular, as well as religious, music was popular during the sixth century, but most of it seems to have disappeared in the turbulence of the early Middle Ages. There was a cultural recovery, however, from the tenth century onward. Poems and songs were presented by wandering scholars, who called themselves Goliards (pp. 208–09). Still later came the troubadours, who composed and sang love songs and romances of chivalry. They, too, used only the monophonic form, with simple accompaniment.

Polyphony ("part" singing) had its beginnings in the tenth century. This more complex form demanded a superior means of musical notation, and during the twelfth and thirteenth centuries the basis was laid for the modern system, with its staff, time signature, and syllables. Meanwhile new instruments were appearing. Most important were the clavichord and the harpsichord, the forerunners of the piano. The pipe organ, which was commonly used to accompany sacred music, underwent successive improvements.

During the Renaissance, polyphony reached its full development in both sacred and secular music. It was applied to religious texts (motets), to Masses, and to performances of the Lord's Passion. The most popular secular songs were madrigals, which were similar in form to motets. Instrumental music (written mainly for dances) also gained favor. The recorder, a wooden relative of the flute, was introduced at this time, while the most common instrument was the lute, similar to a mandolin. Most of the instruments of the period are now obsolete, although we sometimes hear performances of Renaissance music adapted to modern instruments.

The birth of the "modern" style: Monteverdi, Bach

The transformation of music to its "modern" form began rather late in the Renaissance and reached full force during the baroque era of the seventeenth century. So sweeping were their innovations that the baroque composers believed they were bringing about a musical revolution. In fact, they referred to the Renaissance manner as the "old style" (*stile antico*) and to their own as the "modern style" (*stile moderno*).

In contrast to the even-tempered, complex themes of traditional polyphony, baroque compositions were marked by a heavier stress on a dominant melody. Elaborate harmonic chords and dramatic effects were also characteristic, and in order to render a wider range of tonal effects, larger numbers and types of instruments were used: flutes, oboes, trumpets, and bassoons, as well as violas, violins, and the harpsichord. Composers now began to write instrumental music for listening, not just for dancing. Reflecting the growing importance of the bourgeoisie, concerts were held in public halls as well as in the private courts of royalty and nobility. This was a secular age, and secular music now became as important as sacred music.

Perhaps the most important cultural development of the time was the appearance of a new art form: the opera. This "music drama," consisting of expressive speech heightened by melody and rhythm, originated in Italy. Its chief creator was Claudio Monteverdi, who had spent the earlier years of his life writing madrigals and Masses but who in middle age turned enthusiastically to the modern style.

The most appealing of his operas, *Orfeo,* was first performed in 1607. Exhibiting most of the elements of modern opera, it contained the first operatic overture and a number of instrumental passages to heighten dramatic action. Monteverdi, who was also a singer, a viol player, and a conductor, devised an effective combination of instruments to support his operatic themes. The make-up of his ensemble approximated that of the modern orchestra.

Opera did not, however, find ready acceptance outside Italy. More than a century passed before the new art form was taken up north of the Alps. Meanwhile, a prolific German composer was writing in every form except opera. Johann Sebastian Bach (born in 1685) is a giant of the baroque period and one of the great musicians of all time. A devout Lutheran, he composed profound and inspiring scores for religious texts (cantatas and oratorios), Masses, and Passions. Bach was equally talented in secular music, creating superb pieces (chamber music) for performance by small groups at aristocratic courts. He is notable for the power and grandeur of his expression and for his mastery of polyphonic themes.

The classical spirit: Mozart

The death of Bach in 1750 marked the end of the baroque and the beginning of yet another style of musical expression. As in the visual arts, a reaction had set in against the elaborateness and the complexity of seventeenth-century music. The Enlightenment, as we have seen, tended rather to value rationality, clarity, and restraint. In France, the Academy of Music attempted to impose these qualities in a manner similar to that of the Academy of Painting. Melodies and rhythms were simplified, and form rather than content was stressed. Music, the classicists believed, should not be disturbing but should express balance and repose through perfect craftsmanship. The compositions of this era, which were mainly secular, were designed for enjoyable listening. They appealed as much to the intellect as to the heart.

Not surprisingly, instrumental music was more highly regarded than singing. The components of the modern orchestra were well established during the eighteenth century, when the first important symphonies were written. Most popular, however, was music intended for chamber performance, with the string quartet leading the way. The violin emerged as the chief ensemble instrument, the piano as the foremost keyboard instrument.

Among the most gifted of all the classical composers were Franz Joseph Haydn and Wolfgang Amadeus Mozart, both of them Austrian. Haydn, the lighthearted Viennese composer, brought the chamber and symphonic forms to a high point of perfection and in doing so created works of enduring appeal. Mozart, a child prodigy, was composing major works before the age of five. Though he died in poverty in 1791, at the age of thirty-five, he created an astonishing number of magnificent compositions.

Mozart was himself a superb harpsichordist and pianist and wrote many pieces for keyboard instruments. He was a master of all types of composition, however, and displayed the clarity and grace of classicism at its best. But his ultimate triumph was in opera, where his fine understanding of human character combined with his gift for melody to produce immortal works. Among his most popular operas today are *Don Giovanni,* the *Marriage of Figaro, Così Fan Tutte,* and the *Magic Flute.* Though he was a true man of the eighteenth century, trained in classicism, Mozart transcended both the style and the age.

The Revolutions of Liberalism
and Nationalism

10

The eighteenth century—classical, rational, and aristocratic—marked the culmination of a whole epoch of European history. Order, balance, and reason were the passwords of the day. Yet reason, in league with science, was undermining the foundations of the old regime. When the *philosophes* trained the light of reason on the culture and society of this sophisticated age, they exposed all its institutions to harsh criticism. The corrosive impact of the new science on religion has already been described; attacks upon the theory and practice of royal absolutism were also being launched. Clearly, an atmosphere conducive to political and social revolution had developed during the years of the Enlightenment.

The aspiring members of society found the new atmosphere bracing. This was particularly true of the bourgeoisie—businessmen, lawyers, civil officials—who were to play an important role in the revolutionary movements of the eighteenth and nineteenth centuries. In fact, it is in this middle class that we find the fullest embodiment of the forces that had been rising since late in the Middle Ages—capitalism, materialism, secularism, and individualism. In the language of the eighteenth century, the members of the bourgeoisie sought "liberty" and "equality." But these words had a very special meaning for them.

In the economic sense, liberty meant the freedom of enterpreneurs from an inhibiting mercantilism. In the political sense as well, liberty had a narrowly restricted meaning. Voltaire saw it as a prerogative of the educated classes: the rights to speak freely, to publish, to hold property, and to be protected by the law. None of these rights, he thought, had much to do with the working classes, who were generally too "stupid and brutal" even to be aware of such matters. Most of the *philosophes* shared Voltaire's view, and not until a century afterwards did the idea of liberty—full liberty for *all* men—began to take hold.

Similarly, the concept of equality must be understood in its bourgeois context. The middle class, bitterly resentful of the privileges of the aristocracy in law and property, sought to rise to equality of status with the landed nobility; and to this end it advocated, with passion, the doctrines of natural law and universal rights. With few exceptions, however, the members of the bourgeoisie did not want the lower classes to rise to equality with themselves.

What came to be known as "liberalism" was a mixture of these and related concepts, centering around the ideas of individual liberty and equality (in the bourgeois sense) and encompassing a faith in reason and progress. But liberalism was never an integrated ideology; it had a wide range of interpreters. One fact had become clear, however, by the end of the eighteenth century: liberalism was antagonistic to both hereditary privilege and absolutism.

Since those who hold power rarely surrender it voluntarily, a clash of forces became virtually certain. The initial challenge to absolutism occurred during the seventeenth century in England, and the success of that challenge brought into being the first "liberal" state. About a century afterward liberal forces erupted in North America and in France. These three revolutions inaugurated a new political order in Western civilization. Each had its own set of causes, and each followed its own course, but the end result of all three was to extend personal freedom and equality of rights to more and more people.

The liberal movements had a further result: they established the principle of revolution in the modern world. Civil struggles and seizures of power were of themselves nothing new, but the breadth and success of the liberal struggles—and the influence of their apologists, from Locke to Robespierre—made revolution a *human right*. And time would show that the makers of these revolutions could no more restrict this right to themselves than they could restrict the rights of liberty and equality. The collectivist revolutions of the twentieth century—shocking to many heirs of the liberal tradition— found their justification, in large part, in the precedent and rationalizations of the liberal revolutions.

THE ENGLISH REVOLUTION: PARLIAMENTARY SUPREMACY AND THE BILL OF RIGHTS

The English Revolution of the seventeenth century arose from a complex of political, social, and religious tensions. In the wake of the Reformation, religious issues continued uppermost in many minds; and, as most of the king's opponents were of Puritan (Calvinist) leanings, the term "Puritan" became attached to the revolution. This revolution, clearly, was more than a struggle for liberalism, but it shared many of the aims of the subsequent liberal revolutions in America and France. Equally important, John Locke's justification of the English Revolution was to contribute significantly to liberal ideology.

Challenge to the divine right of kings: the Civil War and Cromwell

Why had absolutism fallen into disfavor in England after having been strongly supported since the time of Henry VII? One reason seems to be that the middle class and other commoners had backed the monarch in his efforts to dispel the near-anarchy of feudalism, but once order had been established they were eager to reduce his authority. Tudor despotism died with Elizabeth I in 1603. Her Stuart successor, James I, upheld the royal tradition of divine right. But James was not an Elizabeth or a Henry; he failed to win the personal following they had enjoyed, and Parliament refused to accede to his demands. The House of Commons consisted of elected representatives of the gentry (small to medium rural landholders) and of middle-class townsmen. Most of them were Puritan Dissenters, and they had no affection for the hierarchical Church of England. Moreover, they disapproved of James' foreign policies and his domestic extravagance. When he asked them to approve new taxes to support his undertakings, they stubbornly refused. And so James governed without Parliament during most of his reign.

James' son, Charles I, fared no better. His insistence on his divine right to govern won little response from Parliament. Unable to make Parliament do his bidding on taxes, he resorted to forced "loans" and to controversial extensions of traditional taxes, which fell chiefly upon the gentry and burghers. Their resentment toward Charles was aggravated by what they considered his violation of English constitutional traditions that went back to the Magna Carta of 1215. (In the "Great Charter," the first *written* statement of feudal liberties, King John had accepted limitations upon royal authority and had guaranteed the customary rights of subjects.) When Charles summoned a Parliament in 1640, after a decade of ruling without one, the stage was set for an open clash between the king and his opponents.

The Long Parliament (as it was later called) proceeded to enact measures against the king's ministers and against his exercise of "arbitrary" authority. When, in 1642, Charles tried to arrest the

Parliamentary leaders, the House of Commons responded by raising a citizens' army for its own protection. Charles, with a minority
of the Commons and most of the Lords, then withdrew to Oxford,
while the rest of the members of Commons held London and prepared for war.

The allegiance of the population in the ensuing civil struggle followed no fixed lines of social class or religious affiliation. In the
main, however, Charles was supported by the great nobles, the hierarchy of the Anglican Church, and the Roman Catholics. Parliament was backed by the bourgeoisie, most of the gentry, and by
religious Dissenters. In strictly political terms, the Civil War was a
showdown between two rival power groups and two theories of government. The king and his hereditary lords were defending their
prerogatives and the idea of absolute *monarchy;* Parliament, representing the smaller landholders and businessmen, was fighting for
rule by a broadened *aristocracy.*

In the test of arms, the Parliamentary forces kept control of the
chief cities and seaports and enjoyed the support of the navy. On
land their campaigns were fought by the "new model" army, which
had been organized by Oliver Cromwell—a landowner, a militant
Puritan, and a member of Parliament. The first citizen army to be
recruited in the dawning era of revolutions, this force consisted
chiefly of English yeomen (independent farmers), volunteers ani-
mated by dislike of royal despotism and the established church.
Exhibiting Puritanical zeal and discipline, Cromwell's army decisively defeated Charles' forces in 1646.

But the victorious coalition could not agree on what to do next.
Cromwell and his army fell out with the majority of Parliament
on the questions of church organization and the future of the king.
Presbyterianism supplanted Anglicanism as the state religion for a
few years, but in 1649 a limited sort of religious toleration was decreed. Leadership of the revolution fell more and more upon Cromwell himself. At last he decided that Charles must be executed, on
the grounds that he was untrustworthy and attracted "ungodly"
persons to his cause. When Parliament balked, Cromwell drove out
the members who opposed him. The surviving "Rump" Parliament
of some sixty members put the king on trial and had him executed
in 1649.

The beheading of Charles was a psychological shock to most
Englishmen, who still believed that "divinity doth hedge a king."
The execution was the work of a determined minority, and the
majority of the nation's subjects recoiled from the deed. With the
revolutionaries divided among themselves, Cromwell found that he

could maintain orderly government only through strong personal rule backed by the army. He first proclaimed England a commonwealth (republic), then a protectorate. But no matter what the outward form of government, Cromwell ruled in fact as a military dictator.

The restoration of the monarchy and the Glorious Revolution

The Protector (Cromwell) conducted foreign affairs to the general satisfaction of his subjects, and he advanced the interests of the business class by encouraging trade and shipping. But this was not the kind of state that supporters of the Puritan Revolution had sought. Englishmen learned, as men of other nations would learn again and again, that revolutions can veer off on unexpected courses and that they can be bloody, wretched, and chaotic, often forcing an unhappy choice between disorder and despotism.

Sentiment in England swung steadily toward a restoration of the Stuart monarchy. Shortly after Cromwell's death in 1658, a new Parliament assembled—the first to have been freely elected in twenty years. One of its early acts was to invite the dead king's son, an exile in France, to return as Charles II. He was cheered on his arrival in 1660 by an emotional show of loyalty on the part of his subjects, and the nightmare of regicide and Puritanical tyranny faded into the English past. The Restoration, an era of relaxed tensions and enlarged individual freedom, had begun.

Parliament did not intend, of course, to restore divine right. It made clear to Charles that his was to be a constitutional government, based on the traditional prerogatives of the crown, Parliament, and the people. Though the Anglican Church became once again the established church, it did so in an atmosphere of broader toleration. Bloody revolution and Cromwellism may have been viewed as mistakes, but few desired to turn back the clock to 1600.

Charles II accepted all this, on the surface, though he was suspected of having private reservations. Whatever his convictions, he could not forget the shadow of exile or the block; hence he avoided extreme policies. The same cannot be said of his younger brother, who succeeded him as James II. A convert to Roman Catholicism, James provoked the fear that "popery" might return to England. Moreover he antagonized both the Anglican clergy and the major factions of Parliament, justifying his unpopular acts by reasserting that the king was "above the law."

Though his critics were exasperated by James' behavior, they expected that matters would improve after his death. His heir presumptive was the Protestant Mary, the wife of William of Orange (in Holland). But in 1688 a son was born to the middle-aged English king, who had him baptized a Catholic. Now faced with the prospect of continued reaction and "Romanization," the leaders of Parliament secretly invited William to land military forces in England. After William's landing, James found himself without support and quickly sailed for France, whereupon Parliament, alleging that James had "abdicated," declared the throne vacant and offered it to William and Mary. Thus was the Glorious Revolution of 1688 carried out—glorious because it was decisive and bloodless.

Determined to keep the new rulers in check, Parliament in 1689 passed the Bill of Rights, which enunciated Parliamentary supremacy over the crown and listed specific civil liberties. This historic measure completed the revolution that had started in 1642. It declared that the king could suspend laws, raise armies, and levy taxes *only* with the consent of Parliament; it also provided for frequent meetings of the lawmakers and unrestricted debate within their chambers. The Bill of Rights guaranteed every citizen the right to petition the monarch, to keep arms, and to enjoy "due process of law" (trial by jury and freedom from arbitrary arrest and cruel or unusual punishment). This was a restatement of the guarantees in Magna Carta, but now they applied in fact to a far larger portion of the English population.

The triumph of Parliament in 1689 had a double political significance: it put an end to absolutism and established a governing aristocracy (of property-owners); at the same time, it enlarged the exercise of individual freedoms. These accomplishments prepared the way for democracy in England. In the course of the eighteenth century a "cabinet" system of administration evolved in which ministers were made responsible to Parliament, rather than to the monarch. This presented the world with its first modern example, in a major country, of *representative government*. And the wider enjoyment of civil rights led, eventually, to an appetite for a wider sharing of political power as well.

Locke's justification of revolution

A by-product of the English upheaval was John Locke's political theory, which was destined to have a profound influence on future revolutions. Locke, as we have seen, was sensitive to the scientific, philosophic, and political ideas of his day. He approved of Parliament's fight against absolutism and felt that both the Puritan Revolution and the Glorious Revolution were justifiable. In 1690, in order to satisfy his conscience and that of other Englishmen—and in order to defend the Parliamentary settlement—he published *Two Treatises on Government*. The first treatise rejected the theory of divine right, while the second defended the right of rebellion. Though Locke's political ideas were not original, his second treatise became an ideological handbook for liberal revolutionists everywhere.

Locke believed that the English Civil War could be properly understood and judged only in the broadest context of man, society, and nature. Like his older contemporary, Thomas Hobbes (pp. 354–55), Locke saw the state in a purely secular light and denied that it had been founded by divine action. Both insisted that the presumed condition of man in the state of nature had given rise to an agreement to establish civil government. They shared also an atomistic view of society, regarding it as a collection of self-serving individuals. Starting from these common premises, Hobbes and Locke each attempted to "deduce" universal rules of political behavior and morals.

But there was a crucial difference between some of their assumptions. Hobbes reasoned that men's aggressive tendencies had made life intolerable under "natural" conditions: hence, he argued, men must have turned over *all* their individual rights to the state as a means of securing order. This being so, men are bound to obey the absolute dictates of their ruler. Revolution, therefore, constitutes a breach of contract as well as a return to chaos.

Locke accepted the theory of social contract, but he disagreed with Hobbes about its terms. He held that men are endowed with certain "natural rights," just as physical objects are endowed with certain natural properties (mass, density, shape, and so forth). Men had retained most of their natural rights and powers and had agreed (in the primeval contract) to transfer only *one* power to society: the power to preserve their life, liberty, and property. A society, said Locke, holds this power as long as the society lasts, but it delegates the exercise of the power to political agents. Should any agent push coercive action beyond explicit limits, the society is free, legally and morally, to resist. Who should decide whether a ruler's action is in fact a transgression? *"The people shall judge,"* Locke replied, using as an analogy the relation of a private person to his trustee or deputy. And if, in face of their judgment, a tyrant refuses to mend his ways, the people have the ultimate right to resort to force—to "appeal to Heaven."

Thus, by building on the ancient concepts of "natural rights" and "natural law," on the seventeenth-century style of reasoning, and on appeals to common sense, Locke constructed a "universal" political theory. Though it rested neither on scientific facts nor on actual historical events, it fitted neatly the ideological needs of the Parliamentary side in England's civil struggle. It justified not only acts of rebellion but even the execution of a king. And Locke's atomistic view of society suited the waxing spirit of individualism. In the two succeeding centuries of liberal aspiration and revolution it is clear why the Lockean "myth" proved so useful in the large, historical sense. It was heartily embraced by Thomas Jefferson and other leaders as a self-evident, absolute truth.

THE AMERICAN REVOLUTION
AND CONSTITUTION

Though Jefferson wrote the Declaration of Independence nearly a century after Locke's treatises appeared, he formed a direct intellectual link between the English and the American revolutions. Jefferson crystallized many of the liberal ideas of Locke and the Enlightenment and gave them wider circulation. Liberalism, however, was but one facet of the American Revolution of 1776. That rebellion brought about the first expulsion of a European colonial power, replaced monarchical government with a viable republic, and established the principle and practice of popular sovereignty (democracy). As a result of these achievements, the American Revolution served as a hope and a model for later revolutions around the world.

The American colonies and their aspirations

The overseas expansion of Europe had brought English settlers to the North American continent in the seventeenth century. Most of them, after driving back the Indians and carving homesteads from the wilderness, inhabited the thirteen colonies of the seaboard between Nova Scotia and Florida. By 1750 the white population of these colonies (including settlers from the Continent as well as Britain) amounted to about two million. Viewed from London they comprised but one part of a far-flung empire, for some thirty chartered colonies and companies, in America and Asia, were then subservient to king and Parliament. (The total number of Britain's subjects was approximately fifteen million at the time.)

The colonies were considered valuable chiefly for economic reasons—as a source of raw materials and as a market for exports. But the costs to the mother country for defense and administration probably equaled or exceeded the commercial returns. After 1750, therefore, Parliament tightened up the regulation of trade and the collection of duties. Until this time the colonists had paid little more than the local taxes levied by their colonial legislatures. They had achieved this "immunity" by means of wholesale smuggling and a flagrant disregard of the British Navigation Acts. At the same time, they showed little desire to provide for their own military defense. The Americans thereby gained a reputation in England for lawlessness, and Parliament began to suspect that the Americans were unworthy of trust and incapable of self-government.

Not surprisingly, the colonists resented British efforts to collect existing taxes or to impose new ones. This was especially true after 1763, when the close of the Seven Years' War (known in the colonies as the French and Indian War) brought England victory over France. With French power on the North American continent broken, there was no longer a serious foreign threat to the thirteen colonies. Feeling more secure than before, the Americans grew even more defiant toward their absentee rulers.

Parliament cast about for some kind of tax that the colonists would pay, but the objections were so violent that most levies were repealed soon after their enactment. One exception was a tax on imports of tea; this one Parliament refused to repeal, mainly to symbolize its *right* to tax British subjects everywhere. But the Americans refused to admit that right. "No taxation without representation!" became the rallying cry of colonial protest.

English leaders argued in vain that the colonies enjoyed "virtual" representation, since members of Parliament, in theory, represented, not individual constituencies, but national and imperial interests as a whole. Thus, although many English towns, cities, and individuals had no elected representatives in Parliament, it was asserted that their interests were nonetheless represented there. The argument, though accepted in England at the time, did not impress the Americans. In their own colonial governments, legislators represented *particular* constituencies. This view of representation was firmly rooted in the American experience, and it coincided with the economic interest of the colonists.

The squabble over taxation was only one evidence of the rising antagonism. Actions and counteractions led to a firming up of positions and a heightening of emotions. Though a minority remained loyal to the British flag and British laws, most colonists were moving toward the point of no return. They saw themselves as heirs of the Glorious Revolution of 1688 and the British king and Parliament as tyrants.

The Americans at first sought redress of their grievances, but gradually they began to think of seizing control of their own destiny. The urban middle class took the lead, and soon other groups began to sense that they too would be better off under self-rule. They realized that the British reins of mercantilism would check their economic development and that, under colonialism, their general well-being would always be subordinated to imperial aims. Thomas Paine, a redoubtable revolutionary propagandist, put the situation into a Newtonian perspective. Using with telling effect the language of the Enlightenment, he declared that America's subjection to England was "contrary to reason." He went on:

> There is something absurd in supposing a continent to be perpetually governed by an island. In no instance has nature made the satellite larger than its primary planet; and as England and America, with respect to each other, reverse the common order of nature, it is evident that they belong to different systems. England to Europe; America to itself.

Paine did much to advance the cause of rebellion in America. Later, he aided radicals in both France and England, thus becoming the first international revolutionist of modern times.

War and the Declaration of Independence

By 1774 the colonists had begun to commit acts of violence and sabotage (notably, the Boston "Tea Party"), and the British responded with punitive measures. Parliament passed what Americans called the Intolerable Acts, which closed the port of Boston and virtually rescinded the charter of Massachusetts. The British may have thought that this tough policy would bring the colonists to their senses (or to their knees), but it had just the opposite effect. County assemblies were convened in Massachusetts to protest; one of them declared that no one should obey any part of the acts, which it described as "attempts of a wicked administration to enslave America." Shortly thereafter, representatives from all the colonies assembled at a Continental Congress in Philadelphia. There they drew up a statement of grievances and formed an association to cut off all trade with Britain. The conflict of words had given way to "direct action."

When Massachusetts' British governor ordered its legislature dissolved, the legislators defiantly reconvened and proceeded to raise a defense force of "minutemen." This step was, of course, illegal; it brought into existence a state of armed rebellion. Conciliatory measures were now proposed in Parliament, but it was too late for conciliation. The first clash of arms occurred in April 1775, when British troops set out from Boston to destroy a cache of munitions at nearby Concord. They accomplished their mission but lost heavily to rebel sharpshooters during their return march. The war for independence was on.

The Continental Congress reassembled shortly after the skirmish in Massachusetts. The minutemen around Boston were enlisted as the nucleus of a Continental Army, and George Washington was named as commander in chief. The war dragged on for six years. Britain, though a leading European power, was hampered by long lines of communication, poor generalship, and troubles in other parts of the empire. The colonials were beset by the internal differences that normally plague revolutionists, and the Continental Congress was unable to provide sufficient troops, supplies, or money. Although the rebels fought bravely and endured severe hardships, they could hardly have won without the aid of foreign powers.

The French monarchy, eager to even the score with Britain after the humiliation of 1763, decided to aid the rebels. From the beginning the French had sent officers and arms to the Americans, whose first significant victory, at Saratoga, was won chiefly with French weapons. Impressed by the American success in that battle, the French became formal allies and declared war on Britain. Spain and Holland followed, swinging the European balance in the Americans' favor. The surrender of Lord Cornwallis in 1781, which virtually ended the British military effort, was forced by a French fleet controlling the waters off Yorktown. Two years later, by the Treaty of Paris, the United States of America won recognition as a sovereign territory stretching from the Atlantic to the Mississippi.

The independence of the new government, as well as its bid for allies, had been formally charted in 1776. In fact, the most memorable achievement of the Continental Congress was its adoption of the Declaration of Independence. Drafted by Jefferson, it aimed to justify the resort to force against Britain and to win support abroad as well as at home. It is significant that the Preamble gives as the reason for the preparation of the document "a decent respect to the opinions of mankind . . . ." In 1776 (as today) the influence of foreign opinion on a struggle of liberation could not be ignored.

The declaration is a masterpiece of revolutionary literature tailored to the American cause. Jefferson omitted any mention of the colonists' reluctance to pay their share of defense costs, overlooked the long story of smuggling, civil disobedience, and provocative acts, and gave no hint at all of the deeper motives of the rebel leaders. He knew full well that Parliament had been supreme in England since 1689, yet he shrewdly focused his charges of wrongdoing upon the king. He did so primarily because the king, in an era of despotic monarchs, could readily be painted as a tyrant.

The ringing paragraph that links the American Revolution with universal truths is a paraphrase of Locke, but Jefferson's version is marked by incomparable simplicity, clarity, and power. The flavor of the Enlightenment is unmistakable:

> We hold these truths to be self-evident: That all men are created equal; that they are endowed by their Creator with certain unalienable Rights; that among these are Life, Liberty, and the pursuit of Happiness.—That to secure these rights, Governments are instituted among Men, deriving their just powers from the consent of the governed,—That whenever any Form of Government becomes destructive of these ends, it is the Right of the People to alter or abolish it . . . .

With these deft strokes Jefferson set forth a view of man, government, and revolution that remains an inspiration to believers in human dignity, liberal principles, and progressive social change.

The Constitution of the United States

The Americans emerged from their war of independence with relatively few scars. Serious divisions had opened up within the colonies, but they were moderate compared with those of subsequent revolutions elsewhere. The fact that the enemy was an *absentee* ruler served as a unifying force among Americans of all classes. Even so, there was a minority of die-hard "loyalists" who opposed the "patriots." Subjected to confiscation of their property and rough treatment by the patriots, at least sixty thousand of them fled to Canada. Their departure eased the internal conflict in the colonies, and most of the émigrés, happily, did not return to stir up new trouble.

After independence, the most pressing need of the former colonies was to agree on a governing compact. Each new state drew up a written constitution for itself, but there was disagreement over what form the union of the states should take. The "state-rights" impulse, arising from the experiences of the separate colonies, was very much alive. Many citizens preferred complete autonomy for their states but grudgingly accepted the idea of a loose league as defined in the Articles of Confederation. When the Confederation proved unable to meet the common needs of commerce and defense, the states sent delegates to Philadelphia (1787) to revise the Articles. Instead, they drafted a new constitution aimed at forming a closer union.

The federal Constitution, approved after bitter debate in the thirteen states, was the earliest *written* constitution of a major country—and is the oldest still in use. The very act of Americans in framing their own basic law fired the imagination of European intellectuals. Here was Locke's hypothetical social contract transformed into reality! Here also was a reasoned statement of the new doctrine of popular sovereignty. Starting with a clean political slate (in the spirit of Descartes), the Americans rejected the notion of any privileged persons or bodies. The Preamble identifies the sole source of civil authority in its opening words: "We, the people . . . do ordain and establish this Constitution for the United States of America."

The new document also launched a successful experiment in federalism, in which individuals hold citizenship both in their state and in the nation. The authors of the Constitution tried to strike a balance between powers delegated to the central government and those reserved to the states. With changing conditions, the balance has had to be readjusted through constitutional interpretation or amendment. Thus a peculiar tension was built into American politics in 1787, with results not wholly satisfactory to anyone. Nevertheless, federalism stands as a noble endeavor to harmonize the requirements of centralized planning and power with the desire for local autonomy.

The Constitution was, above all, a charter of eighteenth-century liberalism. It made concrete Jefferson's dictum: "That government is best which governs *least*." Fearing possible tyranny by one man or one body, the framers put their trust in a system of "checks and balances." The best protection against man's urge to power, they thought, is to establish separate political authorities and to leave them in jealous contention. Thus, the states were to keep a watchful eye on the national power; and within all governing units a counterpoise of executive, legislative, and judicial branches was established.

Although the Constitution provides powerful defenses against the invasion of individual rights, fears of an overly strong central government continued to be voiced. And so, at the insistence of many citizens, the Bill of Rights was added to the Constitution in 1791. Comprising the first ten amendments, it spelled out and extended the historic rights of Englishmen. Freedom of worship and freedom from an established church head the list. Every person is also guaranteed freedom of expression, petition, and assembly; the right to keep and bear arms; security of person and home; and due process of law.

By and large, the liberal principles embodied in the Constitution proved well suited to the self-reliant temper of the American people and to the conditions of life during the republic's first hundred years. With no potent enemies on their borders, and with vast resources to be exploited, Americans were free to exercise their ingenuity and talents. Strong government was needed neither for

military defense, for the elimination of counterrevolutionary forces,
nor for the restraint of private power. Not until the end of the nineteenth century, with the closing of the frontier, the swelling of the
population, and the rise of giant industry, did conditions develop
that were less suitable to limited government.

The growth of American democracy

The desire of the founding fathers to maintain checks and balances was frustrated to a substantial degree by the growth of political parties. This development opened the door to "excessive"
power by the people, something the framers of the Constitution had
feared. They had wished to avoid the tyranny of either one man or
many. A majority party, however, by securing control of the various
branches of government, could rise to a position of virtual dominance. An early manifestation of the disrupting effect of parties was
their perversion of the constitutional provision for electing the
President. The Constitution calls for the indirect election of the
chief executive through a college of electors, who are presumably
independent. But parties almost at once began to nominate *lists* of
electors to be chosen by the qualified voters in each state, and the
winning slate was expected to vote as a unit for its party's candidate.

The opening up of the country and the exploitation of its resources brought a steady expansion of government functions in the
United States. This trend gave impetus, in turn, to parties and to
the spirit and practice of democracy. The relation between liberalism and democracy requires close examination. After the successful
challenge to divine-right monarchy in the seventeenth century, the
idea of liberalism had been joined to that of majority rule. Locke
and Jefferson both believed that, *within the limits assigned to a
liberal government,* the individual must submit to the majority.
But there remained an inherent tension between liberal and democratic principles. What if the majority seeks to do something that
the individual regards as an infringement of his "unalienable
rights"? On this question, the strict liberal took the side of the individual, while the democrat supported the decision of the majority.

United States history shows, in fact, a progressive contraction of
individual rights and a corresponding growth in the power of the
majority. Alexis de Tocqueville, a perceptive observer of American
institutions, identified this trend as early as the 1830's. In America,
he reported, the *people* truly govern. Public opinion is king; its
power applies not only to political decisions but to personal convictions and behavior. Tocqueville saw American democracy as the
wave of the future and predicted that it would soon extend to

Europe and the rest of the world. Though stirred by the vigor and promise of America, he feared that the passion for equality and democracy would ultimately stifle individual liberty. His prophecy has not been altogether fulfilled, but the role of democratic government has grown enormously, and the Jeffersonian liberal state has long since passed into myth.

THE FRENCH REVOLUTION: "LIBERTY, EQUALITY, AND FRATERNITY"

The American Revolution helped to spark the French Revolution of 1789, which proved to be the most violent and far-reaching of all the liberal upheavals. Not only did the French Revolution advance liberal ideals; it brought drastic changes in the legal, social, and economic order of France, the largest and most populous country in western Europe. The struggle was intensified by the passionate opposition of privileged groups at home and by the intervention of foreign powers. Even more than the English or American revolutions, it was a watershed in the flow of Western history. As Tocqueville later wrote: "The French Revolution had no territory of its own; indeed, its effect was to efface, in a way, all older frontiers. It brought men together, divided them, in spite of laws, traditions, character, and language—turning enemies sometimes into compatriots and kinsmen into strangers. . . ." Not until the Russian Revolution of 1917 was an uprising again to have such an impact on the modern world.

The Bourbon monarchy and the "old regime"

Living as we do in an age of successive revolutions, it is imperative that we understand the dynamics of social revolt. Scholarly research on the French Revolution, which has been studied more intensively than any other, permits us to know something of the "anatomy of revolution." What were the main causes, phases, and consequences of the movement that began in 1789?

First let us survey the background of the rebellion. The luster of the Bourbon monarchy had dimmed with the passing of Louis XIV, though his heirs continued to sit in the grand manner at Versailles. While preserving its claim to divine-right absolutism, the monarchy grew increasingly ineffectual during the eighteenth century. Louis XV was a capable but pleasure-loving ruler, and his grandson, Louis XVI, was well-meaning but indecisive. Humiliating military defeats and the loss of the French overseas empire undermined royal prestige, while wars, waste, and extravagance brought the monarchy to the edge of bankruptcy. Louis XVI tried to carry through reforms in taxation and administration, but he was frustrated by the privileged classes. Though still capable of arbitrary action, the monarchy could not exercise the absolute authority it claimed. Disclosure of its weakness led to mounting criticism of the regime and nourished the aspirations of dissatisfied classes.

The landed aristocrats sought to regain historic prerogatives that had been stripped away by the crown in preceding centuries. Their resurgent spirit expressed itself through the provincial *parlements* (judicial tribunals), which in 1763 vigorously protested attempts by the king to raise property assessments. The Parlement of Paris went further: it referred to the existence of the "fundamental laws" of France and asserted that no decree of the monarch was valid until it had been endorsed by the Parlement. Thus, the Parlement virtually proclaimed itself the "supreme court" of France. The members of this haughty tribunal (and of the provincial *parlements*) were drawn from noble families and so reflected the desire of the aristocracy to modify royal absolutism in the direction of constitutional government (as in Britain). In short, the nobles hoped to regain their role of political dominance.

Other social classes sided with the aristocracy in its challenge to absolutism, feeling that some advantage would fall to them from a curtailment of royal authority. The French bourgeoisie were especially eager to advance their social and political status. Growing in wealth and education, and sensitive to the winds of change, they longed for higher prestige and more active participation in the affairs of state. Through enlarged political influence they also hoped to do away with the obstructions of mercantilism and reap the fruits of a freer economy.

The peasants, who comprised by far the largest part of the population, were little concerned with prestige or politics. Their lot was a hard one, often marked by famine and disease. What they wanted was more land, emancipation from archaic dues and services to the nobles, and relief from inequitable tax collections. The years 1788 and 1789 were especially poor ones for most peasants (and urban laborers). In their despair, they felt that *any* change in the existing order might result in some good. Though ordinarily lethargic, they now showed themselves ready to act.

The overthrow of the king and the nobles

Though a revolutionary situation existed in France in the 1780's, it took a special chain of circumstances to precipitate the revolution. Having failed to get the revenues he wanted by means of existing laws, Louis XVI was compelled at last to seek additional taxing authority. According to historic precedent, such authority could be granted only by the Estates-General (p. 254). This body, representing the three major estates (classes) of France, had not met since 1614. The king's call for the election of delegates in 1788 created a stir of anticipation, for if the monarch wanted new taxes he would have to make concessions to the assembled representatives.

As planning for the meeting proceeded, however, a nasty split opened up between the nobles and the bourgeoisie. The latter were legally commoners—members of the Third Estate. They resented this medieval classification, which lumped them with laborers and peasants; but, as leaders of the most numerous estate, they sought greater power for themselves in the Estates-General. They demanded that the Third Estate be allowed to send a larger number of representatives to Versailles than the two privileged estates (clergy and nobility) combined, and they insisted that votes be taken by count of *heads* in the total body of representatives. They won satisfaction of the first demand, but the aristocratic Parlement of Paris, to which the issue was referred, decided in favor of the traditional method of voting— *one* vote for each *estate*. It became apparent even before the Estates-General met in the summer of 1789 that rivalry and suspicion between the estates would complicate their dealings with the king.

After the session opened, matters soon came to a head. Unable to persuade the two higher estates to sit and vote with them as one body, the representatives of the Third Estate (most of whom were lawyers) decided to "walk out" on the Estates-General. Stating that they were the only true representatives of the people, they declared themselves to be the "National Assembly" of France. This proclamation (June 17) was the first act of revolution, for it rested on no operative law. A crisis of decision was thereby thrust upon the king.

Louis, forced to choose sides between the nobility and the bourgeoisie, sided with the former. His initial response was to lock the meeting hall of the building where the Third Estate had been sitting. But the action was ineffectual; the Third Estate quickly found another meeting place at an indoor tennis court nearby. There the members swore the "Tennis Court Oath," by which they pledged not to go home until they had drafted a new constitution for France. Within a few days the National Assembly was joined by many priests from the First Estate and by some of the nobles. Having failed to overawe the dissidents with words, Louis next tried to intimidate them by a show of force. Toward the end of June, he called some twenty thousand soldiers to Versailles.

The National Assembly was rescued by the people of Paris. As order began to break down throughout the country, men everywhere began to arm themselves for defense against the king's forces. The excitement in Paris, fed by rumors of troop movements, rose higher and higher. Crowds began to roam the streets in search of weapons, and on July 14 they demanded arms from the Bastille. Though the old fortress was no longer of military significance, it was a hated symbol of despotism. When its commander refused to turn over arms, the mob attempted to push its way in. After an exchange of gunfire, in which about a hundred of the insurgents were killed, the commander agreed to surrender. Then the mob rushed in, lynched the small garrison (including its commander), cut off their heads, and carried them on pikes through the city streets.

Thoroughly alarmed, and doubting that his troops would fire on the people, Louis quickly sent his forces away from Versailles. He played for time by pretending to yield to the demands of the Paris mob and the Third Estate. The king recognized a self-appointed citizens' committee as the new municipal government of Paris and directed the representatives of the privileged estates to sit in the National Assembly. Thus the revolution was saved for the time being and was strengthened by a new and potent influence—the Parisian populace.

Violence broke out in the countryside as well. By late July it was rumored that the landlords were assembling hired ruffians to attack the peasants. While many of the nobles were away at the capital, the peasants seized the initiative. During the "Great Fear" of late summer they vandalized the noble chateaux and destroyed manorial records, thus freeing themselves of stipulated dues and services.

As the king had appeased the Paris mob, the National Assembly now felt constrained to mollify the peasants. Many of the bourgeoisie, as well as the nobles, held landed estates. Frightened by the disorders in the country, they realized that they would have to take drastic action in order to save their families and properties. At a single night session (August 4), the Assembly erased all special privileges in landed property. Liberal nobleman led the way by renouncing their historic rights to peasant fees and labor, hunting on farm lands, tax exemptions and advantages, and special courts of law. A summary decree, approved overwhelmingly, declared that "feudalism is abolished." Thus a drastic overturn in property rights was the first major reform of the National Assembly. The chief losers were, of course, the nobles; the primary beneficiaries were the peasants, who now had a substantial stake in the revolution.

Now the Assembly could turn to its original task: the framing of a new constitution. Although this endeavor was to prove trying and divisive, there was wide agreement on the major liberal principles. These principles were incorporated in the most influential single document of the liberal revolutions: the Declaration of the Rights of Man and the Citizen. Drafted as a preface to the constitution, it served as a guide to the new order.

The declaration was the French counterpart of the English and American bills of rights. It went beyond them, however, in setting forth explicit principles of government. After prescribing the "natural, inalienable, and sacred rights of man," it defined the *duties* of individuals in a social body. "Every citizen summoned or seized according to law ought to obey instantly," but law must be an expression of the "general will." All citizens have the right to participate in the formulation of law, and its administration must be the same for all. "The source of sovereignty is essentially in the nation," reads the declaration; "no body, no individual can exercise authority that does not proceed from it in plain terms."

This emphasis on the general will reflected in large measure the influence of the French-Swiss philosopher, Jean-Jacques Rousseau. It is ironic that the declaration, so clearly the offspring of enlightened rationalism, also bears the imprint of this romanticist. Rousseau had died in 1778, eleven years before the revolution, but his political ideas lived on in his writings. Rousseau's *Social Contract* dealt with the same question of rights and authority that had been treated, in differing ways, by Hobbes and Locke. Though his explanations were obscure and contradictory, Rousseau established the general will as the sovereign entity in organized society.

Upon examination, the "will" of Rousseau turns out to be a vague, mystical concept, bound to "moral principles" and the "welfare of the whole society." The chief difficulty lies in discovering how, in practice, the general will is to be found. There appear to be three possibilities: the general will can be identified with the decision of the majority of citizens (democracy); it can be divined by a charismatic individual (dictatorship); or it can be determined by a chosen elite (one-party rule). Thus the National Assembly, Napoleon, and modern authoritarian parties would each speak in the name of the whole people.

Rousseau's ideas were invoked against all political institutions that rested on divine or historical right rather than on the general will. His arguments gave general philosophical sanction to the French Revolution and served to justify the National Assembly's assumption of sovereign authority. The planners of the new constitution accepted it as their duty to fashion a framework of government that would respond to and articulate the general will of France.

But from the beginning there was sharp disagreement on how the framework should be built. Some wanted the new government modeled after that of England, with an upper and lower house and a king with executive and veto powers. Others, fearing that this arrangement would give undue power to the nobility, wanted a single legislative chamber and a figurehead king.

The rising distrust of Louis XVI tilted the balance toward the unicameral plan. The leaders of the Assembly were properly suspicious of the monarch's loyalty to the revolution; his brother, the Comte d'Artois, had already fled the country, along with many noblemen. These émigrés proceeded to urge foreign powers to intervene in France, and Louis himself hesitated to accept either the Declaration of Rights or the Assembly's decrees abolishing feudalism. Demonstrating their apprehensions about Louis, crowds marched from Paris to the Versailles palace in October and compelled him and his queen to remove to the city.

Moderates in the Assembly, sensing the impending violence, began to fall away from the revolution. Their defection put increasing power in the hands of extremist factions, of whom the most influential were members of the Jacobin Society. The "Jacobin" name was derived from that of a Dominican convent in Paris in which the society met. Founded in 1789, this society soon had local chapters throughout France. By 1793 it had nearly half a million members and had become virtually a government within the revolutionary government. Serving as propagandists and quasi-administrators, the Jacobins were a prototype of the revolutionary parties of the twentieth century.

The constitution completed in 1791 reflected the extremist trend. It provided for a unicameral legislature and a suspensive veto for the king. (He could only *delay*, not prevent, legislation). But at the same time the well-to-do members of the Assembly managed to limit sharply the right of suffrage. Moreover, candidates for the "electoral college," which was to name legislators and administrative officials, had to be citizens of substantial property. (Only fifty thousand men qualified as candidates for the first elections.) The reason proffered for these restrictive provisions was that the great majority of the people were uneducated, but the effect of this constitution was to hand control to the wealthy families of the country.

Louis XVI, who was designated as the titular head of the new government, had sealed his fate earlier in 1791 by attempting to escape from France. Captured near the frontier and brought back to Paris in humiliation, he thus destroyed any serious hopes for a constitutional monarchy. Soon the new regime foundered, the king was deposed, and a new assemblage was called (1792) to draft another constitution. This body, the National Convention, was elected by universal manhood suffrage. It governed France during the troubled years of reform and war and completed its work in 1795 by approving, at last, a republican constitution.

Foreign war and internal disorder

Reaction abroad profoundly affected the course of the revolution. Whereas outside intervention had assured the success of the American Revolution, it had destructive consequences for the French. It stimulated extremism and internal divisions within the revolution, and it helped to bring about panic, dictatorship, and, ultimately, military defeat. The conflict between revolutionary France and the rest of Europe broke out in 1792. Some elements outside France sympathized with the aims and deeds of the revolution, but the most influential groups—the aristocratic and privileged orders—had become increasingly apprehensive. Their feeling was deepened by blood ties with the imprisoned Bourbon royalty and by the agitation of émigrés. Over a hundred thousand aristocrats had left France, but they hoped to return one day to recover their lost positions and lands.

Foreign sentiment was translated into a military threat by the Declaration of Pillnitz (August 1791). In this document, Leopold of Austria, the Habsburg emperor, stated that if the other European powers would join him he would use force to restore the Bourbon rulers to their full rights. Preoccupied with matters in Austria, the emperor was actually reluctant to become involved militarily in the west, but his declaration nevertheless encouraged the émigrés and alarmed the French. It also strengthened the hand of those in France who wished to *internationalize* the revolution—who believed that the reforms could not be made secure in France unless they were also planted abroad.

The more aggressive revolutionary leaders now pressed for an offensive against the reactionary powers of Europe. They pictured their armies carrying the banner of "liberation" into neighboring lands and uniting with native revolutionaries to overthrow established regimes. The impulse to military action gained support also from those leaders who believed that war would restore unity to France and from all individuals who stood to lose should royalist armies invade the country. The government accordingly declared war on Austria in April 1792, thereby launching a period of continental revolution and war that lasted for twenty-three years.

At first the war went against the French, producing fear and disorder in Paris and the provinces. In the autumn a mob rushed the royal palace and massacred the king's Swiss Guard. Later a band of army recruits turned on the Paris jails and seized a thousand or more prisoners who had been rounded up as suspected sympathizers with the aristocracy. After mock trials these unfortunates were put to death. The winds of violence, released by the revolution and whipped by nationalist hysteria, now swept across France. When the National Convention met in September 1792 it faced the immediate problems of disposing of the king, restoring law and order, and prosecuting the war.

Louis' trial for treason opened a major breach between the moderates and the radicals. The leaders of the Convention were all Jacobins, but they were divided into factions reflecting a broad range of philosophy, interest, and temperament. Louis was voted guilty by unanimous decision, but the decree of execution was passed by a majority of only one vote. Half the Convention members thereby marked themselves as regicides; the others were henceforth regarded as halfhearted, even counterrevolutionary. The seeds of mutual distrust and hostility were thus sown within the revolution, and the rival leaders proceeded to devour one another. The guiding spirit of the Convention, the incorruptible zealot Maximilien Robespierre, reigned over the near-anarchy of 1793 and 1794. Revolutionary tribunals were set up around the country to counter lynch law and to stifle local rebellions. At least fifteen thousand fell to the guillotines, usually on charges of treason or sedition.

As foreign peril declined, internal hysteria declined with it. The National Convention, having declared war on England, Holland, and Spain (as well as Austria), approved the conscription of all ablebodied men. (This measure proved to be a fateful precedent for the mass armies of the future.) The French conscripts, fired by revolutionary spirit, soon showed themselves more than a match for their enemies. By June 1794 they had turned the tide of battle and were overrunning the Low Countries. Within weeks the internal foes of Robespierre (both left and right) put an end to his virtual dictatorship. He was outlawed by vote of the Convention and, with many of his associates, was executed.

The fall of Robespierre marked the end of the "Terror" and the return to power of the moderates. It was the moderates, chiefly representatives of the well-to-do, who secured the Convention's approval of the republican constitution of 1795. The government so established (known as the Directory) restricted political power to men of substantial wealth, who were even fewer in number than those who had held power under the constitution of 1791.

The triumphant members of the bourgeoisie could well be satisfied with the trend of the revolution, despite its violence and bloodshed. Their liberal principles and their preeminent political position were guaranteed by the new constitution. Feudal property rights, titles, and special privileges had been swept away, and the chaotic character of traditional administration had been replaced by uniform local units (departments and municipalities) centrally directed from Paris. Freedom of enterprise had been advanced by the abolition of craft guilds and labor organizations and by the scrapping of the mercantilist regulations of the late monarchy.

The clergy, on the other hand, had seen its wealth and influence drastically reduced. In 1790 the properties of the Church had been confiscated as a means of financing the revolution, and the clergy had been placed under a Civil Constitution, with elected priests and bishops and with salaries paid by the state. These measures provoked not only the enmity of most clerics but widespread popular opposition. The clergy, along with remnants of the disgruntled nobility, became a continuing source of counterrevolutionary pressure.

Napoleon and the revolutionary empire

The bourgeois men of property failed, as they had in 1792, to meet the stresses and challenges of national political responsibility. The government of the Directory lacked effective leadership, for the more idealistic reformers of 1789 had either dropped out of public affairs or been destroyed in the rivalry of factions, while the politicians who remained were largely men of expediency and self-interest.

The public spirit had shifted, too. Lofty aspirations had been deflated by disappointment, animosity, and bloodshed. Emotionally exhausted by five years of fevered excitement, many Frenchmen fell into a mood of indifference or cynicism. Political officeholders not only failed to inspire the public but showed themselves indolent, corrupt, and incapable of solving the nation's problems. Challenged from the right by reviving royalist sentiment and from the left by the still-impoverished urban workers, the Directory clung to power only with the aid of the military.

A brilliant young general, Napoleon Bonaparte, was quick to grasp the facts of the political situation. He had first defended the government in 1795 against attacks by royalist mobs. (Afterward he boasted that he had dispersed them with a "whiff of grape-shot.") Two years later his troops were called on to enforce illegal measures that had been taken by the Directory, and in 1799 he connived with some of its own leaders to take over the state by a sudden seizure (*coup d'état*). The conspirators believed that only a strong govern-ment headed by a general could fend off royalism, establish internal order, and defeat France's foreign enemies. Napoleon proclaimed himself "First Consul"; later, after a national plebiscite, he pro-claimed himself emperor (1804). With warm popular support he ruled for fifteen years as a virtual dictator.

Napoleon had made his reputation as a general, but he was more than a soldier; he possessed a keen and wide-ranging intellect. Born on the island of Corsica in 1769, only a year after its annexation to France, he had become a fervent French nationalist. Though he dis-tinguished himself as an officer of artillery, he would no doubt have remained in the junior grades had it not been for the revolution. But the flight of many aristocratic officers opened the grades above him, and the far-ranging wars of the republic offered him uncommon opportunities. (He once dreamed of conquering Egypt and India.) Owing his rapid advancement to the overthrow of the old regime, he heartily declared himself a "son of the revolution."

Napoleon was a master of politics and guile, but there is no reason to doubt the sincerity of his professed devotion to revolu-tionary goals. He despised inherited and artificial privilege and was impatient with the disorderliness of the old regime. He favored *equality of opportunity,* with careers (like his own) open to talent. Interpreting its meaning in his own way, he readily embraced the revolutionary slogan of "Liberty, Equality, and Fraternity."

Napoleon was a child of the Enlightenment as well as of the revo-lution—a skeptic, a rationalist, and a believer in progress. There was a strain of mysticism in him, too, an ever present faith in himself as a man of destiny. Viewing himself as above ordinary men, he felt free from conventional scruples. He was the intellectual and moral heir of Caesar, Machiavelli, and Voltaire. With a firm sense of drama and history, he built an image of himself as the creator of a new Pax Romana—a *Pax Francia.* This image, in turn, was to be transformed into a living myth.

The new master of France had no use for either the old aris-tocracy or the new democracy. Though his various constitutions provided for manhood suffrage, the voters elected only lists of candi-dates from which his government named the legislators and officials. Napoleon saw to it that only men loyal to him and to his purposes were appointed and advanced in office. The democratic façade gave satisfaction to the populace and honor to his favorites, but Napo-leon himself was the real mover. Contemptuous of the democratic interpreters of Rousseau, Napoleon presented *himself* as the articu-lator of the general will of France.

It is inaccurate to conclude that Napoleon snuffed out democracy in France, for it had never existed there before. The great majority of the people—unlettered and uneducated—had enjoyed no political power under either the monarchy or the republic. Napoleon's overthrow of the Directory meant that a propertied aristocracy had been displaced by an enlightened despot. Declaring a general political amnesty, he invited back to France all the émigrés who were willing to work faithfully for their homeland. He called to his service men of widely varying backgrounds (from royalist to regicide) who would cooperate in consolidating the new order. By and large every class gained from his statecraft, but the beneficiaries were the bourgeoisie.

His first task was to secure domestic peace and order. He arranged to have his opponents silenced by means of selective deportations, exposure of alleged subversive plots, and the efficient work of his secret police. Catholic disaffection, springing from the earlier measures that had been taken against the Church, was dissolved by a dramatic concordat (agreement) with Pius VII in 1801. In this agreement Napoleon formally accepted the fact that the Roman Catholic faith was the predominant religion of the French, abandoning the attempt of the previous revolutionaries to supplant traditional religion with a state-sponsored deism or "cult of reason." Church seminaries were reopened, and public religious processions were again permitted. Priests who had submitted to the revolutionary Civil Constitution were left to papal discipline, while those who had remained loyal to Rome were recognized as legitimate.

The pope, in return, accepted the new status of Catholicism in France. He dropped Rome's claims to confiscated church property and gave to the French government the right to nominate bishops. He tried, but failed, to eliminate the toleration of all faiths that had been secured by the revolutionary regimes. Although the settlement was criticized by men on both sides of the dispute, it satisfied the principals and established a peace between state and church in France that lasted for over a century.

Napoleon, privately an unbeliever, recognized the importance of religion to the people and appreciated the advantage of having the Church on the side of the state, but he would not allow it to be the paramount force in the molding of citizens. The state, through its own schools, had to provide for the education and patriotic indoctrination of the young. He endorsed the earlier closing of church schools by the National Convention and put into effect its comprehensive plans for a national educational system. By 1808 his subordinates had completed the structure of state-supported primary and secondary schools as well as public institutions of higher learning.

The entire system, supervised from Paris, remains the basis of French education to this day.

Napoleon also carried through the plans of his revolutionary predecessors for reorganizing French law and administration. His appointed commissions cut through the centuries-old accretion of rules and regulations and brought to completion the Code Napoléon. This compilation of laws and principles relating to persons and property was the product of a gigantic labor of sorting, eliminating, and condensing. The code was to become the new basis of law in major portions of Europe (and America) and is comparable to the ancient Roman codes that inspired it (p. 79). In later years Napoleon regarded the code as his most durable accomplishment. While in exile he wrote, "My true glory is not in having won forty battles; Waterloo has effaced the memory of so many victories. What nothing can efface, what will live eternally, is my civil code."

Under Napoleon, the modern techniques of administering a centralized state took shape. The ancient provinces of France, the local courts and offices, the quasi-private administration of justice—all had been swept away by the revolution. Salaried public officials responsible to the central government now presided over uniform administrative districts. The rationalization of public affairs extended to taxation, public expenditure, and money and banking; the day of the bureaucrat was at hand and, with it, the equality of citizens before the law. All these changes were in keeping with the rationalism of the Enlightenment and with bourgeois ideas of efficiency.

But if Napoleon brought peace, order, and prosperity at home, he wrought turmoil abroad. At the very outset of the revolution a sharp tension had developed between France and the rest of Europe. Any revolution, if it is a true revolution, creates such tension, for it is a threat to established social systems. The privileged classes of Europe, as we have seen, reacted in fear to the events of 1789; the French leaders, in turn, expected to be attacked. In the ensuing warfare the armies of the revolution extended the frontiers of France to the Rhine and to central Italy, but the outcome of the struggle was still undecided when Bonaparte took power in 1799.

His first move in foreign affairs was to break the Second Coalition of powers (Britain, Russia, Austria, Portugal, and Naples), which had come together against France. By swift military strokes and skillful diplomacy, he had achieved this goal by 1802. For the first time in a decade there was peace between France and her neighbors. But it proved to be only an uneasy truce.

Napoleon, in a position of strength, might have dug in on his advanced lines. The French state now embraced more territory than the Bourbons had dreamed of, and Napoleon extended its dominion even further by bringing Holland, Switzerland, and portions of Italy and Germany under his influence. He could have chosen a defensive military posture, against which his enemies might have struck in vain. But the dynamics of the revolution, joined to his own driving ambition, worked against such a strategy. As the heir to what he believed to be universal ideals, Napoleon felt he had to *expand* the new order. His political and military moves led to another break with England, the renewal of the war, and a Third Coalition against France.

Through the tangled diplomacy and military campaigns—from Madrid to Moscow—it became apparent that either Napoleon or his enemies must, in the end, prevail. Defense of the revolution merged, in his mind, with personal and imperial glory, and he began to dream of dominating all of Europe. Napoleon's genius and the confusion of his enemies brought him near to his goal. But the stubborn defiance of the British and their control of the seas, plus the vast manpower and distances of Russia, ensured his downfall.

After abdicating as emperor in 1814, Napoleon was banished to the Mediterranean island of Elba. Escaping shortly afterward, he raised a new army in a foolish gamble against the odds of power. At Waterloo his last minutes as a maker of history ran out. But Napoleon had planted the seeds of a new order in Europe, and the Continent would never again be the same.

THE CONSERVATIVE REACTION

When Napoleon made his dash from Elba in the spring of 1815, the victorious allies were assembled at the glittering Congress of Vienna. Here the crowned heads of Europe and their chief ministers were trying to restore the Continent to what it had been before the revolutionary disturbance. They were chilled by the news that the Corsican was once more at large. For the aristocrats of Europe viewed Napoleon, not as a liberator, but as a vulgar upstart, a destroyer of the culture they were privileged to enjoy. A sigh of relief passed through Vienna when "that madman" was again shipped away—this time to the isle of St. Helena, in the south Atlantic.

Metternich and the "Concert of Europe"

Though there were many signatories to the general settlement of 1815, the management of the treaty was in the hands of the four major powers that had brought about Bonaparte's defeat: Britain, Russia, Prussia, and Austria. Prince Clemens von Metternich, the chief minister of Austria, was the leading spirit of the conference. An aristocrat of distinguished lineage, he had been a career diplomat in the service of the Habsburgs. He had demonstrated his astuteness when Napoleon was at the acme of power (1810) by arranging a marriage between the conqueror and Maria Louisa, daughter of the Austrian emperor. (At the same moment, though Austria was formally at peace, Metternich was working secretly for a new alliance against France.) Then, after Napoleon's disastrous defeat in Russia, Metternich threw Austria's weight against him. Though beaten many times by the French, Austria thus emerged from the wars in a victor's role, and Metternich, to clinch the advantage, persuaded the allies to hold the peace congress in Vienna.

Metternich's cunning was matched by that of the illustrious and unscrupulous Duc de Talleyrand. Talleyrand was loyal only to himself and to France. He had served as a bishop under the old regime, as a statesman of the revolution, and as Napoleon's foreign minister. When it appeared that the French emperor was overreaching himself, Talleyrand proffered secret aid to Napoleon's enemies abroad, thereby preparing a place for himself in the postwar regime. When the emperor fell, Talleyrand urged the allies to restore the Bourbon rulers in France; this, he explained, would accord with the principle of "legitimacy." He hoped, by extending the application of that principle, to hold for France the territories she had possessed before the revolution.

The victorious allies accepted the principle of legitimacy and restoration. The royal succession in France fell to the eldest brother of the executed king, who assumed the title of Louis XVIII. (The late monarch's young son, who had died in 1795, was considered by the royalists as Louis XVII.) The restored monarch, having lived as an émigré in England, was brought back to Paris in 1814 by courtesy of the victors and at once rewarded Talleyrand by appointing him foreign minister.

At Vienna, Talleyrand played skillfully on the differences among the Big Four, thus giving France, the defeated nation, a significant role in the settlement. The chief concerns of the conference were to restore, so far as practicable, the legitimate holdings of all titled rulers and the European balance of power. That balance, which had been established by the Peace of Westphalia, had aimed to secure the independence of European states by preventing one or more of them from gaining preponderant power. In the course of the Vienna conference, for example, Talleyrand joined Metternich and Lord Castlereagh (of Britain) in a secret pledge to go to war should Prussia and Russia carry through their plan of joint aggrandizement in central Europe. When word of the agreement leaked out, a compromise plan was proposed and accepted.

The Congress of Vienna by no means restored the borders of Europe exactly as they had been before 1789; it provided territorial compensations for those states that had contributed the most to toppling Napoleon. The redrawn map of Europe (FIG. *10-1*) was to remain in effect, save for minor alterations, for half a century. The most unstable boundaries proved to be those in central Europe. There, Napoleon had given the *coup de grâce* to the Holy Roman Empire in 1806 and had merged many of the smaller German states into a league of minor kingdoms. Metternich kept this general arrangement, joined Austria to it, and named it the Germanic Confederation. Subject to Austrian control, this grouping forestalled for the moment Prussian aspirations to dominance in Germany.

Metternich was realist enough to know that he could not completely undo the effects of the French Revolution. In France, the dull King Louis felt constrained to grant a constitutional charter that made the country a limited monarchy. The legal, administrative, clerical, and educational reforms of the revolution were retained. And beyond the borders of France the ideas of liberalism could not be altogether erased. Still less could Metternich arrest the rising sentiment of nationalism, which had been strengthened by the revolution's stress on "fraternity." The peoples of Germany and Italy, especially, were impressed by the power and accomplishments of the French nation-in-arms and by the psychological lift that accompanied national solidarity. Their hatred for the conquerors (which succeeded their initial admiration of the French as liberators) also stimulated their own sense of cultural identity. All across Europe, patriotic societies arose to champion the cause of national unity and independence.

But, for the time being, liberal and nationalistic movements were kept under rein. The privileged classes and dynastic states perceived the threats to their interests and agreed at Vienna to guard vigilantly against them. Metternich effected a "Concert of Europe" (in actuality, a Quadruple Alliance of Austria, Prussia, Russia, and Britain) that would use diplomacy and force against moves to change either boundaries or social systems. Accordingly, successive conferences of the conservative powers, under Metternich's guidance, met all threats to the established order. The Metternich System thus provided a type of "collective security" for the existing states of Europe. It functioned efficiently for a while (until the

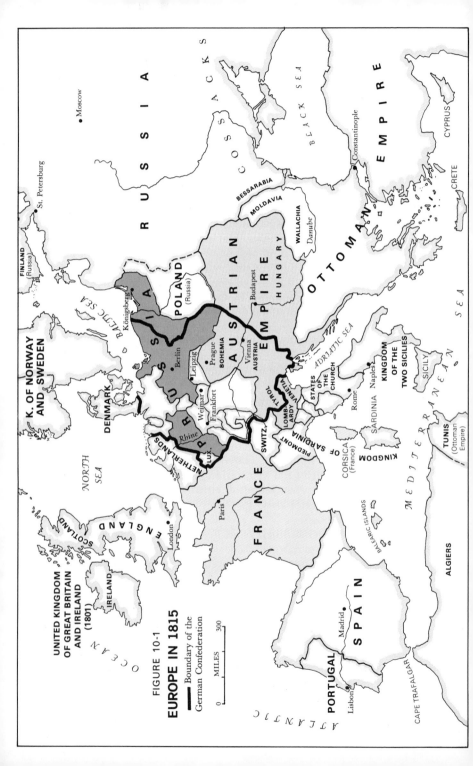

FIGURE 10-1

EUROPE IN 1815

━━ Boundary of the German Confederation

MILES
0   300

middle of the nineteenth century), preserving order and forcing both liberal and national movements underground.

The repudiation of revolution and rationalism: Burke

Opposition to liberal ideas found wide support among the European populace and intellectuals. A long-standing cleavage within Western culture had been deepened by the Enlightenment and widened by the revolution. For generations afterward, those who stressed science and reason, equality and democracy, stood in opposition to those who stressed tradition and sentiment, aristocracy and authority. While some people straddled this broad division, most felt a sense of identification with one side or the other. Through the nineteenth century both sides, paradoxically, appeared to make advances. The liberal forces succeeded in modifying political, economic, and social institutions, and the conservatives made their influence felt in philosophy, the arts, and the general mood of Europe.

During the period immediately following 1815 the conservatives enjoyed a resurgence on all fronts. This was natural enough, for Napoleon, who personified the triumph of the revolution, had fallen. Victory had passed to the defenders of privilege and the old order, and the ideals of the Enlightenment had been dimmed by the ugly realities of revolution, politics, and war. Many who had sympathized with those ideals now recoiled from the bloody cost of implementing them.

One of the most articulate representatives of the conservative point of view was the thinker and statesman Edmund Burke. As an English observer of French affairs he had been one of the first to become alarmed by the events of the revolution. Opposing from the beginning the underlying principles of the revolution, he had feared that those ideas might win favor in his homeland. His *Reflections on the Revolution in France* appeared in 1790 and has remained to this day a primer of conservatism.

Burke's first point of attack was the doctrine of natural rights, which John Locke and the revolutionary leaders had used to justify their actions. David Hume, a skeptical Scottish philosopher, had already demolished the proofs for natural law in his *Treatise of Human Nature* (1740). Though Burke conceded that men might speak of natural rights in an abstract sense, he insisted that such speculation had no bearing on the actual distribution of authority in a civil society. The liberties of Englishmen, asserted Burke, were those that had been slowly forged in the fire of history; he saw them as part of an "entailed inheritance," handed down from generation to generation. And that inheritance was by no means equal for all men. The king, the peers, and every other group within the English social body had the prescriptive right to enjoy the particular privileges and liberties accruing to it from "a long line of ancestors." Burke thus affirmed his belief in aristocracy and attacked efforts made in the name of equality to tamper with legitimate privilege.

Burke warned against undue reliance on human reason. He felt that each man's private stock of reason is pitifully small and therefore a poor guide to action. He much preferred the wisdom deposited in the "general bank and capital of nations and ages"—by which he meant tradition. It is especially presumptuous of reform-minded theorists, thought Burke, to reconstruct institutions out of their own minds; such "progress" as might result from their efforts would prove a cruel disappointment. It is far better, he concluded, for men to follow the "prejudices" (established convictions) that bind them to tried and tested institutions.

Burke reserved his bitterest scorn for the Lockean-Jeffersonian notion of the right and efficacy of revolution. Denouncing the social atomism of both Hobbes and Locke, he conceived of individuals as integral parts of a transcendant organism—*society*. The state he saw as a divinely drawn contract, binding past, present, and future generations. He referred to it as a partnership embracing all human purposes and immune to dissolution by the will of individuals.

The state, being sacred, must be looked upon with awe and reverence. It should not be "hacked to pieces" by would-be innovators; such recklessness can lead only to anarchy. And, Burke felt, the absence of firm social control is "ten thousand times worse" than the blindest and most obstinate government. A devout Anglican, he held to the dogma of Original Sin and rejected the enlightened faith in human goodness and progress. Only by strict social discipline, he believed, is the individual made decent and civilized. Once restraints are broken, men regress to beast-like behavior. Thus, Burke argued, revolution leads to an intolerable chaos, which can be ended only by the imposition of some form of despotism.

Burke did not think, however, that institutions should remain frozen. His organic concept of society led him to think in terms of biological growth, which would permit useless accretions to be sloughed off and new shoots and branches to develop. He was, therefore, a dynamic conservative. He even stated that conditions in a given society might become such that a resort to revolution would be admissible. But it should never be a *calculated action*. Mystically (and dangerously) he asserted that the justification for revolution must be "the first and supreme necessity only, a necessity that is not chosen, but chooses, a necessity paramount to deliberation, that admits no discussion, and demands no evidence. . . ." In other words, he placed his ultimate reliance on *intuition,* thus giving philosophical approval to irrational social action.

Though Burke struck his critics as perverse, contradictory, obscure, hypocritical, and menacing, he gave classic expression to the ideology of conservatism, scoring telling hits on vulnerable points in liberal doctrine. Other conservative writers soon joined him in the assault. The English clergyman, Thomas Malthus, attacked the idea of human perfectibility, which had been propagated by some eighteenth-century writers. Noting the general misery of the poor, Malthus found the explanation in the pressure of population growth. Because of the sexual urge, said Malthus in his *Essay on the Principle of Population* (1798), population tends to increase faster than food supplies. Population growth is restrained only by the "positive checks" of starvation, disease, and war. Seeing no way out of this condition (save the unlikely prospect of sexual continence), Malthus predicted continued suffering for the human race. And without a favorable balance between food and people, the material foundation for happiness (and perfectibility) is missing. Malthus thus called attention to one of the root problems facing the modern world.

A new philosophical synthesis: Hegel

The conservative reaction was also strong on the Continent, where the intellectuals of the Enlightenment were held responsible for the unhappy events of revolution and war. After 1815 liberal writers and critics were regarded with official hostility and general suspicion. The frequent persecution of authors and the suppression of their works were products of the haunting fear of new social upheavals. Defenders of the restored order concluded also that the weakening of religious faith had eased the way to social subversion. They therefore encouraged the revival of religious fervor that had arisen as a reaction to the secularism of the Enlightenment and the revolution. The Roman Catholic Church, traditionally conservative, played a leading role in this renewal of piety, conventional morality, and respect for authority.

European philosophy was affected even more deeply than religion by the reaction against eighteenth-century thought. A German professor, Immanuel Kant, was a key figure in the shift from the outlook of the Enlightenment to that of the nineteenth century. Born in East Prussia, his long lifetime (1724–1804) spanned the confident period of science and rationalism as well as the aftermath of disenchantment. His keen, analytical mind, coupled with a profound moral and religious sense, gave his philosophy its ultimate contours.

Deeply impressed by the achievements of Newtonian science, Kant retained much of the rationalist spirit and methodology. However, he set limits upon its scope and marked off legitimate areas for religion and moral conviction. It was Hume's skepticism that first awakened Kant to the limitations of reason and empiricism as means of knowing. Hume had argued that science has no way of *proving* causal relationships; it can only observe that a certain event is *preceded* by another. This relationship in time and space may be witnessed over and over again; yet the idea of causation remains an inference created by the mind, not a perception of external reality.

Kant carried the point further, asserting that even "perceived objects" are in large measure a reflection of the mind. Locke had previously stated that knowledge comes chiefly from sensation—the result of external stimuli striking our sensory mechanism and registering upon our consciousness. But Kant was critical of this simple explanation. He insisted that our minds, independent of experience (a priori), establish certain categories, which impose their patterns on our perceptions. For example, we have the concept of "time"—which cannot be perceived and is therefore mental rather than experiential. Yet this concept, or category, along with many others, shapes and orders all our observations.

From this Kant concluded that scientific knowledge, though highly useful, is not knowledge of the "real" world but a construct of the human mind, drawn from bits of observation. While science thus provides only a restricted means of knowing about material things, it cannot even address itself to questions that go beyond them. On such issues as the existence of God, immortality of the soul, and moral responsibility, science is dumb. In these vital matters, Kant declared in his *Critique of Pure Reason* (1781), the individual must rely chiefly on his conscience and intuition.

Following Kant's lead, German philosophy in the nineteenth century reached its fullest development in the work of another professor—Georg Wilhelm Friedrich Hegel, an energetic and imaginative man who helped make the University of Berlin a center of philosophic speculation. In response to the doubts and contradictions current among serious thinkers, he attempted nothing less than a complete reconstruction of formal thought. He sought a new methodological approach that would enable him to reconcile opposing philosophic tendencies and bring them into a unified system. He found that approach in the *historical method*.

Hegel steeped himself in the study of history, convinced that true understanding of any subject—whether politics, art, or religion—is derived from examining its historical development. For he saw history as more than a confusing mass of events; underlying the events and guiding them are significant truths. The scholar must employ his talent for synthesis as well as analysis in order to bring these truths to light. It was a postulate of Hegel's thought that a divine and logical plan is the moving though unseen force in history.

This view is related to Greek speculation during the classical age. The Christian philosopher, Augustine, had also seen history as the unfolding of divine will. Hegel's special contribution was his development of the concept of *dialectic* in history. Like Augustine, he saw the continual struggle between opposing forces as the dynamic behind events. But he defined these forces as opposing ideas, which become ever more comprehensive in succeeding stages of the struggle. The dominant idea at any given stage he defined as the *thesis,* which (because it is imperfect and incomplete) calls forth an opposing idea, or *antithesis.* In the conflict between the two, neither is entirely destroyed, but both are absorbed into a new and more comprehensive idea, the *synthesis.* Thus, suggested Hegel, the idea of Oriental despotism had been opposed by the Graeco-Roman idea of limited freedom (aristocracy); both were being supplanted by the German-Christian idea of universal freedom under monarchy. Although discarding the eighteenth-century concepts of progress and reform as naive, he regarded the dialectic of history as leading inexorably to a freer and happier condition for mankind.

Since Hegel saw the development of ideas as the guiding force and the underlying reality of history, he is usually classified (like Plato) as a philosophical idealist—as distinguished from a materialist. "Whatever is rational is real, and whatever is real is rational." But he did not deny material existence; he merely subordinated it to the superior reality of ideas and logic. Man's reason, in the eighteenth-century sense, he discounted, putting in its place the reason of history. Hegel insisted that history provides its own solutions to problems that even the wisest of men can understand only dimly.

The human individual, so precious to the *philosophes,* was reduced by Hegel to a relatively minor role in history. Great men, he thought—in fact, all men—are instruments of the dialectic. But individual leaders can nevertheless accomplish notable deeds: political genius consists in identifying oneself with a developing idea. He would have used this aphorism to explain the greatness of a Caesar, a Washington, or a Bismarck.

Though Hegel stressed the role of logic in historical development, he was at the same time both religious and mystical. He was not an orthodox Christian, but he viewed religious doctrine and ritual as a natural expression of the total life of an age. His system was indeed a synthesis of many elements that had heretofore been regarded as contradictory. It afforded validity, on the one hand, to science, reason, empirical observation, individual freedom, and cultural relativism and, on the other, to religion, faith, intuition, authority, and the absolutism of history. As might be expected, this comprehensive philosophy had a broad appeal; Hegel's books provided stimulus and support for divergent ideas, and Hegelian disciples branched off in many directions.

THE ROMANTIC SPIRIT
IN LITERATURE, ART, AND MUSIC

The reaction against the Enlightenment manifested itself in the arts as well as in philosophy. Here it was to take on the name of "romanticism"—a term that comprehends an extraordinary variety of creative expressions. Common to all of them was an emphasis on emotion and imagination, as opposed to "cold" calculation. Man and the world were to be viewed primarily through the heart rather than the brain. The romantics were rebels, not only against the eighteenth-century cosmology, but against everyday constrictions on the individual and his self-realization. Thus, they fought the conventions of bourgeois morality as well as the conformities imposed by developing industrialism. Most of them desired, at the same time, a mystical identification with God, nature, race, or nation; and they often turned to the past, especially the Middle Ages, for their ideal of culture.

Appeal to the heart: Rousseau

The many-sided nature of romanticism may be seen in the life and works of individual writers and artists. The forerunner was Jean-Jacques Rousseau, whose impact on the French Revolution we have already mentioned. Though he lived during the Enlightenment, Rousseau's career was mainly one of revolt against the dominant intellectual current of that age, but his style and values became increasingly popular after his death, causing him to be known, later, as the "father of romanticism."

A man of little formal education or personal discipline, Rousseau had reacted spontaneously against the eighteenth-century stress on reason and science. Through a stormy and chaotic career, which we know largely through his own *Confessions,* he found time to write hundreds of letters as well as essays and books. His attacks on rationalism struck home, not because he wrote from deep knowledge, but because of the power of his language and his appeal to internal experience. He wrote, he said, from the heart (and to the heart).

Rousseau's antirationalism was expressed characteristically when he opened an important discussion with these words: "Let us begin by laying aside the facts, since they have nothing to do with the matter." He went even further in his *Discourse on the Sciences and Arts* (1750). Science, he declared, gives knowledge to men that they are better off not to possess. The only knowledge worth having is knowledge of virtue, and for this science is not needed; the principles of virtue are "engraved on every heart."

The vogue of Rousseau was due, more than to anything else, to his intense sentimentalism. Readers who were unmoved by the abstractions of science and philosophy responded warmly to his emotional outpourings. In his novel, the *New Héloïse* (1761), the hero is madly in love with one of his pupils, but she must marry another. The two frustrated souls experience protracted temptations and torments that end only with the death of the heroine. The theme of passion and suffering, of morbid introspection, became the touchstone of romantic prose and poetry in the nineteenth century.

Another theme of the *New Héloïse* is Rousseau's criticism of sophisticated society and his exaltation of nature. The hero of the novel seeks relief from his anguish by wandering through a wilderness. This provides the author with an opportunity to fashion eloquent word pictures of lakes, mountains, and flowers, which inspired such romantic nature poets as William Wordsworth.

Rousseau's individualism and his rejection of imposed patterns of behavior are best expressed in his famous *Émile* (1762). This is not really a story but an account of a hypothetical education for life. From infancy to manhood, the fictional Émile is cared for and tutored in a manner contrary to the educational practices of the eighteenth century. Rather than forcing the boy into a succession of studies corresponding to the "knowledge" of the day, his teacher encourages Émile to learn for himself. When the need or desire strikes him, the youngster asks for instruction in reading and writing and in nature studies. Meanwhile he lives a spare, simple, athletic life in the country. The tutor refrains from punishing his pupil for destructive acts, confident that such aberrations will be corrected through the boy's own experience of subsequent deprivation. There are no inherently bad boys, wrote Rousseau; real vices are learned only from "civilized" elders.

There is much of Rabelais in this theory of education, but Rousseau wrote seriously rather than playfully. His permissiveness appealed to romantic individualists and impressed a number of educational reformers (Pestalozzi, Froebel, Dewey). Rousseau's religious sentiments, too, influenced succeeding generations. It was a romantic brand of deism, rejecting theology and sacred books. As taught to Émile (at the appropriate time), this religion consisted of a simple faith in God and immortality. All that needs to be known about the deity and his commandments, wrote Rousseau, can be found in one's heart and in the study of nature.

Poets of nature and humanity: Wordsworth, Goethe

Rousseau's insistence on the divinity and beauty of nature was echoed by the romantic poets of the nineteenth century, especially in England. William Wordsworth was the master of lyric poetry, and his most moving verses deal with the excitement and meaning of wild nature. Generations of school children have recited:

> I wandered lonely as a cloud
> That floats on high o'er vales and hills,
> When all at once I saw a crowd,
> A host, of golden daffodils.

But Wordsworth sensed something beyond the colors and movements of a landscape. His perceptions of nature opened the way to moral and spiritual insights. As he confessed in his "Lines Composed a Few Miles above Tintern Abbey" (1798):

> . . . Therefore am I still
> A lover of the meadows and the woods,
> And mountains; and of all that we behold
> From this green earth; of all the mighty world
> Of eye, and ear—both what they half create,
> And what perceive; well pleased to recognize
> In nature and the language of the sense,
> The anchor of my purest thoughts, the nurse,
> The guide, the guardian of my heart, and soul
> Of all my moral being.

Wordsworth shared Rousseau's contempt for formal learning as well as his passion for nature. In "The Tables Turned," Wordsworth wrote:

> Books! 'tis a dull and endless strife;
> Come, hear the woodland linnet,
> How sweet his music! on my life,
> There's more of wisdom in it.

. . .

> One impulse from a vernal wood
> May teach you more of man,
> Of moral evil and of good,
> Than all the sages can.

> Sweet is the lore which Nature brings;
> Our meddling intellect
> Mis-shapes the beauteous forms of things—
> We murder to dissect.

> Enough of Science and of Art;
> Close up those barren leaves;
> Come forth, and bring with you a heart
> That watches and receives.

Though poetry seemed to be the form best suited to romantic literary expression, romantic prose was also popular with the educated classes of society. Sir Walter Scott, a contemporary of Wordsworth, created the historical novel, choosing the Middle Ages as the setting for most of his books. Novels such as *Waverley* (1814) and *Ivanhoe* (1820) show the drama and imagination that marked his best romances.

In Germany the most prominent literary figure was Johann Wolfgang von Goethe. Born in the middle of the eighteenth century, he grew up during the Enlightenment and lived on into the age of romanticism. Goethe came from a well-to-do family of jurists and administrators; his "conversion" to romanticism took place while he was studying law at Strassburg. He later became a member of the court of Saxe-Weimar, a small German duchy, and remained for most of his life in Weimar, the capital of the duchy, where the duke's patronage afforded him freedom to study, travel, and write.

Goethe's interests embraced the whole range of the arts and sciences, in keeping with the Renaissance ideal of *virtù*. A man of high intelligence and feeling, he transcended as a writer the limits of most romantic authors. But his personal career embodied the spirit of the times, for his life was a succession of passionate amours, many of which he described in his writing. Goethe's lyric poetry reflects his fascination with love, nature, and the macabre. In prose, the most striking expression of his youthful romanticism is the *Sorrows of Young Werther* (1774), which recounts the extravagant sufferings of a forlorn hero tortured by frustrated passion.

Faust, a dramatic poem on which Goethe worked during most of his long life, reflects the conflicts and growth that took place in his personal development. Part One, published in 1808, retells the medieval legend of a learned professor, Doctor Faust, who bargained his soul to the devil in return for youth and power. (This portion was put to music by several romantic composers.) Part Two, which was not published until after the author's death in 1832, carries Faust on a kind of philosophical excursion in search of man's ultimate purpose and way to happiness. The soul of the hero is saved at last because he loves God and mankind and strives, in spite of errors, to serve both. Goethe's Faust serves as a literary archetype of "modern" man—the man who seeks to comprehend and experience the infinite and tries to harmonize his sensual and spiritual urges.

The romantic spirit in literature brought forth an impressive response from Russian writers. As a result of Russia's turning toward the West (p. 352), eighteenth-century Russian literature had been largely imitative of the French. In the nineteenth century, however, it developed its own character. Alexander Pushkin (died 1837) was the first Russian writer to command serious attention in western Europe; his romantic poems and plays are still highly regarded in his homeland. The grand tradition of the Russian novel was started by Nicolai Gogol, whose *Taras Bulba* (1835), a romantic tour de force, recounts adventures and struggles among the barbaric Cossacks. But the finest Russian novelists came later in the century— Feodor Dostoevsky and Leo Tolstoy. Both were concerned primarily with the inner life and struggles of man, while depicting at the same time the color and detail of Russian life. The best known of their works are Tolstoy's epic historical novel, *War and Peace* (1868) and Dostoevsky's profound *Brothers Karamazov* (1880).

Rebellion and romance in painting

The early nineteenth-century reaction against rationalism in philosophy and literature was paralleled in the visual arts by a reaction against the classicism of the preceding century. In France, the main target of the artistic revolt was the classical style that had been established by Jacques-Louis David. David had turned away from the elegant, frivolous works admired by the aristocracy and had sought inspiration in ancient Roman and Greek sculptures. The classical revival in French painting may be said to have begun with the exhibition in 1785 of his heroic painting, the *Oath of the Horatii* (FIG. *10-2*).

The new style, which contrasted sharply with the rococo, became the official style of the French Revolution. David, a middle-class man who sympathized with the radical political reforms of the period, was elected to the National Convention and helped abolish the royal Academy of Painting. The leaders of the revolution regarded art primarily as an instrument of propaganda; they destroyed the

FIGURE 10-2. DAVID. *Oath of the Horatii*. Louvre, Paris. (Giraudon.)

academy because it upheld aristocratic traditions. In its place they established the *École des Beaux-Arts,* which adopted the classical style and sought to impose it on all French painters.

David reached the height of his influence later, under Napoleon. As "First Painter of the Empire," he painted portraits of the new caesar, supervised the national galleries, arranged imperial ceremonies, and saw to the licensing of artists who wished to exhibit their works publicly. After Napoleon's fall, David was ordered into exile, and the Academy of Painting was restored. But David's classicism remained the official style in France for a century afterward.

Romantic painters everywhere revolted against classicism, against official styles of any sort, and against academic rules of painting. One of the earliest rebels was Francisco Goya, a Spanish contemporary of David. Heir to the rich legacy of Spanish baroque painting, Goya preferred it to the restraints of classicism. However, he did not paint in the traditional aristocratic manner, which aimed to embellish or glorify. His portraits of Spanish royalty and nobility are a testament to his extraordinary perception and honesty.

FIGURE 10-3. GOYA. *The Third of May, 1808.* Museo del Prado, Madrid.

Goya's active social conscience also made him sensitive to the tyranny, civil strife, and poverty that he saw on every hand in his native land. (Hundreds of his etchings reveal the cruelty and desperation of the times.) In his painting the *Third of May, 1808* (FIG. *10-3*), he presented an execution scene in the streets of Madrid; Napoleon's soldiers had been attacked by civilians the day before and are here making their reprisal. The horror of war and man's capacity for brutality, a side of the war that David preferred to ignore, Goya chose to dramatize. Though he became more bitter as he grew older, he preserved his integrity and independence to the end.

The romantic style achieved its fullest expression in France during the generation after Napoleon's downfall. Its most brilliant exponent was Eugène Delacroix. After a classical education he decided to become a painter and began his training in Paris, which had now eclipsed Rome as the art center of Europe. He became almost at once an enthusiastic convert to the new style. "If by Romanticism is meant the free expression of my personal feelings, my aloofness from the standardized types of paintings prescribed by the Schools, and my dislike of academic formulas," he wrote later, "I must confess that not only am I a Romantic but that I already was one at the age of fifteen!"

Through the strength of his personality and talent Delacroix made the new style dominant in France, even though it was opposed by the academy critics. He was an excellent draughtsman, but he disregarded formal rules of drawing and achieved his effects mainly through the use of color. He believed that imagination was more important to an artist than knowledge and sought above all to inject excitement and movement into his works. As did Goya, he often played down detail in the interest of sharp focus and strong impact.

Delacroix first gained public attention in 1822 through the showing of his *Dante and Vergil in Hell*. This scene, illustrating a passage from Dante, shows a group of tormented individuals writhing in the dark waters of the River Styx. Friendly critics saw in this work suggestions of the figures of Michelangelo and the colors of Rubens, the antithesis of classical serenity. In his historical painting the *Entrance of the Crusaders into Constantinople* (FIG. *10-4*), Delacroix provoked the emotions of the viewer by contrasting the triumphant invaders with their crouching victims. Responding to the romantic taste for the exotic, Delacroix once traveled to Algiers.

FIGURE 10-4. DELACROIX. *Entrance of the Crusaders into Constantinople.* Louvre, Paris. (Giraudon.)

Some of his most popular works, paintings of lion hunts and of the Moorish court and concubines, grew out of that experience.

The love of nature, which was a central feature of romanticism, was best expressed in painting by the English artists J. M. W. Turner and John Constable. Turner's paintings are visionary rather than realistic. A superb colorist, he invested his landscapes and seascapes with a sense of grandeur and mystery. He often used a sentimental subject for his canvases, as in the *Fighting Temeraire* (FIG. *10-5*), painted in 1839. Many Englishmen were stirred by this picture of the ghostly *Temeraire,* a sailing ship of Lord Nelson's battle fleet, being towed away for destruction. She is led to her inglorious fate by a squat, black tug, symbol of the triumph of steam over sail, iron over timber, efficiency over beauty. Turner showed the ship against a panorama of sky and sea. The time, symbolically, is sunset, and a reddish light is cast on the water. Turner's imaginative treatment of nature proved extremely popular; he sold hundreds of paintings and etchings and built up a fortune during his lifetime.

Constable, Turner's contemporary, approached nature in a different manner. His love of the English countryside was akin to that of his good friend, the poet Wordsworth; but he studied nature with the intensity of a scientist, and, though he finished his canvases indoors, he worked from oil sketches prepared in the open. His paintings were so strikingly different from the familiar studio landscapes of the period that they created a sensation when they were first shown. When the *Hay Wain* (FIG. *10-6*) was exhibited in Paris in 1821, French painters were astonished by its truth to nature, and many set out to imitate Constable's technique.

Constable referred to Turner's works as "airy visions, painted with tinted steam," while he based his own painting on "observable facts." He wanted nature to speak for itself, without artificial effects. Restricting his subjects almost entirely to rural scenes, which he rendered with a sense of intimacy and charm, he painted richly humanistic canvases, with people and animals (as in the *Hay Wain*) gently fitting into a scheme that was clearly designed for man. The general atmosphere of Constable's paintings is often set by his treatment of the sky, which he believed was "the key note, the standard scale, and the chief organ of sentiment."

The Gothic revival in architecture

In nineteenth-century architecture the contention between classicism and romanticism was obscured by a broad eclecticism, under which architectural styles became more and more a matter of individual taste or fancy. This was a time of vast activity in construction,

FIGURE 10-5. TURNER. *The Fighting Temeraire.* Courtesy of the Trustees of the National Gallery, London.

FIGURE 10-6. CONSTABLE. *The Hay Wain.* Courtesy of the Trustees of the National Gallery, London.

especially in the industrial cities—most of the older buildings still standing in Europe today were erected during the nineteenth century. They represent a confusing variety of styles, springing from several architectural revivals. The architect sometimes aimed at a "pure" style, sometimes at a composite one, and sometimes at an original design. But by mid-century, certain conventions had emerged: banks and government buildings, for instance, were usually built in the Greek or Roman manner; churches and colleges, in the Gothic. There were, of course, notable exceptions to the rule, and all buildings, regardless of their design, were affected by a general decline in workmanship.

Of the various styles in vogue, the Gothic is most often associated with romanticism. The Gothic revival first appeared in England before the French Revolution as a reaction to the classical Palladian style (p. 380). Horace Walpole, a man of letters and the son of a noted statesman, wanted to make his country house distinctive from other aristocratic houses. Feeling a romantic affinity with the medi-

FIGURE 10-7. BARRY AND PUGIN. Houses of Parliament. (© 1962 by Charles Rotkin from *Europe: An Aerial Close-up.* Lippincott.)

eval past, he decided to remodel the building in the manner of a Gothic castle. The result was anything but "pure" Gothic, despite the addition of spires and round towers. As with many such attempts, Walpole's creation turned out to be a curious mixture of incongruities.

The romantic movement, after the turn of the century, gave new impetus to the Gothic revival. The outstanding example of this period is the Houses of Parliament (FIG. *10-7*). When the old building burned down in 1834, the lawmakers, remembering that English liberties and Parliament itself traced back to the thirteenth century, decided to rebuild it in the medieval style. At about the same time, across the North Sea in Germany, numerous "medieval" castles began to appear. All over Europe and America the Gothic revival proved popular.

Romanticism in music: Beethoven, Wagner

The eighteenth-century classical style in music, as we have seen, stressed order, grace, and clarity; the nineteenth century cast off restraint and exploited the emotional power of music. The classical style did not disappear altogether, but it was submerged in the tide of romanticism. Ludwig van Beethoven, born at Bonn in 1770, bridged both styles. His early works are similar to those of Haydn and Mozart, and he followed established compositional forms throughout most of his life. But he responded to the romantic spirit, and his later works are marked by heightened drama, suspense, and brilliant climaxes. Unlike some romantic composers, Beethoven never lost control of his themes; his music throbs with energy and strife but is contained within an orderly pattern. For this reason, he is sometimes called a "classical romantic."

Compositions in the romantic style were usually written for the concert hall rather than for the chamber or salon and called for augmented volume and range—Beethoven's orchestra was nearly twice the size of Haydn's. Although few new instruments were introduced, the number of strings, winds, and percussion instruments was enlarged. The symphony became the most popular form, but virtuoso pieces for solo performance also found favor. Melodies were highly expressive and original; harmonies were rich and often dissonant; and rhythms were subject to sudden or subtle manipulation.

The leading composers in the romantic style were an Austrian, Franz Schubert; a Pole, Frederic Chopin; a Frenchman, Hector Berlioz, and a Russian, Peter Ilich Tschaikovsky. More than half the serious music performed today—in the concert hall, on the air, and on records—is by romantic composers. The works of the nineteenth century dominate serious music to a degree unparalleled in any other art.

The culmination of romanticism in music appeared, not in the symphony hall, but in the opera house. Richard Wagner, born in Leipzig in 1813, created a new concept of opera—or music-drama, as he preferred to call it. Wagner personified the deepest yearnings of the romantic spirit. Above all, he stressed the idea of the *unity* of thought and feeling and believed that this unity should be reflected in all art forms. He had contempt for art as mere entertainment or spectacle—"effects without cause." His new conception of opera, which was modeled upon the performances of Greek tragedy, joined poetry, music, scenery, and action into one organic whole.

Wagner's "Ring cycle," a sequence of operas drawn from Germanic legend, best illustrates his conception of form. Here the drama —which is concerned with the curse of gold and the lust for power— is paramount. Voices and orchestra combine to carry foward the powerful themes; instead of writing separate speeches, arias, choruses, and accompaniments, Wagner created an "endless melody" out of all the musical elements. His music is rich and complex, full of passion and suspense, wholly romantic. Whether or not one enjoys it, he must concede the grandeur of its conception and execution.

Italian opera, it should be added, remained close to the tradition established by Monteverdi (pp. 386–87). But it, too, reflected the new stress on emotion and the enlarged capabilities of the orchestra. Giuseppe Verdi, Wagner's contemporary, is probably the most popular of operatic composers. His spectacular and beautiful *Aïda* has been performed more often than any other opera ever written.

THE SPREAD OF LIBERAL DEMOCRACY
AND NATIONALISM

Romanticism in music, art, and literature is generally viewed as part of a broad reaction against eighteenth-century rationalism and liberalism. But neither romanticism nor conservative philosophy— even when coupled with political repression—could stop the advance of liberal reforms. As a matter of fact, some of the romantic artists and writers identified themselves with liberal movements. And the liberal movements gained further strength wherever they associated themselves with the surge of national feeling.

The revolutions of 1830 and 1848

The struggles for liberal democracy and national unity and independence followed a general pattern in Europe during the nineteenth century. In the first decade after the Congress of Vienna, most of the uprisings were quickly suppressed (as in Naples, Spain, and Russia). Revolutionary successes were achieved only beyond the seas, where the Spanish and Portuguese colonies of Latin America gained their freedom by 1825. But waves of revolution continued to break across Europe, notably in 1830 and 1848. The first impressive victory for the liberal forces came in France in 1830.

Even with the restoration of the Bourbon king, Louis XVIII, in 1814, France had preserved the principal reforms introduced by the revolution and Napoleon. Louis reigned as a constitutional monarch, with a legislature that represented the restored nobility and well-to-do members of the business class. Though the narrowly restricted suffrage displeased the majority of citizens, the political arrangement was very close to what the moderate bourgeoisie had sought in 1789. That arrangement was threatened, however, when Louis was succeeded by his younger brother, Charles X, in 1824.

Charles had been an unyielding enemy of the revolution, a militant leader of the émigrés who had aroused European nobles and princes to attack revolutionary France. After becoming king, he and his reactionary friends moved to turn back the clock. They sought perpetual annuities for the nobles whose lands had been confiscated during the revolution, the reestablishment of the feudal rule of primogeniture, and a resurgence of clerical influence in education and politics. Charles himself, proud and stubborn, was contemptuous of the popular criticism his measures provoked. When the elective Chamber of Deputies refused, in 1830, to bend to his will, he broke the constitutional charter that had been issued by Louis XVIII. By decree, Charles dissolved the Chamber, censored the press, and altered the franchise to strengthen the power of the old nobility.

Paris responded to this show of despotism by throwing up barricades in the streets. This July Revolution lasted only a few days, for the troops and police refused to fire on the populace. Charles, who had no desire to share the fate of Louis XVI, promptly abdicated and left for England. The insurgents now found themselves divided on what to do next. The revolutionary workmen, students, and intellectuals who had hoisted the tricolor at the city hall (in place of the Bourbon fleur-de-lis) demanded that the monarchy give way to a republic. The bourgeois politicians, however, opposed such a change, feeling that their interests would be safer under a constitutional monarchy. What they wanted was a different kind of king, one who would serve their purposes. The politicians found such a man in Prince Louis Philippe, who, though a relative of the Bourbons, had fought on the side of the revolution in 1789. They persuaded the aged and respected national hero, the Marquis de Lafayette, to support Louis Philippe, which made the "left-wing" Bourbon acceptable to those who had wanted a republic.

The reign of Louis Philippe brought a modest extension of liberal and democratic practices. Though the number of voters was still only a small fraction of the total citizenry, it was double what it had been before. The chief significance of the July Revolution was that it decisively ended the threat of counterrevolution in France and shattered the principle of legitimacy, hallowed at Vienna in 1815—Louis Philippe became king upon the *invitation* of an elected Chamber of Deputies. The French thus struck a blow against the Metternich System, and their success emboldened liberals and patriots elsewhere.

The first uprising outside France occurred in the Belgian Netherlands. This territory, for centuries under either Austrian or Spanish control, had been joined to the independent Dutch Netherlands by decision of the Congress of Vienna. Metternich and his colleagues had hoped that a united Netherlands would serve as a barrier to the French, whose rulers had frequently sent armies northward toward the Rhine. But there were deep-seated frictions in the cultural relations between Dutch and Belgians: the Dutch were predominantly Protestant, while the Belgians were mainly Catholic; and the French-speaking population of southern Belgium (Walloons) resented the required use of the Dutch language. Discontent with the unyielding Dutch monarch, William I, led to street riots in Brussels shortly after the July uprising in France. At first the Belgian leaders demanded only local autonomy. But when William took up arms against them they declared for complete independence.

Metternich and his allies in central Europe would have moved against this eruption of nationalism in the Low Countries had they not been occupied with threats nearer home. With French and British backing, the Belgians managed to hold off the Dutch king. Finally, in 1831, an international conference in London provided for an independent Belgium, with a German prince (Leopold of Saxe-Coburg) as constitutional monarch. In 1839, King William at last recognized the new state, and its independence and neutrality were guaranteed by the major European powers.

Polish patriots, meanwhile, had tried and failed to reestablish the independence of their homeland. After long diplomatic maneuvering at the Congress of Vienna, Poland had been turned over to Russian control as a separate kingdom under the personal rule of Nicholas, the Russian tsar. Early in 1831 the Polish diet of nobles rejected him as their king, and Nicholas sent in a large army to crush the brave but divided Polish forces. Revolutionary stirrings also arose in 1830 in various parts of Germany, Italy, Spain, and Portugal. In almost every case, they were put down by force, as they had been in Poland. But the widespread agitation demonstrated that liberal nationalist impulses were waxing throughout Europe, kept in check only by political repression and military measures.

In Britain, where substantial change could be brought about through legislation, liberal ideas and practices made a striking advance. Even during the 1820's Parliament moved away from a mercantilist economy toward free international trade. It also gave to Catholics and dissenting Protestants political rights equal to those of Anglicans. But the most significant single act was the Reform Bill of 1832, which altered the franchise and the system of representation in the House of Commons. In response to shifts in the English population, this bill assigned seats to the growing urban centers of the North and the Midlands at the expense of districts in the South.

The individual right to vote remained tied to property ownership, but more lenient requirements almost doubled the number of eligible voters—to nearly a million. The new voters were chiefly of the middle class, to which the Reform Bill gave a share of power in Commons roughly equal to the landed gentry's. It also opened the door to progressive liberalization and democratization during the ensuing decades. Although the British achieved this transformation without revolution or civil war, at critical moments the use (and threat) of violence was no doubt decisive. In 1832, for example, the Reform Bill was driven through Parliament under the pressure of street demonstrations and signs of impending insurrection. The controlling powers showed sufficient resilience to yield at such times rather than face the barricades.

On the Continent the strongholds of privilege proved more obdurate. Rather than submit to change, or attempt to guide its course, the conservatives generally sought to repress it. Liberal and nationalist discontent continued to build up, however, and another series of explosions detonated in 1848. In France, Louis Philippe, the "citizen-king," had become exceedingly unpopular. Voting rights remained limited to a small fraction of citizens, and many of the bourgeoisie, as well as workingmen, became increasingly discontented. The critics of the government fell into two groups: the radicals, who wanted to discard the monarchy and establish a republic with universal suffrage, and the liberals, who wanted only an extension of the franchise. Had Louis Philippe yielded to the liberals, he could have gained broader support and kept his crown. But he stubbornly rejected any constitutional change, and in February 1848 the streets of Paris bristled once again with barricades.

In a virtual repetition of the events of 1830, the royal troops refused to march against the people, and the king discreetly sailed for England. The victors were again split between monarchists and republicans, but this time the disagreement developed into deeper civil conflict. The republican leaders of Paris were concerned about social as well as political reforms. They spoke for the swelling number of workingmen, many of them unemployed, who had been drawn into the industrial centers. The victims of low income, insecurity, and poor working conditions, these "proletarians" were generally anticapitalist and antibourgeois.

In 1848 the republicans overcame monarchist opposition and forced the proclamation of a republic. They then arranged for the election by universal manhood suffrage of a Constituent Assembly to frame a new basic law for France. The assembly, which met in May, no doubt represented the prevailing sentiment of the nation as a whole (outside Paris). It favored democratic political changes but no substantial social or economic reforms. This view was assailed by the aroused workingmen of the city, most of whom wanted the government to establish industrial workshops as a means of providing employment.

Fearing that the majority of the assembly would spurn their demands, groups of workers attacked the assembly and set up a provisional government of their own. An ugly class war was thus precipitated in Paris, and some ten thousand were killed or wounded in several days of bloody street fighting. The regular army, which was called upon to defend the assembly, crushed the revolt and thereby incurred the bitterness of most of the urban workers. The defeated insurgents concluded that the army had been used to sustain the "exploitation" of laborers by the capitalist class. The bourgeoisie, for its part, was shaken by the specter of social revolution.

After those bloody "June Days" the assembly drafted a new constitution that provided for a president with strong powers. It decided to call for his election at once, even though the final work on the constitution had not been completed. Of the four well-known candidates who entered the presidential contest, the victory went to the one who promised the most to both sides in the civil struggle. Prince Louis Napoleon Bonaparte, a nephew of the famous Corsican, represented himself as standing for both social *order* and social *change*. Playing upon his family name, he swamped his rivals and became president of the Second Republic in December 1848. Three years later, he engineered the dissolution of the legislature and had himself elected for a new term of ten years. In 1852 this shrewd politician proclaimed the Second Empire, taking the title of Napoleon III.

The cycle of revolution and counterrevolution was repeated beyond the borders of France. In central Europe liberal demands were mixed with nationalist aspirations. Revolutionaries rushed into the streets in a dozen capitals, proclaiming political rights and calling for the unity and independence of their national groups. Monarchs and ruling classes were at first frightened by these demonstrations and generally responded by issuing concessions or new constitutions. But the revolutions lacked the internal cohesion and the organized force to sustain them. When it became clear that they could be stopped by military action, the authorities recovered their composure, withdrew their concessions, and put down the rebels with troops and police. In the course of the uprisings the peasants were freed of serfdom and manorial obligations, but liberal reforms and progress toward national self-determination were checked.

Nevertheless, the movements of 1848 had significant consequences. The Austrian Empire felt the greatest shock, a warning of things to come. Until 1848 Prince Metternich had remained the arch symbol of legitimacy and conservatism. Yet the liberal uprising in Vienna so unnerved him that he hurriedly resigned as imperial chancellor and departed for London. The flight of Metternich brought joy and hope to the advocates of change everywhere. These feelings were premature, however, for within two years imperial troops had suppressed the disturbances in the Habsburg domains, and Metternich could return to his beloved Vienna to compose his memoirs. But he was no longer in power, and the Metternich System was broken.

Nationalist aspirations, though frustrated, were intensified throughout central Europe. Hungarians, Czechs, Italians, Serbs, Croats, and Rumanians became more restive within the Austrian Empire. Many Germans, meanwhile, were looking toward the creation of a large, Pan-German state. The various German territories (including Austria proper) sent delegates to Frankfort in 1848, with the aim of setting up a German federal union. This Frankfort Assembly could not reach agreement, however, on the type of constitution to draft for such a union. Upset by the political reaction that had set in by 1849, the assembly produced no tangible results. Nationalist sentiment had nonetheless been stirred, and within a generation a united Germany would be forged by the more "realistic" methods of diplomacy and war.

The liberal ideal: Mill

The immediate aims and actions of the liberal and nationalist movements reflected their maturing ideologies. The liberal demands were for extension of the franchise, free expression, judicial guarantees, and constitutional checks on arbitrary power; the nationalist demands were for the political union and independence of distinct cultural groups. Neither set of aims can be fully understood without a knowledge of its underlying system of thought.

Nineteenth-century liberal thought was the culmination of a trend that had originated in the Renaissance, or even as far back as the later Middle Ages. It was represented in succeeding stages by men like Rabelais, Erasmus, Locke, and Jefferson. Central to the thinking of these men was their stress on human personality and its untrammeled development. This ideal could be realized, they believed, only through each man's exercise of personal *freedom*. The nature of freedom and the proper conditions for its exercise had been elaborated prior to the French Revolution; after Napoleon, those views had to be substantially modified.

Nineteenth-century liberals were bitterly aware that something had gone wrong with the revolution—"Liberty, Equality, and Fraternity" had led to carnage and dictatorship—but they clung to the same basic beliefs, while seeking out the mistakes that had been made. They became more respectful of history than their liberal predecessors had been, observing that man's rationality is not sufficient to overcome, in a short time, the inertia of long-standing institutions and habits of thought. They were also more wary of popular tyranny, concluding that the will of the majority can be as wrong and oppressive as that of a despot. Many liberals emphasized, finally, that freedom must be tempered by morality if it is not to go astray. Thus the nineteenth-century liberals held that a *chastened* doctrine of liberty is the best means to individual happiness and the fulfillment of man's potential.

On the Continent, liberal voices were generally overpowered by those of the conservatives and romantics. In England, however, they remained vigorous, and liberal speeches and writings accompanied the advance of political reforms. John Stuart Mill was the foremost spokesman of nineteenth-century liberalism. His conceptions of personal freedom, precisely and eloquently expressed, have had a persistent appeal to men everywhere who admire the ideal of liberty.

Mill was a follower of Jeremy Bentham, the founder of a philosophy called "utilitarianism." According to Bentham, who took an atomistic view of mankind, the most plausible criterion for social actions is "the greatest good of the greatest number" of individuals. Mill defended this view, explaining that the calculation of the "greatest good" must take into account qualitative differences in human satisfactions. He believed that the highest satisfactions can be attained under conditions of personal freedom, and he set out to specify the optimal conditions and to work for their achievement. His closely reasoned *On Liberty* (1859) remains the classic exposition of the historic liberal view of individual rights in relation to society.

Mill embraced Aristotle's thesis that the purpose of man's life, as perceived by reason, is the harmonious development of his faculties. This end, declared Mill, requires two conditions: "freedom, and a variety of situations." He would give to each individual, therefore, the utmost freedom in relation to society and the state. Like John Locke, he distinguished between freedom and license, for the latter means interference with someone else's freedom. Each man's liberty he regarded as sacrosanct—"the only purpose for which power can be rightfully exercised over any member of a civilized community, against his will, is to prevent harm to others." He justified this position, not by resort to the outmoded doctrine of natural rights or the social contract, but on the utilitarian ground that freedom is essential to the greater happiness of the individual and the species.

Mill abhorred the drift toward absorptive bureaucracies and cultural conformity. The state itself, he insisted, is worth no more than the individuals who make it up: "a State which dwarfs its men, in order that they may be more docile instruments in its hands even for beneficial purposes, will find that with small men no great thing can really be accomplished. . . ." It is by cultivating individual diversity, concluded Mill, that human beings become noble and enrich social life. As each person becomes more valuable to himself, he is capable of being more valuable to others. He thus "strengthens the tie which binds every individual to the race, by making the race infinitely better to belong to."

Mill opposed the assumption of services by the government, even when done for the benefit of individuals. He preferred that citizens and groups act upon their own initiative and forestall the "deadening hand" of centralized power and uniformity. But his paramount concern was the preservation, at any cost, of liberty of thought and discussion. This, he thought, is crucial to the health of the individual and society. He denied the right of any government, popular or despotic, to interfere with free expression: "If all mankind minus one were of one opinion, and only one person were of the contrary opinion, mankind would be no more justified in silencing that one person, than he, if he had the power, would be justified in silencing mankind." The evil of forbidding the expression of an opinion is more than the injury to an individual, Mill asserted; it hurts the human race, and it hurts those who dissent from the opinion more than those who hold it. "If the opinion is right, they are deprived of the opportunity of exchanging error for truth; if wrong, they lose, what is almost as great a benefit, the clearer and livelier impression of truth, produced by its collision with error."

The nationalist ideal: Mazzini

While many men, especially in England and France, applauded Mill's sentiments, there were others who subordinated individual freedom to nationalism. In Italy and Germany, still "geographical expressions" rather than national states, the aspiration for national unity and prestige overshadowed all other aims. Freedom, like every good thing, was seen to be rooted in the *nation*. Unlike Mill, who took England's power for granted, the nationalists on the Continent did not glorify the individual, "unfettered" by the state; they regarded the building of a powerful state as the necessary means to full nationhood and individual realization. Hence in Germany and Italy the moving ideology was national liberalism (or liberal nationalism). Its peculiar form and flavor, in the first half of the century, were expressed by the Italian patriot Giuseppe Mazzini. Though inspired by the humanitarian and egalitarian ideals of the Enlightenment, Mazzini was caught up in the romantic and nationalist fervor of his own generation. In him, the "religion of liberty" became the "religion of the fatherland."

The nationalist ideal, as described by Mazzini, was linked to a sentimental concern for all mankind. Mazzini described his feeling in a series of essays, *The Duties of Man,* written at mid-century and directed to the Italian working class. "You are men," Mazzini told his readers, "before you are citizens or fathers." The "law of life" requires that individuals embrace the whole human family in their love, confessing their faith in the unity and brotherhood of all peoples. But the lone individual, declared Mazzini, is powerless to work for the benefit of mankind: "The individual is too weak, and Humanity too vast." Effective action requires fraternal cooperation among individuals who can work together—men of a common language and culture—in other words, a nation. Starting with this line of reasoning, Mazzini went on to glorify the nation as an instrument divinely ordained for serving humanity. Ironically, many of his readers, then and later, became so attentive to the glory of the nation that they forgot his precept of a prior duty to mankind.

Mazzini saw the independent nation as a promoter of individual liberty and equality. "A Country is a fellowship of free and equal men. . . . The law must express the general aspiration, promote the good of all, respond to a beat of the nation's heart." But, in fact, the push for national strength through unity often eroded freedom, especially when freedom involved dissent from national objectives. Nationalism could readily become statism, as it did north of the Alps. The historian Heinrich von Treitschke, writing later in the century, declared that man's first duty is *obedience to the state*. This influential professor at the University of Berlin gave academic and philosophical respectability to the German drive for discipline, unification, and dominance.

The achievement of national unification: Bismarck

The unsuccessful liberal-nationalist uprisings of 1830 and 1848 had failed because of inadequate organization and power. It is significant that the eloquent Mazzini, who labored tirelessly to rid Italy of foreign occupation, spent most of his years as a revolutionary exile. But his patriotic propaganda paved the way for the diplomatic and military exploits of others, notably Count Camillo di Cavour and Giuseppe Garibaldi. Though his liberal ideals were far from realized, Mazzini lived to see the achievement of a united Italy in 1870.

But in Germany the practical means to national unification were most forcefully demonstrated, and the consequences for Europe and the world were most profound. After the disappointments of 1848, German nationalists looked for more effective means of bringing their dreams to fulfillment. One of them, Count Otto von Bismarck, was sure he knew the way. Born into an aristocratic landowning family, he rose to power as a statesman in the Prussian kingdom. In the tradition of Frederick the Great, Bismarck admired autocracy and militarism. He had despised the liberal leaders of 1848 and had urged the Prussian king to use the army to restore order and civil obedience. (Many German liberals later supported Bismarck, however, because his methods proved effective in building national power.)

He set out, after 1848, to make Prussia the dominant German power. His desire was both to glorify Prussia and to unify Germany. He was convinced that the German princelings would never join together through their own efforts, and he had only contempt for what the "people" might accomplish. The important decisions and acts had to be taken, he thought, by the ruler and ministers of the leading German state, Prussia. "Not by speeches and majority votes," declared Bismarck, "are the great questions of the day decided—that was the mistake of 1848 and 1849—but by blood and iron." Acting upon this conviction, he proved to be Europe's shrewdest practitioner of the art of power politics.

Appointed chief minister to the Prussian king in 1862, Bismarck determined to remove, by diplomacy and war, whatever stood in the way of German unification. Austria was clearly the chief obstacle, for Metternich had contrived to establish and maintain Austrian dominance in central Europe, and he and his successors looked with distaste and apprehension upon the ambitions of Prussia. Prussia collaborated with Austria in a military campaign to take the provinces of Schleswig and Holstein from Danish control, but the two powers quarreled over disposition of their conquests. In 1866 the argument turned into armed conflict, and Prussian troops invaded Austria and her allied German states. European diplomats were dismayed by the efficiency of the Prussian military machine, which Bismarck had created at heavy expense. After the conclusion of the Seven Weeks' War, defeated Austria yielded its control over northern Germany to Prussia. Metternich's Germanic Confederation was abolished, and Bismarck raised in its place the North German Confederation, under the presidency of the king of Prussia. This new political grouping had a firm economic foundation, for Prussia had previously led the way in establishing a customs union (*Zollverein*) that included most of the German states outside Austria.

It was now France's turn to be apprehensive, for the French, like the Austrians, had traditionally opposed a strong and united Germany. Aggressive factions in both Prussia and France viewed a military showdown as inevitable. Though the French emperor, Napoleon III, and Bismarck himself were not committed to war, diplomatic maneuvering and insults led, in 1870, to a declaration of war by France. The whirlwind Franco-Prussian War was another brilliant success for the Prussian armies, resulting in the death of one empire and the birth of another. Napoleon, humiliated by defeat and capture, lost his throne, and William I of Prussia was proclaimed the emperor of a united Germany. Four south German states, which had remained aloof from the North German Confederation, took their places in the proud new empire (FIG. *10-8*). Bismarck, now the imperial chancellor, had achieved the central ambitions of his career: Prussia was supreme in Germany, and Germany was supreme in Europe.

During the Franco-Prussian War, Napoleon III had recalled his troops from Rome, where they had been protecting the territory and political independence of the pope. (Rome was all that was left of the States of the Church.) The French withdrawal permitted the newly created kingdom of Italy to send in forces and annex Rome,

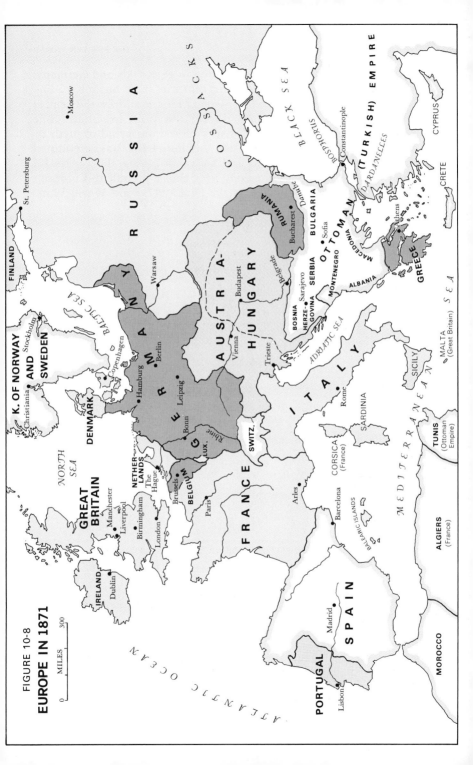

FIGURE 10-8
EUROPE IN 1871

MILES
0   300

thereby completing national unification in 1870. Italy and Germany, both of which had been divided for centuries, now became leading members of the European state system. This would be the central fact of international relations during the years to follow. The greater power, Germany, which had achieved unity and strength by the methods of authority, discipline, and militarism, was determined to exact compensation for her late arrival as a state. The successful revolutions of national unification were thus a prelude to European and global struggle, climaxed by the First and Second World Wars.

The Impact of the Machine

11

All through the nineteenth century, revolutions aimed at political and social reform engaged the attention of Europe. These were sporadic movements that rose and declined at various times and various places. Less noticed, but unceasing, was the developing *technological* revolution heralded by the coming of the machine. The political and social movements had many parallels in history. But the machine set Europe on a totally *new* and irreversible course.

Although many primitive machines had been contrived before 1800, until that time food and commodities all over the world had been produced mainly by human and animal power and by hand tools. After 1800 they were produced increasingly by powered machinery; technological development, once begun, never stopped. Today the use of machines has passed beyond the abundant creation of goods; machines are extending and replacing human functions of every sort. Machines (and the scientific knowledge that lies behind them) have given us power for good and evil that separates us qualitatively from the men and societies of all preceding ages.

One of the effects of the machine was to transform the conditions that had given rise to historic liberalism. As we saw in the preceding chapter, liberal ideas and institutions made striking progress during the nineteenth century, despite the countercurrents of conservatism and romanticism. "Free enterprise" and the encouragement of individual initiative spurred the invention and development of machines. Yet, ironically, those very machines, by altering the structure of production and the organization of society, were to make the doctrine of liberalism obsolete. That doctrine had been nurtured in the eighteenth century, in a society that was predominantly rural and in which the units of production were small. The principle of laissez faire (let alone) could not successfully meet the problems that were to arise from mass production, class conflict, urbanization, and the concentration of private power. The twentieth century, which liberals had predicted would be a century of widening freedom for individuals, would in fact be an age of huge corporate organizations and ever more powerful governments.

THE INDUSTRIAL REVOLUTION

The Industrial Revolution was unplanned. Perhaps the most remarkable thing about it is that it ever happened. True, the fund of scientific knowledge on which early machine technology rested had reached substantial dimensions by the end of the seventeenth century, and Europe possessed the raw materials necessary for industrialization. But the transformation of an agrarian, hand-tool society into an industrial one is not something that comes about automatically. It is, in fact, an extraordinary development, and there is reason to believe that industrialization came when and where it did only because of an unusual set of circumstances.

The agrarian transformation

It was in England that these circumstances first materialized, and it was there that the Industrial Revolution, for better or for worse, began. Preceding and accompanying it were significant changes in agriculture. In the course of the eighteenth century the large landlords had substantially increased their holdings and revenues by accelerating the practice of land enclosure, which had been proceeding since the end of the Middle Ages. Under the old manorial regime, the lord's tenants had enjoyed access to the common lands of pasture, meadow, and woodlot. By successive acts of enclosure, these lands were gradually removed from common use and assigned to individuals. Over the same period the open fields of cultivated strips were transformed into consolidated plots and fenced in for individual use. In the process of redistribution, the landlords usually gained additional arable land, while the tenants often found that they could no longer eke out a living.

Although the redistribution brought hardship to thousands of farm families, it put large tracts of land under more efficient management. Whereas the typical small farmer clung to old-fashioned ways, the more ambitious landlords were willing to experiment with improved methods. They tried new farming implements and better fertilizers, planted soil-renewing crops, and developed scientific breeding. The result was a sharp rise in output. This revolution in agriculture created a large pool of displaced farm workers who desperately sought employment. Some hired themselves out to successful farm operators; others turned to spinning or weaving. They were ready to go wherever they could earn better wages.

At about the same time, British traders were discovering lucrative new markets. By 1750 Britain had built up a globe-circling empire supported by a large navy and merchant fleet. Rich profits beckoned to traders who could increase their exports. Woolens merchants, whose business was well established, were in a favored position to do this; all they needed was a larger output of woolens. There was a brisk demand for cotton goods, too. If English cottons could be made competitive in price with oriental imports, quick fortunes could be reaped in the cotton-textile trade.

The mechanization of industry

A series of inventions gave the textile merchants what they were looking for and led to the general mechanization of industry in England. The first breakthrough, about 1760, was a hand-powered, multi-spindled spinning wheel (jenny). Soon afterward came Richard Arkwright's water frame, which spun many strong threads at once. Advances in spinning were soon matched by the development of powered weaving looms.

The logic of events led next to the building of factories. Spinning and weaving under the domestic system (p. 228) were to persist for many years, but the new machines were not well suited to household use. They represented a substantial capital investment, and they had to be operated around the clock. Moreover, they required a source of power, which at first was available only near swift-running streams. For these reasons, and for reasons of maintenance and supervision, power machines were set up in special establishments. Arkwright launched the first spinning mill in the 1770's, and within a few years he was employing hundreds of workers who attended thousands of spindles. Other entrepreneurs soon followed his example.

The greatest boost to the building of factories was the development of an efficient steam engine, which furnished a flexible, mobile source of power. The story of the steam engine is one of subtle and continuous interplay between science and technology. The chief advances appear to have been made by artisans, but they could not have succeeded without the aid, direct or indirect, of accumulated scientific knowledge.

The steam engine, initially, was a practical response to a problem in coal-mining. For deep shafts to be operated efficiently there had to be some way to pump out the water that drained into them. Thomas Newcomen invented the first working machine for this purpose about 1700. Later in the century James Watt and others made radical improvements on Newcomen's invention. By 1800 the steam engine had become the chief source of power in the new factories and was being adapted to both water and land transportation. The heroic "age of railways" was launched in 1830, when George Stephenson's famed locomotive, the *Rocket,* made its first run on the Liverpool and Manchester line. Within a generation thousands of miles of track had been laid in Europe and America.

Although the new production techniques took shape only gradually, with a host of major and minor inventions, it was clear by the middle of the nineteenth century that industrialization was the wave of the future. Machines would become more and more efficient and versatile, new power sources would be tapped, undreamed-of miracles of transportation and communication would appear. There is no doubt that in the long run industrialization raised standards of living and lightened the burden of manual toil. But working conditions in the early factories were miserable, hours were unconscionably long, and wages were meager. The factory-owners beat down the workers' protests and ploughed profits back into more efficient machines. Capital accumulation and investment were thus wrung out of the unhappy laborers, whose only choice was to work or starve.

THE BUSINESS CORPORATION
AND CAPITALIST EXPANSION

As industrial operations grew in scope and size, entrepreneurs found it necessary to raise capital from sources other than their own profits. Up to mid-century the single proprietorship and the partnership were the principal forms of business organization, but after that time those forms proved less and less able to command the amounts of risk capital needed. Large undertakings, calling for heavy initial investment in buildings and equipment, required the pooling of money from hundreds or thousands of individuals. The apparatus that businessmen developed for raising and controlling such funds was called the *limited company* in England, the *corporation* in the United States. Its antecedent, the joint-stock company, had first appeared in the seventeenth century as a means of financing commercial and mining ventures.

The structure and control
of the corporation

The distinctive feature of the corporation (or limited company) is the financial protection it gives its stockholders. The joint-stock company had sold transferable shares and had served as a means of risk-sharing, but the stock-owners collectively had been liable for debts incurred by the enterprise. The corporation, on the other hand, is an ingenious legal invention, a fictitious "person" created by statute. It is authorized to hold property, incur debt, and sue and be sued, without liability on the part of the stockholders—should the assets of the corporate "person" be dissipated, the stockholders lose only whatever investment they have in their shares, but whatever other property they own is immune from liability.

"Limited liability" is of first importance, since it permits individuals far removed from the control of a business to invest in its stock without danger of losing their other property. They delegate direction of the firm's operations to a small body, the board of directors, who are elected (usually routinely) by an annual vote of the shareholders. The board, in turn, chooses the executive officers. So long as the managerial group (the directors and the executives) produce profits for the stockholders, they normally remain in control.

As corporations grew in size (especially after 1900), and as shareholders became increasingly numerous and dispersed, more and more power gravitated to the managers. The historic link between property *ownership* and property *control* was dissolved by the giant corporations of the twentieth century—a process that has been aptly referred to as the "managerial revolution."

The modern corporation, whose development was a direct response to the large-scale use of machines, has become the main functioning unit of Western capitalism. Since large corporations affect the lives of people everywhere, it is worth examining how they function. The typical large corporation is owned by thousands of stockholders, whose primary concern is with regular dividends or an increase in the value of their stock. It employs thousands or hundreds of thousands of people, provides commodities for millions, and pays taxes to national, state, and local governments. Its total assets may run into hundreds of millions of dollars; its gross income may exceed the revenue of many states and nations. Yet this vast economic empire is *controlled* by a small group of managers, who can hold their power indefinitely. Their decisions, made within the limits of law, finance, and consumer adaptability, determine the flow of investment, research, and development—as well as the tastes and habits of the public.

The global scope of capitalism

The large corporations, from the very beginning, usually had important interests overseas. They sometimes sought to eliminate competition in world markets through private international agreements; and by extending their investments abroad, they controlled the rate of economic growth in many lands. Industrial capitalism thus became an international phenomenon, with money and business seeking the highest rates of return, and with a growing cosmopolitan elite of bankers, promoters, owners, and managers.

Risk capital was drawn to "backward" countries by the promise of extraordinary profits. Labor was cheap in those countries, the demand for capital was high, and in some cases rich resources were awaiting exploitation. Overseas investments also facilitated the development of an interdependent global economy geared to the interests of the industrial countries. Thus European capital built railways in Africa that brought out raw materials that were processed in Europe and distributed to markets around the world.

The industrialists of Great Britain had the jump on those of other nations. By 1914, British private investments overseas amounted to more than $18 billion. French capitalists were next, with some $7 billion. These figures are a fair index of the two nations' comparative penetration and influence in the "backward" continents. (United States investors had only $3 billion committed overseas in 1914; by 1960 the figure was close to $70 billion.)

As early as 1900 some thoughtful men began to ask whether the concentration and expansion of economic power could go on without seriously disturbing political relations within and among nations. The tycoons knew well enough that their wealth was shaping politics both at home and abroad. They saw nothing wrong in this; in fact, they felt their political influence was essential to the untrammeled development of the world's resources. Buttressed by the doctrines of economic liberalism, they believed they could serve mankind best by the unrestricted pursuit of profit.

Economic liberalism: theory and practice

Such political and economic views were quite different from the doctrine of mercantilism, which had prevailed up to the end of the eighteenth century. Mercantilism held that economic activities should be used to strengthen the state and that the state, in turn, should guide industry and commerce. The Scotsman Adam Smith had been the most effective critic of mercantilism during the eighteenth century. His classic *Wealth of Nations* (1776) attacked the system and called for a new order of "liberal" economics. Basing his conception on Hobbes' atomistic view of man and the widely held idea of natural law, he argued that there exists a "natural" economy geared to human selfishness. Each man, if left free to follow his own nature and interests, will be led by an "invisible hand" to promote the economic welfare of all.

Smith's writing had reflected the general optimism of the Enlightenment, but later theorists—the developers of "classical" economics—presented a darker outlook so far as the working class was concerned. Thomas Malthus contributed to this pessimism with his *Essay on Population* (p. 421). However, the "dismal science" (economics) did not dishearten the captains of trade and industry. On the contrary, it furnished them with respectable and compelling rationalizations for seeking profit when and where they could and for working toward the elimination of unwanted government interferences. They were generally successful in striking down controls that were not to their liking and in promoting government action that favored their interests. Toward the end of the nineteenth century and on into the twentieth, the latter practice became increasingly common as economic and political realities moved further away from the models of Adam Smith. The liberal doctrines nonetheless persisted—as a kind of mythology—to be invoked or ignored as economic advantage dictated.

THE REACTION OF LABOR
AND GOVERNMENT

"To every force, there is an equal and opposing force." Those familiar with Newton's Third Law of Motion should have expected that bigness in enterprise would call into being an opposing force (or forces). And, indeed, by the turn of the century Big Business was being confronted by Big Labor and Big Government. The "autonomous" individual found his liberty of action ever more hedged by the decisions and operations of huge "autonomous" organizations.

The appearance of trade unions

The long hours, low wages, and poor working conditions characteristic of the early factories gave rise to bitter discontent. In some respects conditions were little worse than those prevailing under the domestic system of production. But the factory system, by bringing large numbers of workers together, made workers more aware of their common plight and gave them a sense of what their *united* power might be. Alone, the laborer was at the mercy of a large employer. With a surplus of hungry workers seeking jobs, the employer could run his factory without the help of any particular wage-hand. The wage-hand, however, often had no place to turn should he lose his job. In the early part of the nineteenth century, therefore, there was no bargaining over wages and hours; they were set by the employer, and the worker could either take them or leave them.

Collective action for the purpose of bargaining with employers or influencing legislation offered some promise of relief to the laborers. They discovered, however, that whenever they tried to organize the odds were against them. Local "trade clubs" had existed in England before the Industrial Revolution, but only in a few skills (printing, tailoring, weaving) and only in certain communities. When artisans tried to organize on a wider basis, their combinations were broken up by the joint action of employers and the state. Generally viewed by the courts as conspiracies, trade unions had been prohibited by statute in both France and England by 1800. Governments feared that they might lead to riots or uprisings; employers feared that they might lead to higher costs. Subsequent legislation in England (1825) allowed unions to exist but closely limited their activities.

Workers themselves were far from unanimous in their support of unions, due at least in part to the harsh punishments meted out by employers to workers suspected of belonging to such organizations. The taint of conspiracy was no doubt another discouraging factor. Nevertheless, by the middle of the nineteenth century, steps had been taken in England to organize some skilled workers on a nation-wide basis. The cotton operatives, for example, began to gain recognition for their associations and to develop modern collective-bargaining procedures (supported by the power of strikes). Many legal battles still had to be fought and won by British labor unions, but by 1900 two million workers (skilled and unskilled) had been organized into effective bargaining associations. A similar pattern of struggle—legal, economic, and political—developed in the United States and in other industrial countries.

The trend toward state intervention

Many workers looked to legislation as a means of remedying certain evils of industrialism. Some believed that legislation was a helpful supplement to direct economic action by unions; others thought legislation might make direct action unnecessary. In England the laboring classes themselves had virtually no political power until after mid-century; even before that, however, a combination of other social groups succeeded in bringing about some needed reforms through legislation. Responsible observers had come to realize that protective measures by the state (contrary to the doctrines of economic liberalism) were essential to the health and safety of the nation.

Reform legislation was initiated by the Tory party, which represented primarily the interests of the landed aristocracy. Since the landowners did not usually have large investments in industry, they could afford to promote humane treatment of factory workers. Numerous intellectuals and humanitarians, without respect to party, also supported the Tory proposals. And it is only fair to add that some of the industrialists themselves, after accumulating their fortunes, endorsed reforms. Factory-owners as a group, however, bitterly fought all proposed restraints on their freedom to conduct their enterprises as they saw fit.

A series of Parliamentary acts, beginning in 1833, alleviated the worst conditions in British industry. Employers were forbidden to hire children under nine years of age, and the labor of those under eighteen was restricted to nine hours a day. Women and children were excluded from mine labor, and better hours and safety devices were required in the mines. Government inspectors were provided to ensure that the regulations were observed. After wage-earners themselves gained the right to vote (in 1867), additional measures were enacted for their protection and welfare.

Germany was several decades behind England in industrial growth, but in the latter part of the century she took the lead in social legislation. Conditions in mines and factories were similar to those in England, and laws regulating safety, age of employment, and hours of labor were passed in due course. Labor unions, intellectuals, and religious groups helped bring about these reforms. After Bismarck became imperial German chancellor in 1871, he used social legislation as a means of improving the nation's health, ensuring his own popularity, and stimulating the loyalty of citizens to the new German state. The crowning regulatory measure was the Industrial Code of 1891, which guaranteed uniform protection to workmen (with respect to hours and conditions) throughout the German Empire. Equally significant were paternalistic laws providing for sickness and accident insurance and old-age pensions for workers. The German social-insurance code of 1911 became a model for other industrialized countries.

In adopting measures of this nature, the United States was at least a generation behind western Europe—though in another field of government intervention, America was ahead. Giant industrial enterprise developed by leaps and bounds after the Civil War; by 1890 mergers, trusts, and other forms of combination were eliminating competitors and reaping exorbitant profits. Many liberals, labor-leaders, populists, and small entrepreneurs became frightened by the specter of concentrated economic power. They demanded legislation to check the expansion of monopoly and to keep enterprise "competitive and free."

Thus, in the name of liberalism, the power of the American state was called up as a counterforce to Big Business. The Sherman Anti-trust Act of 1890 declared illegal "every contract, combination, or conspiracy in restraint of interstate commerce." The passage of this law was only the starting point of a long and tortuous contest in which government has sought to protect the public against the excesses of "private" economic power. A related action by the federal government was the imposition of a graduated income tax, which was enacted in 1913 over the frantic opposition of corporations and wealthy individuals.

URBANIZATION AND STANDARDIZATION
OF SOCIETY

Personal freedom was further eroded by the concentration of population in large cities. This had been foreseen by the classic liberal Thomas Jefferson, who had written in 1800, "I view great cities as pestilential to the morals, the health, and the liberties of man." Population congestion calls forth regulation as a means of organizing essential services and protecting citizens from the trespasses of their neighbors. Although the move from farm to town had begun in the later Middle Ages as a response to the revival of commerce, for centuries the flow was insignificant. It was the Industrial Revolution, along with an unprecedented rise in population, that brought about the real expansion of European cities.

Population figures before 1800 are only estimates, but it is evident that the number of people in Europe had risen very slowly until that time. The nineteenth century saw a startling increase, however. From 1800 to 1900 the population of western Europe grew from about 150 million to about 270 million—an increase greater than that of the preceding *ten* centuries. The increase cannot be explained by a change in birth rates, for these remained fairly stable. The lowering of the *death* rate was the decisive factor, and this resulted from several causes. Increased food production (prompted by agricultural improvements), advances in sanitation, and control of epidemics were the most important of these. In addition, the Industrial Revolution provided more purchasing power in the manufacturing countries, and that power was used to import more food from overseas.

By 1900 Germany, with 56 million, had the largest population of any western European nation. France was next, with 39 million; then Britain, with 37 million, and Italy, with 32 million. The most striking growth, everywhere, was taking place in the cities. At the start of the Industrial Revolution there were only 4 English cities of over 50,000 inhabitants. By 1850 there were 31, and half the population of Britain was living in cities—a proportion unprecedented in European history. Manchester, in the coal-and-iron Midlands, was the largest and best known of the new industrial communities. Formerly a market town of 25,000, it had grown to half a million by 1850. Its civic officials, like those of other urban centers, lacked the authority and organization they needed to meet the city's needs.

By accelerating the shift from farm to city, the factory brought to near-completion a trend that had persisted for many centuries, carrying Western man from a world in which he was surrounded and dominated by nature to one more of his own making. And the man-made environment was ugly. The cities lacked sewers and paving. Housing for workers was cramped, rickety, and drab. Into the crowded, soot-blackened tenements poured the refugees from rural poverty—strangers in their own land. The chronic urban maladies of alienation, disease, and crime have persisted into the twentieth century.

Cities, in time, also brought much that was positive: better education, medical care, theaters, libraries, and merchandise from all over the earth. Even these advantages, however, were shared unequally, and the poor man felt deprived in the presence of riches he could not buy. Moreover, he seldom found the satisfaction in his daily labor that had brought meaning to the life of the craftsman in earlier times. The factory system reduced him to an appendage of a machine and subjected him to its rigid discipline. Narrowing specialization of tasks chained him to deadening, repetitive motions. The worker, like his machine and all its parts, became a standardized, replaceable cog in a production line that turned out standardized, replaceable things.

Mass production and maximum profits required not only standardized commodities but mass demand. In order to keep capital and plant capacity working up to their full potential, advertising was developed to force feed natural desires. Organized "buy" appeals supported and expanded the media of mass communication—overcoming local resistance and tending to make the demand for goods uniform and universal. As the twentieth century proceeded, the individual was to be viewed increasingly as a *consumer* of goods (*homo consumens*), a permanent target of the commercial persuaders. His daily choices (conscious or not) were to be governed to a mounting degree by shrewdly devised, omnipresent propaganda.

When mechanization was applied to the art of salesmanship as well as to production, it weakened many time-honored habits and customs. Mass culture thus came into being essentially as we know it today—conformist, passive, and malleable. It was geared to one constant and dominant value: concern for *material* things. The materialism and secularism of the West, on the rise since the Renaissance, had reached new heights by the beginning of the twentieth century. Man's acquisitive nature had always opened him to the lure of worldly goods. The machine now enabled him to produce wealth "beyond the dreams of avarice," and the new salesmanship ensured that such dreams would never cease.

THE DEVELOPMENT OF SOCIALIST THOUGHT AND ACTION

The impact of the machine provoked a wide range of intellectual responses. Ever since the Industrial Revolution, men have been grappling with the vast problems and the vast promise of technology. In alternating moods of gloom, bewilderment, and hope, they have sought to understand where the machine is leading them and how to adapt it to human ends. Since the machine was identified in the nineteenth century with the system of industrial capitalism, that system became the focus of analysis and criticism.

The first reactions were to the factories themselves. Sensitive observers in the early nineteenth century could hardly have anticipated the infinite ramifications of modern technology, but they were immediately disturbed by the dislocations and miseries affecting the working class. Beyond the low wages, the oppressive working conditions, and the wretched housing was the deprivation caused by cyclical unemployment. Operating, in the main, according to "natural economic laws," nineteenth-century capitalism was a dynamic, unstable mechanism. Good times, or booms, alternated with bad times, or depression, and the periodic crises appeared to grow worse and worse. The wage-earner, whose daily bread depended on his pay envelope, was hardest hit when the factories laid off workers. Under the doctrines of economic liberalism he was destined to suffer for as long as the system endured.

We saw earlier in the chapter that many workers turned to unions and social legislation to protect themselves and their families. But some workers and intellectuals became convinced that reform within the system was insufficient. The only hope, they believed, for a better economic life and a just society lay in a radical change of the system itself. Most of these dissenters, though their ideas ranged across a broad spectrum, may be classified as *socialists*.

Utopian socialism

Among the socialist thinkers of the nineteenth century the major division was between "utopians" and Marxists. The former, who included a wide variety of social critics, belonged to a tradition reaching back as far as Plato. Their general approach was to turn from the evils apparent in the existing order and to seek in their imagination something closer to their ideal of life and society. Some of these thinkers were influenced by the *Utopia* of Sir Thomas More, written in the sixteenth century. Sir Thomas despised the grasping, callous landlords and entrepreneurs of his day; for the island Utopia (literally, "no place") he envisioned a planned society of common ownership, tolerance, and equality.

In France, the utopians pursued two distinct lines of thought. The Comte de Saint-Simon proposed a reorganization of society from the top, with state ownership of the means of production and control by a national board of scientists, engineers, and industrialists (technocrats). The purpose of industry would be *production* rather than *profit,* and workers and managers would be rewarded according to individual merit. In his chief work, the *New Christianity* (1825), Saint-Simon stressed philanthropic motives: "The whole of society ought to strive toward the amelioration of the moral and physical existence of the poorest class; society ought to organize itself in the way best adapted for attaining this end." Saint-Simon's writings drew the sympathetic attention of numerous European intellectuals. His disciples in France, some of whom became prominent in politics, were among the first modern advocates of a nationally planned society.

Charles Fourier, a younger contemporary of Saint-Simon, took a different tack. Resisting the idea of centralized economic control, he favored the creation of thousands of autonomous production units, which he called "phalanxes." Limited in size to four hundred families, each phalanx would contain a residential hotel, school, market, health service, and other public facilities—in addition to its own farms and manufacturing plants. All these were to be community property, and the rule governing labor and distribution would be: "From each according to his ability; to each according to his needs." (The Marxists were later to appropriate this slogan.) Surplus production would be exchanged for other goods by barter between the phalanxes; within each plant workers would change jobs often, in order to mitigate the effects of performing repetitive tasks.

Fourier anticipated many of the problems of industrialism and believed that the free association of cooperative producers was the

soundest way of meeting them. His ideas attracted numerous followers, and a few isolated phalanxes were actually established in America—notably Brook Farm, near Boston. Each phalanx had its own
internal problems, and each was doomed to failure. Success for
Fourier's plan would have required the development of an extensive
system of phalanxes, and there was scarcely a chance that this could
have come into being.

The efforts of Robert Owen, an industrialist and utopian planner,
failed for the same basic reason. A successful cotton-mill owner in
New Lanark, Scotland, Owen was distressed by the poverty, ignorance, and immorality of his employees. He determined to change
matters and succeeded in setting up a model factory and community in New Lanark. He was not satisfied, however, with his own
local reforms and aspired to reform the whole industrial order.

Owen observed that the factory system had not freed men—it had
enslaved them. Under the operation of laissez faire, the worker's
condition had fallen to a level lower than it had been under feudalism. Morals had deteriorated along with material standards, and the
traditional ties of compassion between master and servant had
snapped. Owen had fair success in promoting remedial factory legislation, but this served only to check the worst abuses. After failing
to persuade factory-owners to emulate his example at New Lanark,
he proposed that the poor be organized into cooperative, self-
sufficient villages.

Owen's plan won commendation in the British press and in Parliament, but nothing more. Abandoning his appeals to the leaders
of government and industry, he next turned to the working people
themselves. Out of his efforts grew several producers' cooperatives,
including one at New Harmony, Indiana. Founded in 1824, this
venture (like the others) lasted only a few years. Owen nonetheless
left his mark on public thought and on the struggle to ameliorate
the harshness of industrialism in Britain. But it took another, more
rigorous thinker to produce a tougher brand of socialism that would
meet the capitalist system head on.

Scientific socialism: the synthesis of Marx

Karl Marx brushed aside utopian ideas as sentimental and quix-
otic; in this he shared the opinion of most of the capitalists of his
time. Marx's study of history told him that events are shaped by
underlying economic developments rather than by idealistic reformers, and he believed that these developments were leading toward
the collapse of capitalism. Therefore, he insisted, the proper task of
workers and intellectuals is to grasp the trend of history and to

participate in its forward movement. While accepting some of the observations and principles of Owen and Fourier, he felt that their appeals distracted men from the "correct" course of thought and action.

It was in this sense that Marx and his followers regarded his own doctrine as "scientific." Marx set forth certain hypotheses in Newtonian fashion and sought to validate them by the empirical evidence of history. Like Newton, he was not primarily an inventor of ideas; his achievement was a monumental synthesis. Materialist, rationalist, libertarian (though not in the bourgeois sense), and revolutionist, Marx was an heir of the Enlightenment who also incorporated the leading scientific, economic, and philosophic ideas of the nineteenth century—evolution, struggle, and historicism. But, reflecting the romantic spirit of the age, Marxism contains strong elements of faith and feeling as well as of reason and science.

Born in the Rhineland of a middle-class Jewish family, the youthful Karl attended the universities of Bonn and Berlin. His father was a lawyer, and he began to prepare for the same profession. Soon, however, he became absorbed in the study of history and philosophy and would have liked to have qualified himself for a professorship. But he knew that his liberal political views precluded his chances of winning a university appointment, for this was the period of the conservative reaction in Germany. Caught up by the revolutionary stirrings of the 1840's, he turned instead to journalism and pamphleteering.

With his lifelong friend and collaborator, Friedrich Engels, Marx organized revolutionary groups in Germany and wrote the *Communist Manifesto* of 1848. After participating in the insurrections of that year in the Rhineland, he escaped to London, where he remained for the rest of his life. He was one of the first critics to stress the *international* character of working-class movements—thus placing himself in opposition to the mounting spirit of nationalism in Europe. From London, Marx continued his association with revolutionary movements in various countries, helping to found the First (socialist) International in 1864. And he spent long hours in the British Museum pursuing his study of history and economics.

The most famous product of his labors, *Das Kapital* (Capital), appeared in part before his death and was completed by Engels. It consists chiefly of theory and analysis and is closely related to the writings of the classical liberal economists. While Marx scorned their ignorance of history, he respected their understanding of the dynamics of nineteenth-century capitalism. Working largely from their stated "laws" and principles, he concluded that all economic value derives from human labor, that the capitalist unjustly appropriates a portion of this value, that the system promises nothing but misery to the laborers, and that it contains contradictions that ensure its own destruction. But Marx's economic conclusions were perhaps the least original, least valid, and least significant of his ideas. His enormous influence was to come from the fact that he was able to join his criticism of capitalism with a revolutionary program based on a unified concept of history, politics, and morals.

The philosopher Hegel gave Marx the key to his comprehensive view. History is an unceasing process, said Hegel, governed at any moment by the struggle between a dominant idea and its opposing idea (p. 423). This was a relatively simple explanation that imputed order and progressive purpose to the bewildering tangle of events. Marx was excited by Hegel's dialectic principle, but he had no taste for the notion that *ideas* are the prime forces in history. After much study and reflection, he concluded that the "mode of production" is actually the determining circumstance in any given society; its opposing force arises from technological developments that are no longer compatible with established institutions. In Marx's own words:

> In the social production which men carry on they enter into indefinite relations that are indispensable and independent of their will; these relations of production correspond to a definite stage of development of the material powers of production. The sum total of these relations of production constitutes the economic structure of society—the real foundation, on which rise legal and political superstructures and to which correspond definite forms of social consciousness. The mode of production in material life determines the general character of the social, political, and spiritual processes of life. It is not the consciousness of men that determines their existence, but, on the contrary, their social existence determines their consciousness.

Thus did Marx "turn Hegel upside down." The flow of history and the growth and interrelation of ideas and institutions, thought Marx, are all shaped by the evolution of the mode of production (historical materialism). And this evolution had passed through four identifiable epochs: "the Asiatic, the ancient, the feudal, and the modern bourgeois methods of production."

Engels later sought to modify the rigor of Marx's economic determinism, which Marx no doubt had overstated. What he meant, explained Engels, was that the economic factor is "the strongest, most elemental, and most decisive." But to postulate determining roles for *various* factors is to weaken the special claim of historical materialism. Even non-Marxian historians concede that the system of production is an important factor (of variable weight) in the sum of "determinants" of a given culture.

Marx saw the "class struggle" as one aspect of historical materialism—an idea that had special significance because of its relation to the actual struggles of working people in the nineteenth century. Each mode of production, he said, serves a particular "ruling" class, which takes advantage of its opposing "exploited" class. The ancient world had its masters and slaves; the feudal age, its nobles and serfs; the capitalist age, its bourgeois and proletarians. (This last word, from its Latin root, signifies "propertyless" and was applied by Marx to the swelling numbers of industrial wage-hands.) Marx believed that the ruling class of each epoch devises laws and institutions to guarantee its continued exploitation of the opposing class. The state itself thus becomes a mechanism of suppression. The executive of the nineteenth-century capitalist state, he declared, was "a committee for managing the common affairs of the whole bourgeoisie."

Social revolutions occur, according to Marx, when a new mode of production—maturing within the framework of the old—bursts the fetters of established laws and relationships. The agents of the revolution are the "new" class, which is destined in time to become the ruling class. Thus, he argued, the bourgeoisie had promoted the liberal revolutions, thereby paving the way for a new economic order—and a new ruling class. But the bell had tolled for the bourgeoisie, as it had earlier for the European nobility. The potential of expanding technology could not be realized within the structure of private capitalism; and the capitalist system of production, beset by increasingly severe crises, was stumbling toward its end. In accordance with the dialectic principle, the expiring system had already brought into existence the class that would overthrow it and that would build a new order upon the ruins. This class, the proletariat, was being drawn into the industrial centers in ever larger numbers. All it needed in order to help history along was Marxist instruction and organization.

Though Marx had bitter feelings toward the bourgeoisie and regarded its exploitation of the proletariat as the most naked in history, he felt that it had played, in preceding centuries, a progressive role. This was in keeping with his (and Hegel's) conception of history as moving inexorably toward higher and higher goals of human fulfillment. Marx approved the liberal revolutions, whose results were chiefly *political*. The freedoms gained were of primary benefit to the entrepreneurial class, but they also enhanced the opportunities of the exploited class to work for *social* revolution. Political freedom was meaningless to the hungry and the homeless, thought Marx, but it was a step toward achieving a new order of production that could provide a decent living for all—and would liberate the worker from humiliation and servitude. Only after those changes had been brought about could the individual realize the potential of his manhood, the goal Marx desired for all men.

Marx predicted that the mounting clashes between the proletariat and the bourgeoisie would culminate in the triumph of the working class. This victory would bring an end to the historic class struggle, for all individuals would then be incorporated into one body of workers. Liquidation of the defunct social order and public appropriation of the instruments of production would be carried out under a temporary "dictatorship of the proletariat." This would be followed, in turn, by an intermediate period of "socialism" during which individuals would "work according to their ability and receive according to their output." Socialism would lead eventually to pure "communism."

Once communism had been attained, the state would "wither away," Marx deduced, because in the absence of class struggle there would be no reason for its existence. Thus would come into being, for the first time in civilized history, "true" liberty for all. In the vaguely outlined communist society, voluntary associations would plan and carry out production; each individual would "work according to his abilities and receive according to his *needs*"; private persuasion and restraint would supplant police, prisons, and war.

Critical observers of human nature, from Aristotle and Augustine through Montaigne, Hobbes, and Voltaire, would no doubt have felt that such a sketch of an earthly paradise was highly unrealistic. Even if we grant a measure of scientific validity to Marx's analysis of the past, his vision of the future was indeed a romantic one. If accepted at all, it must be accepted on faith. Indeed, the followers of Marx have found in his doctrines a kind of religion; they have called it the *religion of man*.

Their "god," the prime mover, is dialectical materialism, and Marx is its prophet. There are Marxist apostles and saints—as well as despised heretics. The sacred books are his writings, which are defended by dialectical theologians. The "visible church" is the party, and the true believers must have unquestioning faith in its gospel and its works. The Day of Judgment is the day of revolution. The Marxist heaven is the classless society to come.

This analogy with conventional religion is intended to suggest the atmosphere of Marxism and to stress the fact that it constitutes an all-encompassing view of man and the universe. This is a crucial point to grasp if we are to understand the appeal of Marxist doctrine over the past century. At a time when the foundations of "old-fashioned" Christianity and liberalism were being undermined, Marx created a new cosmology related to the salient facts, theories, and hopes of the new industrial age. Its promise appealed to the working poor, but it appealed also to many intellectuals who felt alienated from industrialism and were groping for some kind of total reorientation. Partial critiques and actions based on a pastiche of traditional values (as in utopianism) left such people unsatisfied. Marxism presents itself as a comprehensive ideology and a psychological equivalent to traditional religion. The fact that it contains ambiguities, errors, and contradictions does not distinguish it from other comprehensive belief systems. If we employ the term "myth" to mean a large construct that men believe to be true and by which they try to understand and act, the Marxian myth has served during the past century as a principal alternative to the Christian and Lockean myths.

The interpreters of Marx: revolutionary and evolutionary

As with all great myths and dogmas, Marxist "truth" has been open to differing interpretations. The early Christians discovered that disagreement over doctrine was one of their most serious problems, and that problem has persisted to the present day. The followers of Marx, similarly, have been divided by heresy (and schism). Had capitalism faltered and collapsed during the nineteenth century, as Marx himself expected, the split among his followers might have been less profound. But the established order proved much tougher, much more resilient, than he had anticipated. Reform laws and unions strengthened capitalism (as did Marxist criticism), improved the distribution of purchasing power, and alleviated the condition of the workers. The rich were getting richer, as Marx predicted, but the poor (at least in the West) were *not* getting poorer. And in the United States, the young giant of capitalism, no substantial revolutionary fervor or class consciousness materialized among wage-earners.

How did the Marxists cope with this indefinite postponement of the day of revolution? Again, one is reminded of the parallel with the Christians of the second century, who had to face the fact that the Second Coming was evidently not going to happen right away. Some decided to "overthrow" the world by withdrawing from it, but most decided to make their peace with the world—to remain "in" it, if not "of" it. Marx had considered two possible paths to the overthrow of capitalism: one by legal means, the other by force. He did not specifically exclude either, and he recognized the potential power that an extension of the suffrage would hold out to the working class. But he leaned toward the view that the ruling class was unlikely to surrender its property through democratic processes and that resort to violence must ultimately be expected.

After Marx's death (in 1883) the capitalist states showed no signs of tottering, and most socialist workers tended to make their peace with the system. True, a small group of Marxists stuck by the dogmatic line, scorning "legalism" and "gradualism." But the larger group recognized that such a stand would not appeal to the bulk of workers in the existing situation. They stated frankly that Marxist doctrine would have to be revised if it was to continue as a major force.

The revisionists mapped a much longer (and different) road to the ideal society. They stressed democracy, parliamentary methods, and class cooperation as means of achieving further reforms. Eduard Bernstein, a German socialist, was the leading spokesman for this view. (The Fabian socialists of England, though non-Marxist, held a similar tactical position.) The broad term "social democratic" can be applied to most of the labor parties in European politics after 1890, who represented the "evolutionary" wing among the heirs of Marx. The "revolutionary" (orthodox) faction remained significant only in eastern Europe, where the absence of representative government precluded change by peaceful, legal methods. It was there, in a relatively backward country, that the revolutionary Marxists would achieve the first great victory of socialism.

THE ACCELERATING POWER
OF SCIENCE AND TECHNOLOGY

It is clear that the impact of the machine, the central subject of this chapter, was wide and deep. Before the end of the nineteenth century, the machine had altered the means of production, had promoted the urbanization and standardization of society, and had stimulated the development of Big Business (and the counterforces of Big Labor and Big Government). Industrialism also had intensified the social division between the rich and the poor, had created a significant segment of alienated intellectuals, and had brought into being new ideologies and forces aimed at overturning capitalism. Meanwhile the machine and the science and technology from which it sprang were progressing at an accelerating rate, foreshadowing still larger consequences for man and society.

The surge of inventions

The connection between pure and applied science cannot always be observed directly. This was true, as we have noted, in the development by Newcomen and Watt of the early steam engine. But during the nineteenth century, more and more industrial firms recognized the connection and sought to exploit it; the large corporations (and governments) began to invest substantial sums in research and development.

Thousands of new products and processes were derived from the laboratories of chemists, physicists, and biologists. But breakthroughs of immediate consequence to industry were often achieved by inventors who were not professional scientists. Henry Bessemer, an English metallurgist, invented a radically simple method of converting pig iron into steel. His method was improved by research chemists, and by the end of the century steel had largely replaced iron for rails, bridges, and other types of construction where superior tensile strength is required. The dynamo, which turns mechanical energy into electrical energy, made it possible to lay out vast power grids. The electric motor and the steam engine were shortly joined by the internal-combustion engine, which, fueled by hitherto untapped petroleum resources, revolutionized transportation. Oil and other raw materials were also used, through chemistry, to produce an infinite variety of drugs, foods, textiles, plastics, and explosives.

The inventions of the past hundred years are now commonplace. Most of them, like the automobile and the airplane, began as crude and unreliable machines. But once launched, they underwent rapid improvement. Today most Westerners take for granted jet airliners, atomic submarines, earth satellites, automatic machinery, radio, television, records, movies, telephones, refrigerators—and, of course, the indispensable electric light! Taken together, these marvelous devices have profoundly altered traditional views of the world, attitudes toward work and leisure, and personal and social habits.

Advances in the physical and medical sciences

Accompanying this dazzling technology were prodigious leaps in pure science. The scientific revolution of the seventeenth century had lost none of its force: the organization of science became even wider and better supported. As more and more trained minds were focused on the riddles of nature, their combined efforts and findings rose at a geometric rate.

Physical scientists continued to build on the foundations of Galileo, Newton, and Boyle. One of the most significant subjects of their investigations was that of energy. Experimenters verified the equivalence of heat and energy and enunciated two basic laws of thermodynamics. The First Law states that the total energy (or heat) in the universe remains constant, though it is continually changing its form. The Second Law states that energy systems tend toward degradation (heat, for example, flows from a hotter body to a colder one); hence, the amount of *useful* energy is diminishing in the universe. These generalizations, supplementing the Newtonian laws of motion, gave fresh perspective to physicists, chemists, astronomers—even philosophers.

The first correction or modification of Newton's laws was made by the mathematician Albert Einstein, who first stated his Special Relativity Theory in 1905 and later elaborated it into a General Theory. Though he recognized that Newtonian physics "worked" well enough for mundane purposes, Einstein believed that it did not truly describe the universe of nature and that it could lead to hopeless error in cosmic calculations. Newton and his disciples had conceived of space and motion as *absolute.* They postulated the existence of an "ether," a vague kind of immovable substance that fills the void, and by reference to which all changes of positions could be measured absolutely. But experiments in the late nineteenth century proved that no such substance exists, thus destroying any fixed basis for reference.

Einstein met this puzzlement with a radically different approach. Matter and motion are not absolute entities, he declared, but are *relative.* They can be measured only from a given point or system in time and space. (What is the velocity of a fly buzzing about inside a speeding aircraft?) Einstein postulated, further, that objects have a *space-time* dimension that affects their length, breadth, and thickness. Bodies moving toward or away from a given point have different proportions of extension and mass with respect to that point. The alterations are imperceptible in ordinary motions, but they become significant as bodies approach the speed of light. The speed of light is the one constant he found in the universe; it remains the same for all physical systems. Though Einstein's theory, expressed in mathematical terms, was incomprehensible to the average man, it exploded many of the fundamental assumptions of scientists. It reminded them (and laymen) that the scientific myth, too, while eminently practical in its applications, is by no means absolute or immune to change.

At about the same time, the theory of matter was moving toward its current formulation. Until a century ago men had believed that matter was solid, although the ancient Greek Democritus had theorized that it was reducible to invisible, indivisible particles. John Dalton, an English schoolteacher, accepted this general notion but found that each chemical element was composed of atoms of a different weight. Scientists later postulated the *molecule,* a somewhat larger unit, consisting of atoms of different weights. All material substances, they concluded, are made up of molecules.

As molecular theory advanced, physicists further theorized that the molecules are separated from one another and are in continual motion. Increases in heat cause the molecules to vibrate more rapidly; increases in pressure slow them down. But the "solidity" of objects dissolved still further when Ernest Rutherford and Niels Bohr introduced their model of the atom (about 1910), which they conceived of as a miniature solar system, containing a nucleus of one or more protons with encircling electrons. These infinitesimal particles were explained as units of electrical energy. Later research would show the atom to be more complex than Rutherford or Bohr had at first believed, but their essential concept remains the basis of atomic physics today.

More immediately practical uses flowed from discoveries about the nature of light and electromagnetic waves. Newton had observed that when sunlight passes through a prism it spreads into a band of colors—red at one end and indigo at the other. Scientists of the nineteenth century discovered that each chemical substance, in the gaseous state, will yield a characteristic spectrum distinct from every other. Spectrum analysis was developed as a tool for chemists—and for astronomers in studying the sources of celestial light. The production, reception, and explanation of electromagnetic waves by Heinrich Hertz (about 1887) pointed the way to Guglielmo Marconi's wireless and all that followed in the field of radio communications. Another German, W. K. Roentgen, discovered X-rays soon afterward. His contribution raised additional questions about the nature of matter and proved of enormous value in medicine and technology.

Notwithstanding the advances in physical science, the nineteenth century was preeminently the century of biological and medical progress. Drawing upon seventeenth-century descriptions of cellular structure in plants, Theodor Schwann developed the cell theory to explain organic matter. It was realized by about 1835 that all living things consist of tiny cells, whose health and growth determine the physical fate of the total organism, and a special branch of biology (cytology) was established for the comprehensive study of cells. Embryology and bacteriology also became specialized fields of inquiry.

From the former, the study of organisms from the time of conception to birth, came the theory of recapitulation, which holds that each individual, while in embryo, repeats the evolutionary stages of its species. This theory was to have implications not only for biology but for theology and philosophy as well.

Bacteriology, an outgrowth of the germ theory of disease, opened for examination the world of microorganisms. These tiny forms of life had been seen through the primitive microscopes of the seventeenth century, but little attention was given to them until after 1850. It was a French chemist, Louis Pasteur, who first theorized that bacteria (germs) were the cause of many deadly illnesses. Physicians knew of the existence of bacteria but thought them the result, rather than the cause, of disease. After years of ridicule, Pasteur at last had the opportunity to demonstrate the validity of his theory and the practice of preventive inoculation. His first successful test was against an epidemic of anthrax in sheep.

Once the germ theory was accepted, it led quickly to the identification and treatment of countless bacteriological and viral diseases, as well as to antiseptic procedures in surgery and to general improvements in hygiene and sanitation. No development in science can match the importance of the germ theory in its effect on the world's death rate—and the consequent upward curve of human population.

THE CHALLENGE OF DARWIN'S
THEORY OF EVOLUTION

The discoveries about bacteria raised no serious controversy after Pasteur's classic proofs. But the emerging theory about the origin of *man* provoked bitter disputes that continue to rankle a century afterward.

New perspectives in human biology

The work of Charles Darwin may be compared with that of Isaac Newton, who lived two centuries earlier. As Newton completed the overturn of ancient conceptions about the physical universe and its governing principles, so Darwin completed a revolution of thought with respect to the earth's creatures—the human species, in particular. The theory of the transformation of species was not original with him; it had, in fact, been suggested as early as the seventeenth century. Prevailing opinion until about 1850, however, had supported the idea of the "immutability" of species within a "Great Chain of Being." A Swedish botanist, Carolus Linnaeus, was in part responsible for the persistence of this idea. His comprehensive work as a classifier (in the 1730's) helped to develop the notion that all creatures had been ordained into a neat and permanent scheme. Linnaeus assumed, and most of his readers believed, that all members of a particular species could be traced back to an original pair formed at the time of Creation.

Before the nineteenth century, there had been insufficient evidence either to prove or disprove the immutability thesis. But by 1850 cumulative discoveries in comparative anatomy, embryology, and geology were converging toward one inescapable conclusion. Even before Darwin published his *Origin of Species by Means of Natural Selection* in 1859, the theory of transformation had been endorsed by a number of naturalists and philosophers. Darwin focused his life's work upon that theory and securely established it on the basis of his extensive observations, collected data, and reasoned explanations.

Though the evolutionary theory raised many thorny problems, it won acceptance because it accorded better with known facts than did the competing theory of "special creation." According to Darwin all forms of life are descended from one or a few primeval creatures. Each individual (and the species of which it is a part) has come into existence as the result of an unbroken competitive struggle. Continuing slight variations in physical endowment give an advantage to some creatures over others; the losers in the struggle become extinct, while the winners transmit through heredity their distinctive qualities.

Without the concept of geologic time, Darwin could not have convinced even himself, for the process of "natural selection" required a sweep of millenia beyond human imagination if it was to produce, in tiny gradients, the kind of transformation that carried upward from plankton to mammals. But Charles Lyell, an English geologist, had opened the door to Darwin's theory. Prior to the appearance of Lyell's *Principles of Geology* in 1830, leading geologists had held that the earth's history had been relatively short and that the earth's configuration had undergone sudden and drastic changes ("catastrophism"). Lyell succeeded in reversing this conception, holding that geologic change had been slow and gradual ("uniformitarianism") and that the earth's age ran into hundreds of *millions* of years.

Second only to Lyell in direct influence on Darwin was Thomas Malthus, whose *Essay on Population* offered a key to the process of natural selection. Malthus pointed out that reproduction in animals (including men) advances at a rate that outstrips the supply of food. Hence, the fate of mankind, and of all nature's creatures, is one of struggle for survival. This point was crucial to Darwin's doctrine, for without struggle there would be no *selection* (and rejection) among variants.

The least satisfactory portion of Darwin's theory concerns the mechanism by which superior characteristics are transmitted to succeeding generations. He believed this to be essentially a matter of passing along to offspring the physical characteristics of superior individuals. He understood only dimly the mechanism of heredity and the fact that the gene supply is independent of the other physical characteristics of individuals. Only *widespread* mutations in *gene composition* can make for evolutionary change. This fact was established by the experiments of the Austrian botanist Gregor Mendel and by later researchers in the new science of genetics.

Darwinism in philosophy and social thought

Whatever may have been Darwin's limitations and his debts to other scientists, he fully deserves the acclaim that has been his. He combined a stirring new vision of living creatures with the courage to promulgate and defend his ideas. What others had hinted at or shied away from, Darwin at last expressed openly and honestly. Although his theory provoked criticisms from all segments of the community, by the close of the century it had become generally accepted among educated people.

At first the more severe attacks came from theologians and Christian laymen who were upset by Darwin's rejection of "special creation." Though he argued that the divine hand can (and does) work its will through evolution, his critics preferred to think that man had been fashioned directly in God's image. The Copernican theory had dwarfed the importance of man's earth in the heavens; the Darwinian theory now reduced man himself by associating him with animal evolution. Moreover, it contradicted the literal reading of the Book of Genesis. It is small wonder that many Christians were shaken by yet another blow to their faith and pride.

On the other hand, there were philosophers, statesmen, industrialists, and theologians who welcomed the doctrine and sought to extend it beyond the biological realm. Herbert Spencer, a brilliant and self-educated advocate of evolution, was one of those most excited by Darwin's writings. It was he who coined the ambiguous phrase "survival of the fittest" to describe the governing principle in nature and, more significantly, he asserted that the principle applies not only to creatures and constellations but to human institutions, customs, and ideas as well. All of these, he reasoned, have their cycle of origin, growth, competition, decay, and extinction. Thus there can be no "absolutes" of religious or moral truth; there is only the passing truth of those ideas that have evolved and that have (so far) *survived.*

These convictions, however, did not drive Spencer to mechanism or atheism. As did some theologians of his day, he adapted his faith in god to the new facts of science. Behind the universe of the senses, he believed, there must exist a supernatural power—one that man cannot comprehend. He believed, however, that moral standards can be established on the basis of what men *do* know. Spencer propounded a "science" of ethics based on the principles of natural evolution: moral acts are those that contribute to man's adaptation and progress. The perfect moral man, he concluded, is "the completely adapted man in the completely evolved society."

Spencer's philosophy of morals did not pass unchallenged in the nineteenth century. If morality is geared to the evolutionary processes of nature, what becomes of man's moral responsibility and freedom? What has science to do with ethics? Even if Darwinism explained the development of man's moral sense, it could not prescribe a particular code of behavior. A further objection was that nature itself had been shown by Darwin to be ruthlessly amoral. How, then, could nature serve as a foundation for morals?

The "tooth-and-claw" character of organic evolution does indeed present nature in a mixed light. Some saw magnificence in it; Darwin himself found it thrilling:

> Thus, from the war of nature, from famine and death, the most exalted object which we are capable of conceiving, namely the production of the higher animals, directly follows. There is grandeur in this view of life . . . from so simple a beginning endless forms most beautiful and wonderful have been, and are being evolved.

But this creation so admired by Darwin had been achieved through monstrous waste and universal conflict. The beneficent Mother Nature of the tender romantics had revealed another and terrible face.

It soon became clear that Darwinism could be interpreted and applied in conflicting ways. All could agree on one central point: the idea of a static world, of fixed relations and values, had been overthrown and replaced by the idea of perpetual change and struggle. But how men should think and act in relation to the struggle, especially human struggle, was a question that drew profoundly different answers.

Philosophers of Hegel's school viewed Darwin's theory as a confirmation of the dialectical idea in history. Romantics saw in it the internal and external torments of their own souls. Among theologians, Calvinists most often found support for their teachings in Darwinism, for their doctrine of human salvation by election is paralleled, in nature, by the survival of the few and the destruction of the many. As one Calvinist teacher put it, Darwinism is to science as Calvinism is to theology: it serves as a foe of sentimentalism and optimism and as a check on the reign of law and the trust in reason.

The implications of Darwinism for social action had far-reaching consequences. After reading the *Origin of Species*, Karl Marx declared that it furnished a "basis in natural science for the class struggle in history." He hoped that it would help to overturn supernaturalism and bring support to his revolutionary appeals. Marx gave Darwin a copy of *Das Kapital*, but it is doubtful whether the scientist read it. While Darwin sought to avoid controversy outside his own field of study, he rejected the notion that his theory was connected with socialism. He was, rather, inclined to agree with the classical economists of his time, who saw the social struggle as a "natural" expression of human competition. Like them, he opposed interference with the system of laissez faire, no matter what the motives might be. As his friend, Herbert Spencer, explained, "The poverty of the incapable, the distresses that come upon the imprudent, the starvation of the idle, and those shoulderings aside of the weak by the strong, which leave so many 'in shallows and miseries,' are the decree of a large far-seeing benevolence."

John D. Rockefeller once employed an attractive metaphor to explain how natural selection worked to the advantage of all. The man who had built Standard Oil into a giant monopoly by beating out his competitors compared his work with the breeding of a lovely flower. The American Beauty rose, with its splendor and fragrance, could not have been produced, Rockefeller told a Sunday-school audience, except by sacrificing the buds that grew up around it. In the same way, the development of a large business is "merely survival of the fittest . . . merely the working-out of a law of nature and a law of God."

Rockefeller and other titans of industry were unashamed advocates of what was later called social Darwinism. Essentially, it condoned a no-holds-barred struggle of "all against all," in the manner of the jungle. And the idea readily passed from one of battle among individuals to one of battle among races and nations. Darwin's theory strengthened the convictions of slave-owners, racists, militarists, and extreme nationalists. Many individuals, including some respected philosophers, glorified war as a cosmic pruning hook for improving the health of humanity. "It is not only a biological law," declared a famous general, "but a moral obligation, and, as such, an indispensable factor in civilization."

The absurdity of this statement points up the risk of transferring theories that may be valid in their original context to areas and problems of a different kind. It does not follow, because nature and the lower animals operate in a cruel and blind fashion, that men cannot devise rational and constructive ways of living together.

Development of the social sciences

The nineteenth century saw the prestige of science rising to its apogee. Generals, industrialists, statesmen, theologians, and philosophers sought to ally themselves with scientific doctrines. And social thinkers of various sorts, not included in the mushrooming branches of natural science, tried to model their methods of inquiry upon those of mathematics, physics, or biology—and, in the process, to establish for themselves definable disciplines that might draw the kind of respect paid to natural science.

The Frenchman Auguste Comte was the first to use the term "sociology" as a designation for the "science of society." A disciple of Saint-Simon (p. 461), Comte was inspired by lifelong reformist zeal. He shared with Saint-Simon the view that society is best managed by "experts," but he believed that the experts needed a more reliable body of knowledge about man and his social relations than was at hand. Scorning "knowledge for its own sake" and narrow academic specialization, Comte believed that learning should *serve man,* and he felt that all studies should be oriented to that purpose.

He asserted that the most useful knowledge is the sort that rests upon empirical evidence—"positive" knowledge, he called it—which was to be found in his day only in the natural sciences. But empirical methods can and must, he insisted, be extended to "social" science; human conduct is neither random nor altogether unpredictable, and it can be quantified, analyzed, and classified. From the emerging social "laws," the proposed managers of society would be able to draw guidance for social regulation and planning.

Comte died in 1857 before he could complete his ambitious studies directed toward reconstructing knowledge and society. (Before breathing his last he is said to have sighed, "What an irreparable loss!") But the foundations of sociology had been laid, and they were extended by the energetic Herbert Spencer. At about the same time, a companion discipline, anthropology, came into being. This word means, literally, the "study of man," but the study has focused upon physical evolution, prehistoric cultures, and comparative social institutions.

Where anthropology tended to analyze and classify the *externals* of human conduct, observed over time and geographical space, a separate discipline (psychology) concentrated on the *internal* aspects of behavior. Wilhelm Wundt established the first laboratory (in Leipzig) for the controlled observation and testing of human and animal subjects. A Russian, Ivan Pavlov, soon afterward gained worldwide notice by his remarkable experiments with dogs. He discovered the "conditioned reflex," a principle that could be extended to humans. (Seekers after profit and power were shortly to make use of Pavlov's discovery in mass advertising and propaganda.)

By 1900 psychology was moving in several directions. Followers of Pavlov's experiments developed a conceptual view called "behaviorism." Believing that man's thought and actions can be understood on a purely physiological basis, they dismissed as meaningless such concepts as "mind" and "soul." They studied the various systems of the body—nervous, glandular, muscular—and the mechanisms of stimulus and response and subjected them to measurement. From the accumulation of such data the behaviorists hoped to develop "positive" knowledge of man's nature. Most theologians, philosophers, and humanists found these ideas repugnant. They argued that man's true essence was spiritual rather than physical—or, if only physical, that it was infinitely more complex than the behaviorists imagined.

Other investigators, meanwhile, were trying to penetrate the dark interior of man by means of psychoanalysis. The Austrian physician Sigmund Freud was a bold leader in this effort to plumb the subconscious and unconscious depths underlying thought and action. His methods were neither quantitative nor statistical but, rather, clinical. Each human subject was probed, by means of free discourse and dream recollection, for clues to his inner self. (The broader philosophical and social significance of Freud's thought will be developed in Chapter Thirteen.)

We have reviewed the emergence of new social disciplines in the nineteenth century, along with the startling advances in the natural sciences. It should be noted also that the established disciplines dealing with human relations were deeply influenced by the trends of the times. Political economy, which traced back at least to Adam Smith and the eighteenth century, reached its classical development in the formulation of economic "laws." In addition, economists of the nineteenth century established a "scientific" vocabulary, statistical techniques, and instruments of prediction.

Historiography, one of the most ancient disciplines concerned with human affairs, flourished in the nineteenth century. Much of the writing, though marked by erudition and high literary merit, was essentially romantic and nationalistic. An effort to apply "scientific" methodology centered in Germany, where Leopold von Ranke launched the objective school of historiography. He announced that he and his students would describe the past "as it actually happened." Sentiment and national bias were to be set aside, and historical documents were to be collected and interpreted in a rigorously critical fashion. Near the end of the century the scientific vogue was carried by historians from German to American universities.

Ranke wrote some laudable histories, and his stress on methodology was wholesome for the discipline. He did not convince all historians, however, that it is possible to reconstruct a single, true picture of what "actually happened." Serious philosophical and practical objections have been raised against his assumptions, and most twentieth-century historians have concluded that the account of individuals and societies can never be told with anything like the precision of natural science. There are indeed "lessons" of history, but they are interpreted in different ways by different writers and cultures. The muse of history, as a matter of fact, has never felt at ease among the social sciences. She is more at home with the humanistic disciplines, especially philosophy, literature, and the arts.

LITERATURE AND ART
IN THE MACHINE AGE

Writers and painters responded sharply to the changes in civilization triggered by science and the machine. They developed, by the middle of the nineteenth century, new goals and modes that would eclipse romanticism in European literature and art.

Expressions of social ferment:
Dickens, Ibsen, Shaw

The new trend in literature was known as "realism." It started in France with Honoré Balzac, who began writing successful novels in the 1830's. (His collected works were later published as the *Human Comedy*.) Balzac placed under sardonic scrutiny men and women of all stations in society. A keen observer, he set the style of meticulous and insightful reporting of human strengths and foibles that dominated French literature for the rest of the century and spread to neighboring countries.

In England, realism spotlighted the social effects of the Industrial

Revolution. Charles Dickens, one of the most popular authors of the era, called the attention of his readers to the cruelties and hardships suffered by the urban working class. In the *Pickwick Papers* (1836) he exposed the grim debtors' prisons; in *Oliver Twist* he revealed the horror of the English workhouses. Though his many novels range widely over general human themes and problems, they have a strong note of social protest; the world of Dickens' characters is not dissimilar to Karl Marx's image of a misshapen capitalist society. Dickens' books contributed, no doubt, to the reform legislation of the nineteenth century.

The Continental writer who addressed himself most directly to contemporary problems was a Norwegian, Henrik Ibsen. Though he is today recognized as one of the prime molders of modern dramatic form and technique, his reputation at first rested largely upon his social dramas. The son of a once-prosperous businessman, Ibsen grew up in alienation from his own society, especially from the new bourgeoisie. He became disturbed by the psychological and moral repercussions of his changing society.

In the *Pillars of Society* (1877), he illuminated the corruption and hypocrisy he had discerned among "established" Norwegian families. Succeeding plays dealt with such issues as female emancipation (*A Doll's House*) and the conflict between commercial interests and honesty (*An Enemy of the People*), eliciting reactions of indignation and animosity from their middle-class audiences. In his subsequent works, Ibsen abandoned his challenges to the social system and created memorable portraits of individuals.

George Bernard Shaw, the versatile Irish author, was among Ibsen's admirers. He appreciated the intelligence and purpose that Ibsen had brought to the nineteenth-century theater, and he turned his own pen to the cause of social criticism. To Shaw, nothing was sacred; he even pilloried Shakespeare for lacking a social message for his own time. One of the most prolific of writers, Shaw composed nearly fifty plays during the course of his long life. Virtually every one of them contains Shavian satire and gospel; his characters, accordingly, tend to be two-dimensional, serving mainly as bearers of intellectual argument.

The relation of literature to social questions during the latter part of the nineteenth century is suggested by the fact that Shaw was a self-taught economist and one of the founders of English socialism. "In all my plays," he once stated, "my economic studies have played as important a part as a knowledge of anatomy does in the works of Michelangelo." The drama that first attracted sharp (and hostile) attention was his *Widowers' Houses* (1892), a condemnation of slum landlordism. This was followed by *Mrs. Warren's Profession,* showing the economic roots of modern prostitution, and *Arms and the Man,* satirizing the military profession. Later dramas dealt with such matters as poverty, eugenics, war, and the nature of religious faith. By 1915 Shaw's fame was established around the globe, and in 1925 he was awarded the Nobel Prize for literature.

The response of the artist:
Monet, Cézanne, Van Gogh

In the plastic arts, social protest was explicit in the works of only a few individuals. Most prominent among them were two French artists of the realist school: Gustave Courbet and Honoré Daumier. Both rebelled against the romantic tradition, sympathized with the poor, and felt that art should correspond to social actualities. While Courbet stressed the simple and truthful representation of nature, Daumier rendered countless portrayals of the squalor and despair of the working class. Daumier is best known for his thousands of lithographs caricaturing all segments of French society; they comple-

FIGURE 11-1. DAUMIER. *The Third Class Carriage.* The Metropolitan Museum of Art. Bequest of Mrs. H. O. Havemeyer, 1929. The H. O. Havemeyer Collection.

ment the word pictures of his contemporary, Balzac, in depicting the "human comedy." One of his masterpieces in oil, the *Third Class Carriage,* suggests his power and sensitivity (FIG. *11-1*). He experienced in his own life the deprivation and adversity recorded by his art—he died a pauper in 1879.

Daumier's artistic techniques, particularly the "unfinished" effect of his canvases, persisted beyond his death. They influenced the style of "impressionism," the most important development in nineteenth-century painting. The impressionists, however, had nothing to do (as artists) with social satire or protest. They tended to be strictly formal, wishing to record images on canvases with optical fidelity and without concern for any kind of message.

The whole trend of painting after 1870 was toward "art for art's sake." This signified, perhaps, an even deeper sense of alienation than that which inspired social realism. Rather than trying to speak for the downtrodden or to change society, most artists now turned their backs on society, seeking escape into an autonomous world of

FIGURE 11-2. MONET. *The Gare St. Lazare.* Louvre, Paris. (Giraudon.)

art, where the painter could impose whatever rules he desired upon elements of his own creation.

Claude Monet represented most fully the aims and achievements of impressionism. He desired to record physical appearances as he immediately perceived them. In order to do this faithfully, he disciplined himself to suppress his prior knowledge of the shape and detail of things—a break with traditional painting. Fascinated by the change in appearances resulting from alterations in light, Monet insisted on working in the open air, putting his visual impressions to canvas in rapid strokes, almost as though he were making a sketch. As the eye, in glancing, sees only a few objects clearly, he deliberately left major areas of his pictures blurred or "unfinished." (FIG. *11-2*).

This absence of sharp definition in Monet's work at first provoked the scorn of critics. In 1874, along with other painters of the new style, he exhibited a picture of a harbor seen through morning mists. He called it *Impression: Sunrise*. From this title, an unfriendly observer coined the term "impressionists" as a label for these upstarts. The pejorative connotation, however, was in time to disappear as critics and public alike grew to appreciate the special aims and terms governing this kind of painting. Some of the impressionists, perhaps in self-defense, associated their techniques with the rigorous method of scientific observation, then generally in vogue. Most, however, simply ignored their critics and yielded to the delight of producing their riches of color and tone.

The ultimate success and popularity of the impressionists gave all artists a fresh sense of freedom and power. Any chosen combination of forms and colors might now be considered a legitimate work of art. Shattered were the restrictive dogmas that required "dignified" or "worthy" subjects, "correct drawing," "rules of perspective," and "balanced composition."

Impressionism itself, however, was a beginning, not an end. Toward the close of the nineteenth century there came new stirrings in art—largely reactions to impressionism. Paul Cézanne, who came to Paris in 1861, had adopted many of the techniques of the new school. He objected, however, to what he regarded as the airy, transient quality of impressionist paintings and longed to combine the luminosity of their coloring with more substantial forms.

As may be seen in his *Still Life* (FIG. *11-3*), one of hundreds of such studies that Cézanne painted, he strove to develop the elements of mass and solidity in his works. As a means of furthering this aim, he subtly shifted eye levels in reference to various objects in the painting, thus creating multiple planes of perspective on a single canvas. He also distorted the natural shapes of objects and avoided symmetrical or repetitive lines. These shrewdly devised techniques make his paintings a source of persisting interest and pleasure.

While Cézanne sought to rearrange nature into what he considered a more satisfying equilibrium of light and form, a younger artist, Vincent Van Gogh, had different objectives. Like Cézanne, Van Gogh learned the brush techniques of the impressionists. But he was not really interested in the outward appearances of things; he wanted to express his own deep feelings about nature and life. Van Gogh was the precursor of the modern school of "expressionist" painters.

Extraordinary spiritual and mental stress marked Van Gogh's brief life. The son of a Protestant minister, he had, from youth, an urgent missionary impulse. In later years he sensed a divine creative force within nature and all forms of life; this force he sought to manifest in most of his paintings. His works were the products of an emotional frenzy that passed into recurrent mental illness.

FIGURE 11-3. CEZANNE. *Still Life.* National Gallery of Art, Washington, D.C. Chester Dale Collection.

FIGURE 11-4. VAN GOGH. *Wheatfield with Blackbirds.* Collection: Vincent Van Gogh Foundation, Stedelijk Museum, Amsterdam.

Finally, when he found himself no longer able to paint, he took his own life (1890).

But in the years before his death, especially during a final sojourn at Arles, he produced a series of remarkable canvases. Exhilarated by the sun-drenched countryside of southern France, he painted it with fervid excitement, applying color with greater vigor and freedom than had any painter before. He did not try to imitate the hues of nature; the colors represented his feelings. Yellow, his favorite color, was his means of expressing the immanent love of God. Blue, pale violet, and green expressed rest or sleep.

A striking example of Van Gogh's last works is *Wheatfield with Blackbirds* (FIG. *11-4*), finished just before his death. It presents "vast stretches of corn under troubled skies," expressing, as he wrote, "sadness and the extreme of loneliness." Such was the final response of a great and sensitive talent to the closing years of the nineteenth century.

Imperialism, World War,
and the Rise of Collectivism

12

As the twentieth century opened, scientific technology gathered momentum. At the same time, powerful economic, political, and military developments were converging toward a decisive crisis, the crisis of the First World War (1914–18). That ruinous struggle marked the beginning of a profound change in Western civilization. Change in history is continuous, but future scholars will doubtless confirm that a radical transformation was wrought in the West during the half-century following the First World War. As a result the basic conditions and concepts of life today are far different from what they had been before 1914.

In this chapter we will see how the calamity of world war arose and how drastic were the developments it precipitated. Chief among these developments was the breakdown of the liberal order in Europe and the rise of collectivist social systems. In the concluding chapter, we will see how the Second World War accelerated the change in Western civilization and furthered the transformation of the entire globe.

IMPERIALISM AND EUROPE'S
WORLD DOMINION

The expansion of Western society, which has left indelible marks upon a large portion of the earth, began at the close of the Middle Ages. Overseas exploration and colonization proceeded steadily from the sixteenth century into the eighteenth and then, about 1750, slowed down for a time. For more than a century thereafter, western Europe was preoccupied with its own political and social stirrings and with the absorbing process of industrialization. But after 1870 new colonial ventures were undertaken in Asia and Africa. Since these ventures differed in some respects from earlier colonial efforts, they are often referred to as the "new" imperialism.

Imperialism itself is as old as history. Broadly defined, it is any form of control exercised by one group of people over others beyond the group's own borders. It thus includes a wide variety of impositions, from outright occupation and enslavement to the exercise of covert and subtle influence. Imperialistic adventures fill the accounts of our most ancient writers—Homer, Herodotus, and Thucydides. By far the most successful imperialists of ancient times were the Romans; the Pax Romana brought order and prosperity to the Mediterranean world for several centuries.

Imperialism, no matter what its form, has been of three main types. Roman imperialism was in most instances *beneficent:* it provided for a sharing by the conquered in the advantages of empire and a movement toward common political rights. A second type is clearly *exploitative:* as with Cortez in Mexico, it aims primarily at using the resources and peoples of another land for the benefit of the conquerors. A third type of imperialism is almost wholly *destructive:* the ancient Assyrians, Huns, and Mongols brought only plunder, cruelty, and devastation to their victims.

Motives for nineteenth-century expansionism

The imperialism of the late nineteenth century was exploitative; its impact (intended and unintended) was shattering. What was it that moved Europeans to strike out across the seas and impose themselves and their technology upon the peoples of Asia and Africa? The economic motive, nourished by the growth of industrial capitalism, was certainly powerful. We saw in the preceding chapter how surplus profits found their way to "backward" countries (p. 454). The urge to secure raw materials, markets, and investment opportunities gave a mighty impetus to overseas penetration.

J. A. Hobson, an English socialist, wrote an influential analysis of the economic causes of expansionism. His book *Imperialism* (published in 1902) attacked the system of overseas exploitation as "a depraved choice of national life, imposed by self-seeking interests." Hobson suggested that the system had grown out of the maldistribution of profits from industry. Since wage-earners lacked the purchasing power to buy all they produced, manufacturers had to go abroad to sell their output and invest their profits. He argued that the elaborate mechanism of colonial administration and defense was wasteful and dangerous, that economic problems could be better solved by providing higher wages and better social services at home. By these means the domestic market would be expanded, and capitalists would have better opportunities to invest their funds. In effect, Hobson was urging a change in policy that would make British capitalism conform to humanistic aims.

Vladimir Lenin took a different tack. As a Marxist dialectitian, he did not think it possible for "reformers" like Hobson to alter the preordained course of capitalism. He accepted Hobson's analysis of imperialism, but he viewed imperialism as the inevitable last stage of capitalism. In *Imperialism, the Highest Stage of Capitalism* (written in 1916) Lenin declared that profits flowed overseas because they produced a higher rate of return there. And only in a colony under formal political control did investments yield their maximum return, which is why colonies had expanded so swiftly, concluded Lenin. They had extended the life of capitalism only by bringing into existence new proletariats. But now that the globe had been parceled out, the capitalist states were being driven by their economic systems to wage imperialist wars against one another. These, he prophesied, would be followed by proletarian revolutions, the establishment of socialist states, and the demise of imperialism. Though Lenin's thesis is inadequate, its partial confirmation by events and its acceptance by communist leaders throughout the world have made it enormously influential.

The economic motive, no matter how interpreted, was only one of the forces behind imperialism. Probably more important was the drive for national power and prestige. European nationalism had come of age by 1870, as we saw in Chapter Ten. Germany, proud and militant, had set out to find her "place in the sun." It is no accident that the renewed scramble for colonies began at about the time that Germany and Italy became unified nations. The pride and effort that go into achieving self-determination for a nation (nationalism) can lead easily to the desire to control other nations and peoples (imperialism).

The balance of power in Europe itself seems to have stabilized after 1870, and the field of maneuver shifted overseas. The military and naval chiefs of rival nations sought strategic fueling stations, fortified bases, and sources of critical raw materials. They looked to colonies also as reservoirs of combat troops. But, above all, many Europeans came to regard overseas possessions as the measure and substance of national power and glory.

Now intellectuals began to speak and write of their nation's "civilizing mission." Many members of the upper and middle classes sought careers in the colonial establishments, where they could lord it over the natives. Ordinary citizens fell captive to jingoistic phrases like "advance of the flag," the "white man's burden," and "Manifest

Destiny." Men, women, and children of all classes studied the new global maps that showed their nation's overseas possessions in distinctive imperial colors. And, as the vocal minorities that protested against imperialism on practical or moral grounds were swept aside as small-minded or unpatriotic, the triumph of chauvinistic nationalism accelerated the mad race for colonies.

Devices of penetration and exploitation

Imperialism did not always mean colonies; control could be informal as well as formal. In fact, many economic and political experts preferred informal control, since it was cheaper and enabled a nation to avoid many risks and responsibilities. Prior to 1870 the British, with their maritime and financial predominance, had been particularly adept at securing economic privileges abroad. But informal and formal relations were woven together into a single fabric of empire, the central purpose of which was commercial penetration and dominance, political and cultural influences being secondary. The British imperial strategy was consistent: trade with informal control if practicable, trade with rule when necessary. The United States pursued a similar strategy in the Western Hemisphere, where it was the predominant power. Though it annexed Puerto Rico and established ultimate legal authority in Cuba (1898), the United States controlled the rest of the Caribbean republics through "dollar diplomacy," aided, when necessary, by the Marines.

When competing states began to challenge British economic privileges in particular areas, Britain responded by seeking formal and exclusive arrangements. Thus after 1870 its Foreign Office sought treaty rights, spheres of interest, and colonies. Germany and Italy, as well as the older European nation-states, joined in the sweepstakes. All employed various devices for gaining a foothold or an advantage and backed up their efforts by the threat or use of military force. The undeveloped or declining countries of Asia and Africa found themselves helpless before this combined onslaught. As in the case of earlier confrontations between Europe and the non-Western world, the Europeans held the advantages of aggressive purpose, superior organization, and advanced technology.

The new assault on Africa illustrates the methods of imperialist penetration. The Dark Continent, except for a few coastal strips, remained virtually unknown to the outside world until 1870. The first white man to explore the interior was a Scottish physician and missionary, David Livingstone, who spent some thirty years among the natives doing medical and religious work and traveling the upper courses of the great rivers. When Livingstone was reported in

Europe and America as being "lost" in the jungles, a New York newspaper sent a reporter to find him—as a journalistic stunt. Henry Stanley "found" the good doctor in 1871, decided to conduct further travels of his own, and later publicized his adventures in a book called *Through the Dark Continent*. More important, Stanley perceived the possibilities of extracting wealth from central Africa. He succeeded at last in interesting King Leopold II of Belgium in his promotional plans.

Belgium, a small country that had gained its own independence only a generation before, had no overseas possessions. Leopold's venture was entirely private—in keeping with the individualistic, freebooting spirit of the times. He formed a private company, with himself as president, and sent Stanley and other agents into the Congo region. Taking the view that the African interior was open for sale to the white man, Leopold acquired "possession" of an enormous area by making "treaties" with hundreds of tribal chieftains. The documents were usually "signed" after the Belgians handed over trifling gifts to the bemused native leaders. The Congo Free State, as it was styled by an international conference, was subjected to the personal rule of Leopold. Its boundaries embraced an area equal to that of the United States east of the Mississippi River.

Though Leopold ascribed scientific and humanitarian purposes to his venture, his prime purpose was personal gain. His eye was fixed on the booming industrial demand for rubber: the Congo had rubber trees and a large supply of native laborers. But the natives were ridden by tropical diseases and proved unresponsive to European work incentives; they could be forced to work only by the harshest methods.

Leopold's agents used up the trees and the natives of the Congo without compunction. And though the annual value of its rubber exports reached ten million dollars by the year 1908, Leopold did not make the rubber operations there self-sustaining. He used much of the income for personal extravagance and borrowed huge sums from the Belgian government. In return, he mortgaged the Free State to the government, which took it over at his death. As the Belgian Congo the region received somewhat better treatment, but it remained a notorious example of human and material exploitation.

Leopold's taking of the Congo attracted the attention of other European states to the prizes of Africa. A conference was called in 1885 to give some order to the carving up of the remainder of the continent. Certain ground rules were agreed on: a nation with possessions on the coast had prior right to the related hinterlands; but in order for a claim to any territory to be recognized, it must be

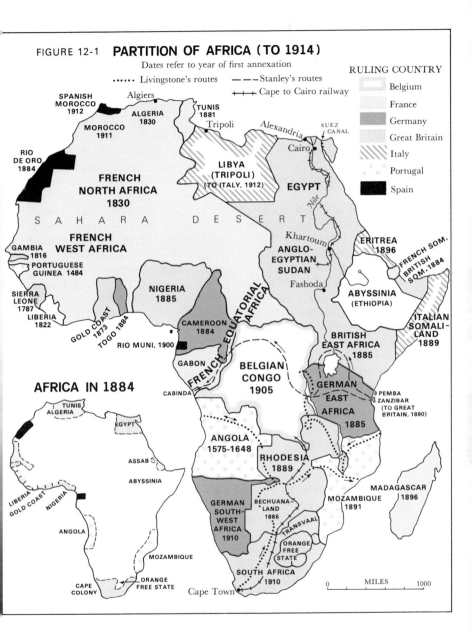

FIGURE 12-1 **PARTITION OF AFRICA (TO 1914)**

Dates refer to year of first annexation

RULING COUNTRY

•••••• Livingstone's routes ——— Stanley's routes

+—+—+ Cape to Cairo railway

Belgium
France
Germany
Great Britain
Italy
Portugal
Spain

SPANISH
MOROCCO
1912

Algiers

TUNIS
1881

Tripoli

Alexandria

SUEZ
CANAL

ALGERIA
1830

MOROCCO
1911

RIO
DE ORO
1884

LIBYA
(TRIPOLI)
(TO ITALY, 1912)

EGYPT

Cairo

FRENCH
NORTH AFRICA
1830

S A H A R A   D E S E R T

Nile

Khartoum

ANGLO-
EGYPTIAN
SUDAN

ERITREA
1896

FRENCH
WEST AFRICA

GAMBIA
1816

PORTUGUESE
GUINEA 1484

Fashoda

FRENCH SOM.
BRITISH
SOM. 1884

SIERRA
LEONE
1787

LIBERIA
1822

NIGERIA
1885

ABYSSINIA
(ETHIOPIA)

GOLD COAST
1873 1884

TOGO 1884

CAMEROON
1884

ITALIAN
SOMALI-
LAND
1889

RIO MUNI, 1900

FRENCH EQUATORIAL AFRICA

BRITISH
EAST AFRICA
1885

GABON

BELGIAN
CONGO
1905

AFRICA IN 1884

CABINDA

GERMAN
EAST
AFRICA
1885

PEMBA
ZANZIBAR
(TO GREAT
BRITAIN, 1890)

TUNIS

ALGERIA

EGYPT

ANGOLA
1575-1648

RHODESIA
1889

ASSAB

ABYSSINIA

LIBERIA

GOLD COAST

NIGERIA

MADAGASCAR
1896

MOZAMBIQUE
1891

GERMAN
SOUTH-
WEST
AFRICA
1910

BECHUANA-
LAND
1885

ANGOLA

TRANSVAAL

MOZAMBIQUE

ORANGE
FREE
STATE

CAPE
COLONY

ORANGE
FREE STATE

SOUTH AFRICA
1910

Cape Town

MILES

0   1000

supported by the presence of administrators and soldiers. The conference agreement was thus a signal to all competitors to move in with
civilian and military forces. Within twenty-five years Africa had been
completely staked out by the Europeans (FIG. *12-1*).

The methods employed were similar to those used by Leopold's agents. White men trekked into the interior in search of chiefs who would sign treaties. The chiefs seldom understood what the treaties meant or had the authority to transfer rights—either to sovereignty or to property—but the white men acted as if they did. These "rights" were then transferred to some European government, and a colony was thereby established. The only serious difficulties arose when rival nations secured overlapping grants in the same region. Such problems were usually referred to European capitals for settlement.

In Asia the situation was different. There were no "dark," unoccupied zones. China, for example, was an ancient empire, quite adequately charted and administered. What the Europeans wanted there initially were trading privileges. They coveted the luxury goods of China (silks, precious stones, porcelain), and they wanted to secure them in exchange for their factory-made products. Unfortunately the Chinese did not want such commodities. The one article they would buy in substantial quantities was opium, which was grown in India and sold by British merchants. When China tried to check the importation of this insidious drug, Britain opened hostilities. (This was the so-called Opium War of 1841.)

The treaty forced upon the Chinese at the end of the Opium War was a precursor of countless impositions on that unhappy country. According to the treaty's terms the opium trade was to be resumed with no further interference. In addition Britain demanded and won possession of the strategic Chinese city of Hong Kong. Within the next few decades other countries made their own demands. Under the "treaty system" a dozen Chinese port cities were opened to European traders (FIG. *12-2*), and in each port city the leading European powers were allowed to establish their own settlements, immune from Chinese jurisdiction. European nationals, under further agreements, were allowed to travel inside China subject only to the laws of their own homeland. The Chinese government was deprived of sovereign control over its own external commerce when the European powers required that no tariff of more than 5 per cent be levied on imports and that the permitted duties be collected by Europeans. A good portion of this revenue was then siphoned off as "war indemnities" to the invaders. Small wonder that the Chinese felt growing resentment toward the "foreign devils"!

No matter what technique the Europeans used to impose their control, the results were disastrous to native institutions and morale. Although Westerners are seldom aware of the unsettling effect of their technology when it is loosed upon traditional cultures, histori-

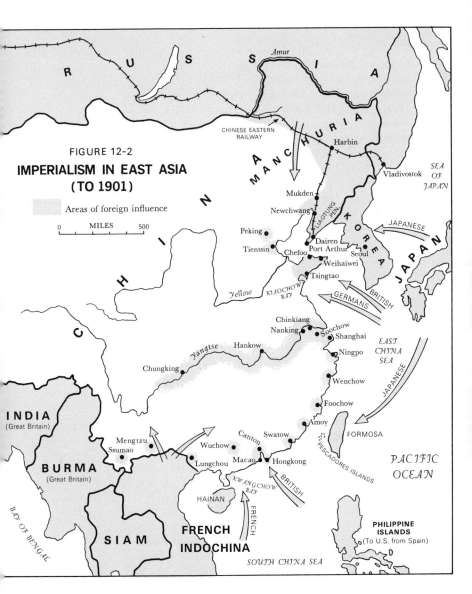

FIGURE 12-2

**IMPERIALISM IN EAST ASIA
(TO 1901)**

Areas of foreign influence

0 MILES 500

ans and anthropologists generally agree that modern industrial
civilization has been the most disturbing cultural force ever known.
It breaks down and transforms pre-machine social organization,
habits of life, and ways of thought. In this sense, the damage brought
by imperialism was the result as much of unplanned cultural trauma
as of the planned exploitation of man by man.

China suffered the full consequences of economic and social dislocation. Before the British broke in, there had existed a kind of balance between farming and handicrafts. A merchant class had arisen in the cities, and some large-scale workshops had been set up. China had had a lively export trade in silks and porcelains, and her splendid craftsmen had been kept busy. But the entry of cheap manufactured goods in the nineteenth century undermined the entire structure. Finally, by building factories in the free ports and using cheap "coolie" labor, the Europeans ruined the old Chinese handicrafts, upset the balance of the economy, and demoralized the labor force. Quick fortunes were made from these enterprises by foreign traders and manufacturers, but the cost to the Chinese people was beyond measure.

The Japanese, long isolated on their islands, were more fortunate. Though they could not exclude industrialism, they managed to develop it themselves without disruptive interferences by foreigners. They jealously guarded control over their finances and tariffs, and in an extraordinary national effort they modernized their economy and were able by 1890 to meet the Westerners on their own terms. Asians, generally, learned a lesson from the Japanese experience. Today most Asian leaders prefer to build their own national economies, in accordance with the character and needs of their own societies.

The partitions of Asia and Africa

The concessions of trade and treaty ports by China failed to satisfy imperialist appetites, and the major powers continued to jockey for advantage. The Russians, who for centuries had been expanding eastward across Siberia, reached the Pacific about 1850, where they founded Vladivostok (Ruler of the East) and then turned their attention to Manchuria and Korea, both of which had close historical ties to China. The Japanese, also infected by the virus of expansionism, shortly revealed that they had plans of their own in this area. They drew China into war over contested rights in Korea in 1894, and their Western-style army won easily. China was compelled to cede to Japan the large island of Formosa, as well as her claims to Korea (FIG. *12-2*).

The Europeans were astonished by this demonstration of Japanese will and strength. Now that it appeared that China might be falling prey to avaricious neighbors, they determined to protect their interests by seizing control of whatever territories they could. The Germans, French, Russians, and British pressured the Chinese government to yield vital coastal zones, in addition to their respective settlements in the treaty ports. Only suspicions and disputes among the great powers saved the rest of China from complete dismemberment at this time.

The intervention of the United States, which had become a Pacific power in 1898 when it took the Philippines from Spain, had only a minor effect on the situation. The Americans feared that their commerce with China would be cut off if the foreign interests already there succeeded in spreading their territorial holdings. The secretary of state, John Hay, therefore pushed vigorously (1899) for the acceptance of an "Open Door" policy in China, which would guarantee the "territorial integrity" of the country against further incursions and extend to *all nations equally* the commercial privileges that had been wrested from the Chinese government.

Britain supported the Open Door policy, for it promised to counter the threat of more annexations by China's neighbors. The other contending powers viewed it coolly, however, for they hoped to pounce upon portions of the faltering empire. Ignoring the Open Door principle, Japan in 1905 secured a free hand in Manchuria; in 1912 Britain assumed paramount rights in Tibet; and in 1913 Russia established a protectorate over Outer Mongolia.

Meanwhile the rest of Asia had been gobbled up. In 1883 the French had created a protectorate in Annam, which was later combined with adjoining territories to form French Indo-China. The British had begun to plant settlements in India back in the seventeenth century; in the nineteenth century the crown assumed direct control of the Indian government and extended its grip to Burma and Malaya. The Dutch widened their earlier lucrative holdings in the East Indies, while Persia and Afghanistan were split into British and Russian spheres of influence (1907).

As for Africa, the entire continent had been partitioned by 1914. France held most of the bulge of West Africa, which was largely desert; the British held the richest lands, running from Cape Colony in the south to Egypt in the north. The main possessions on the lower coasts and in the central region were those of Portugal, Belgium, Germany, and Italy (FIG. *12-1*).

At last this era of fabulous conquest came to an end. The new imperialism had added five million square miles to the British empire. (In 1900 Queen Victoria ruled nearly four hundred million subjects, with overseas territory forty times larger than the home island.) French possessions had expanded by almost as much; substantial though lesser areas had been acquired by Germany, Belgium, Portugal, and Italy. And Russia, Japan, and the United States had joined the list of imperial powers.

The moral issue aside, imperialism brought some advantages to the colonial peoples. Roads, railways, sanitation, hospitals, missionaries, and schools were introduced into "backward" countries, while tribal wars and gross superstitions, where they existed, were suppressed. Most significant, "modernization" was brought to the non-Western world—though it might have come in a less coercive fashion. But these benefits scarcely balanced the physical and psychic damage inflicted by imperialism upon the subject peoples. It left them with a pervading sense of confusion, defeat, and degradation.

In 1914 Europe stood at its peak of power and arrogance. But its outward thrust had intensified the forces that were pushing the Western nations toward war among themselves. Europeans purported to take care of the problems of "backward" peoples, but they proved unable to solve their own. Europe was soon to explode in a frightful conflagration, leading to the demise, later, of the enormity of colonialism.

THE FIRST WORLD WAR
AND THE DECLINE OF EUROPE

The two "world wars," one starting in 1914 and the other in 1939, are closely linked. Both were products of the prevailing international political system, which had been legitimized by the European powers. The First War ended not with a stable peace, but with a truce; the Second War was its nightmarish sequel. It was 1914, rather than 1939, that was the major turning point of modern history. For the events of that year set in motion an irreversible shift in the affairs and prospects of Western civilization.

Yet on the eve of 1914 there were few who could see what the future held. The trend of surface events had indeed been deceptive. The advance of science, liberal institutions, and material welfare was indisputable. The decades before 1914 had been a time of expansiveness and optimism, with the promise of the Enlightenment apparently on the verge of fruition. Given another half-century of peace, it seemed that education and reform might secure the goals of liberalism for Europe, if not for the world.

Looking back, however, it seems evident that such an outcome was most unlikely. The existing peace was shaky; and, even without the blow of war, it seems doubtful whether a liberal order could have prevailed. For there was another, gloomier side of the European picture. Technology had created forces that were dissolving the foundations of liberalism, and imperialism had opened wounds, both in Europe and overseas, that continued to fester.

There was, too, a rising romantic mood, irrational and illiberal, associated with mystical ideas of racial purity and national "soul." But Europe's fatal flaw was excessive nationalism—especially as it became associated with militarism and alliances among the great powers.

Nationalism, militarism, and the alliance system

By the close of the nineteenth century, the nationalist ideal of Mazzini (p. 444) had hardened into a self-centered and self-destroying passion. Its characteristics were the same in every Western land: the people of each nation believed in their own superiority, sovereignty, and peculiar mission in the world, and, consequently, they held the advancement of national power and glory to be the supreme aim of individual and collective life.

Nationalism, the "religion of the fatherland," was in fact the true faith of most Europeans at the turn of the century. Each nation viewed itself as the chosen instrument of God; its founding fathers and heroes were the apostles and martyrs; its political charters were revered as holy texts. The flag was the sacred symbol of each nation, and saluting and pledging allegiance to the flag and visiting historic shrines were prescribed rituals.

The armed forces of each nation became the principal embodiment of its sovereign spirit and honor. They served, at the same time, as the ultimate means of pursuing national aims; both pride and interest, therefore, moved statesmen and citizens to respect and strengthen the army and navy. Bismarck, building on the military tradition of Frederick the Great, had pursued this policy in Prussia. His forces had dismayed the rest of Europe as they paved the way to the creation of the German Empire in 1871. The other powers had worked to catch up militarily as rapidly as possible: all except Britain adopted universal male conscription and military training. Competition in weaponry accompanied the rise of huge standing armies; by the end of the century Europe had become a bristling camp. Nationalism and militarism were thus fatefully joined.

Stated simply, militarism is the belief that preparation for war provides sound moral training and the best safeguard of peace and the national interest. Militarists scorn diplomacy, except when it is used as an expression of force. They aim, therefore, to build ever stronger military power—greater, if possible, than that of any likely combination of enemies. "Peace through strength" is their slogan. (But strength is *relative,* and each nation wants to be the strongest.) When the European peoples embraced militarism in the nineteenth century, they embarked upon an unrestricted arms race. All were caught up in it; for though a nation might never hope to win such a race, it dared not fall behind.

Unwilling or unable to work out accepted principles of peaceful coexistence, the European powers were left to the lethal consequences of their own nationalisms. For in relations between states there was no enforceable law comparable to that which existed within states. Since each sovereign power recognized no authority superior to itself, the ultimate recourse was to war. The situation then, as now, has been aptly called *international anarchy*. There is only one fundamental difference today: the weapons of war have become infinitely more destructive.

Metternich's Concert of Europe (p. 417) had been an attempt to deal with the problem of international anarchy by harmonizing the interests of the great powers. But this idea, basically incompatible with nationalism, was doomed from the start. During the course of the nineteenth century, a few far-seeing individuals tried earnestly to modify the sovereignty principle, strengthen international law, and establish international judicial tribunals. Peace conferences were called, notably those at The Hague (the Netherlands) in 1899 and 1907. Representatives of twenty-six nations, assembled at The Hague, tried and failed to agree on a proposal for arms limitation; but they did take steps to codify the "law of war" and pledged not to use poison gas or other weapons that were considered especially inhumane. They also created an international court of arbitration to which countries might (by joint agreement) submit disputes for adjudication. It is worth noting also that numerous "peace societies" were formed in various parts of Europe during the prewar period.

These efforts were forerunners of more substantial moves toward replacing anarchy with international order. But they were not taken seriously by the responsible statesmen of that era. These men believed that the only path to security, beyond keeping their own nation strong, was to enter into alliances with "friendly" powers. Thus nationalism and militarism led to the alliance system of the late nineteenth century. Like the arms race the alliances were competitive, and they were meaningful only in relative terms. The European states did not find safety from war in either arms or alliances. The pursuit of both served only to make the conflagration hotter and more widespread after it flared up.

The road to war

Though most of Europe's leaders, even as late as 1914, declared that war was unthinkable, we can see now that war was built into the existing international system. The pronouncements of the statesmen of that time give persuasive evidence of the human proclivity to indulge in wishful thinking—to cling to comforting myths rather than face disturbing realities. Some said war would not happen because it was "too expensive," or "too frightful," or "too irrational." But we know now that those characteristics of war do not prevent it. The research of countless scholars on the origins of the First World War constitutes a well-documented case study of how international anarchy leads, in fact, to international conflict.

Until 1914 there had been some grounds for optimism about keeping the peace in the fact that a number of crises had been settled without resort to force. But the pressures for war were cumulative, and the right type of crisis at the right time was virtually certain to strike the igniting spark. Many countries were working at cross-purposes internationally; Germany, however, held the chief initiative. Its triumphal unification in 1871 made it the dominant power on the Continent. The eyes of European diplomats were fixed upon the Germans, watching what they would do and how far they would go. The subsequent acts of other powers were closely related to German actions.

It was Bismarck who launched peacetime alliances, as a means of maintaining Germany's hegemony in Europe. His motives were no doubt defensive; he feared that the French, stung by their defeat in the Franco-Prussian War, would seek military revenge. And so he arranged an alliance with another vanquished rival, Austria-Hungary, in 1879. Italy joined this agreement a few years afterward, making the Triple Alliance. Its public terms provided for military assistance by the partners if any one of them was attacked by two or more powers. Secret understandings, however, called for general diplomatic and military collaboration.

The isolation of France, shrewdly cultivated by Bismarck, was broken soon after the Iron Chancellor fell from office in 1890. His fall was due in part to the ambitions of the new German emperor, William II, who replaced Bismarck's cautious, continental policy with a policy that would propel Germany into her "rightful" place as a *world* power. The emperor's policy was an open challenge to Britain, which Bismarck had sought to keep neutral in European affairs. Britain responded by developing closer relations with France.

Britain's island security and world position had depended for over a century upon her superiority on the seas. But Kaiser William, convinced of the importance of sea power to overseas commerce, colonies, and national prestige, was determined to have a great navy as well as the world's finest army. Beginning in 1898, Germany began to make huge expenditures for her fleet of warships. Britain, alarmed, reacted with still larger sums, insisting on the principle that her navy remain the equal of any other *two*. And, though traditionally committed to "splendid isolation" from European entanglements, the British now began to consider European alliances to counter the rising power of Germany and the Triple Alliance.

The French, meanwhile, had not forgotten 1870, and they, too, were seeking military partners. They looked first to the power on Germany's eastern border. Russia—autocratic, conservative, and orthodox—was ideologically and socially at the farthest remove from liberal and progressive France. But internal differences between states do not necessarily stand in the way of common goals in foreign policy. Already linked to each other by substantial French loans to the improvident tsarist regime, the two countries entered into a Dual Alliance in 1894. The action confronted Germany with the threat that Bismarck had most feared—the possibility of a two-front war. From this time until 1914, the governments of Europe studied the military, diplomatic, and economic moves of the various powers with a view toward measuring their effects upon the two opposing alliances. Any development that might decisively shift the balance of power between them could precipitate immediate and general war.

Britain found herself swinging ever closer to France and Russia. The French *revanchists* (revenge-seekers) acceded to British advances in Africa and persuaded Russian diplomats to settle long-standing disputes with the British in the Middle East. For their part, the British were growing more apprehensive with each belligerent gesture by the kaiser. They made no formal military commitments, but after 1907 there existed a "close understanding" (entente) between Britain, France, and Russia. British and French military officers began to carry on informal staff conversations. The Dual Alliance was thus extended into a Triple Entente. That understanding was to grow firmer as trouble erupted in the Balkans.

The Balkans and the strategic straits (Dardanelles and Bosphorus) had been objects of great-power interest for more than a century. The Ottoman Turks, who at one time had threatened central Europe (p. 218), continued to hold most of southeastern Europe, as well as the Middle East, until after 1815 (FIG. *10-1*). The subject nationalities in the Balkans, mostly Slavic, differed in language, religion, and general culture from their Moslem rulers, and they began to respond to the spirit of nationalism that was spreading through Europe. The Greeks, for example, had won their independence in 1829, and the Rumanians, Bulgars, and others were waiting for a chance to throw off the Turkish yoke. Slavic efforts to gain independence were supported by Russia, Austria-Hungary, Britain, and France—all of whom hoped to snatch for themselves some property from Turkey, the "sick man of Europe." Intervention by these countries complicated Balkan affairs by feeding a dreary sequence of wars, treaties, conferences, and more wars. It was the grasping of the great powers, combined with the nationalist ferment in southeastern Europe, that furnished the tinder for the First World War.

The Russians had three objectives in the area: to liberate their brother Slavs, to win control of the Black Sea coasts, and to secure a warm-water outlet for themselves at the straits. The tsar nearly achieved these objectives in 1878, when he invaded the Turkish Empire and crushed its forces. But Austria and Britain demanded, upon threat of war, that the Russians moderate their peace terms. At the ensuing Berlin Conference, presided over by Bismarck acting as an "honest broker," Russia gained only a few harbors and border territories, plus an indemnity. But Rumania, Serbia, and Montenegro were recognized as independent states, and Bulgaria secured autonomy under the Turkish sultan. Russia thus emerged as the protector of the Balkan peoples, having released them from the arbitrary rule of a crumbling empire.

The alarmed sultan now tried to arrest the decay of Turkish strength by inviting German experts to reform his army and finances. He tried, at the same time, to play off the great powers against one another. But he was obliged to pay a price: in return for their continuing diplomatic aid against Russia, he had to permit the British to occupy Cyprus and the Austrians to administer the provinces of Bosnia and Herzegovina. Egypt, nominally a part of the sultan's empire, was occupied by the British in 1882 as part of their colonial design in Africa. The island of Crete broke free from Turkey in 1896. Only a remnant remained of the moribund empire, and that was disposed of by the settlement that ended the First World War.

The conflicts in the Balkans reflected the deadly clash of incompatible national aims. Russia, as we have seen, wanted to make the Black Sea a Slavic lake by controlling its outlet at Constantinople. But Britain considered Russia's southward push a threat to its own line of empire, which ran through the Mediterranean to India, and therefore sought to keep Russia bottled up. Austria-Hungary, and Germany, too, had designs on the Balkans. Austria, which wanted to expand trade and influence in the region, resented mounting Russian prestige there. And the Germans were building a Berlin-to-Baghdad railway to open up the Middle East and India to German economic and political penetration. This ambitious project required understandings with the Balkan states through which the railway passed, as well as with the sultan. Britain, Russia, and France regarded the German enterprise as a source of unwelcome aid to the Turkish Empire and as an incursion into their own spheres of interest.

The most serious and irrepressible conflict, however, was between the Slavic nationalists and the polyglot empire of Austria-Hungary. The Habsburg rulers realized that their empire, consisting of a dozen nationalities, would fall apart if they failed to contain the nationalistic forces that were rising within it. The little state of Serbia posed the most immediate threat. The Serbs, a Slavic people who had secured their independence in 1878, had an ambitious sense of national mission and wanted to unite all the "South Slavs" into a single political unit. Some of these South Slavs dwelled in the provinces of Bosnia and Herzegovina, which Austria annexed in 1908. The leaders of the "Greater Serbia" movement launched a program of agitation and subversion in an effort to win the allegiance of their fellow Slavs and to bring about their liberation from Austria.

The statesmen in Vienna were justifiably apprehensive. A Serbian success would pull important territories away from the Austrian Empire. Still more dangerous was the force that such a success would set in motion. The Magyars (Hungarians) had already gained autonomy within the empire (in 1867), but the Czechs, Poles, Rumanians, and other minorities were still treated as subordinate peoples. They, too, were aroused by nationalist feelings and were eager to split the Habsburg domain into independent national states. The potentially explosive situation also had obvious implications for the alliance system, on whose stability the general peace of Europe seemed to hang. If Austria-Hungary were to come apart, the Triple Alliance would be decisively weakened. Germany, the senior partner of the alliance, therefore kept in anxious touch with Vienna. On the opposing side, the Russians did all they could to encourage the Serbs.

The Serbian nationalists, knowing that their country was militarily weaker than the Austrian Empire, resorted to terror and assassination to further their "holy" cause. Their efforts reached a climax in the streets of Sarajevo, Bosnia, in June 1914, when a young extremist assassinated the Archduke Francis Ferdinand and his wife. World leaders were shocked by the murder, and the Austrian government decided to use the occasion for a showdown with Serbia. Assuming that the Serbian government was implicated in the assassination plot, Vienna fired off a harsh ultimatum to Belgrade. The Serbs accepted in substance all but one of the demands. But the Austrians rejected their response as unsatisfactory, broke off diplomatic relations, mobilized the imperial army, and declared war on Serbia. The small Slavic nation, having received reassurances from Russia, also mobilized.

The responsibilities of the great powers in the face of this grave threat to European peace are difficult to assess. Germany, for reasons already suggested, had advised Austria to move ahead. Russia, having made a commitment to the Serbs, felt she could not back down. France, determined to preserve her alliance with Russia, admonished Moscow to be firm and to avoid any compromise that might cause a loss of prestige for the Triple Entente.

The decisive step in widening the war was the tsar's order to mobilize the Russian army. A week or more was needed before an army could be made ready for battle, and German leaders decided that they could not stand idly by while Russian mobilization proceeded. They dispatched a telegram demanding that the Russians halt their call-up within twelve hours. Failing to receive a positive reply, the Germans declared war on Russia on August 1, 1914. As Paris ordered mobilization, Berlin declared war on France as well. The conflagration that "nobody wanted" had at last broken out.

Though Britain had made no public commitment to aid France, her ministers had privately undertaken to help if the French were attacked by Germany. Parliament put aside any reluctance it might have had to make good this undertaking when the Germans, according to their prior war plan, invaded Belgium. Britain, as one of the guarantors of Belgian neutrality and security, now had a legal basis for action. Parliament declared war on Germany on August 4. Japan, Britain's partner in the Pacific, soon entered on the Allied side, while the Turks, renewing their struggle with Russia, joined the Central Powers. Italy, nominally a member of the Triple Alliance, did not enter the war at once, taking the position that her military obligation to her partners (Germany and Austria) was binding only if they were attacked. Italy remained neutral until 1915, when secret promises of postwar rewards induced her to come in on the Allied side. Many smaller nations were gradually drawn into the war (at least formally), but they did not influence its outcome.

The course and consequences of the war

The strategy of the First World War was basically simple. The Allies, with control of the seas, were sure of winning a long war of attrition. The Central Powers sought a quick, decisive victory based on superior technique and superior forces in being. They enjoyed the advantage of interior lines of communication, which meant that they could concentrate their forces swiftly on chosen sectors. The

Germans, who wished to avoid dividing their army between west and east, had planned to strike an overwhelming first blow against France and then turn against the Russian forces, which would be slower in mobilizing. In executing their plan, the German generals did not hesitate to violate an earlier pledge of protection to Belgium (which they now called a "scrap of paper"), explaining that the invasion was a matter of "military necessity."

The powerful German strike westward, which aimed to roll up the French army in a grand wheeling movement, stalled at the Marne River, near Paris. After the first few weeks, the battle changed from one of movement to one of fixed positions. Now the advantage shifted to those who were on the defensive. Trench warfare, with its barbed wire, machine guns, artillery barrages, and bayonet charges, became a routine of carnage for the next four years. A few surprises, such as the use of tanks (by Britain) and poison gas (by Germany), were introduced in the hope of breaking the stalemate on the ground. Above the lines, airplane pilots engaged in free-wheeling "dog fights," but with negligible effect on the action below. Advances were measured in yards and were paid for in thousands of dead and maimed.

On the eastern front the Germans were more successful. The soldiers of the tsar, brave but poorly supplied, suffered disastrous losses and were virtually out of the war by 1917. This military loss to the Allies was more than balanced, however, by the entrance of the United States on their side in 1917. By bringing in fresh troops and equipment, and by pledging the resources of their continent, the Americans assured the Allies of ultimate victory. Bowing to the inevitable, the Germans at last responded favorably to President Woodrow Wilson's offer of a moderate settlement on Allied terms—a "peace without victory." In November 1918 they agreed to lay down their arms.

At the peace conference, which met at Versailles and other suburbs of Paris, separate treaties were arranged with each of the Central Powers. None of the defeated powers was given any effective voice in the settlements; it turned out to be a victors' peace after all. France, Britain, and the United States laid down the conditions, which were severe. Delegates from the Central Powers protested vehemently, but they were compelled to accept under threat that the war would be renewed. With a fine *revanchist* touch, the French arranged for the signing ceremony to take place in the Hall of Mirrors at Versailles, where, in 1871, Bismarck had proclaimed the German Empire.

The most reprehensible part of the Versailles Treaty, from the

German point of view, was the "war-guilt" clause—which stated that Germany and her partners accepted responsibility for *all* loss and damage caused by the war. The Germans did not feel that they alone were to blame, and the historical facts indicate that other powers shared the responsibility. The guilt clause no doubt reflected popular sentiment in the Allied countries, which had been fed virulent propaganda by their wartime governments. It was put into the treaty in order to justify huge reparation claims by the victors, but it served only to arouse among the Germans a violent and lasting hatred of the settlement.

Under the territorial provisions of the treaty, Germany lost the provinces of Alsace and Lorraine (which she had taken from France in 1871), her overseas colonies, and valuable lands on her eastern frontiers. She also had to surrender most of her merchant shipping and to dismantle her armed forces. The treaties with the other defeated powers provided for the remaking of the map of central and eastern Europe, for now three empires (the Russian, Austrian, and Turkish) were in partial or total dissolution. The guiding principle in drawing the new frontiers was that of "self-determination" for nationalities. Seven new states (FIG. *12-3*) came into being: Finland, Esthonia, Latvia, Lithuania, Poland, Czechoslovakia, and Yugoslavia. (The last named fulfilled the dream of the Serbian patriots, who had started it all at Sarajevo.) Austria and Hungary were separated and reduced to small, landlocked states. All that remained of the Turkish Empire was the Republic of Turkey, limited to Constantinople (in Europe) and Asia Minor.

Despite the general application of self-determination, the problem of nationalities continued to plague Europe. The diverse cultures had become so entwined that every fixing of boundaries seemed to leave minority enclaves within a larger national group.

The deeper consequences of the war went far beyond the treaties and the breaking and making of states. The war had inflicted a catastrophic loss of lives and treasure from which Europe never recovered. Of the more than forty million men mobilized, some seven million were killed and three million were totally disabled. Total civilian casualties, direct and indirect, amounted to millions more; economic costs ran into trillions of dollars.

France was the hardest hit. During the first year of war, the French soldiers defended their homeland with a reckless courage due as much to the foolhardy tactics of the generals as to the bravery of the men. French military theorists before 1914 were committed to the doctrine of the offensive: "Attack"—always and everywhere. With disastrous results for the French, this doctrine was put to test

FINLAND

Helsinki

Leningrad
(St. Petersburg,
Petrograd)

NORWAY

SWEDEN

Oslo

Stockholm

ESTONIA

LATVIA

*NORTH
SEA*

BALTIC SEA

DENMARK

Copenhagen

Memel
LITHUANIA

UNION OF
SOVIET
SOCIALIST
REPUBLICS

Danzig

EAST
PRUSSIA

G E R M A N Y

POLISH CORRIDOR

The
Hague

NETHER-
LANDS

Berlin

Posen

Warsaw

Brussels

BELGIUM

Rhine

Kiev

LUX.

POLAND

UKRAINE

Paris

ALSACE-
LORRAINE

CZECHOSLOVAKIA

Prague

GALICIA

BESSARABIA

FRANCE

Munich

Vienna

Budapest

Berne

SWITZERLAND

AUSTRIA

HUNGARY

R U M A N I A

S.
TYROL

ISTRIA

Milan

Fiume

BOSNIA

SERBIA

Belgrade

B A L K A N S

Bucharest

Danube

I T A L Y

Y U G O S L A V I A

ADRIATIC SEA

Rome

MONTE-
NEGRO

BULGARIA

Sofia

Constantinople

*BLACK
SEA*

BOSPORUS

ALBANIA

G R E E C E

T U R K E Y

Naples

*AEGEAN
SEA*

DARDANELLES

Athens

FIGURE 12-3

**PEACE SETTLEMENTS
IN EUROPE, 1919**

TERRITORY LOST BY:

Germany

Bulgaria

Austria-Hungary

Russia

0   MILES   300

MEDITERRANEAN SEA

at a time when offensive techniques were decisively inferior to defensive techniques. In the first sixteen months of fighting, France lost three-quarters of a million men—half her total losses in the war. Such casualties were unprecedented. During the first traumatic year, nearly one family out of two received the dreaded message announcing the death of a loved one in action. As the struggle wore on, a sense of doom and despair spread across embattled France.

After 1916, a year in which the British suffered the highest losses in any single offensive (at the River Somme), all the combatants realized that such wholesale squandering of lives was futile. Yet the daily slaughter went on to the end, resulting in the destruction of half a generation of young men. The spirit of Europe, especially of its surviving aristocracy, was broken. The youth who lived through the war, and wondered why, regarded themselves as the "lost" generation. The old creeds and slogans had for them become mockeries; traditional morals, manners, and standards seemed, at best, irrelevant.

Men and morals were not the only casualties of the war. The liberal order, which in 1914 had appeared firmly established, was badly damaged. France and England, the leading liberal states, were crippled by the ordeal. In addition to irreplaceable losses in manpower, their world positions had been shaken. In prosecuting the war, both nations had found it necessary to liquidate a large portion of their overseas investments. Moreover, the spectacle of Europe at war with itself dispelled the awe with which colonial peoples had viewed their conquerors. The Western powers had given them reason to hope that they might one day send the foreigners packing.

The loss of physical and psychic power by the liberal states was equaled by the damage to their professed ideals and institutions. Liberalism was rooted in the Enlightenment, with its optimistic faith in man, reason, nature, and progress. But this faith had been crushed in the agony and futility of the war. Could liberalism survive as a viable ideology after its supporting faith had collapsed? Disenchanted Europeans were unsure. Some drifted into skepticism, cynicism, or nihilism; others were drawn toward socialism or toward a new and more virulent strain of nationalism.

The war had undermined specific liberal institutions as well. This was most evident in the economic sphere, where "free enterprise" had been jealously guarded during the nineteenth century. Every nation at war was forced to clamp controls on business; just as the draft on manpower was compulsory, so was the call on economic resources. Raw materials, exports and imports, banking, wages, prices—all had been regulated in the pursuit of victory.

Laissez faire principles had been ignored "for the duration," and the experience and implications of government planning and direction carried into the future. The war had also disrupted the intricate mechanism of international trade, and a chain of dislocations after 1918 marked the end of laissez faire. It was demonstrated time and time again that private enterprise, both domestic and international, was not "self-regulating" in the public interest. To maintain employment and save business from mass failures, government intervention was to prove essential.

The World War was fought, declared President Wilson, "to make the world safe for democracy." As he surveyed Europe from Versailles in 1919 he might well have thought that the goal was within the reach of mankind. Prussian militarism had been defeated, venerable empires had been reduced to ruins, and monarchies had been toppled. Democracy (as well as nationalism) appeared triumphant. Yet Wilson and other men of liberal-democratic convictions were to suffer bitter disappointment. For most of the new democracies were only superficially democratic, and the older democracies were soon to lose their liberal character. Moreover, the shock and after-shock of the war were to open the doors of revolution in several countries. From the underground of the nineteenth century sprang the promoters of new social orders—men who were radically opposed, in theory as well as in practice, to both liberalism and bourgeois democracy.

COMMUNIST COLLECTIVISM: THE RUSSIAN REVOLUTION

The most comprehensive term applicable to the entire range of antiliberal ideologies and systems is "collectivism." Collectivism opposes liberalism (or individualism) most directly on the issue of the degree and scope of individual freedom in society. The liberal idea assigns priority to the goal of the *maximum freedom of each individual* from any kind of restraint. Each person is to be "let alone," to decide and to do for himself what he pleases, so long as he does not injure the life or property of others. The collectivist idea, on the other hand, assigns priority to the goal of the *harmonious and efficient functioning of the whole society*. In pursuit of this goal, collectivist systems restrict the freedom of individuals in some respects and assign many important areas of decision-making to bureaucratic organizations and, above all, to the state. The organizations and the state may be controlled in various ways—from autocratic to democratic—but, no matter what the forms of control may be, the individual in a collectivist system is bound by the decisions of others in many spheres of life.

In modern interdependent societies, the matters subject to "collective decision" tend to be highly inclusive. And so we must distinguish the collectivist state from the political absolutisms of the past, where both the intention of the ruler and his means of control were relatively limited. Comparisons with all earlier polities have, in fact, little relevance. We can comprehend modern collectivism only in relation to the scientific, technological, and social conditions of the twentieth century.

Collectivist systems have shown considerable variety, arising from their different ideologies, principles of action, and historical settings. They have come into being through one or the other of two modes of development: revolution or evolution. The former mode has appeared in countries where peaceful change has been blocked and where experience in liberal democracy has been slight, while the latter mode has grown directly out of liberal democracy and has involved little or no violence. All collectivist developments have had at least this much in common: they have been positive responses to the failures of liberalism and to the predicaments of modern industrial society.

Russia before the revolution

Paradoxically, the first collectivist regime was established in a country where modern forces had scarcely started to develop. Autocratic Russia was a century or more behind the changes that had swept over western Europe. In 1917 the position of the Romanov Dynasty was not far different from what it had been more than two centuries earlier under Catherine the Great (p. 352). It resembled, in its pretensions and ignorance, the Bourbon monarchy of France in 1789.

Russia had created a vast empire, stretching eastward from central Europe to the Pacific. East of the Ural Mountains the sparse population consisted of various Asiatic peoples, some of whom were seminomads. In European Russia (which then included Poland and the Baltic lands), the population was settled and dense; in 1900 it totaled about a hundred million. More than 80 per cent of these people were peasants, and most of them had only recently been freed from serfdom (1861). They held more than half the arable land of the country, either as individual owners or through their village organization (*mir*), and they had gained limited political rights. Nevertheless, they remained largely illiterate and uneducated and were regarded by the landed aristocracy (less than 10 per cent of the population) as an inferior caste. Over all was the heavy hand of the Russian Orthodox Church, which resisted Western ideas and supported the tsar's "divine" rule of Holy Russia and its empire.

Western influences had nevertheless reached into Russia. The late nineteenth century saw the rise of a new social element, the intelligentsia, made up of educated members of the aristocracy and the small urban middle class. Though the intelligentsia usually identified themselves with Slavic traditions, they were familiar with Western books and ideas. Writers like Tolstoy and Dostoevsky were members of this group. Their popularity in the West reflected the growing commonality of culture. Russia also produced composers, philosophers, and poets of stature, as well as some outstanding mathematicians and scientists.

The Industrial Revolution served as the chief spearhead of Westernization. After 1880, with the help of outside funds, the capitalist pattern of economic growth began to take shape in Russia. Substantial investments went into factories, mines, and railroads, and Russia became active in the world trading system. Capitalist development, however, was still limited in comparison with that of England or Germany. Industrial wage-earners constituted but a small fraction of the total labor force in 1914, and their working conditions resembled those in England fifty years earlier. The proprietary class was very small and had to share the economic field with numerous state-owned enterprises.

Though in theory an absolute monarch, Nicholas II was beset by a wide range of domestic criticism and opposition. Around 1900 the rising business class, in combination with liberal aristocrats, had formed a party known as the Constitutional Democrats. Eager to follow the example of western Europe, they wanted to convert Russia's autocracy into a liberal, constitutional regime. At about the same time, two radical parties were founded—the Social Revolutionaries and the Social Democrats. The former, drawn mainly from the intelligentsia, was an agrarian party; its goals were to give more land to the peasants and to strengthen the functions of the *mir*. The Social Democrats were a Marxist group, also chiefly intellectuals. They viewed the peasants as hopelessly backward and believed that social change would have to follow the Marxian conceptual pattern—that is, the growth of capitalism, followed by the ascendancy (and triumph) of an urban proletariat.

In 1905 a body of protesting workers had gathered in front of the tsar's Winter Palace in St. Petersburg and had been fired on by troops. This "Bloody Sunday" set off insurrections across the country that were supported and used in various ways by the opposition parties. As a means of restoring order, the tsar promised a constitution and civil liberties and agreed, further, to the creation of an elected legislative body (duma). Thus, by 1914 some concessions had been made to demands for political and economic reforms, but discontent still seethed among most classes of the population. Only by means of a hated secret police was the tsar able to repress the opposition. Even so, some revolutionaries resorted to terrorism, and no public official was safe from assassination. The grandfather of Tsar Nicholas (Alexander II) had been killed by a bomb, and Nicholas' prime minister was shot and killed in 1911.

The collapse of the tsarist regime and the triumph of Lenin

Russia's military disasters in the First World War opened the way to revolution by laying bare the inadequacy of the tsarist administration and heaping disgrace upon the regime. Soldiers and sailors, poorly supplied and hungry, at last refused to continue the hopeless fight against the Germans. In March 1917 food riots and strikes in Petrograd (formerly St. Petersburg) led to mutinies among the garrisons of the capital. The tsar, then at the front, abdicated upon the advice of his generals; thus the Romanov Dynasty ended, and Russia became a republic. A provisional government, composed chiefly of the reformist leaders in the Duma, now assumed power. This government was challenged, however, by the Petrograd Soviet of Workers' and Soldiers' Deputies, a body representing the radical parties. The country's future now hinged upon the struggle for power between the provisional government and the Soviet.

In April, Vladimir Lenin arrived in Petrograd. The son of a middle-class bureaucrat, Lenin had enjoyed a comfortable childhood. But at the age of sixteen, after the execution of his elder brother for alleged complicity in a terrorist plot, he had thrown himself into opposition to the tsarist regime (1886). Depending on his friends for sustenance, he made revolution his life career. Lenin spent most of his years in exile—first in Siberia and later in western Europe.

An early convert to Marxism, Lenin worked to make the Russian Social Democratic party a strictly disciplined, revolutionary organization. The revisionist wing of the party appeared to outnumber Lenin's faction, but at a meeting in 1903 he temporarily secured majority support for the radical position. His followers thenceforth called themselves Bolsheviks, from the Russian word meaning "majority"; their reformist rivals came to be known as Mensheviks (minority). In 1912 the Bolsheviks broke away completely from the Social Democratic ranks and formed an independent revolutionary party. They changed their name to "Communist" in 1918.

During most of the war Lenin promoted international Marxist activities from Switzerland. His return to Petrograd in 1917 was facilitated by the Germans, who hoped that his activities there would help to subvert the new government and take Russia out of the war—which is precisely what Lenin succeeded in doing. First, however, he had to wrest power from the provisional government, which was making an earnest effort to restore internal order and uphold Russia's obligation to her allies to continue fighting the Germans. But conditions grew steadily more desperate in the country. Though Russia's economy had not developed to the point where a proletarian revolution in the Marxian pattern could be expected, Lenin became convinced that the war had opened a short-cut to socialism. He saw that the bulk of the Russian people wanted three things above all: peace, land, and food. The provisional government, headed after July by Alexander Kerensky, a Social Revolutionary, had failed to satisfy these longings.

Lenin's road to power was through the Petrograd Soviet. Local soviets (councils) had first appeared during the insurrections of 1905; these "spontaneous" bodies had presumably spoken for the peasants, urban workers, and soldiers. Similar councils were formed in the crisis of 1917, and the Petrograd Soviet began to act as a shadow government. Though the Bolsheviks were a minority within the Soviet when Lenin arrived, he saw that the Soviet could be a potent agency for seizing control of the state. He adroitly outmaneuvered his opponents (the Mensheviks and the Social Revolutionaries), and his emphatic promises of peace and land won growing popular support for the Bolsheviks. In October 1917 Lenin's faction won the upper hand in the Soviet and elected Lenin's close ally, Leon Trotsky, chairman. As Kerensky faltered and as soldiers once more began to desert their units, Lenin decided to move against the provisional government.

The seizure of power (on November 7) was carefully planned and swiftly executed. With the support of the Petrograd garrison, a revolutionary force seized the telephone exchanges, power plants, and railway stations of the capital. The cruiser *Aurora,* stationed on the Neva River, trained its guns on the Winter Palace and fired the signal for the main attack. Kerensky found no troops to defend his government; he escaped, and the rest of his ministers fled or were captured.

On the afternoon of the coup, according to plan, Lenin arranged a meeting in Petrograd of delegates from soviets in other parts of the country. This "all-Russian" congress, controlled by the Bolsheviks, declared the provisional government at an end and assumed full authority. It approved decrees for an immediate peace and for the distribution of land to the peasants. It also elected a Council of People's Commissars to conduct the government, with Lenin at its head. These formalities could not conceal the fact that a small faction, shrewdly and boldly led, had moved into the deteriorating situation and had assumed command. Thus was established the world's first communist state under the first "dictatorship of the proletariat." Could such a government, facing enormous internal and external problems, keep itself in power? Its only organs of administration were the party, the soviets, and the council of commissars. The commissars established a secret police and authorized the raising of a Red Army. The war commissar, Trotsky, was to be its builder and leader.

The Communists' first test was not long in coming. Former tsarist generals organized and led counterrevolutionary forces ("Whites") in several regions of the country. They were joined by property-owners, reactionaries, liberals, and constitutionalists, and by anti-Bolshevik revolutionaries as well. In addition, Allied military contingents gave aid to the Whites against the Reds. (The Allies were trying to keep Russia in the war and desired to help strangle communism.) But after two years of frightful civil war, marked by mass terror on both sides, the hardened Communists emerged victorious.

The Red triumph owed something to the indomitable will of Lenin and to the military and organizing genius of Trotsky. And it owed something to the confusion and cleavages among the counterrevolutionary groups and their association with foreign powers. But in the last analysis it owed most to the attitude of the common people. Some of the commoners, to be sure, opposed the new regime. But the majority sensed that a White victory would probably lead to the withdrawal of land from the peasants and to a restoration of the old order of autocracy, caste, and privilege. Though they feared the Communists, they preferred them to the reactionaries. And popular support, in a fluid, guerrilla-type struggle, proved decisive. After 1920, with the bloody ordeal over, Lenin and his party sought to bring order out of chaos.

Building a socialist society

The task of pulling together a battle-torn country and at the same time overhauling its social structure was staggering. The ravages of civil strife had brought more distress than had the war against the Central Powers. During the fight with the counter-revolutionaries, the regime had resorted to crude expedients—later dignified by the term "war communism." These included the conscription of workers into labor battalions and forced deliveries of food by the peasants. Lenin was eager to start building socialism, but economic conditions were still so bad in 1921 that his plans had to be deferred.

Food was the primary problem; drought had made matters worse by bringing famine to large areas of the country. Something had to be done quickly to spur the efforts of farmers and to encourage them to market their produce. The New Economic Policy (NEP) aimed at doing just that. Launched in 1921, it removed restrictions on the ways in which land could be held and operated. (The peasants now possessed *all* the arable land; in accordance with the Soviet land-distribution decree of 1917, the farmers of each community had divided the landlord's property among themselves.) Now they were permitted to hire laborers and to sell or lease land as they saw fit. Forced deliveries of food were stopped, and the growers could market as they wished. The NEP was also extended to industry and commerce. While the state kept its grip on public utilities and other large industries (which had been nationalized in 1918), it encouraged private entrepreneurs to undertake new business ventures.

This temporary reversion to capitalistic methods brought about some recovery of production. But it fell short of the hopes and promises of the Communists. By 1928 output was at about the same level as it had been in 1913, and the momentum of the New Economic Policy seemed spent. Meanwhile, in 1924, the revered Lenin had died, and his former colleagues were maneuvering to succeed to his authority. Trotsky was the best known and probably the most talented. He, better than anyone else, expressed the impatience of the party with respect to economic development. In 1926 he openly criticized the NEP, complaining in particular about the new bourgeoisie and the affluent landowners (kulaks). He called for the collectivization of agriculture in the interest of greater efficiency, for the vigorous expansion of heavy industry, and for a master plan for balanced and rapid economic growth.

Trotsky, who also urged the promotion of Marxist revolution in countries beyond Russia, could not gain the support of the majority of the party. Joseph Stalin, who held the post of party secretary, had quietly and skillfully built a following for himself as Lenin's heir. He appealed to those who wanted to concentrate on the revolution inside Russia, to men who looked inward, rather than to the world. The party congress expelled Trotsky in 1927; he was first sent to Siberia and then deported. During his years of exile he attacked the Stalinist regime as a perversion of Marxist ideals and tried to develop the "true" international revolutionary movement. Branded a communist heretic ("deviationist"), Trotsky was assassinated in Mexico in 1940—probably by agents of Stalin.

With Trotsky and other rivals out of the way, Stalin in 1928 embarked on the building of "socialism in one country." He announced the party's initial Five-Year Plan, which concentrated on the collectivization of farming and the accelerated development of industry. State-controlled planning proved to be the most significant communist contribution to modern economics. It was the realization of a concept that had been worked out by Marx's collaborator, Friedrich Engels, many decades before. Engels had noted that planning was indispensable to the efficient operation of individual factories and industries. The logical and ultimate goal, he thought, was the creation of a unified and comprehensive *national* plan, embracing all parts of the economy. Though Soviet plans have encountered failures as well as successes, the idea behind them has taken hold, in greater or lesser degree, in many countries of the world. Since planning from above necessarily impinges upon individual freedom of decision and action, it is clearly a *collectivist* phenomenon.

Stalin's first plan ran into near-ruinous resistance. His agents toured the Russian countryside, joining private farms into large collectives of a thousand or more acres each. Strictly speaking, the farmers of each collective, as a "cooperative" unit, retained possession of the land, but the individual farmer no longer controlled any portion of land as his own. The poorer peasants usually submitted to the merging of lands without much grumbling; but the richer farmers, the kulaks, who possessed many acres, animals, and capital improvements, fought collectivization bitterly.

The government at last decided to coerce the recalcitrant landowners and brutally liquidated, as a class, some two million kulaks and their families. Most were shipped off to farm lands in Siberia; others were forced into submission; and some were killed. Many of them, in a final act of defiance and sabotage, destroyed their animals and implements before yielding. These heavy losses contributed to renewed food emergencies in the early 1930's. Nevertheless, the collective-farm program was driven through, and in the long run it increased agricultural efficiency and output. The collectives, properly managed, could make better use of machinery and scientific methods than could the single-owner farm. They were also in keeping with socialist theory: the collectives reduced private property and created a kind of agrarian proletariat.

While the painful transformation of the countryside began to assure a reasonably stable food supply, giant strides were being taken in industry. The rate of growth in the decade of the 1930's surpassed that of any Western nation during any ten-year period. Much of the new development was located east of the Urals, in central Asia, where it altered the life and culture of a vast region. It was the ability of socialist planning to achieve rapid modernization (without outside capital) that captured the attention and respect of other underdeveloped countries. The successes, of course, were trumpeted to Russian workers and peasants, who developed a fierce pride in Soviet material accomplishments. They found deep satisfaction in the feeling that "backward Russia" was at last catching up, scientifically and industrially, with the West. Access to education and the arts was also extended, and Soviet children enjoyed far greater opportunities than their fathers had.

The price of all this, in addition to the early years of bloodshed, expropriation, and privation, was the domination of life by the Communist regime. The Orthodox Church was stripped of its former influence, and other traditional faiths were barely tolerated. (Marxism became, in effect, the state religion.) There was no free press, free speech, free unions, or freedom of assembly. Political power remained a monopoly of the party, which was sustained by the feared secret police. In these respects, the atmosphere resembled that under the tsars. But the new government was more efficient, used modern tools of control, and succeeded in deadening virtually every nerve of resistance.

The major political institutions of the new state had been formed before Lenin's death. According to the constitution of 1923, the Union of Soviet Socialist Republics (U.S.S.R.) was a federal, democratic state. The former Russian Empire had embraced some fifty nationalities, and the Communists wrestled with the question of how to relate them to the new government. They wanted to preserve indigenous languages and customs, while guarding against separatist tendencies. Lenin decided upon the federal principle (borrowed from the United States) as the most suitable answer. Each major nationality became a constituent republic (or an autonomous region within a republic). By 1940 there were sixteen republics; by far the largest was the Russian Republic, which contained over half the U.S.S.R.'s total population of two hundred million. The Ukrainian Republic had about half as many inhabitants as the Russian Republic, and the White Russian (Byelorussian) about one-tenth. Most of the other republics were relatively small, with from one to six million inhabitants each.

Each republic had its own organs of administration for internal affairs. The highest body in the federal structure was the Supreme Soviet, which was composed of two chambers: a Council of Nationalities, representing the republics on a basis of numerical equality, and a Council of Union, representing them according to population. The Supreme Soviet held ultimate legal authority and enacted national legislation. However, this body met for only a short time each year, when it elected a Presidium, to which its functions were delegated. The Supreme Soviet also chose the Council of People's Commissars, whose members served as the executive heads of the federal government.

The real and pervading power of the U.S.S.R. lay in the Communist party, rather than in the agencies of the state. It was not a party in the liberal-democratic sense but a disciplined organization whose mission was to run the country. In fact, the constitution of 1923 authorized it to carry out this special role. Thus, while one did not have to be a party member to vote or stand for office in the Soviet Union, party representatives determined whose names would be placed on the ballot. Within the party itself, organization and authority followed the principle of "democratic centralism": officers and delegates to higher bodies were elected at succeeding levels—from the level of the smallest "cell," to intermediate bodies, to the All-Union Party Congress, which normally convened every other year. Though the congress was recognized as the highest party authority, actual control resided in its Central Committee, to which the congress delegated power. After the time of Lenin, power tended to gravitate more and more to the top. And once policy was decided upon there, it was the duty of every Communist to work for its fulfillment. Without the party organization and its carefully selected membership, the machinery of the state could never have transformed, as it did, a country so huge that it covers one-sixth of the land surface of the earth.

International communism

Although the Bolsheviks succeeded in "building socialism in one country," they were less successful in spreading socialism abroad. As Marxists, they believed in and worked for world revolution (as Trotsky had urged), but they made little headway in that direction. Marx himself had imparted to socialism its international character, regarding national states as narrow creations of the exploiting bourgeoisie. In 1864 he had organized the First (socialist) International. During the rest of the nineteenth century, however, the international socialist movement had proved feeble and faltering. It was troubled by internal dissension—ideological and personal—and, ultimately, by the divisiveness of rival patriotisms. The Second International, which succeeded the First, foundered in 1914. An association of the socialist parties of many nations, it fell to pieces during the war. Although a minority stuck to their convictions and refused to support their war governments, most reformist socialists supported the "patriotic fronts" of their homelands.

Lenin, who interpreted the war as a culmination of capitalist imperialism, scorned the reformist parties as bourgeois. In 1919 he invited dissident left-wing socialists throughout Europe to join the Soviet Communist party in forming a Third International. This, Lenin declared, would be a "pure" successor to Marx's original organization. Free of the reformist socialists, it pledged itself to worldwide revolution and the dictatorship of the proletariat.

Left-wing socialists of other countries, impressed by Lenin's stand and by the Russian Revolution itself, readily accepted Moscow's leadership. During the 1920's the methods of the Soviet party were adopted by the new association. Tight organization, centralized control, and the name "Communist" were imposed on the international body and on each of its constituent parties. As a result, sharp hostility arose between rival groups of Marxists outside the Soviet Union. The reformist socialists viewed with horror the violence employed by the Communists, especially under Stalin, and despised the dogmatism to which members of the Soviet party were subjected.

Having alienated the preponderant majority of Marxists outside the Soviet Union, the Third International (now known as the Comintern) had little chance of success. It was the reformist (democratic) socialists, strengthened by their break with revolutionary Marxism, who made impressive gains in the Western nations. After the failure of several communist-led uprisings after the war, the reformists helped advance collectivism by legal and democratic means in France, Germany, Scandinavia, and Britain. Despite the predictions of Marx and Lenin, proletarian revolution was clearly not imminent in the industrial countries of the West.

Meanwhile, communist parties, with Moscow's support and direction, were at work (usually underground) in fifty or more countries. Though they failed during the 1920's and 1930's to bring about successful revolutions, they served as an apparatus of foreign agitation and espionage for the U.S.S.R. The principal international influence of communism came not through the activities of the Comintern (which merely frightened the bourgeois capitals) but through the fact that the Soviet Union *existed* as a world power. Collectivists of all shades could point to it as a concrete alternative to liberalism and capitalism. Though they objected to certain characteristics of the Soviet Union, they could use it as a working example of state planning and cooperative social principles.

FASCIST COLLECTIVISM:
THE REVOLUTIONS IN ITALY
AND GERMANY

The fear of communism helped push several European nations into revolutionary collectivism of another sort. In Italy and Germany, the fascist revolutions sprang from two conditions: a social crisis that arose in the wake of the First World War and the inadequacy of liberal-democratic government. (Wherever governments effectively met their problems, they were able to resist subversion.) Moreover, the revolutions in Italy and Germany were propelled by violent nationalisms exacerbated by the frustrations of the war. Whereas the communists focused on *class* and interclass struggle, the fascists stressed the *nation* and international struggle.

There is another significant difference between the two kinds of collectivist revolution. The communist uprisings in Europe had been prefigured by decades of Marxist organization, propaganda, and threats of action. (Bolshevism was unwelcome but not unexpected.) Fascism, on the other hand, came as a surprise. As an explicit doctrine, it had no ideological founders, no authoritative books, and no forces in evidence before 1918.

Its explosive appearance can now be understood as a climax of potent ideas and passions, some open to view and some hidden, which were opposed to liberalism, democracy, and rationalism. Though revolutionary, fascism had a broad appeal to privileged groups as well as to ordinary people. Its militant nationalism aroused all patriots, and its support of class interests (including those of the military) satisfied men of property and power. This relation of fascism to national spirit, class, and power makes it a persisting (though latent) threat to capitalist democracies everywhere. Fascism, we should remember, was destroyed in its national strongholds only by external military force (in the Second World War); should internal crises recur in the industrialized countries of the West, existing regimes will find fascism a greater threat than communism. The relative ease with which fascists can take over a nation is demonstrated by the historical example of Italy.

Fascism in Italy: Mussolini

Italy after 1918 provided an ideal setting for the rise of fascism. Its parliamentary institutions, less than fifty years old, had never evoked much loyalty or enthusiasm from the people. Even before the war Italians often complained of graft and inefficiency in government, and the Italian legislature seemed incapable of dealing with the acute economic challenges of the 1920's. The majority of citizens, suffering from postwar inflation and unemployment, were thoroughly disillusioned with the nineteenth-century precepts of liberty, reason, and progress. Moreover, they were bitterly disappointed over Italy's role in the war. Though they finished on the side of the victors, their armies had experienced hardship, losses, and humiliating defeats. And at war's end, the Allies gave Italy only a portion of what they had promised as a reward for Italy's entering the conflict on the Allied side.

Many voters turned to the socialists in the hope that they would do something about the worsening economic situation. The elections of 1919 gave the Socialist party one-third of the seats in the national Chamber of Deputies; with the Catholic Popular party, the Socialists might have developed a viable program for the country. Mutual distrust between Catholics and Marxists made such cooperation impossible, however, and the socialist trade unions began to take direct action. In 1920 unionists occupied a number of factories and tried unsuccessfully to operate them. The workers soon withdrew, but their action had given the propertied classes a fright. In the following year the Socialist party split over the question of whether or not to join the communist Third International, thus losing what chance it might have had of becoming a dominant political force. It was upon this scene of confusion, discontent, and fear of bolshevism that Benito Mussolini presented himself as the national savior.

A shrewd propagandist and politician, Mussolini might be regarded as the Lenin of the Italian revolution. But, unlike the Russian hero, he did not find it necessary (as we shall see) to seize power by military force. Born into a socialist family, the son of a blacksmith, Mussolini was a man of the laboring class. He went to school to become a teacher but turned to journalism and radical agitation. In 1912 he secured the position of editor of the Socialist-party newspaper in Milan and gained a reputation as a dynamic radical leader. As a Marxist he had initially opposed war and had escaped military conscription by going to Switzerland; but in October 1914 he reversed himself by advocating Italian entrance into the war against Germany. For this he was expelled from the party and from his newspaper. Whereupon he founded a journal of his own, which he used to publicize his new convictions and to advance his political career.

Mussolini served in the war as a corporal until he was injured in an accident in 1917. Resuming the editorship of his paper, he tried to stir popular support for the flagging war effort. He turned wholly against socialism after the Russian Revolution, growing more and more militant and nationalistic. He opposed the floundering parliamentary regime of his own country; the legislature, he declared, was a congeries of special interests and selfish individuals who lacked the desire and the ability to serve the national interest. Mussolini, like many other veterans of the war, became enamored of violence as a way of life and as a means of securing change. He started organizing his followers into paramilitary, black-shirted units (*fasci di combattimento*—hence the name *fascist*). These units took it upon themselves to engage in street fighting with socialists and others they disliked, to smash opposing party and newspaper offices, and to assassinate some of the opposing leaders. The Black Shirts thus came to be regarded as the fighting arm of the new social movement.

Mussolini next organized his forces into a fascist political party, even though he had only contempt for the parliamentary party system. In the national election of 1921 he and his followers won thirty-five seats in the Chamber of Deputies. As their leader, Mussolini indulged in nationalist appeals and attacks on socialism. He began to gain widespread support, especially from the shopkeeper and white-collar class, but from the rich as well. Young people were strongly attracted by the uniforms, parades, mass rallies, and incitements to action. During 1922 his Black Shirts drove the legally elected socialist governments from Italy's northern industrial cities, and later that year a huge Fascist assembly in Naples called for a march on Rome.

The constitutional king of Italy, Victor Emmanuel III, was now faced with the prospect of black-shirted bullies converging upon his capital. His prime minister, unable to secure an effective parliamentary majority, urged him to declare martial law. But the king decided to do otherwise; he invited Mussolini to come from Milan and form a new ministry. The Fascists, camped near Rome, marched on the city while Mussolini arrived by sleeping car to take over the government.

The new leader, who preferred his party title of *Duce* (leader), was not long in consolidating his position. The parliamentary deputies, who had surrendered to the Black Shirt threat without a fight, quickly voted Mussolini dictatorial power for one year. During that time he altered the election law to allow the party that received the most votes (even though less than a majority) to take *two-thirds* of the seats in the chamber. A Fascist victory was thus assured (again, by "legal" means), and in the election of 1924 the party won about 70 per cent of the total national vote. Despite its unclear aims and its fondness for violence, the party received the support of many moderates who hoped that they could exercise a restraining influence upon the Duce. Within a few years he had virtually eliminated all opposition and had established a fascist state.

The collapse of Italian democracy was clearly due to its own failures, but Mussolini's triumph resulted from a variety of factors. Critical among them was the backing of the army and the great industrialists of the country. Mussolini did not have to create a new army (as did Lenin), though his Black Shirts became a permanent military corps. The regular army swung readily to his standard. Many of its high officers had had fascist sympathies from the beginning, and the Duce's glorification of militarism and his extravagant support of the army evoked their fervent loyalty.

The industrial leaders, for their part, had been uncertain about Mussolini at first. They approved his smashing of the Socialist party and the unions, but they were apprehensive about his intentions toward business. In 1925 the associated industrialists signed an agreement with the Duce. In return for their support of the Fascists, the industrialists were given a recognized status under the regime and the authority to regulate the nation's industrial affairs. The major employers in agriculture and commerce were later afforded similar status. Together with hand-picked labor and professional bodies, these regulatory groups comprised what Mussolini called the "corporate" state. In theory this state represented a harmonization of all the legitimate economic and social interests of the country. In fact the corporate state was an instrument of the dictator, through which he permitted the leading capitalists to administer the nation's economic life.

Mussolini completed his edifice of power by negotiating an alliance with the pope. Ever since the move for national unification had begun, in the middle of the nineteenth century, state and church in Italy had been at loggerheads. After lengthy and difficult discussions, Mussolini and Pius XI signed the Lateran Treaty and Concordat of 1929. By their terms, the pope gained sovereignty over the area of Vatican City, which includes St. Peter's Basilica and its immediate environs. The Church also secured a special position in the educational system of the country. In return, Pius gave his weighty support, and that of the Italian clergy and laity, to the Fascist state. Mussolini was himself a devout atheist, but like Napoleon before him he sealed his position as dictator by a bargain with the Church.

Though Fascism stressed action and was anti-intellectual in tone and character, it nevertheless possessed a distinctive ideology. In the beginning, as Mussolini himself admitted, it was largely a negative movement: *against* liberalism, democracy, rationalism, socialism, and pacifism. This negative feeling flowed from Mussolini's personal experience and that of countless other Europeans during and after the war. They had been cast adrift, disenchanted by false hopes of progress and happiness. Faceless in a mass society, they also felt alienated from *themselves*. The Fascists found an answer to this emptiness by invoking extreme nationalism. One could get an emotional lift by forgetting one's plight as a person and by giving oneself to something larger and grander—the nation. Mussolini and his associates developed this idea into the myth of the "organic state."

Drawing upon the political tradition of Edmund Burke, the Fascists asserted that the state is a living entity, transcending the individuals who compose it. Though personal liberty in Italy was under the control of state authority, they held that the individual's power was magnified through association with the body of citizens. This view contrasted sharply with liberal and Marxist conceptions of the individual and the state. "The state," declared Mussolini, "is a spiritual and moral fact in itself . . . ." It encompasses every sphere of life; it alone can "provide a solution to the dramatic contradictions of capitalism." And, as a living organism, the state must *expand* in order to manifest its vitality. This meant a continuous and disciplined will to power, which required forced unity within the nation, militarism, imperialism, and war.

The fascist myth repudiated the liberal reliance on reason and supplanted it with a mystical faith. Stridently anti-intellectual, it held that the "new order" would spring from the conviction of the "heart." Fascists therefore looked upon intellectuals in general as outmoded and suspicious characters, unduly concerned with their private cerebral aberrations. Yet most Italian intellectuals willingly cooperated with the Fascists, thus confirming Mussolini's view that they were lacking in integrity and courage. The few who opposed the regime were either silenced or forced into exile—the Fascist secret police struck down any active opposition.

Most ordinary Italians accepted Fascism with enthusiasm. The individual, who formerly felt alone and unneeded, enjoyed a new sense of "belonging"; this feeling of personal identification and participation was buttressed by the paternalistic measures of the regime and by various other devices. Many categories of workers wore distinctive uniforms, and elaborate public rituals were staged in the great squares of Rome and other cities. By 1930 Fascism appeared to have gained the firm support of most of the Italian people, as well as the admiration of many conservatives abroad.

The political institutions of Italy underwent a steady evolution under Mussolini. The corporate associations, which guided economic affairs, gradually became the basis for political representation in the national legislative body. But the true power in all spheres was the Fascist party, headed by the Duce. The party resembled, in many ways, the Communist party of the Soviet Union. It was the only legal party; it consisted of only a fraction of the total citizenry; and its members were carefully drawn from the ranks of elite youth organizations. Corresponding to the Communist Central Committee was the Grand Council of Fascism. Its members, however, were appointed directly by Mussolini, rather than being elected by a representative party body. They generally held high offices in the government in addition to their party positions; this connection, too, paralleled the interlocking of party and state that was characteristic of the Soviet system.

Fascist ideology offered an explicit justification for government by an elite. While the Marxists taught that the state and its office-holders would gradually disappear after the abolition of capitalism, the Fascists advanced the idea of *permanent* control by an elite guided by its natural leader. Special criteria were applied to the selection of party chieftains. They had to be men of rare intuitive power, capable of rising above self-interest and of sensing the character and aspirations of the nation. Their superiority, the Fascists boasted, derived mainly from action rather than thought: it was basic that they should have borne arms for the fatherland, taken part in the Fascist revolution, and participated in building the new order.

The Nazi compound of fascism and racism: Hitler

Just as the ideas of communism could not be confined to the U.S.S.R., so the fascist philosophy spread quickly across Europe—and the world. It won a substantial following in Austria, Portugal, Spain, and Argentina; but its world-shaking triumph was in Germany. Here fascism as a doctrine merged with deeper and older forces in the Teutonic tradition; here the fierce words of elitism and imperialism turned into deeds of genocide and devastating conquest.

Germany's humiliation at Versailles, coupled with severe economic problems after the war, prepared the ground for Adolph Hitler and his National Socialists (Nazis). The Germans adopted a democratic constitution in 1919, but its success was unlikely from the start. The new government was inexperienced, it suffered from the usual stresses and divisions within liberal states, and it was associated with the crushing military defeat. (In the closing days of the war, the German generals had shrewdly withdrawn and left the country's surrender to a liberal civilian government hastily appointed by the kaiser.) Unlike the parliamentary regime in Italy, the German Republic did not collapse in the years immediately after the war. But it failed to win the full allegiance of the people, and in little more than a decade it fell under the weight of its unsolved problems.

One of its problems was Adolph Hitler, who had been born of middle-class parents in a small Austrian town. Early in life he had become an ardent German nationalist, and, though he spent some of his formative years in Vienna, he found its cosmopolitan atmosphere especially distasteful. A moody drifter, he did not find a place for himself until the outbreak of the First World War. When he enlisted in the German army, Hitler experienced the comradeship and discipline of military life and exulted in his service to his adopted fatherland.

In 1919, embittered by the war's outcome, he went to the Bavarian capital of Munich, where large numbers of unemployed veterans and political dissidents had congregated. There he joined a budding group that called itself the National Socialist German Workers' Party and shortly became its leader (*Fuehrer*). This new role provided an outlet for Hitler's deep-seated animosities and aspirations. He attracted to the National Socialist banner others who shared with him an intense nationalistic feeling and a hatred for Jews. Among his supporters were Hermann Goering, a swaggering pilot-hero; Dr. Josef Goebbels, a university-trained journalist; and General Erich Ludendorff, an arch-conservative and Germany's chief military commander during the First World War.

Hitler committed himself fully to the life of politics and national "regeneration." Though he had but limited formal education, he had an intuitive grasp of the issues that were disturbing his fellow Germans. And, like Mussolini, he had a gift for demagogic speech. The early 1920's were a time of ferment and disorder in Germany;

street clashes and insurrections were commonplace. In 1923 Hitler led an attempted coup (*putsch*) against the Bavarian state government. It was stopped in the streets of Munich by police fire, and the Nazi party seemed to be crushed by subsequent government reprisals. Hitler was imprisoned for nearly a year, during which time he wrote *Mein Kampf* (*My Struggle*), the statement of his life and creed. Upon his release from prison, he refounded the party. For a while it made little headway, but financial support from Rhenish industrialists enabled Hitler to purchase newspapers and periodicals through which he could spread Nazi propaganda.

The international economic crisis of 1930, a product of the dislocations stemming from the World War, gave the German revolutionary parties their great opportunity. Rising numbers of unemployed workers were looking desperately for a way out. Many of them found "jobs" as brown-shirted Nazi storm troopers, similar to Mussolini's Black Shirts. The party gained electoral strength steadily during the years of economic hardship. And when at one point it ran out of funds, representatives of German industry came to the rescue. In January 1933 Hitler received from them a promise to pay the wages of his storm troopers and the party's debts. In return the Fuehrer agreed to leave big business alone. The German industrialists (like those of Italy) thus preserved what they viewed as a "bulwark against communism" and insured themselves against the event of a Nazi victory in the elections.

A few weeks later Hitler succeeded in persuading the aged president of the republic, Paul von Hindenburg, to appoint him head of the government (chancellor). The Nazis had the largest number of elected delegates in the legislature (Reichstag), but they still did not have a majority. However, when the Reichstag building was mysteriously burned, Hitler used the event to declare a suspension of constitutional guarantees. He banned the Communist party and had its leaders imprisoned; the Social Democrats were the only opposition party left. The Nazis, with the support of collaborating parties, then passed the Enabling Act of March 1933, a crucial measure that gave the government power to rule by decree for a four-year period.

Soon afterward Hitler outlawed all parties save his own, following the Fascist example; by mid-1933 his political opponents were either in jail or in exile. A year later, after Hindenburg's death, he assumed the office of president in addition to that of chancellor. This act was ratified in a vote of overwhelming approval by the German electorate. Thus, the paranoiac Austrian became the sole ruler of one of the most educated and civilized nations of the world.

He proceeded, with the cooperation of the army and leading industrialists, to marshal the country's manpower and resources. Hitler's aim was to make Germany the most powerful nation in Europe and, ultimately, the world.

Nazism had much in common with Italian fascism. Both rested on the myth of the organic state, the importance of struggle and will, the glorification of militarism, an insistence on authority and discipline, rule by an elite, and a mystic faith in the leader. But in Germany there were added elements of violent racism, neoromanticism, and nihilism. The first two were largely out of the nineteenth century; the last was mainly an excrescence of the war and took the form, essentially, of a mindless lust for power.

Like the Fascists, the Nazis had contempt for reason and for intellectuals. Hitler saluted the values of the German peasantry and asserted that those values were the foundation of Nazi ideology. Yet under Hitler the country became increasingly industrialized and urbanized. Paradoxically, the Nazis overcame the disruptive reality of technological change by manufacturing a belief in the myths of bucolic purity and racial superiority. Millions became converts to the Nazi faith during the 1930's. It suited the traditional romantic yearnings of the Germans, offered a total view of life in place of fragmentation and emptiness, and appealed strongly to national and racial pride. Finally, it released the urge to violence. Nazism led, by successive steps, to the inhuman treatment of the Jews, to the infamous death camps, and to the catastrophes of the Second World War.

DEMOCRATIC COLLECTIVISM:
EVOLUTION OF THE WELFARE STATES

While collectivist societies built on authoritarian lines were taking shape in Germany, Italy, and the U.S.S.R., the shift from liberalism was proceeding in a different manner in the democratic countries of the West. In the Scandinavian lands, France, Great Britain, and the United States, the major prewar social institutions appeared to hold firm. But none was secure from the disturbances unleashed by the war or from the ceaseless march of science and technology.

In response to these forces, the governments in the West became more and more interventionist in domestic affairs. The tension between democracy and liberalism has already been noted (pp. 402–03); in the decades following the war, democratic government penetrated steadily into "private" preserves. As its authority expanded, the democratic state left behind many of the precepts and practices of liberalism. It created, though without deliberate intent, a *democratic collectivism*. Some called this "creeping socialism," but a more appropriate term is "welfare state."

A European example: Britain

Events in Britain after the war illustrate the evolution of a welfare state. This country had been identified, more than any other, with the historic liberal spirit and principles. John Locke and J. S. Mill were among a host of Englishmen who had developed and propagated liberal ideas both at home and abroad. Britain in the nineteenth century had stood as the citadel of capitalism and free trade; furthermore, her people enjoyed a singular tradition of stability. Prior to 1914 one would hardly have expected this nation to move toward any form of collectivism.

Yet, as we have seen, even before the war the British had traveled a substantial distance away from liberalism. Trade unions had become a force between the individual worker and his employer; Parliament had passed numerous laws regulating industrial conditions. By 1914 the foundations had also been laid for compulsory national insurance, which protected workers against the costs of accident, sickness, unemployment, and old age. The revenues to support such programs were to be derived in large measure from progressive income taxes.

The First World War brought in its train new problems that demanded further action by the government. During the war itself, impositions and regulations were viewed as a matter of necessity; the experience no doubt made it easier for the British to accept growing state intervention in the postwar period. Though England had suffered severe losses of manpower and wealth during the struggle against Germany, her most pressing problem at war's end was to recover her financial and trading position in the world. British investments overseas had been largely liquidated, and many British markets had been taken over by American and Japanese firms.

It is a truism that Britain must "export or die," and both statesmen and industrialists tried to improve the island's competitive position. One obstacle to this effort was Britain's obsolescent industrial plant. Another was organized labor: the unions, accustomed to abnormal wages during the war, would not agree to lower wages afterward. For these principal reasons Britain failed to regain the lost markets, and after 1921 the country fell into a chronic depression that lasted until the Second World War. Unemployment and privation became a way of life for several million Britishers.

Organized labor grew into a powerful force in British politics during the 1920's. The unions, in combination with moderate socialists, had formed the Labour party in 1892. By 1924 it had the largest number of seats in Parliament and stood as a challenge to the dominant Conservative party. Labor discovered, however, that its exercise of political power did not guarantee a better living for workers or a solution to the country's economic dilemma. The domestic policies of Labour governments did not, in fact, depart sharply from those of Conservative governments. Both parties conceded that they could not rely on "automatic" economic forces to produce recovery. The protection and advancement of the public well-being demanded continuing and widening intervention by the state.

As the British depression grew deeper during the early 1930's, laws were passed that ended the traditional policy of free trade. Tariffs were enacted, especially to guard the home market against imports from the United States. (This action was explained as a countermeasure against high tariffs in America.) The government also abandoned the gold standard (1931) and devalued the pound sterling in terms of other currencies. The latter step was taken as a means of facilitating British exports, but it was shortly negated by corresponding devaluations of other national currencies in capitals around the world. When key industries, like coal, proved unable to compete, they were voted subsidies by Parliament. Extensive plans were also laid by the government for the general development of British industry and agriculture.

The American experience: Roosevelt

Democratic governments on the Continent were forced to adopt measures similar to those adopted in Britain. But the most sweeping movement toward the welfare state took place in the United States, which had become, as a consequence of the First World War, the leading capitalist country of the world. During the 1920's, the nation recoiled from its military adventure overseas and from the domestic controls imposed during the mobilization for war. It was the decade of "normalcy," a word coined by the amiable and easygoing President Warren Harding. Though laissez faire was more of a shibboleth than a reality, the power of big business and high finance was seldom checked by the ruling Republican party.

Normalcy, however, soon proved anything but normal, and the government of the United States, during the 1930's, was pushed into the kind of intervention that had become characteristic of other Western democracies. The economic boom of the postwar years had brought temporary prosperity to the nation, but the boom was driven by artificial and unstable forces. In the spectacular stock-market crash of 1929, many of the inflated values were wiped out within a few hours. More serious, the crash signaled the onslaught of the Great Depression—a long and bitter experience for millions of Americans. During that ordeal they discovered the underlying shortcomings and helplessness of the "free" economy.

President Herbert Hoover, the Republican leader, was in office when the crash came. A competent administrator and a well-meaning humanitarian, Hoover never understood that a system and an epoch had ended. Although he approved limited government measures to assist certain financial institutions and railroads, he held stubbornly to the view that business in general would recover by itself. But the facts of the situation did not correspond to Hoover's view. While he was telling an apprehensive public, repeatedly, that recovery was "around the corner," production and employment spiraled downward. They struck bottom during the winter of 1932–33. By then, physical production had fallen nearly 40 per cent from the 1929 level; wages were down by the same proportion; farm income was reduced to half. Construction had virtually ceased, and about fifteen million men were out of work.

Depressions were by no means a new phenomenon in capitalist countries. The ups and downs of the business cycle had been carefully studied if little comprehended. This depression, however, was the worst in history, and there was reason to believe that "normal" recovery forces were unlikely to prove effectual. This was due to several factors: the rigidity of price and wage structures, rapid technological advances in industry (which displaced workers), and the near-hopeless situation of farmers, who were producing for a depressed and uncontrollable world market. Given enough time, some kind of balance in the economy would no doubt have emerged through "natural" forces. But the economy had grown so complex and interdependent that these forces would have been too slow. So many men (and families) would have been crushed in the process that the strain on the social system would have proved intolerable.

In the presidential election of 1932 the American people turned to Franklin D. Roosevelt, who promised that he would *act* in the crisis—that he would lead the federal government in an attack on the depression as if it were an attack on a physical enemy. The temper of the country was such that, had he not promised to act, more radical leaders might well have gained a mass following. After an overwhelming electoral victory for the Democrats, Roosevelt launched the first Hundred Days of his "New Deal" program. This program marked an advance from the traditional policy of limited government interference to one of positive acceptance by the government of responsibility for the general welfare.

The New Deal was new only to a degree, since it built on the ideas and policies of earlier progressives as well as on the wartime experience of industrial mobilization. But Roosevelt realized that the challenges were now vastly greater in scope and that they demanded a new boldness. He proposed remedies in a frankly experimental and pragmatic fashion, with no developed ideology. The New Deal was not anticapitalist; on the contrary, it aimed at *preserving* and *strengthening* the capitalist system. Recognizing the interdependence of social and economic forces, the New Dealers turned their attention to all aspects of national life: finance, agriculture, industry, labor, foreign trade, natural resources, public works, education, and personal security.

Roosevelt categorized his measures under the headings of relief, recovery, and reform. Those measures were too numerous and extensive to describe here. The significant thing is that most of the programs *worked,* and they placed the government in a new and permanent relation to the social and economic life of the country. Though FDR was castigated by his opponents as a devil and a "traitor to his class," he was really an agent of irresistible (and irreversible) change.

The democratic welfare state, in America as in Europe, has not lost sight of the individual. In a technological, mass society, it is simply doing what must be done if the individual is to be adequately protected and served. In certain respects, Western men have less freedom now than they did in the nineteenth century. On the other hand, the affluence and economic security made possible by advances in technology and social organization offer them new dimensions of freedom—in leisure, travel, education, the arts, entertainment, and material consumption.

Man's hope for a better life through technology is threatened by his construction of ever more deadly weapons. Some observers thought that the lesson of the First World War would lead to a scrapping of the "war system" for settling international differences. Instead, the war unleashed more virulent forces of nationalism and hatred that led to another and more terrible struggle.

THE SECOND WORLD WAR
AND ITS LEGACY

When President Woodrow Wilson led the United States into the European conflict in 1917, he had declared that it was a "war to end war." As the costly struggle neared its close, Wilson launched a determined effort to make his promise come true. He urged the Allies to accept his peace program (the Fourteen Points), which included the principles of national self-determination and "open covenants, openly arrived at." The crowning edifice of his proposed peace was a formal association of nations to guarantee the "political independence and territorial integrity" of all states and thus put an end to international anarchy. After the defeat of the Central Powers, Wilson himself journeyed to Paris to take part in the settlement. At his special insistence the covenant of the League of Nations was written into the Treaty of Versailles in 1919.

The failure of the League of Nations

Most of the European statesmen at Paris, still nationalists to the core, had little enthusiasm for the League. They approved it largely to please Wilson, who, in turn, made concessions on other important issues. To Wilson, the League was the redeeming feature of a treaty that in many respects seemed harsh and unjust to the defeated peoples. He believed earnestly that the League, once established, could correct such injustices and lay the foundation for a warless world. Ironically, the Treaty of Versailles, including the

League covenant, was later ratified by all the Allied governments *except* the United States. Its defeat in the Senate was due to a combination of rigid nationalism, disillusionment with the late "crusade" in Europe, and partisan politics.

Whatever chance the League may have had to fulfill its high purpose was crippled by America's failure to approve and join it. Both Germany and the Soviet Union were excluded from membership for a number of years; hence, the organization was far from being universal. Nevertheless it had some staunch advocates, and it carried on in the hope that the United States would one day become a member. During the boom of the twenties, however, most Americans became absorbed in making money and showed a declining concern for the problems of the world. The miseries of the depression turned them even more inward. By 1933 the United States was clearly committed to an independent course in foreign affairs.

The League assumed many useful international functions, including the conduct of plebiscites in disputed territories, the repatriation of war prisoners, and the provision of aid for refugees. Through subsidiary agencies and commissions it also facilitated the exchange of scientific and cultural information and the collection of social and economic statistics. Its sponsorship of disarmament conferences proved completely fruitless, for the participating nations viewed proposals for arms reduction as another aspect of the continuing power struggle.

The primary purpose of the League, as conceived by Wilson, was to *prevent war*. The covenant required that member states submit their disputes to arbitration and, if that failed, to the Council of the League. The council, which consisted of representatives of the principal countries, could, by unanimous vote only, call for economic or military action by member states against any aggressor state. The principle underlying this provision was that of "collective security." This was a simple idea, one that Wilson fervently believed in. It held that if all "peace-loving" countries acted together (collectively) against any violator of the peace, the violator would be overwhelmingly defeated. Potential aggressors, once convinced that collective action against them was a certainty, would refrain from initiating acts of conquest.

Collective security might have worked if the leading powers (including the United States) had put an overriding priority on restraining aggressors. Unfortunately, the idea was never taken seriously in the major capitals. In and out of the League, each nation continued to pursue its own particular aims and refused to act except where its own immediate interest seemed to be threatened.

Furthermore, a number of powers (notably Japan, Italy, and Germany) were conniving to support one another's seizure of territory. The balance between countries wishing to preserve territorial boundaries and those prepared to use force to break them proved to be too even for the collective-security idea to succeed.

Japan was the first country to test the will of the League's members. In 1931 her soldiers occupied Manchuria, driving out the legitimate Chinese authorities. Responding to China's appeal, the League sent an investigating commission to Manchuria, which concluded in 1932 that Japan was guilty of aggression and recommended appropriate action. But the Council of the League could not agree on sanctions. Britain, with extensive interests in the Far East, was reluctant to offend the Japanese, who had a powerful Pacific fleet. Unable to secure a commitment of assistance from the United States should sanctions lead to war with Japan, the British decided that nothing should be done. And Britain was the most influential member of the League and its council.

The exultant militarists in Tokyo, having successfully defied the League, strengthened their grip on Japanese politics and prepared for more ambitious conquests. Had the League and the United States joined in imposing sanctions on Japan, that island nation would have been compelled to back down. Instead, the League's failure encouraged aggressors in both Asia and Europe. Hardly more than a decade after the First World War, the Wilsonian hope for collective security lay shattered. The powers were already on the road to the Second World War.

Fascist conquests and defeat

Benito Mussolini viewed the League's failure with special satisfaction. In keeping with the fascist ideology of militarism and imperialism, he was seeking to expand Italian control in Africa. During the 1920's he had attempted by negotiation to gain a foothold in Ethiopia. But the Ethiopian emperor, Haile Selassie, had stubbornly refused. Mussolini, after observing the impotence of the League, decided to move by force of arms. He first secured his rear by an agreement with France in 1935 and then sent troops and planes to Ethiopia.

Selassie's tribesmen, armed with primitive weapons, could not hold out against the artillery and aerial bombardment of the Italians. Within a year Ethiopia was defeated and formally annexed to Italy. In this affair, Britain had been more deeply aroused than in the case of Manchuria; she had persuaded the Council of the League to call for economic sanctions against Italy, the declared aggressor.

The measure was only partially effective, however, and Mussolini continued to receive supplies from Germany. Italy resigned from the League in 1936; Japan and Germany had already pulled out.

By now it was becoming clear that these three nations were linked in a plan of wide-ranging conquest. The "Rome-Berlin axis," joining the two fascist states of Europe, was formalized in 1936. In the following year the militaristic and quasi-fascist government of Japan joined Germany and Italy in signing an Anti-Comintern Pact. The pact was intended, ostensibly, to check the spread of communism; actually, it constituted a general defensive-offensive military alliance. And the strongest member of the alliance, Germany, was feverishly preparing to strike. In 1935 Adolph Hitler had announced his decision, in defiance of the Treaty of Versailles, to rearm Germany. His army (Reichswehr) and air force (Luftwaffe) were growing steadily in strength. Though he proceeded cautiously at first, Hitler continued to violate the 1919 settlement. His troops crossed into Austria in 1938, and the Fuehrer announced the incorporation of that state into the new German Empire (the Third Reich).

Britain and France were thoroughly alarmed by this time, but popular antiwar sentiment and political incompetence kept them from responding effectively to the German threat. The Soviet Union seemed to be the only power that could check Hitler. France had concluded a defensive alliance with the Soviets in 1935, but the agreement proved short lived.

One reason for the collapse of the Franco-Soviet alliance was the failure of France and England to honor their treaty obligations to defend Czechoslovakia. At Munich, in September 1938, the two Western powers accepted Hitler's demand for a portion of Czech territory. Joseph Stalin's suspicions of the West were aggravated by this act of appeasement. The Soviet dictator feared (rightly) that some British diplomats were secretly hoping that Hitler would smash eastward into the Soviet Ukraine, thus locking in mortal combat the two great land powers of Europe. Such a struggle could serve the British interest by reducing or eliminating both the Nazi and the Soviet threats to the West. Stalin chose to forestall a German invasion by working out a deal with Hitler: the Nazi-Soviet Nonaggression Pact of 1939 came as a shock to British and French diplomats. It provided, in return for mutual pledges of nonaggression (and territorial concessions to the Soviet Union), that Stalin would not interfere with Hitler's next territorial seizure.

The ink was hardly dry on the pact when the Nazis, without warning, pounced on Poland on September 1, 1939. In a desperate effort to deter or contain Hitler, the British and French had previously given their pledge of assistance to the Poles. This time they stood by their word and declared war on Germany. The Second World War was under way. Poland was crushed militarily within a week as the Germans displayed new tactics of mobile warfare. Fast armored columns, supported by aircraft and paratroops, paralyzed and enveloped the opposing armed forces. So successful were these tactics that the Germans appeared to be invincible.

In 1940 France fell before the German blitzkrieg, and Italy formally joined the war. Hitler, ignoring his nonaggression pact with Stalin, savagely attacked the Soviet Union in 1941. In Russia and elsewhere in eastern Europe the Germans not only sought swift military victories; they launched a ruthless program of exterminating all Jews and a portion of the Slavic peoples, whom they regarded as racially inferior (*Untermenschen*). Soon after the German attack began, pursuing their own conquests in Asia, the Japanese struck the United States Pacific fleet at Pearl Harbor. By 1942 all the major powers were involved in war by land, sea, and air.

The fascist forces, having seized the initiative, scored astonishing gains at first. But the combined resources of their opponents were vastly superior, and in the end the Allies won unconditional victory. Soviet manpower and American airpower were among the decisive factors. In the last year of the war, British and American bombers turned more and more to attacks on the enemy civilian population. (The Allies were not the first to bomb cities, but they did so now on an unprecedented scale.) Mass raids on Hamburg and Dresden were among the deepest horrors of the war, and virtually every Japanese city was reduced to ashes by giant bombers.

The new kind of war was demonstrated most dramatically by the dropping of the first atomic bombs on Hiroshima and Nagasaki, which had been spared for this special purpose. Each of the two bombs (small in power by present-day standards) incinerated many thousands of men, women, and children. These ingenious devices of mass killing hastened the "total" victory of the Allies in 1945; more significantly and ominously, they marked a decisive turn in the evolution of all-out warfare—from attacks aimed primarily against combatant forces to attacks upon the centers of human habitation.

The emergence of new power balances and the Cold War

At the end of the war, Japan was stripped of empire, Germany was divided, and fascism was destroyed in the defeated countries. The states of western Europe, which a generation before had dominated global affairs, had now fallen to the rank of secondary powers. The Soviet Union, though it had suffered enormous losses and dam-

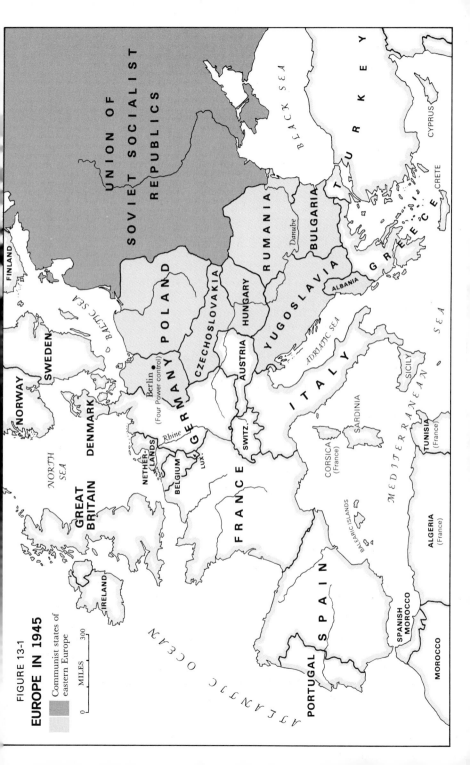

FIGURE 13-1
EUROPE IN 1945

Communist states of
eastern Europe

MILES
0   300

age from the Nazi invasion, extended its political control in both Asia and Europe (FIG. *13-1*). Untouched at home by the ravages of battle, the United States emerged as the predominant military and economic power of the world.

President Franklin Roosevelt, the principal leader of the Allied coalition, had anticipated this new distribution of power. During the war he had joined in top-level conferences with the redoubtable British leader Winston Churchill and with the wily Stalin. By working in unity, despite grave differences and difficulties, the Big Three had succeeded in defeating their common enemies. Roosevelt hoped that when the war was over the major powers could continue to cooperate for peace as they had cooperated for victory. The key to this accomplishment, he thought, was American-Soviet understanding.

It was in part to develop such understanding and cooperation that Roosevelt proposed a new international organization, the United Nations. Its general outlines were endorsed by the Big Three at the Yalta Conference (1944), and the organization came into being formally a few months after Roosevelt's death in 1945. In planning it, Roosevelt had sought to avoid what he regarded as the "visionary" aims of his predecessor, Wilson.

Though the United Nations was similar in structure to the defunct League of Nations, it was not based on the obsolete principle of collective security. Nor was it conceived as a world government or anything approaching it. The organization, thought Roosevelt, might be a *step* in that direction, but its immediate function was to serve as an instrument that would enable the two "super-powers" (the U.S. and the U.S.S.R.) to maintain world order. This was a practical, short-range objective that might have been achieved had Roosevelt lived.

Within a few months of the President's death a chill descended on East-West relations; as this chill deepened into the "Cold War," hopes for cooperation evaporated. The reasons for the deterioration in relations have been acrimoniously debated by statesmen and scholars. On the Soviet side there was fear and suspicion of the Western powers, tracing back to their intervention in Russia after the Bolshevik Revolution (p. 513). During the struggle against Hitler the Soviet leaders had developed a cautious trust in Roosevelt, but they had little faith in the word or intentions of Churchill. Shortly after Roosevelt died, Churchill had proposed to the new American President, Harry Truman, that crucial understandings about Allied occupation zones for Germany be repudiated by the Western powers. Truman turned down the proposal but soon joined with the British in converting the Western occupation zones into an independent German state (the Federal Republic). As it became clear that the United States had decided to restore and rearm West Germany (contrary to the wartime agreements), Stalin displayed more determination than ever to keep under communist control the countries that his troops had "liberated."

On the Western side there persisted a deep-seated fear of communist expansion. This fear also traced back to 1917, but now it was exacerbated by the presence of Soviet power in central and eastern Europe. Churchill and Truman protested vainly against Stalin's failure to provide free elections (as he once had promised) in Poland, Rumania, Bulgaria, and Hungary. Their apprehensions rose when communist-assisted guerrilla fighters threatened the Western-oriented government of Greece in 1947. President Truman responded vigorously by dispatching military and economic aid to Athens. More important, he pronounced a general American policy of communist "containment," which pledged military assistance to *any* regime threatened by "armed minorities or by outside pressure." In support of this policy, he launched a multi-billion-dollar program of economic aid to western Europe (the Marshall Plan). In 1949 Truman concluded a twelve-nation military alliance (the North Atlantic Treaty Organization) for unified defense against the presumed Soviet threat.

Meanwhile Churchill added his voice to those of some American leaders who believed that Stalin desired to march across western Europe. (As early as 1946 Churchill had spoken of the "Iron Curtain" and had urged the United States and Britain to unite their forces against the Russian "menace.") Actually there is no evidence that the Russians were planning a military attack, and the circumstances strongly suggest that they were not. The Soviet people and leaders were sick of war and were so absorbed in rebuilding their battered homeland that they were hardly in a position to undertake such a struggle. Stalin, moreover, was well aware that Truman had sole possession of the deadly A-bomb and that he had demonstrated (at Hiroshima) his readiness to use it.

The American nuclear monopoly was the most decisive single fact in world politics after the war. It caused anguish in Moscow, where leaders feared that some American generals might gain backing for a "preventive" war against Russia. There is no evidence to sustain their fears, but Soviet scientists nevertheless worked feverishly to build a bomb of their own as a counter to the American weapon. This they succeeded in doing in 1949, much to the consternation of scientists and political leaders in the United States.

Soon it became evident that the Russians were a match for the Americans in sophisticated technical undertakings. When the United States exploded its first hydrogen (fusion) device in 1952, the government revealed that the energy released was hundreds of times greater than that of the Hiroshima (fission) bomb. Within a year the Soviets announced the explosion of their own hydrogen bomb, and in 1957 they became first in space by rocketing *Sputnik* into orbit around the earth. In a real sense, these Soviet demonstrations lent a degree of stability to the international situation. With each side in the Cold War capable of destroying the other (with aircraft or intercontinental missiles), a new kind of balance was struck—albeit a "balance of terror."

No balance, however, could last for long, because the power alignments and the nature of power itself were continually changing. The bi-polar world of American and Soviet power began to dissolve soon after it appeared. Stalin died in 1953, and his place in Russia was taken by Nikita Khrushchev, who unfolded a policy of internal relaxation and "peaceful coexistence" among states. Marshal Tito of Yugoslavia, though a communist, exerted leadership that was increasingly independent of Moscow. After an anti-Soviet uprising in Hungary in 1956, all the Soviet "satellite" states displayed greater freedom of action.

Most weighty in the change within the communist bloc has been the growing power of China. In 1949 Mao Tze-tung led the Chinese party to victory over Chiang Kai-shek's Nationalists, bringing the most populous country on earth under the Red banner. After a period of dependency on Russian aid, the Chinese began to regard Mao as the principal ideologist of Marxism and Peking as the true capital of proletarian revolution. Communism, once viewed as a "monolithic" force, has thus become a loose alliance of states that give priority to their *national* identities and interests. As nationalism proved stronger than liberalism in the nineteenth century, so it has countered communism in the twentieth.

The Atlantic alliance (NATO) has been similarly transformed, due in large measure to the swift recovery of western Europe (aided by the creation of the Common Market). While the western European nations have become reconciled to relatively minor roles in the world, they have felt a mounting urge to reassert their traditional character and independence. France in particular, under the guidance of President Charles de Gaulle, has experienced an economic, political, and cultural resurgence. French leaders desire to reduce or eliminate the pervading influence that American statesmen, generals, and businessmen have exerted in Europe since the war, and de Gaulle has acted openly against the dominant role of the United States in NATO. By 1963 he had established, independently, a French nuclear striking force, and in 1966 he ordered United States military forces and bases out of France. He has also turned a cold shoulder on Britain, whom he regards as a partner of America in Europe.

A contributing factor in Europe's mounting spirit of independence has been the virtual disappearance of the earlier fear of Russia. The American-Soviet "balance of terror" cast a protective cloak over Europe, and Kremlin policy after Stalin's death has given no indication of a desire for military adventure. Britain, whose scientists shared atomic secrets with the United States during the Second World War, developed its own nuclear force in the late 1950's. The subsequent spread of atomic weapons to France and to China (1965) further contributed to the equalizing of military strength and the consequent diminution of single-power influence.

All treaty organizations, blocs, and alliances have become, in consequence, less solid and predictable. The United Nations remains an important forum of political discussion and debate; but it, too, is no longer taken seriously as a "collective" power. The international scene is now characterized by growing national independence and a wide spectrum of socio-political systems. There is no evidence of a trend toward a unitary world or even a world police force. Each nation desires to go its own way, without interference in its internal affairs by any other power. This development appears to be a regression to the kind of international anarchy that prevailed before the First World War. A new world war, of incomparably greater horror, can be avoided only if the peoples and leaders of the world break decisively with traditional ways of conducting international relations.

THE GLOBAL SWEEP OF NATIONALISM AND MODERNIZATION

The trend toward collectivism, either through revolution or evolution, was accelerated during and after the Second World War. Total war, as waged by the main combatants, called for the total organization of the human and nonhuman resources of each country. When the fighting stopped, some of these controls were relaxed in the democratic welfare states. But the collectivist patterns persisted and were borrowed by the defeated countries after their own social systems were dismantled. The most dramatic expansion of collectivism, revolutionary style, occurred in Asia, when communism, after long and devastating wars, triumphed on the mainland of China (1949).

All of Asia and Africa—the "underdeveloped world"—has continued in ferment. The old system of colonialism is finished, and the emerging nations, almost without exception, have come under the rule of collectivist regimes. This development is tied closely to the rising spirit of nationalism and the spreading passion for modernization.

The liquidation of colonialism

Even before the end of the Second World War, nationalist leaders in the various colonies were planning for independence. As we saw in Chapter Twelve, the original impact of European intruders upon native cultures had been shattering and traumatic. Within a few decades after 1870, millions of people and millions of square miles had fallen under Western control. The natives had reacted in awe, confusion, and hatred, but they were pretty well convinced that the white man could not be driven out.

The Second World War, even more than the First, dissipated their feelings of apathy and despair. Though the British and French made free use of colonial troops and resources during the war, native leaders were mightily impressed by the defeats that the Western powers suffered. Nations under French rule took heart when France collapsed before the German attack in 1940; all of Asia was surprised when British and Dutch troops succumbed to the Japanese in 1942. The bluff and mystique, not to mention the substance, of white imperial power had been stripped away before the war ended. Between 1945 and 1960 most of the peoples of Asia and Africa gained their independence. The swiftness of European colonial acquisition was more than matched by the swiftness of its dissolution.

The spurt to independence outran the hopes of many native leaders, not to mention the fears of the colonial powers. Men like Mahatma Gandhi (India), Achmed Sukarno (Indonesia), and Kwame Nkrumah (Ghana) found that the latent force of nationalism in their countries, once unleashed, was irresistible. It is not surprising that the new spirit of native pride has sometimes been carried to excess. Though newly independent peoples have forgotten and forgiven much of the colonial past, they retain a residue of bitterness toward their former masters that can readily be kindled. And since the masters have been of the white race, this underlying antagonism carries with it racial overtones.

For their part, Western political leaders have sought to salvage what they could from the colonial wreckage. The British appear to have taken the most realistic and enlightened view. For many decades, the component parts of the traditional British Empire had been evolving into a Commonwealth of Nations. Self-governing countries, like Canada and Australia, were sovereign states but linked in friendship and cooperation with Britain. Recognizing that they could no longer play the role of masters, Britain's leaders sought to transform once subject peoples into friendly allies. They hoped thereby to retain a measure of political influence around the globe and to benefit from established ties of commerce and culture. In keeping with such aims, the British offered leadership training to a selected few in the colonies. These natives, usually educated in Britain, have aided in the transition of their homelands to independence and to Commonwealth association.

The liberation of India from British rule was the largest single step in the liquidation of colonialism. The subcontinent, with its four hundred million people, had been granted limited autonomy before the Second World War. This had not satisfied Indian nationalists, however, and at the war's end they insisted on full independence. Winston Churchill, representing British conservatives and old-fashioned imperialists, would have delayed the granting of independence. But the Labour party, which came to power in 1945, favored a clean break with the colonial past. The chief obstacle arose from the demand by Moslem leaders in India for a state separate from the Hindu majority. At last, in the hope of avoiding widespread violence, the British agreed (1947) to partition the colony into two successor states. The larger, mainly Hindu, portion of the subcontinent took the name of India; the smaller, mainly Moslem, portion was called Pakistan. Both, by their own action, became members of the Commonwealth.

Britain followed a similar liberation policy with respect to Ceylon, Burma, and Malaya. In Africa, too, the British took appropriate steps to prepare their colonies for independence. Acting swiftly, they ended their treaty rights in Egypt in 1954 and granted independence to the Gold Coast (Ghana) in 1957. Within a brief time most of Britain's remaining African colonies made the transition to membership in the Commonwealth (and the United Nations). With few exceptions, these new states are now being governed by representatives of their black majorities.

France took a different tack in dealing with its colonies by offering to absorb them into a "French Union," which would integrate overseas territories with metropolitan France. This approach proved a failure; it appealed only to a limited number of natives who had been educated in French schools and who had come to respect and admire French culture. But Charles de Gaulle, who had led the "Free French" movement during the war, had promised the colonies that assisted him a free choice of status after peace was restored. They chose independence, though most of them have affiliated themselves with the French Community, an association resembling the British Commonwealth.

In two areas—Algeria and Indo-China—the French resorted to war in a vain attempt to hold power. After brutal fighting and heavy losses, they were at last compelled to withdraw from both. Algeria became independent in 1962. Portions of Indo-China—Laos and Cambodia—won their independence in 1954, but the remainder —Viet Nam—was partitioned by an international conference and soon fell into a prolonged and bloody civil struggle. Its agonies were intensified when the United States intervened to forestall a possible communist victory in the southern half of the divided country. Viet Nam after 1960 became a testing ground for the projection of American military strength into the former colonial world. It also became a pivot in the global struggle among the super-powers and their rival ideologies.

The smaller colonial states—the Netherlands, Belgium, and Portugal—tried to regain or hold on to their colonies after the Second World War. The Dutch, who had lost their rich holdings in the East Indies to the Japanese, sought to reestablish their control. But they were compelled in 1949 to recognize the newly formed state of Indonesia, with a population of nearly a hundred million. Belgium made virtually no preparation for the transition of the Congo to independence, but in 1960 the rising tide of nationalism in Africa forced the Belgians to agree to premature freedom. The result was chaos. The Portuguese, meanwhile, remained determined to keep their grip on the vast territories of Angola and Mozambique, which they continue to view as Portuguese provinces. It seems clear, however, that it will be only a matter of time before the last vestiges of colonialism are swept from the globe.

The liberated nations have faced new problems from the outset, for political independence did not bring them, automatically, prosperity and happiness. It has become the responsibility of native leaders to deal with the grave challenges of hunger, ignorance, and internal strife. They have found, too, that they are seldom free of external influences and controls. They are still bound to the economic structures imposed earlier by the colonial states: to a substantial extent their countries have continued to serve the purposes of foreign capital ("neo-colonialism").

As the leading capitalist and industrial power, the United States has exercised the major influence in the emerging nations. Its large corporations have put billions of dollars into overseas enterprises; the American government, through economic and military aid, speaks with a strong voice in most capitals. On a lesser scale, the Russians and the Chinese have sought influential roles for themselves. The new nations find that the hand of the colonial ruler has been replaced by a complex of forces arising from vested economic interests and the strategic clash of great powers.

Rising material expectations: economic and social development

It is under these tensions that the new leaders are trying to satisfy their peoples' "revolution of rising expectations." Even as their own pride was kindled, earlier, by the pride of their conquerors, the former colonials are dazzled by Western affluence and technological mastery. Though glad to see the foreigners depart, they are impatient to learn their ways and enjoy their material advantages.

What, specifically, do the new nations desire? Their goals are often ambivalent, for they value their traditional institutions and at the same time want to modernize their societies, aspiring to retain their cultural identity while adapting Western techniques to their own patterns of life. They have not always succeeded; in the encounter between the old and the new, the old is generally destroyed. The ancient institutional structures of Asia and Africa have proved no more capable than those of Europe of withstanding the impact of technology.

The emerging countries wish first of all to gain economic independence, for political sovereignty is hollow so long as foreigners govern the economy. In most instances there has been only one practicable means of transferring control: nationalization. Foreign owners, supported by their home governments, have naturally resisted this process.

Nationalization has proceeded at a different pace in each liberated country. In China, the communist revolution took over all major sectors of the economy. Elsewhere, most of the new regimes have practiced some degree of socialism, though a number have continued to protect established business interests, both foreign and domestic. A salient example is Cuba, where political independence from Spain (achieved in 1898) had not led to economic independence. Fidel Castro's revolution of 1958 took the decisive step of nationalizing agriculture and industry, both of which had been owned in substantial part by Americans. Cuba thus became a model of a "national-liberation movement" directed against a native political regime.

The underlying aim of Castro's movement, as of other efforts to uproot the vestiges of colonialism, is to put the resources of his new nation at the disposal of its own people. But Castro and the other leaders have been well aware that continued independence and the effective use of resources depends on improved education, that universal literacy is essential if their purposes are to be understood and their programs successfully carried out. They stress technical education in particular, so that the young men and women of each new nation can operate the complicated machines that promise a better future. Ignorance is associated with the miseries and humiliations of the colonial era; "backwardness" must be overcome at all costs. The new leaders have found that the cost of education is high indeed and that resources are often unequal to requirements.

The "revolution of rising expectations" extends to all the wonders and comforts that the advanced countries have displayed to the underdeveloped lands. It is one of the tragedies of the twentieth century that millions of people have been stirred to crave things that lie beyond their reach. Communication by mass media is mainly responsible: magazines, films, radio, and television project images of the affluent West into the world's continents of poverty. Spurred by mounting nationalistic pride, the poor of those lands see no reason why they should not share in a richer life. They want more of everything—food, housing, medicine, comforts, and travel— if not for themselves, then for their children.

The cruel fact is that the resources of the new nations will hardly suffice to meet the subsistence requirements of their expanding populations. Even to assure subsistence (and to keep hopes alive for more than that), these nations must pursue vigorous economic development. Their leaders know the specifics of the challenge, and their peoples have a general sense of it; so there is unremitting pressure for whatever steps (or systems) may be necessary to achieve development.

Time is a key factor in economic growth. And if production is to be increased fast enough, it will almost certainly require central planning and supervision. Whether the changes are introduced by evolution or revolution, it seems clear that the efforts will be mainly collectivist. China and India seem to represent the chief alternatives: "communism" or "democratic socialism." The smaller nations are watching to see which one achieves its development goals—and at what price. The experience of the two giants of Asia will deeply influence the course of all new nations around the globe.

RADICAL RECONSTRUCTION
IN WESTERN PHILOSOPHY
AND RELIGION

The sweep of events in the former colonial territories, as well as the convulsive wars that preceded them, have had marked repercussions on the West. They have influenced to some degree the profound readjustment of ideologies growing out of new discoveries in science (since about 1900). The common denominator of the new discoveries is that the universe is not as *knowable* or as *orderly* as man had previously believed. Educated persons have been painfully absorbing the truth that Newton's world-machine is as much a construct of the human mind as is the theistic cosmos of Dante.

The Einstein theories and quantum mechanics contradict the older concept of "absolute" physical laws. It is not just a matter of the complexity of things or the limits of observation; the new physics points to a radical disjunction between the way things behave and our ability to conceive of them. How can we imagine space that is at once finite and unbounded? Or light that is at once particle and wave? The specialized researchers, of course, continue to produce prodigious amounts of data that can be put to practical use. But our spiraling knowledge carries us ever farther from a comprehensible view of the universe as a whole.

Philosophers, reflecting the new skepticism of the scientists, have virtually abandoned efforts to explain objective "reality." They generally agree that no such explanation is possible. The two most influential schools of philosophy in the twentieth century are those of the "linguistic analysts" and the "existentialists." The former hold that nothing significant can be said about "being in general"; they focus attention, therefore, on limited intellectual problems, especially the applications of symbolic logic. The existentialists insist that man's very humanity prevents him from seeing things *in themselves.*

As in all times of change, traditional myths and ways die hard. Optimistic liberalism, born of the Enlightenment, still persists--especially in the United States. As we saw in Chapter Twelve, liberalism in Europe had become discredited by 1919; and the void there was filled, in part, by Marxism, fascism, or extreme nationalism. These faiths, however, have also proved to be false or inadequate.

Some Western men, in disillusionment, have returned to traditional religion. The crimes and horrors of world wars and revolutions have heightened their awareness of "evil" and man's "sinful nature." Hence, certain religious leaders have rekindled Augustinian precepts and called for a resurgence of orthodoxy and ritualism. But neither this effort, nor the more permissive "status" Christianity, nor old-fashioned fundamentalism has satisfied the intellectual challenge of the times.

The implications of depth psychology: Freud

The source of the twentieth-century challenge lies as much in the new psychology as in the new physics. John Locke's simplistic view of the mind has been more completely superseded than Newton's mechanics. The Aristotelian and Christian views of man as an organism are now seen as inadequate, if not distorted. The giant of modern psychology is Sigmund Freud, whom we referred to in Chapter Eleven as a pioneer in the discipline. Freud was a practicing physician whose initial interest was in curing the mental ailments of his patients. In the course of his clinical work, however, he discovered aspects of the human mind and personality that had long lay hidden. Freud published his significant *Interpretation of Dreams* in 1900, but his broader impact on thought was not felt until after the First World War.

Though Freudian psychology has been disputed and amended, much of its substance has gained acceptance. Freud held that man is by no means a rational machine, consciously directing his appetites and will. On the contrary, reason plays a relatively minor and subordinate role in most individuals, for the conscious life and its expression form a veneer covering the "real" person. Beneath the surface lurk unconscious and subconscious desires, or drives, which are the chief engines of motivation. There is, of course, important interplay among the various levels; but Freud concluded that reason is more likely to serve as an *instrument* of the unseen drives than as their *regulator*. In any event, a realistic view of man must assign a limited place to his conscious mind; it must recognize that man is dominated by deep-seated drives (e.g., for sexual gratification, love, power, death), physiological responses, and acquired attitudes.

Society, wrote Freud in *Civilization and Its Discontents* (1930), compels the individual to repress many of his "natural" desires. In a highly organized civilization, these repressions exact a heavy toll from the individual; yet, without some repression civilization would be impossible. The "normal" person sustains the traumatic damage without breaking down, but the neurotic (or psychotic) succumbs to some degree. The Freudian conception of man and his relationship to society poses a sharp challenge to traditional morals, religion, and politics. All these have rested on a base of rationality and inhibition. It now appears that they are not geared to psychological reality and may therefore be dangerously false. Freud believed that human personality would suffer even under "enlightened" behavioral codes, because there exists an ineluctable conflict between personal drives and the social order. Hence, utopian dreams can never be fulfilled, and the goal of perfect individual happiness is a tormenting mirage.

Rejection of traditional systems and values: Nietzsche, Sartre

Friedrich Nietzsche, the German philosopher, died in 1900; but he was a contemporary of Freud and shared many of his views on man's nature. And the impact of both men was most strongly felt in the twentieth century. Nietzsche's influence was perhaps wider than Freud's, for he challenged not only the traditional conception of man's nature, but the entire institutional and ideological heritage of the West. When he said, "God is dead," he meant not only the God of the Judaeo-Christian faith but the whole realm of philosophic absolutes from Plato down to his own day. Since all human values had been linked to those ultimate and eternal values, they crashed to earth with "God's death." Facing the void alone, thought Nietzsche, men pursue one goal: *power*. Thus would Nietzsche explain the ceaseless drive for power by individuals and nations, especially in our own times.

Nietzsche's most revealing work is his most poetic *Thus Spake Zarathustra* (1884). In it he allowed his unconscious self to speak freely, without regard to rational organization. The book is a flowing stream of images, symbols, and visions, some of which have not yet been fully fathomed. In *Zarathustra* and his other works, notably *Beyond Good and Evil,* Nietzsche ranged over the condition of man and his relation to the universe. He was one of the first thinkers to stress the *absurdity* of human existence: the inability of man's reason to comprehend his surroundings—though he is destined to try. Man, said Nietzsche, is distinguished from all other creatures in that he alone has "broken free" of nature and posed the question of his own meaning.

All existing systems, whether based on reason or revelation, appeared false to Nietzsche. He focused his attack upon the bourgeois civilization of the late nineteenth century: upon science, industrialism, democracy, and Christianity. As an untamed individualist (who eventually went mad), he rejected theism, mechanism, and any other idea that would deny freedom. What he hated most was the reduction of men to specialized functionaries and their subjection to a Christian ("slave") morality. He longed for a return to the heroic Greek ideal of the "whole man." This goal could be achieved, thought Nietzsche, only by the overthrow of contemporary values and the release of determined individuals ("supermen") to recover their wholeness through disciplined struggle and sacrifice. The philosopher left unanswered many practical questions concerning just how these aims could be accomplished. His importance lies primarily in his bold challenge to "sacred" beliefs and in his shrill protest against the smothering of the individual by the herd.

A thinker of different temper was Søren Kierkegaard, a Danish theologian-philosopher. Though he was born a generation earlier than Nietzsche, the influence of both was felt at about the same time. Writing from widely separated points of view, they were the forerunners of twentieth-century existentialism. It was, in fact, Kierkegaard who gave special meaning to the word "existence" (though his works were scarcely read until after the First World War). He defined "existence" as a unique attribute of human beings. They alone exist "outside" nature, possessing the power to contemplate the universe and to *choose* what they will believe and how they will act. This very freedom, thought Kierkegaard, charges man with responsibility and anxiety (*Angst*). Man must suffer anxiety, for he can never be certain about the consequences of his own free choice.

Kierkegaard, like Nietzsche, attacked the rationalism and determinism inherent in Hegel's philosophy. He branded as ridiculous the generalization that the world is rational and that it represents the unfolding of a divine plan. How can man, a particular part of an uncompleted scheme, know what the completed form will be? If the world *is* a system, only God can know it! It follows, therefore, that no individual can presume that he occupies a specific place in a known scheme of things. Every man must act, rather, from day to day, as best he can, perpetually unsure of the consequences.

Though Kierkegaard has exercised profound influence upon Christian theologians, his writings have appealed also to men of agnostic or atheistic leanings. Such men have been impressed by Kierkegaard's assertion of man's nakedness and loneliness in the universe—"condemned to be free." They see the individual increasingly submerged and depersonalized by the forces of modern society: rational economic organization, mechanization, bureaucratization, and the high level of abstraction encountered in most phases of living. Following this observation, the secular existentialists seek to awaken in each man a sense of his *individuality* and the possibility of an "authentic" life.

Jean-Paul Sartre, more than any other writer, has brought the existentialist view to the educated public (through *Nausea, No Exit,* and other works). Sartre, partly through his experience in the French Resistance against the Nazis, came to believe that personal commitment and action were essential to genuine living. He felt this especially during the war, in his daily decision-making and risk-taking. He proved to himself that, even in extreme situations, man possesses the *irreducible liberty* of saying "no" to overpowering force. Such a force, Sartre inferred, might be an occupying army—or it might be the conformist, collectivist cultures in which modern men reside. The individual's freedom to say "no," even to "disaffiliate" himself from the system, is his ultimate defense against being swallowed up as a person.

Each man's existence, declares Sartre, is prior to any "essence," or abstraction. Sartre feels, with Nietzsche, that the death of God has left each man *free* to make of himself what he will. This belief in freedom, however, clearly contrasts with the optimistic, rational liberalism of the Enlightenment. Sartre holds that each man, to realize himself, must live faithfully according to his own values in the face of an aimless and painful universe. If the world is *absurd* in human terms (as Sartre believes), the first requirement is to recognize the absurdity and man's freedom within it.

Revision in Christian theology: Kierkegaard, Tillich

The blow to "systems" and "absolutes" in philosophy has been paralleled by a rethinking of Christian cosmology. We have seen that Søren Kierkegaard opened the way to philosophic existentialism; he was the pioneer also of profound theological changes. A deeply committed Christian, Kierkegaard insisted that *rational* proofs for the existence of God were irrelevant. The elaborate logic of Aristotle, Aquinas, or Descartes left him unconvinced. In order to become a Christian, asserted Kierkegaard, one must make an inward choice: a *leap of faith*. All other human choices, he insisted, are subsidiary. And that crucial one has to be made without knowledge of whether it will lead to salvation or damnation. Thus, a true Christian lives in a kind of despair.

The leading theologians of the twentieth century have advanced, in their own way, this fundamental concept of Kierkegaard's. While respecting the value of reason in connection with scientific and practical affairs, they have insisted that it cannot answer the ques-

tions of "ultimate concern." Karl Barth, an influential Swiss Protestant theologian, has concluded that there is no *straight line* from
the mind of man to God: "What we say breaks apart constantly
. . . producing paradoxes which are held together in seeming unity
only by agile and arduous running to and fro on our part." Rather
than preaching that there are compelling reasons for believing in
God, religious thinkers now tend to say: "This community of faith
invites you to share in its venture of trust and commitment."

In addition to viewing religious faith as a matter of internal
commitment instead of something objectively proved, the theologians of the twentieth century have sought to reconstruct the
ancient symbols and myths. They perceive that the traditional
Christian image of God and the universe has crumbled under the
bombardment of scientific findings and historical scholarship. The
"vision of reality" expressed in the Biblical formulary no longer
serves as a credible frame of reference for educated people. If Christianity is to endure as a meaningful testament, it will have to create
an imagery compatible with up-to-date knowledge.

To modern religious thinkers, this is another way of saying "God
is dead." For the theologian Paul Tillich, the phrase meant simply
that the ancient image of God has passed into history. This does
not mean that Christianity is obsolete, but that it must find, as it
has found in the past, forms and concepts to convey its message to
the living. The idea of a Supreme Being—"out there," or "up there"
—is not an essential part of Christian truth. Tillich insisted that
God is depicted erroneously as a special *part* of creation, when God
is, in truth, Ultimate Reality itself. Modern men, Tillich suggested in his *Shaking of the Foundations* (1948), must look for God
as the *ground of all being,* as the *depth* and *center* of their lives.

The ecumenical movement: Pope John XXIII

Though the Protestant churches have been more absorbed than the
Roman Catholic Church in theological reappraisal, both branches
of Christianity have given serious attention to closer relations with
each other. The period following the Second World War, especially,
has been marked by a diminution of sectarian hostility and a sense
of Christian oneness. This is due in part to the consciousness that
all churches are challenged, as never before, by secularism in general and Marxism in particular. Religious leaders can plainly see
that interfaith antagonisms are shunting more and more people
into agnosticism and that a more united front would strengthen
the appeal and power of Christianity.

On the Protestant side an important step was taken in 1939 with the formation of a provisional committee of the World Council of Churches. The Second World War interrupted the committee's work, but in 1948 the World Council was formally established at Geneva. One of its primary purposes has been to bring some two hundred separate denominations into closer association. It includes in its supporting membership most Protestant churches, Anglicans, and Eastern Orthodox groups. The Roman Catholic Church held aloof at first but later opened formal relations between the Vatican and Geneva.

The accession of Pope John XXIII in 1958 gave decisive impetus to the ecumenical movement. As leader of the largest organized body of Christians, John was in a position to strengthen greatly the unity movement. He did so with the full force of his warm personality. Though he did not abandon the papal claim to being the "one shepherd" of the Christian flock, John broke down centuries-old barriers to communication with Protestants. At the same time he launched a sweeping program for *aggiornamento* (bringing the Church up to date). This included a fresh attitude of humility and affection toward the "separated brethren" (no longer "heretics")—and toward "men of good will" beyond the fold (no longer "atheists"). John opened windows and let fresh air into the Vatican, while introducing a new era of hopeful dialogue between the Roman Church and all other Christian groups.

The most complete expression of Pope John's thought and feeling was his encyclical *Pacem in Terris,* issued in 1963. This document, an extraordinary appeal to reason and decent sentiments, calls for the harmonious coexistence of all faiths and social systems. John's work for peace, both religious and secular, was carried on after his death by Pope Paul VI and the second Vatican Council (1963–65). Paul has dramatized the new responsiveness of the papacy by breaking its historic confinement to Rome and embarking on flying visits to the Holy Land, India, and the United Nations headquarters in New York.

THE REVOLUTION IN ARTS
AND LETTERS

Literature and art have been deeply affected by the twentieth-century transformation of world society, thought, and faith. We saw in Chapter Eleven how writers and artists reacted to the impact of machine civilization during the nineteenth century. Some mirrored society, some advocated reform; still others turned inward upon themselves. In every age the arts are intimately involved in contemporary life; as they respond to events, they in turn influence events.

The search for a new language of expression: Joyce, Eliot

Contemporary literature may be thought of as that written since the First World War. (We noted at the beginning of Chapter Twelve that 1914 marked a crucial divide in the course of Western civilization.) The past half-century has brought radical innovations in the forms of writing; the content has brought daring new insights into the human condition.

The key to contemporary literature is its emphasis on *subjectivity*. As in modern psychology, philosophy, and religion, the tendency has been away from seeing the individual as an object geared to an orderly and purposeful environment. The new view holds that each man is unique and can be comprehended only through his *internal* experiences. The contemporary author feels, therefore, that he must assume a position quite different from the traditional one.

In the past, writers controlled their stories from the *outside*, furnishing dialogue and action for their characters. This technique hardly touched the subjective life. The new-style author desires to penetrate more deeply the mind of his characters, to enter into their private thoughts. The reader, then, also becomes intimate with their internal experiences. The effect is sometimes accomplished by the "stream-of-consciousness" technique in which the author puts down words in the way that ideas appear to the mind. The result is a running jumble of sense and nonsense, a collage of past, present, and future.

Numerous literary experiments have been tried in the endeavor to communicate the "inner truth." In many of these, preconceived plots and firmly drawn characters are missing. The Aristotelian model of dramatic structure and other such models have been abandoned as artificial. The moment-by-moment, *existential* reality is all. As one modern critic has commented:

> Recent novelists tend to explore rather than arrange or synthesize their materials; often their arrangement is random rather than sequential. In the older tradition, a novel was a formal structure composed of actions and reactions which were finished by the end of the story, which did have an end. The modern novel often has no such finality.

James Joyce was a pioneer of the new literature. Born in Dublin, he had abandoned his homeland and his Catholic faith to live in self-imposed exile on the Continent. He made *himself* the subject of his work, and by scrutinizing his own experience he sought to understand the general human problems of his times. In *A Portrait of the Artist as a Young Man* (1916), he drew upon the first twenty years of his life.

The hero of Joyce's novel, Stephen Dedalus, struggles with major crises during his youth. In early years he is indoctrinated with religion, and a love affair at sixteen brings on a period of tormented guilt feelings. During his years in college, Stephen at last abandons religion, turns his back on conventional society, and commits himself to the artistic life. His departure from Ireland is also a symbolic rejection of his cultural heritage and a seeking for goals and forms of his own making. The escape does not bring him contentment; it is only the beginning of a lonely and bitter search. In his narrative Joyce dealt hardly at all with action but was preoccupied with the association of the words that flow through consciousness.

In his later works, notably *Ulysses,* Joyce continued to draw from his personal experience. In doing so, he developed further his unorthodox use of language. In its complexity and obscurity his prose reflects the loneliness and alienation felt by many artists (and others) in the contemporary age. He was an inspiration to writers of his own and later generations. Many of them, using a variety of styles, have explored his method of "interior monologue."

The preeminent poet of the contemporary period is American-born T. S. Eliot, who, like Joyce, became an expatriate. Eliot found his spiritual home in England, and he found deep meaning in the Christian religion. The writings of Eliot, like those of Joyce, are introspective, allusive, and rich in symbols and imagery.

Eliot moved to London in 1914 and soon began to write poems and literary criticism. His early works reflect a profound disenchantment with modern civilization, a sense of its emptiness and sterility. The *Love Song of J. Alfred Prufrock* (1917) was followed by other poems in the same mood, notably *Gerontion,* the *Waste Land,* and the *Hollow Men.* These are erudite works, full of echoes from the literary past. With subtle irony and linguistic sensitivity, Eliot stripped bare the corruption within Western culture. These "confessional" poems attribute the breakdown to the loss of the religious spirit; after Eliot's confirmation in the Anglican faith, he began to write more hopefully (if penitentially) about man's condition. If the waters of God's grace have dried up within us, he said in effect, we must discover how to make them flow again. In a bid to reach a wider public, he turned to the theater; his most successful dramatic work, a modern "morality" play, is *Murder in the Cathedral* (1935).

The drama, like prose and poetry, has come under subjectivist and experimentalist influences. Such notable playwrights as Eugene O'Neill, Tennessee Williams, and Arthur Miller have dealt with ancient themes in new ways; they have not hesitated to alter methods of staging, as well as plot, form, and dialogue. The current "theater of the absurd" reflects meaninglessness and the failure of human communication. The Irishman Samuel Beckett is perhaps the best known of the "absurdists." In *Waiting for Godot* (1948), his characters find themselves trapped in a nonsense world of neither "logic" nor "decency."

The private world of painters and sculptors: Picasso, Moore

The man of letters may not always perceive (or report) his world in balance and wholeness, but he generally reflects the salient ideas and feelings of his times. The sense of alienation and disgust, the abandonment of belief in order and purpose, the preoccupation of the individual with himself—all these have been dominant themes in contemporary literature. We ignore these literary signals at our peril, no matter how smooth material civilization may seem on its surface. And the same message has been issuing from the visual arts. Painters, considerably earlier than writers, had begun to withdraw into themselves (p. 482). The artistic ferment of the late nineteenth century became a storm of rebellion as the twentieth century proceeded.

Pablo Picasso, a Spaniard who makes his home in France, is the giant of modern art. His productive life has spanned the major developments in art since Cézanne and post-impressionism. A gifted draftsman, trained at the Barcelona Academy of Fine Arts, Picasso began painting in a fairly conventional manner. The *Old Guitarist,* produced in 1903, illustrates his early, expressionist interest in portraying the poor, the derelict, and the alienated (FIG. *13*-2). Through his distortion of bodily contours and his careful attention to composition, Picasso quickly achieved mastery of the expressionist style. But he moved restlessly on through successive experiments (he calls them *discoveries*). From Cézanne he took the idea of building solidity into his works, of reducing natural subjects to their component "cubes, cones, and cylinders." Picasso thus became a leading exponent of "cubism," perhaps the most fecund movement in painting during the first half of the twentieth century.

Though it has spawned numerous varieties, cubist art involves, essentially, a breaking down and reordering of nature. For example, in Picasso's treatment of a violin (*Le Violon,* FIG. *13*-3), he not only took the instrument apart, he showed the parts at whatever angle

FIGURE 13-3. PICASSO. *Le Violon*, 1913. Hermann and Margrit Rupf Foundation. Museum of Fine Arts, Berne.

FIGURE 13-2. PICASSO. *The Old Guitarist*. Courtesy of The Art Institute of Chicago. Helen Birch Bartlett Memorial Collection.

FIGURE 13·4. PICASSO. *Guernica*. On extended loan to The Museum of Modern Art, New York, from the artist, Pablo Picasso.

and in whatever degree of distortion he desired. More correctly, he projected onto the canvas his own thoughts and feelings about a violin, about handling and looking at it. At the same time, he arranged the pictorial elements in an aesthetically pleasing composition. The finished work, then, is Picasso's private, disciplined response to the idea of a violin. Like Joyce's literature, Picasso's painting is radically subjective, personal, unique: it is not a copy or an imitation of something, but a *special creation* of the artist.

Such inward-oriented creations have not been easily understood by the general public. If alienation induced artists to paint private and cryptic visions, such paintings only lengthened the distance between them and the public. But informed and sensitive laymen have been able to grasp Picasso's meaning. They have understood, too, that his technique could be more than a graphic reduction of objects to geometrical forms; it might also signify the disintegration of traditional culture and values. The latter possibility is starkly realized in Picasso's *Guernica* (FIG. *13-4*), a commemoration of the bombing of a small town during the Spanish Civil War (1937). The rebel fascist general Francisco Franco had used German bombers in a terror raid against the civilian population. (The attack was a prelude to the mass killings of the Second World War.) Picasso, who was both antifascist and antimilitarist, responded by painting this large canvas, in black, white, and grey. It is a masterful protest—utilizing techniques of cubism and expressionism— against the indiscriminate and hideous character of modern war.

Social protest, however, has seldom been the motive of contemporary painters. They are generally absorbed in problems of their craft, especially the problems of form. Since the Second World War, the principal trend has been abstractionism—work completely divorced from any external point of departure. A Russian, Vassily Kandinsky, had begun to paint such works as early as 1911. His researches into the psychological properties of color, line, and shape led him to conclude that a "pure" art, devoid of representation, could be developed. This would be visual art on its own terms, corresponding to the purely auditory art of music.

Though the new idea has taken various forms, perhaps the most exciting is abstract expressionism. This combines spontaneity with nonobjectivity and has been most forcefully advanced by an American, Jackson Pollock. Pollock employed unorthodox techniques in order to express most fully his vigorous feeling for lines, shapes, and colors. He preferred to begin painting with no preconceived pattern in mind, allowing one stroke to lead to another and responding almost subconsciously to his strong inner tensions. He spoke of his

designs as creating themselves; he did not know what the final
appearance would be while he was "still in the painting." In order
to achieve desired effects, Pollock sometimes worked from a scaffold
—pouring, spraying, and dripping his paints upon a large canvas
below. His techniques were regarded as extreme by some of his fellow artists; others have gone beyond him in even freer uses of pigment and plastic materials. These far-out efforts, some sincere and
some for sensation, have created an "art of the absurd."

Similar trends can be observed in sculpture, where conventional
representation has also been abandoned. The greatest modern sculptor, the Englishman Henry Moore, is comparatively conservative in
this respect. Many of his figures, though distorted, do suggest a
subject. His primary interest, however, lies in the materials and
forms. One of Moore's best-known works is his *Recumbent Figure,*
done in 1938 (FIG. *13-5*). The figure suggests the idea of woman, or
the female principle; but it is at the same time a remarkably fashioned stone landscape—and a three-dimensional, created object.
(Moore devoutly believes in "truth to materials"; the figure therefore remains *stone*, while suggesting *woman*.) The sculptor, by freeing himself from the obligation to reproduce naturalistic details,

FIGURE 13-5. MOORE. *Recumbent Figure,* 1938. Courtesy of Henry Moore
and The Tate Gallery, London.

can concentrate on curves, texture, and the balance of masses. The characteristic "hole" in Moore's figure points up the advantage of this kind of artistic freedom. The aperture attracts interest, increases the number of visible curves, and improves the play of light and shadow.

Technology in architecture: Wright, Gropius

Architecture has been affected far less than painting and sculpture by the philosophical and psychological currents of our time. This is due, no doubt, to the inherently utilitarian character of architecture. Yet there have been striking innovations, spurred by the availability of new materials of construction. The twentieth century is one of the great ages of architecture.

Contemporary building is notable not only for its unprecedented quantity, but for its distinctive style as well. We have seen that architecture in the nineteenth century was a mixture of "revival" styles, none of which derived from the spirit or technology of the times. During the 1890's a number of designers in Europe and America began to express dissatisfaction with the state of architecture. They pointed to the incongruity of putting up a structure by means of modern engineering methods and then covering it with a façade of "historical" ornamentation. They complained at the same time of the workmanship of the façades, for craftsmanship in building was a casualty of the Industrial Revolution.

Frank Lloyd Wright, an American, was the pioneer of a new architecture. He concluded that the machine was here to stay and that the crafts could not be rescued. One should break entirely, he asserted, with the forms and decorations of the past. One should try to utilize whatever kind of beauty the machine is capable of producing and allow *"form* to follow *function."* An authentic style is one that provides the kind of space suited to a particular kind of human activity (work, rest, or play); its beauty will lie in the character of the building materials themselves. Because his structures were designed around the needs and desires of the individuals who occupied them, and because they preserved the natural appearance of the materials, Wright called his style "organic."

Wright began building residences at the turn of the century. In order to achieve the freest flow of space inside and to join that space with its natural surroundings, he made shrewd use of the cantilever method of construction. The cantilever, an outgrowth of the post-and-lintel method of the ancient Greeks (p. 38), provides for an *unsupported extension* of the horizontal members. Traditional construction materials, like stone, wood, or cement, can be used only in a limited way as cantilevers. But steel or ferro-concrete (concrete reinforced by steel rods or mesh) can be boldly employed in this method of building.

Wright's "Falling Water House" (1936) is a spectacular example of organic architecture employing cantilevered elements (FIG. *13-6*). This home, built over a rustic waterfall, appears to grow out of its surroundings. Inside the house, free space and a sense of contact with nature are maintained. While Wright is especially respected for his designs of private dwellings, he also created impressive structures for public and industrial uses.

Outside the United States, leading architects have been deeply impressed by Wright's "functional" ideas. Perhaps the most influential among them is a German, Walter Gropius. He designed his school of art and architecture (the Bauhaus, at Dessau) according to the new principles (FIG. *13-7*). Though it appears conventional today, it provoked spirited controversy when it was built in 1926.

FIGURE 13-6. WRIGHT. Falling Water. (Hedrich-Blessing.)

FIGURE 13-7. GROPIUS. Bauhaus. (Courtesy of the Museum of Modern Art, New York.)

FIGURE 13-8. MIES VAN DER ROHE. Seagram Building. (Ezra Stoller Associates.)

Gropius, like Wright, emphasized that fidelity to function is the first principle of architecture; a good *design* in an object (no matter what it is) ensures its *beauty*. His Bauhaus became a model of what today is called the "international" style. Especially as applied to large buildings—factories and offices—this style aptly expresses the precision and efficiency of the machine age.

The most brilliant architect in the international style is Gropius' contemporary, Ludwig Mies van der Rohe, who holds that function alone is not enough to assure beauty. His stunning skyscrapers please the eye because of their balanced proportions, richness of materials, and painstaking details. His shimmering glass walls hang upon frames of cantilevered steel. Mies' masterpiece, the Seagram Building in New York (FIG. *13-8*), has been appropriately described as "dignified, sumptuous, severe, sophisticated, cool, consummately elegant architecture for the twentieth century and for the ages."

In lesser hands the "glass box" of the international style has often been undistinguished and monotonous. In recent years this decline

FIGURE 13-9. LE CORBUSIER. Notre Dame du Haut. (George Holton-Photo Researchers.)

has led to a turning away from the stereotype and a searching for more imaginative, if less efficient, designs. The French architect, Le Corbusier, has produced some striking examples of an architecture that appears to *reject* the machine. His mountain chapel near Ronchamps, France, completed in 1955, is startling and mysterious in its sculptured masses (FIG. *13-9*). Lacking in symmetry or evident plan, its interior suggests a primitive sacred cave. Numerous other contemporary architects have subordinated function to evocative forms. But most of them have one thing in common with Wright and the internationalists: they have abandoned the backward-looking imitativeness of the nineteenth century and are committed to an architecture that is modern both in spirit and materials.

Novel patterns of tonality and rhythm: Schoenberg, Stravinsky

The radical change that swept through the visual arts around the turn of the century affected music as well. Though romanticism continued to dominate concert and operatic performances, composers began to embrace new aims and methods. Some turned to impressionism, which was inspired in part by the movement in painting. Musical impressionism, as developed by the Frenchman Claude Debussy, was anticlassical as well as antiromantic. It sought to record the composer's fleeting, transitory responses to natural phenomena (clouds, sea, moonlight). Departing from traditional patterns of melody, tone scales, and rhythms, Debussy's music has a dreamy, iridescent quality.

As in painting, impressionism in music was followed by expressionism. The expressionist composer was not interested in responding to his environment; he sought, rather, to record musically his inmost, even subconscious feelings. (This motive corresponds to the literary subjectivism of Joyce.) The Viennese composer Arnold Schoenberg was one of the earliest expressionists. Just before the First World War he turned from the large orchestral productions of the nineteenth century and began writing string quartets and other forms of chamber music. Abandoning traditional tonality, Schoenberg stressed melodic distortion and the chance coincidence of notes—often producing a harsh cacophony. Later in life he adopted a unique tone scale of his own invention. Musically, Schoenberg was not unlike Van Gogh or Picasso in seeking vigorous and disturbing means of expression.

The contemporary composer, like the contemporary painter or sculptor, has freed himself from the traditions of his craft and chooses whatever musical elements he wishes. The result is an unbounded diversity of individual styles. One of the best known and most successful of the moderns is Russian-born Igor Stravinsky. A younger contemporary of Schoenberg, he, too, worked with conventional forms before discarding them. He also decided to ignore public tastes (as the painters were doing) and to write "abstract" music to suit his own ideas. The salient characteristics of his mature works are stress on polyphony, free use of dissonance, and quickly changing rhythms. Stravinsky's compositions bear as little resemblance to those of Haydn or Mozart as Picasso's paintings bear to those of Watteau or Reynolds.

THE END OF THE BEGINNING:
A NEW EPOCH OF MAN

Music and the arts furnish auditory and visual confirmation that Western civilization has entered upon a new epoch. Some writers have introduced the term "post-modern" to characterize it. But what has come into being since 1914 (both in the West and in the world as a whole) is more than a change in phase. *It marks a break as decisive as that between pre-civilized and civilized times.* Man has finished with a world in which he was subordinate to the forces of nature. He stands on the threshold of a new world—one largely of his own making and subject to his own control.

The radical mutation in human culture

Though we are but dimly aware of the deeper meaning of this change, we may readily note the obvious contrasts between the cultures of the nineteenth and twentieth centuries. Contemporary literature, the arts, philosophy, and religion show a disjunction from their pasts in both form and content. In the sphere of politics and economics, varying types of collectivism prevail in place of liberalism and laissez faire capitalism. In relations between the West and the rest of mankind, the growing self-assertion of peoples has succeeded white domination.

But the distinctiveness of contemporary civilization derives from more than mere shifts in patterns and relationships. Totally new elements have developed in human culture. One is the factor of *acceleration* itself: changes in every aspect of living are proceeding, it appears, by geometric progression. Before we are able to identify a given problem and approach it, the problem changes or is obscured by new problems. No previous generation has faced the prospect of dwelling indefinitely in a cultural centrifuge.

The machine, originally a simple tool, is in large part responsible for the bewildering rate of change. It has culminated in "automation," a system of integrated machines that eliminates human labor. Human *thought* is also being replaced in some situations by more and more ingenious computers ("thinking machines"). The ultimate impact of these and other technological developments can hardly be imagined. Science has unlocked cosmic powers for the use of human society. The widening fields of genetics, weather control, synthetic chemistry, and nuclear energy are some of the indicators of man's expanding ability to manipulate himself and his environment.

Jet aircraft and rockets have annihilated distances on earth and have projected men, for the first time, into space. No one can predict how far man will go or what he will find there; we know only that science fiction is fast becoming reality—and that no suggestion can be dismissed as too far-fetched. Meanwhile, a Damoclean sword hangs over life itself. Nuclear, radiological, chemical, and bacteriological weapons have passed the level of "overkill"—and their use could put an end to the human species.

The challenge of survival and mastery

The new epoch confronts man with the most radical challenge of his million-year existence. Can he preserve himself from self-destruction? Can he control his new power so as to create a better life for all? Having "overcome" nature, man must now overcome himself—that is to say, his traditional values and institutions. For man's history has been marked by endless competition and warfare, but it now appears that he must learn to *cooperate* in order to *survive*.

In this perspective, current differences over ideologies and national interests appear relatively unimportant. Arguments and disagreements will undoubtedly persist, but they will have to operate in a framework where war has been abolished. The abolition of war, and the construction of a system of international relationships to replace war, will by no means be easy. The attempt, in fact, may fail, in which case civilization as we know it will perish. But there is no more pressing task for men to pursue—if they desire to go on living.

If war can be abolished, men could then work toward improving the life of all the inhabitants of the planet. The accomplishment of this goal will require many things, but it will mean, first and foremost, a modification of the principles of national sovereignty and national privilege. The idea of the welfare state, now generally accepted within modern nations, would have to be extended; the new imperative is a welfare *world*. Intergovernmental agencies for economic planning, financing, education, and communication—on a global basis—are indispensable if the poor of the world are to have a chance to develop.

A welfare world would impose restrictions on the current freedoms and privileges of some individuals and nations. Western man, who has succeeded in using much of the globe for his own purposes, may find this prospect uninviting. But the challenge cannot be ignored. Perhaps Western man can find compensation in the excitement and adventure of the new epoch he has created. In any event, he cannot turn backward; he now shares with all peoples the burden of godlike knowledge—and a common fate.

Recommended Further Reading

History embraces everything that men have said or thought or done. So in our search for the record of our yesterdays there is no substitute for the widest possible reading. The most rewarding reading, no doubt, is in the original writings of the past. Many such writings are cited in this book and can be read as individual works. (Most are available in paperback.) For practical reasons, however, a judicious selection of portions of original works may better fit the needs and desires of the majority of students. Several suitable anthologies are available; especially recommended is the paperbound set prepared to accompany this book: *Classics of Western Thought* (Harcourt, Brace & World, 3 vols., 1964).

In addition to original source materials, many secondary works are of great value and interest. The authors of such works attempt to sort out and interpret man's experience in the light of later events and differing points of view.

The books recommended in the list below are secondary works, chiefly by modern authors; titles followed by the date of publication (in parentheses) are available in *hard covers* only. Fortunately, a great many books of high quality and appeal are available in *paperback,* and almost all the titles recommended here may be found in paperback editions. They have been chosen for both their authority and their readability. Titles are arranged to correspond to the *chapter headings* of this book.

1. The Greek Beginnings

ORIENTAL ORIGINS OF CIVILIZATION

V. G. Childe, *Man Makes Himself;* Sir L. Woolley, *The Beginnings of Civilization;* and H. Frankfort, *The Birth of Civilization in the Near East,* are all brief accounts by leading authorities; J. Finegan, *Light from the Ancient Past* (2nd ed., 1959), discusses the archaeological background.

THE AEGEAN BACKGROUND OF WESTERN CIVILIZATION

J. W. Alsop, *From the Silent Earth* (1964), is a colorful account of Bronze Age Greece by an enthusiastic amateur archaeologist. C. W. Ceram, *Gods, Graves, and Scholars* (1952), provides a lively account of modern excavations in the Aegean area. M. Smith, *The Ancient Greeks,* is a short, well-written introduction to the eleventh through the third centuries B.C.

THE CITY-STATE

N. D. Fustel de Coulanges, *The Ancient City,* a century-old classic, is still valuable. K. Freeman, *The Greek City States,* is a recent survey, and Sir A. Zimmern, *The Greek Commonwealth,* is an interesting account of fifth-century Athens. H. Mitchell, *Sparta,* is clear and scholarly.

GREEK RELIGION

For a general appraisal of the Greeks, see G. L. Dickinson, *The Greek View of Life,* by an enthusiastic admirer, and Sir M. Bowra, *The Greek Experience,* an admirable summary of the Greek achievement. These accounts may be balanced by E. R. Dodds, *The Greeks and the Irrational,* or by M. I. Finley, *The Ancient Greeks, An Introduction to Their Life and Thought.* H. D. F. Kitto, *The Greeks,* is a readable short account.

Specifically on religion, H. J. Rose, *Religious Life in Greece and Rome,* is brief but lucid on the civic cults; A. Festugière, *Personal Religion among the Greeks,* deals with less formal aspects of worship.

THE FOUNDERS OF WESTERN PHILOSOPHY

Of the many treatments available, B. Russell, *History of Western Philosophy,* may be recommended for its lively style; W. K. C. Guthrie, *Greek Philosophy from Thales to Aristotle,* provides more detail. A. E. Taylor, *Socrates: The Man and His Thought,* is an excellent brief introduction.

GREEK LITERATURE

T. A. Sinclair, *History of Classical Greek Literature, Homer to Aristotle,* and H. C. Baldry, *Greek Literature for the Modern Reader* (1951), are standard surveys.

ARCHITECTURE AND SCULPTURE

Of the many available accounts, J. Boardman, *Greek Art;* G. M. A. Richter, *The Sculpture and Sculptors of the Greeks* (2nd ed., 1950); A. W. Lawrence, *Greek Architecture* (2nd ed., 1962); and F. Chamonix, *The Civilisation of Greece* (1965), are authoritative treatments with excellent illustrations. For art in general, a sound work is H. W. Janson, *History of Art* (rev. ed., 1967); a compact introduction and manual of art history is D. G. Cleaver, *Art: An Introduction.*

THE DECLINE OF THE GREEK CITY-STATES

W. W. Tarn and G. T. Griffith, *Hellenistic Civilization* (3rd ed., 1952), is outstanding in authority and interest.

ALEXANDER THE GREAT AND THE WIDER SPREAD OF GREEK CULTURE

A. R. Burn, *Alexander the Great and the Hellenistic Empire,* is a good brief survey.

2.   *The Roman Triumph and Fall*

THE RISE OF ROME

R. H. Barrow, *The Romans,* and C. G. Starr, *The Emergence of Rome as Ruler of the Western World,* are good scholarly surveys.

THE OVERTHROW OF THE REPUBLIC

Starr, above, and F. R. Cowell, *Cicero and the Roman Republic,* are valuable brief accounts; J. F. C. Fuller, *Julius Caesar: Man, Soldier, and Tyrant* (1965), is a scholarly work by a military officer.

THE IMPERIAL FOUNDATIONS

C. G. Starr, *Civilization and the Caesars,* and H. Mattingly, *Roman Imperial Civilisation,* are recent, readable books by outstanding scholars.

THE APPROACH TO ONE WORLD: PAX ROMANA

C. Bailey, ed., *The Legacy of Rome* (1923), which contains essays by several experts, is still valuable. J. Carcopino, *Daily Life in Ancient Rome,* is a spirited account by a French scholar.

ROMAN CHARACTER AND THOUGHT

H. Mattingly, *The Man in the Roman Street* (1947), describes the empire as it appeared to the common man. H. J. Rose, *Religious Life in Greece and Rome,* and F. C. Grant, *Ancient Roman Religion,* are standard accounts. M. Grant, *Roman Literature,* and E. Brehier, *History of Philosophy: The Hellenistic and Roman Age,* are authoritative.

ROMAN LAW

P. Grimal, *The Civilization of Rome* (1963), and A. H. M. Jones, *The Later Roman Empire, 284–602* (3 vols., 1964), have chapters on the law.

ARCHITECTURE AND ENGINEERING

Sir M. Wheeler, *Roman Art and Architecture,* and G. Daniel, *The Art of the Romans* (1965), are both excellent; L. S. de Camp, *The Ancient Engineers* (1963), Chs. 6–7, is a nontechnical account.

DIVISION OF THE EMPIRE AND FALL OF THE WEST

E. Gibbon, *The Decline and Fall of the Roman Empire* (3 vols.), is a monumental classic of historical literature (available also in a one-volume abridgment by M. Hadas). A. H. M. Jones, *The Decline of the Ancient World* (1966), is a work of the highest authority; F. Lot, *The End of the Ancient World and the Beginning of the Middle Ages,* is the masterpiece of a distinguished French scholar. On the Germanic invaders, see J. B. Bury, *The Invasion of Europe by the Barbarians.*

3. *New Roots of Faith: Christianity*

SOURCES OF CHRISTIANITY

I. Epstein, *Judaism,* is a historical presentation by a rabbinic scholar; A. Robertson, *The Origins of Christianity,* is by a scholarly rationalist.

THE LIFE AND TEACHINGS OF JESUS

A. Schweitzer, *The Quest for the Historical Jesus,* is a classic work by the great humanitarian; H. Daniel-Rops, *Jesus and His Times* (2 vols.), is a standard account by a Roman Catholic author.

THE EARLY CHURCH AND ITS EXPANSION

J. G. Davies, *The Early Christian Church;* R. H. Bainton, *Early Christianity;* A. Deissmann, *Paul: A Study in Social and Religious History;*

and E. J. Goodspeed, *Paul,* are all works of deservedly high reputation.

THE GROWTH OF CHRISTIAN ORGANIZATION AND DOCTRINE

E. Hatch, *The Influence of Greek Ideas on Christianity,* and A. D. Nock, *Early Gentile Christianity and Its Hellenistic Background,* trace the impact of the pagan environment on the new sect; R. H. Bainton, *Early Christianity,* is a recent general introduction, with select documents.

THE WORLDLY VICTORY OF THE CHURCH

H. Mattingly, *Christianity and the Roman Empire;* A. H. M. Jones, *Constantine and the Conversion of Europe;* and C. N. Cochrane, *Christianity and Classical Culture,* deal with various aspects of the rival traditions. H. Pope, *St. Augustine of Hippo,* is by a Paulist scholar.

EARLY CHRISTIAN MONASTICISM

C. Dawson, *Religion and the Rise of Western Culture,* and E. S. Duckett, *Gateway to the Middle Ages: Monasticism,* are the works of, respectively, a Catholic and a Protestant historian.

4.   The Creation of Europe:
Political and Social Foundations

EUROPE IN THE EARLY MIDDLE AGES

C. Dawson, *The Making of Europe,* and H. St. L. B. Moss, *The Birth of the Middle Ages, 395–814,* are stimulating studies of both East and West and their respective cultures; J. M. Wallace-Hadrill, *The Barbarian West,* is brief and readable; Einhard, *Life of Charlemagne,* is by a leading member of Charlemagne's court.

THE RIVAL CULTURE OF BYZANTIUM

Besides Dawson and Moss, above, S. Runciman, *Byzantine Civilization,* is a useful account by a leading authority. A. Grabar, *Byzantium from the Death of Theodosius to the Rise of Islam* (1966), is comprehensive.

THE BOOK AND SWORD OF ISLAM

Besides Dawson and Moss, H. A. R. Gibb, *Mohammedanism,* is an excellent introduction; A. J. Arberry, *The Koran Interpreted,* and D. T. Rice, *Islamic Art,* are useful; and T. Andrae, *Mohammed: The Man and His Faith,* is brief and up-to-date.

THE EMERGENCE OF MEDIEVAL INSTITUTIONS

C. Dawson, *The Making of Europe,* continues to be valuable; S. Painter, *The Rise of the Feudal Monarchies,* and J. B. Morrall, *Political Thought in Medieval Times,* are standard works.

FEUDALISM

M. Bloch, *Feudal Society,* and F. L. Ganshof, *Feudalism,* are works of high scholarship, while S. Painter, *French Chivalry,* and G. S. Thomson, *Life in a Noble Household,* are in a lighter vein.

MANORIALISM

H. S. Bennett, *Life on the English Manor;* G. G. Coulton, *The Medi-*

eval Village; and E. Power, *Medieval People,* deal primarily with English conditions.

THE RISE OF TRADE AND TOWNS

H. Pirenne, *Medieval Cities,* is brief and readable, though Pirenne's basic thesis remains controversial. S. L. Thrupp, *The Merchant Class of Medieval London,* is an interesting account of commercial activities.

5. The Flowering of Medieval Culture

THE MEDIEVAL CHURCH

F. Heer, *The Medieval World,* is a first-rate account of the period 1100–1300, with chapters on such topics as urban, intellectual, and courtly life as well as on religion. A. Daniel-Rops, *Cathedral and Crusade,* and M. Baldwin, *The Medieval Church,* are by Catholic authorities.

CHRISTIAN ART

C. R. Morey, *Medieval Art* (1942), is the best comprehensive treatment; J. Beckwith, *Early Medieval Art,* includes the Romanesque style; and E. Mâle, *The Gothic Image: Religious Art in France of the Thirteenth Century,* is authoritative and detailed. H. Adams, *Mont-Saint-Michel and Chartres,* is a classic synthesis of medieval culture as a whole.

THOUGHT AND EDUCATION

D. Knowles, *Evolution of Medieval Thought,* by a distinguished Catholic scholar, is a most readable introduction; F. C. Copleston, *Medieval Philosophy* and *Aquinas,* are valuable works by a learned Jesuit. C. H. Haskins, *The Rise of the Universities,* is a general survey.

LANGUAGE AND LITERATURE

For a general history of the new vernacular literatures, see W. T. H. Jackson, *Medieval Literature.* G. G. Coulton, *Chaucer and His England,* and T. G. Bergin, *Dante,* are excellent biographies.

WEST AND EAST: THE CRUSADES

S. Runciman, *History of the Crusades* (2 vols.), is complete and readable, while R. Pernoud, *The Crusades,* and J. A. Brundage, *The Crusades, Motives and Achievements,* are good shorter accounts.

THE MEDIEVAL SYNTHESIS

H. O. Taylor, *The Medieval Mind* (2 vols., 4th ed., 1949), is an admirable general survey. C. G. Crump and E. F. Jacob, eds., *The Legacy of the Middle Ages* (1926), is a collection of essays on diverse topics.

6. The Transformation and Expansion of Europe

DISSOLUTION OF THE MEDIEVAL SYNTHESIS

J. Huizinga, *The Waning of the Middle Ages,* is a work of subtle insight, dealing mostly with the Low Countries and France.

THE NEW ECONOMY

H. Pirenne, *The Economic and Social History of Medieval Europe,* is a good introduction; D. Landes, *The Rise of Capitalism,* and R. de Roover, *The Rise and Fall of the Medici,* provide greater detail. A. von Mertin, *The Sociology of the Renaissance,* deals with the new society in Italy.

THE NEW GEOGRAPHY

C. E. Nowell, *The Great Discoveries and the First Colonial Empires,* is a good survey; B. Penrose, *Travel and Discovery in the Renaissance, 1420–1620* (1952), deals with the opening up of Asia, Africa, and America.

THE NEW POLITICS

D. Hay, *The Italian Renaissance in Its Historical Background,* and J. B. Morrall, *Political Thought in the Middle Ages,* Chs. 5, 7, and 8, are good introductions; J. N. Figgis, *Political Thought from Gerson to Grotius,* and J. R. Hale, *Machiavelli and Renaissance Italy,* give more detail.

7. *The Renaissance: Upsurge of Humanism*

THE RENAISSANCE VIEW OF MAN

M. P. Gilmore, *The World of Humanism, 1453–1517,* is a comprehensive study of the age; P. O. Kristeller, *Renaissance Thought,* is a summary of the classical, scholastic, and humanist strains. B. Cellini, *Autobiography,* is a unique record by a contemporary artist. M. M. Phillips, *Erasmus and the Northern Renaissance,* is a brief, readable study; and H. Baker, *The Image of Man,* deals with the ideal of the gentleman.

THE REVOLUTION IN ART

H. Woelfflin, *The Art of Italian Renaissance,* and B. Berenson, *The Italian Painters of the Renaissance,* are celebrated; N. Pevsner, *Outline of European Architecture,* and P. J. Murray, *Architecture of the Italian Renaissance,* are also authoritative. J. A. Symonds, *Life of Michelangelo,* is a biography by a famous man of letters; and K. Clark, *Leonardo da Vinci,* is by an outstanding art historian.

LITERATURE AND DRAMA

H. O. Taylor, *The French Mind;* A. Gide, *Montaigne;* and E. Dowden, *Shakespeare, His Mind and Art,* are all valuable.

8. *The Reformation: Division and Reform in the Church*

BACKGROUND OF THE REFORMATION

G. L. Mosse, *The Reformation,* and E. H. Harbison, *The Age of the Reformation,* are brief but excellent; R. H. Bainton, *The Reformation of the 16th Century,* is a fuller study.

THE REVOLT OF LUTHER: JUSTIFICATION BY FAITH

R. H. Bainton, *Here I Stand,* and J. Maritain, *Three Reformers* (1929), are excellent biographies by a sympathetic Protestant and a distinguished Catholic, respectively.

CALVIN AND THE ELECT: PREDESTINATION

G. Harkness, *John Calvin and His Ethics,* is a reliable biography. For doctrinal matters, see also J. T. McNeill, *The History and Character of Calvinism.*

HENRY VIII AND THE CHURCH OF ENGLAND

A. P. Pollard, *Henry VIII,* and T. M. Parker, *The English Reformation to 1558,* are standard accounts.

THE ROMAN CATHOLIC RESPONSE: REFORM AND REAFFIRMATION

H. Daniel-Rops, *The Catholic Reformation,* is a lengthy Catholic study; B. Kidd, *The Counter Reformation* (1933), is a shorter work by an Anglican scholar; and T. Maynard, *St. Ignatius and the Jesuits* (1956), is a brief Catholic study of a powerful figure.

HISTORICAL SIGNIFICANCE OF THE REFORMATION

P. Smith, *The Age of the Reformation,* Vol. II, Ch. 14, is a masterly critical summing up. Another excellent summation is K. Holl, *The Cultural Significance of the Reformation.*

ART DURING THE REFORMATION

G. G. Coulton, *Art and the Reformation* (1928), is a good general study; H. Hibbard, *Bernini,* is a valuable specialized account; E. Mâle, *Religious Art: From 12th to 18th Century,* covers the period authoritatively.

9. *Science and the New Cosmology*

NATIONAL AND INTERNATIONAL DEVELOPMENT

D. Ogg, *Europe in the 17th Century,* and C. J. Friedrich and C. Blitzer, *The Age of Power,* are excellent general studies. For particular countries: A. Guerard, *France in the Classical Age,* is brilliant; S. B. Fay, *The Rise of Brandenburg-Prussia,* and B. Pares, *Russia,* are more detailed scholarly studies; N. Mitford, *The Sun King* (1966), is a readable, reliable, and sumptuously illustrated account of Louis XIV and his court.

THE SCIENTIFIC REVOLUTION OF THE SEVENTEENTH CENTURY

Among the many first-rate accounts, A. R. Hall, *The Scientific Revolution, 1500–1800;* T. S. Kuhn, *The Copernican Revolution;* and L. Fermi and G. Bernardini, *Galileo and the Scientific Revolution,* are of the highest authority. H. Butterfield, *The Origins of Modern Science,* is popular in the best sense and readable; and A. N. Whitehead, *Science and the Modern World,* is the noted work of a brilliant philosopher.

THE IMPRESS OF SCIENCE ON PHILOSOPHY: THE ENLIGHTENMENT

F. Copleston, *A History of Philosophy,* Vol. IV, is valuable on Descartes; F. E Manuel, *The Age of Reason,* and Part 2 of J. Bronowski and B. Mazlish, *The Western Intellectual Tradition,* are stimulating introductions. Among the longer works, K. Martin, *French Liberal Thought in the 18th Century,* and P. Gay, *The Party of Humanity* (1964) and *The Enlightenment* (1966), appear for the defense; while C. Becker, *The Heavenly City of the 18th Century Philosophers,* and P. Hazard, *European Thought in the 18th Century,* tend to be critical.

THE RATIONAL SPIRIT IN LITERATURE AND ART

P. Smith, *History of Modern Culture,* Vol. II, is excellent for the whole field. H. N. Brailsford, *Voltaire,* and J. Wain, *Alexander Pope,* are attractive biographies of the two leading writers of the period.

THE CLASSICAL AGE OF MUSIC

P. Collier, *History of Modern Music,* provides the general background. A. Schweitzer, *J. S. Bach,* and A. Einstein, *Mozart: His Character, His Work,* are splendid biographies.

10.   The Revolutions of Liberalism and Nationalism

THE ENGLISH REVOLUTION: PARLIAMENTARY SUPREMACY

AND THE BILL OF RIGHTS

G. P. Gooch, *English Democratic Ideas in the 17th Century,* is a comprehensive and sound analysis; C. Hill, *The Century of Revolution, 1603–1714,* is a recent stimulating survey; G. M. Trevelyan, *English Revolution, 1688–89,* is an older work of high authority. M. Ashley, *Oliver Cromwell and the Puritan Revolution,* and M. Cranston, *John Locke* (1957), are reliable biographies of two leading figures of the century.

THE AMERICAN REVOLUTION AND CONSTITUTION

J. R. Alden, *The American Revolution, 1775–1783,* and E. S. Morgan, *The Birth of the Republic,* are excellent general accounts. On the Constitution, M. Farrand, *Framing the Constitution of the U.S.,* is standard.

THE FRENCH REVOLUTION: "LIBERTY, EQUALITY, AND FRATERNITY"

C. B. A. Behrens, *The Ancien Régime,* is a good study of the background; G. Lefebvre, *The Coming of the French Revolution,* is an outstanding work by a noted French scholar; C. Brinton, *A Decade of Revolution: 1789–1799,* is a readable, scholarly survey; Brinton, *Anatomy of Revolution,* compares the English, French, and American movements. F. Markham, *Napoleon,* and H. Butterfield, *Napoleon,* are excellent studies of the emperor; and P. Geyl, *Napoleon: For and Against,* deals with various interpretations in a lively fashion.

THE CONSERVATIVE REACTION

H. Nicolson, *The Congress of Vienna,* is an attractive study; P. Viereck, *Conservatism Revisited: 1815–1949,* contains a sympathetic account of Metternich and his supporters. On Burke, R. Kirk, *The Conservative Mind,* is a well-written, partisan introduction. On Hegel, H. Marcuse, *Reason and Revolution: Hegel and the Rise of Social Theory,* is a highly esteemed analysis of a complex subject.

THE ROMANTIC SPIRIT IN LITERATURE, ART, AND MUSIC

M. Praz, *The Romantic Agony,* and C. M. Bowra, *The Romantic Imagination,* are works of a high order. For an introduction to the vast literature on Rousseau, E. Cassirer, *The Question of Jean-Jacques Rousseau,* is superior. M. Brion, *The Art of the Romantic Era,* is outstanding.

THE SPREAD OF LIBERAL DEMOCRACY AND NATIONALISM

L. T. Hobhouse, *Liberalism,* is a short book of distinction; H. Kohn, *The Idea of Nationalism,* and B. C. Shafer, *Nationalism: Myth and Reality,* are two of the best works on the subject; and B. Ward, *Nationalism and Ideology,* is a global approach to the origin and spread of nationalism. G. Salvemini, *Mazzini,* is a sympathetic biography of the romantic nationalist; W. N. Medlicott, *Bismarck and Modern Germany* (1965), is a brief and balanced work. A. M. Schlesinger, Jr., *The Age of Jackson,* is a vigorous study of American democracy in this period.

11. The Impact of the Machine

THE INDUSTRIAL REVOLUTION

T. S. Ashton, *The Industrial Revolution, 1760–1830,* and P. Deane, *The First Industrial Revolution,* are valuable brief studies.

THE BUSINESS CORPORATION AND CAPITALIST EXPANSION

P. F. Drucker, *The New Society: Anatomy of the New Industrial Order,* is the work of a readable economist; M. Dobb, *Capitalism Yesterday and Today,* is a popular account; T. C. Cochran, *The American Business System, 1900–1955,* is a brief perspective by a historical scholar; and J. K. Galbraith, *American Capitalism,* presents the views of a perceptive and critical economist.

THE REACTION OF LABOR AND GOVERNMENT

C. J. H. Hayes, *A Generation of Materialism, 1871–1900,* puts the whole subject in historical framework; E. H. Carr, *The New Society* (1951), is a brilliant and provocative account of the growth of planned economies and mass democracy in the 20th century.

URBANIZATION AND STANDARDIZATION OF SOCIETY

L. Mumford, *The Culture of Cities* (1938), is a masterly and colorful account of the influence of the machine on modern urban life; E. Mayo, *Human Problems of an Industrial Society,* is a short study of human reactions to industrialism; S. Giedion, *Mechanisation Takes Command* (1948), is a summary of the influence of the machine on industry, agriculture, and the home.

THE DEVELOPMENT OF SOCIALIST THOUGHT AND ACTION

H. Becker and H. E. Barnes, *Social Thought from Lore to Science* (3 vols.), is a comprehensive work by well-known sociologists. In J. A. Schumpeter, *Capitalism, Socialism and Democracy,* a leading economist treats of Europe and America. I. Berlin, *Karl Marx: His Life and Environment,* is a balanced biography; E. H. Carr, *Studies in Revolution,* contains absorbing sketches of nineteenth-century revolutionists.

THE ACCELERATING POWER OF SCIENCE AND TECHNOLOGY

J. Bronowski, *The Common Sense of Science,* is an explanation of the essential nature of science by a distinguished scientist. T. C. Cochran and

W. Miller, *The Age of Enterprise,* is a social history of industrial America; and J. Ellul, *The Technological Society* (1965), presents an original and stimulating analysis by a French sociologist of technology in the West.

THE CHALLENGE OF DARWIN'S THEORY OF EVOLUTION

A. D. White, *A History of the Warfare of Science and Technology,* is a modern classic; J. S. Huxley, *Evolution: The Modern Synthesis,* is by a distinguished biologist.

LITERATURE AND ART IN THE MACHINE AGE

G. Masur, *Prophets of Yesterday,* is a study in European culture in the generation before the First World War; H. R. Hitchcock, *Architecture: 19th and 20th Centuries* (1955), is a brief but authoritative account; S. Hunter (ed.), *Modern French Painting, 1855–1956,* is comprehensive.

12.   Imperialism, World War, and the Rise of Collectivism

IMPERIALISM AND EUROPE'S WORLD DOMINION

J. A. Hobson, *Imperialism,* is rather old but still valuable; De L. Jensen, *The Expansion of Europe: Motives, Methods and Meanings,* is a recent survey.

THE FIRST WORLD WAR AND THE DECLINE OF EUROPE

H. Baldwin, *World War I,* and B. H. Liddell-Hart, *The Real War, 1914–1918,* are brief but readable works by military experts.

COMMUNIST COLLECTIVISM: THE RUSSIAN REVOLUTION

H. Seton-Watson, *The Decline of Imperial Russia,* sets the stage; E. Wilson, *To the Finland Station,* is a spirited survey of the revolutionary tradition from the French Revolution to Lenin's return to Russia in 1917; B. D. Wolfe, *Three Who Made a Revolution,* presents a fascinating comparison of Lenin, Trotsky and Stalin; A. G. Meyer, *Communism,* is a balanced and scholarly treatment of Communist theory and influence.

FASCIST COLLECTIVISM: THE REVOLUTIONS IN ITALY AND GERMANY

C. J. Friedrich and Z. K. Brzezinski, *Totalitarian Dictatorship and Autocracy;* W. Halperin, *Mussolini and Italian Fascism;* and G. L. Mosse, *Crises of German Ideology,* deal with the ideological origins of the Fascist movements. A. Bullock, *Hitler: A Study in Tyranny,* is a life of the *Fuehrer.*

DEMOCRATIC COLLECTIVISM: EVOLUTION OF THE WELFARE STATES

D. Thomson,. *England in the 20th Century, 1914–1963* (1964), deals briefly with the welfare state in England. W. Leuchtenburg, *F. D. Roosevelt and the New Deal: 1932–1940,* and T. H. Greer, *What Roosevelt Thought* (1958), treat the nature of the Roosevelt revolution and its central ideas.

13.   Global Transformation: A New Epoch of Man

THE SECOND WORLD WAR AND ITS LEGACY

R. Aron, *The Century of Total War,* presents the reflections of a distinguished French commentator on our current dilemmas. In C. Wilmot,

The Struggle for Europe: History of World War II, a critical Australian journalist views the war.

THE GLOBAL SWEEP OF NATIONALISM AND MODERNIZATION

R. L. Heilbroner, *The Great Ascent: The Struggle for Economic Development in Our Time,* is a good general treatment; more basic is R. Emerson, *From Empire to Nation: End of Colonialism in Asia and Africa.* B. Ward, *The Rich Nations and the Poor Nations,* deals with four revolutionary ideas at work in the world today. E. H. Carr, *The Soviet Impact on the Western World* (1946), is a short book of unusual interest.

RADICAL RECONSTRUCTION IN WESTERN PHILOSOPHY AND RELIGION

W. W. Wager, *European Intellectual History Since Darwin and Marx,* is excellent on the whole subject; E. Fromm, *Escape from Freedom,* is a famous psychological interpretation of mass movements. W. Barrett, *Irrational Man,* gives a clear analysis of existentialism; P. Roubiczek, *Existentialism: For and Against,* presents two views of the same philosophy. J. Robinson, *Honest to God,* is a widely discussed expression of the religious uncertainties of an Anglican bishop.

THE REVOLUTION IN ARTS AND LETTERS

On literature, E. Wilson, *Axel's Castle,* is a famous study of imaginative literature, 1870–1930; and S. R. Hopper, *Spiritual Problems in Contemporary Literature,* is a stimulating investigation. On art, A. Neumeyer, *The Search for Meaning in Modern Art;* H. L. C. Jaffe, *Twentieth Century Painting;* and W. Gropius, *New Architecture and the Bauhaus,* are especially valuable.

THE END OF THE BEGINNING: A NEW EPOCH OF MAN

K. E. Boulding, *The Meaning of the 20th Century,* deals with the transition to a new order growing out of science and technology; R. L. Heilbroner, *The Future as History,* convincingly outlines the shape of things to come; G. Myrdal, *Beyond the Welfare State,* deals with the new imperative of international planning. H. Brown, *The Challenge of Man's Future,* places man and his prospects in cosmic perspective; R. P. Weeks, ed., *Machines and the Man,* is a useful collection of articles about the implications of automation; E. Fromm, *May Man Prevail?,* is an excellent account by a noted psychologist of the central problem of world politics; N. Cousins, *In Place of Folly,* outlines the threat of man's new weaponry.

Index

A page number in italics indicates an illustration. No separate number is given for related text on the same page.

Dates in parentheses following title or country of rulers are dates of reign. Other dates are birth and death dates.